THE AGE OF THE EXPERT IS HERE

MASTER EXPERT

HOW TO USE **EXPERTSHIP** TO ACHIEVE PEAK PERFORMANCE, SENIORITY AND INFLUENCE IN A TECHNICAL ROLE

ALISTAIR GORDON & DOMINIC JOHNSON

Published by Expertunity Press

MASTER EXPERT

NATIONAL LIBRARY OF AUSTRALIA

A catalogue record for this work is available from the National Library of Australia

Master Expert: how to use Expertship to achieve peak performance, seniority and influence in a technical role.

Published by Grant Heinrich
Edited by Graeme Philipson and Susan Ryan
Design by Ronnoco - ronnoco.com.au
Cover by Jodie Laczko

ISBN 978-0-6450466-3-2 (Print)
ISBN 978-0-6450466-4-9 (EBook)

(C) HFL Leadership and Expertship Press

Program enquiries programs@expertunity.global

expertship.com

"LEADERSHIP"

is for people leaders.

"EXPERTSHIP"

is for subject matter experts.

The journey to
EXPERTSHIP MASTERY
is long but ultimately
rewarding and
life-changing.

Table of Contents

Table of Figures

Preface

THIS BOOK IS WRITTEN for technical subject matter experts who want to make a much greater impact.

It has one simple objective: to help every expert be the best possible expert they can be and assist them on the road to Expert Mastery. This book is for you if you are an expert who:

- Wants to reduce or eliminate low-level work and operate at a more strategic, value-adding level.
- Wants to be more influential in their organization and beyond.
- Wants to be involved in initiatives that can make a difference.

We have been working closely with experts in many fields, such as IT, finance, risk, HR, engineering, marketing, medical, science, etc., for several years, and we've yet to meet an expert who hasn't shared these objectives. Every expert wants to be the best in their field. Every expert wants to add as much value to their colleagues and their organization as possible.

Traditionally, authors of books like this make some opening promises to readers to entice them to read on. Here are ours. We promise that:

- The following pages will positively challenge your view of yourself as an expert and as a colleague, and expand your view of the value you do and could add.
- You will look at the role of an expert much differently than you currently do.
- That reading this book alone will help you add greater value or operate at a higher level, with the caveat that this will take application. We will encourage and advise you on how to build a Personal Growth Plan, which will enable you to act on the ideas that resonate with you in these pages.
- Attaining the highest level of capability as an expert isn't easy, but it's very possible and hugely fulfilling.

> *"Hone your skills, sharpen your thinking, and add the extra value."*

In this book, we use the word Expertship, which may feel unfamiliar. Expertship is a new word, aligned with but quite different from leadership. Leadership is defined as the action of leading a group of people or an *organization.* Expertship is defined *as the insightful application of expertise, leading to optimal outcomes.*

But even if the word Expertship is unfamiliar, the challenges, complexities, responsibilities and opportunities that experts face every day in their workplaces will not be.

Working globally with over one thousand experts in large organizations, we have developed an Expertship model—a clearly defined description of the Expertship capabilities that experts need to master. Using this Expertship model as a foundation, we have also developed a series of personal growth activities that enable the experts we work with to achieve their full potential. This means becoming *Master Experts.*

> ### *"Only mastery of both technical and enterprise skills leads to becoming a Master Expert."*

Master Experts are held in the highest esteem by both their technical colleagues and all others in their organizations. They have a seat at the top table, are thought leaders and change catalysts. These are the outstanding professionals who are reinventing our world and striving to make it a better place for everyone. Master Experts deliver extraordinary and enduring value.

In this book, we make the assumption that you are technically very competent. But we also make the case that technical skills alone will not transform you into the best expert you can be. Your *technical skills* need to be supplemented with what we call *enterprise skills* in order for you to achieve maximum impact and influence. You'll find that while perhaps one-third of the book focuses on elevating the way in which you deploy your technical skills and knowledge, two-thirds of the book focuses on helping you understand and master enterprise skills, such as commercial acumen (market context) and engaging and influencing stakeholders.

Only through the mastery of both technical and enterprise skills will you become a Master Expert.

Over the past few years, we have learned a lot about working with experts. In fact, we've become the experts on experts. We know, for example, that the experts who would most benefit from understanding and embarking on the journey to Master Expert initially resist participation. Firstly, they believe they're already as expert as they can be. Secondly, they don't understand the value enterprise skills bring. Thirdly, they may have attended "leadership" programs in the past that, for the most part, did not take into account the complex world in which experts operate.

We're glad to report, however, that those who do start the journey inevitably discover that this approach to Expertship helps every expert add more value. Everything we do, particularly in our face-to-face programs, is based on social learning. This is where we learn from one another. Those who graduate from these programs are convinced that exploring, understanding and enhancing Expertship is a pivotal and positive course of action in their professional lives.

Participants in our programs realize that they have an opportunity to add a lot more value to their organizations. They have used the program to significantly change the way they approach their role and deal with their many stakeholders. Experts also grow as people, with many reporting a positive impact on their personal, as well as professional, lives. We hope to encourage similar breakthrough thinking, behavior and positive outcomes by writing this book, although text cannot replicate the collective social learning and camaraderie of a live learning experience.

It's not possible in a single book to look at everything we cover in the public and in-house programs we run for experts. Instead, we have attempted to provide an overview of what it takes to be a Master Expert and the steps you can take to grow your skills, knowledge and mindset to increase the value you add to your organization (or any future organization). We will show you how to increase both your own value and the level of fulfillment you feel by practicing your expert skill at the highest level possible.

We will show you how to be the best expert you can be.
We hope you rise to the challenge and become a Master Expert.

ALISTAIR GORDON
DOMINIC JOHNSON

June 2021

PART | 01 |

ABOUT
EXPERTSHIP

CHAPTER 01

The Age of the Expert

EXPERTS ARE BECOMING MORE and more important to the organizations that employ them. Increasingly, we live in the Age of the Expert.

Most organizations rely on an increasing population of talented technical experts who do ever more specialized work. This work typically keeps the organizations functioning. In other words, the expert's work is *mission critical*, even though, for a considerable portion of the organization's workforce, their work is often invisible. Experts are increasingly at the epicenter of innovation and value creation in their organizations. If they aren't, they ought to be.

Ask any chief information officer, chief risk officer, head of engineering, or indeed the chief of any technical function, and they'll tell you that finding the right technical *experts* is extremely difficult and often very expensive. Thus, hanging on to the best experts and keeping them happy is imperative.

However, our research and our experience of working with many technical experts around the world shows that many experts are *not* happy.

Experts are often deployed in the same technical role for many years, roles that frequently become unchallenging and uninteresting for the expert over time. Experts are often constrained by their workload and the lack of understanding of their ability to add extra value—value they know they could create for their organization *if* they were given the chance. Experts often lack any semblance of a well-thought-out career path. People leaders have well-developed *leadership* pathways in most medium to large organizations, while experts typically have no *Expertship* pathways.

In short, many high-performing and high-potential experts are *career stuck*.

This book is all about helping experts in this predicament get unstuck.

It's about helping experts around the world achieve their aspirations, fulfill their very significant potential to make a difference, and find fulfillment, challenge and passion in their work.

It's a book that challenges expert readers to become Master Experts.

"Around the world, experts are not as happy at work as they should be."

The Edward Predicament

EDWARD IS A BUSINESS analyst in a finance department and has been with his organization for seven years. Edward's job has constantly evolved over the years. He started out putting together accurate reports for divisional heads, but recently, he has been undertaking much more complex tactical and strategic financial analysis for these same stakeholders. Edward loves the analysis aspect of his work and wants to be in a position to be part of the conversation the wider organization has about what to do with the insights raised by the data he has collected and analyzed. He wants to be seen as a businessperson who is also a financial analyst, rather than being seen only as a financial analyst. Over the past two years, because of the quality of the work he's clearly capable of, these senior divisional heads have asked Edward to do more and more analysis, almost doubling his workload. Because he loves the work and believes it will lead to a more senior position, Edward has fulfilled all requests.

When we first met Edward, he had recently had his annual performance review with his manager, Alex. He told us that this annual review had been a mirror image of the six that had gone before. Alex had scored Edward a mid-level performance ranking (a "3", which is described as "meets expectations"). Given the quality of his work and the doubling of his workload, Edward is fuming about the rating. He argues that he delivers work far beyond his position description almost every week. He manages a far higher workload than his peers and is completed trusted by Alex to manage complex tasks. Edward believes, at a minimum, he should be scored a "4" ("exceeds expectations") or even a "5" ("significantly exceeds expectations").

Defining who experts are

Our definition of an expert is a knowledge worker who has a deep domain knowledge in a particular specialty. Many experts don't regard themselves as experts and feel uncomfortable being described as such, but that's how others think of us. We say "us" because the authors of this book are perceived to be experts in our field. We're experts on experts. All experts have knowledge in an important field and are generally highly respected for having such knowledge and experience by the wider organization. Experts hail from a very wide range of technical domains, such as science, law, engineering, marketing, medical, human resources, technology and so on. At first glance, these may seem like quite different knowledge domains with little in common, but first appearances are deceptive. Technical experts, regardless of their domain, have many things in common, as we will discover.

Edward tells us that the annual performance review is virtually the only performance conversation he has with his manager each year. He tells us that "Because I'm performing, because I work independently, because I cause no problems, because my stakeholders are happy with my work, because I am in fact a high performer and low maintenance, my manager focuses on putting fires out elsewhere, knowing he doesn't need to spend time on me." Edward reports that the review discussion centers around key performance indicators that were set at the beginning of the year, which are now out of date. Many more tasks and undertakings have been added, none of which are reflected in the structured process of the annual review. We hear this quite a lot from high-performing experts.

"Edward has come to believe he will never be promoted."

When we ask Edward why he thinks Alex, his manager, only scores him a "3", Edward provides a number of theories. Firstly, he thinks that his manager doesn't really understand the complexity of the work he now completes on a day-to-day basis. Secondly, he believes his manager has virtually no visibility of the more complex and challenging work Edward does for senior business divisional leaders. Thirdly, given the first and second theories, Alex does not really understand how Edward's skills and the value he adds have increased. Finally, Edward admits that he believes his manager is a little "old school" and that Alex scores almost all of his reports a "3", so Edward would need to do something extraordinary and very visible to get a higher rating. This is another sentiment we hear quite often from high-performing experts.

Most of the meetings Edward has with his manager are short, sharp, and task-related. The items Edward wants to discuss aren't on the agenda. These are:

- Why does he get allocated more and more work without either additional reward or any recognition?
- Why has he scored a mid-ranking rating when all of his senior stakeholders clearly have high confidence in Edward's abilities and potential by entrusting him with increasingly complex and important analysis?
- Why isn't Edward's career trajectory a topic of regular conversation?
- Why, in fact, does his manager show *no interest* in how Edward is feeling about his role or career path?

The Great Paradox of Experts: the more expert you are, the less likely you are seen to be capable of or available for greater responsibilities.

When we ask him if he has raised these issues directly with his manager, Alex, he tells us that he does so repeatedly and that Alex promises to explore these issues soon, but he never does. Edward explains that Alex awkwardly ends these conversations as quickly as he can.

Edward has come to believe he will *never* be promoted.

He lists many reasons for this contention. Firstly, there is no obvious successor in place. He's the only person in the organization who does precisely what he does, which is a typical scenario for experts. Secondly, he feels he's taken for granted by his manager and the wider organization. He believes that everyone just assumes he has no ambition. "They think that because I enjoy the parts of the work that involve detail, I'm going to be happy to be a technical analyst for the rest of my career," he tells us. Thirdly, there is no defined career path for him unless he decides he wants to lead a team of people in the finance department. Edward isn't sure this is a path he wants to take, and since he's got no experience with leading people so far, he doubts he would ever be offered or entrusted with such a role.

He is *career stuck.*

Edward is highly ambitious. He's keen to progress to greater level of responsibility, a more fulfilling role, and he believes he's capable of adding significantly more strategic value to his stakeholders and the organization.

He wants to grow his influence and his income. He *knows* he can add so much more value to his organization. But he can't see a way forward. It would be fair to say that when we met Edward, he was extremely frustrated and considering his options. He believed that leaving the organization was possibly his only way out of his present predicament.

> *"The more brilliant the expert becomes, the more career stuck they can be."*

The Great Paradox of Experts

EDWARD'S SITUATION IS ALARMINGLY common. There are millions of experts around the world just like Edward. They're career stuck and feel they could add much more value if provided the opportunity.

And there are thousands of organizations that aren't getting the full organizational value from their experts that they could and should.

Edward is an example of what we call the *Great Paradox of Experts.* The more expert he becomes, the less likely it will be that he will be promoted to wider responsibilities. He's becoming increasingly difficult to replace and the organization grows more and more dependent on him in his *current* role. The last thing the organization wants is for anything to change. Edward is a technical star, and this is what the organization wants him to remain, regardless of what Edward wants.

This Great Paradox of Experts is something we have continuously encountered while working with experts. The more brilliant some experts are at their chosen specialty, the more career stuck they become. They have reached an apparently impervious *technical ceiling*.

> *"The next step is to invest in building mastery of enterprise skills."*

Typically, how experts tend to resolve this issue is in one of two ways. The first solution is they leave the organization, believing the only way to get promoted is at another enterprise. This is the *grass is greener on the other side of the fence* philosophy, which, of course, may or may not be true. The second solution is they stay at their current organization but become withdrawn, cynical, and increasingly unhappy.

Both of these resolutions are poor for the organization, as the experts become high maintenance and difficult to manage or have to be replaced. Neither one is necessarily the optimal resolution for the expert either.

But there is a *third way*, and that's why we have spent three years writing this book. Thousands of experts have already adopted this third way, often with outstanding personal and organizational rewards.

In order to break through these technical ceilings, experts need to change the way in which they think, operate and connect. Experts like Edward need to progress from performing at *Expert* level to what we describe in detail in this book as *Master Expert* level. Key transitions include:

- A shift from tactical support to strategic support.
- A shift from departmental focus to an organization-wide focus.
- Replacing jargon-filled communication with cut-through, plain-language messaging that everyone in the organization can understand.
- A shift from designing solutions for the now to designing solutions for the future.
- Replacing transactional stakeholder relationships with transformative stakeholder relationships.
- A shift from a reactive workload strategy to being proactive about which work is prioritized.
- Replacing a mostly internal focus with a much broader external focus.
- A shift from delivering ordinary value to their organization to delivering extraordinary value.

In short, they need to build their mastery of Expertship—the practice of being the very best expert they can be.

The Path to Expertship Mastery

THE PATH TO MASTERY is littered with gifts. Great fulfillment in the work we do as experts. Greater recognition of the value of the work we do. Greater influence over those who shape strategy and can provide funds and resources. Greater learning and less repetitive work. Greater challenge and greater achievement.

Mastery is achieved, that is, breaking through the technical ceiling is achieved, by simultaneously maintaining technical excellence and supplementing technical skills with *enterprise skills*. In many organizations, these are called "soft skills," but we don't like that name because there is nothing soft about them.

What are these enterprise skills? While we describe these in detail in Chapter 2, here is a brief overview. They include: advanced stakeholder management skills, elevated change agility skills, and best-in-class collaboration skills and techniques. Additionally, there are comprehensive market context skills, which means understanding the complex environment in which our organization exists, advanced consulting skills, advanced influencing skills and strong commercial or community acumen.

In order to progress past being a technical analyst, Edward needs to learn this new set of skills that will help him leverage his technical abilities to a much greater extent. In order to contribute value to those business conversations, he needs to understand the business, his business colleagues, and his business's customers and competitors. In fact, until he masters this knowledge and these skills, he can't add great value.

Edward, as many experts have, has, up to this point in his career, mostly invested in building his technical skills. And he has done this brilliantly. The next step, however, is to invest in his enterprise skills.

Master Experts are masters of both sets of skills (see Figure 1.1), allowing them to escape the constraints of technical ceilings.

The Expertship Model

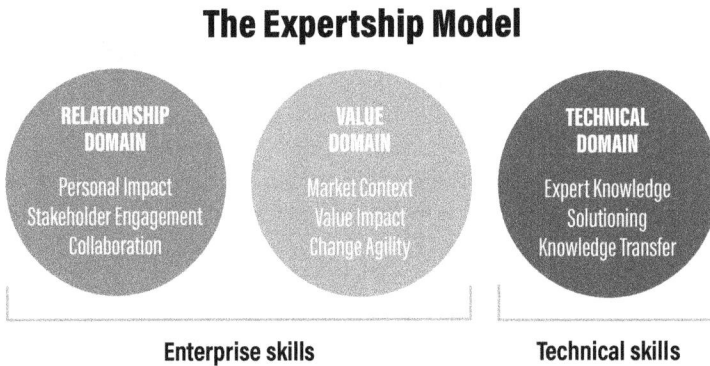

RELATIONSHIP DOMAIN	VALUE DOMAIN	TECHNICAL DOMAIN
Personal Impact Stakeholder Engagement Collaboration	Market Context Value Impact Change Agility	Expert Knowledge Solutioning Knowledge Transfer

Enterprise skills   **Technical skills**

FIGURE 1.1: Technical and Enterprise Expert Skills

Why Do Technical Ceilings Exist?

AS EXPERTS, WE MIGHT consider the existence of a technical ceiling as profoundly unfair and clearly someone else's fault—like Edward's manager, for example, or those folks in human resources.

Sadly, some of the blame lies at our door, however unwittingly. Experts can give off confusing signals that are misunderstood by the rest of the organization.

For example, experts are rarely seen by the rest of the organization as ambitious. This is because most experts don't aspire to be people leaders. In fact, many of the experts we work with couldn't imagine a more appalling role, filled with vacuous meetings and not getting work done. The problem is that the definition of ambition in many organizations is defined by how rapidly you rise through the ranks and how many employees report to you. Executive potential is defined by the scope of control over employees rather than by the potential to add extraordinary value, which is the role many experts play or aspire to.

In a recent survey conducted by the authors, 87 percent of experts said they felt they could contribute more value at a more senior level if only they were given the opportunity to do so. Our experience in working with experts is that most are very frustrated that they lack the influence, authority, and resources to be able to transform productivity and enterprise capability. If experts lacked ambition, they wouldn't be frustrated.

To make matters worse, in many organizations, experts are typecast as people who lack the social or management skills to operate outside their own specialty or to fulfill senior roles within the organization. Many managers and human resources folk believe that experts are "not good with people," and some openly say so with irritating regularity.

These colleagues have formed this view based on observations over time, where they have seen experts favor cold hard facts and clinical analysis to the exclusion of relationship building and maintenance. But it's not that experts are inherently handicapped or lacking the skills to address this common shortfall. Experts are, in most cases, left-brained. Essentially, we're instinctively attracted to and focused on procedural, factual, detailed and rational content, which is often the very reason why experts are very good at certain aspects of their jobs.

> *"It's a trait of many experts that*
> *we love a good argument."*

Our experience is that once armed with the right tools and skills, experts can be brilliant at building high-value relationships with non-technical people across their organizations. They just need to be convinced that mastery of these skills is important and then understand how to master these skills.

Another strongly held view of experts is that they have poor collaboration skills. In other words, we aren't easy to work with. Well, in fairness, many of us aren't, but again, this isn't because somewhere in our DNA, someone decided we were born difficult. The majority of experts tend to be quite introverted. We're quiet and independent. We like working alone. And, because we're experts, we can see into the future and predict problems with the proposed solutions our colleagues bring to us. Combine these three factors and suddenly we can appear to be, without realizing it, a group of sullen, uncommunicative and difficult people.

One of the authors worked in a mobile applications development organization some years back. His experience of highly technical IT folk was completely different from the description above. In meetings, the designers and engineers were animated, passionate, and if anything, overly communicative. In fact, it's a trait of many experts that we all love a good argument. We value debate, the exchange of ideas, and possibly being found to be wrong because it leads to more learning. This team was very supportive of new ideas and solutions.

But often, this is a side of experts that only our own technical peers see. Experts can, when provided with the right environment, tools and motivation, be as effective at building relationships and displaying emotional intelligence as any of their non-technical colleagues in the organization.

A further damaging but popularly held perception is that experts care more about their profession than they do about their employer. In other words, when introducing themselves to others, they may be more inclined to identify as "I'm in IT" (or finance, or law) than "I work for XYZ organization."

Experts are hired by organizations for their expertise. But the more we use our expertise, the more it seems we can become distanced from the rest of the organization. We can be typecast as specialists because that's consistent with our behavior. We're accused of being unable to see the bigger picture because, in some instances, other people's interactions with us are only at the technical level. In some cases, of course, because we're so focused on the technical side of our role, this accusation of failing to see the big picture may be true.

> *"Many experts operate and interact with the organization almost entirely from a technical perspective."*

This image of experts becomes self-reinforcing. The organization sidelines us and, as a consequence, we feel unloved, unwanted, undervalued and taken for granted. So, we hang out with others who are similarly sidelined, our tribe. And because we relate to the tribe more than the whole employee group, when we're asked at a barbeque what we do, instead of saying we work for XYZ firm, we say we "work in IT." This misconception about how experts relate to the organization has serious implications for both experts and their managers. We discuss this in much more depth throughout this book.

Finally, another common criticism of experts is that we operate in our own little technical bubble, and we don't understand "the organization." Here's the thing: a high proportion of the experts who attend our programs are "guilty as charged." They demonstrate a significant lack of critical knowledge about their organization and its strategic challenges and competitors (or, in the case of the public sector, substitutes).

This criticism is often valid because most experts focus on the acquisition and application of *technical* knowledge. They operate and interact with the organization almost entirely from a *technical* perspective. If they attend courses to expand their knowledge and skills, these will usually be on the technical side. This appears to make sense because of the role experts are typically asked to play: providing objective, emotionless analysis by leveraging facts and data and offering their technical expertise.

It's a classic Catch-22: the expectations of experts' contribution are restricted to technical inputs based on their area of specialty, and so that's where we focus our attention in terms of knowledge and skills acquisition, which guarantees we'll not be invited, expected or permitted to make broader contributions.

How Do Enterprise Skills Help Experts Break Through the Technical Ceiling?

WE HAVE NOW WORKED with more than a thousand technical experts from a wide range of professions, and we've got some wonderful news. Experts, in our experience, once convinced of the value of mastering enterprise skills, approach doing so with military precision. In the vast majority of cases, this results in extremely positive outcomes. This is because experts, by their very nature, are smart. We're also usually capable of great focus and are ambitious to make a greater difference. Many experts are surprised at the transformative nature of mastering a much broader skill set.

> *"This is a book you never knew you needed about things you never imagined were important."*

Richard Silberman, an insurance broker, told us: "Before I came across Expertship, I honestly thought there was something wrong with me. Expertship helped me realize that I am far from being alone. There was nothing wrong with me. I just hadn't learned the right skills."

Sweta Telkar, an SAP applications expert, told us: "Expertship has done a lot for my confidence. It helped me understand my positive and negative traits, and helped me be more in tune with myself. I had always felt that I was unable to articulate what I wanted to say. Exposure to Expertship has done a lot for my confidence. To be more effective, it was about me having enough business knowledge to be able to challenge the business. It helps us all realize our potential."

Aphra Hanlon, a program integration manager, told us: "Expertship taught me that just because you're articulate, that doesn't necessarily make you a good communicator. Different people think differently and have different motivations. A study of Expertship taught me how to communicate with other people on their terms."

Kellie Wills, a senior messaging engineer, told us: "Understanding Expertship really turned on a light for me. It made me realize there was so much more to being a technology person than the technology. I really got a lot out of the stuff on Personal Impact, which is essentially how other people see you."

Dave Brown, a project director, told us: "So often in my career, I have felt that the other person didn't understand what I was saying, while at the same time, I had a feeling I didn't understand them. A study of Expertship really changed that. Expertship has given me tools I can really use."

Lidia Jukic, senior corporate counsel, told us: "I found studying Expertship enabled me to develop a way of thinking that made for a more collaborative environment. I didn't previously appreciate just how much I have the potential to influence change in the organization. It equipped me with the insights and the tools to become a much more effective member of both the legal team and the overall organization. It helped me refine my skills and become a trusted advisor."

Tony Horton, a senior Unix administrator, told us: "I absolutely believe a study of Expertship changes people's lives. I realized I need to stop being 'the guy who can't be wrong.' I feel now that my relationships with people at work are way better, and I am more accepting of other people."

Tony also did us the honor of reading a beta version of this book, and when we asked him to write a short description of it, he wrote this: "The book you never knew you needed, about things that you never imagined were important. Finally understand why things are so hard to get done, and what you need to do to make it easier."

> *"There are three levels of Expertship, and Master Expert is the highest level."*

All of these executives have applied themselves to make the transition from expert to Master Expert. And the progress they have made in their careers is a testament to the fact that what's holding experts back isn't nature but nurture.

The Three Levels
of Expertship

MASTER EXPERT
- Strategy
- Transformative
- Far horizon
- Leading, proactive
- Innovating
- External focus

EXPERT
- Tactical, some strategy
- High value transactional
- Near and mid horizon
- Following, reactive, some proactive
- Continuous improvement
- Department focus

SPECIALIST
- Tactical
- Transactional
- Near horizon
- Following reactive
- Task orientated
- Internal focus

DERAILERS
- Closed mindset
- Unresponsive
- Past horizon
- Disconnected
- Blame orientated
- Self-focus

INCREASING VALUE ADD

FIGURE 1.2: The Three Levels of Expertship

A Model for the Age of Experts

THIS BOOK EXPLORES THE three levels of Expertship, defined in our Expertship model (see Figure 1.2). This model describes what high-value contributions are possible when a combination of technical and enterprise skills is deployed. During Edward's review process, his manager, Alex, does have a capability framework, which is a description of behaviors that make experts successful, to refer to. Most organizations have such a framework for people leaders, but not for their experts. With the publication of this book, we remedy this problem.

Many experts arrive at our programs, and indeed at these very pages, believing they're as expert as they can be. They have arrived at this conclusion by measuring their technical prowess against all others. Their assessment of their status doesn't include measuring their mastery of enterprise skills.

The concept of being a Master Expert is new to many but quickly makes sense. Most experts we work with have very clear goals.

- They want to reduce or eliminate their low-level work and operate at a more strategic, value-adding level.
- They want to be more influential in their organization and beyond.
- They want to be involved, front and center, in transforming their organization through innovation.
- They want to be involved in initiatives that can make a difference.
- They'd like a career path that reflects this greater ability to make a contribution beyond purely technical advice.
- They'd like to be seen as a Master Expert in the organization and more broadly in their field.

If these aspirations resonate with you, then this book was written for you.

We often start our programs by asking experts to undertake a self-assessment, and we suggest you also do so when starting to read this book.

You'll see the assessment in Figure 1.3. We invite all of our participants to read the descriptions in the boxes carefully and then circle the box that's most appropriate to the level at which they're currently operating.

The assessment is a simple one based on the Expertship model, which is the underpinning model in this book. The Expertship model has three domains: Technical, Value, and Relationship. Each of these domains has three capabilities.

- **Technical Domain**: Expert Knowledge, Solutioning, and Knowledge Transfer.
- **Value Domain**: Market Context, Value Impact, and Change Agility.
- **Relationship Domain**: Personal Impact, Stakeholder Engagement, and Collaboration.

	RELATIONSHIP DOMAIN		
	Personal Impact	Stakeholder Engagement	Collaboration
MASTER EXPERT	Highly empathetic and inspirational. Takes ownership for business outcomes. Manages own and others' emotions effectively. Drives for results.	Proactively builds networks across and beyond the organisation. Strategic partner status. Manages conflicting priorities.	Models teamwork, collaboration and focuses on outcomes. Communicates excellently across stakeholders. Presents brilliantly. Diplomat - negotiates win-win outcomes.
EXPERT	Empathetic. Takes ownership for technical outcomes. Manages own emotions effectively. Engages beyond minimum results.	Builds effective relationships within immediate domain. Trusted technical partner status. Manages conflicting departmental stakeholder priorities.	Active team member. Expert advisor. Communicates well as functional representative. Presents efficiently. Negotiates from technical position.
SPECIALIST	Aims to establish personal credibility. Takes ownership of allotted tasks. Developing ability to manage own emotions. Delivers acceptable results.	Manages a small, effective network related to current mandate. On-demand technical supplier status. Struggles with conflicting priorities.	Active individual contributor. Technical advisor. Communicates as a technical staffer. Rarely presents. Responds to results of negotiations.
DERAILING	Disengaged and cynical. Blames others for unachieved outcomes. Poor at managing own emotions.	Operates within a limited network. External networks focused on profession. Talented but difficult to deal with.	Disconnected and distant from team. Communicates using impenetrable jargon. Seeks outcomes that are personally favourable.

VALUE DOMAIN			TECHNICAL DOMAIN		
Market Context	Value Impact	Change Agility	Expert Knowledge	Solutioning	Knowledge Transfer
Advanced knowledge of global organisation. Strategically and politically savvy. Understands competitors. Deep customer focus. Across global trends.	Generates long-term, strategic, business-orientated recommendations. Focuses on creating long-term customer value. Shapes solutions that deliver competitive advantage	Promotes positive change culture. Change catalyst. Articulates compelling case for change. Leads change. Confidently addresses concerns.	Advanced, comprehensive knowledge. Thought leader. Next practice.	Complex problem identification. Anticipates problems. Leads the shaping of technical and business solutions to future proof the organisation. Innovative.	Champions culture of knowledge sharing; sharing freely. Coaches technical cohort and wider organisation. Prioritises own and others' personal growth.
Advanced knowledge of local organisation. Customer focus. Strategically limited. Limited and local competitive focus. Across local trends.	Generates short-term, strategic, business-orientated recommendations. Focuses on creating immediate customer value. Shapes solutions that deliver technical advantage.	Models supportive change mindset. Identifies and promotes change initiatives. Executes change with professionalism and commitment.	Comprehensive knowledge. Current. Best practice.	Accurately identifies most problems. Swift response. Shapes timely and accurate technical and business solutions. Adaptive.	Promotes value of knowledge sharing; sharing when asked. Coaches technical cohort. Owns personal growth and encourages others.
Departmental knowledge. Tactical focus. Professional not market insights.	Delivers short-term, tactical, technical-orientated recommendations. Focuses on creating internal customer value. Shapes solutions that deliver internal technical benefits.	Models an ability to embrace change. Identifies and promotes individual change initiatives. Contributes dutifully.	Developing knowledge. Current. Early practice.	Accurately identifies common problems. Reactive response. Shapes technical solutions. Systematic.	Recipient of knowledge sharing. Deploys a directive training style. Owns own personal growth.
Siloed view of role and department. Internal focus. Operates in technical bubble. Trend blind.	Delivers technical solutions with little long-term value. Inability to create customer value. Delivers short-term technical fixes.	Demonstrates a closed mindset towards change. Actively resists change initiatives. Reacts subjectively and emotionally.	Incomplete knowledge. Out-of-date. Past practice.	Identifies problems from past experience. Slow response. Jumps to known solutions. Inconsistent.	Resists knowledge sharing activities. Fails to contribute to coaching/sharing. Considers emerging experts a threat.

FIGURE 1.3: The Expertship Self-Assessment

We encourage you to score yourself against each of these nine capabilities. You have four levels to choose from: Derailing Expert, Specialist, Expert, and Master Expert.

In order to complete the assessment, you will read the various behaviors that need to be commonly demonstrated at each level and then determine the level at which you're currently operating. Since this is a self-assessment and no one else will see it, be tough on yourself.

Of course, each expert will have their own strengths and growth opportunities, but we often see experts hover their pens over the *Master Expert* level, before choosing to circle the box below it, *Expert*, instead. In each instance, the Master Expert level requires us to commonly demonstrate elevated contributions to our team and organizations.

It's very rare that an expert would consider themselves at the *Derailing Expert* level, but in many instances, the experts we work with hold their hands up to one or more derailing behaviors. It's quite possible to rate ourselves at *Expert* level and yet still have a derailing behavior that we need to expunge.

Having had these stretch performance standards set by the Expertship model, most of the experts we work with almost immediately aspire to get to *Master Expert* level.

Indeed, the most common reaction to being shown the Expertship model is for experts to ask us why no one had shown them this performance model for experts previously. A few years ago, the authors could find few organizations that had adopted this type of performance chart for their high-value individual contributors, but more and more organizations in this age of Experts are recognizing the need to introduce such a capability framework to allow for career pathing for experts. Some have simply adopted this model.

The Edward Evolution

DURING OUR WORK WITH Edward's organization, and with Edward himself, we introduced the Expertship model to both Edward and his manager, Alex. It now continues to form the basis of all career and personal growth conversations that Edward is involved with. Alex has used the model as a basis for conversations with a broad range of experts in his finance department.

In the early conversations that Alex had with Edward, Edward concluded he didn't have a particular desire to be promoted into a people leadership role, but he did want to be promoted—rewarded and recognized—for his greater technical contribution. He also wanted to rise above being someone who provided analysis and be more involved in decision-making in the organization. Edward wanted to transform his relationships with divisional heads from being a supplier to a partner.

In order for Edward to achieve these goals, there needed to be a clearer understanding of how his work should be both assessed and rewarded, with both his manager and the wider human resources team.

With Edward's permission, we spoke at length to his manager, Alex, who told us that providing feedback for the very technical individual contributors in his department was the most difficult part of his entire job. Alex cited a range of reasons for this being the case. He admitted that when it came to the very technical aspects of Edward's role, for example, he didn't have either visibility or technical know-how to be able to adequately assess Edward's work, just as Edward suspected. With all of his individual contributors, Alex worked on the basis that if there were no complaints from his individual contributors' stakeholders, things were fine. This is where the "meets expectations" rating emanated, the score that had riled Edward to such a great degree.

> *"By explaining how we worked with Edward and Alex,*
> *readers will get a sense of how to use this book."*

When it came to how Edward operated as a colleague, we heard Alex state several concerns. Alex explained that, from his perspective, Edward operated very autonomously and rarely interacted with other members of the department. Alex told us that Edward had a reputation among his finance colleagues as being aloof and too busy to be interested in what everyone else was doing, or indeed help in times of high demand. Alex also expressed concerns about Edward's attitude toward him as a manager. "He's very independent and quickly gets defensive when I ask him what he's working on," Alex told us.

We asked Alex how he had communicated this feedback to Edward. Well, he hadn't. Why not? Alex was concerned about how Edward would react. In fact, he was sure Edward would react negatively. Alex didn't want to rock the boat and wasn't really sure how to address the issues about teamwork, since nothing about this was part of Edward's key performance indicators.

This state of affairs is very typical. On the one hand, we have a high-performing, dedicated but autonomous technical expert, and on the other, an uninformed and nervous manager. This is how what we call "feedback-free zones" occur. Many experts experience them.

He could see that in the technical domain, he performed very well, operating at full Expert level and with some elements of operating at Master Expert level. But Edward could also see that he had performance gaps. He was low in Market Context and also in Collaboration.

	RELATIONSHIP DOMAIN		
	Personal Impact	Stakeholder Engagement	Collaboration
MASTER EXPERT	Highly empathetic and inspirational. Takes ownership for business outcomes. Manages own and others' emotions effectively. Drives for results.	Proactively builds networks across and beyond the organisation. Strategic partner status. Manages conflicting priorities.	Models teamwork, collaboration and focuses on outcomes. Communicates excellently across stakeholders. Presents brilliantly. Diplomat - negotiates win-win outcomes.
EXPERT	Empathetic. Takes ownership for technical outcomes. Manages own emotions effectively. Engages beyond minimum results.	Builds effective relationships within immediate domain. Trusted technical partner status. Manages conflicting departmental stakeholder priorities.	Active team member. Expert advisor. Communicates well as functional representative. Presents efficiently. Negotiates from technical position.
SPECIALIST	Aims to establish personal credibility. Takes ownership of allotted tasks. Developing ability to manage own emotions. Delivers acceptable results.	Manages a small, effective network related to current mandate. On-demand technical supplier status. Struggles with conflicting priorities.	Active individual contributor. Technical advisor. Communicates as a technical staffer. Rarely presents. Responds to results of negotiations.
DERAILING	Disengaged and cynical. Blames others for unachieved outcomes. Poor at managing own emotions.	Operates within a limited network. External networks focused on profession. Talented but difficult to deal with.	Disconnected and distant from team. Communicates using impenetrable jargon. Seeks outcomes that are personally favourable.

VALUE DOMAIN			TECHNICAL DOMAIN		
Market Context	Value Impact	Change Agility	Expert Knowledge	Solutioning	Knowledge Transfer
Advanced knowledge of global organisation. Strategically and politically savvy. Understands competitors. Deep customer focus. Across global trends.	Generates long-term, strategic, business-orientated recommendations. Focuses on creating long-term customer value. Shapes solutions that deliver competitive advantage	Promotes positive change culture. Change catalyst. Articulates compelling case for change. Leads change. Confidently addresses concerns.	Advanced, comprehensive knowledge. Thought leader. Next practice.	Complex problem identification. Anticipates problems. Leads the shaping of technical and business solutions to future proof the organisation. Innovative.	Champions culture of knowledge sharing; sharing freely. Coaches technical cohort and wider organisation. Prioritises own and others' personal growth.
Advanced knowledge of local organisation. Customer focus. Strategically limited. Limited and local competitive focus. Across local trends.	Generates short-term, strategic, business-orientated recommendations. Focuses on creating immediate customer value. Shapes solutions that deliver technical advantage.	Models supportive change mindset. Identifies and promotes change initiatives. Executes change with professionalism and commitment.	Comprehensive knowledge. Current. Best practice.	Accurately identifies most problems. Swift response. Shapes timely and accurate technical and business solutions. Adaptive.	Promotes value of knowledge sharing; sharing when asked. Coaches technical cohort. Owns personal growth and encourages others.
Departmental knowledge. Tactical focus. Professional not market insights.	Delivers short-term, tactical, technical-orientated recommendations. Focuses on creating internal customer value. Shapes solutions that deliver internal technical benefits.	Models an ability to embrace change. Identifies and promotes individual change initiatives. Contributes dutifully.	Developing knowledge. Current. Early practice.	Accurately identifies common problems. Reactive response. Shapes technical solutions. Systematic.	Recipient of knowledge sharing. Deploys a directive training style. Owns own personal growth.
Siloed view of role and department. Internal focus. Operates in technical bubble. Trend blind.	Delivers technical solutions with little long-term value. Inability to create customer value. Delivers short-term technical fixes.	Demonstrates a closed mindset towards change. Actively resists change initiatives. Reacts subjectively and emotionally.	Incomplete knowledge. Out-of-date. Past practice.	Identifies problems from past experience. Slow response. Jumps to known solutions. Inconsistent.	Resists knowledge sharing activities. Fails to contribute to coaching/ sharing. Considers emerging experts a threat.

FIGURE 1.4: Edward's Self-Assessment

We have provided Edward's self-assessment against the Expertship model in Figure 1.4.

Over the course of six months, Edward and Alex transformed their relationship and their effectiveness as a finance team.

They built a Personal Growth Plan (see Chapter 50, *Building a Personal Growth Plan*) for Edward, and Alex was able to provide Edward with many opportunities to build up his broader knowledge of the market context of the business and its strategy (see Chapter 26, *Why Market Context Matters So Much*). Edward himself was determined to study both his own organization (see Chapter 27, *Becoming a Student of Your Organization*) and its competitors (see Chapter 28, *Becoming a Student of the Competition*). Alex and Edward agreed that Edward should play a more active role in collaborating with other colleagues in finance, and that in doing so, he would improve the outputs he provided for his stakeholders (see Chapter 22, *The Many Team Roles of Experts*). They also discussed building proactive stakeholder engagement plans for key divisional heads and agreed to undertake a Stakeholder Health Check (see Chapter 12, *Expert Stakeholder Strategy*) on a few stakeholders where the relationship was potentially broken or sub-optimal. Finally, for this first Personal Growth Plan, they agreed Edward should review how he currently spent his time and where he believed he ought to (see Chapter 9, *The Expert Energy Engine*), and also deploy some tactics to make this happen (see Chapter 10, *The Art of Saying No*). We might note that every growth objective Edward chose was building his *enterprise skills* rather than his *technical skills*. This is very typical of the Personal Growth Plans we see from experts.

Alex himself agreed that he had some growth to work on. He agreed that he needed to listen more carefully to his team and stakeholders (see Chapter 20, *The Power of Listening*), and that he needed to become much more active in helping his team plan and develop their careers (see Chapter 49, *Building a Talent Factory*).

In explaining how we worked with Edward and Alex, readers will get a sense of how to use this book. You can read it from start to finish, or, and most experts deploy this approach, you can self-assess and then turn directly to the chapters on the relevant topics. The book is designed to be a flexible reading experience.

Our Mission: Change the Expert World

CHANGING THE EXPERT WORLD by helping every expert evolve into a Master Expert is a big objective. We estimate that there are 40 million technical experts in the world, so this is quite a lofty goal. Our approach to this mission is attempting to help one expert at a time.

The challenge for many experts is that the burning platform, the immediate need to learn and deploy advanced enterprise skills, isn't readily apparent. As we discussed earlier, there is a danger that experts will play the victim, expecting others to change before they do.

In Samuel Beckett's famous play, *Waiting for Godot*, two characters (Didi and Gogo) wait for the arrival of someone named Godot, who never arrives. We sometimes see this scenario play out for experts. Many of us are waiting for the wonderful day, at some unknown time in the future, when everyone else in the organization will suddenly have an epiphany and realize that we're outstanding contributors, worthy of adoration and investment, who should be elevated to rock star status.

In our programs, we meet many experts who hold this view. We typically start this conversation:

Facilitator: *So, you've chosen to wait for the rest of the organization to see the error of their ways and change their thinking about experts?*
Expert: *Yes.*
Facilitator: *How long have you had this as your strategy?*
Expert: (Pause) *Er, ten years or so.*
Facilitator: *How successful has this strategy been? Seen any changes?*
Expert: (Further pause) *Er, no. No change. It's going badly.*
Facilitator: (Deliberately long pause, allowing the expert to contemplate the significance of their answer) *Given the current lack of progress, would you be open to considering an alternative strategy?*
Expert: (Grudgingly) *I suppose so.*
Facilitator: *Are you sure? You don't sound sure. Perhaps you could continue with your current strategy and something will change soon?*
Expert: (Having processed the conversation because they're smart) *I wasn't sure, but now you've put it like that, continuing with the same strategy would be madness, right? So, what's the alternative?*

Einstein once said that insanity is doing the same thing over and over and expecting a different result. This is, in effect, what many experts are doing. And Einstein was right—it's insane!

The first mindset experts have to change is *our own*. Then, and only then, will we be in a position to influence a change in mindset in others about the way in which experts are experienced and valued across every organization. That's our modest mission with this book: a global change that helps every expert be the best expert they can be and helps organizations everywhere acknowledge their value accordingly.

Let's begin.

TAKING ACTION

Growing Our Expertship

THROUGHOUT THIS BOOK, AT the end of each chapter, we will make some suggestions for actions you might wish to take to build your Expertship skills. Here is the first:

▶ START WITH A ROBUST SELF-ASSESSMENT

Later in this book, we describe a variety of assessments you can undertake to establish the current level of your expertship. But we recommend starting with some personal reflection. Undertake the same exercise that Edward did. Assess where your current behavior sits on each of the nine capabilities of Expertship by using the grid in this chapter. Ask yourself:

- After examining the behaviors at each level of each capability, where do my *typical* behaviors rank? Specialist, Expert, or Master Expert?
- As much as I would like to be generous to myself, am I being robust in my assessment? Do I really exhibit those Master Expert behaviors every working day?
- Looking at the lowest ratings, what skills and behaviors do I need to master in order to be able to rate myself, in the future, at a higher level? (If you aren't sure, read the relevant chapters of this book (see Chapter 3 for a guide).

CHAPTER 02

The Expertship Model

A roadmap for aspirational experts

In this chapter, we will explore:

- The three levels of Expertship, and why the highest level, Master Expert, the title of this book, requires a roadmap for experts to follow and master.
- How the Expertship model provides a complete description of the skills, experiences and mindsets that are required to reach Master Expert level.
- Each of these capabilities, in addition to their respective expert roles, are introduced in this chapter and explored in greater depth later in the book.

THIS CHAPTER IS ABOUT helping experts understand how good they are at their jobs. Superfluous, you say? We already know how good we are—because we're experts!

The reality of the situation is that most experts we work with operate in a feedback-free zone. They either don't get any feedback or they discount the feedback they do get because it's offered by people who don't understand the complexity of what they do.

In this chapter, we're going to provide a proven and valid method that will enable every expert reading this book to begin the process of assessing how good they are. We answer these critical questions:

- What do I actually need to do to be good as a Master Expert?

- How do I, or others, objectively measure my capability? Against what scale? Against what criteria?
- How do I escape from my feedback-free zone and get objective and constructive feedback that's news I can use?

In Search of Expectation Clarity

IF EXPERTSHIP IS A description of what experts do, then defining exactly what that is for all experts is a much larger undertaking. Most experts will imagine that what we do is very specific to our own particular role.

This is typically true when we consider the technical aspects of our roles. But beyond our detailed technical knowledge and skills lie *enterprise skills,* which are the capabilities that enable us to apply our technical knowledge to great effect.

Over the last five years, we've worked with over a thousand experts, asked each of them this question, and then captured their answers. In workshops around the world, we've asked them to describe the capabilities and attributes of the best experts they've worked with. We've also asked them to describe what characterized the worst experts they have worked with. The results, regardless of country or culture, are remarkably consistent.

"What are the attributes and skills of the best experts you have worked with?"

Taking into account all of these responses, we defined and then refined a capability model, which we've called the Expertship model.

At its highest level, you'll see it represented in Figure 2.1 below. Experts need to be good at three things: technical ability, creating value, and managing relationships effectively. We call these the *three domains of Expertship.*

Of the three domains, we have classified two as enterprise skills and the other as technical skills. Historically, experts have focused on achieving a very high capability in the technical domain, but this book is about how to reach even higher levels of expertise and value by mastering both of the enterprise domains as well as our already acquired technical skills.

The Expertship Model

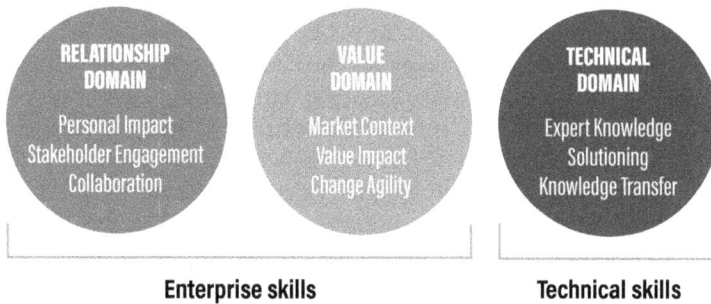

RELATIONSHIP DOMAIN	VALUE DOMAIN	TECHNICAL DOMAIN
Personal Impact	Market Context	Expert Knowledge
Stakeholder Engagement	Value Impact	Solutioning
Collaboration	Change Agility	Knowledge Transfer

Enterprise skills   **Technical skills**

FIGURE 2.1: The Three Domains of the Expertship Model

The **Relationship Domain** covers capabilities such as:
* Identifying which key relationships and stakeholders are integral to your success.
* Understanding the needs and motivational drivers of these stakeholders.
* Effectively engaging and influencing these stakeholders.
* Relationship building and collaboration skills, i.e., building trust, advanced listening skills, mastering courageous conversations, and building impactful coaching skills that allow for knowledge transfer.
* Having positive personal impact by developing a genuine and effective personal brand.

Underpinning all of these is an understanding of what typically makes human beings tick.

> *"Underpinning the Value domain is an understanding of the levers that make your organization successful."*

Many experts in technical roles have had little or no exposure to this kind of material. They have *under-invested* in building stakeholder engagement and interpersonal skills. In our experience, most experts can easily learn the concepts and techniques required to quickly become extremely capable in these areas.

The **Value Domain** covers capabilities such as:
* Understanding the context in which your organization operates and the trends and pressures that impact its current and future operation.

- Understanding, where relevant, the competitive environment of your organization, as well as its strengths and vulnerabilities in comparison to rival organizations. In the public service sector, this often means identifying alternative services the community that are a substitute for yours and the impact this might have on your organization.
- Understanding how internal and external customers choose what products and services to buy and consume, and why.
- Being curious and very informed about future trends on all of the above aspects of market context, and thereby being able to operate strategically over the long term by developing plans and initiatives that position your organization for future success.
- Understanding how, in this context, you, as an expert, can deliver the most value to your organization (for today and tomorrow).
- Understand the expert's role in driving and supporting change initiatives that enable the organization to succeed in the future.

Underpinning all of this is a commercial and community awareness, and an understanding of the levers that make your organization successful.

Typically, this is the weakest domain for existing expert performance, but it's also the greatest opportunity for experts to grow their capability. In the Relationship domain, experts build relationships that help them get things done effectively, while prowess in the Value domain helps experts decide what to do and why, as well as how to add the most value.

Finally, there is a **Technical Domain**, which covers capabilities such as:
- Identifying which key information sources are critical to our success.
- Maintaining and providing access to information sources for key stakeholders across the organization, thus reducing their dependence on us.
- Understanding how stakeholders prefer to consume information and applying the relevant versioning processes and policies.
- Maintaining currency of our expert information and ensuring its currency in the future.
- The ability to create new knowledge from the insights we receive from various information sources.
- The ability to solve complex problems quickly, which we call "solutioning."
- The ability to build the capability and self-reliance of the wider organization by effectively sharing knowledge.

Underpinning all of these is an understanding that information is valuable. Many of the experts we work with naturally consider this capability one of their strengths. But while they may be assessed positively by their peers in terms of having great technical knowledge, they're typically rated less enthusiastically when it comes to making their knowledge accessible to others.

Using the Expertship Model

IF LEADERSHIP IS WHAT people leaders do to lead people, then Expertship is what experts do to ply their trade. The Expertship model describes these capabilities.

> *"A tool for many tasks: how best might*
> *we use the Expertship model?"*

People leaders have had capability frameworks available to them to act as a roadmap for their professional growth for decades. Technical experts have had competency frameworks available to them as well, but these have typically been exclusively used to describe *technical* competence. For example, one of our client organizations uses a very detailed project management competency framework. This described the technical processes involved in project management. Professional bodies often have detailed technical competency frameworks (the engineering profession is a good example). All of these frameworks describe the technical skills required, but not the *enterprise skills* that we include in our framework (see Figure 2.3).

The Expertship model is designed to assist experts, their managers, and their colleagues with understanding what it is to be a Master Expert. The model is used in many organizations for a variety of purposes:

- **Self-reflection and asssessment by individual experts**: as you will see in detail in this book, every behavior is described, explained and explored, enabling experts to self-audit.
- **Reflection and assessment by managers**: managers often can't put their finger on the precise behaviors that, if mastered, will catapult their experts to a higher level of performance. The detailed descriptions in the model help them identify what is missing or what could be boosted.
- **HR teams, for shaping bonus and performance frameworks**: who is really doing high-value work and creating new value for the organization, and how do we measure this fairly?
- **Learning and development teams**: using the model to assist in the design of programs that help experts build their capability and worth.
- **Expertship coaches, like the authors**: we use the capability framework to help us frame conversations with experts and help our coachees find strengths to build on and gaps to address.

The Three Levels of Expertship

EVERYONE, REGARDLESS OF THEIR line of work, needs a description of what "good" looks like. This is as true for experts as it is for people leaders. We might argue that it's even more necessary for experts because they're frequently measured (and measure themselves) only in technical terms.

In sports, a variety of measures are quoted (via statisticians) to reflect how well one player's performance compares with another. In many sports, there are also different levels of play.

The Expertship model has three levels of capability (see Figure 2.2). These describe the levels at which experts typically operate, and a fourth level describes the *derailing* behaviors that get in the way of experts performing well.

> *"Derailing behaviors: which behaviors get in the way of being a great expert?"*

Specialist

THE LOWEST PERFORMANCE LEVEL in the Expertship model is Specialist. Those we have worked with who profile at this level are often starting out in their expert career or have possibly recently switched roles into a new or adjacent technical specialty. They typically perform very transactional work that's directed to them by others.

Acquiring knowledge, skills and experience is often the main focus of their attention, in addition to learning from mistakes and shadowing more experienced experts to understand how and why they operate in the way they do. The work specialists carry out tends to be highly transactional, focused on making things work properly today, and usually has a strong internal focus. Many specialists work in backroom roles, with little external contact with those outside their department or the organization. Specialists are typically learning their trade.

There is nothing inherently wrong with operating at the Specialist level of Expertship. It's simply a stage on the way to greater mastery of the expert's chosen domain expertise. Most experts operating at the Specialist level have a burning ambition to attain a higher level of capability as quickly as possible.

It's important to note that, traditionally, these experts have imagined that this will be achieved purely through the acquisition of more *technical* expertise. But consideration of the Expertship model shows them that broader *enterprise* skills also need to be acquired. This is an insight that usually accelerates their career for reasons we'll discuss throughout this book.

Expert

THE SECOND LEVEL OF Expertship is the Expert level. At this level, we're describing very capable experts who typically have a lot of experience, skills and knowledge.

The work done by experts at this level varies widely. Plenty of tactical and transactional work still needs to be completed, but occasionally, this will be supplemented with some strategic or longer range work. Much of the work is still reactive rather than proactive, but greater exposure to colleagues outside the technical department and possibly outside the organization takes place. At the Expert level, there will be a focus on continuous improvement and productivity outcomes. However, the main focus will remain at the departmental rather than what we call the Enterprise level.

The vast majority of experts we have worked with over the last few years have profiled at the Expert level of the Expertship model. And most of them felt they were operating at the highest level of Expertship possible. For many, it was a rude awakening that we had defined a level of Expertship above the Expert level.

Master Expert

THE MASTER EXPERT IS working on tasks and projects that are strategic rather than tactical, transformational rather than transactional, and on the far horizon rather than the near horizon. Master Experts are proactive and determine their own work and priorities because the organization sees they can identify the value they can add better than any one else. Master Experts operate across the enterprise, with stakeholders at senior levels of the organization and outside of it. They're focused on both internal and external customers. Given this description, it will be no surprise to read that they're often at the center of innovation projects and frequently act as a catalyst for change. They dream up the future and then get buy-in from the rest of the organization to fund and create it. Most experts aspire to reach this level of influence and impact.

The Three Levels of Expertship

INCREASING VALUE ADD

MASTER EXPERT
- Strategy
- Transformative
- Far horizon
- Leading, proactive
- Innovating
- External focus

EXPERT
- Tactical, some strategy
- High value transactional
- Near and mid horizon
- Following, reactive, some proactive
- Continuous improvement
- Department focus

SPECIALIST
- Tactical
- Transactional
- Near horizon
- Following reactive
- Task orientated
- Internal focus

DERAILERS
- Closed mindset
- Unresponsive
- Past horizon
- Disconnected
- Blame orientated
- Self-focus

FIGURE 2.2: The Three Levels of Expertship

What Are Derailers?

A DERAILER IS AN expert behavior that gets in the way of our progress. We call them derailers because they're like a train coming off a railway track. We call these behaviors derailers rather than weaknesses because weaknesses are often viewed as structural and unchangeable. By comparison, once an expert is aware of the impact a derailing behavior can have on their ability to get things done and deliver value, they can quickly adjust that behavior.

> *"Improvement science: how do experts escape the feedback-free zone, and what's the payoff?"*

Derailers develop for a range of reasons. They can develop when a particular skill or talent is deployed too often. For example, some experts like to remind their colleagues and stakeholders of how expert they are, and they tend to do this frequently. This can be because they lack awareness or don't understand the negative impact a particular behavior has on their colleagues and other stakeholders.

Experts are renowned for "knowing best" because they are, after all, the experts. This means they can stop listening to alternative points of view, particularly if that point of view is expressed by someone who isn't perceived to be an expert in their domain. Many experts do this unconsciously.

In the Expertship model, we have called out a range of behaviors or habits we see as derailers. We do this at a granular level, chapter by chapter, throughout this book. But in summary, they can include behaviors such as having a closed mindset, being unresponsive to client requests, being focused on the past or what has worked before, a lack of connection with critical stakeholders, a blame mentality, and being very much focused on their own needs rather than the needs of their department, the wider organization, or external stakeholders, such as customers.

What Is Your Level?

OUR WORK AS EXPERTS is highly complex. As you might expect, determining what level you operate at as an expert is complex, too.

We have already introduced you to the three high-level domains: the Relationship domain, the Value domain, and the Technical domain.

Each of these domains is comprised of the three capabilities, broad knowledge, and skill sets that describe how experts operate. These capabilities are shown in Figure 2.3

In the **RELATIONSHIP DOMAIN**, the three capabilities are:
- **Personal Impact**: the capability to influence people positively, being self-aware, empathetic and adaptive, and making individual and collective results happen.
- **Stakeholder Engagement**: the capability to build and maintain mutually rewarding stakeholder engagements across a variety of internal and external stakeholders.
- **Collaboration**: the capability to act as a valuable member of the team, whether virtual or co-located, and taking on an Expertship and/or leadership role when required or appropriate.

In the **VALUE DOMAIN**, the three capabilities are:
- **Market Context**: the capability to acquire, retain, refresh and leverage contextual organizational, competitive and customer knowledge effectively.
- **Value Impact**: the capability to identify, articulate and realize tangible ways of adding commercial or community value, demonstrating an active engagement in improving overall organizational performance.
- **Change Agility**: the capability to act as a change catalyst and lead change initiatives effectively.

*"The Nine Capabilities: Which do I need
to work on the most, and why?"*

Using the Capability Framework to Self-Assess

BY WAY OF AN example, one expert we worked with, Trevor, was, without doubt, operating at Master Expert level in two areas of the Expertship model.

When it came to the Expertship capability of Expert Knowledge (in the Technical domain), he had more knowledge, skills and experience in his domain, which was a specialized field of information technology, than most others in his field, and he was *applying* this knowledge strategically and innovatively on a daily basis. He was the go-to person for the enterprise, and no new technology projects were advanced without getting his input and advice. This is the mark of a Master Expert.

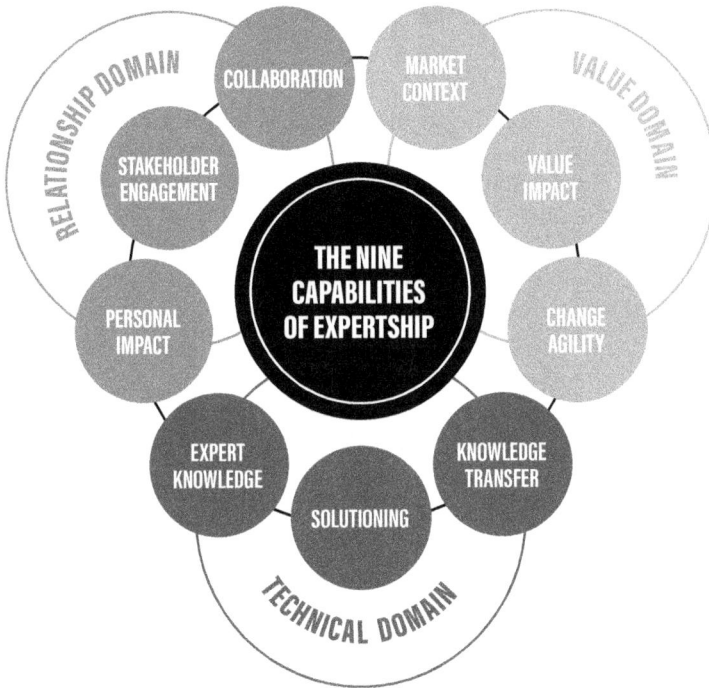

FIGURE 2.3: The Nine Capabilities of Expertship

The same could be said for the Expertship capability of Solutioning. Whenever there was a problem that was out of the ordinary or difficult to solve, Trevor was the person everyone went to for solutions. Similarly, when the business was trying to predict future challenges and problems, Trevor's input into future solutions was sought out enthusiastically. Trevor was known for being able to see round corners when it came to anticipating potential problems with applications and infrastructure in the future. Surely a Master Expert.

While it appears Trevor is on track to be rated Master Expert, it turns out that things aren't quite so rosy in the Relationship domain. Trevor took a close look at the behaviors described at Master Expert level under Stakeholder Engagement and identified that he operated only at the Expert level. He also noted that he was probably guilty of several derailers when it came to stakeholder engagement as he had poor external networks and could sometimes be "difficult to deal with." He concluded that he was operating only at Specialist level when it came to the Stakeholder Engagement capability.

Trevor was, in many ways, quite typical of what we regularly see. In the past few years, we have conducted over one thousand 360-degree multi-rater assessments using the Expertship model (the feedback tool is called *Expertship360*), and many of those assessed score strongly in the Technical domain capabilities, but less well in the Relationship domain capabilities. Typically, the lowest ratings are seen in the Market Context and Value Impact capabilities.

Trevor's example demonstrates that experts operate at different expert levels in different Expertship capabilities. Our overall rating is an average of all nine capabilities, and most of us need to be operating at Master Expert level in five or more capabilities to achieve the status of being a Master Expert, which is the very best expert we can be.

> *"Many hundreds of experts have increased the value they add, thereby accelerating their careers quickly and effectively."*

Interestingly, these results are independent of technical specialty (for example, IT or legal) and aren't typically affected by the industry (such as healthcare or financial services).

Until exposed to the Expertship model, most experts were unaware of the importance of the Market Context and Value Impact capabilities in ensuring they master their overall effectiveness as an expert. Without operating at a reasonably high level in these two capabilities, it's impossible to reach Master Expert level overall.

In each chapter that covers a specific Expertship capability, we offer you an opportunity to self-assess your level. In the final chapter of this book (Chapter 50), we describe how to build a Personal Growth Plan that helps you increase the level at which you operate, thus increasing your value to your organization and your marketability to other organizations.

This may sound complicated and a lot like hard work, but it really isn't. Many hundreds of experts have successfully navigated this path, quickly accelerating their careers and considerably boosting the value they add.

The Structure of the Expertship Model

EXPERTS WORK IN HIGHLY complex environments, so you might expect the Expertship model to be reasonably complex as well.

We've already introduced you to the three domains of Expertship: Technical, Value and Relationship (Figure 2.1). We have also, in Figure 2.3 illustrated the nine associated capabilities, three each under each domain.

In order to help experts understand the precise behaviors required on the journey to mastery, the final level of granularity in the model is the expert roles. In total, there are 27, and each capability has three of these expert roles. You'll see them listed in Figure 2.4 under the relevant capability.

In this book, 27 of the chapters are devoted to an in-depth look at each of these expert roles, focusing on their importance and the skills that are required to fulfill them. In each of these chapters, we list detailed actions that experts can take to build their mastery in these roles.

Behaviors Set the Standard

THE EXPERTSHIP MODEL IS designed to provide experts with an objective assessment tool. When we first start working with experts, most tell us that very few conversations take place between themselves and their managers about levels of performance. Both the experts and their managers tell us they need a properly researched and validated guideline of what unsatisfactory (derailers), good (Expert level) and outstanding capabilities (Master Expert level) look like.

As you will see as you progress through this book, we're very specific about the core behaviors that are considered Expert level and those that are considered Master Expert. The model provides an objective assessment because the real test is binary. We can ask ourselves "Do I do this consistently, or not?" Phrases like "I'm quite good at this" are eliminated.

A prime example is Angela. She is an expert we worked with early in our Expertship journey. She worked in information technology teams. Angela considered herself a strong collaborator, but she reported ongoing frustration because despite her wanting to collaborate with others, they didn't seem to want to collaborate with her.

The Expertship Model – A Roadmap for Master Experts

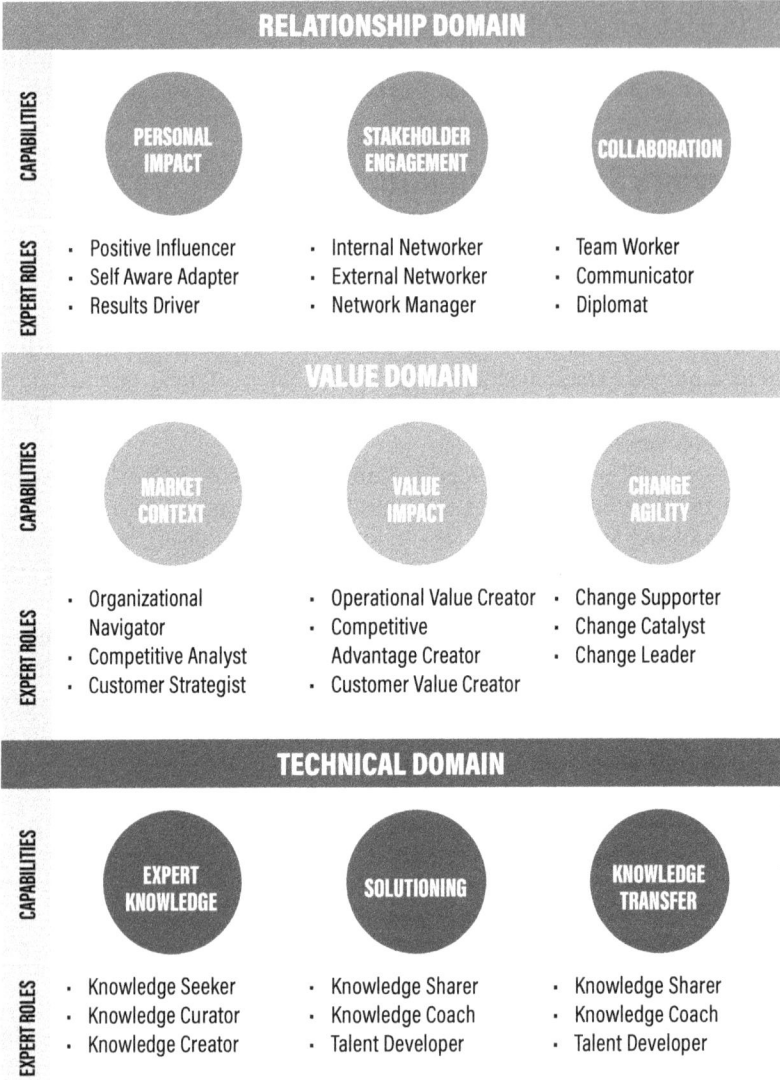

RELATIONSHIP DOMAIN

CAPABILITIES

PERSONAL IMPACT

STAKEHOLDER ENGAGEMENT

COLLABORATION

EXPERT ROLES

- Positive Influencer
- Self Aware Adapter
- Results Driver

- Internal Networker
- External Networker
- Network Manager

- Team Worker
- Communicator
- Diplomat

VALUE DOMAIN

CAPABILITIES

MARKET CONTEXT

VALUE IMPACT

CHANGE AGILITY

EXPERT ROLES

- Organizational Navigator
- Competitive Analyst
- Customer Strategist

- Operational Value Creator
- Competitive Advantage Creator
- Customer Value Creator

- Change Supporter
- Change Catalyst
- Change Leader

TECHNICAL DOMAIN

CAPABILITIES

EXPERT KNOWLEDGE

SOLUTIONING

KNOWLEDGE TRANSFER

EXPERT ROLES

- Knowledge Seeker
- Knowledge Curator
- Knowledge Creator

- Knowledge Sharer
- Knowledge Coach
- Talent Developer

- Knowledge Sharer
- Knowledge Coach
- Talent Developer

FIGURE 2.4: The 27 Expert Roles of Expertship

Angela decided to focus on the expert role of Communicator from the Collaboration capability. Angela examined the behaviors described at each level in the expert role (Chapter 24, *Next Level Communication*). We have reproduced the behavior chart in Figure 2.5. She concluded, as a self-assessment, that she was operating at the Expert level.

Angela recognized that she probably didn't listen to others as much as she could, and she certainly didn't use storytelling techniques. She also reflected that she probably used a quite directive and telling communication style in project meetings, rather than the consultative and inclusive communication style recommended in the behavior chart. Angela was also concerned that she was seen by others as opinionated and close-minded because she was clear about what she wanted everyone to do for her. This behavior was listed as a derailer in the model.

Angela had never previously seen behaviors listed as they are in the behavior chart, so she had not self-assessed against them. She had previously considered herself to be operating at a very high level as a communicator but could now see there were significant opportunities for her to master more advanced communication skills, which would make her a much more effective expert and colleague.

Working with her coach, Angela shaped a Personal Growth Plan to begin to address the issues her self-assessment had identified.

In each of the chapters that relate directly to an expert role, you'll see a behavior chart like the one above. This enables you to self-assess against the highest level of behavior, Master Expert, and then consider what actions you can take to reach that level. This book is designed to be actionable, so in each of these chapters, we make several suggestions as to things experts can do to build their skills in each of these roles.

We have also published a more detailed Expertship Growth Guide that lists more than 100 growth opportunities in far more detail than we're able to go into in this book. This publication is available for sale from our website, *expertship.com*.

In the next chapter, we'll provide some advice on how to quickly extract value from this book.

Capability: COLLABORATION
Expert Role: COMMUNICATOR

MASTER EXPERT

- Brings to life complex technical concepts/terms via compelling storytelling in accessible language.
- Inspires and consults, promoting inclusive processes whereby everyone is heard.
- In-demand presenter across the organization and externally due to their ability to combine technical and business concepts.
- Advanced listening skills.
- Embraces diversity of thought when discussing complex issues.
- Communicates assertively, balancing courage with consideration.

EXPERT

- Translates technical concepts/terms into practical and accessible language to increase others' comprehension.
- Employs a variety of influencing techniques to gain commitment to ideas and plans.
- Takes the lead in delivering effective presentations on behalf of function.
- Good listening skills.

SPECIALIST

- Communicates predominantly using technical language.
- Uses rational and policy arguments when influencing technical groups; rarely consults with the wider organization.
- Rarely takes the lead in technical presentations

- Communicates almost exclusively using technical language/jargon.
- Favors rational persuasion as primary influencing strategy.
- Comes across as closed-minded and opinionated, either by talking far more than listening or by being non-communicative.

DERAILING

FIGURE 2.5: Detailed Behaviors for Communicators

TAKING ACTION

Growing Our Expertship

THINKING ABOUT EXPERTSHIP IN general, here is a suggestion for an action you might wish to take to build your Expertship skills:

▶ ANALYZE THE BEST OF YOUR COLLEAGUES

Most of us are lucky enough to have worked with experts who are exemplary professionals and have the respect of, and ability to influence, not just their technical peers but many senior non-technical colleagues across the organization. They are Master Experts. We might ask ourselves:

- How do they do it? What specific behaviors, skills, or even mindsets do these Master Experts deploy to achieve this impact and influence?
- What knowledge do they possess and leverage that I don't have?
- In which particular areas of the Expertship model do they excel? Which behaviors seem to have the most impact (particularly among our non-technical colleagues)?

This analysis can be extremely valuable if it's ongoing. Careful observation can help us discern what it is that these Master Experts do differently that we can learn from. The braver of those among us might even ask these Master Experts to mentor us.

CHAPTER 03

How to Get the Best From This Book

Which chapters should you read, and why?

In this chapter, we will explore:

- Why this is a big book and how to navigate it successfully.
- How to self-assess and then pick the chapters and topics that are most immediately relevant to you.
- How scanning the pictures isn't cheating but actually a good idea!

THIS BOOK IS STRUCTURED into separate sections dealing with each of the nine capabilities.

You don't have to read them in the order we have set. In fact, readers are encouraged to investigate the various capabilities in the order that they feel are most relevant to them and offer the most immediate opportunities for professional growth. But in order to do that, you need to know what each of these capabilities and expert roles is about, so we've created a quick summary in this chapter to help you decide where to start.

We also encourage you to look at the chapters on the areas where you feel you're already very competent. Our experience from working with hundreds of experts is that many of us aren't quite as expert as we think we are, or we discover there are opportunities to become more expert that we had not previously considered, even in areas we believe to be our strengths. Expert Knowledge is a particlarly good example of this (Chapter 38).

This Book is Big—and Here's Why

THE WORLD OF EXPERTS is complex, and there's a long list of things experts have to be good at to do an excellent job. It's our hope that many thousands of experts will read this book, and each one of you will have your own unique needs. So, in order to make this book valuable for everyone, we've decided to be really comprehensive in covering the skills experts need to master on their way to adopting Master Expert behaviors.

However, the good news is that the book is designed so that each of the chapters can stand alone and can be read in any order. Each chapter has an "In this Chapter, We Will Explore" introduction, which enables you to very quickly scan through and find the topics you're most interested in. You can also flick through the book and look at the charts. A picture paints a thousand words, so if one piques your interest, you can quickly read the accompanying sections of text. As executive coaches, the authors do this all the time!

We encourage all of the experts we work with to identify and start with what is often referred to as the "low-hanging fruit." These are the three or four capabilities that, with little effort, offer opportunities to add a lot more value. At least one of these opportunities should be building on an existing strength (such as teaching others how to do something we excel in). Others will be gaps in our skills that could be quickly addressed for maximum advantage.

Taking into account the context of your role, your aspirations to add more value in particular areas, and the size and disposition of your organization, this list of opportunities will be different for every expert.

Certain opportunities will jump out at you as quick wins. Others may appear to be opportunities that will take time and effort to master but will provide a long-term career advantage. Most Personal Growth Plans are a rich combination of both.

Every one of these capabilities is examined in detail in the relevant chapter, and suggestions are offered on how to build upon an existing strength or build a capability up to Master Expert level.

So, here is a 10-minute overview of everything in the book.

THE RELATIONSHIP DOMAIN

THE RELATIONSHIP DOMAIN HAS three capabilities: Personal Impact, Stakeholder Engagement, and Collaboration (Figure 3.1).

	RELATIONSHIP DOMAIN		
CAPABILITIES	**PERSONAL IMPACT**	**STAKEHOLDER ENGAGEMENT**	**COLLABORATION**
EXPERT ROLES	· Positive Influencer · Self Aware Adapter · Results Driver	· Internal Networker · External Networker · Network Manager	· Team Worker · Communicator · Diplomat

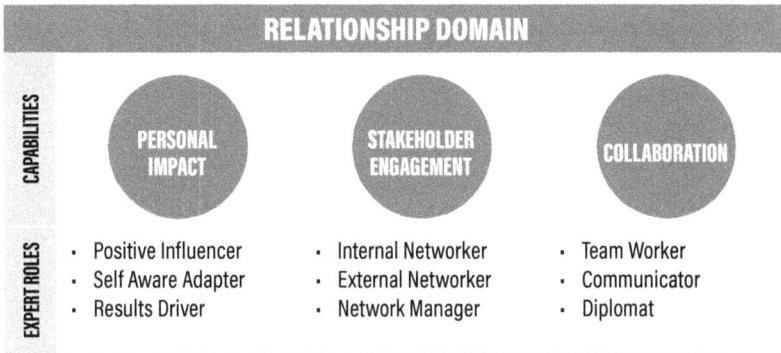

FIGURE 3.1: The Relationship Domain, Capabilities and Expert Roles

Personal Impact

THE CAPABILITY OF PERSONAL Impact deals with the ability of the expert to effectively influence others positively, their self-awareness of the impact they have on others, their empathetic and adaptive demeanor, and their ability to make individual and collective results happen. The three expert roles are:
- **Positive Influencer**: makes positive contributions, avoids cynical and disengaged behavior, and is inspiring and warm, with a can-do attitude.
- **Self-Aware Adapter**: is aware of their position within the organizational context, very aware of their personal impact on others, and is caring.
- **Results Driver**: demonstrates a results orientation, combining advanced prioritization and on-time delivery of agreed outcomes and value.

Chapters 4 to 11 explore these roles and the behaviors that underpin them.

Stakeholder Engagement

THE CAPABILITY OF STAKEHOLDER Engagement deals with how the expert has to build and maintain mutually rewarding stakeholder relationships across a variety of internal and external stakeholder groups. The three expert roles are:
- **Internal Networker**: develops a large and diverse network of stakeholders and colleagues across the organization, both locally and globally.

- **External Networker:** develops a high-quality external network that's multi-lens and transformational.
- **Network Manager:** is effective and efficient at managing and maintaining a large network of colleagues and stakeholders and is proactive and strategic in doing so.

Chapters 12 to 18 explore these roles and the behaviors that underpin them.

Collaboration

THE CAPABILITY OF COLLABORATION deals with the ability of the expert to act as a valuable, proactive member of their teams, whether virtual or co-located, and their ability to take on a leadership role when required and appropriate. The three roles:

- **Team Worker:** is a culturally effective team player, from local and technical to global and organizational.
- **Communicator:** displays advanced communication skills, ranging from rational influence and technical descriptions to sophisticated influencing skills, along with both technical and business fluency.
- **Diplomat:** enables fast and informed decision-making, manages negotiations, all while taking a facilitative leadership approach and supporting win-win prioritization and outcomes.

Chapters 19 to 25 explore these roles and the behaviors that underpin them.

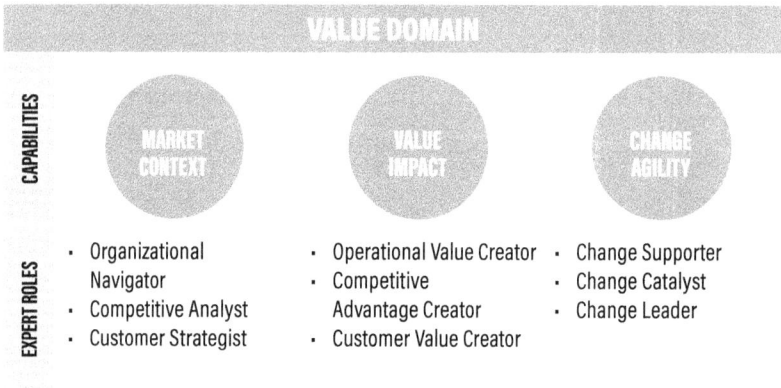

VALUE DOMAIN

CAPABILITIES

| MARKET CONTEXT | VALUE IMPACT | CHANGE AGILITY |

EXPERT ROLES

- Organizational Navigator
- Competitive Analyst
- Customer Strategist

- Operational Value Creator
- Competitive Advantage Creator
- Customer Value Creator

- Change Supporter
- Change Catalyst
- Change Leader

FIGURE 3.2: Value Domain—Capabilities and Expert Roles

THE VALUE DOMAIN

THE VALUE DOMAIN COVERS areas such as:

- Understanding the context in which your organization operates and the trends and pressures that impact its operation.
- Understanding, where relevant, the competitive environment of your organization. This includes your organization's strengths and vulnerabilities in comparison to rival organizations. In the public service sector, this often means identifying alternative services the community use as a substitute and the impact this might have on your organization.
- Understanding how internal and external customers choose what products and services to buy and consume, and why.
- Being curious and very informed about future trends on all of the above aspects of market context, and thereby being able to operate strategically and long term by developing plans and initiatives that position your organization for future success.

The Value domain has three capabilities to be mastered. These are Market Context, Value Impact, and Change Agility (see Figure 3.2).

Market Context

THE CAPABILITY OF MARKET Context deals with the ability of the expert to acquire, retain, refresh and deploy contextual, organizational, competitive and customer knowledge consistently and effectively. The three roles:

- **Organizational Navigator:** understands and traverses the entire organization and makes contributions at departmental, organization-wide and, where relevant, global levels.
- **Competitive Analyst:** understands the competitive landscape from a broad external business and community perspective.
- **Customer Strategist:** deploys customer-centric thinking and action that's applied to both internal and external customers, as well as those who are current, prospective, and future customers.

Chapters 26 to 29 explore these roles and the behaviors that underpin them.

Value Impact

THE CAPABILITY OF VALUE Impact deals with the ability of the expert to articulate and realize tangible ways of adding commercial or community value, thus demonstrating an active engagement in improving overall organizational performance. The three roles:

- **Operational Value Creator**: creates real value, ranging from incremental technical initiatives to organization-wide efficiencies.
- **Competitive Advantage Creator**: creates a real competitive advantage, ranging from incremental change initiatives to breakthrough initiatives.
- **Customer Value Creator**: creates value for customers and stakeholders, ranging from internal customer value-adds through to external customer value breakthroughs.

Chapters 30 to 33 explore these roles and the behaviors that underpin them.

Change Agility

THE CAPABILITY OF CHANGE Agility deals with the ability of the expert to act as a change catalyst and lead change initiatives effectively. The three roles:

- **Change Supporter**: champions productive change, avoids a closed and negative mindset, and instead embraces change constructively and positively.
- **Change Catalyst**: generates organizational change initiatives and acts as a catalyst to make things happen.
- **Change Leader**: leads change initiatives where required and inspires and manages teams through change.

Chapters 34 to 37 explore these roles and the behaviors that underpin them.

THE TECHNICAL DOMAIN

THE TECHNICAL DOMAIN COVERS areas such as:

The Technical domain has three capabilities to be mastered. These are Knowledge Expert, Solutioning, and Knowledge Transfer (see Figure 3.3).

TECHNICAL DOMAIN

	EXPERT KNOWLEDGE	SOLUTIONING	KNOWLEDGE TRANSFER
CAPABILITIES			
EXPERT ROLES	• Knowledge Seeker • Knowledge Curator • Knowledge Creator	• Knowledge Sharer • Knowledge Coach • Talent Developer	• Knowledge Sharer • Knowledge Coach • Talent Developer

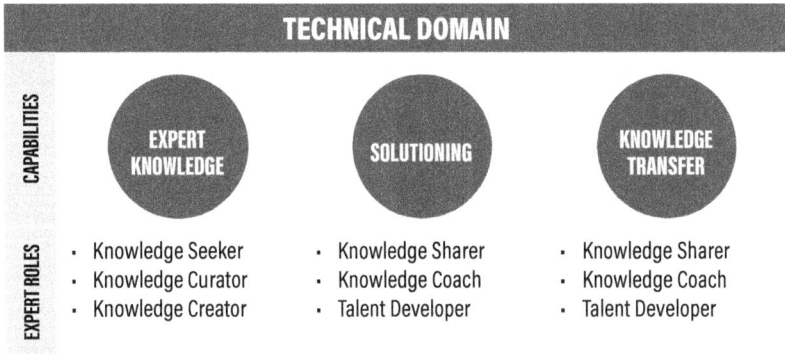

FIGURE 3.3: Technical Domain—Capabilities and Expert Roles

Knowledge Expert

THE CAPABILITY OF KNOWLEDGE Expert deals with how experts acquire, retain and grow the deep specialist knowledge and experience they require to do their jobs effectively. This is more complicated and requires more deliberate effort than most experts allocate.

If your knowledge is all inside your head, then you're definitely not operating at Master Expert level. Rather, you're a single-point-of-failure risk for your organization and colleagues. The three roles:

- **Knowledge Seeker**: ensures that the organization has correct and up-to-date knowledge in their technical domain.
- **Knowledge Curator**: makes sure that the relevant knowledge is readily available in accessible versions to stakeholders and colleagues who need it.
- **Knowledge Creator**: takes existing knowledge and experience and leverages insights into new knowledge.

Solutioning

THE CAPABILITY OF SOLUTIONING deals with the ability of the expert to solve complex technical problems effectively and quickly via insightful diagnosis, shaping long-term solutions that improve processes and create opportunities. The three roles:

- **Problem Identifier**: understands where and why problems occur by deploying objective and complex analysis.
- **Active Responder**: responds at an appropriate speed to requests, is proactive rather than reactive, and predicts where requests will come from, and why.
- **Problem Solver**: sees problems through to resolution and works toward delivering long-term, organization-wide solutions.

Chapters 42 to 45 describe these roles and the behaviors that underpin them.

Knowledge Transfer

THE CAPABILITY OF KNOWLEDGE Transfer deals with developing increased expertise in others and encouraging the application of this specialist knowledge to facilitate overall increased organizational capability. The three roles:

- **Knowledge Sharer**: ensures knowledge is disseminated effectively across the organization to the relevant parties.
- **Knowledge Coach**: helps colleagues understand and make best use of our (the expert's) specialist knowledge.
- **Talent Developer**: ensures that both ourselves and our colleagues are involved in continuous learning and we actively identify and develop future talent.

Chapters 46 to 49 explore these roles and the behaviors that underpin them.

TAKING ACTION

Growing Our Expertship

THINKING ABOUT EXPERTSHIP IN general, here is a suggestion for actions you might wish to take to build your Expertship skills:

▶ CALCULATE YOUR GROWTH OPPORTUNITIES

Having read the above outline, if you're still no wiser as to where to start reading, then here is a suggestion: on our website, at *expertship.com/ growth*, we have constructed a simple Growth Calculator. It allows you to answer some questions and receive a report that helps you identify the most important capabilities to master first. It's a password-protected tool, so you'll need to have purchased this book to access the calculator.

PART | 02 |

THE RELATIONSHIP DOMAIN

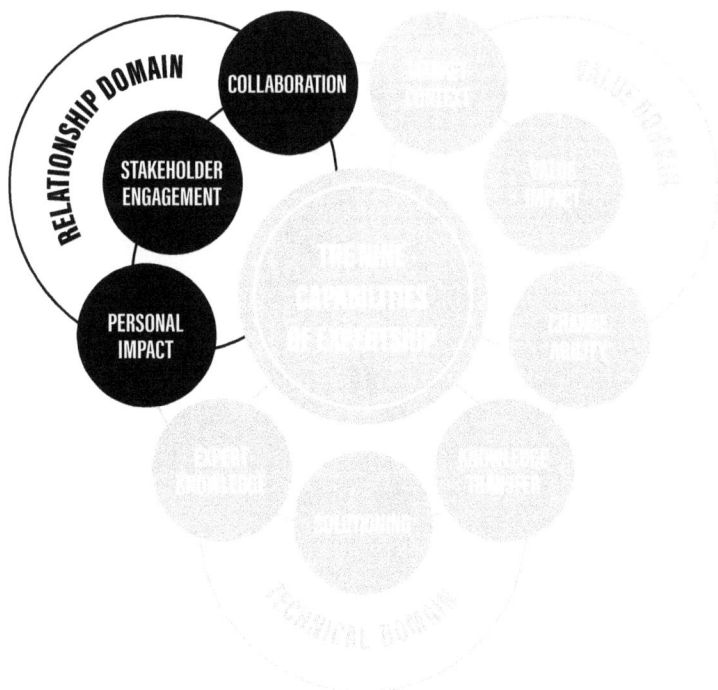

"The MASTER EXPERT influences people positively, is self-aware, empathetic and adaptive, and makes individual and collective results happen.**"**

MASTERING PERSONAL IMPACT

RELATIONSHIP DOMAIN

COLLABORATION

STAKEHOLDER ENGAGEMENT

PERSONAL IMPACT

"When dealing with people, remember you are not dealing with creatures of logic, but creatures of emotion."

Dale Carnegie

CHAPTER | 04 |

Exploring Our Personal Brand

How do our colleagues experience us? Should we care?

IN THIS CHAPTER, WE WILL EXPLORE:

- What is a personal brand, and how is it formed? Which information sources are perceived to be the most credible, and why?
- Why should what colleagues think of us matter? What difference does it make to our work as experts? How do we understand how others see us? How do we conduct a personal brand audit?
- How long does it take to change our personal brand?
- How can we shape a brand that will enable us to optimize our impact and influence?

WE SPEND PLENTY OF time later in this book exploring what makes colleagues or stakeholders tick—particularly those who we need to engage with and influence so we can produce more effective outcomes.

In this early chapter, the focus is on *ourselves*. Looking from the inside out, we form opinions about those we work with. Are they "good" to work with (and we'll explore what "good" means more precisely in these pages)? Are they reliable? Do they know what they're talking about? Do they work well with others? Do they have the right connections to get things done? The combination of all of these factors makes up what we think of them. It's their personal brand.

Whether we like it or not, we all have a personal brand. It's what people think of us, not how we think of ourselves. Our personal brand might be something we've intentionally cultivated and designed, but it's more likely to have grown organically from people's experiences of us.

> *"Your brand is what people say about you when*
> *you are not in the room."*
> *- Jeff Bezos -*

In Figure 4.1, we explore the information sources that our colleagues and stakeholders depend on to assess our personal brand. The graphic was compiled using data from hundreds of experts who were asked this question. We asked participants to list and then categorize the information sources that their colleagues use to determine who they are and what they are like (their *personal brand*). We then ask participants to identify and assess the most important sources of information—that is, those they rely on most and perceive as the most credible.

As we can see from the graphic, experts, just like everyone else, assess others based on their interpretation of a variety of things. Like all of us, experts have many sources to choose from, such as others' behavior, interests, perceived motives, capabilities, apparent priorities, and their reputation. We all take into account how those we're assessing speak and dress and *their* interpretation of others' motives and interests. These impressions shape how everyone relates to their colleagues.

Some information sources are far more important than others. In the graphic, the larger the circle, the more important that information source is. You can see that we have described the sources as either firsthand (we have directly experienced the person), secondhand (we have heard from someone who directly experienced that person) or thirdhand (we have heard a report from someone we don't know who experienced that person). By definition, when we hear secondhand or thirdhand experiences, we're getting a filtered version of what happened. It's colored by the preconceptions, values and standards of the person or persons providing that information.

Hearsay is quite influential. Before experts have personally seen their colleagues in action, it's the closest source of information, particularly if the hearsay is coming from a colleague we know to be reliable and to have sensible judgment. But this is still secondhand knowledge. Thirdhand knowledge (typically "media") is reliable only to the extent that we believe the source to be credible. People's direct, firsthand experiences with us are always at the top of the credible and to-be-believed list.

Capability: PERSONAL IMPACT

Personal Brand: HOW DO COLLEAGUES JUDGE US?

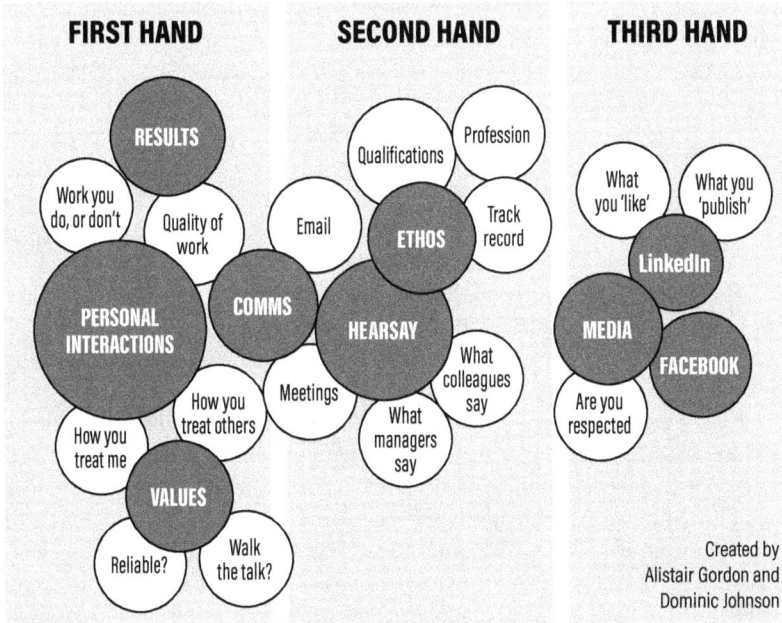

FIGURE 4.1: Sources of Information for Our Personal Brand

The natural cynicism of experts comes to the fore when we ask them how much of what people write about themselves on LinkedIn, for example, they take at face value (Answer: not much.) If the *Wall Street Journal* wrote an article about us, most of our colleagues would consider this highly credible. On the other hand, if our local paper runs a puff piece about our good work cleaning up a beach nearby, our colleagues might pat us on the back but tell us that it was probably a slow news week.

> *"Email turns out to be a major factor in what we think of someone's personal brand."*

Easily, the most meaningful and convincing source of information is the evidence our colleagues see with their own eyes. It might be a little scary to think about this, but when we're on show, our colleagues are making lasting judgments about us. Were we rude to Judy by putting her and her opinion down aggressively? That's seen as a negative. If someone else was putting Judy down, did we step in and make sure we discussed the idea, not attack the person who suggested it? That would typically be seen as a positive. When we last promised to deliver something for Jack by Friday afternoon, did we follow through? A positive. Or did we make a list of excuses, which let Jack down and put his project behind schedule? That's a negative, particularly so if Jack was not convinced by the excuses.

When we discussed with participants what they "know" about particular celebrities, this "seen it with our own eyes" phenomenon really comes into focus. People are more inclined to judge someone by what they have seen them do, rather than what magazines and tabloid television are telling us they did. With the popularity of video-based social media platforms and YouTube, it's pretty easy to take a long look at someone in action and make our own mind up about their authenticity and values.

In the workplace, we're constantly on show and our colleagues are judging us by how we treat them and others, the quality of our work, whether we do what we say we're going to do, whether we walk our talk, and how we communicate, both verbally and digitally, with others.

In our Expertship programs, we find that email turns out to be a major factor in how we perceive someone's personal brand, because so much of our communication with colleagues these days is electronic. HP did a study several years ago that proved most people can't interpret the tone of an email correctly. The study showed respondents were wrong as often as they were right, but most people we have worked with believe they can accurately spot whether someone is being rude, direct or dismissive in an email. Whether this is true or not isn't relevant. These judgments, correct or otherwise, contribute positively or negatively to our personal brands.

Auditing Our Personal Brand

A QUESTION FOR US to consider when we think about our personal impact (and the impact we aspire to) is: how are we currently doing? In other words, how self-aware are we of the impact we currently have on others?

In our programs, we ask experts to consider the three boxes described in Figure 4.2, the Personal Brand Audit.

Box 1 in this graphic asks us to consider what we think our personal brand is. This judgment is made based on what we currently know. We always ask participants to complete this exercise (and we invite you to do so now as well) after examining the information sources our colleagues use to determine their view of us. How have we behaved in recent meetings? Were we overly critical of a colleague in public recently? Have we visibly gone out of our way to help someone recently? Did the conflict we had with a project manager get wider airplay than we might have imagined or wanted?

Capability: PERSONAL IMPACT

Personal Brand Audit

1

**What I THINK
my current
personal brand is**

2

**What I KNOW
my current
personal brand is**

3

**What I DESIRE
my current
personal brand to be**

FIGURE 4.2: A Personal Brand Audit

Notes made in this box aren't about what we would *like* our personal brand to be. Instead, we have to see ourselves through the eyes and experiences of others. It's a look in the mirror. This exercise in self-reflection is a critical success factor for executives everywhere, but it's particularly important for experts, as we typically believe that our technical excellence is the main contributor to our personal brand. This is only part of the equation, however. Just as important is the impact we have on others. The key question to consider is: how informed am I about the impact I am having? We're constantly reviewing the impact others have on us, but are we putting ourselves under the same spotlight as often?

One way of auditing oneself is to take a look at the traits listed in Figure 4.3. This data is from a range of surveys the authors have conducted over the years to gather feedback from the wider organization about how they experience poor and good experts. The list provides a useful checklist for us to consider how we're likely to be viewed by stakeholders beyond our own technical cohort.

Some of the positive aspects in this list are particularly challenging for experts.

Are we really open-minded, for example, when we're presented with something that challenges what is widely accepted in our domain? Are we open-minded when a colleague offers a "gut feeling" or is such a notion quickly dismissed as not being based on data?

Do we really operate with an organizational focus, or are we too entrenched in our technical bubble? Do we generously give up our time to gently mentor and coach more junior colleagues? Or are we just too busy and senior, so we provide advice in an expedient and grumpy manner because we're irritated by the interruption? Given that we're experts and we know best, do we really demonstrate humility?

> *"Is it true that experts are very poor at receiving and listening to feedback?"*

Succession planning is of particular importance. Many experts assume that their organization values them *only* for their technical capability and experience, so they actively hoard knowledge rather than sharing it in order to maintain their hegemony.

Being seen as a technical guru in our own technical group, but as an arrogant, unhelpful and rude colleague beyond our own department isn't the personal brand we want to have. The opinions of stakeholders for whom we're supposed to be adding value are probably more important than those of our technical peers.

Capability: **PERSONAL IMPACT**

How Experts are Experienced

NARROW SPECIALIST	MASTER EXPERT
· Close-minded	· Open-minded
· Grudgingly helpful	· Keen to help
· Knowledge hoarding	· Knowledge sharing
· Superior	· Humility
· Negative about past	· Creating a better future
· Dispersed knowledge	· Centralized knowledge
· Supplier	· Partner
· Technician	· Colleague
· Telling, advising	· Mentoring, coaching
· Tight technical network	· Multi-disciplinary network
· Depowering	· Empowering
· Maintaining dependence	· Building independence
· Forever	· Succession planning
· Technical focus	· Organizational focus
· Defined by knowledge and expertise	· Defined by creating great outcomes
· Technical awareness and thinking	· Commercial awareness and thinking

FIGURE 4.3: How Experts Are Experienced

This runs contrary to the typical but self-serving idea that the views of our technical sisters and brothers are more important than those of the wider organization because they're more informed about what we do. Our technical family is more informed about the technical capabilities we have, but they're usually much less informed than stakeholders in the wider organization about our enterprise capabilities and the value we're actually creating for the organization.

Once we're in an objective state of mind to conduct this task, experts are usually quite self-aware of our own existing personal brand. There are some blind spots, of course (things that others know about us that we don't see), but in general, experts can accurately identify 80 percent of their existing personal brand.

Box 2 in Figure 4.2 is for capturing what our personal brand *actually* is. It isn't possible for us to complete this box independently. We have to depend on feedback from others to populate it. In most of our expert programs, we conduct what is called a 360-degree survey. This is where we (as participants) invite a range of stakeholders and colleagues to provide feedback in a structured manner, based on a series of questions, on how well we're performing in their eyes. In our particular tool, *Expertship360*, the questions are based on the Expertship model that forms the basis of this book.

There is a myth we hear expressed more often than we would like: that experts don't like and respond negatively to feedback. The authors' experience, and indeed those of the various Expertship coaches we work with, is very much the opposite. We've found experts to be open, analytical, and keen to understand feedback from these tools. Very often, they tell us that this is the first structured feedback they have ever had (most 360-degree surveys measure the effectiveness of people leaders and therefore feel misaligned when used on experts).

Those positing that experts are dismissive of feedback from others are perhaps confusing their reaction to ad-hoc, uninformed commentary, which all experts are sometimes subjected to. Experts' reactions to this type of feedback are typically negative. In the authors' experience, however, experts' responses to properly structured, reliable and comprehensive data are usually very open and proactive. They consider these data to be "news they can use."

Feedback can be much more informal than using a structured tool, of course. Informal feedback can be gained by asking the same few questions to a range of colleagues. "Expertship excellence, it turns out, gets noticed. Master Experts are always in demand."

> *"Expertship excellence, it turns out, gets noticed.*
> *Master Experts are always in demand."*

Box 2, when properly populated from valid sources, will show us the gap between what we *think* our personal brand is and what it *actually* is.

In our experience, there is no consistent theme to describe this gap. Sometimes, experts are too hard on themselves and are pleasantly surprised by positive feedback from stakeholders. Other times, they discover that activities they consider themselves very proficient in are being assessed quite differently by their stakeholders. Often, different groups of stakeholders have quite different opinions: the technical cohort report that Jack is tremendously good at solutioning, while the removed stakeholders, those out in the business who are the eventual recipients of the value we create, report that the solutions that are vanilla and lack value. These differences of opinion are always explored carefully and typically provide some very useful insights.

Box 3 in Figure 4.2 is perhaps the most interesting. It describes what we *desire* our brand to be. In our experience, the experts we work with almost always have something new and challenging in this box that isn't contained in Box 1. This, by the way, is true for all of the executives we've worked with, whether they're experts or not. Take a few minutes to think about what you might add to this box. If you're struggling, think about what your answers to these questions might be:

- What would I desire my colleagues to say about me at my leaving party? Which colleagues and stakeholders would I want to be keen to stand up and say something positive about me?
- What legacy would I like to leave for my colleagues, team and department? What would I want people to remember about me when I am no longer in the picture?

By way of an example, the authors have asked themselves the same question about readers at the conclusion of reading this book.

What would we like you to take away as a consequence of investing your valuable time into reading this text? How will you remember the experience? How long will you remember the experience? By getting clarity about what the "end game" is for us personally, we can check whether we're on track as we write each chapter. We can also step back and look at this text holistically and ask "Is this good enough to ensure we achieve our objective?"

As experts going about our day-to-day work for our organization, we can ask similar questions. Did that meeting create lasting value? Did I mentor that junior associate in such a way that the lesson will stay with them for a long time and help them with their career? Did that stakeholder hugely benefit from my interaction with them, and consequently, will his/her memory of me be positive and enduring?

Our questions here relate to the long game: what do I want my brand to be at some undefined stage in the future? You might wish to choose a shorter horizon. By the end of the year, or even the end of the quarter, what do I want people to say about me? Regardless of the time horizon you choose, you can begin to work on building a positive personal brand immediately.

Remember that your "leaving party" might be to move to a new role within the same organization, and that event might not be as far away as you think. This will be particularly true if you can make the transformation to Master Expert, as everyone wants a Master Expert on their team or project. A large proportion of those who have attended our Expertship programs have ended up working in new areas, or on larger projects, or have taken on new responsibilities. Expertship excellence gets noticed.

Building Our Self-Awareness

RICHARD FEELS READY FOR a promotion. He feels he's a natural choice for the role of technical team leader. He's the most experienced technician, with the most significant depth and breadth of expertise.

What he's not aware of is that he's viewed by his manager and stakeholders as being excessively negative. Consequently, he's the last person they would ever think of appointing to a team leadership role. Additionally, they were also sure, given his attitude toward existing managers, that Richard wouldn't want such a role. How did Richard end up with such a reputation?

Richard's reputation has developed over a number of years as a direct result of his behavior. His nickname is "Mr Negative." Richard expresses negativity on a consistent basis, constantly worrying about impossible deadlines, technical complications no one else has voiced, future issues that might be created if we take a short-term view of the solution, and so on. He's extremely bright, so he's highly skilled at destroying others' ideas and suggestions with rapier-like clinical, rational arguments.

Richard considers his own opinion so obviously correct that he, without really realizing it, tends to be extremely dismissive of others' ideas and suggestions. This comes across to colleagues as plain arrogance. People who work with him have learned that if they don't want to have their ideas dismissed and criticized, then it's better to avoid him.

As far as project managers and Richard's own manager are concerned, he has generated a lack of trust. They couldn't confidently entrust him with the responsibility to execute a key responsibility because Richard is likely to focus on telling them about all the implementation challenges they're bound to encounter.

They don't think Richard believes he can deliver, so they worry that he won't. On occasions when Richard hasn't delivered, he tells people loudly that "the deadline was impossible, and he told them so." This is a further concern for the team leaders he works with because he's not taking ownership of issues and is quick to lay blame elsewhere.

"What do colleagues know about us that
we don't know about ourselves?"

Richard is the victim of his own lack of self-awareness. He fails to appreciate the links between his behavior and his reputation, which ultimately form his personal brand. While he might see himself as being a respected authority in his particular technical field, the rest of the ecosystem he works within doesn't place the same premium on his specialist knowledge. Instead, they identify him as being difficult to deal with based on their experience of Richard's attitudes and behaviors.

What should Richard do?

Richard, devastated to hear from his manager that he wouldn't be considered for the team leadership role, confided in a friend, Margot, who also did some part-time coaching.

Margot suggested they use a self-awareness tool called the Johari Window, which was created by psychologists Joseph Luft and Harrington Ingham in the early 1960s. We describe the Johari Window in Figure 4.4

The Johari Window consists of four quadrants. Quadrant 1, the area of open activity, refers to behavior and motivations known to both the self and others. It's the area that is open for all to see. In Richard's case, both Richard and those he works with can see his technical expertise and problem-solving skills.

Quadrant 2 is the blind area, where others can see things in us of which we're unaware. In Richard's case, others can see the impact his direct and challenging behaviors have on those he works with, while he cannot (he is blind to this).

Quadrant 3, the avoided or hidden area, represents things that we know about ourselves but which we don't reveal to others. Examples of this are hidden agendas, or perhaps matters about which we have sensitive feelings. In Richard's case, he's inwardly devastated to learn he isn't being considered for promotion, but he doesn't show these feelings to anyone (except Margot). To others, he comes across as not really caring one way or the other. Richard doesn't share his paralyzing fear of failure either, which accounts for quite a lot of his negative positioning around getting things done.

Quadrant 4 is the area of unknown activity—a mystery. Neither the individual nor others are aware of certain behaviors and motives.

Richard might have, for example, a deep-seated distrust of salespeople, but neither he nor others have realized this. Sometimes, there are strongly ingrained beliefs that underpin our behaviors, and these are just as surprising to us as they are to those who know us. One belief the authors identify in many experts is a lack of awareness about their self-confidence. For example, although wildly confident when talking about their technical domain, they can lack confidence when talking about themselves. In particular, they often dread discussing subjects where they might lack distinguished expertise, as if others will discover this and conclude that they're an imposter. Understanding why this is the case is often a breakthrough moment for experts on the journey to Master Expert.

Margot and Richard discussed how to populate quadrant 2. They agreed Richard would need to get some feedback. For quadrant 3, he would also need to explore what he knew about himself that others didn't, and whether or not that might be useful to disclose.

Over the course of a few weeks and many informal discussions, where Richard found he had to work hard to get people to provide him with open and honest feedback, he learned about the way in which his colleagues typically experienced him. As he did so, quadrant 2 shrank and quadrant 1 expanded (see Figure 4.4).

With Margot's help, Richard began to realize that he was ambitious and wanted to progress from a career perspective, but this was something other people didn't know about him. One reason identified was that Richard was constantly so dismissive of people in authority that everyone assumed he didn't aspire to such a role.

Now significantly more self-aware, Richard began to think about how to learn to curb his more negative behaviors. He taught himself to find something positive to say, something genuine, about a colleague's point of view or suggested action before being critical or countering their idea. He worked hard to action many more questions about others' ideas before judging their idea and found, unexpectedly, that these ideas, once explored, had much more validity than he had previously believed.

In the past, he had been unaware of how often he interrupted people in order to make his own point, so he successfully stopped doing this. He asked some of his closest colleagues to point out to him when he did so, in public if necessary, and he found that he was able to change the habit more quickly than he might have imagined.

On the suggestion of his manager, Richard began mentoring and training some of the junior team members—something he would never have made time for in the past. His manager had positioned the suggestion as being an audition for whether, at some stage in the future, Richard could train and inspire a team. Knowing what was at stake, Richard threw himself into doing the best mentoring job he could.

As weeks turned into months, Richard's colleagues' perception of him slowly changed. They took a much more positive view of him for two reasons. Firstly, he was much more pleasant to be around and to work with as he was also showing real interest in what his colleagues were doing, as well as their opinions and ideas. And he was helping more junior people to develop. This was a positive change.

Secondly, his colleagues were impressed by the commitment, energy and determination that Richard was demonstrating by trying to make these changes. They saw him as someone who had asked for feedback and was then attempting to do something about the negative feedback he had received. Richard won their respect for the vigor he was deploying to be a more positive colleague. This is a phenomenon the authors see on a regular basis. It's not only the actual changes experts make to their behavior but the effort they put in that is respected by those around them.

The example of Richard leads us to several significant questions. Is our personal brand, whether consciously or unconsciously produced, delivering us the results we desire? Do people react favorably to our personal brand? Does our brand give us access to key people or privileged information that we need to excel in our role and create value? Does our personal brand bring us opportunities—or does it forever consign us to the role of technical specialist?

Capability: **PERSONAL IMPACT**

Johari Window: How well do we know ourselves?

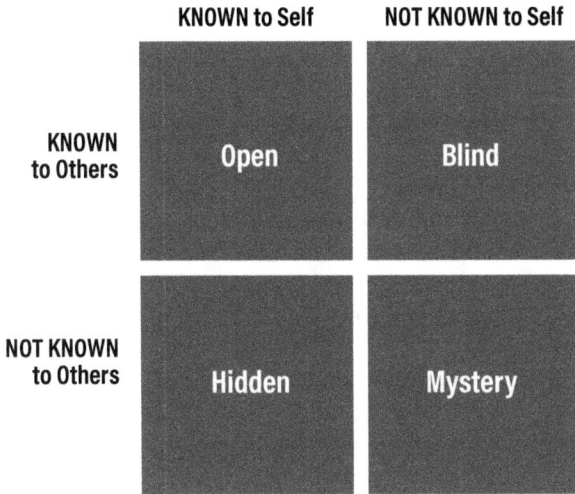

Created by Joe Luff and Harry Ingham

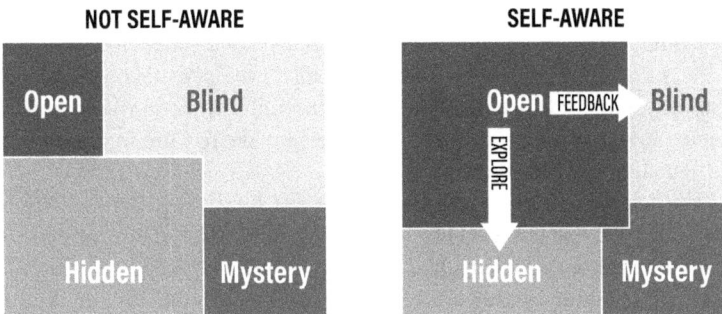

FIGURE 4.4: Johari Window—How Well Do We Know Ourselves?

And furthermore, is our desired personal brand genuine? If, for example, we want to be known as a helpful colleague, are we naturally helpful?

Brand Stereotypes

SOME PROFESSIONS OR ROLES come with their own brand associations. In the world of experts, these are often unhelpful stereotypes, like "all accountants are boring bean counters" or "all IT people are propeller heads with no people skills." Even if we're an expert in one of these stereotyped roles and we're not thought of in such ways, we still need to consciously work on fostering a more positive brand.

Many of these stereotypes are subconscious. Our colleagues won't realize they're assuming, for example, to quote one common myth, that because we're in IT, we're not good with people. Or because we're in IT, we can immediately fix any technical problem our colleagues may have with any other type of technology.

We can contribute to these stereotypes, reinforcing others' existing perceptions, by using impenetrable technical jargon. Or, instead of wearing typical business attire, we might wear T-shirts and jeans, clothing that aligns us with our craft rather than our organization. The lack of business attire may convey a disinterest in being business-like or customer-focused. We might inadvertently convey that we're rebellious and more interested in being casual (or perhaps even slovenly) than focused.

Some of these clues also predispose our colleagues to a certain judgment of our importance and whether we're worth investing time with.

The impressions people form of us are developed unconsciously and organically, but we can help shape them through our actions and behavior. We need to determine the impression we would like to form in others' minds and then align our behaviors accordingly.

As an example, one of the experts we coached was a terrifically gifted coder in the IT department. He had very creative ideas about how to solve identified customer problems by developing some very clever software. Tim was a typical T-shirt, jeans, and very battered sneakers type of guy. And this was the attire he wore when he attended meetings to promote his ideas to more senior leaders in the business. He didn't get traction.

We asked Tim what was getting in the way of him accessing the resources he required, which time away from his main responsibilities. He developed a good list of the reasons, many being highly subjective ("they are idiots" or "they don't get it" and so on), and some being more measured ("I don't think they take me seriously" or "they don't actually see the value in what I am proposing").

With some re-thinking, Tim shaped his proposal to connect it to executing the new strategic drivers that had recently been introduced—the organization needed to be more customer-centric. Tim was able to show that his software would achieve this objective by improving the customer experience (speed and access) and also providing the organization with better customer data (which options interested the customers and which ones didn't). This addressed relevance and buy-in.

What wasn't addressed was the extent to which the senior leaders took Tim seriously and trusted him to execute an important business initiative. We asked Tim if he felt that the senior leaders saw him as one of them. Tim quickly identified that the way he dressed to attend these meetings was completely different from everyone else in the room.

Tim strenuously pushed back at changing his dress. He felt that it demonstrated bias and immaturity for senior leaders to "judge the book by its cover" as he put it. We explored why these leaders might not have trusted him, and he concluded that they erroneously didn't feel safe because he looked like he didn't care about how he looked. The senior leaders subconsciously connected this to sloppy work, which was, ironically, the most unlikely thing any of Tim's technical colleagues would ever say about him as his code was meticulous.

Eventually, Tim's commitment to moving his project forward outweighed his irritation at having to conform from a dress perspective. He didn't wear a suit and tie. Instead, he procured a business shirt and smart slacks, then proceeded to present his initiative professionally, connecting his idea to the organization's strategy. And as a final flourish, Tim banished any technical jargon from his presentation and used the language that repeatedly appeared in the organization's strategy documents. After several meetings, he eventually got approval to proceed.

> *"'Your reputation precedes you' has become a cliché."*

Some changes in our personal brand are relatively easy to notice and shift. For instance, if we start asking more high-level and business-oriented questions, people will form an impression that we're more commercially and strategically oriented and not a one-dimensional tech-head. But other changes dig more deeply into our core identity and motives. These require a more thorough level of analysis and possibly a reframing, such as exploring what intentions or motivations are prompting us and others to behave as we do.

Are Brands Personal?

WE USE THE PHRASE "personal brand" rather than "professional brand" for a good reason. It's easy to provide yourself with a glowing reference if you only look at your brand through a professional lens. "I have X years' experience. I am very competent at Y. I earn Z. I have seniority over A. I am on the Q project teams because my skills and knowledge are valuable to the business."

But our qualifications aren't our brand. They're merely a collection of information about us, usually from our perspective, that people may or may not be aware of or regard as significant. Our brand is what people who work with us see and feel. It's how they experience us, both as a colleague and as a human being.

They may or may not know we have a PhD in astrophysics, but they do know that we were considerate (or dismissive) to a colleague in a recent meeting when they disagreed with our point of view.

They may or may not know or care how many years' experience we have, and they may or may not consider this important. But they'll remember when a project team we were on was struggling and whether we offered to help or simply blamed others for the problems.

They may or may not recognize us as senior to them in the organization. They may or may not think this is important. But they'll remember how we responded when they asked us for our advice and whether we adopted a superior manner or guided them to the possible options to solve the problem.

We might assume that others will suspend judgment until they experience us directly, but they often meet us having heard quite a bit about us first. "Your reputation precedes you" has become a cliché.

If an expert has a major meltdown in a meeting and leaves the room yelling and screaming, how long does news of this event take to become widely known in the organization? A couple of minutes. How long does it take for people to forget the meltdown? Years, if ever.

We need to consider this when it comes to our personal brand. There is a saying that we're only as good as our last result. Four great results followed by a disaster means that the disaster is the current view, despite the fact that we've been successful 80 percent of the time. You might think that's not bad, but people remember the most recent 20 percent.

Most of our personal brands aren't consciously designed. They emerge over time based on others' aggregate experiences of us. They're often strongly shaped by certain significant events that take precedence over others. Our behaviors, the language we use, the quality of our work, and even our attire all combine to form a general picture in others' minds about who we are, what we do, what value we add, what we stand for, what they can expect from us, what we care about, and so on.

Personal brands can evolve positively over time as a consequence of a sustained and intentional effort, such as in Richard's case. Experts, like everyone else, are responsible for the impressions that people form about them over time. Master Experts always consciously work on behaving in a way that helps them achieve their ideal personal brand.

Progressing to Master Expert level typically involves giving increased attention to how you relate to others. It also relates to your attitude toward the organization's commercial realities. It involves a shift from being reactive to being proactive. A lot of it has to do with moving up the value chain and partnering with others in the organization.

TAKING ACTION

Growing Our Personal Impact

IF GROWING YOUR PERSONAL impact skills is something you think would benefit you, then here is a suggestion for action you might wish to take to build your Expertship skills:

▶ DELIBERATELY SHAPE A PERSONAL BRAND

As we have established in this chapter, we all have a brand, whether we have consciously fashioned it or it's simply the aggregate sense people have made of us. A positive brand ensures that people will relate to us in ways we would welcome. A negative brand will consistently undermine our optimal involvement and contributions. Questions we might want to ask ourselves:

- Have I assumed that my personal brand revolves solely around my subject matter expertise?
- Am I viewed as unidimensional—only interested in certain things?
- Am I known as arrogant and opinionated or as a pleasure to work with?
- Am I known as a valued and vital strategic contributor or simply a propeller-head with deep knowledge in only a narrow and specialized topic?
- How would I like my stakeholders and colleagues to think of me? What would I like them to say about me?
- To what extent is there a gap between what I want them to say and what they might currently say?

Most experts will discover a gap between their desired brand and current brand. They'll check the validity of their own assumptions by asking for feedback from colleagues. They'll make a short list of the new behaviors, knowledge, mindsets they need and set up a plan to develop these new capabilities in order to enhance their personal brand.

"In a very real sense, we have two minds, one that thinks and one that feels."

Daniel Goleman

CHAPTER | 05 |

The Brand Power of Emotional Intelligence

Can we combine factual objectivity with compassion and emotional understanding? Is it worth the effort?

IN THIS CHAPTER, WE WILL EXPLORE:

- What is emotional intelligence, and what impact does it have?
- Is emotional intelligence learnable?
- The key insight: there are six emotional intelligences.
- Barriers that experts face when it comes to taking into account feelings as well as facts.

LEAH IS A CORPORATE lawyer. Every time her organization enters into a contract, she needs to review the terms and sign them off. More than three-quarters of the time, there are issues with the proposed arrangements, which means she has to temporarily stop the deal from progressing until they've been fixed.

This makes Leah unpopular. But one of the reasons people leave it until the last minute to consult her, which is part of the problem, is that they find her clinical analysis of the agreement's faults to be soul-crushing.

Leah would prefer to be engaged earlier, and in particular, she would like to be involved in the initial negotiations as she believes she could prevent some of the problems that regularly occur. However, she's reconciled herself to the fact that last-minute consultations are merely an inalienable hazard of the work that she does. It's what she's paid to do.

"Can someone learn to be professionally likable?"

Stephanie, also a corporate lawyer, faces similar challenges but has worked hard to hone her interpersonal skills. Working with a coach, she has refined a way of letting her clients down softly. Rather than issuing a blunt "No," followed by a clinical description of how the proposed terms are faulty and unacceptable, Stephanie now resists judgment and schedules time to talk further with the stakeholders to understand what they're trying to achieve with the contract. She calls this "taking time to save time." Clients now actively seek her out at the early stages of the contract preparation, and largely because of this, the initially proposed terms and conditions of contracts are much improved in their quality and conformity. This saves Stephanie time and builds positive relationships with stakeholders.

Are these merely personality differences that are inherent? Can someone learn to be likable? To find the answer, let's look at the concept of emotional intelligence and ask what it has to do with being a Master Expert.

What Is Emotional Intelligence?

DAVID MCCLELLAND, A PSYCHOLOGIST at Harvard University in the 1960s, posited that a set of "emotional competencies" were a more significant predictor of workplace performance than a person's intelligence quotient (IQ). The idea was extended significantly by his student, Daniel Goleman, as an "emotional quotient (EQ)."

Goleman popularized the term in his bestselling 1995 book *Emotional Intelligence – why it can matter more than IQ*. It has since become a widely used concept in psychology and business.

Much work has been done to define these emotional intelligences, and yes, there are more than one, since these early works. The authors like using the Genos model, which is described in Figure 5.1.

The Genos model describes six key EQ competencies, published by Genos International. The capabilities described in the orange circles are the six emotional intelligences. Yes, that's right, there are six distinct emotional intelligences, which we describe in Figure 5.2.

Proponents of the importance of emotional intelligence believe that the progressive mastery of these competencies is correlated with success in many fields, such as professional, athletic, academic, personal, social, and so on.

There is ample evidence to suggest that they're right. One new study shows that people's earning capacity increases significantly with improved EQ.

IQ covers logical thinking in areas like problem solving, mathematics and linguistics, and by the age of 10 or 11, it's more or less fixed. There is little we can do about our IQ, but fortunately, we know that EQ is something that can be learned and continually developed throughout our lives.

EQ is very important for experts, as those who lack strong people skills will only get so far, even with their incisive questions and market insights. If experts lack emotional intelligence, the broad mindset and skill set that we're about to unpack could well alienate stakeholders, even as they go about trying to do good.

Capability: PERSONAL IMPACT
The Genos Model Of Emotional Intelligence

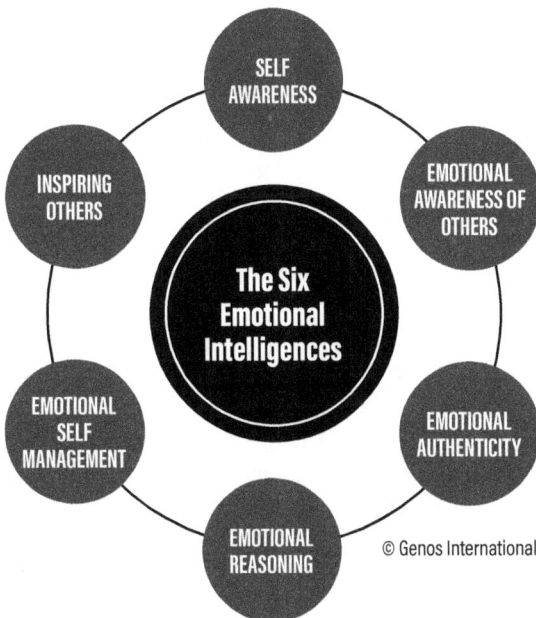

FIGURE 5.1: The Genos Model of Emotional Intelligence

Experts typically need to have a relatively high IQ to acquire expertise in their given field. They usually need a tertiary education in a rules-based discipline. In fact, some people believe and argue that "people skills" (as emotional intelligence is often termed) aren't essential to the discharge of their responsibilities. In fact, many of them even argue that having a few rough edges is the price that others should be willing to pay for their expert "genius."

But it's rare that the expert's value proposition stems purely from some specialized knowledge of a given field. They also need to be able to work with others to ensure that the benefits of their expertise are realized.

The willingness of people to engage with them is a pivotal aspect of the expert's effectiveness. The expert's ability to understand what drives their stakeholders is a fundamental success factor in their capacity to consistently deliver relevant value.

Too many experts don't understand this important fact or have chosen to ignore it. For instance, if Leah increased her self-awareness (one of the foundational emotional intelligences, see Figure 4.4, the Johari Window), she might recognize how grumpy she can often appear when she feels pressured because a client has set a very short deadline.

She might also appreciate that this grumpy exterior is the primary deterrent to her stakeholders engaging her in a timely fashion. She might better recognize that when she feels under pressure, she often becomes snappy and dismissive, finding fault with something or someone rather than being more cooperative.

"Conveying warmth, flexibility, and a willingness to collaborate elicits trust and reciprocity in stakeholders."

Digging even deeper, she might learn that the reason she feels so frustrated with tight deadlines stems from a desire to perform flawlessly, which is often threatened when she feels she is under pressure.

Increased self-awareness, such as knowing our triggers and how we react when triggered, is a prerequisite for increased emotional self-management (another of the six emotional intelligences). The impulse to be critical may never go away. The ability to check that instinct, recognizing its problematic effects on others' emotions and motivations, and shift to a coaching mindset and methodology, keeping our frustrations and our expressions of them in check, usually means we have to master our emotional instincts.

Capability: PERSONAL IMPACT

The Genos Six Emotional Intelligences

EMOTIONAL SELF-AWARENESS	This refers to a person's capacity to identify what they are feeling, the potential triggers of those feelings and the behaviors that typically follow. The person might then have the capacity to curtail the impact of negative emotions and behaviors, and accentuate positive behavior.
EMOTIONAL SELF-MANAGEMENT	Self-management is the capacity to control and manage your emotions and impulses, to restrain yourself even when provoked by problematic emotions.
EMOTIONAL AWARENESS OF OTHERS	This refers to the capacity to read the emotions of others and respond effectively, to understand or predict likely feeling that others will have, and thus have the opportunity to influence them.
EMOTIONAL AUTHENTICITY	This refers to the ability to openly and effectively express oneself, honoring commitments and encouraging this behavior in others
EMOTIONAL REASONING	This refers to the ability to combine the information in our own feelings, and those of others, with facts and other information to make decisions.
EMOTIONALLY INSPIRING OTHERS	This refers to the ability to positively influence the way others feel through problem solving, providing feedback and supporting others' work

(C) Genos International, with adaptations from Expertunity.

FIGURE 5.2: The Six Emotional Intelligences

We can learn this mastery. Patience is like a muscle. As it's exercised, its capacity grows. It's not that Stephanie doesn't also experience frustration and the instinct to criticize and find fault. It's that she has learned how to contain and transform problematic emotions and their associated behaviors. Because she relates differently to her clients, they relate differently to her.

Stephanie has learned to put herself in the shoes of her clients. That's not something we can easily do if we're becoming overwhelmed by feelings of frustration. Stephanie conveys a willingness to support and be of service to her clients, whereas Leah makes them feel like they're an irritation or a hassle, like naughty or dumb school children.

By conveying warmth, flexibility, and a willingness to collaborate, Stephanie elicits trust and generates the instincts of reciprocity in her stakeholders. There is an atmosphere of mutual respect. Stephanie's clients experience the exchange as rewarding and become inclined to put their best efforts into their ongoing working relationship. As a consequence of this approach, the outcome is typically that everyone's needs are more likely to be met.

At the heart of the research on emotional intelligence are insights gleaned from anatomical research about the brain. The neocortex (the brain's prefrontal lobe) is where rational thought takes place. But this sits atop the limbic brain, which is an older part of the brain where feelings prevail. The capacity to think rationally and dispassionately is dependent upon the limbic brain being in a pacified state. If there is a heightened emotion of some sort, such as a negative emotion like fear or anger, then the capacity of the rational brain to function optimally is compromised. We lose the capacity to fully discriminate or discern and to fully consider the consequences of our actions and the degree of our subjective bias.

"Our ability to understand future customer requirements depends, to an extent, on emotional intelligence."

It's not that experts inherently lack emotional intelligence. It's just that it's not necessarily what we've been trained to exercise. Some of this is the product of the training methods that are common nowadays. At school, we learn how language has a set of rules to follow, such as how grammar works, but there are no classes on how to communicate with or relate to others.

Many of the fields in which experts work have a rational or scientific bias. Practitioners are instructed and trained to subjugate or eliminate the possible contamination of decision-making with their own or others' subjective feelings. Experts often work in fields where there are right and wrong answers, and great importance is placed on being correct and on the disciplined following of set procedures.

Experts may even feel that their professional integrity is at stake if they aren't seen to be the upholders of precision, exactness, and a disciplined execution of the methodology. IQ and EQ aren't mutually exclusive, but because many experts are primarily concerned with accuracy and due process, they may not take into consideration how others are feeling, and this can have a big impact on uptake and commitment, therefore impacting execution and benefits realization.

Imagine an expert who has a low awareness of how their behavior is impacting others (poor emotional self-awareness) and is unable to identify how others are feeling (poor emotional awareness of others). Despite their knowledge or expertise, they can be viewed as difficult to work with or unengaging. And this directly affects their effectiveness as an expert.

EQ and Relationships

EMOTIONAL INTELLIGENCE IS THE foundation of our application of the many impact areas in the Expertship model.

Our ability to understand future customer requirements depends, to an extent, on emotional intelligence. In other words, empathizing with their emerging felt needs. Our ability to work closely, proactively and effectively with stakeholders leans heavily on our emotional intelligence. Our ability to help colleagues through change programs is underpinned by our ability to understand our colleagues' emotional states.

Our personal brand is made up of both our capabilities and our knowledge, as well as our temperament or personality. That includes our perceived motives and interpersonal style. Most of the time, we're not consciously thinking about how we perceive others or how they perceive us, but we do base our inclination to engage with others on things like warmth, trust, and our collaborative instincts.

> *"Inspiration also relies heavily on the ability to articulate a case that is rationally sound and emotionally compelling."*

If a person feels averse to engaging with an expert, they'll likely not do so, even at the cost of non-compliance or in subversion of their best interests or those of the organization.

If an expert is going to engage effectively with stakeholders, then they need their trust. An emotionally unaware expert may avoid developing certain stakeholder relationships, either because of shyness or a desire to remain aloof, or because of unexamined tensions in those relationships.

The emotionally illiterate expert might recognize as valid only the functional requirements of stakeholder groups and lack any empathy or insight as to what really motivates them, such as their desire to feel important, valued, or cared for. An expert lacking emotional intelligence may have no idea where to start regarding how to engage those stakeholders.

One of the primary ways in which an expert might increase their Personal Impact is through their ability to influence others. This is especially critical in the many situations where they don't have the authority to mandate their suggested solution to a problem. They have to influence without exercising formal authority.

The emotionally illiterate expert may feel tempted to cite professional authority as an influencing tactic, such as a valued research conclusion in their given field, and then wonder why those they're seeking to influence don't treat such a conclusion as definitive despite their own obvious lack of relevant experience and judgment.

Sophisticated forms of influence, such as inspiring others, require insights into others' values and stated and felt needs. Inspiration also relies heavily on the ability to articulate a case that is rationally sound *and* emotionally compelling.

The Six Emotional Intelligences

LET'S EXPLORE EACH OF these six emotional intelligences in summary. A detailed explanation of each one appears in the later sections of this chapter under the relevant Expert Role.

- **Self-Awareness**: A person's capacity to identify what they're feeling, as well as the potential triggers of those feelings and likely behaviors that typically follow, so that they might then have the capacity to curtail the impact of negative emotions and behaviors and accentuate the positive. Self-awareness is the foundation of all the other EQ competencies.
- **Emotional Self-Management**: Self-management is the capacity to control and manage our emotions and impulses, to restrain ourselves even when provoked by problematic emotions.
- **Emotional Awareness of Others**: This refers to the capacity to read and acknowledge the emotions of others and respond effectively, and to understand or predict the likely feelings that others will have and thus gain the opportunity to perhaps influence them.
- **Emotional Authenticity**: This refers to the ability to openly and effectively express oneself, honoring commitments and encouraging

this behavior in others. Being authentic is vital if we're to foster trust in others.

- **Emotional Reasoning:** This refers to the ability to use the information in feelings, our own and those of others, and combine it with facts and other information in decision-making. Emotional Reasoning refers both to a thought process as well as the manner in which such thoughts are conveyed, whether verbally or in writing.
- **Inspiring Others:** This refers to the ability to positively influence the way others feel through problem solving, providing feedback and recognizing and supporting others' work. This is the mature fruit of all of the other aspects of emotional intelligence. It's the ability to positively influence another's thinking and feeling and prompt them to shift their behaviors in accordance with worthy goals.

The Expert Roles of Personal Impact

THE EXPERT CAPABILITY OF Personal Impact in the Relationship domain describes the three roles an expert must play, all of which require emotional intelligence:

- **The role of the Positive Influencer:** the extent to which experts demonstrate warmth, empathy, and a positive influence on people, as well as a can-do attitude toward challenges and solutions.
- **The role of the Self-aware Adapter:** the extent to which experts are highly aware of their own and other impacts on others, be humble, and be capable of adapting to others and new situations.
- **The role of the Results Driver:** the extent to which experts drive results and real-world outcomes, consider wide interests, take ownership of results, and manage time, priorities and challenging conversations effectively.

In our experience, when it comes to Personal Impact, most experts are punching well below their weight. They have a huge opportunity to increase their mastery of Expertship and reach their full potential. We argue that experts, the authors included, have too often allowed these prejudices against us to develop. It's up to us to actively ensure we receive the recognition that we and our work deserve.

Experts are essentially the custodians of the organization's unique knowledge base. We're the people who make things work. It's one of the great tragedies of modern business life that we're not more recognized and that our career paths are limited. But it's time to accept the hard truth that much of the responsibility for this lies with us. We have contributed to the status quo, and only we can change it.

So, are you prepared to take on the Expertship challenge? Are you willing to take an objective view of your level of Expertship? Are you prepared to master the techniques and strategies described in this book? Are you ready to reframe your expert brand and expand the value you can add to your colleagues and the wider organization?

The quickest way for us to get people thinking differently about experts is by acting differently ourselves—one expert at a time.

TAKING ACTION

Growing Our Emotional Intelligence Skills

IF THIS IS AN area in which you believe you should build your capabilities, here is an action we suggest you might take:

▶ UNDERTAKE AN EMOTIONAL INTELLIGENCE SELF-ASSESSMENT

Experts with suboptimal emotional intelligence tend to lack both the personal discipline to be individually effective as well as the interpersonal smarts to engage with and influence others. The expression of problematic emotions tends to be one of the biggest derailers. Questions we might ask ourselves are:

- Would there be value in undertaking an emotional intelligence assessment (such as the free test in the book Emotional Intelligence 2.0 by Bradbury and Greaves)?
- Should I invest in a more extensive assessment? One in which the views of my colleagues are included, such as the Genos International EQ test. (We highly recommend this.)
- What ad-hoc feedback might I be able to gather about how I interact with other colleagues around my emotional intelligence?
- Are there some gaps that are obvious to me from reading this chapter?
- Does my organization have some existing tools I could leverage to inform the extent of my current emotional intelligence?

"Attitude is a little thing that makes a big difference."

Winston Churchill

CHAPTER | 06 |

Being a Positive Influence

How can managing the way in which our views are experienced transform our influence?

IN THIS CHAPTER, WE WILL EXPLORE:

- Whether experts are naturally negative, and if so, why?
- What are the impacts of being overly critical, even if we're right?
- What key techniques can we master that will enable us to deliver accurate and objective analysis and critiques but continue to positively engage with colleagues?

THE FIRST EXPERT ROLE in the Personal Impact capability is that of Positive Influencer. This expert role deals with the extent to which experts demonstrate warmth, empathy, a positive influence on people, and a can-do attitude toward challenges and solutions. The behaviors at each level of Expertship for this expert role are described in Figure 6.1.

At an immature level, experts tend to be empathetic toward their own technical cohort but struggle to be empathetic with broader stakeholder groups. They can articulate arguments in a clinical and rational manner, which can appear negative and indifferent when saying "no." Early stage experts will be highly motivated to achieve technical mastery but typically struggle to connect work to the organizational vision and mission. They'll perceive their scope for personal impact to be within the confines of their own narrow technical team.

Experts derailing in this capability often are experienced by others from outside their technical domain as condescending and egotistical, whether they mean to be or not. They represent themselves as disengaged and cynical, often full of criticism for their organization and many colleagues. They're demotivated and sometimes have that impact on others. They don't feel or attempt to feel connected to the vision and mission of the organization.

The Master Expert, on the other hand, exudes personal warmth, empathy and patience when dealing with colleagues from both inside and outside their technical domain. They present as positive and "can-do," even when facing challenges or finding solutions is difficult. Their connection to the vision and mission of the organization is inspirational for those around them. This positive mindset leads to a constant stream of opportunities and positive connections, both within the organization and external to it. The positive influencer is in demand.

Are We Light or Dark?

HOW DO PEOPLE EXPERIENCE us? As a positive influencer or a negative naysayer? Light or dark?

At a recent workshop, we encountered a participant named Steve. Every time he spoke, which was often, he went on and on about some decision that his organization had made that he didn't like. He spoke in the most dismissive and damning ways about his managers' and co-workers' lack of intelligence and poor work ethic. Every time he opened his mouth, it seemed to suck all the oxygen out of the room. Everything was so dark and hopeless. He was blissfully unaware of the effect he was having on the group. His situation may have been difficult, but his attitude was not helping matters and was leading to his further marginalization.

> *"Steve realized he often had good thoughts about things, but he rarely expressed them."*

Steve was a good example of how someone with a low level of self-awareness and poor social skills can miss vital cues that they have fallen into a negative way of seeing and relating to the world. Steve may well have been one hundred percent right in his assessment of decisions and policies, but in the end, his negativity resulted in no one listening. It can take a lot of discipline and resilience to maintain an optimistic mood when things around us are deteriorating. But it's important, if we're to sustain a positive personal brand, that others are happy to engage with us. Unrelenting negativity gets in the way.

Many experts are perceived by others to be cynical, perfectionistic, dismissive, or critical—all negative traits. Even if their gripes have merit, others might prefer not to engage with them. They would much rather deal with people who are solution-oriented, positive and cheerful, rather than those who are negative, cynical or judgmental.

Changing these sorts of bad habits requires a lot of self-awareness. We need to notice if we're expressing negativity. We need to resist the urge to be overly critical. We need to be aware that other people are reacting unfavorably. The rights and the wrongs of the situation are rarely likely to be as important as our engagement and connection to the people we work with.

Steve subsequently responded well to feedback. He recognized that even if his criticism was sometimes justified, it was counter-productive for him to be constantly seen as critical. Expressing hopelessness and negativity did him and his reputation, which is his brand, no good at all.

He also realized that he very often had good thoughts about colleagues, projects and organizational achievements, but he rarely expressed them. The negatives always got first airplay. He resolved to first exhaust all the opportunities to positively influence the situation instead of resorting to expressions of cynicism.

Steve achieved this change by mastering two new skills: the art of self-management and the art of advanced listening.

Mastering Self-Management

HOW DO WE MASTER a positive mindset if we're not wired to or don't currently feel that way about our role?

At the Master Expert level, the ability for us to find and articulate the positives over the negatives is a key capability. And in our experience, it's one of the toughest transitions some experts have to make.

> *"Self-management implies a mastery over our emotional urges."*

The insights that will arise from increased self-awareness will typically provide us with the impetus to change our responses. Impulse control or deferred gratification is at the heart of self-management.

We might still feel stressed or disinclined to engage in a conversation that might result in conflict, but self-management involves not allowing our natural avoidance instinct (prompted by feelings of fear) to cause us to put off having such a meeting. This entails developing the courage to face the potential discomfort inherent in conflict.

Capability: PERSONAL IMPACT
Expert Role: POSITIVE INFLUENCER

MASTER EXPERT

- Exudes personal warmth, empathy and patience when dealing with colleagues from outside their technical domain.
- Presents as positive and "can do," even when challenging thinking and solutions.
- Inspirational—exudes passion for the vision and mission.

EXPERT

- Appears supportive and patient toward those who lack technical depth.
- Articulates arguments in a measured way, presenting as constructive even when saying "no."
- Motivational—articulates the vision and mission of the organization effectively.

SPECIALIST

- Empathetic toward technical cohort but struggles to be empathetic to broader stakeholder group.
- Articulates arguments in a rational manner, which can appear negative when saying "no."
- Self-motivational—struggles to connect work to the vision and mission.

- Can present as condescending and egotistical when dealing with colleagues from outside their technical domain.
- Presents as disengaged and cynical.
- Demotivational—does not connect work to vision and mission of the organization.

DERAILING

FIGURE 6.1: Positive Influencer Behaviors

Courage isn't the absence of fear. It's the possession of enough mastery of our emotions that our decisions aren't entirely dictated by fear but driven by our commitment to a noble goal. A person with emotional self-mastery will subjugate the feelings of fear to the anticipation of feeling satisfied with having tackled a difficult conversation.

The development of such discipline can begin with making and keeping small promises to ourselves, such as making a commitment to an exercise program or getting up at a particular time each day.

If a lack of self-awareness is a failure to recognize what's going on (more on this later in the chapter), a lack of self-management is the failure to take appropriate action.

Experts who lack self-management may show up in the following ways:

- Scatty, disordered and always late, these people have no fail-safe system to deliver on their commitments and are usually inadequately prepared.
- Overloaded, no clear sense of priorities, and can't say "no."
- Angry outbursts, low self-control, excessive or disproportionate emoting of any kind, and conveying a victim mentality.
- Hypercritical, disproportionately focused on what's wrong, never encouraging, and never catches people doing things right.
- Over-talking. These people have an uncontrollable urge to dominate the conversation (because *we* are the expert, and we need to prove it).
- Being overly sensitive or defensive (being triggered).

These examples may illustrate both gaps in self-awareness as well as self-management. The over-talker, for instance, would likely be oblivious to the fact that no one else has been able to get a word in edgewise for the last 15 minutes. Such behavior would be indicative of a lack of self-awareness, insufficient restraint (self-management), and low social awareness (missing others' cues).

> *"Advanced listening skills are a foundational capability of Master Experts."*

Self-management implies mastery over our emotional urges. Just as someone on a special diet resists the urge to snack on forbidden foods, someone who has decided to become more of a listener than a teller will notice when they feel an urge to speak and take action to regulate that urge so they only speak when absolutely essential. A person with low self-discipline will not be able to suppress the urge, even if they happen to possess sufficient self-awareness to notice what's happening.

With more and more research on the brain and neuroscience being published every day, it's becoming increasingly obvious that the supposed distinction between (rational) thinking and emotions is unhelpful and inaccurate. Our brain's rational centers (the prefrontal lobe and neocortex, among others) are built on top of and wired into our emotional centers (limbic brain, amygdala, etc.)

Most of our thoughts have some feeling stimulating them. If we're not conscious of these feelings and therefore in a position to exercise some discretion about what actions we allow those feelings to prompt, then our lives tend to become a product of instincts and impulses over which we're exercising very little conscious direction.

Experts who are strong in self-management:
- Are more focused, self-disciplined and productive.
- Are more proactive and strategic, resisting the allure of urgency.
- Are more resilient and of stable temperament.
- There are a number of ways we can build our self-management:
- Planning/prioritization. We can reflect on how we would like to design our lives and then plan and act accordingly (see Chapter 9, *Energy Management*).
- Reframing negative self-talk and thinking (narrating).
- Taking up some form of stress-release habit, such as meditation, exercise or slow breathing.
- Visualizing our preferred future and aligning our behaviors and plans (time) accordingly.

As we discuss in Chapter 19 on Collaboration, and also in more detail in Chapter 17 of this book, advanced listening skills are a foundational capability of Master Experts. (See the *Five Levels of Listening*, Figure 20.1).

In order for Steve to become a positive influencer, he needed to understand the opinions and belief systems of his colleagues and understand what they were attempting to achieve.

The ability to listen intently and ask gentle but probing questions in order to elicit an even greater depth of insight about where his colleagues were coming from enabled Steve to shape his discussions with them in a much more positive, collaborative, and eventually influential manner.

TAKING ACTION

Growing Our Positive Influencer Skills

IF THIS IS AN expert role in which you believe you could add greater value, here are some high-level suggestions for actions to take:

▶ EXPLORE MORE HOLISTIC INFLUENCING STRATEGIES

Experts often rely on a limited range of influencing strategies. Being rationally inclined, we might lean toward an exclusive or primary approach, which is characterized as "rational persuasion." This is purely facts, sound reasoning, tight logic, and so on. Such a methodology may not always prove effective as logic and reasoning aren't the only factors driving people's decision-making. We might need to take into account the emotional feelings that our stakeholder is experiencing. Questions for us to ask ourselves:

- What are some recent situations where we'd have liked to have increased influence? What got in the way of us influencing successfully? What influencing tactics did we use?
- What alternative influencing tactics could we have used?
- Did we properly explore how our colleague was feeling as well as thinking?
- Did we properly explore the impact our proposal or suggested approach might have on our stakeholders? Did we consider their reality as well as our own?
- Did we properly listen to their suggestions or reasons for wanting to approach the problem differently? Or did we simply imagine we were right and they were wrong?
- If we were faced with the same situation again, how might we tackle it differently?
- Define the outcomes that would naturally result from you developing increased influence. Identify which methods of influence (see Stakeholder Engagement, Chapter 3) you have historically sought to employ in this situation that haven't proven sufficiently impactful. Identify which alternative tactics you could experiment with next time.

▶ ENGAGE PEOPLE BY LINKING PROPOSALS TO THEIR FELT NEEDS

If proposals aren't effectively positioned so as to positively impact the felt needs of our colleagues, then they tend to be seen as irrelevant or low value. In the competition for finite time and resources, they lose out to propositions that more obviously address felt needs. Questions we might like to ask ourselves:

- How much time do I spend seeking to engage others and eliciting their buy-in to a project or initiative?
- Do I proactively position my proposal or recommendation to demonstrate how their commitment to it or adoption of it will heighten the likelihood of their own needs being addressed?
- Am I clear on what their felt needs really are? Have I asked them directly or merely assumed I know?
- Am I clear on how my proposal or recommendation sits in their priority queue of things that need doing or are important to them?
- Have I explored their needs beyond mere functional requirements? Examples might be:
  - The need to feel safe and secure.
  - The need for comfort, balance or convenience.
  - Perceived value for money.
  - The need for a certain quality of life.
  - The need to feel adequately resourced and equipped.
  - The need to feel supported, cared for, and to belong.
  - The need to feel a sense of achievement, progress, recognition, importance, as well as being heard, being trusted, and feeling autonomous.
  - The need to feel stimulated and have a sense of variety.
  - The need for a sense of meaning and purpose.
- Am I listening intently to the words and behaviors of my colleagues to deduce what their unfelt needs might be?

▶ INCREASE YOUR SELF-AWARENESS

Commit to becoming more aware of the effect you have on others. When experts lack self-awareness, they can often exhibit behaviors that undermine their relationships with others. Questions we might ask ourselves:

- Do I really know how I am experienced by colleagues?
- Have I really thought about the impact my actions (and inaction) have on my colleagues and broader stakeholders?
- Have I sought feedback from others about when I am effective and when I am not? Have I had the courage to seek really honest feedback and encouraged this in others?
- Have I created an environment where my colleagues feel safe giving me feedback? Have I considered exactly what I need to do in order to create such an environment?
- Have I spent time reflecting on which situations create emotional triggers for me and result in sub-optimal emotional behavior? Have I reflected on what alternative responses I'll choose in the future?
- Have I considered what actions will and will not build trust between myself and key stakeholders?

CHAPTER | 07 |

Being Self-Aware and Adaptive

How does heightened self-awareness of our impact on others lead to better outcomes?

IN THIS CHAPTER, WE WILL EXPLORE:

- What are the key attributes of someone who is self-aware about how they're being experienced by others?
- What techniques can we deploy to become naturally much more self-aware?
- How do we build the capability to put ourselves in others' shoes and understand their emotional state? How does this help us add real value to our teams and organization?

THE SECOND EXPERT ROLE in the Personal Impact capability is that of Self-Aware Adapter. This expert role deals with the extent to which experts are highly aware of their own impacts on others, to be humble, and to be capable of adapting to others and new situations.

The behaviors at each level of Expertship for this expert role are described in Figure 7.1.

At immature levels, experts tend to be focused on developing their ability to manage their own emotions. They'll be learning to be aware of their personal impact on others, hopefully looking for and positively responding to feedback from colleagues. They'll be focused on how they communicate rather than adapting to the way others communicate or make sense of incoming communication. Early stage experts may come across as self-important while they're trying to establish their expert credentials.

Experts who are derailing are typically very poor at managing their own emotions. They're known for being combustible and moody. Focused on their own situation, they'll not care about or even be unaware of the personal impact they're having on others. They often quickly shoot down ideas that they don't agree with in a negative, combative manner. Typically, they'll have little notion of how they're being negatively experienced by others.

The Master Expert, on the other hand, demonstrates superior ability when it comes to managing their own emotions and helping others manage theirs. They're very aware of and constantly monitoring the impact they have on others, and they care about making a positive impact on their colleagues and stakeholders. They demonstrate a willingness and superior ability to adapt their communication style to engage effectively with others. And as expert as they are, they're known widely as humble.

Mastering Self-Awareness

MASTERING SELF-AWARENESS IS A critical milestone on the way to expert mastery. The ability to stand back and observe the impact our beliefs and actions are having on ourselves and those around us enables us to adapt our actions to have a greater positive impact. Without awareness, we can't find our way to a place where we're adding more value.

> *"If we lack of self-awareness, it means that we just haven't noticed how we come across to others."*

One practice that may help is regular reflection. Ask yourself these questions: How am I feeling right now? How was my mood during the day? How did those moods influence my behavior? Were there any problematic exchanges with other people? Can I identify what triggered those exchanges? What is it about those triggers that provokes such reactions? What was I feeling when I said or did that?

Capability: PERSONAL IMPACT

Expert Role: SELF-AWARE ADAPTER

MASTER EXPERT

- Excellent at managing own and others' emotions.
- Aware of their personal impact on others.
- Willing and able to adapt communication style to engage effectively with others.
- Shows humility.

EXPERT

- Manages own emotions effectively.
- Aware of their personal impact on others.
- Some ability to adapt communication style to others.
- Shows humility.

SPECIALIST

- Developing ability to manage own emotions.
- Learning to be aware of personal impact on others.
- Focused on their own communication style.
- May present as self-important while establishing expert credentials.

- Poor at managing own emotions.
- Does not care about, or is unaware of, personal impact on others.
- Quickly shoots down ideas they don't agree with in a negative manner.

DERAILING

FIGURE 7.1: Self-aware Adapter Behaviors

Over time, you will probably observe patterns that repeat. Experts who lack self-awareness commonly show up in the following ways:

- Negative/cynical, focusing on why things will be difficult to implement.
- Impersonal/aloof, in their own world, preoccupied with their own considerations.
- Arrogant/judgmental, they think that they're smarter than everybody else.
- Prickly/temperamental and easily triggered.
- Unhelpful/non-responsive, absorbed in their own agenda.
- Becoming a pleaser, avoiding all risk of conflict, saying yes to every request, and depending on others' approval.

It's rare that these behaviors are intentional. If we lack self-awareness, it means that we just haven't noticed how we come across to others or how we're showing up. And when we finally do become aware, possibly by taking notice of the eighteenth piece of feedback, we may have little insight into why we present like this and therefore also lack insight as to how we might change.

An inability to recognize our own feelings will hamper our capacity to recognize feelings in others. Experts can often struggle to legitimize other people's feelings because they may see them as somehow contrary to reason and therefore potentially problematic, containing biases, and so on.

Experts who score highly in self-awareness:

- Are measured, composed and balanced.
- Are considered in their viewpoints and aware of/on top of their own biases.
- Can adapt their style (of decision-making, communicating, and so on) in line with the situation.
- Are fully present.
- Handle change more adaptively.

There are a number of different ways we can develop our self-awareness. We can:

- Start paying more attention to the feedback we receive. This might be direct (e.g., someone telling us that they think we're rude) or indirect (e.g., someone grimacing when we criticize their ideas for the third time in a meeting).
- Pay more attention to our own behaviors, moods or even bodily sensations. For example, you might observe that you're a bit snappy with a colleague. Or, if you think that you're overloaded with work, you might push back on requests more aggressively. This might be seen as developing an awareness of your triggers and habitual responses.

- Do an audit. There are many self-assessment tools and personality tests that we can take (such as DISC, 15FQ+, Myers Briggs, Genos EQ, StrengthsFinder, and many more) that all provide perspectives on understanding our innate tendencies.
- Solicit formal feedback, either in writing, verbally or via a 360-degree tool, which can be very enlightening. As a technical expert, you may find Expertship360 to be the most relevant tool because it measures the behaviors of experts rather than people leaders. These tools make it easier for people who have a perspective of our conduct to identify what they do and don't appreciate about working with us. Warning: don't do this unless you're committed to taking action accordingly. Asking people for their feedback creates an expectation that you're prepared to act on that feedback (assuming it's consistent from many parties). If you don't take the corresponding actions, you will likely do further damage to your personal brand.
- Keep a diary. This entails spending a few minutes each day on evaluating key events and interactions and how they have affected us. Evaluating how we responded can be a very powerful way of paying closer attention to what's going on emotionally. According to C.S. Lewis, "The more you listen to your conscience, the more it demands of you."
- Reflect on and develop a statement of personal mission and values.
- "It's surprising how effectively we can read others if we simply *pay attention.*"

> *"It's surprising how effectively we can read others if we simply pay attention."*

Emotional Awareness of Others

MASTERING EMOTIONAL AWARENESS OF others comprises the ability to put yourself in another person's shoes and develop a sense of what they're feeling, their priorities and their needs. For experts who want to be more influential, getting really good at understanding how others are feeling is a breakthrough capability.

Contrary to popular belief, we're all inherently capable of empathy, at least in principle. It's surprising how effectively we can read others if we simply *pay attention* to what people say, their tone of voice, and their body language.

Other practices, such as paraphrasing what others have said or reflecting back their feelings, can prompt the development of an empathic frame of mind. We need to listen for the essential meaning and associated feelings rather than merely filtering for facts. Of course, we can also engage in a more structured understanding of others' needs and feelings through exercises such as eliciting feedback or conducting surveys.

There are a number of ways that a lack of awareness of others can play out with experts. These include being viewed as:

- Opinionated or a poor listener and not appreciative of others' needs to feel heard or to be able to express their opinions and needs.
- Running our own agendas and not being committed to mutual or collective outcomes.
- Task-focused and committed to some output or standard of performance, regardless of whether others can relate to it.
- Lacking people skills, prone to being blunt, lacking tact and consideration.
- Insular, withdrawn or excessively shy.

"Are we worrying about things we can't possibly hope to influence? Is this increasing our frustration?"

These traits could also represent deficits in self-awareness and self-management, as well as awareness of others. The development of empathy (the ability to put oneself in others' shoes) is a very strong theme in this book. Empathy lies at the heart of all relationship building. Without it, we won't be able to ask the right questions or elicit full and honest answers due to a lack of psychological safety.

Experts who rate highly in the emotional awareness of others:

- Build more trusting relationships that are grounded in mutual understanding (reciprocal partnerships).
- Have a better read on the social and political climate.
- Have greater insight into stakeholders' felt needs, concerns, perspectives and expectations.

There are a number of ways in which we can develop our awareness of others:

- The chapters in this book on Collaboration and Stakeholder Engagement contain numerous tools and tactics to increase mastery in this area.

- Make a deliberate point of building and paying attention to rapport when meeting with others. Pay attention to body language and other non-verbal cues.
- Practice reflecting back, paraphrasing and summarizing what others have said to their satisfaction.
- Utilize various personality style frameworks (e.g., DISC, Myers Briggs, Team Roles) to get a better sense of where others are coming from.
- Look for cues as to others' motivations.

Worrying About Things We Can't Influence

ARE WE WORRYING ABOUT things we can't possibly hope to influence? Is this increasing our sense of frustration and making us come across as unduly negative?

A useful framework is the circle of influence framework introduced in *The 7 Habits of Highly Effective People* by Stephen Covey (see Figure 7.2).

Personal Impact
THE CIRCLE OF INFLUENCE

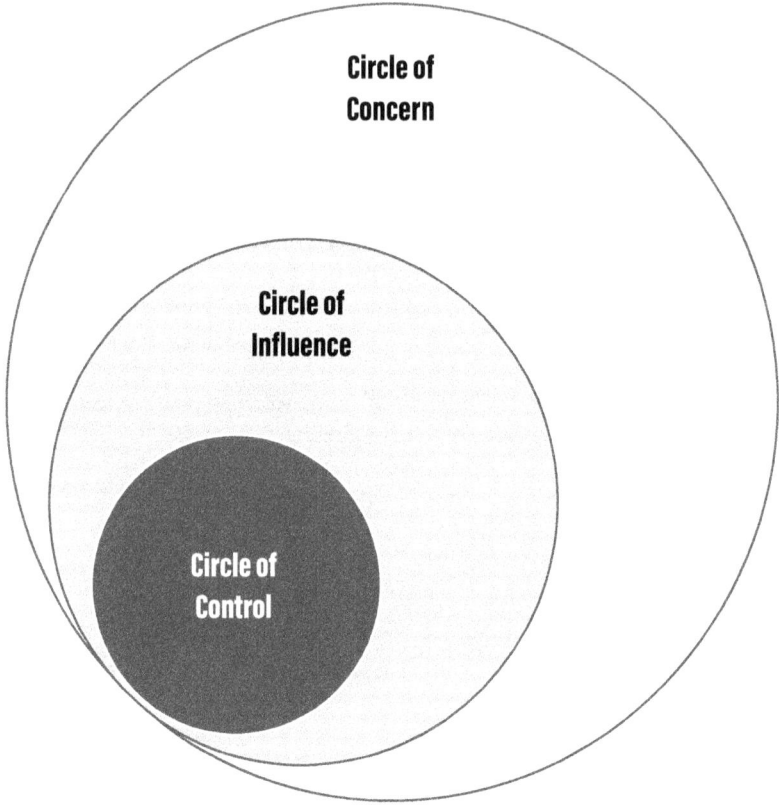

Adapted from Stephen Covey, *7 Habits of Effective People*

FIGURE 7.2: The Circle Of Influence

Covey argued that you can direct your attention either to the things that you're concerned about but have no control over (the Circle of Concern) or to the things over which you have a high degree of control and influence (the Circle of Influence).

You will get a very different result for each circle. If you direct your attention to things beyond your control or influence, you're likely to feel frustrated and disempowered. You may feel overwhelmed and despair that the situation is beyond your remedial powers. On the other hand, if you focus on matters you can do something about, you will feel more hopeful and develop a sense of ownership.

For example, Ed has just learned that his recommendation that the business invests in a particular software package was refused at the finance meeting.

Many people, when faced with a disappointment like this, might be tempted to express their frustrations publicly by criticizing the decision-makers or those who failed to adequately sell the merits of the proposal, and could just become discouraged.

Discouragement, the sapping of our courage, is the natural consequence of focusing on matters beyond our control or influence. It just reinforces a sense of being powerless against larger realities.

Some people have developed the habit of focusing on their Circle of Concern (things that bother them but which they can do little about) to the point that they have convinced themselves that they have no control over anything. Everything seems like a lost cause. It's almost like they find any expressions of hope to be intolerable and feel compelled to extinguish the perceived false hopes of anyone who might voice them. Many experts who people believe to be skeptics or cynics exhibit these tendencies.

On the other hand, Ed could choose to focus on his Circle of Influence.

- "Okay, that's disappointing. Let me find out what criteria was applied and see if I can sharpen it up next time."
- "Let me find out which decision-makers I need to get closer to next time."
- "Let me work on my proposal writing skills."

At the very least, Ed will feel less like a discouraged victim. And there's a good chance that by pursuing well-chosen positive strategies, he will also increase the likelihood of getting a superior outcome next time. Certainly, he won't repel people from wanting to have a conversation with him, as is the case with the person wallowing in a cynical Circle of Concern.

Growing Our Ability to Adapt

THE FINAL FIRST VERSIONS of this book were written in 2020 in the middle of the COVID-19 global pandemic. Surely, if any single event provided an example of how important it is to be able to quickly adapt to new circumstances, this was it. And interestingly, it has quickly become a fine example of how quickly individuals, teams, and whole populations can adapt quickly if there is a clear need. Many ways of living and working changed overnight.

This chapter has focused on our ability as an expert to adapt our communication and interpersonal style to our stakeholders and colleagues, the better to build win-win relationships with them.

More generally, the ability to adapt to new circumstances is a broader skill that requires mastery. We discuss these themes in the chapters dealing with change and market context.

It's perhaps worth noting that when organizations are looking to hire very senior executives these days, the ability to quickly adapt and pivot is a key attribute most head-hunters are looking for. This applies to experts as much as general leadership positions.

TAKING ACTION

Growing Our Self-Aware Adapter Skills

IF THIS IS AN expert role in which you believe you could add greater value, here are some high-level suggestions for actions to take:

▶ FOCUS ON YOUR CIRCLE OF INFLUENCE

- Stressing about matters we have very limited or no ability to control is a waste of valuable energy. We can easily fall into the trap of feeling disempowered because we lack formal authority. Getting past this and focusing on what we can influence is both positive and fulfilling. Questions we might like to ask ourselves:
- Have I distinguished between the things that concern me but which I can't do much about (things in my Circle of Concern) and the things I can do something about (things in my Circle of Influence)?
- Regardless of feeling overwhelmed and paralyzed by how complex and challenging the circumstances are, do I focus positively by considering all the moves I could make?
- Have I identified stakeholders and colleagues I could partner with to extend my circle of influence?

▶ PRACTICE APPLYING EMPATHY

Experts who don't listen effectively are likely to be seen as arrogant, not understanding, and uncaring or indifferent. Not listening properly can often lead to experts jumping to solutions before getting the whole story, or at least having stakeholders feeling heard. Questions we might like to ask ourselves:
- How good am I really at listening? Do I truly seek to understand? Or am I overly keen to get to solutions via making assumptions about what I have heard?
- Whenever stakeholders express heightened emotions (e.g., frustration), do I listen and respond empathetically?
- Am I constantly using paraphrasing to make sure I have understood?
- Do I regularly get buy-in from stakeholders or is trust an issue? Will practicing empathy help me understand both facts and feelings better so I can produce elevated results?

"There are two kinds of people, those who do the work and those who take the credit. Try to be in the first group; there is less competition there."

Indira Gandhi

CHAPTER | 08 |

Being a Results Driver

How do we ensure we get the right things done, for the right reasons, in the right order, so we have maximum impact?

IN THIS CHAPTER, WE WILL EXPLORE:

- What are the key contributing factors to getting things done, and what skills and processes should we deploy?
- How do we make decisions, and is it the way we imagine?
- How do we build the capability to inspire colleagues to action?

THE THIRD EXPERT ROLE in the Personal Impact capability is that of **Results Driver**. This expert role deals with the extent to which experts demonstrate a results orientation, combining advanced prioritization, on-time delivery of agreed outcomes and value creation.

The behaviors at each level of Expertship for this expert role are described in Figure 8.1.

At an immature level, experts tend to deliver acceptable results or productivity in line with expectations. They consider the interests of both themselves and others. Strongly task-focused at this level, they tend to take responsibility for allocated tasks. It's likely that, at an immature level, experts will still be learning to manage their own time effectively.

Experts derailing in this capability are routinely making excuses for lack of delivery. They may well consider their own interests above all other interests and be mostly focused on their own agenda. Derailing experts here will regularly blame other colleagues or departments for unachieved outcomes. They may prefer to work alone and may fail to maintain effective contact with the rest of the team. Or they may suffer from paralysis by analysis if they feel they don't have enough data or evidence, and they'll sometimes refuse to make decisions until every last piece of available evidence from anywhere in the world is gathered and considered. In the meantime, the world is passing them by.

The Master Expert, on the other hand, strives relentlessly for results and delivers real-world outcomes. The consideration they show for stakeholders goes far beyond immediate departmental colleagues and themselves, taking into account the interests and agendas of the wider organization and customers. Experts operating at the highest level take ownership for the achievement of both technical and corresponding business outcomes. They manage their time effectively, focusing on important and urgent matters but favoring the important. In order to achieve this level of impact and value creation, they tend to regularly and artfully deploy the courage to have timely, transformative conversations with colleagues.

What Generates Results?

AS EVERY EXPERT KNOWS, consistently getting the results we want isn't easy. There are so many barriers, such as distractions, competing agendas and requests for resources, and time pressures, all of which make focusing on the key objectives very difficult. Sometimes, we feel it's impossible. The simple act of getting the right things done in the right order can be very taxing.

> *"The simple act of getting the right things done in the right order is very taxing."*

In the next few chapters, we'll explore some critical enterprise skills that Master Experts use to make a substantial impact and get things done.

In this chapter, we'll explore the ability to make decisions and inspire people to take action.

In Chapter 9, we'll explore the Expert Energy Engine, which is the ability to successfully manage our time and energy. In our programs, our participants consistently tell us that this concept is one of the biggest takeaways for them.

In Chapter 10, we'll explore the subtle but critical art of saying "no," without actually using the word "no." It isn't possible to prioritize unless we're saying "yes" to some projects and tasks and "no" to others.

Capability: PERSONAL IMPACT

Expert Role: RESULTS DRIVER

MASTER EXPERT

- Relentlessly drives results and delivers real-world outcomes.
- Considers the interests of the wider organization and customers.
- Takes ownership for technical and associated business outcomes.
- Manages time effectively to focus on important and urgent matters but still favors the important.
- Deploys courage in having transformative conversations with colleagues.

EXPERT

- Frequently engages beyond minimum requirements.
- Considers the interests of self, others and the organization.
- Takes responsibility for allocated technical outcomes.
- Manages time effectively to focus on important and urgent matters in equal measure.
- Helps others manage time and priorities.

SPECIALIST

- Delivers acceptable results or productivity in line with expectations.
- Considers the interests of self and others.
- Takes responsibility for allocated tasks.
- Learning to manage their own time effectively.

- Constantly makes excuses for lack of delivery.
- Paralysis by analysis—unable to make a decision.
- Considers the interests of self above all other interests, focused on own agenda.
- Generally blames other colleagues or departments for unachieved outcomes.
- Prefers to work alone and can fail to maintain effective contact with the rest of the team.

DERAILING

FIGURE 8.1: Results Driver Behaviors

In Chapter 11, we'll explore the key Master Expert skill of having courageous conversations in an effective and timely manner.

This is the ability to find sufficient time, apply energy to tasks, make the right decisions, and inspire our colleagues to contribute, and it's also the courage to call out colleagues who aren't contributing. All of these skills are the building blocks that enable Master Experts to excel at driving results.

In many instances, they might appear to be things we already know or feel we already should know. Who hasn't, at some stage, done a course or read a book on time management? Making decisions just comes naturally, right? After all, don't we already have a reputation for telling it like it is and calling out colleagues directly for poor thinking, discipline or work?

Perhaps, but in the next few pages, we'll all audit ourselves and question whether we're carrying out these tasks at best practice level?

"The decisions we make are far more complex than they seem when you consider the processing involved."

In our experience, the advice in the next few chapters have the power to change your working life, and perhaps even your personal life, forever.

Let's begin with decision-making.

Advanced Decision-Making

WHAT MAKES DECISION-MAKING ADVANCED?

There are a range of measures in our minds that make a decision-making process advanced:

- Knowing what we have decided.
- Ensuring everyone shares the same understanding as to what has been decided and have bought into the plan.
- Everyone knows why it has been decided and accepts the rationale to be sound. This implies that we can describe the decision-making process and explain what options were not chosen, as well as articulating which options were chosen.
- The ability to describe the decision-making criteria applied, as well as the underlying assumptions, contingencies and dependencies of making the decision.
- Being able to assess objectively, at a later date, whether the decision was a good one. Having an understanding of why it was or wasn't a good decision. This might involve checking our criteria and assumptions to identify whether they were the right ones. This also implies that, at

this later date, we can remember why we made the decision. For more complex or important decisions, did we document our process?

This entire process might sound like it's a little over-engineered, right? Few of us think we have the time for such painstaking and thorough thinking.

However, for smaller decisions, it turns out that most of us can find the time to think things through, which saves us time in the long run.

Michelle was a senior marketing executive at a fast-global moving consumer goods firm. She was super-successful at building great campaigns, fostering positive distributor relationships, and helping drive the organization's key brands forward. As a consequence, Michelle was asking to step into the country manager role and needed to recruit someone to replace her as marketing director.

Simple, eh? Well, perhaps not so simple. Most recruiters will tell you that an incumbent trying to hire their replacement is fraught with danger. Firstly, we tend to look for a facsimile of ourselves, when that is probably not what the organization needs as we already have one copy of us. Secondly, we tend to look for the finished article—the version of ourselves that is ready to be CEO rather than the version of ourselves we were when we stepped into that more senior role for the first time. We find it very hard to remember *that version* of ourselves, or perhaps we don't want to.

We met Michelle after she had hired a replacement named Joanne. Michelle felt she had made a mistake and was seeking to exit Joanne and start all over again. We asked for some examples of where Joanne was significantly underperforming. She described some key media-selection decisions on a major campaign where, according to Michelle, the choices took far too long to make and ended up being "all wrong." We asked Michelle to share with us her decision-making process for selecting media choices A (her own) over media choices B (Joanne's).

> *"That snap decision you made—was it really a 'snap' decision?"*

"I just made it," Michelle initially told us. "I mean, it's obvious you would choose options A over options B." When we asked her why, Michelle immediately listed out seven complex reasons why she would choose A over B, including the right target audience, the right volume of audience, the right quality of editorial, the right price point, the opportunity to get editorial and competitions featuring their products, and so on. These were Michelle's decision-making criteria. We asked Michelle why she had chosen those criteria. She told us it was years of experience of running hundreds of campaigns.

This decision-making at the speed of light is a phenomenon we often see among very experienced experts in their field. From the outside, it appears as if it's a simple process, but it's actually very complex processing of multiple options and data points, loaded with judgments about what worked in the past and what didn't, and why. These are all compressed into, in Michelle's case, a frown, some notations on a file, and then a decision.

Readers will discern what came next. We asked Michelle whether Joanne had access to all of the same past data points and decision-making criteria. ("No.") We asked Michelle whether Joanne was as experienced as Michelle. ("Well, clearly not.") We asked Michelle whether she had taken Joanne through all of this gathered experience prior to tasking her with choosing the media for this campaign. ("No.") Why not? ("It would have taken far too long. I'm busy."). Ah. This is a common story. We deal with the ability to really master *knowledge transfer* in Chapters 46 to 49.

The reason we tell this story here is to demonstrate that decision-making by experts is actually quite complex, but it's also very rapid. It doesn't seem like lots of time was spent choosing option A or B, but actually, years of accumulated experience automatically feed into the decision-making process. Think of a snap decision you might have made in the last week or so. Was it really a snap decision? "There are significant benefits to using a decision-making grid."

> *"There are significant benefits to using a decision-making grid."*

On the one hand, Michelle has made the decision that Joanne isn't up to the role she has been hired for. On the other hand, Michelle hasn't thought about how much help Joanne might need to make good early decisions about media selections. Both of these things are actually wrong.

Making Complex Decisions

IF MICHELLE WANTED TO effectively explain to Joanne how she had made the decision, the best way of doing so would be to develop a decision-making Grid design to help her make this decision (see Figure 8.2).

A decision-making grid lays out the decision-making criteria, providing a voting system that allows decision-makers to compare different options and thus reach a decision. If we examine the design of the grid, we can see exactly how it's done. This grid can be deployed to make any decision.

Criteria. Arranged at the top of the chart, the criteria are the tests that options need to pass in order to be selected. We've added in what might have been in Michelle's mind. Target Audience "reach" (traffic), followed by cost per thousand, which is a typical measure of digital advertising cost, and so on. If we were making a decision about buying a residential property, we might include the number of bedrooms, whether or not it has a garden, if it's close to schools, shops, transport and so on. Making sure you have the right criteria, and listing them in order of importance from left to right, is essential to making a good decision. When we're purchasing an expensive item, for example, we might imagine functionality and cost are the main criteria, but often things like cost of maintenance, product life, cost of future upgrades and general running costs can be just as important.

Scores. Having ascertained the rating each media option has across all the criteria, Michelle can now add up the scores. She is using a simple system (2 points for a High, 1 point for a Medium, and no points for a Low rating). Her weighting means that any rating in columns 1 and 2 get double scores. The end result is that Media B is the clear winner, scoring 15 points.

> *"Many experts bristle at the suggestion that their decisions are anything but objective."*

There are significant benefits to using a decision-making grid for an expert, particularly when we're making complex decisions. By creating a grid, we have a tool that can:

- Help us make the decision in the first place, and this is particularly true if a group is making a decision.
- Help us understand the relative value of the criteria we should be using to make the decision.
- Explain the decision more easily to a wider group, and this is particularly useful when explaining a decision to a non-technical group.
- Help us build the decision-making capability of others (such as Joanne).
- Have a documented reference point as to why we made the decision, which we can refer back to later.

For many of our decisions, we have to make assumptions, so a documented grid is a good way to capture those assumptions and re-check them later on. Often, when we make a decision that doesn't turn out right, we struggle to remember how we made the decision and have no real way of figuring out how we made the wrong decision. With the help of a decision-making grid, we can see clearly which assumptions worked out and which didn't.

Capability: PERSONAL IMPACT

Decision-making Grid

CRITERIA	CRITERIA MEASURES High, Medium and Low rating definition H – 2 pts, M = 1 pt, L = 0 pts	OPTIONS		
		MEDIA A	MEDIA B	MEDIA C
1 TARGET AUDIENCE REACH (TRAFFIC)	H: Over 1 million M: 0.5 to 1.0 million L: Below 0.5 million WEIGHTED (X2)	M	H	L
2 COST PER THOUSAND	H: Less than $1 CPC M: $1 to $3 CPC L: Over $3 CPC WEIGHTED (X2)	H	H	L
3 BRAND ALIGNMENT	H: Upmarket M: Mid-market L: Mid- to low-market	L	H	H
4 PREMIUM PLACEMENT	H: Yes, available and exclusive M: Yes, available (non-excl) L: Not available	H	M	H
5 FREQUENCY	H: Audience turnover 8 x a month or more M: 4 x to 8 x a month L: Below 4 x a month	M	M	M
6 EDITORIAL PLACEMENT	H: Yes, available unpaid M: Yes, available but paid L: Not available	M	M	H
7 COMPETITIONS	H: Yes, available unpaid M: Yes, available but paid L: Not available	M	H	M
	SCORES	11	15	8

FIGURE 8.2: Decision-Making Grid

One of the authors worked some years back with an executive team that had made a decision to spend $100,000 on an initiative, which then didn't achieve the goal. A year later, when reviewing the decision (a meeting at which the author was in attendance), the executive team argued for over an hour about why they had made the decision a year before, what criteria had been used, and even what outcomes they were expecting. It turned out that several executives had thought the decision was made to achieve different goals. If they had used a decision-making grid, everyone would have had clarity, both then and when reviewing the decision a year later.

Is Gut Feeling Valid?

ANOTHER CRITICAL INSIGHT ABOUT decision-making that we need to understand is that regardless of the decision, very often, we're making emotional decisions about issues without realizing it. This is the "gut feeling" we mentioned previously. Gut feelings are real. They're a store of emotions that tell us whether option A feels right, or whether option B does. Daniel Goleman does a great job of explaining this simply in his talk to Google University, which you'll find on YouTube.

Many experts bristle at the suggestion that their decisions are anything but objective, evidence-based, and untainted by unconscious bias of some form. But the data supports the view that gut feeling is a crucial factor in the way we make decisions.

This is exactly why deploying emotional reasoning, one of the six emotional intelligences (see Chapter 5), is very important for experts. Experts with a high emotional reasoning capability have the ability to tune into those gut feelings and determine whether it's appropriate to apply it to this particular decision or not. And that is harder than it sounds.

Emotional Reasoning

THIS EMOTIONAL INTELLIGENCE REFERS both to a thought process as well as the attempt to convey such thoughts, whether verbally or in writing. There are a number of ways in which immature experts may exhibit insufficient emotional reasoning:

- A failure to anticipate (or recognize as legitimate) others' likely reactions to our assertions.
- Communication that fails to adequately engage or inspire.
- Proposals and business cases that may be fact-laden but are bereft of passion or strategic connection.
- Emotionally driven decisions that fail to account for personal bias.

Facts are safe, finite, and predictable. Yet as we have now described several times, research suggests that all decisions involve the emotional brain, too. Ignoring or simply failing to master the emotional dimensions of decision-making means we'll be blind to these significant influences in the decision-making process.

Experts with advanced emotional reasoning:

- Are more persuasive, influential and inspiring because they can explain the *why* behind the decision, not just the *what*. They're also prepared to take the time to do so and will not move forward until colleagues understand the overall context of the decision. This builds buy-in and commitment.
- Are more articulate about subjects outside of their technical knowledge. When it comes to making a decision about asking for funding for a specific project, the Master Expert will see beyond the technical case for the investment and be able to link it to corporate strategy and organizational benefits. They'll be thinking about how other senior executives will be thinking about their proposal and will shape it accordingly.
- Make more rounded decisions, taking into account both the salient facts as well as their and others' feelings. Where are our colleagues' opinions and feelings coming from? What are they based upon? Do they perhaps have some insight or data that we don't have?

Is it possible to build up our emotional reasoning? There are a number of actions we can take, and there is a lot of literature around this topic now. Some simple techniques include:

- We can make a deliberate point of gauging our own and others' feelings as part of the decision-making process.
- We can put ourselves in the shoes of others and intentionally try to make a case that would be compelling from that frame of reference.
- We can develop a comprehensive vocabulary that describes emotions so that we can recognize and describe all shades of feelings.

Inspiring Engagement, Commitment and Change

THE ULTIMATE CAPABILITY OF a successful Results Driver is being able to convince colleagues to engage and commit to the path being proposed. Inspiration means that our colleagues *want* to follow the path we have formulated (often in association with others), which is a powerful motivator that ensures things get done.

Inspiration and engagement are the mature fruits of all the other aspects of emotional intelligence. They allow us to positively influence others' thoughts and feelings and then prompt them to shift their behaviors in accordance with the organizational or project goals. When experts lack this capacity, they:

- Rub others the wrong way, triggering their resistance.
- Fail to motivate others to change and even trigger others' demotivation or resistance.
- Work in isolation more than collaborating or compete excessively or inappropriately.
- Become over-reliant on formal authority structures (escalation), policies and systems rather than practicing the art of persuading people to do things on their own merits.

Experts who are strong in this capability:

- Tend to have greater influence.
- Develop lasting and productive/rewarding relationships.
- Negotiate win-win outcomes and resolve conflict constructively. This includes being open to shifting their own views if presented with compelling evidence that they may be wrong.
- Collaborate effectively.

Authenticity

BEING AUTHENTIC IS VITAL if we're to foster trust in others. Subconsciously, we're all reading others' intentions and determining whether or not those intentions are honorable. Our antennae for picking up something fake or disingenuous are highly developed, even though the process is typically subconscious, primal and instinctive. When we feel that someone is being genuine and is extending trust to us by being themselves, then we tend to be at ease around them. If we perceive the opposite, we tend to be guarded.

There are a number of ways in which a lack of authenticity can show up:

- Coming across as closed-off or guarded through a lack of personality, being non-expressive, withdrawn, or overly private.
- Non-committal and unwilling to take a stand or to "get their hands dirty," or being aloof, distant or disinterested.
- Untrustworthy or lacking integrity.
- Closed-minded.
- Passive-aggressive.
- Evasive.

Becoming authentic involves being comfortable expressing oneself, including one's feelings, in an unedited fashion. It's about being candid in a manner that others appreciate and that fosters trust. Candor, for example, in sharing our decision-making grid to explain decisions and policy positions. We're willing to take risks and be vulnerable, thus signaling that we're trusting and operating in a safe environment.

Experts who have significantly developed their capacity to be authentic:
- Earn others' trust more rapidly.
- Create an environment wherein information flows easily.
- Engage in courageous conversations.

How we can develop our authenticity:
- Practice the courageous conversations methodology detailed later in Chapter 11.
- Find a way to put what we're feeling into words and take a risk in disclosing it.
- Take responsibility and avoid the temptation to blame.
- Clearly state our expectations and provide timely and courageous feedback.

TAKING ACTION

Growing Our Results Driver Skills

IF THIS IS AN expert role in which you believe you could add greater value, here are some high-level suggestions for actions to take:

▶ PRACTICE A STEP-BY-STEP PLANNING PROCESS

Without a planning discipline that prioritizes high-value strategic activities over those that are merely urgent, experts get caught up in the day-to-day demands at the expense of long-term effectiveness. Questions we might like to ask ourselves:

- Am I getting trapped in humdrum day-to-day activities instead of acting strategically?
- Have I assessed what my key strategic priorities are? Are they expressed as meaningful, proactive, well-defined, high-impact goals in each of my most important roles?
- Have I adopted a step-by-step planning process that enables me to assess the value I'm adding and where my time and energy shouldn't be invested?
- What conversations are needed with key stakeholders to reset expectations and communicate my larger directives?
- Have I identified a sensible operating rhythm for my role?

▶ TAKE OWNERSHIP OF IMPROVING KEY ORGANIZATIONAL RESULTS

When experts don't seem aware of or committed to improving organizational results, we're seen as marginal players. To avoid this, we need to become (and be seen as) active players and owners of key organizational metrics. Questions we might like to ask ourselves:

- Which organizational KPIs do I have the ability to influence?
- How aligned are my contributions with creating a positive impact? How could I improve this alignment?
- How does the organization currently track and report any uplifts in those metrics that I can reasonably attribute to my inputs? Do I

have visibility of these measures? Do I measure and report my own performance against them? If not, why not?

- Do I need to develop internal, forward-looking metrics to measure my contribution to key organization goals?

▶ ACT WHEN COURAGEOUS CONVERSATIONS ARE NECESSARY

Failing to tackle challenging conversations in a timely and effective way means that issues often end up unaddressed, including our needs not being met. This can lead to resentment and looking weak and ineffectual. Questions we might like to ask ourselves:

- What is my default position when it comes to courageous conversations? Do I refrain from expressing my concerns or needs, or do I find a way to express my needs, concerns and observations in a manner that balances courage and consideration?
- What key courageous conversations have I been putting off, and why? What has got in the way of tackling them confidently and effectively?
- What courageous conversations have I had recently, and how did they go? Effectively? Or did they damage relationships and my personal brand? If so, why? How could I improve my delivery and effectiveness?
- Do I spend time using models, such as the I-GRROW (Chapter 48) and OFFICER (Chapter 11) models to plan these conversations?
- What opportunities are there for me to immediately increase my influence and impact, including the timely resolution of issues?

"In order to carry a positive action, we must develop here a positive vision."

Dalai Lama

CHAPTER | 09 |

The Expert Energy Engine

How do we spend the right time on the right tasks to increase the value we add to the organization?

IN THIS CHAPTER, WE WILL EXPLORE:

- The resources we have at our disposal that are in least supply are time and energy. It's impossible to create more of them... or is it?
- Techniques to assess where we currently spend our time and energy and where we would like to invest these resources to create greater value for the organization.
- The Expert Energy Engine, and how to deploy it effectively to regain control of our own time and energy.

ONE OF THE PRIMARY shifts between the lower levels of Expertship and operating at Master Expert level is the shift from a focus on immediate, responsive, short-term tasks to one characterized by longer term, strategically oriented, proactive initiatives. This is an easy thing to describe, but in the authors' experience, it's a very difficult transition for most experts to make.

Many experts tell us that they feel inundated with a deluge of requests that don't represent the best use of their time and capabilities. They don't feel like they have the right or liberty to decline many of these requests as there generally isn't an alternative resource available or an alternative department that can complete the task. The net effect is that the volume of immediate tasks keeps experts tied up and distracted from the more significant value-adding activities that they might otherwise engage in, which also provide them with greater fulfillment.

Spending the right amount of time on the right things for the right reasons is a defining talent of Master Experts. Many call this skill "time management" or "advanced prioritization." We like the idea of "energy management" since we don't, in reality, manage time. We simply choose what we direct our energy (our time and attention) toward. We determine what is most deserving of our energy and, when required, direct appropriate levels of energy toward the appropriate tasks.

The frustration for experts comes not just from the fact that our skills are wasted on basic tasks but from people wasting our time and sapping our energy. Experts need lots of energy to be innovative and creative. Spending energy on low-value tasks destroys our ability to have the right amount of energy available to make a bigger difference.

> *"In most organizations, the amount of expert work is increasing, but expert resources are reducing."*

Let's take Peter as an example of the many experts we meet. He receives upward of 400 emails a day. This can take up to 50 percent of his workday, with a further 25 percent (on average) of his day being consumed by meetings of one sort or another. This leaves him, at best, with two to three hours to actually produce all of the work outputs that he's paid to deliver, and that includes him working through until 6.30 p.m. or later four nights per week. These unpaid additional hours aren't in his contract, but Peter feels the culture of his organization expects this additional effort from him.

Peter feels that he's constantly behind in most of his projects and is struggling to meet deadlines he didn't set and often was not consulted about. He needs coffee to get through the day, he no longer gets to the gym, and he rarely spends quality time with his family. When he finally arrives home weary from the day, he reclines on the couch in front of the TV until it's time to go to bed. After a few hours of sleep, it all kicks off again the following day.

Peter's story isn't uncommon. With our digital devices connecting us 24/7 to the office and the often unreasonable expectation of a prompt response to all digital communication, all employees, experts included, are maxing out in terms of their capacity to process and properly attend to all of the information and requests coming at them.

Most organizations don't have an over-supply of qualified experts, and invariably, the volume of inbound requests for the expertise of experts is completely disproportionate to the number of experts available. In most organizations, the amount of expert work is increasing, but expert resources are reducing. These factors create a focus that is reactive and typically more transactional, with the experts responding to the tactical requirements of others, who are often oblivious as to what sorts of value the organization might truly derive from its experts if they were otherwise directed.

As experts, we alone might realize the contribution we could make that might be of greatest value. Oftentimes, those we report to don't have adequate knowledge to see where our time is being wasted. Therefore, it's our responsibility as experts to take charge of where our time is spent. We cannot depend on anyone else to sort this out for us.

Many of the experts we work with believe it simply isn't possible to gain control of their time and their energy. They believe organizational design and poor management have consigned them to a life of overworked misery forever. We beg to differ.

Changing the Polarity

AS WE DISCUSS IN many chapters of this book, experts live complicated and multi-faceted professional lives. We typically have many masters, most of whom never talk to one another. We have responsibilities on multiple projects simultaneously, which mysteriously all have deadlines that clash. We have huge workloads and not enough time to complete them. We have no one obvious to delegate these tasks to.

> *"The Expert Energy Engine helps experts take back control of their working lives."*

We all know this, but perhaps it hasn't dawned on all of us yet that we have far more agency than we might suppose and, as such, share responsibility for our lives feeling so out of control, overwhelmed by workload and responsibility, and misunderstood.

Effective prioritization of our energy on activities that add high value is actually our responsibility. If we wait for multiple masters to sit down and plan this all out for us, we will be waiting forever. And indeed, many of us have been waiting forever.

The **Expert Energy Engine** (see Figure 9.1) is a seven-step process to help all experts take back control of their working lives—and often their wider lives as well. There are many time-management models out there, and we've morphed some of the best into our process, which is designed specifically for experts. The following seven steps represent a 15 to 20-minute planning process that is to be conducted weekly, or at least regularly.

Capability: PERSONAL IMPACT

The Expert Energy Engine

1. ALIGN OUR VALUE TO STRATEGY/MISSION
Consider how your role contributes to the execution of the organization's strategy. Where can we add the most value and why?

7. RE-AUDIT ENERGY LEVELS AND GOAL OUTCOMES
Periodically review where energy/time is being spent against existing and changing priorities.

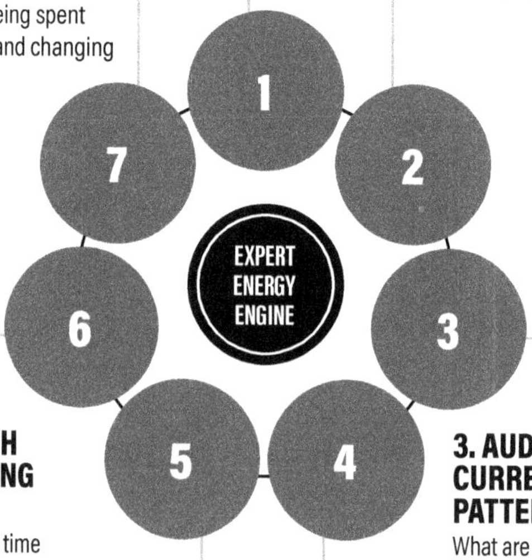

2. IDENTIFY HIGH-VALUE KEY ROLES
What are the big-picture things we are employed to do?

6. ESTABLISH AN OPERATING RHYTHM
Allocate energy / time to key priorities, and build an effective monitoring system; fine tune operating rhythm.

3. AUDIT CURRENT ENERGY PATTERNS
What are we currently spending our energy on? How does this profile match our key value-creating roles?

5. SET GOALS - SHORT, MEDIUM, LONG
Determine a range of short- to long-term goals for how our contribution will be measured as successful, and validate with key stakeholders.

4. RESET PRIORITIES & EXPECTATIONS
Select priority areas of contribution – the places where we intend to spend our energy – and negotiate new expectations among stakeholders.

FIGURE 9.1: The Expert Energy Engine

Step 1: Align Our Value with Strategy/Mission

Our planning session needs to begin with thinking through how our role contributes to the execution of the organization's strategy and purpose. Where can we add the most value, and why? What are our long-term goals and measures of success?

This is our 70,000-foot question. It connects the work we do with how we directly or indirectly help the organization we work for execute its strategy and achieve its purpose or mission. Did you know that the idea of a 70,000-foot perspective comes from the height a U2 spy plane flies at, giving it a 550 km view of the horizon, which is a very long way out in front (see Chapter 48 for our graphic on this concept)?

We might want to start with an even wider lens, looking at where, as an expert, we want to contribute holistically, and then consider the contribution we're making to our current organization as a milestone along that road. The broader our thinking can be about contribution at this stage, the better. This is because we're seeking our "true north," which is where, in the bigger picture, we're going and why. The idea is to invest a few minutes, whether each week or month, but at least once a quarter, reflecting on how effectively our time and energy are currently being devoted to achieving high-value impact.

Key questions: What do we want to achieve overall? What things matter most to us? We could explore such questions from a whole-life perspective if so inclined, or we could simply consider such questions from within a purely professional frame of reference. What do we ultimately want to deliver by way of value? What's our vision for ourselves and our function(s) over the next two or three years? Naturally, such reflection sits alongside evaluative questions, such as "To what extent are we on track?" This sort of personal inquiry helps inform our long-term goal setting and eventually cascades down into setting targets for the week ahead, as well as the necessary summoning of the discipline it will take to execute these and push back on distractions from our preferred focus.

Step 2: Identify High-Value Key Roles

The second step is to consider all of the different roles in which we would need to be active in order to make headway toward our overall contributions to the execution of the organizational strategy or purpose.

These can include roles outside of work, such as spouse, parent, neighbor, community volunteer, and so on. Our energy levels at work are likely to also be significantly impacted by the extent to which we're using our non-work time productively.

At work, most experts have multiple roles. We may have a primary role that is specified in our job description, but this only represents one aspect of what we actually do and are expected and need to do.

> *"One expert amended this to 'helping others solve technical problems that they ought to be able to solve themselves.'"*

We may have several responsibilities or projects, all of which need some degree of input, and some, even high-value ones that happen to not be urgent, may be suffering from neglect or under-investment. There may be all kinds of informal roles, such as coach, knowledge curator, thought leader, networker, innovator, and so on, that warrant our attention. The purpose of this step of the process is to brainstorm all of our roles and then to determine which of them are of the highest value and would benefit from the setting of specific goals to be accomplished within a given time period. Typically, it's the coming week, but sometimes it's over a longer period. What would success look like in the long term, medium term, and possibly short term?

Step 3: Audit Current Energy Patterns

In this third step, we assess where we're currently spending our time and our energy. There is only one way to do this: conduct a simple audit by measuring for several weeks what tasks and activities we're actually spending our time on. Our advice to experts isn't to over-engineer this process. Simply use a spreadsheet or pencil and paper to note down what time has been spent throughout the day. We recommend doing this four times throughout the day: mid-morning, lunch, mid-afternoon and at the end of the workday. We can usually estimate quite accurately what we have spent the last two to three hours on.

Having worked with many experts and people leaders in the last few years, the authors can attest to both the value and the surprise involved in this exercise. We suspect you won't quite believe how quickly you can identify huge portions of time that get wasted each week. Or at least how much time is spent relatively unproductively as our attention was diverted from our highest priorities.

Once a clear pattern has been established, it's possible to start categorizing activities and tasks. For example, one category of energy consumption that chews up an inordinate amount of time might be "helping others solve technical problems."

One expert amended this to "helping others solve technical problems that they ought to be able to solve themselves." This expert reacted to the insight that this activity was taking up 20 percent of her time by spending a month mentoring and training this group of colleagues. The end results were that this category of energy consumption diminished by over 75 percent. This investment in *knowledge transfer* really paid off (see Chapter 46). These categories of sub-optimal tasks will vary depending on the role of each expert.

Once we're clear on where we actually spend our time (usually alarmingly different from where we previously thought we spent our time), then we're ready to embark on the next step.

Step 4: Reset Priorities and Expectations

This step is where the hard work begins. Taking the results of our work in step 2, identifying where we can add the most value, and combining this work with the results of step 3, where we spend our time, most experts need to reset their priorities. To do this, we've come up with a simple list:

- What do we need to do more of?
- What should we continue doing?
- What must we stop doing?

This last question is where there is usually a requirement for some courageous conversations (see Chapter 11). In order to allocate more energy to high-value activities, we have to stop doing low-value activities, even though these may be activities that our stakeholders have grown accustomed to us delivering for them. The courageous conversations will be about resetting the expectations of these stakeholders because, given our new priorities, we regretfully no longer have the resources to complete these tasks for them. Following each of these steps is critical for this to be effective. Without established high-value alternative activities that are connected to the organizational strategy and purpose, we can't plausibly argue the case for ceasing or reducing the delivery of service to others.

Letting stakeholders down gently is a subtle art and calls for careful planning. We suggest using the I-GRROW model, which is described in Chapter 48).

Step 5: Set Goals - Short, Medium, Long

We have now worked out which roles we need to focus on. The next step involves establishing very specific goals to be achieved within each role across various timeframes.

What constitutes short, medium and long term will vary by role. Often, achieving long-term goals requires some very specific actions and outcomes to be achieved, usually by the end of this week or month.

This planning process requires us to identify something that represents a stride forward, focused activity leading to a worthwhile outcome that likely wouldn't otherwise be undertaken or delivered. For instance, if we want to add more value to our technical cohort and increase others' capability or commitment, perhaps with a view to delegating some lower value responsibilities to these colleagues, then we might set ourselves a goal to coach these colleagues.

The long-term goal is for them to become trusted and competent in carrying out new activities. A short-term goal might be to gain their buy-in, develop a coaching plan, and commence coaching sessions. For example, "I will work with Angela on refreshing her Lean Sigma skills with a view to her picking up project X from next month onward." And we would do the same (set a worthwhile goal) for each of our other prioritized roles.

We recommend starting with long-term goals first, then contemplating what steps need to be taken to eventually achieve that goal. On a weekly basis, we recommend that you identify and diarize one high-value goal for each of your key roles and build the entire week around these priorities.

Step 6: Establish an Operating Rhythm

The next step, which, in our experience, is one that most experts don't give enough attention, is to start populating our calendar with suitable time allocations for carrying out the necessary activities in support of the goals we have set in the previous step.

"How do we defeat the energy thieves?"

The idea is that the things that matter most should not be at the mercy of the things which matter less. These critical tasks must claim a place of priority in the calendar before the week fills up with less important or less valuable stuff. For many of the experts we work with, this is a significant behavioral change. Often, experts use their diaries only for meetings and reminders, not for allocating time to specific tasks.

Over time, this kind of approach will allow for a gradual displacement of lower value activities with elective high-value activities. It's never going to be possible to do everything, but this method will mean that our focus can truly be on the highest value actions rather than being deluged by lower value tasks and having our true (but often unprioritized), potentially highest contribution eclipsed. Now the other things will have to make way for our chosen (and, because of excellent stakeholder engagement, *agreed*) priorities.

One of the authors, Alistair, has a reasonably complex role. He's the leader of the business, and he's allocated 25 percent of his time to this task. He's also a working consultant (25 percent), the chief marketing strategist (20 percent), and has an important business development role (30 percent).

Alistair has established that his natural operating rhythm is monthly. That is, in any one week, he can't achieve this balance between all of these roles. Some weeks, for example, he's running Expertship programs all week, but over the month, balance is achievable.

He uses color coding in his diary so he can easily identify which of these roles are being under- or over-serviced.

There are some months, of course, where consulting commitments overtake marketing activity. While this isn't a perfect state of affairs, at least it's instantly visible using this system. It enables us to rebalance our activities in the following months.

It's important to note that while we're busy trying to establish an operating rhythm that matches our chosen high-value roles and goals, others in the organization, those with quite different agendas, are busy trying to steal our energy and time. We have some suggestions on how to defeat *energy thieves* in the next chapter. Energy thieves don't do this deliberately, of course. In fact, they might actually have tasks that ought to take precedence over ours.

> *"Did we just go flaky?*
> *Is there a pattern of flakiness we could*
> *learn from?"*

The first five steps of the Expert Energy Engine are progressive methods of identifying and scheduling priorities. But a plan isn't, in itself, a cause for celebration until it's executed. A plan is no guarantee of execution or that benefits will be realized, though it typically heightens the likelihood of execution. More so than if we never conceptualized what exactly we want to happen. If we have a plan to conduct a coaching session with Angela on Thursday at 4 p.m., we have a greater fighting chance of pushing back on others' requests for our time at that moment than we would if we only had a vague notion that we would coach Angela at some point.

Of course, that doesn't mean that we slavishly stick to the plan, regardless of situations arising. If there is a genuine crisis that warrants our attention, we can always adapt and reschedule with Angela.

Stephen Covey famously suggests "exercising integrity in the moment of choice." Exercising integrity means "making choices that are consistent with one's values." If the plan is well-conceived then exercising integrity will usually involve pushing back on the less important matter that has arisen and sticking to our chosen focus. But it's entirely possible that something more important but not envisioned deserves our attention. In this case, we accommodate but quickly reschedule the delayed priority.

Step 7: Re-Audit Energy Levels and Goal Outcomes

At the outset of the next planning cycle, we can reflect on the previous week or month's plan and its execution. Did we achieve all of the planned goals? Yes? Do we feel a sense of progress and accomplishment? If not, why not? Do we need to go deeper in our goal setting? If we didn't achieve our goals, why was that? Was it because of legitimate but unanticipated priorities that came up? Or did we just go flaky? Is there a pattern of flakiness that we could learn from? What do we need to do next time to ensure that the coaching session with Angela goes ahead? Is repair work needed in our relationships?

Can you imagine what kinds of results and progress we could make if we made a habit of undertaking this seven-step planning process regularly, whether weekly or monthly, over the next few months? More and more of our time will be invested in high-value activities, gradually displacing low-value activities. We'll be proactive, strategic, and develop our brand accordingly. We'll be building capability around us. Taking timely preventative action. Investing in relationships. Experiencing increased quality of life. And the top payoff is that we'll experience less stress.

There is, of course, one fundamental consequence of this analysis and planning. We're going to have to say "no" to some of our stakeholders more often. That's not comfortable or easy, particularly if they have gotten used to us simply delivering whatever they want, whenever they want it.

The next chapter is focused on the subtle but critical art of saying "no."

TAKING ACTION

Growing Our Energy Management Skills

IF THIS IS AN expert skill in which you believe could help you add greater value, here is a high-level suggestion for actions to take:

▶ REGULARLY AUDIT WHERE YOU SPEND YOUR TIME

- It takes far less time than many experts believe, but keeping a register of where we're spending our time and energy is a great way of saving time.
- Deploy a simple system that suits your working rhythm to capture what you're spending your time on.
- Assess regularly whether the percentage of time between major key performance indicators (KPIs) is on track or needs adjustment.
- Explore with your leaders what percentage of time ought to be spent on each KPI and discuss key conversations that need to be had with stakeholders to rebalance your energy allocations.
- Build clear and compelling narratives that can be deployed when you need to decline tasks. Help stakeholders understand why you're required to spend energy on alternative activities rather than the ones they would like you to complete.
- Identify a sensible operating rhythm for your role and assess weekly whether you're sticking to it. If not, why not? What is getting in the way?

CHAPTER | 10 |

The Art of Saying No

How do we learn to say "no" without upsetting stakeholders?

IN THIS CHAPTER, WE WILL EXPLORE:

- How we typically think about refusing people, and how it impacts our overall effectiveness.
- The excuses we make and now need to avoid.
- Six simple techniques to say "no" without saying the word "no."

TIME THIEVES. EVERY ORGANIZATION has them. And the vast majority of experts we have worked with over the past few years are guilty, ourselves included, of giving them oxygen. For a variety of reasons, we have simply not learned how to say "no" diplomatically and effectively.

In our programs, the authors invite experts to list what gets in the way of them doing high-value work. The results of this question are very predictable, whether our program was staged in New York, London, Singapore or Sydney.

In no particular order, experts typically list most of these barriers:
- Too many meetings
- Meetings without outcomes
- Too many stakeholders with differing priorities
- Firefighting, spot fires (unplanned work)
- Interruptions
- Too many emails

- Excessive reporting
- Managers changing the goalposts
- Lack of necessary resources
- Unrealistic deadlines
- Insufficient training on new systems or processes
- Simply too much work (very high workload)

Do these sound familiar? Across literally hundreds of groups that the authors have facilitated, it's remarkable how similar these lists are.

"The art of saying 'no' is one skill that separates mere experts from Master Experts."

Whether the experts are from IT, legal, engineering, science, finance or audit, it appears to be a standard condition of professional life for most experts. But it doesn't need to be. We work with expert groups to help them define solutions to these barriers. Setting priorities linked to strategy and purpose (see previous section) is a critical process they offer as a solution, along with managing meetings more effectively and not attending meetings that don't really require them (see the chapter on collaboration for a more detailed analysis of Master Expert behavior when it comes to meetings).

A third solution is even simpler: say "no." But doing so, our experts tell us, is never simple.

When we ask experts to list their reasons for being unable to say "no," the list is as predictable and consistent as the barriers to getting things done. They are, again, in no particular order:

- We believe saying "no" creates conflict.
- We want to please our colleagues and stakeholders.
- We want to look like we're doing a good job.
- We worry about the pressure saying "no" creates.
- We don't want it to seem like we don't know how to do the work.
- Saying "no" is career limiting.
- We find what they're asking us to do interesting or challenging, so we have FOMO (fear of missing out).
- We can't say "no" to our manager.
- We don't have license to say "no."
- We don't know how to say "no" diplomatically.

Do these reasons for avoiding refusing specific tasks sound familiar? An interesting observation that groups make is that when we're actually saying these things to ourselves, in our minds, they sound sensible and plausible.

When we list them on a flip chart at a workshop, however, they sound less convincing. It's the avoidance of conflict and the hubris of "we can do anything" that drives many of these self-talk excuses.

In Figure 10.1, we break down the solutions and alternatives to these excuses. But let's focus for a moment on the art of saying "no," which is a critical Master Expert capability. It's a skill that separates mere experts from Master Experts. It's the ability to objectively look at our workload and say that task is important and must be done, and that task is less important and will have to be deferred or declined. It the ability to make this case and to influence people effectively. This is actually what this book is all about.

It's the ability to understand that, within large organizations, there will always be too many projects and crazy deadlines. The reason for this is there are thousands of different agendas and there are careers on the line.

As experts, it's our duty, and a key professional responsibility, to help the organization prioritize, because the way in which organizations are structured makes it very difficult for experts to do this in isolation. General Manager A wants to be promoted to Executive General Manager before General Manager B. This natural tension leads General Manager A to insist that his/her project is more important than any proposed by General Manager B.

For us, as experts, to believe that common sense or reason will break out in this career-driven, ego-driven, silo-driven madness is, in itself, madness. We have to be the calm, objective, reasoned, strategically aligned voice—not the shrill, victim-based, subjective, emotional, derailing, immature voice. It's our choice. As we say in the last box in Figure 10.1, we need to grow up. We need to say it like it is, but say it nicely. Say it *diplomatically*.

Another way to look at it is that those asking us to do non-important work against unrealistic deadlines, the *time thieves*, are, in effect, unreasonably stealing our time and energy. Inviting us to a meeting where our contribution is likely to be limited to one item for five minutes means, by definition, if the meeting is an hour long, they're stealing 55 minutes of our very valuable time. We have choices. We can let them or we can push back. We'd like to suggest a rule, a mantra, if you like, that should police our behavior in this respect.

We either learn to say "no" diplomatically or we stop moaning about the pressure and overload of work we have accepted. It's our fault. It's our responsibility. We either master the ability we have to manage stakeholder relationships, "win-win" rather than "they win and we always lose," or we accept that we don't have that skill and will quietly suffer as a consequence.

Capability: **PERSONAL IMPACT**

The Art of Saying "No"

	TYPICAL REASONING	REVISED REASONING	ALTERNATIVE RESPONSE
1	Saying no creates conflict	Saying yes now will also result in conflict later – usually worse	"If I take this on something else will have to be left undone"
2	We want to please our colleagues and/ or stakeholders	Saying yes – overcommitting – will result in someone else's displeasure sooner or later	"My existing focus and commitments are (x)"
3	We want to look like we are doing a good job	Over-committing on lower priority work is doing a bad job	"My strategic mandate is (x) and this, unfortunately, doesn't fit"
4	We worry about the pressure saying no creates	Saying yes when we should say no is what creates pressure	"If I agree to this, we risk quality issues due to excessive overload"
5	We don't want to appear weak or that we don't know how to do the work	Actual brand damage results from being over-extended, missing deadlines, poor quality rush jobs or colluding in being engaged at a lower than optimal level	"Let me equip and train others to do this. It's not my optimal focus"
6	Saying no is career limiting	Constant under-delivery or being grumpy limits one's career	For managers, list work, show calendar – they need to decide what gives
7	Fear of Missing Out (FOMO)	Lack of sufficient knowledge transfer results in our not having capacity	Plan for future projects we wish to be part of by delegating now
8	We can't say no to our manager (or certain stakeholders)	Managers/stakeholders will expect and ask until we push back. They expect us to alert them when we reach our limits	List work, show calendar, negotiate trade-offs – involve them in deciding what gives
9	We don't have the license to say no	We may earnestly believe this but it's not true. It is our right and responsibility to prioritize	Change mindset – it is my professional responsibility and right to say no
10	We don't know how to say no diplomatically	We can start thinking and behaving differently – and practice	Get adult. Say it like it is. Nicely

FIGURE 10.1: The Art of Saying "No"

The Best Way to Say "No" is to Never Use the Word "No"

AS WE DEMONSTRATE IN the chart, there are many ways to say "no," and all of the best techniques avoid using that word entirely. Once we get into the knack of using some of these techniques, there's no stopping us. Not only are they effective, but they're also a lot of fun.

Technique #1: "Yes, but …"

- In your mind: "There is simply no way I am doing that…"
- Out loud: "Yes, I can see that it's a very important task for you to have us complete, but… I have these other priorities to complete and I have been told not to take anything else on…"

Technique #2: Timeframing

- In your mind: "No way. That isn't a key task and a priority for me…"
- Out loud: "Yes, I possibly could do it, but unfortunately, not until after the holidays…"

Technique #3: Independence building

- In your mind: "You have to be joking… I can't believe you don't know how to do that yourself…"
- Out loud: "Okay, I can see it's very important to fix that problem. How about I get a colleague to show you how to do it, so you'll never have to wait for me to be available if the problem occurs again…"

Technique #4: Remote negotiation

- In your mind: "If I say "yes" to this, stakeholder X will have to wait another week for their work…"
- Out loud: "Okay, I can do it for you. But first, you need to go and see Stakeholder X and get their agreement that your task should take precedence over hers/his. Okay? Let me know how it goes…"

Technique #5: Referent authority

- In your mind: "Please no, not this low-end task again…"
- Out loud: "Ah, I'd love to do that for you, but my manager has told me to stop doing that type of work. She/he has asked me to prioritize other activities…" (i.e., take it up with my manager)

Technique #6: Strategic professionalism

- In your mind: (your turn, choose a thought that you regularly have…)
- Out loud: "Yes, well, I could do that for you, but if I did, I would be failing to prioritize properly and failing to do tasks that I have been set that have strategic importance…"

All fun apart, the answers we provide should be authentic and properly thought through. Experts aren't encouraged to say "no" regardless of what they're being asked to do. Being truly collaborative means listening carefully to what our stakeholders want and considering whether or not what they want us to do is more important.

Similarly, on many occasions, experts tell us that the work proposed is part of their strategic remit, but the element that creates the pressure is the unreasonable deadlines or short notice that stakeholders insist upon. The ability to challenge the deadline rather than the task is another skill we can benefit from acquiring. The ability to agree with stakeholders that deadlines should be jointly agreed, taking all workloads into account, rather than unilaterally imposed, is an important stakeholder conversation to have. Remember, most stakeholders can't see the full remit of an expert's work. They can only see how long it takes an expert to do *their* work.

None of these conversations are easy, particularly in the first instance.

All of which means we need to master another art: that of conducting effective *courageous conversations* in which we deal with conflict effectively, fairly, and for the greater good of all.

TAKING ACTION

Growing Our Ability to Push Back When Appropriate

IF THIS IS AN expert skill that you believe could help you add greater value, here is a high-level suggestion for actions to take:

▶ EXPLORE YOUR INNER "NO" SETTINGS

- Using the chart in this chapter, ask yourself which mindset or beliefs mostly govern the decisions you make to say "yes" to stakeholders when you would much prefer (and believe it's the right thing) to say "no."
- Make a note of the *regretted yeses* that derail your workload and have the greatest impact. Start planning how you might effectively and authentically push back diplomatically on those requests. What support might you need ahead of time to do so?
- Run the movie: run a replay of a typical conversation and reimagine it using some of the techniques in this chapter. What might you say, and what might your stakeholder say in return? Prepare for likely responses and practice how you will sensibly answer their questions and deal with their concerns.
- Having made a list of tasks you really want to push back on, take action, and then review that list in a month's time. How well did you do? Did the new tactics work? If not, why not? What tactics might you deploy instead?
- Don't give up if it really is important for you to decline that work.

CHAPTER | 11 |

Mastering Courageous Conversations

Using both courage and consideration to have the conversations that matter and make a difference.

IN THIS CHAPTER, WE WILL EXPLORE:

- What gets in the way of us having timely courageous conversations?
- What techniques can we deploy to help us find the courage we need to address difficult issues with colleagues? What are the payoffs?
- What is the best and most effective way of starting the courageous conversations we need to have with colleagues?

WHAT GETS IN THE way of us having courageous conversations?

Between us (the authors, with over 30 years of running Expertship and leadership programs), we must have asked this question a thousand times, and the answer is nearly always the same for both people leaders and experts. Participants we work with report almost universally that they have a fear of such conversations. Experts, along with many leaders, feel uncomfortable telling a colleague something they presume the colleague doesn't want to hear or will struggle to digest. Most of us worry about our colleagues' reactions, which we *always* assume will be awful. Many of us worry we will upset the person we're having the conversation with, thus ruining our relationship with them. We're fearful of the resistance we might encounter, which we mostly over-imagine. We might be wary of seeming like we're imposing our will or opinions, or have taken exception to those that we have witnessed doing so.

> *"Our colleague remains oblivious to a poor, derailing,*
> *possibly career-limiting behavior because we were too*
> *worried about how they might feel if we told them."*

Capability: **PERSONAL IMPACT**

Courage and Consideration

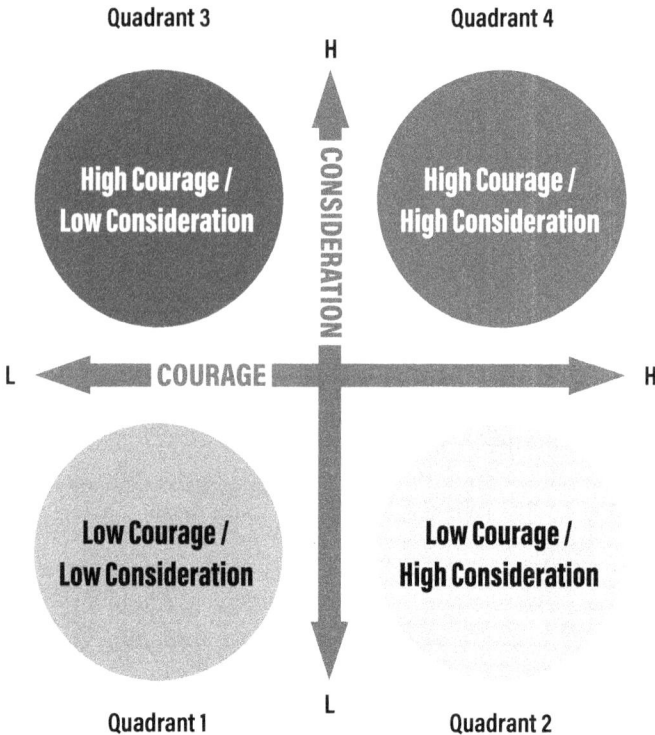

Adapted from Stephen Covey, *7 Habits of Effective People*

FIGURE 11.1: The Courage and Consideration Model

We're concerned about our part in the problem—particularly if we have put off the conversation far too long. Avoiding the conversation for as long as possible, hoping the problem will go away, is the most common tactic deployed by the thousands upon thousands of the participants we have worked with. We feel we need lots of time to prepare for the conversation and that we need lots of time for the conversation. We fear we don't have the communication skills to execute the conversation effectively.

While we're aware of all our reasons for not having the courageous conversations we need to have, we're also very aware of the impact of not having these courageous conversations.

Tasks fail. Rework is required, sometimes many times. Relationships fail. Projects fail. Products fail. Services fail. Careers fail. Whole organizations can fail.

If we consider the working environments and cultures that we have experienced or read about that are the most successful at creating and sustaining value for customers or the community, a culture of telling it like it is, constructively and with consideration, is almost always vital.

The payoffs for this type of culture, even if it's a micro-culture inside a larger organization, are huge. This will be a culture of trust. This will be a culture of learning. This will be a culture of focus and performance. This will be a culture where people work together to produce outstanding outcomes. Courageous conversations have to be in place for it to be a culture of innovation.

In her standout book, *Fierce Conversations*, Susan Scott sums this up in a single sentence. "It isn't the real conversations you should be afraid of, it's the unreal conversations."

"They'll be upset with us for not telling them…"

All of the reasons for avoiding important conversations come down to *balancing* consideration for the other person and the courage to tell it like it is (see Figure 11.1, the courage and consideration model). Low courage is when our orientation toward these courageous conversations is in quadrants 1 and 2. In this case, typically, the required conversation won't happen. If our orientation is more toward high courage (quadrants 3 and 4), the conversation will likely happen, but the outcomes will vary, depending on the amount of consideration shown. Let's explore the courage and consideration model, and while we do so, let's personally audit where we typically sit.

Quadrant 1: Low courage, low consideration. With low courage, we're unlikely to risk the conversation, so our low consideration doesn't really come into play. This quadrant is for experts who are passive observers, unwilling to step into action. Such strategies don't result in either parties' needs being articulated and explored. As such, it's unlikely that anyone's needs are satisfactorily addressed. Both parties end up living with sub-optimal outcomes, making do with the current situation. Very often, it's lose-lose.

Quadrant 2: Low courage, high consideration. If we show too much consideration for the other party's situation and insufficient courage, then we'll probably avoid the conversation or broach the subject so indirectly that it's unlikely our needs will be met or that our points of view will register with others. We're generally overly attentive to the other party's needs, feelings, perspectives and interests, and we tend to under-represent our own. This often means a problem continues to fester or our colleague remains oblivious to a poor, derailing, possibly career-limiting behavior because we were too worried about how they might feel if we told them. The truth is, of course, that they'll eventually be upset with us because we didn't tell them their behavior was a problem. "I thought you were my friend," they'll complain. "Why didn't you mention it?" We typically end up resenting the other party for not changing whilst being culpable for not earnestly speaking our truth (lose/win). Another common foible is "rescuing." At the first sign of the others' irritation or distress, we abandon our position and focus on placation.

Quadrant 3: High courage, low consideration. Too much courage and insufficient consideration and we'll likely deliver the message in such a direct and inconsiderate way that the message will be lost. A direct and uncompromising delivery style is so confronting for many feedback recipients that they respond to the critical tone of the delivery rather than the actual content of the message. This is incredibly common. The speaker represents their own position, needs and interests without exploring or even considering the needs, feelings, perspectives and interests of the other party. Others either push back similarly, resulting in a tug of war or an impasse, or they capitulate. We get our way but liquidate any goodwill in the relationship (win-lose).

Quadrant 4: High courage, high consideration. In this orientation, we have mustered the courage to have the conversation, but we have also carefully shaped the way in which we communicate the message to ensure it lands with consideration and takes into account the other party's perspective, needs, feelings and interests. Experts (and any colleagues) who have mastered this skill add great value to their colleagues, their teams and their organizations. Real conversations take place with real and usually very positive outcomes. Such exchanges typically build relationships and lead to satisfactory outcomes for all parties involved (win-win).

We'll examine some techniques for getting this right shortly. But first, let's look at an uncomfortable example of a courageous conversation.

The Billy Dilemma

IN OUR WORKSHOPS, WE choose topics for courageous conversations that are universally challenging wherever in the world we might be. One example we use is providing feedback to a colleague, Billy, that their serial missing of agreed deadlines is very disruptive for others and reduces the likelihood that they'll be invited to work on other projects, which is career limiting. It's the type of courageous conversation that we imagine can go very wrong. For example, the other party may believe we're accusing them of being incompetent—or worse, unreliable, half-hearted or lazy. It can also appear self-serving (*please make sure you do the work you do for me on time*). We imagine our colleague pushing back, explaining how their workload is unmanageable (*you simply have no idea how busy I am*), insisting they never agreed to that deadline or stating that it was imposed on them and they knew it was unrealistic at the outset.

This missing of deadlines has been going on for months. Among the project team, you've been elected to have the courageous conversation. How do you approach it?

> *"This technique of rejecting the 'do nothing' option is a crucial part of getting our minds and hearts right."*

In our workshops, we tend to focus the groups on what the intent of the conversation is. What are your intentions? Good or bad? Are you trying to help Billy or are you simply being critical? Most participant groups conclude that our intention should be to help, although there are usually some dissenting voices arguing that Billy is a poor fit for the project, team or organization and should be removed from his position immediately.

What would be the outcome, we ask, if you avoided the conversation? That is, if you allowed the situation to continue. What is the impact on Billy if he continues to have a reputation for non-delivery, late delivery or poor results?

We ask the participants to list out the consequences, and as you might imagine, they're reasonably negative. Colleagues avoid working with Billy. They don't give credence to any commitments Billy makes and some roll their eyes when these commitments are made in meetings. Some colleagues gossip behind Billy's back, discussing his lack of competence. Most participant groups we work with determine quite quickly that the right thing to do is to address the issue with Billy as quickly as possible because it's having such a negative impact on Billy's relationships, career and personal brand.

The I-GRROW model is discussed in detail in Chapter 48, but it's worth briefly reviewing the first stage of this conversation and coaching planning tool. The "I" stands for "Intent." This element of the planning tool is designed to help us get our minds in the right state to have a courageous conversation.

"What is the best way to start a courageous conversation?"

After careful consideration of Billy's predicament, we've agreed that our intent is to be *helpful*. Since no one else has stepped forward courageously, we're about to be the most helpful anyone has been to Billy in a while. Having ascertained our intent and that we're actually doing the right thing, we muster the courage. We get there partly through considering the option of "doing nothing" and rejecting it. This technique of weighing up the "do nothing" option is typically a crucial part of getting our minds and hearts right so we're able to have courageous conversations, especially since the ramifications of taking no action usually aren't justifiable. There are risks either way so we might as well embrace them.

Once committed to engaging in the conversation, our planning is often more about being considerate now that we have mustered the courage. Let's explore how to start a courageous conversation.

When we ask people to roleplay a conversation with Billy in our programs, it's quite extraordinary (and usually quite amusing) to observe the lengths to which participants will go round and round in circles before actually addressing the issue. It turns out that starting a conversation, even when you have summoned up the courage and intent to have it, is one of the hardest things to do.

How to Start a Courageous Conversation: The OFFICER Model

MANY YEARS AGO, ONE of the authors, Dominic, created the OFFICER model, which is featured in Figure 11.2, to help address this issue. He leaned heavily on the great work done by Susan Scott in her seminal book *Fierce Conversations*, which we would highly recommend to every expert.

The OFFICER framework is designed to describe how we might be able to convey the rawest of messages in a manner that integrates both courage and consideration. In Billy's case, the OFFICER model might work like this.

Outline. Billy, I want to have a conversation with you about something that I think will really help you in your work here. This is a statement of intent; it's about where we're coming from.

Billy's likely response, quite possibly not verbally expressed at this stage, is: "Okay, I'm listening, you seem to be coming from a positive space."

Facts. Have you noticed people disrespecting you and being dismissive of you when you make commitments to complete work? Have you noticed new projects starting up without you being invited to join the team? Have you noticed colleagues getting very irritated with you when, for whatever reason, you don't meet an agreed deadline? I certainly have, and I know the reason why they do this. It's because, for whatever reason, you make promises about completing work and almost always fail to meet them. I know this because many people have told me this independently.

Billy's likely response—again, possibly not verbalized: *I have noticed those things. I had thought it was because they have no idea how busy I am.*

Feelings. "Billy, I am feeling both very concerned about telling you this, as I'm worried about your reaction, but I also feel as a colleague that it's the right thing for me to do to tell you, just in case you aren't aware of this. And I know that telling you this might result in you feeling very bad about the message and probably the messenger, too. But I feel it's negatively impacting your reputation among colleagues and thought you would want to know."

Capability: **KNOWLEDGE TRANSFER**

The OFFICER Model

1	**O**UTLINE	It can be useful to give careful consideration to how the topic is initially raised – often better to emphasize the positive outcome sought rather than the issue that needs to be addressed.
2	**F**ACTS	Feedback is rarely effective when it is merely a matter of subjective viewpoint. It is typically much more effective to provide some concrete examples of what needs to change – where possible, even measures.
3	**F**EELINGS	It may seem counter-intuitive, but it can often be useful to express one's feelings about the subject. This can provide an indication to the other party of the extent to which one is concerned. The speaker identifying their feelings prior to initiating the conversation can also be a useful reflective practice. Are they proportionate?
4	**I**MPLICATIONS	What are the advantages of changing? Or the consequences if things don't change?
5	**C**ONTRIBUTION	Has the person providing the feedback contributed in some way to the issue? Or is there a contribution that the person providing feedback is willing to make?
6	**E**VIDENCING INTENT	What happens from here on out? Is it about earnest collaboration? Time for escalation?
7	**R**ESPONSE	At the conclusion of one's opening statement, explicitly solicit the perspectives of the other person.

FIGURE 11.2: The OFFICER Model

Billy's likely response: Almost certainly silence because Billy will be processing this feedback. Possibility of anger, push-back, everything we had worried about at the beginning of this conversation.

Implications. "Billy, I feel that this inability to deliver work in the time when you have committed to is getting in the way of you making a brilliant contribution here, and I wanted to make sure that you were aware of it so that you could address it and make the sort of contribution everyone realizes you're capable of."

Billy's likely response: *"Okay, I need to go away and consider this."* Or. *"How dare you?"* Or. *"I don't believe you!"* Or no response at all.

Contribution. "I feel bad about not mentioning this before, and I apologize for taking so long to do so. If there is anything I can do to help, please just ask."

Billy's likely response: *"Okay."* (Typically, still processing ...)

Evidence Intent. "Billy, any clarification needed? I am happy to have a further meeting with you to discuss this once you have processed it..."

Billy's likely response: Many possibilities at this stage...

And finally...

Response. "Billy, what's your response to this?"

Billy's likely response: Pause. There will definitely be a pause while Billy considers how to respond. This is a time for us to be quiet, wait patiently, and *not* fill the space with more talk. As Susan Scott says: "Let the silence do the heavy lifting."

> *"This is a time for us to be quiet, wait patiently, and not fill the space with talk."*

Billy's likely response could be positive ("Thanks for telling me. That took some courage") or negative (simply walking away upset or challenging your right to even have the conversation) at the time. But, *over time,* the likelihood is that Billy will come to thank you for the conversation.

Even if the relationship is damaged by the conversation, we have to ask ourselves: did we do the right thing? Was our intent pure? If it was, then we did what we could, and the responsibility for future difficulties lies with Billy, not us.

One of the authors has, with several employees, had to have a courageous conversation about their performance at work that led to the employee leaving the organization. The employees' responses at the time were negative, but, *in every instance,* some weeks and months afterward, the employee in question thanked the author for their candor, honesty, and intent to help improve their performance, advance their career, and point out derailers.

Courageous Conversations in an Expert World

IN THE EXPERT WORLD, these conversations are often about resources, priorities, and different approaches. They're frequently had with people who may be senior to us organizationally, but where we're the senior party in terms of technical expertise. The same combination of courage and consideration is important.

Simply telling General Manager A that their proposed project is a vanity project and doesn't have our support, and indeed that we won't execute it, is very courageous, but the lack of consideration will be damaging to our personal brand and the long-term relationship.

Simply telling our manager that we're just too busy rarely cuts it today's corporate world. Everyone is too busy. We have to be able to convey and demonstrate that we're happy to be busy, but we have to be selective about what we're busy with so that we create the maximum value for the whole organization. We have to make choices, to prioritize, and we have to demonstrate that we have done so in an aligned fashion, not just on the basis of the work we want to do or like doing.

Refusing a colleague our time and effort because their work isn't important to us is courageous but lacks consideration.

Conflict or disagreement with colleagues isn't inherently bad. Indeed, constructive conflict is often essential or highly valuable, particularly in situations where experts are coming together to find new solutions. The trick is to accept that the parties have differences and are prepared to explore what is generating those differences of opinion with curiosity rather than a desperate need to win the argument.

It's possible to converse about difficult subject matters or areas of contention without causing relationship fracture or tension, which is the primary fear that typically leads people to avoid such conversations. Doing so effectively generally requires putting some careful thought into how to initiate the conversation and a combination of both courage (to say what needs to be said, to risk saying something that the other party might find disagreeable) and consideration (a palpable sense of warmth and support that predisposes the other party to engage constructively and not become defensive or hostile).

Courageous Conversations: Tricks of the Trade

CAN WE OFFER SOME simple tricks of the trade and insights that might help us all remember to have courageous conversations with consideration as early as we can?

Planning is the High-Percentage Play

Using the OFFICER model to plan an opening of a courageous conversation is a winning strategy. The more we plan and think, quickly, about the conversation, the greater the chances of it going well. However...

Speed is of the Essence

If we spend too long planning, we'll lose the opportunity to have the conversation soon after the event that triggered the need to do so. The closer the conversation occurs to the actual event, the better it usually goes. The guilt that builds up in us by waiting too long to have the conversation simply makes us avoid the conversation even longer. And then we're culpable. If a colleague does something that warrants a courageous conversation (fails to deliver by their deadline, poor quality work, refuses a request, goes in a different direction than was previously agreed), best practice is to call it out straight away. But with consideration. Over-preparing until we somehow have a fail-safe opening paragraph could be a subconscious avoidance tactic aimed at managing the high levels of discomfort being triggered by the prospect of a conversation that we're dreading.

Courage in the Morning

Our advice to all the colleagues we work with is: if possible, try to arrange courageous conversations for the morning. First thing. It means we don't put it off. It means we don't have to carry around the worry of it all day. But more importantly, it gives the parties time to come together later in the day and follow up on the discussion, resolve issues, process each other's perspectives, expressed feelings, potential implications, and then discuss. Very often, our colleagues need to go away and process the issue we have raised. Morning meetings mean that they have time to do that, so issues don't fester overnight. There's a good chance that both parties are more resilient when fresh and rested than later in the day when other stressors have had a chance to impact our moods.

On a Percentage Basis, They Work Out Okay

Those conversations that we view as difficult or uncomfortable are rarely as troublesome in practice as we might imagine them to be. The vast majority of participants we have asked about this over the years accept that when the courageous conversation inevitably happens, the outcome is usually far better than had anticipated. In many cases, the recipient of our uncomfortable message had been *expecting* the conversation (see next tip).

Remember, We're Signaling

Once we decide that we need to have a courageous conversation with a colleague, our connection with them subtly changes, often in ways that we don't notice but are very apparent to them. We might start avoiding them subconsciously because we aren't ready to have the conversation. We might unconsciously show our irritation toward them. Our language might marginally change when communicating with them. We might even stop communicating with them! In many ways that we don't notice, but our colleagues do, we're signaling troubled times ahead. And having done so, the longer we avoid having the conversation, the more fraught and worried our colleague might become.

People Can't Disagree With Feelings

As experts, we love to have extended arguments about who has the best set of facts. We also worry that someone might disagree with our set of facts, or have better facts than us, or offer a different interpretation of the same facts. But often, courageous conversations are about feelings. And if we feel disenfranchised, or let down, or angry, or irritated, that's how we feel. However much of an expert our colleague is, if we feel angry, they have to accept that we feel angry. The Feelings part of the OFFICER model is a powerful friend in these conversations.

Contribution (in the OFFICER Model) is Super-Important

Before commencing a courageous conversation, it's important for us to contemplate what our contribution has been to the issue or problem and prepare ourselves to be honest about it. In our Billy conversation, we apologize for delaying the communication. Often in expert work, we've contributed to a problem by providing an incomplete brief or making assumptions that weren't right. It's rare that our colleague is 100 percent at fault and we're 100 percent innocent.

Across Cultures, Dual-Communication Works

As many experts work in international teams, some difficult conversations have to take place across video conferencing or the telephone, sometimes across culture and language barriers. We encourage the use of a call accompanied by a written document, such as the OFFICER model written out, if you like. This can be emailed at the same time. This is particularly useful if we're communicating with someone whose native language is different from ours. The ability to read what we're saying as well as listening to it helps reduce misunderstandings.

Testing, Testing—As If It Were Me

A final acid test is to put ourselves in the conversation as the other party and imagine how we would respond to the approach we're planning. Would we find it reasonable? Would we respond well to the approach we're taking? It's an important principle we believe in on the journey to Master Expert: we treat colleagues as we ourselves would want to be treated.

TAKING ACTION

Growing Our Ability to Have Effective Courageous Conversations

IF THIS IS AN expert skill that you believe could help you add greater value, here is a high-level suggestion for action to take:

▶ MAKE A DATE TO HAVE A COURAGEOUS CONVERSATION

- What conversations have you have been meaning to have with colleagues that you've been avoiding? Make a list.
- Which conversation meets the criteria of least stressful (and/or potentially risky) but will have the most impact? Choose that conversation.
- Explore the reasons why you have been avoiding the conversation. Work on establishing your intent.
- Use the OFFICER model to plan the opening of the conversation.
- Think through what the positive outcomes of the conversation might be if it were to go well. Keep these firmly in mind during the conversation.
- Run the final test: how would I react if it were me?
- Schedule the conversation and execute it. Display and deploy courage and consideration.
- Post-conversation, run an audit. What went well and what could have been done better? What did I learn?
- Choose the next conversation on the list… and repeat the above steps.

"The Master Expert builds and maintains mutually rewarding stakeholder engagements across a variety of internal and external stakeholders."

MASTERING STAKEHOLDER ENGAGEMENT

RELATIONSHIP DOMAIN

STAKEHOLDER ENGAGEMENT

"A stakeholder is anyone who can ruin your day."

Anon

CHAPTER | 12 |

Expert Stakeholder Strategy

Who are the most important professional people in our lives, and what's our strategy for effectively engaging with them and fostering their optimal participation in what we're seeking to achieve?

IN THIS CHAPTER, WE WILL EXPLORE:

- Why is understanding who our stakeholders are, and how we interact with them, important? How does this help us become better experts?
- Why expert stakeholder groups are more complicated and broader than those of other employees.
- What is strategic stakeholder engagement, and why is it an important skill set for experts?
- What would it take for stakeholders to be optimally engaged with the various initiatives we're driving?

IF YOU'VE MADE IT this far in the book, you know we have established one thing very clearly: as experts, we're different. This difference is expressed perhaps most clearly when we explore who our stakeholders are in comparison with typical *people* leaders.

> *"A stakeholder is anyone*
> *who can ruin your day."*

Most organizational structures have evolved with the exclusive intention of facilitating the delivery of the organization's primary activities, services and products to the consumer. There is a clear chain of command that is focused on the assignment of performance targets and holding people to account for delivering against them. Decision-making powers, including authority over allocation of organizational resources, tends to *flow down* these operationally focused hierarchies. Experts are rarely afforded the same powers and representation as those driving core organizational results. Formal lines of authority are often expressed in the form of an organizational chart (also called an *org chart*), as in Figure 12.1.

Capability: **STAKEHOLDER ENGAGEMENT**

A People Leader's Organizational Chart

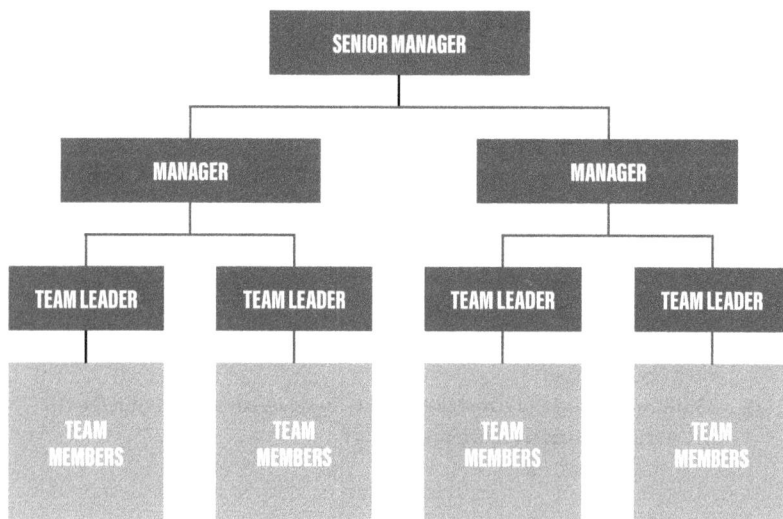

FIGURE 12.1: A People Leader's Organizational Chart

If only the life of an expert was so simple! Our expert roles rarely sit in such well-organized hierarchies. In fact, figuring out where experts sit on an organizational chart is a real challenge for most organizational development people. Often, they can't put us on the lowest rung on the organizational ladder (where "individual contributors" sit) because we're too senior—and occasionally too well-paid. But on the other hand, many of us don't lead teams of people so we can't be put at the management level either.

What to do?

> *"Experts had better embrace this uniqueness.*
> *Indeed, we should leverage it."*

On many organizational charts, experts are placed off to one side, often within specialized functions or teams euphemistically referred to as "shared services" or some such term. It's not intuitive to the person drafting the organizational chart what kind of access, representation, authority or resources an expert needs. The fact is: we're weird. And well, we'd better embrace this uniqueness rather than moan about it. Indeed, we should *leverage* it. Being slightly outside a defined chain of command could have advantages. We ought to be able to approach anyone without them suspecting that we're in some way usurping a manager somewhere in the chain. Most experts don't use this advantage enough or lack the enterprise skills to make the conversation count. All too often, access to senior leaders is viewed as something reserved for others in the leadership hierarchy.

An organizational chart for experts is much more complex, multilayered and fluid than that of people leaders. With that in mind, rather than a chart, we've chosen to represent it as an *operating environment* (see Figure 12.2).

Capability: STAKEHOLDER ENGAGEMENT
The Expert Operating Environment

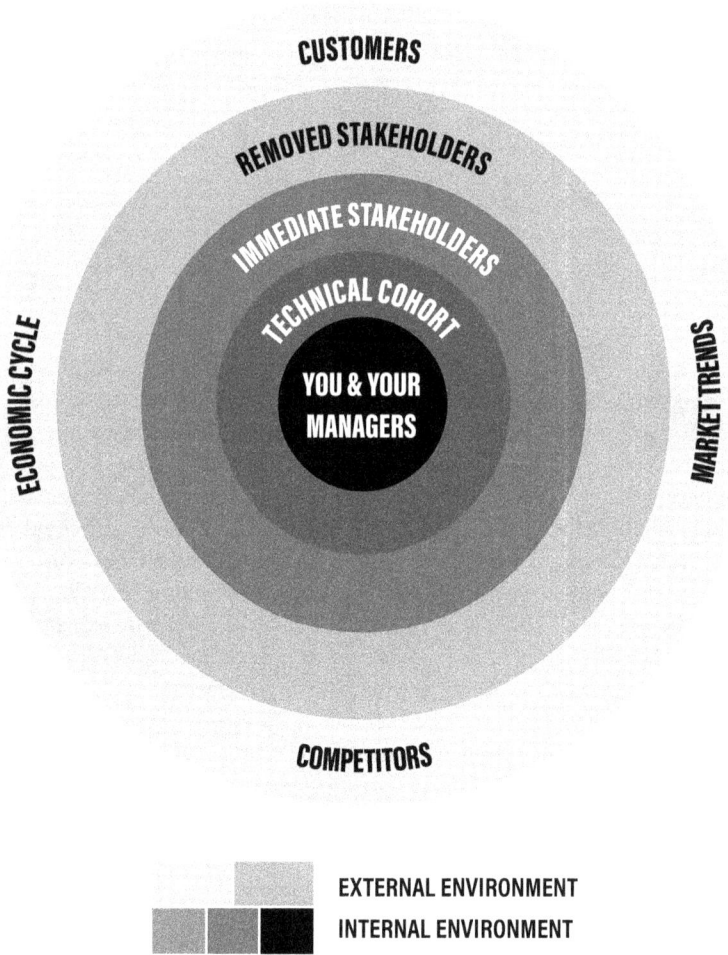

FIGURE 12.2: The Expert Operating Environment

A unique feature of an expert's organizational chart is that we often communicate and work with colleagues at all levels of the organization, frequently reach out to stakeholders who are in other departments or other organizations. This means a feature of us being the best experts we can be is that we have to adopt a sophisticated expert stakeholder strategy. The reality is that every expert's organizational chart is quite different.

> *"The organization doesn't typically recognize experts as vital voices to include in key decisions."*

When we ask experts to list all of their stakeholders, we find that they can effortlessly place 60 or 70 colleagues on a stakeholder map. If we give experts a little more devoted time, the number of stakeholders typically reaches over one hundred. That is, let's face it, a lot of relationships to initiate, maintain, optimize and nurture. And of course, most of us don't do so because we don't believe that we have the time—and perhaps because we haven't thought about the most efficient way to do it or the value in doing so.

That's what this chapter is all about.

But before we delve into stakeholder engagement, a few more thoughts on how we're *different* from people leaders. Our uniqueness has multiple impacts, even on the allocation of space within a building. This is because our status isn't clear, which means teams of experts sometimes get less "prime real estate"—we're typically situated away from the action, away from access to senior leaders, and so on—than other more obviously value-adding teams, such as sales, for example. As experts, we know the meaning (and look) of the "back room."

Key information flows around the organization, but the expert population is not necessarily viewed as a vital recipient of certain data, nor as a vital voice to include in key discussions. This is often reflected by where senior management "park us" on the floor plan.

This isn't an ideal situation for us because, ultimately, our success depends upon building a complex web of effective alliances across the organization.

All experts need to be proactive in changing this state of affairs rather than being passive or even grumpy about it and waiting for years for the rest of the organization to wake up to the value we create.

At the Master Expert level, we have to be proactive in identifying which key individuals and teams across it's vital we connect with, understand and engage with. This often entails gaining access to stakeholders who would not be obvious to others, including the stakeholders themselves.

Defining Stakeholders

THE WORD "STAKEHOLDER" HAS become much more common in recent years. In fact, it's now used so freely in most business environments that it's in danger of losing its true meaning. Put simply, a stakeholder is anyone who has an interest, or a "stake", in the success or failure of our enterprise. The origins of the word come from gambling. In the early 18th century, a stakeholder was the person who held the stakes of two gamblers in a bet and then paid the winner.

We interact with, depend upon, and deliver for many varieties of people every day. Their commitment levels and expectations shape almost everything we do. They might be someone whose positive commitment or disposition is pivotal to our success. We might rely on their labor, their financial support, their decisions or their endorsement—or even all four. They could also be someone who, if not satisfied or feeling somehow threatened, could make life difficult for us.

They could be the intended beneficiary of what we're doing. They could even be someone who simply stands to gain or lose through what we're doing or anyone who might impact our work, such as a key decision-maker who we barely ever connect with and might not even have direct access to. All of these people could prove to be a critical stakeholder to engage with.

> *"Politically astute experts recognize that the success of all enterprises rests upon a network of goodwill."*

A more popular description of a stakeholder among experts we have worked with might be "anyone who can ruin our day." As experts, we tend to have a lot of these people floating around us.

Given the nature of our work, in larger matrix organizations, the number of possible stakeholders we have, visible or invisible, is scary.

Politically astute experts recognize that the success of all enterprises rests upon a *network of goodwill*. It makes sense, therefore, that we proactively identify who all the critical parties are, what their needs are likely to be, how they'll likely see and respond to the enterprise (and specifically the initiatives), and where we might depend upon them being engaged. Having conducted such an analysis, we can then formulate and execute engagement strategies to get those stakeholders favorably inclined and contributing as desired.

In this chapter, we'll explore how to do this effectively, how to get on the front foot, and how to make our most vital stakeholder engagements super-effective.

Stakeholder Engagement in Play

LET'S EXPLORE HOW STAKEHOLDER engagement can play out positively and negatively in a real-world situation.

Meet Marsha. She is a software architect who builds functionality in a software application used by customer-facing operations staff. In her early career, Marsha's stakeholder map was limited to members of her technical cohort, the business analysts who took the briefs from the operations team and passed them on to her, and her manager. These relationships were almost purely transactional in nature. She was operating, at this time, at the Specialist level in her stakeholder engagement because her networks were limited, single-lens, very tactical, and she was mostly reactive in the way she interfaced with them.

After a few years working with the application, Marsha started to expand her network. Her stakeholder map now featured other senior IT managers, not just her own manager. She had extended her influence out to other IT management team members, including those in networking, server management and testing. More importantly, she had started building closer relationships with the operations team.

This began with her working with some individual contributors involved in testing, and then working more closely with operations managers. She began to attend meetings where briefs were taken by the business analysts, a process from which previously she had been excluded. Marsha also reached out to other shared services providers, such as her HR business partner and the finance business partner, who was responsible for financial reporting, budgeting and, crucially, procurement for IT services.

But her relationships were still mostly *time-bound transactional* projects. At this stage, Marsha had progressed from Specialist to the Expert level. She had broadened her internal network in her organization, become more multi-lens, and started to manage stakeholder engagements more proactively. But there was still room for growth.

Today, Marsha has grown a significant internal network, including senior operations managers, a broad spectrum of IT staff, and a wide cohort of end users in the operations team, all of whom inform her software architecture and coding decisions. She has also started to build effective relationships with people who do what she does in other parts of the global business, implements networking best and next practice, and shares innovations from her team with the broader organization. And, against her introverted nature, she has started networking outside her organization, joining broader interest groups and exploring how other industries and professions operate, think about and deal with challenges.

> *"Engagement entails evoking people's discretionary effort and stimulating them to be positively disposed to contributing to our efforts."*

She's heading to Master Expert level. Marsha has advanced from **local and narrow** to **broad and global** in terms of her organizational network. Her network quality has become more multi-lens, and networking outside of her organization will build her ability to see things strategically and in the context of broader market forces. Additionally, her network management has definitely moved from purely reactive to much more proactive.

The results of Marsha's active cultivation of new engagements are that she is much better known across the business, the quality and relevance of her work has improved as more insight is brought to bear on what the business really wants, and she is seen by those around her as more valuable and as possessing significant future potential.

Marsha's journey is one that every expert can take. If we have the drive, energy, commitment and technique.

From Management To Engagement

ENGAGING WITH STAKEHOLDERS REQUIRES more than merely identifying and managing them. Engagement entails evoking people's discretionary effort and stimulating them to be positively disposed to contributing to our efforts. Indeed, we dislike the phrase *stakeholder management* because it implies that all stakeholders can be managed, and as every expert knows, this is definitely not the case. We also hear from experts that the more they attempt to *manage* some stakeholders, the more obstinate they become.

> *"Stakeholder engagement is more of an emotional and/or psychological state than a purely rational one."*

An outstanding outcome of a Master Expert brilliantly engaging a stakeholder might, for example, be having an important economic stakeholder positively inclined to prioritize the funding of our projects. Or a key decision-maker whose sanction we depend upon feeling positively predisposed to making a favorable decision informed by all the relevant criteria. In other words, someone who listens to and respects our opinion, has clarity about our needs, and is sympathetic toward them. Or someone whose contribution of time and effort our outputs depend on striving with all their might to fulfill our needs or expectations of them. These are the type of stakeholder engagements we dream of having because they directly contribute to the value we can create for our organization.

As experts, we're often one step removed from end users or customers, but we similarly hope to create a sense of satisfaction, loyalty and even advocacy for our services and efforts.

It is, of course, a mistake to assume that stakeholders are automatically favorably disposed toward us. Among the experts the authors have worked with, in many cases, the opposite is true. Experts tell us all the time that the very people they feel their services can help in the organization resist their proposals and suggestions. These people usually imply that the experts don't understand their needs or the pressure they're under. Sometimes, of course, this is painfully true.

We can't, as experts, even rely on our stakeholders' basic emotional warmth toward our needs and proposals, even if these needs and proposals are based on a logically sound case or pragmatic reasoning. For example, in many of the large finance or IT teams we have worked with, no one appears to have any time for personal interaction that builds connection and warmth as it's simply not part of the culture. In these highly technical environments, stakeholder engagement tends to be transactional and a race to secure resources.

Defining engagement

Engagement is an attitudinal state presupposing high levels of trust and commitment toward a relationship.

A stakeholder who has been positively engaged will consider the expert his or her ally with a sense of shared purpose. There will be a sense of the expert being of value. The stakeholder will be inclined to support or advocate for the expert and will take pleasure in providing a service or funding that the expert needs.

Such a level of engagement is worth its weight in gold—especially because, as experts, we often cannot exercise or rely on formal authority, power, representation and control of resources. We need to build a network of goodwill across the human ecosystem in which we operate. Others' engagement cannot be taken for granted or simply assumed, no matter how much logical sense it makes. Engagement has to be worked at.

Typically, when stakeholders see an alignment of interests, they strive for mutual benefit. In the absence of perceiving such interests being met, engagement will almost certainly be lower than we would desire. In really problematic cases, there could be active disengagement, where there is a perceived conflict of interest or some form of antipathy. Such disengagement often arises from stakeholder needs or expectations remaining unmet, even though they might have never been officially articulated or contracted for.

If we don't intimately know what the needs of our stakeholders are, it's very difficult to build a clear alignment of interests and therefore positive engagement. Stakeholders going without their key needs being met often creates tension, and the human mind typically forms an attitude toward those it sees as in some way responsible for such needs remaining unmet. Therefore, identifying and addressing *felt needs* is a shrewd and proactive strategy for a Master Expert to adopt as it often highlights opportunities to engage specific stakeholders around the needs they're already passionately committed to addressing.

As experts, we don't just strive to *have* stakeholder relationships. We aspire to build stakeholder engagements.

The reality is that, just like everyone else in the organization, we're always competing for finite amounts of time, energy, attention and resources. Prioritization of decisions is often driven by tribal loyalties, traditions, and affinities that exist in the organization, not on cold, hard logic. The conclusion we must draw, because all of the evidence suggests that this is now clearly the case, is that stakeholder engagement is more of an emotional and/or psychological state than a purely rational one. This means, as experts, we need to pick up our game and start building effective engagement with our stakeholders. These relationships need to be strong on many levels in order to succeed.

How to Improve Stakeholder Engagement

WE CAN INCREASE THE likelihood of a stakeholder feeling engaged, favorably disposed, and inclined to strive to help us by satisfying one or more of the following criteria:

- Connection. Demonstrating a clear connection between the initiative we're seeking to engage the stakeholder in and one of their most keenly felt needs, and then satisfying such needs. Linking our initiative to the more efficient execution of the organization's strategy may be one way of doing this. While offering the initiative as a solution to one of the key challenges the stakeholder faces may be another. Alternatively, we can frame the initiative as a way to win new customers or get greater satisfaction scores from the community. We call this "joining the dots."

> *"If the only time we reach out to a stakeholder is when we need something, then that's not a relationship. It's a transaction."*

- Contribution. Illustrating how their involvement, support or contribution delivers a tangible and sought benefit or perceived value and then delivering accordingly. To warrant the effort to deliver their contribution, the stakeholder needs to believe in the sought benefit or perceived value. So, we might ask a stakeholder in the finance department to talk to our project team about the way in which finance reporting is conducted. We'd have to be clear about the benefits of the finance executive spending time doing so (providing context, building understanding, creating an opportunity to ask questions directly to finance, making sure finance's interests were taken into account, and so on). The ideal approach here is for us to test whether the stakeholder sees the benefit in the same way as we do. In practice, they often don't, and that's helpful to know.
- Relationship. Developing a relationship with the stakeholder that is characterized by a high level of trust, shared interests, values and

purpose, as well as emotional warmth and mutual empathy. Later in this section, we explain Stakeholder Health Checks, an ideal method for building trust and empathy. Another method is simply to make sure that we understand what keeps that stakeholder awake at night and taking that into account in our dealings with them. We can also ask them for feedback on what we could do better. This openness tends to be well received and builds trust and warmth. The stakeholder can see we're striving to do our best for them.

Stakeholder Mapping

WE'RE ALL WORKING IN human enterprises with many different types of stakeholders. But how do we decide who's got more at stake than others? Who is the beneficiary of what we do? Who is the main contributor? What is it we're depending on from each of our stakeholders? Are we just small dots on their landscape? Or are we as significant to them as they are to us?

Relationships often just develop organically, which could mean that unless we have intentionally reached out to somebody and cultivated a connection with them, there is no relationship. If the only time we make contact is when we need something from them, the relationship is transactional, single-direction, and unlikely to be optimal. When we consider the stakeholders who treat us like this, we don't exactly get enthused when they contact us, do we? And yet, our research suggests that this style of relationship among experts is the norm rather than the exception.

> *"Many experts are stuck in a destructive reactive cycle, unable to free themselves from the shackles of incoming work – all of which is urgent and important."*

However, what if we put a proactive relationship engagement strategy in place? We could find out what they need, what they're passionate about, what they're committed to, and what their concerns are. We can learn what happens if those concerns or needs aren't met. Would that, for example, affect their commitment levels?

Capability: **STAKEHOLDER ENGAGEMENT**

A Sample Stakeholder Map

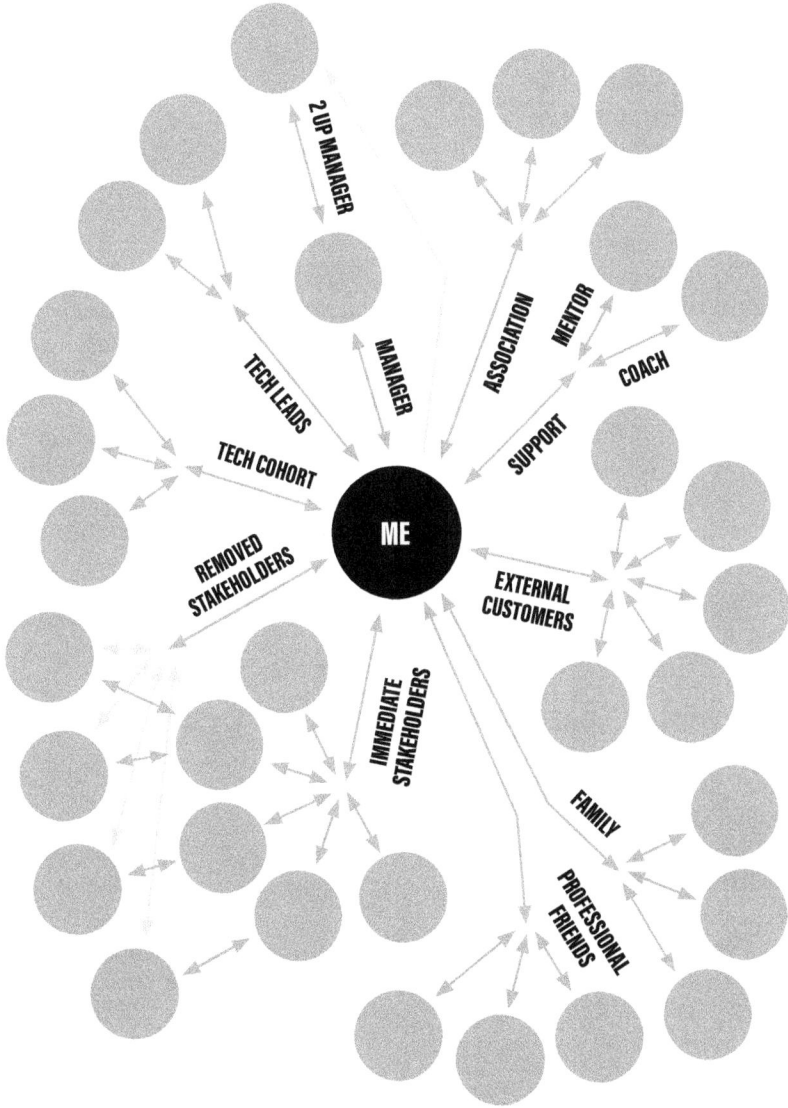

FIGURE 12.3: A Sample Stakeholder Map

One activity we have found very helpful is building a stakeholder map (see an example in Figure 12.3) While most employees working in large organizations have complex stakeholder maps, in our experience, experts often have even more complex stakeholder maps. We have complicated and multifaceted reporting lines; we have membership in numerous cross-disciplinary teams; we interact with international colleagues in different time zones; and we often report to multiple managers who have conflicting agendas. We typically have an extraordinarily high number of relationships to keep in good working order and an impossible number of "clients" to service, many of whom express insatiable demand.

If we don't take a strategic approach to determining which relationships to focus on (and which we can reasonably de-emphasize), and if we don't explore the keys to getting high engagement levels, then the whole situation becomes unmanageable. At the outset, most experts we have worked with rarely have a clear and holistic view of their entire stakeholder map. Rarely have they prioritized the most vital relationships. And they often have no strategy for maintaining relationships while busy on other projects.

Indeed, how they spend their time is often dictated by others, leaving them stuck in a destructive reactive cycle, unable to free themselves from the shackles of incoming work, all of which is urgent and important to those requesting it. The result is that many experts don't focus on activities that add the most value. And as a consequence of this, some critical stakeholder relationships become broken and need to be fixed.

Developing a stakeholder map is a simple enough process, but we'd like to offer some advice on how to get maximum value and insight from the exercise.

A Strategic Approach to Stakeholder Engagement

HERE IS A FIVE-STEP strategy for improving stakeholder engagement (see Figure 12.4).

Step 1 – Identify

The first step is to populate a stakeholder map. Essentially, this is a mind map of all the relationships we have. We need to understand who all of our stakeholders are in order to prioritize them later. For a detailed description of how to go about this, see our primer in the next chapter of this book.

Step 2 – Prioritize

The next step is to prioritize. The large number of stakeholders we have identified can't all be equally important. Some require or deserve more time and attention from us than others.

While we may well have senior people on our maps, key colleagues elsewhere along the value chain may be the stakeholders we most heavily rely on to bring our work to life. Whose needs and commitment levels matter most of all? For whom, or with whom, can we create the most value? Who needs to be aware of the value we have created? Upon whom do we depend the most to continue creating value?

When undertaking this exercise "live" in our workshops and coaching pods, we encourage our participants to start by identifying their top five most important stakeholders. Once they have done this, we ask them to consider the criteria they used to make this decision. The ensuing discussion is usually quite insightful. Typically, seniority isn't the primary consideration in the expert world. Sometimes it's the most demanding stakeholders who make the list, ahead of those stakeholders for whom we could add the most value. Or stakeholders who are the most visible (local). Or stakeholders who we enjoy working with. None of these criteria ought to be in play for a Master Expert.

Ensuring that the right stakeholders are prioritized for the right reasons is a critical early task once a stakeholder map has been compiled.

Step 3 - Understand

Next, conduct a Stakeholder Health Check. We cover how to do this in detail in the next chapter. Essentially, we're seeking to understand several things:
- What is the current condition of each stakeholder relationship, and why?
- What are trust levels like, and why?
- How frequently do we interact, and is that optimal?
- To what extent do we and the stakeholder get what we both need and expect from each other?
- What are the stakeholder's needs, and ours? To what extent are they aligned? This needs analysis can include both *functional needs* (such as a report or information) and *implicit human needs*, e.g., the need to be valued, to feel cared for, to progress, and so on. Which needs are most keenly felt and, therefore, easiest to motivate the stakeholder to act on?

Step 4 - Build

Armed with the insights from the above analysis and health check, it's time for us to build engagement by developing an engagement strategy. What do we have to offer these stakeholders that might be appealing to them? How might we initiate a conversation? What proposition are we taking to them? Ideally, how often should we connect?

Capability: STAKEHOLDER ENGAGEMENT

An Expert Stakeholder Strategy

IDENTIFY	**SCOPE**	· Internal / External · Local / Global · Current / Future
	TACTICS	· Individual not team-focused · Absentees?
PRIORITIZE	**SCOPE**	· Categorize by importance · Categorize by type · Categorize by frequency
	TACTICS	· Map to key performance requirements, key projects
UNDERSTAND	**SCOPE**	· Our needs / their needs · Our measures / their measures · Our derailers / their derailers
	TACTICS	· Stakeholder health checks · Advanced needs analysis
BUILD	**SCOPE**	· Find win-win settings · Establish success metrics
	TACTICS	· Identify early wins · Build trust & understanding
OPERATE	**SCOPE**	· Establish operating rhythm · Agree communication protocols · Measure effectiveness
	TACTICS	· Celebrate wins · Analyze failures

Capability:
KNOWLEDGE EXPERT

FIGURE 12.4: An Expert Stakeholder Strategy

Undertaking stakeholder health checks tends to generate a to-do list, which is a way of moving forward with stakeholders. Establishing what would be defined as a great success for the stakeholder relationship, what our priorities should be, and what both we and the stakeholder are committed to and passionate about are all vital questions when creating a win-win stakeholder relationship.

Not every stakeholder will be willing to offer up their innermost felt needs because these might be quite personal (for example, showing insecurity with "I don't want to get fired" or personal ambition with "I want to be promoted or paid more"). To get to this level of understanding, we need to be able to ask penetrative questions in a highly diplomatic manner. We need to build trust. Truly understanding the needs of our stakeholders may take *many* conversations over time.

One way to fast-track building trust is to share our own motivations and concerns. This requires us to trust first and be vulnerable. This isn't an emotionally comfortable zone for many experts. It takes courage and technique, but it also pays big dividends.

Step 5 - Rhythm

Having put all the right building blocks in place, the stakeholder engagement needs to find its operating rhythm. We want the arrangements (meetings, connections, information sharing and so on) to become natural and effective for both parties. We need to ensure we're checking in with appropriate frequency, celebrating what's working, and quickly rectifying what isn't. We also need to be aware that many circumstances change quite quickly, which will impact the prioritization and value each party might want to give to the engagement. It'll certainly result in needs or expectations shifting, so we have to be prepared to reset and recast where necessary.

For some stakeholders, the rhythm might be a daily check-in. For others, once a quarter (or longer) might suffice. Some stakeholders are happy with regular email updates. Others might find face-to-face interactions more effective (whether physical or via video conference).

Some stakeholders may want to have a discussion about every decision. Others will be happy to be informed that "this is what we intend to do" and agree that if we don't hear from them within a specified time limit, then we go ahead and act with assumed approval.

One thing is for sure: a one-size-fits-all approach certainly doesn't work in this environment. We need to adapt to stakeholders, and them to us.

TAKING ACTION

Growing Our Stakeholder Engagement Skills

IF THIS IS A capability in which you believe you could grow your skills and knowledge to add greater value, here is a suggestion for action to take:

▶ ACTIVELY ORIENT YOUR ROLE AROUND DELIVERING VALUE TO KEY STAKEHOLDERS

- We have to understand who our most important stakeholders are and focus on the work that matters most to them. We can sometimes end up with a default focus on others' demands rather than a clear sense of purpose or mission. Questions we might like to ask ourselves:
- Have I conducted a thorough analysis of who my most important stakeholders are? Or who they should be?
- Have I spent enough time with those stakeholders to understand what value they would like from me? Have we had a big-picture conversation and not just a current-work-in-progress discussion?
- How would I measure whether I am adding value to the right stakeholders for the right reasons at the right time?
- To what extent do I have a clear sense of purpose and mission in my role? To what extent am I fluent in articulating my clear purpose, particularly in moments when I need to demonstrate intregrity around prioritizing work?
- Am I spending enough time thinking about where I spend my time, as well as on whom and what I spend it and why? As priorities change, do I adapt quickly enough and communicate these changes broadly enough?

CHAPTER | 13 |

Stakeholder Mapping

Who do we work with, and why?
Who should we be working with, and why?
And why aren't we?

IN THIS CHAPTER, WE WILL EXPLORE:

- How to develop complex stakeholder maps that help us understand who our stakeholders are and assign levels of importance to them.
- How to identify stakeholders we don't have on our stakeholder maps but should have.
- What are Stakeholder Health Checks and how do we execute them?

THIS CHAPTER IS A simple how-to primer on building stakeholder maps and conducting Stakeholder Health Checks. Undertaking this exercise might take an hour of your time, but we believe it's a critical step on the way to becoming a Master Expert.

Can you make a list of all of your stakeholders? This sounded like a simple question to Chiang Yu Mei, an engineer based in Singapore. Warming to her task, she quickly drew up a stakeholder map containing 32 people. We have a rule that maps must contain people rather than teams because every relationship is individual.

Invited to take a look at the maps created by other experts, Yu Mei quickly discovered that she had missed listing her family, her manager's manager, the entire project team she had worked with the previous quarter, her friends from her national engineering body, and her past manager who had moved companies. Within an hour, Yu Mei was looking at a complex web of relationships comprising over 80 people—and every few minutes, she was adding further stakeholders that she had forgotten.

When we asked Yu Mei who she interfaced with within her organization but outside of her own country, she was able to add a further 20 colleagues located around the world, from New Zealand to Japan to India. This is very typical of the modern expert. In a recent survey we conducted, 67 percent of experts had remits that were international. But the phrase "out of sight, out of mind" is very relevant here.

Yu Mei's experience is typical for most experts, whose *undeveloped* stakeholder maps contain between 70 and 90 colleagues.

A developed stakeholder map will focus on ensuring all external stakeholders and all future stakeholders have been added. Our next challenge for Yu Mei was this: "Who would you like to have on your stakeholder map who isn't there today, and why?"

The conversations around this question get quite intense and future-focused. We asked Yu Mei:

- Who do you want your manager to be in three years' time?
- Thinking of important meetings you hope to be involved with in three years' time, who will be the other participants?
- Who will be the leading lights in your technical field in three years' time? Are they on your radar now, and will they be included in your map?
- Who will be your most important stakeholders in three years' time? How long will you have known them? Where and how will you have first met?

"Who ought to be on our stakeholder maps that we haven't met yet?"

Using the stakeholder map to focus on the future goes to the heart of what mastering Expertship is about. Far from accepting our lot in life, a life of being underappreciated and underutilized, if we want to maximize the value creation we're capable of and reach our potential, we need to plan for it. We talk in other chapters about the skills and knowledge we'll need in the future, but this chapter is about ensuring that we have the contacts to help us be the best expert we can be.

Yu Mei had to consider who she hadn't met yet but ought to be on her stakeholder map. And she had to consider how she might go about meeting those people, such as through networking or outreach.

One participant delighted us by adding the name of an as yet unborn grandchild because he knew in his heart that once that child had arrived, they would be an extremely important stakeholder in his life.

To identify all of your stakeholders, we recommend you, just like Yu Mei, invest some time into building your stakeholder map.

Building Your Stakeholder Map

EXPERT STAKEHOLDER MAPS ARE usually more complex than those belonging to people managers, who tend to have simpler and more linear relationships. Experts tend to move around the organization and work with different levels of people in different areas. This means we need heightened stakeholder management skills. Our process includes five steps:

- **First Identification**: adding all our stakeholders to the map.
- **Prioritizing (identifying the most vital relationships)**: those that are the most important to our success as an expert.
- **Understanding (undertaking simple Stakeholder Health Checks)**: identifying which relationships might need to be optimized and where the possible misalignments might be (needs, interests, expectations, agendas).
- **Future-proofing**: identifying stakeholders who aren't on our maps but we're going to need in the future.
- **Building and implementing engagement strategies**: identifying actions that will help us optimize the leverage and value we get from our stakeholders (and they get from us).

> *"Mind maps, not lists, because we're always adding new members and mind maps allow us to do that seamlessly."*

Over the years, we have helped hundreds of experts develop comprehensive stakeholder maps and have developed these suggested guiding principles for getting the best outcome. We'd encourage you to follow them.

STEP ONE: Identify the population of your stakeholder map

There are some standard categories of stakeholders that are reasonably easy to think of and are quick to map. We have captured these in Figure 13.1. Things we might want to consider:

- *This is an iterative process* that is best completed across a period of time. In our normal course of work, we will continue to think of key stakeholders who might not initially come to mind when we first sit down to do this. In our experience, we're shocked by some of the people we "forgot" and who are crucial to our success at work.

- *Don't be dominated by seniority*, as some of our most important stakeholders may be junior colleagues or colleagues located remotely who do critical work that enables us to create value. A helpful exercise is to think of the last few projects we have completed and all who were involved.
- *Start off with the present.* Ask who should be on our stakeholder map today? Later on, we provide some examples of questions to ask about future-proofing your stakeholder network.
- *Think internally and more broadly. Think of the stakeholders we have across the entire organization.* Many of us forget about colleagues from other departments who we turn to in times of need. These could perhaps be finance business partners, colleagues in HR, or IT experts.
- *Go back in time* and ask who, over the past year or so, has allocated work to us or requested our help, and who was it that influenced them to involve us? The first group *immediate stakeholders,* the people we complete work for or depend upon, and the second group are *removed stakeholders,* the eventual recipients of the value we create or upstream contributors.
- *Think externally. Who do we rely on?* Not just for technical support or career advice but for motivation and inspiration. Readers may be surprised by the number of experts we have worked with who forgot to put their family on their stakeholder map. Most of us will have business colleagues who do different jobs in different organizations but who we nevertheless use as a sounding board. Our personal friends and family are often a great source of support, encouragement and advice. These are all key stakeholders who contribute in many different ways to us being great at what we do.
- *Think about the stakeholders who are impeding us.* We need to think beyond the people who help us in our work and include unhelpful or disengaged colleagues. These may well be the stakeholder relationships that need the most repair, opening up new avenues for us to create value.

> *"The person who allocates key experts to key projects can change our year for the better or worse."*

We have a couple of additional guidelines that we encourage you to follow:
- *People, not teams.* It's important to include the names of individual people on our stakeholder maps. For example, we might put Mark and Terri on our map, both of whom are in HR, rather than just a

circle that says HR. Why? Because our relationships with Mark and Terri will be different, and when we come to assess the health of our stakeholder relationships, we need to be able to differentiate between them. We don't have relationships with HR; we have relationships with Terri and Mark.

- *Mind maps, not lists.* A fluid, graphic style of representation helps us to see connections and omissions more clearly than a simple linear list. We don't have to finish listing team members before moving on to other categories if we use a mind map because we can always return and add new team members as they occur to us. The mind map also helps us graphically represent the importance and health of these relationships later on in this process.
- If we're typical technical experts, we'll have between 60 and 100 individuals on our stakeholder maps by the end of this process. We'll also be constantly adding new names over the next few days as new additions occur to us.
- If we take the average, which is 80 stakeholders, we can observe that this is a lot of relationships to maintain. Most of us will be doing this sporadically and reactively, risking that some key relationships may not be nurtured to the degree that would yield optimal results.

STEP TWO: Identify the most important relationships

If we have between 60 and 100 stakeholders on our map, we need to assess where best to spend our time, and which relationships are the most important to initiate, focus on and/or optimize. In our programs, given time constraints, we invite experts to choose their five most important stakeholders. You might choose more.

On our maps, we use thicker lines to represent greater importance.

In terms of gauging which relationships are the most important, these criteria might be helpful:

- *Qualify importance using value, not seniority.* The importance of a relationship in the expert domain isn't necessarily determined by seniority, the size of a colleague's pay package, the length of their job title, or how much time we spend working with them. The criteria we advocate is the extent to which this colleague enables us to add value at Master Expert level.
- *Don't mistake noisy for valuable.* Some of our stakeholders will be vocal and communicate all the time, but that doesn't qualify them as a critical stakeholder—although they might wish that it did, and that might even be their goal. Sometimes, quiet stakeholders can have the most impact on our work.
- *Don't confuse frequency of contact for importance.* There may be stakeholders we work with every day, but our most important

stakeholder relationships might be with people we see and hear from rarely, but when we do, it really matters. The person who allocates key experts to big projects, for example, will not impact us very often, but when they do, they can change our year for the better or worse by including or excluding us.

Capability: STAKEHOLDER ENGAGEMENT
Who are my Stakeholders?

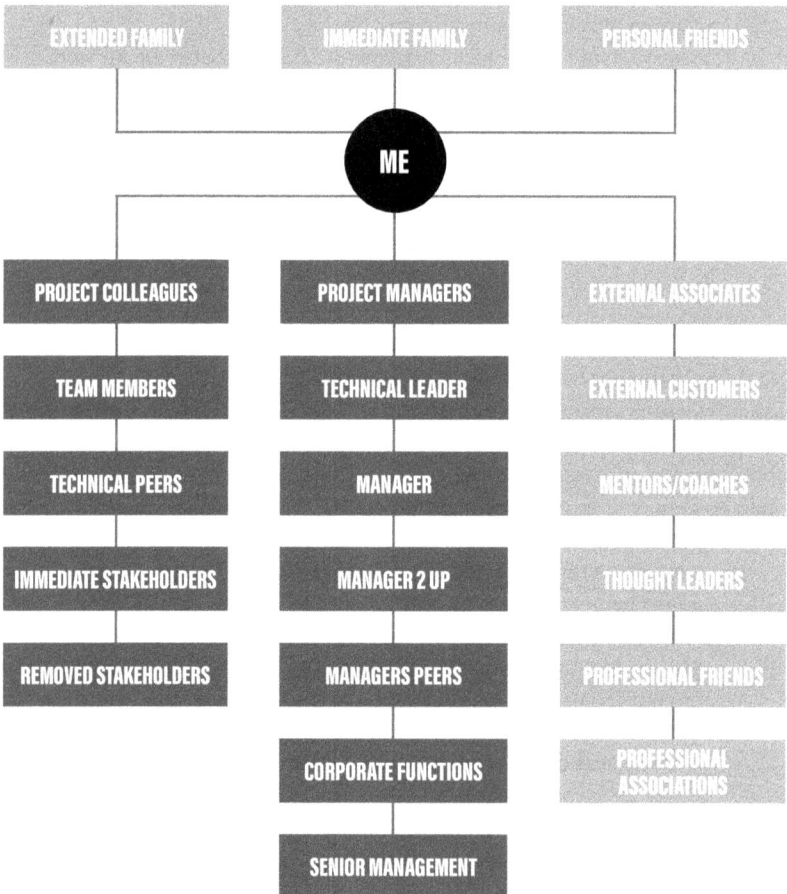

FIGURE 13.1: Who Are My Stakeholders?

STEP THREE: Undertake Stakeholder Health Checks

Once we've constructed our stakeholder maps and identified our most important stakeholders, it's then time to run objective health checks on those relationships.

We recommend using the *Stakeholder Health Check* template described in Figure 13.2 (electronic versions of this template are available on our website – *expertship.com*.) This template helps us conduct a detailed analysis of each of our critical stakeholder relationships. There are ten lenses included in the template. There may be additional lenses that you might wish to add, depending on the stakeholder relationship.

While we need to consider the relationship from our standpoint, we also suggest that we stand in our colleague's shoes for a moment to consider how they might evaluate the health of their relationship with us from their perspective.

"Avoid assumptions by hearing it 'from the horse's mouth.'"

Some suggested rules we encourage readers to follow:

- *Don't make assumptions.* It's expedient but dangerous to assume you know what your stakeholder's viewpoint on any of these questions is. We've all been in situations where we've had lightbulb moments of clarity when working with people. Moments when we've discovered that they actually want X, while all the time we've assumed they wanted Y. In fact, it would be fair to say that misunderstandings form the basis of very many conflicts in the workplace. In Expertship language, it means the stakeholders haven't done the foundational communication and alignment work we're describing here to make sure that (a) they are both on the same page when it comes to needs and/or (b) they know and have agreed to disagree where alignment isn't possible.
- *"From the horse's mouth."* To avoid making assumptions, only populate the parts of the health check that describe stakeholders' perspectives and needs if you have actually *asked them the direct question and have heard them say what they want out loud* and have heard them *say what they want out loud.* You need to hear it from the horse's mouth, as the saying goes.

Stakeholder Health Check

RELATIONSHIP:	IMPORTANCE:
PURPOSE	**What is it? Level of clarity?**
1 From my perspective	
2 From my stakeholder's perspective	
SUCCESS MEASURES	**What are they? SMART goals?**
3 From my perspective	
4 From my stakeholder's perspective	
5 From the organization's perspective	
DE-RAILERS	**What are they? Impact?**
6 From my perspective	
7 From my stakeholder's perspective	
HYGIENE FACTORS	**What are they? Impact?**
8 Do we trust each other?	
9 Do our aspirations enhance or inhibit us?	
10 Do our individual styles align or clash?	
OVERALL SCORE	**1 = Extremely poor, 10 = superb**
11 Does this relationship need work?	1 2 3 4 5 6 7 8 9 10
12 Action Plan	

FIGURE 13.2: The Expert Stakeholder Health Check Template

This, of course, requires a mature conversation between the parties. We often get asked what an expert should do if the relationship has been in existence for a long time. Surely it's awkward to suddenly ask these questions? Doesn't it imply that the questions should have been asked long ago? As we've discussed previously, what we all have on our side as experts is that change is the new normal. This provides us with numerous potential entry points for a long-overdue conversation.

For example, "I'm just checking in to see if anything has changed. I've been working on these assumptions, but given time has passed, why don't we do a double check? Something is bound to have subtly changed in our worlds and it would be good for our relationship if both of us know what these changes are, their impacts, and how we might need to modify the way we're working together or the goals we're trying to achieve." This can be a 15-minute conversation. Or it could be a relaxed lunch appointment. Or it could be a formal stakeholder reset meeting. Whatever it is, the longer the stakeholder relationship has existed without confirmation of currency, the sooner the meeting needs to happen.

Emails to conduct this work should be avoided.

In Figure 13.3, we look at each lens in the Stakeholder Health Check template in turn and suggest some questions.

STEP FOUR: Future-proof your stakeholder map

We suggest this as a separate step from creating our current stakeholder map because it makes it easier (and it's more strategic) to start with where we are now in terms of our stakeholder relationships. We can then contemplate where we would like to be in three years' time.

Where we "want to be" is, of course, a very personal choice. Typically, experts we've worked with don't want to enter management or run large teams. They want to be more influential. They want to work on high-impact projects, initiatives and innovations.

They want to rid themselves of some of the "grunt work" they do. This is work that is highly repetitive, uninteresting, low value, no longer challenging, and could reasonably be carried out by others.

Some of the future thinking that needs to be done will be about what needs to happen to make existing stakeholder relationships more valuable to all parties. This might involve repairing or super-charging these connections.

But the purpose of this book is to map a way forward for experts who want to become Master Experts, and this means we have to take a very strategic, long-term view of what we want our stakeholder map to look like in three to five years' time.

Lens 1	Purpose of the relationship from my perspective	What is the aim of the relationship? What am I hoping to get out of the relationship that makes it worthwhile?
Lens 2	Purpose of the relationship from my colleague's point of view	What is the aim of the relationship? What am I hoping to get out of the relationship that makes it worthwhile?
Lens 3	Success factors from my perspective	What is the aim of the relationship? What am I hoping to get out of the relationship that makes it worthwhile?
Lens 4	Success factors from my stakeholders' perspective	What metrics would my stakeholder use to determine the success of this stakeholder relationship? What would poor, satisfactory and excellent actually look like from their perspective?
Lens 5	Success factors from an organizational perspective	What metrics would my stakeholder use to determine the success of this stakeholder relationship? What would poor, satisfactory and excellent actually look like from their perspective?
Lens 6	Derailers from my point of view	What behaviors or outcomes do I not want to see from my stakeholder? What actions by my stakeholder are detracting, time-consuming, or downright irritating?
Lens 7	Derailers from my stakeholder's point of view	What does my stakeholder NOT want from me? What about me is irritating? What types of outcomes would be perceived as blockages or derailers in this relationship from their point of view?
Lens 8	Hygiene factor 1 - Do we trust each other?	To what extent is trust between the two of us evident? Do we keep our commitments to each other? Do we have each other's backs? Is trust in the relationship sufficient that we could give each other challenging feedback?
Lens 9	Hygiene factor 2 - What are our career goals/motivators?	Are our career goals and motivations aligned or in conflict? Can we create win-win personal outcomes for ourselves, as well as win-win organizational outcomes?
Lens 10	Hygiene factor 3 - Do our personal styles align?	Are they compatible or in potential conflict? Do we both need to consider the ways in which we operate differently, such as our level of detail, speed of action, risk profile, change profile, and so on?

FIGURE 13.3: The Expert Health Check – Possible Questions

STEP FIVE: Action planning

Having followed the first four steps, the stakeholder mapping exercise will certainly have given us quite a bit to think about. But it will also have prompted one or more of the following actions:

- We'll have identified a critically important stakeholder relationship that we've now realized is overdue for some attention or is sub-optimal in some way.
- We'll have identified a stakeholder relationship that's much more important than we had realized. We'll have recognized that we need to prioritize spending more time on this person.
- We'll have identified several stakeholders who are very demanding of our time and attention, who we've likely been over-servicing. We know we need to develop a strategy for passing this relationship over to someone else or curtailing it in some other fashion.
- We'll have discovered vital stakeholders with whom we've little or no relationship, so we need to work hard to build a win-win connection as soon as possible.

There is no need to despair if our action list is much longer than this. Revisiting and re-activating stakeholder relationships is one of the most common personal growth objectives experts announce when completing our Mastering Expertship program. In some cases, participants wish to repair relationships that have been broken or in some way sub-optimal for many years. The difference these resets can make is very significant and worth the effort.

In the following chapters, we explore the interpersonal tactics we need to deploy to build the stakeholder relationships we'll need to forge a bright, interesting, and challenging future.

TAKING ACTION

Growing Our Stakeholder Engagement Skills

IF THIS IS AN area in which you believe you could add greater value, here is an obvious suggestion for an action to regularly take, if you haven't so far:

▶ BUILD A COMPREHENSIVE STAKEHOLDER MAP AND REFRESH IT REGULARLY

- Since experts work in highly complex ecosystems that are shifting and adapting all the time, regularly developing and refreshing our stakeholder maps is actually a critically important activity. Master Experts work hard to get a handle on their stakeholder groups and to take a strategic approach to prioritization. All of the key questions we might like to ask ourselves are included in the chapter above.

"Every so often, it is not just what you know that is important, but also who you know."

Anon

CHAPTER | 14 |

Building Internal Networks

Are we proactive enough in reaching out and building win-win relationships inside our organization?

IN THIS CHAPTER, WE WILL EXPLORE:

- What categories of internal stakeholder are there?
- How to identify stakeholders we don't have on our stakeholder maps but should have (and why).
- What interactions be engineered with stakeholders to build better relationships with them?

THE FIRST OF THE expert roles under Stakeholder Engagement is Internal Networker. This expert role deals with the extent to which experts build a broad internal network of stakeholder engagements, create clarity about needs, and are consistent in our delivery of quality outcomes.

This expert role focuses on the breadth of our internal networks and the extent to which we've created strong engagement across these networks. The behaviors at each level of Expertship for this expert role are described in Figure 14.1.

At the immature level, experts are likely to be managing only a small (but perhaps growing) network that is almost exclusively directly related to their current mandate. This might be our technical cohort or our immediate stakeholders, like the people who generate or assign us work and those whose efforts we depend upon.

Experts at this level will demonstrate knowledge of and be responsive to the specific needs communicated by key immediate stakeholders. They'll allocate time based on incoming mandates from stakeholders and be mostly in a reactive mode.

Derailing experts will operate within a limited and exclusive network, maintaining only those relationships that are personally useful. They'll take a transactional, self-centered view of stakeholders, seeing these relationships as a means of getting things done and focusing only on their own personal needs. They'll overlook less obvious stakeholders and may well be operating with an outdated understanding of their stakeholders' needs.

> *"Our manager's manager is an important stakeholder.*
> *We ignore them at our peril."*

The Master Expert will proactively build and manage a network of effective relationships across the organization that reaches well beyond the requirements of their mandated work. They'll demonstrate a strong grasp of the current and emerging needs of both their immediate and removed stakeholders across and beyond the organization. They'll have a reputation for consistently satisfying stakeholder needs and delivering value over and above their expectations.

A key skill will be the ability to strategically prioritize time and attention between the relationships that are important to the current mandate, as well as those that inform future mandates.

Internal Stakeholders

AS WE DISCUSSED IN the last chapter, not all stakeholders are created equal. And different categories of stakeholders, once understood, need different engagement strategies. For most experts, there are four categories of stakeholders. Let's look at each of these in more detail.

Managers

Managers are the most obvious stakeholder group, one to which we're all in many different ways beholden.

Most experts have at least one formal manager but often have complex relationships with other colleagues. These may include those leading the project teams we're members of or global technical gurus in our area of specialty who, while we don't report to them, wield significant influence over our technical decisions and career paths.

Capability: STAKEHOLDER ENGAGEMENT

Expert Role: INTERNAL NETWORKER

MASTER EXPERT

- Proactively builds and manages a network of effective relationships across the organization.
- Demonstrates a strong grasp of the current and emerging needs of key immediate and removed stakeholders across the organization.
- Consistently satisfies and exceeds stakeholder needs.
- Strategically prioritizes time and attention between the relationships that are important to the current mandate and that may inform future mandates.

EXPERT

- Builds and manages a network of effective relationships within their immediate operational domain.
- Demonstrates a strong grasp of the current needs of key immediate stakeholders across the organization and is proactive in understanding all needs.
- Consistently satisfies stakeholder needs.
- Prioritizes time and attention on the relationships that are most important to the current mandate.

SPECIALIST

- Manages a small but growing network of relationships directly related to the current mandate.
- Demonstrates knowledge of the needs communicated by key immediate stakeholders and is reactive to those specific needs.
- Allocates time as directed by incoming mandates from stakeholders.

- Operates within a limited and exclusive network, maintaining relationships that are personally useful.
- Takes a transactional, self-centered view. Views relationships as a means of getting things done and focuses only on personal needs.
- May miss less obvious stakeholders or be operating with an outdated understanding of needs.

DERAILING

FIGURE 14.1: Internal Networker Behaviors

It's quite typical for us, as domain subject matter experts, to have a manager who doesn't really understand the nuts and bolts of what we do. In these instances, managing us is often as difficult for them as being managed by them is for us.

We suggest you purchase a copy of this book and subtly leave it lying around near their cubicle. The feedback we get from managers of experts is that the Expertship model is equally useful for managers of experts as it is for experts themselves. Your life will almost certainly improve if you take this initiative.

Our stakeholder maps should include everyone we have a relationship with, even if for only part of our role. This can include technical leaders of the functions in which we operate. Our manager's manager is also an important stakeholder in our career. We ignore them at our peril.

Technical Cohort

Our technical cohort is best described as the experts we work alongside in our technical domain. It's important to note that many members of our technical cohort might not actually work with us on the same projects. For example, a group of software architects might sit together and share the same skills but work on quite disparate projects and rarely work together.

But we're a tribe. We share the same difficulties and challenges in our work, we constantly learn from one another, and we very often nod understandingly when a technical cohort colleague is complaining about an out-of-control stakeholder, whether immediate or removed. Or our manager, of course.

Members of our technical cohort can be a source of valuable information or a source of considerable distraction.

"In the past, we've been more interested in how things work than how people work. Stakeholder engagement requires us to study the latter."

Immediate Stakeholders

Immediate stakeholders tend to be the people we interact with on a regular basis:

- Those who request our input or services.
- Those to whom we deliver advice or services.
- Those we collaborate with—or upon whose inputs we depend.
- Those who make decisions that directly impact us.

With immediate stakeholders, it's likely that we've developed a sense of their needs, expectations, concerns, and points of view, although this is sometimes merely a tacit impression that we've formed but not confirmed directly with them.

It could be that we've overlooked, misconstrued, or misjudged them and their needs. We might be making assumptions that are mistaken or are, at the very least, incomplete. We need to actively check in with them and test such assumptions. We can do this by conducting a health check, as described in Chapter 13.

Removed Stakeholders

Removed stakeholders are those who are indirectly impacted by what we do, but with whom we have less contact. They may be less obvious for that reason, so it may take some rigorous thinking to identify them and their needs. Removed stakeholders might include:

- End users of our solutions and services.
- Others who are impacted in some way but are not necessarily intended beneficiaries. Often, these more remote stakeholders may have good reason to feel that their needs are somehow threatened.
- Other departments or individuals in the organization who might have potentially aligned or conflicting interests.
- Less obvious decision-makers who might, for instance, have an interest that is affected by our work or upon whom we possibly depend.

While it might be tempting to think of removed stakeholders as a lower priority, this isn't always the case. Sometimes the key to developing greater influence within an organization is understanding the formal and informal lines of power and building alliances with stakeholders of strategic significance.

Immature experts are often unaware of the needs of the various stakeholder groups with whom they interact. To build more mutually beneficial partnerships, we all need to develop a relationship-oriented lens rather than an exclusively task-oriented lens. In some instances, developing a relationship-oriented lens is a radically different worldview than the one we've developed or expressed in our career to date. In fact, for many of us, we've been much more interested in how *things* work than how *people* work. Advanced stakeholder engagement requires us to study the latter.

Internal Activations

ONCE WE'VE ESTABLISHED WHO our stakeholders are, we have to think through what the appropriate engagement strategies might look like. These would obviously vary dramatically depending on which stakeholder we're thinking about.

A significant challenge is that we often don't have regular contact with these important stakeholders. In these instances, we need to determine ways to maintain the relationship. This might be a cup of coffee or a phone call. It might be a quarterly email check-in. It might be an agenda-free meeting (see Chapters 19 to 21 on Collaboration).

Two activations are worth a quick mention.

Meeting With a Removed Stakeholder

A COMMON MISTAKE AMONG experts is believing that some categories of stakeholders don't want to talk to them or are otherwise "off-limits." This is particularly true when it comes to dealing with *removed stakeholders* who are often the end recipients of our services but with whom we rarely meet or interact. We find that once experts take the plunge and reach out to these stakeholders, they discover that the stakeholders are often delighted to meet with "the real expert" and are prepared to invest time in the relationship.

They're even more delighted to discover that, as experts, we're interested in getting a good understanding of the trials, tribulations and challenges our removed stakeholders face. They instinctively know that the more we understand them, the better we'll be able to help them. Don't assume that they consider these interactions a waste of time. The only situation where it isn't a valuable experience for removed stakeholders to do so is when the expert arrives and behaves in a derailing manner, boring them with what we've been up to and explaining at length how expert we are.

> *"Start-up meetings are an opportunity*
> *to check in on the big stuff."*

Those operating at Master Expert level are on the front foot when it comes to building their influence and partnerships across the business. They don't wait around for the stakeholders to engage them. They know what all of their stakeholders expect, what they need, and the health of each relationship.

Some key questions for meetings with removed stakeholders might be:
- What are the challenges you face in your current role?
- What challenges does the organization face in your area? How are competitors or substitute services addressing those challenges?
- What additional or different value will your customers or communities look for in the future, and why?
- What do you feel you and your team waste time on?
- What would you and your team like to spend time on but can't because of other responsibilities?
- What are the concerns that keep you awake at night?

Removed stakeholders might not have answers ready the first time you ask, but you'll have added value to the relationship by asking them. In our experience, at the second meeting, clients often say something like "I have been thinking about your questions about what future value our community will want, and I think it is…" Voltaire suggested that you should judge a person not by the answers they provide but by the questions they ask. It's a famous quote for good reason!

Start-Up Meetings

ANOTHER HIGH-VALUE STAKEHOLDER ENGAGEMENT meeting is the start-up meeting. These occur at the beginning of a new project or engagement, or at the beginning of a new stage of a project. Start-up meetings are the opportunity to check in on the big stuff before we dive into the details. As experts, we often want to get into the detail straight away and miss this opportunity to go to 70,000 ft and clarify the strategic alignment and impact we hope the project will have. These meetings are an ideal opportunity to build relationships rather than just focusing on the task.

We need to have our 70,000 ft questions ready in order to prevent these meetings from almost immediately focusing on the task or jumping to the solution. Posing these questions helps all of the meeting participants take a step back and look at the whole project that sits before them.

- What does success look like in both the short and long term? What impact do we hope this project will have?
- What does our organization expect of us?
- What roles will we each play? How do we expect each other to add value to the group? How will we collaborate brilliantly together?
- What constraints, if any, are the parties working under?
- How do we hold each other accountable? What happens if, instead of adding value to one another, we're creating problems for each other?
- What are our working styles, and are they in concert or misaligned? How do we cope with different styles?

The ability to deal with these higher level operating rules of engagement early in the relationship usually means that conflicts are dealt with faster and there is greater clarity around the environment in which each colleague is operating. Information and insights gathered at this point can be very helpful later in the project if (and when!) it hits speed bumps.

TAKING ACTION

Growing Our Internal Networking Skills

IF THIS IS AN expert role in which you believe you could add greater value, here are some high-level suggestions for actions to take:

▶ TAKE ADVANTAGE OF EXISTING ORGANIZATION NETWORKING FORUMS

- Those who don't take advantage of natural gatherings to organically and informally meet and build relationships with stakeholders typically face the challenge of only engaging with stakeholders when they want something from them. This is not a recipe for fostering trust. Questions we might like to ask ourselves:
- What is stopping me from actively participating in my organization's networking event, including social occasions such as Friday night drinks? How might I overcome these?
- If I do attend these events, do I tend to hang out with people I know rather than seeking out intelligence from people I don't know (and who don't know me)? How would I introduce myself to people I don't know? How would I get *them* talking?
- Am I ready to answer the basic questions colleagues ask about me in a more fluent and interesting way? How do I present myself well without being over- or under-confident?
- Do I have my three or four trusty conversation starter questions at the ready? Will they help me gather additional insights so I can understand what is going on in the wider organization?
- What measures am I going to adopt to force myself outside my comfort zone and start meeting some people who I don't know but who might be valuable sources of information?

▶ GET ON THE FRONT FOOT

Failing to reach out or initiate engagement with key stakeholders has consequences. The result will be a more passive or an altogether unengaging co-existence combined with low visibility of their needs. Low visibility means we will struggle to add real value and may indeed deliver work that does not meet the precise needs of the stakeholder. Or they might fail to deliver on what we need from them. Some questions we might like to ask ourselves:

- Do I have an important stakeholder with whom I have yet to build any substantial connection? If so, what has stopped me from developing a stronger connection with this stakeholder? Do my answers to such questions sound like excuses?
- If my goal is to get a meeting in their diary, perhaps a 30-minute coffee meeting, in order to interview them about their goals and challenges, how might I go about it? What response am I expecting? If I get that response, how will I handle it? Is there a genuine (and perceived) benefit for the stakeholder in meeting me? For example, is it obvious that gathering deeper insights allows me to better meet their needs?
- Have I explained clearly to these types of stakeholders the loss of opportunity that results from me not being aware of their needs and the context in which they're asking for work to be completed? Can I articulate these clearly, and are they valid and of shared importance?
- Would it be reasonable to put myself under pressure and set a deadline to achieve this goal?

▶ CONDUCT A STAKEHOLDER ANALYSIS

Without conducting a deeper analysis of our stakeholders' needs and preferences, there's a possibility that we will be engaging with them purely at a functional level with little or no insight into what really makes them tick. This can cause tensions or, more often, missed opportunities to better collaborate or satisfy each other's needs. Some questions we might like to ask ourselves:

- Which of my stakeholders would most benefit from me conducting a proactive needs analysis?
- In terms of preparation, which answers on the Stakeholder Health Check template (Figure 13.2 on page 206) am I least sure about and need the most insight? Which questions should I be asking? How will I frame the intent behind asking such questions?
- What has changed at my end of the relevant projects and/or programs of work that might impact on the stakeholder, and how will I communicate this diplomatically?

CHAPTER | 15 |

Building External Networks

Are we proactive enough about reaching out and building win-win relationships outside our organization?

IN THIS CHAPTER, WE WILL EXPLORE:

- What categories of external stakeholder are there?
- What is the value of active engagement in external organizations?
- What stops us from engaging externally? And what can we do about it?

THE SECOND EXPERT ROLE in Stakeholder Engagement is **External Networker**. This expert role deals with the extent to which experts build a broad external network beyond their organization's boundaries and understand and meet the needs of external stakeholders.

This role covers all of our networks, ranging from an internal approach and transactional style to an external approach and transformational style. The behaviors at each level of Expertship for this expert role are described in Figure 15.1.

> *"You need a strategic network because the forces that drive change in your field will come from outside your current world."*

At the immature level, experts tend to have stakeholder networks that are almost entirely internal, and they have little or no connection to stakeholders external to the organization. The expert's focus is on immediate, internal relationships. Experts who are derailing here will be operating very much in their own limited internal bubble and will show no interest in the affairs, challenges or needs of external stakeholders.

The Master Expert, on the other hand, actively networks beyond the boundaries of the organization to build alliances. Because of this external stakeholder contact, Master Experts possess a strong grasp of the current and emerging needs of key stakeholders external to the organization. Consequently, they'll strategically prioritize their time and attention toward relationships that might add future value.

In their Harvard Business Review article on networking, Hill and Lineback make the point that external networks are a critical success factor if experts are to be on top of any forthcoming disruptive change in their industry. "You need a strategic network because the forces that drive change in your field will probably come from outside your current world."

> *"Most of us have mentors—formal or informal—*
> *whether we realize it or not."*

External Stakeholders

SO, WHO ARE THESE external stakeholders? Below, we suggest some categories you may wish to consider. This list is not exhaustive.

External Associates

Colleagues who work in different organizations but with whom we interact on a business-as-usual (BAU) basis. Building a deeper relationship with these stakeholders, rather than just transacting with them, often leads to these associates being rich sources of information and perspective. We may need to also share our perspective with them, so the relationship is valuable both ways.

Many experts have contact with external associates who they have since stopped working with regularly. Because we aren't in contact with them for BAU, maintaining and nurturing these relationships is harder, takes more time, and requires a disciplined approach.

Capability: STAKEHOLDER ENGAGEMENT

Expert Role: EXTERNAL NETWORKER

MASTER EXPERT

- Actively networks beyond the boundaries of the organization to build alliances.
- Has a strong grasp of current and emerging needs of key stakeholders external to the organization.
- Strategically prioritizes time and attention on the relationships that might add future value.

EXPERT

- Occasionally networks beyond the boundaries of the organization.
- Demonstrates limited knowledge of current needs of key stakeholders external to the organization. Little or no visibility of future needs.
- Does not spend time on relationships that may have future value.

SPECIALIST

- Network focus is almost completely internal.
- Little or no connection to stakeholders external to the organization.
- Focuses on immediate internal relationships.

- External relationships are typically in the professional domain and focused on technical knowledge and developments.
- Future value is defined as personal career value rather than organizational value.

DERAILING

FIGURE 15.1: External Networker Behaviors

Over the years, the authors have learned that waiting until we have a precise need before we interact with these stakeholders doesn't really work. They get irritated that we only called because we have an agenda. And it may be that they don't have any specific perspective on the precise topic we want to research. Having catch-ups with these associates with no agenda, however, means a more relaxed conversation. It also allows the conversation to go off on tangents that may well be very valuable. We often run networking sessions with some of our clients with only one agenda item: each guest shares something they've learned over the last two or three months. These sessions are universally regarded as extremely useful by attendees, and we always learn heaps from them, too.

> *"The worst supplier relationships have a*
> *master/slave dynamic going on."*

Supporters

This group of stakeholders is here to help us. Not every expert has a coach, although we'd encourage every expert to consider investing in one at some point (or ask the organization to do so on our behalf). This is particularly the case if we're focused on committing to the journey from expert to Master Expert.

In this category, we're describing the stakeholders who are outside our usual BAU circle (normal working group) as external, even if they're still internal to the organization. Any external-from-us sounding board is extremely helpful in providing feedback as we master and deploy new skills and thinking.

Most of us have mentors—either formally or informally—whether we realize it or not. We discuss the difference between coaching and mentoring in Chapter 49. Mentor relationships can be internal or external to the organization.

Other supporters may be colleagues in other departments who are supportive of our projects.

Family

Family members are possibly the most critical stakeholders, but they're often left off stakeholder maps because we imagine that our stakeholders are only those connected directly with our work. However, our families are directly connected to our work.

If we work too much, we don't see our family. If we're frustrated at work, this plays out at home. If we're feeling insecure at work, that impacts us at home. In contrast, if we're happy and fulfilled at work, have our work/life balance properly organized, and can look forward to a positive future with our employer, then the positive impacts on our family are many.

Is it worth contemplating how we manage these family stakeholder relationships? We might answer questions about how our day was at work, but do we discuss in detail how our last three months have been, what we'd like to change, or even what new thinking and skills we'd like to apply having read this book? And how often are we genuinely inquiring about our family members' perspectives and needs rather than merely assuming that they're understood and being addressed? A relatively modern English language saying comes to mind: "A problem shared is a problem halved." In the USA, they add "A job shared is a job doubled." We talk at length about this in Chapter 29.

Customers

External customers should always be on the stakeholder map of an expert, even if we don't know any. This category gets included so as to remind us that we need to have external customers in our network in order to inform how the eventual recipients of the value we create through our Expertship perceive and consume that value.

Suppliers

Very often, external suppliers are critical stakeholders in the world of experts. Their ability to know what we need and supply it in a timely fashion has a huge impact on our ability to get things done. The best supplier relationships are collaborative and have at their foundation a win-win agreement. The worst are combative, conflict-driven, and usually have a master/slave dynamic going one way or another.

Professional Associations

Most professions have professional bodies or organized groups of like-minded professionals coming together to discuss best practice and work on defining next practice.

Time spent with these stakeholders tends to suffer when we get busy, but most of us have had the experience of taking the time to get out and see what everyone else is doing and enjoying, as well as how they're benefiting from the experience. Associations are also a great source of market context for experts.

> *"Our advice: don't just follow thought leaders—engage with them."*

At Master Expert level, experts really leverage these organizations, carefully researching where the best forums and conferences are for the latest trends, ideas, thinking and solutions. They'll be involved in multiple associations, and some of these will be where one profession intersects with another since this is often where new knowledge frontiers are explored.

Being active in such associations is usually a worthwhile endeavor, rather than just being a passive consumer of their knowledge sharing. By doing so, experts build powerful external relationships that can be leveraged far more than those of a bystander. It also means that rather than just attending events, we can get involved in starting to shape them.

Experts

How many experts do you have on your stakeholder map? If part of the purpose of an external network is to ensure we're up to date and familiar with the latest thinking about our professions, then following experts is crucial.

But why should they be on our stakeholder map? Our advice isn't just to follow experts but to engage with them. For many of us, the ultimate test of whether we're Master Experts is whether we're considered experts in our profession, first in our organization, then in our locality, and then worldwide. This isn't possible without sharing ideas with others. Most experts don't sit in a dark room dreaming up new concepts and approaches. They talk to a huge number of people and gradually synthesize all these conversations into new thinking.

If our eventual aim is to be known as an expert, then we need to hang out with some.

Invisible Stakeholders

In the course of conducting our programs in Expertship, we've discovered an important group of stakeholders that most experts have: *invisible stakeholders*. Typically, experts are, at best, peripherally aware of these players in their work life, and they rarely appear on the first draft of our stakeholder maps. Very often, but not always, they are external stakeholders.

> *"Sometimes you don't need to run a health check to know a relationship is broken."*

For each of us, our invisible stakeholders will be unique, but some of the following questions may help us bring them into the light.

- When we want to be considered for involvement in a new, exciting project, who is it that influences whether we get the gig or not? This question often teases out stakeholders like HR business partners, the peers of our manager, or an end user of our services with whom we have never previously been involved.
- When we completed our last project, who was involved peripherally and without whose involvement the project could not have succeeded? This question often teases out junior and seemingly unimportant colleagues who nevertheless play a small but critical role in getting

something done. Again, this might be a junior lawyer who approves a piece of legal text quickly or a procurement manager who approves a critical purchase.

- When we last proposed a solution to a problem being experienced by the business, with whom did the business consult about whether or not our proposed solution was optimal? This question often teases out external advisors to our decision-makers, such as other consultants, external accountants, friends who operate in the same space, a revered blogger, or a colleague who has undertaken a similar project in another organization. In some cases, this may not be a person at all. It could be a trusted website or media outlet, for example.

Resetting a Poor Stakeholder Relationship

IN THESE CHAPTERS ABOUT stakeholder engagement, we have discussed the idea of running Stakeholder Health Checks (see Chapter 13). But sometimes, you don't need to run a health check to know a relationship is broken. The most difficult relationships to mend are typically those with external stakeholders. Let's take a look at what might work by using the experience Alex shared with the authors.

Alex is a subject matter expert in pension products and services. As such, he has to interface with a broad range of complex stakeholders, including the internal managers who hold him responsible for shaping products and services that generate high demand and are profitable, the internal stakeholders who hold him responsible for compliance (such as the legal and compliance teams), the external stakeholders who administer the products and funds he shapes, and, of course, eventually, the investors themselves who have put their hard-won pension funds to work in Alex's platforms.

> *"Alex and Sam had little in common and didn't really like each other."*

At the end of one of our Expertship programs, Alex committed to fixing a clearly broken stakeholder relationship. He explained to his coach that his relationship with Sam, a senior executive and important stakeholder at an external organization, was broken at every level.

It was clear to Alex that Sam didn't know what Alex needed, or why, or when, and Sam had no idea what behaviors created havoc at Alex's end because these behaviors were commonplace and were clearly delivered oblivious to their impact. Similarly, however, Alex realized that he had no good information about what was critically important to Sam. In fact, they'd never had the conversation. Alex realized that he'd made a critical error: he'd assumed he knew what Sam required.

The relationship was also on the rocks for other reasons. The project they were working on together (a partnership between their organizations) was well behind schedule and both sides blamed each other. Furthermore, Alex's style was introverted. He preferred to operate in a slow, careful, thoughtful and considered manner. Meanwhile, Sam was very extroverted, wanted the discussions and decisions to be fast, and tended to jump quickly to a solution. Alex and Sam had little in common and didn't really like each other.

But the challenge was on. Alex invited Sam for a coffee and, in his own words, "hit the reset button." Using the Stakeholder Health Check template, he asked Sam to imagine they were meeting for the first time and would be working on the project together. He then began to explore Sam's needs, KPIs, operating style, pressures, definitions of success, as well as his motivations.

At the end of these gently asked but penetrative questions, Alex fed back to Sam what he had heard Sam say success looked like to him. "Yes, you've absolutely got it," Sam replied.

Alex then took the advice of Susan Scott (author of *Fierce Conversations*) and let the silence do the heavy lifting. After a short pause, Sam started asking the same questions of Alex. That half-hour coffee meeting turned into an hour. Expectations and working style were agreed, frustrations were shared, interdependencies were explored and understood, and the relationship was reset.

"It's now one of the best working relationships I have," Alex told us later. "We've built respect and understanding, and this is gradually turning into a very trusting relationship. As soon as I know I can't deliver something, I tell Sam immediately. He's my first call. And he returns the favor."

"Where we have conflicting KPIs, which is often, we get together to work on the problem and then go back to our respective masters to reset expectations, which generates a workable compromise. It's how every stakeholder relationship should be."

Alex admits that he was extremely nervous when he proposed the coffee meeting. He had no idea of how Sam would react, and like many difficult conversations we have to conduct, he'd imagined the worst outcome as likely. But after an initial period of skepticism, Sam warmed to the process and the increasing good communication and outcomes. He understood Alex's intent was pure.

"It was my worst relationship on my stakeholder map but one of the most important, and that's why I chose to work on it," Alex told us. "I'm very glad I did, and so is Sam."

Alex's story is very similar to many we have heard and shares two common strands: we need to have the courage to make a start and we need to have a technique in place to achieve a good result.

TAKING ACTION

Growing Our External Networking Skills

IF THIS IS AN expert role in which you believe you could add greater value, here is a high-level suggestion for action to take:

▶ ACTIVELY PARTICIPATE IN WELL-CHOSEN NETWORKING EVENTS

- Without deliberately networking beyond the boundaries of our own organization, we could end up with a narrow, somewhat institutionalized view of the world. Some questions we might like to ask ourselves:
- Am I clear on the benefits of actually extending my network? Can I set measurable goals for the benefits I want to achieve? What specific knowledge, contacts and experiences am I trying to collect, and why?
- How much time am I willing to invest in building my external network? Can I allocate a particular amount of time per month or week? How many events will I attend?
- How do I choose events to participate in judiciously? Where will I most likely encounter my target stakeholders? What criteria am I going to establish that will help me make a "go" or "no-go" decision?
- What is my follow-up strategy for the people I meet who I think would be valuable to my network? How will I reconnect with them? What value can I bring to them?

CHAPTER | 16 |

Managing Our Networks

Are we proactive enough about maintaining internal and external relationships?
How do we do this efficiently?

IN THIS CHAPTER, WE WILL EXPLORE:

- When we have far too many stakeholders to maintain regular personal contact, how do we effectively stay in touch?
- How do we find time to identify and recruit new stakeholders?
- What tactics are available to us that don't take much time but have a high impact?

THE THIRD EXPERT ROLE in the Stakeholder Engagement capability is that of Network Manager. This expert role deals with the extent to which experts strategically and effectively manage stakeholder engagements, manage conflicting priorities, and anticipate future needs.

This expert role covers the scope of the service relationships we have with stakeholders. It involves a shift from operating in a reactive and tactical manner to proactively managing our stakeholder engagements and considering their strategic, long-term value. The behaviors at each level of Expertship for this expert role are described in Figure 16.1.

At an immature level, experts will tend to interact with key stakeholders as on-demand technical suppliers. They'll react to immediate needs. Immature experts will not yet be adept at managing conflicting priorities and requirements and will be dependent on interventions from others to resolve them. Derailing behavior in this role is indicated by being perceived by key stakeholders as unapproachable, difficult to deal with, and regularly unavailable. Services are provided inconsistently and unreliably.

The Master Expert, however, tends to interact with key stakeholders as a strategic partner and trusted technical expert. Their relationships with stakeholders always generate mutually beneficial outcomes. The Master Expert is adept at anticipating future needs and manages conflicting priorities and requirements across stakeholders for win-win organization-wide outcomes.

> *"Our stakeholder ecosystems are not static.*
> *They are constantly changing."*

Master Experts also actively keep their stakeholder map current. Our stakeholder ecosystems are not static. They are constantly changing. We need to routinely update our stakeholder maps to ensure that we can be our most effective. Since, as we have discussed, we can't rely on formal structures to help us navigate the organization and dictate where we spend our time, we need to use our stakeholder maps as a guide. It's easy for us to fall into the trap of relying too much on formal structures when creating our stakeholder maps.

Proactive Stakeholder Management

ARTY IS A JUNIOR digital marketing executive at XYZ Corp, a large entertainment enterprise, where he's part of a recently recruited team. Just a few months in, Arty became frustrated by the lack of a clear digital marketing strategy across XYZ Corp in the country he operated in. Most of his work was a last-minute afterthought—an addition to existing and more traditional marketing campaigns. His frustration was that he didn't see his colleagues in the organization imagining how digital marketing could do things differently and make a difference.

> *"Arty's plan revolved around figuring out*
> *why executives would want to engage."*

Capability: STAKEHOLDER ENGAGEMENT
Expert Role: NETWORK MANAGER

MASTER EXPERT

- Relationship with key stakeholders is as a strategic partner and trusted technical thought leader.
- Relationships always generate mutually beneficial outcomes.
- Anticipates future needs.
- Manages conflicting priorities and requirements among stakeholders for win-win, holistic organization-wide outcomes.

EXPERT

- Relationship with key stakeholders is as a trusted technical partner, providing timely advice and direction.
- Relationship mostly generates mutually beneficial outcomes.
- Anticipates current needs.
- Manages conflicting priorities and requirements among stakeholders for win-win, department-wide outcomes.

SPECIALIST

- Relationship with key stakeholders is as an on-demand technical supplier.
- Reacts to immediate needs.
- Is not yet adept at managing conflicting priorities and requirements.

- Perceived by key stakeholders as difficult to deal with and unapproachable.
- Service is provided inconsistently and unreliably.

DERAILING

FIGURE 16.1: Network Manager Behaviors

After compiling his stakeholder map at one of our Expertship programs, it was clear to Arty that while he had strong immediate networks among the marketing and IT team (effectively, his *technical cohort*), his connection with the rest of the business was almost non-existent (*immediate and removed stakeholders*). After a long discussion about market context, Arty also realized that he didn't know enough about where XYZ Corp was going, and why.

Arty set a personal growth goal after the Expertship workshop to try build some effective relationships with senior business leaders, both in his organization and externally. The purpose of this was to educate them on how digital marketing could make a difference in XYZ Corp.

His Expertship coach, Craig, worked with Arty to discover the strategies that would enable this personal growth target to be achieved. They quickly agreed that exposure to senior executives and their long-term plans for the organization would help Arty be more productive and see where more value could be added. But there was a challenge: why would senior executives want to take meetings and connect with a new junior member of the marketing team?

Arty and Craig formulated a strategy that would enable the first connections to take place.

Arty's plan is represented in Figure 16.2.

As we can see, Arty took a classic Master Expert approach to the development of the strategy. He went to market context first and focused on understanding the strategy of XYZ Corp. Armed with this information, he planned to get meetings with senior executives. The plan was to then use the data captured to develop insights on where digital marketing could add value. Once opportunities were identified, Arty was going to run pilots with sponsors and build a business case, where appropriate, for a wider rollout of the campaigns.

> ### "Most of us have the opposite of Arty's problem— we have too many stakeholders."

A lot of Arty's plan revolved around building stakeholder engagements with identified executives or their deputies. And part of building those engagements included working out why they might be interested in engaging with him.

During the process, Arty discovered that many people in the organization were willing to meet with the digital team—more than he had anticipated. Digital was something most people wanted to understand better. However, neither the CEO nor the CFO agreed to meet with him, but they did ask members of their team to connect with Arty. In the end, these executives were able to present the CEO and CFOs views to Arty and describe the challenges faced by the business.

Capability: **STAKEHOLDER ENGAGEMENT**

Arty's Engagement Plan

STEP 1	**Company Strategy**	• Grow from country of origin • Organic sales • Possible acquisitions • Innovation – new products • New services • New audiences	**ARTY'S TO-DO LIST:** 1. Understand what strategy means in detail 2. Explore current 'go-to-market' approach 3. Ask: can digital help?
STEP 2	**Target Key Stakeholders**	• CEO – drives growth strategy • CFO - $$$ and risks • Sales directors • Marketing directors	**ARTY'S TO-DO LIST:** 1. Develop meeting pitch 2. Develop questions 3. Ask: can digital help?
STEP 3	**Insights**	• Growth is slower – behind target (Need!!) • Partnering overseas difficult because no XYZ Corp profile (Marketing! Digital!) • XYZ Corp doesn't invent anything – it commercializes	**ARTY'S TO-DO LIST:** 1. Shape possible digital campaign for international 2. Shape possible campaign for local inventors 3. Review digital sales channel and marketing
STEP 4	**Engagement Strategy**	• Local sales – test pilot, partner with sales; did it work? • Partnering overseas – test with pilot, any incoming enquiries? From where? • Inventors – test pilot with product development team; any incoming?	**ARTY'S TO-DO LIST:** 1. Carry out pilots 2. Document results 3. Make business case if worth it 4. Ask for time with relevant decision makers 5. Get budget 6. Get results

FIGURE 16.2: Arty's Engagement Plan

Once Arty understood the challenges the business leaders were facing, in particular the ones that were really worrying them, he could begin to tailor his propositions to highlight where digital could help.

The growth agenda was stalled, so could digital assist in building sales? He thought so. The innovation agenda was stalled, but it turned out that despite innovation being a big target in the strategic plan, XYZ wasn't actually very good at it. Their successes had come from taking other people's inventions and innovations to market. Could digital assist with this? Again, Arty thought so.

International growth was also stalled. Despite identifying some potential partners, these organizations weren't responsive because no one had heard of XYZ Corp in these territories.

Arty worked on some campaign ideas with his colleagues in marketing and then approached a variety of stakeholders to run small pilots. He ran three in total, each addressing a key stakeholder need. One didn't work, but the other two showed signs of promise. Working closely with his stakeholders, he crafted a business proposal and his sponsors backed these plans. Arty eventually got in front of the CEO to present one of his campaigns—and it was approved!

A month or so later, Arty and members of his team were invited to a meeting to discuss innovation strategy. The CFO had suggested someone from the digital team should be present. Taking a strategic approach to stakeholder engagement had got his role noticed, especially because he was adding value.

Arty got traction because his proposals were directly aligned with more effectively executing the organization's strategy. This meant he got funding. But he got a lot more than that. Six months on, he has doubled the number of internal stakeholders on his map, and nearly all the new additions are in business roles, both in his home country and internationally. He's now regularly invited to strategy sessions by many departments because the CEO has insisted that a digital lens would now be considered for all of the organization's initiatives. More importantly, he feels he's adding significantly more value, learning all the time, and is a highly engaged member of the organization.

Strategic alignment is a sure way to get the attention and engagement of stakeholders.

But there are personal considerations that we also need to consider as we manage our network.

Managing a Large and Complex Network

ARTY'S PROBLEM IS THE opposite of that experienced by most experts, who generally feel they have too many stakeholders and not enough time to sustainably engage with them.

A typical expert might have between 100 and 120 active stakeholders, which is far too many to maintain regular personal contact with. This means experts need to think strategically about how they can keep in touch while still managing their heavy workload.

Taking a tip from retail, we suggest that experts consider deploying a category management process to help build and manage a stakeholder communication strategy. Essentially, we create categories of stakeholders, determining the amount of time and energy we have available to communicate with them, and then select relevant and workable communication strategies that fit the category and the time available.

For example, here is what a set of categories and possible communication strategies might look like:

Category 1: Core Current Stakeholders (85 percent of my time)

Description: People we're consistently working with on current projects and as part of business as usual (BAU).

Objective: Ensure that we're spending at least some time on building the relationship and staying aligned, so we're not just being dominated by the task.

Challenge: Most of our time is spent working on immediate tasks with these stakeholders. Occasionally, we need to hit the pause button, go to 70,000 feet, and check in on the bigger picture.

Possible network management solutions:

- Regular stakeholder health checks, perhaps quarterly. Are we still aligned, are we still serving each other well, are we achieving the results we hoped? Has anything changed?
- Quarterly kaizen meetings, which are incremental innovation conversations. How could we be working together more efficiently? Is there any work that is now redundant or low value? Could we replace it with higher value work?

Category 2: Non-Current VIP Stakeholders (7 percent of my time)

Description: Most likely, these are removed stakeholders who are the eventual recipients of the value we create or sponsors of our work.

Objective: Somehow stay connected and informed about their priorities, including any changes in priorities. Remain front of mind for them.

Challenge: They're quite inaccessible and busy, as are we. Generally, we meet when projects begin or when there is a problem, but we want a richer relationship than that.

Possible network management solutions:

- Seek them out at regular internal network events.
- Read everything they circulate and, where possible and relevant, comment on it or provide feedback. Find a reason to connect.
- Ask their advice about work priorities and direction from time to time. Let them know what projects you're prioritizing.
- Use them as connectors. "I'm looking for help with X or Y. Do you know anyone relevant?"

Category 3: Future VIPs (5 percent of my time)

Description: People we want to connect with in the future, but with whom we're yet to build a relationship.

Objective: Leverage their knowledge and influence in the future to build our professional impact.

Challenge: They don't know who we are and may initially have no interest in connecting with us. Because they're future contacts, we don't have time to invest in "recruiting" them.

Possible network management solutions:

- For internal future stakeholders, arrange an introduction through a third party.
- Seek them out at internal networking events.
- For external future stakeholders, seek them out at external network events.
- Identify the associations they're most active in and join them.
- Provide considerate feedback on their thought leadership.
- Reach out directly to tell them why you would like to connect.

Category 4: Sporadic Colleagues (3 percent of my time)

Description: People we've worked with on projects that have finished.

Objective: Stay in touch because we might work together again or have opportunities and information for each other.

Challenge: Virtually no time available to connect face to face so it's easy to fall out of touch.

Possible network management solutions:

- Seek them out at internal network events.
- Quarterly one-line emails, such as a pro forma relaxed email asking how they are and what they are up to.
- Post in the project's WhatsApp group or have some type of social media interaction. Definitely connect on LinkedIn, which means

taking the time once a week to scroll the news feed and see who has posted what.

- Captains of industry catch-ups. One of the authors uses these to catch up with good friends who also run businesses. We discuss what we have learned over the last six months, and the conversation is always dynamic, useful and motivating.

We can see that the vast majority of the time is spent dealing with current stakeholders, via business as usual, but still with a specific call-out on periodically checking in on the big picture.

Only 3 percent of the time is spent on sporadic associates, but this time is spent carefully connecting with them all and staying in touch.

We see experts who circulate a quarterly email newsletter updating their colleagues on what they have been up to. Depending on the quality and length of the prose, this may or may not work for most experts.

We've also seen experts deliberately find something of high quality (research, an article, a book review) that is relevant to their network. Sharing this allows them to offer high value but also stay in touch.

The most important aspect is being deliberate. We need to understand who we need to communicate with, how often, and then find a low-maintenance way to have a high impact.

TAKING ACTION

Growing Our Network Manager Skills

IF THIS IS AN expert role in which you believe you could add greater value, here are some high-level suggestions for actions to take:

▶ BE A CONNECTOR

- Our stakeholders don't exist in a vacuum. They're part of a network where there are likely advantages to being connected with each other. By introducing stakeholders when we think they could both benefit from engaging with each other, we're actively promoting tighter collaboration between all. Some questions we might like to ask ourselves:
- Which of my internal stakeholders don't know each other but face similar challenges in their roles and might benefit from exchanging experiences? How would I motivate them both to meet or connect?
- Which of my external stakeholders are in the same situation?
- Which of my stakeholders need to work more closely together but currently don't? How can I help them connect and work more collaboratively? What's in it for them? What's in it for me?
- Which of my stakeholders know someone I would like to be connected to? How would I find this out? How would I approach my stakeholder and ask for an introduction? How would I frame the request in such a way that it's clear there would be value in the connection for all parties?
- Which stakeholders do I and others have, but others have a better level of engagement with them than I do? How can I leverage their knowledge of our in-common stakeholder to improve my engagement with them?

▶ PERIODICALLY SURVEY STAKEHOLDERS

We operate in a highly dynamic environment where priorities and challenges change all the time. Failing to frequently update our understanding of stakeholders' changing needs, preferences and priorities means we run the risk of missing emerging requirements and having our services and solutions become outdated and obsolete. Some questions we might like to ask ourselves:

- How often do I elicit feedback on my services and update myself on stakeholders' felt needs, priorities, plans and challenges?
- Is there a way for me to automate this process via surveys? Or do I need to institute quarterly check-ins?
- How often would it be relevant or useful to re-check assumptions, priorities and challenges of stakeholders? What would they think is a good frequency?
- How could I use consolidated data from many stakeholders to shape my and my team's direction, priorities and services?

CHAPTER | 17 |

What Motivates Stakeholders?

Are we thinking deeply enough about what is really motivating our stakeholders?

IN THIS CHAPTER, WE WILL EXPLORE:

- What are the typical deep human motivators that often drive extra effort and commitment?
- How do we recognize them in people?
- Without manipulating our colleagues, how do we leverage our understanding of these motivators to build win-win stakeholder relationships?

OUR STAKEHOLDERS HAVE BOTH functional needs (some data in a report, a technical solution or a piece of advice) and psychological needs (the need to feel important, to feel connected, a sense of achievement and progress). Just as the emotional brain trumps the rational brain in general, our deeper human motivations, when attended to, are more motivating and engaging than functional requirements alone.

For example, we may wish to command a big salary because, rationally, we think we're underpaid in comparison to market rates. As such, we'll be rationally motivated to seek higher pay. But we might want to use that extra pay to purchase a family home, for example. Perhaps a larger home with a garden where we can bring up the kids. This emotional motivation is likely to be stronger than simply getting an increase in our paycheck.

One of the key strategies for achieving higher levels of engagement with stakeholders is for us to consciously attend to their most keenly felt needs. They're highly motivated to address these felt needs and will welcome allies in this regard.

So what are the categories of motivation? And how do we recognize what motivates our stakeholders?

There are many models of motivations, some much more complicated than others. In Figure 17.1, we describe a simple but useful model of seven common human motivators.

Achievement as a Motivator

This is the need to achieve, excel and succeed. A stakeholder with this type of need will set goals that are challenging but realistic. These goals have to be challenging so that the person can feel a sense of achievement. However, they also have to be realistic, as stakeholders believe that when a goal is unrealistic, its achievement is dependent on chance rather than personal skill or contribution.

> *"A strong need for affiliation can interfere with a stakeholder's ability to lead teams, run projects, make decisions, and their objectivity."*

These colleagues are highly motivated by stretch targets or goals that appear difficult but possible. Because the achievement of the target is the most important thing to them, they're likely to work collaboratively and collegiately. Achievement-motivated stakeholders don't necessarily need recognition or praise, but some colleagues motivated by achievement also need the recognition component—and some will get grumpy if it isn't forthcoming. If our stakeholders talk about their achievements, then it's likely that recognition is important. However, if they quietly achieve, this probably isn't the case.

If our stakeholder has a strong achievement motivation, then our strategy is to focus on the achievement of outcomes and the inherent worthwhileness of various tasks. Achievement-motivated colleagues embrace difficult tasks with relish. If our stakeholders are imbued with strong achievement motivation, they're often easier to engage as they're already quite driven and require little encouragement from us to fulfill their responsibilities and tasks.

Indeed, if they're struggling to achieve, their natural reaction is to tell their colleagues and ask for help.

Affiliation as a Motivator

This is the need for friendly relationships and human interaction. There is a need to "feel liked," "cared for," and "accepted" by others, as well as a sense of belonging. A stakeholder with a high need for affiliation is likely to be a team player. They'll perform best in a co-operative environment where interaction among colleagues is frequent and positive. A strong need for affiliation can interfere with a stakeholder's ability to lead teams, run projects, make decisions, and their objectivity.

Capability: STAKEHOLDER ENGAGEMENT
What Motivates us?

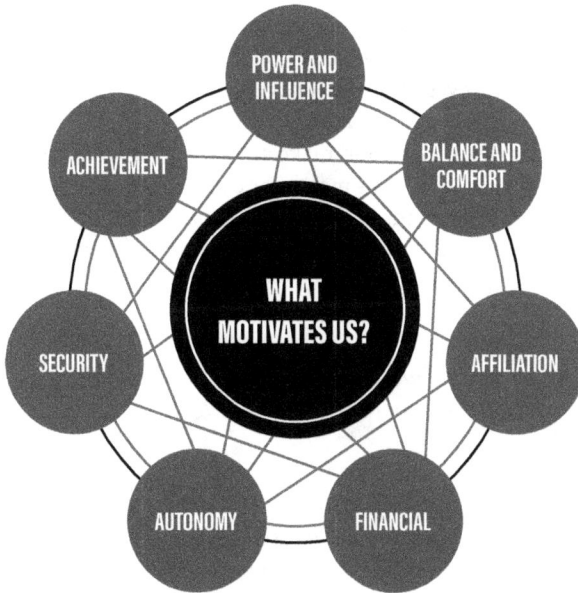

FIGURE 17.1: What Motivates Us?

The "need to be liked" prompts affiliation-motivated colleagues to make decisions, whether about business or about people, that increase their popularity, rather than necessarily furthering the interests of the organization. On occasion, they may defer a decision or make a decision to avoid possible conflict.

There's also an occasional downside with affiliation-motivated colleagues whereby they distract other people from their work because they're so keen to socialize. However, on strongly technical teams, they're very often the social glue that pulls the team together and forces the group to socialize.

If our stakeholder is affiliation motivated, they'll always be willing to meet and talk thing through. They will also consistently suggest we add other people into the mix who might have some interest. Communication is usually their strong point, but we might find some of these meetings superfluous or long-winded. Strong agendas, clear timelines, shorter meetings, and a focus on outcomes as well as relationships are the approaches we need to take to get the benefits of their communication abilities without the downsides.

As an additional note, affiliation-motivated stakeholders are very useful in helping us understand the motivations, concerns and aspirations of other stakeholders. They know everything about everyone.

Power and Influence as a Motivator

This is the need to lead others and make an impact. In some models, this motivator is referred to as "ego." This motivator can exhibit itself in two ways. The first is the stakeholder needs to have and demonstrate personal power, more power than those around them, which may be viewed as an undesirable trait.

> *"Power and influence motivations can be used, unfortunately, as a force for bad."*

In these instances, the stakeholder isn't concerned with outcomes but with their position. Many experts are accused of having this motivator by those in the wider organization. The whole concept of being an expert is that we know more than others. This is the source of our power. Occasionally, experts like to emphasize their superior knowledge or influence when it comes to technical decisions. Stakeholders with this win-lose motivation need to win at the expense of others.

The second type of power and influence motivator is the need for institutional power. People with this need want to direct the efforts of their team to further the objectives of their organization. They're ambitious without needing to win at the expense of others.

Power and influence motivations can be used as a force for good. Unfortunately, they can also be used as a force for bad (i.e., used to disrupt and disengage team members and destroy team spirit). In their worst incarnation, ego-motivated individuals set colleagues against one another, hoping to benefit from the conflict.

Given that the most disruptive behavior of ego-motivated colleagues is their focus on "I," our strategy should always be to focus on the "we" and the team. What are we all trying to achieve for our organization and our customers? If our stakeholder is motivated by ego, we have two choices. We can give in to it, or we can reframe issues around risk and reward so that the stakeholder can see an alternative route to success and achieving their goals that doesn't involve simply forcing everyone to do what they say.

Balance and Comfort as a Motivator

This is a need for a comfortable and low-stress work environment. People with this motivation are keen to maintain a sensible and rewarding work/life balance. They'll generally have a more laid-back and relaxed style. They tend to be less concerned about making an impact, advancement and getting ahead in an organization. They'll be concerned about doing a good job, but they'll also be focused on sensible and achievable workloads and making sure realistic timeframes are set. They'll strongly push back on hours outside work, particularly if this isn't rewarded with days in lieu or is announced at short notice.

There is a tendency for our participants on programs to paint colleagues who are motivated by balance and comfort as lazy and afraid of hard work. We tend to see a different dynamic. These colleagues work very hard while they're at work and avoid distractions. They simply prefer predictability and order over chaos and disorder.

> *"For autonomy-motivated colleagues, their independence is a strength, but it can also result in poor communication."*

They're able to pinpoint with a high degree of accuracy how long tasks will take and they're very realistic. Their time management and organization skills are usually highly tuned because they want to get their work done and then get out of there. They make excellent project managers and are the best time-management trainers. They can lead projects and people very effectively, provided that they're properly resourced.

If our stakeholders are motivated by balance and comfort, they're likely to be very valuable, productive and dependable team members, but we'd better get our own act together. We'll need to offer really clear briefs, sensible deadlines, and deliver our work to these stakeholders on time because that's what they want to do for others. If we're delivering work that they'll then pass on to removed stakeholders, we can expect constant pressure to meet deadlines until the work is done.

We'll demotivate them by requiring rework, particularly if the rework is a consequence of a poor briefing from us. Asking them to deliver work at the last moment is another derailer in terms of our engagement with these stakeholders. They'll also likely be turned off by anything that appears to create significant disruption.

Autonomy as a Motivator

This is the need for individual accomplishment and expression. These stakeholders and colleagues are generally creative and "out-of-the-box" thinkers. They have a desire for independence and a propensity toward self-sufficiency. They'll perform best if they're free to create and express themselves. They're comfortable with taking risks and "bending the rules," even if it means adding a little stress. While they like working with people, they prefer to work alone.

Generally speaking, stakeholders and colleagues who are autonomy-motivated are high achievers and very valuable team members. They tend to be highly productive, with an ability to come up with innovative "out there" solutions when others have been stumped.

But there may be some downsides. Their independence is a strength, but it can also result in poor communication with us and other project team members they're involved with. Insisting on regular check-ins and proper documentation is essential, and if we have it in our power, we need to agree that the ability to work on their own on projects, which is their preference, will only be granted if these check-ins and proper communication with the team is maintained. However, anything that appears to limit their freedoms may be resented.

> *"Security-motivated colleagues are likely to be quite risk-averse. This can be both a blessing and a curse."*

Boundaries need to be clearly defined. There are many famous anecdotes about autonomy-motivated experts who were asked to go off and design a green square button and arrived back weeks later with a bright-orange circular button. They might argue that their design is superior, and it may well be, but it wasn't what the client asked for.

If our stakeholder or a colleague we depend on is motivated by autonomy, then setting clear rules of engagement is crucial to making the relationship work.

Security as a Motivator

This is the need for stability and predictability. Therefore, the focus will be on aspects of the work environment that provide that security. These stakeholders will perform best if there is structure and consistency, and if they can operate in their "comfort zone." The need for security and structure will therefore limit creativity and will block the generation of breakthrough ideas.

These stakeholders will be risk-averse. They'll explore almost everything that could possibly go wrong, and these concerns will often outweigh the possible upsides in their decision-making.

Anything new is a challenge for security-motivated colleagues and stakeholders because new means something to be mastered, and what happens if that new activity can't be mastered? "New" threatens the comfort zone they were previously operating in.

Many stakeholders are, of course, risk-averse, but this isn't necessarily because they're motivated by security. Senior executives in public companies or secretaries of major government departments understandably need to take the risk profile of new initiatives seriously as the public and commercial backlash for mistakes can be very significant. So, we need to explore whether there is a rational and sensible reason for their inaction or risk aversion or if it's irrational and emotional. In the latter cases, the likelihood is that the stakeholder is motivated by security.

> *"It isn't possible to neatly classify each stakeholder as belonging to one of these seven primary motivators."*

In the world of experts, these stakeholders have to be motivated in a counterintuitive fashion. Typically, we have to use authentic and valid arguments to persuade them that inaction is actually more dangerous than making a decision. We also need to ensure that any proposals we make have properly considered the risk of failure and put emergency buttons and risk-mitigation processes in place so that if things do go wrong, they'll be quickly and effectively managed.

Financial Reward as a Motivator

Financial reward is the least abstract form of recognition. Generally, this is how stakeholders motivated by money measure how they're valued for the work they perform. These people are likely to work harder and/or smarter if they believe their efforts will lead to valuable rewards. Therefore, the amount of effort generated depends on the value of the reward, the amount of effort they view as necessary, and the probability of receiving the reward.

Many experts consider financial reward a hygiene factor. In other words, that they should be paid a reasonable amount for the expertise that they're contributing. In our experience, not very many experts are motivated by financial incentives alone.

But plenty of our colleagues and stakeholders in the wider organization may be. They're reasonably easy to spot as they're always talking about financial remuneration of profits and margins (because they're remunerated against those goals) or they consistently provide evidence of expenditure, such as being well dressed, driving a nice vehicle, and so on.

Stakeholders motivated by financial reward take some convincing when asked to do activities that don't have an associated reward. So, our role is to make sure that these stakeholders can see the connection between what we're asking them to do or fund and the enhanced performance of the budget, team, division or organization. Or indeed, the extent to which the initiatives we're proposing will add to customer satisfaction and greater sales, which in turn will lead to better organizational performance.

Classifying Our Stakeholders

AS YOU READ THE seven descriptions above, you probably asked yourself what your motivators are. It may be that the answer isn't entirely clear. If this is the case, you're very typical. Most experts we have worked with struggle to choose only one key motivator. Our descriptions are relatively simple, but we're all very complex human beings.

It isn't possible to neatly classify each stakeholder as belonging to just one of these seven primary motivators. Generally, people have a number of these in play at any point in time. Typically, they may have a primary motivator, with one or two close runners-up. But your primary motivator may be more conspicuous because we, if so motivated, send signals indicating our desire to address such *needs*.

> *"Life is simply too short to be working on the wrong things for the wrong reasons."*

Our stakeholders will be no different. Several factors will be in play as we seek to understand their aspirations and motivations and effectively collaborate.

The idea of conducting this analysis isn't to box people in or manipulate them. We're simply searching for clues as to where there might be some potential alignment of interests. If we have a key stakeholder who has been notoriously difficult to engage, it might be worth seeing if we can develop greater insight into what might incline or disincline us both.

The further complication is that motivations change fast. If our stakeholder wins the lottery, then it's unlikely they will continue to be financially motivated. If a stakeholder or colleague suddenly has an older parent who needs looking after, achievement might take a back seat while balance and comfort and security come sharply into play.

We need to be aware of changes in how our stakeholders and colleagues behave and what they're positively or negatively responding to.

Signs, Symbols and Conversations

ONE OF THE MOST common questions experts ask us is how to identify the motivators of individual stakeholders. The answer most frequently offered by groups of experts is the obvious one: we could just ask them. This assumes two things, neither of which might be true. Firstly, that our stakeholders know what deeply motivates them or can describe it using the simple categories we have provided above. In reality, most can't. Secondly, it assumes that our stakeholders are prepared to share such personal information with us.

We run the risk of actually making our stakeholders wary of us, as they might be afraid that we're preparing to unreasonably manipulate them into agreeing to support our project or point of view.

A more sensible and diplomatic approach is to start by observing our stakeholders carefully. Once we have the seven simple motivational categories in mind, it's surprisingly easy to spot the signs and symbols that suggest what is important to our colleagues.

> *"What would outstanding professional success look like in three and five years?"*

Beyond observation, it's authentic and professional to ask colleagues we're involved with what "success" looks like for them on this project, in this stakeholder relationship, and eventually, perhaps as trust gets built, what success looks like for them in terms of their career and life. Sometimes, it really helps to gradually share what *our* aspirations and felt needs are. In this scenario, we share first.

Aspirational Clarity

WE ENCOURAGE THE PARTICIPANTS of our programs to gain clarity on what their own aspirations and motivators are. As coaches, we often find that even very experienced and successful experts aren't quite clear on what their motivations and long-term goals really are.

Defining this aspirational clarity is hugely beneficial. It helps us to decide whether a job, opportunity or project will propel us toward our long-term goals or actually distract us. By understanding what motivates us, we'll be able to assess whether we will enjoy a project or hate it, which is a good predictor of our likely level of engagement and motivation during the project. Life is simply too short to be working on the wrong things for the wrong reasons. We ask those we coach to ask themselves the following questions:

- What would outstanding personal success look like in three years and five years?
- What would outstanding professional success look like in three and five years?
- Are these two sets of goals connected? If not, why not?
- What measures will you use to track whether you have achieved this success? (The answer to this question is rarely the size of your bank balance.)
- Do you have a clear plan for achieving these objectives? Or, are you simply hoping that "things will work out"? Hope, in our experience, is generally not a successful strategy.
- Have you discussed all of these questions with your family or partner? Are you strategically aligned? If not, why not?

As experts, we don't typically get much help from our organization with figuring out the road to success. As previously discussed, there is plenty of organizational focus on "leadership pipelines" (career paths), but it's much rarer to find an organizational focus on "expert pipelines."

We have to take control and ownership of our own career planning and destiny. And as we do so, we find that this enhances our ability to observe and consider the motivations and life aspirations of others. Because we've asked ourselves the hard questions, we're more able to identify the signs and symbols that help us understand and engage with the motivations of others.

Understanding others' motivations can provide insight into how we might best seek to engage them or whether something that we're doing naturally risks disengaging them.

If we observe that their engagement is relatively low, then we can create engagement strategies that consider:

- Will they naturally respond to being made to feel important or that achieving a particular result might increase their status and career advancement opportunities? Such strategies might be effective with those motivated by power and influence.

- Does the initiative afford them a chance to feel that worthwhile progress is being made? This might assist with the engagement of those who are motivated by achievement.
- How about feeling safer? This might work for a security-minded stakeholder.
- Less cumbersome and complex? This might work for those who strongly value balance and comfort.
- Will people feel more connected and cared for? This might appeal to affiliation-oriented individuals.
- Does improved financial performance, and even individual financial appeal to financially motivated individuals?
- Or offer more freedom and less red tape, which might win over those inclined toward autonomy.

Or we might at least recognize the factors that might cause individuals to disengage or even actively resist:

- Does our preferred approach leave people feeling less important or make them feel incompetent? This might violate the needs of someone motivated by the desire to feel powerful and influential.
- Does our preferred approach offer little by way of meaningful, measurable progress? Are deadlines routinely missed? This might turn off the achievement-driven individuals.
- Are there (perceived or actual) sizable and unmitigated risks? This could cause a security-minded person to be very wary.
- Does our approach potentially lead to more complexity and inconvenience, even if just in the perceptions of others? This could be a big issue for the individuals motivated by balance and comfort.
- Does our approach seem to reduce positive cultural/relational experiences? This could prove a turn-off for affiliation-oriented individuals.
- Will it be costly or offer little financial upside? This could result in the disengagement of those who are financially driven.
- Does our approach appear to limit freedom, agency or individual flair? This could feel like an encroachment on the expectations of those who are driven by a need for autonomy.

TAKING ACTION

Growing Our Motivational Skills

IF THIS IS A capability in which you believe you could add greater value by growing your skills, here is a high-level suggestion for an action to take:

▶ GET TO KNOW PEOPLE BETTER

- If our relationships are purely transactional, we'll never build the required trust in stakeholders to build a truly win-win engagement. Creating time to have a more informal and personal connection with our stakeholders allows us to understand who they are, what motivates them, and more directly connect with their felt needs. Questions we might want to ask ourselves:
- How well do I actually know my key stakeholders from a work perspective? Do I know about all aspects of their role, how their work is measured, what challenges they face in their role, and the extent to which my work is important to them?
- How well do I actually know my key stakeholders from a personal perspective? Do I know where and how they live, with whom, and what their interests are outside work?
- Have I asked my colleagues about their professional and personal goals?
- Have I got a system to capture this data so I remember it and can reference it next time we catch up?
- Am I capturing this extra information with a genuine interest in understanding my colleagues and with a willingness to help them, or am I just using the relationship as a way to forward my career. If the latter, will this build or destroy trust?

CHAPTER | 18 |

Intelligent Networking

It's time to stop seeing networking as socializing and start seeing its real potential: advanced intelligence gathering

---

IN THIS CHAPTER, WE WILL EXPLORE:

- How do we create purpose and value in our networking activities?
- What simple techniques can help us relax and engage with interesting people at networking events?
- How does the concept of paying it forward transform inauthentic networking into advanced relationship building?

ELSEWHERE IN THIS BOOK, we've talked about the power of networking to inform our knowledge about the organization we work for and the market context in which it operates. In the expert role of network manager (Chapter 16), as we might expect, networking also plays a big part.

Using our networks for intelligence gathering is a critical success factor, and making sure that we use networking opportunities to meet and diplomatically interrogate those from other functions and perspectives is Master Expert behavior. But networking can also help us build much more extensive networks. We can leverage people we know and, provided we give them a good reason, persuade them to introduce us to others we would like to know. This skill is particularly useful for building our external (and often future-focused) networks (Chapter 15).

As Arty discovered (see the case study in Chapter 16), setting a target to add the CFO to our inner network might not be immediately achievable, but by setting the goal, Arty was able to meet people who reported to the CFO and still achieved most of his objectives.

Experts love to have structure, so let's consider this model (see Figure 18.1) from Linda Hill and Kent Lineback (Harvard Business Review 2011) on the different types of networks that we might need.

The Operational Network – Work

OUR OPERATIONAL NETWORK IS about connecting with the colleagues and stakeholders required to do our work well. We could consider it our *work* network. They may be close by and in our department (our technical cohort) or in other departments of our organization.

As experts, we're likely to have informal reporting lines with most in our operational network, relying on our influencing skills to get work done and our consulting skills to ensure the work we're doing produces the outcomes our stakeholders are looking for.

The Development Network – Growth

THIS IS OFTEN UNDERDEVELOPED, ironically, on the many stakeholder maps we see in our programs. The development network consists of those we rely on to progress our capabilities and career and those who act as a sounding board for advice when we're faced with difficult situations, decisions or choices. We could consider it our *growth* network. This group can include coaches, mentors, professional associations, external experts in our field, global thought leaders, friends, random network connections, even media outlets or commentators. This is the group that we depend on to help us grow as experts and professionals.

Capability: STAKEHOLDER ENGAGEMENT
The Three Networks Experts Need

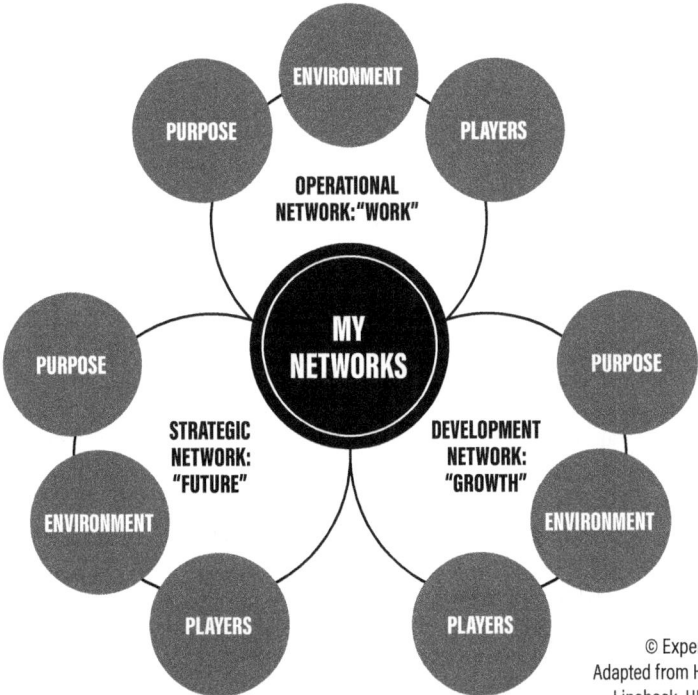

© Expertunity.
Adapted from Hill and
Lineback, HBR 2011

	PURPOSE	ENVIRONMENT	PLAYERS
OPERATIONAL NETWORK: "WORK"	Getting work done efficiently, maintaining capacity	Contacts are internal and orientated toward current demands	Non-discretionary, prescribed by task, clear who they are
DEVELOPMENT NETWORK: "GROWTH"	Enhancing personal and professional development, intelligence	Contacts are external and orientated toward current and future demands	Discretionary, not always clear who is relevant; diversity is positive
STRATEGIC NETWORK: "FUTURE"	Informing future priorities and challenges; creating buy-in	Contacts are internally and externally orientated toward future demands	Discretionary, future-focus essential, internal and external, global

FIGURE 18.1: The Three Networks Experts Need

The Strategic Network – Future

AS YOU MIGHT HAVE guessed, given the recurrent themes in this book, the strategic network is Master Expert territory. It's often the least developed of our three networks because it doesn't develop organically, while operational and development networks can. We have to make a commitment to deliberately building our strategic network and allocated time to doing so.

"Our strategic network is the most eclectic and difficult network to develop."

Members of this network are often outliers. They aren't critical to anything we currently have going on, but we rely on them to help us imagine and prepare for the future of our domain. They could be individuals from organizations who focus on thought leadership, like futurists. They could be contacts who are in industries that are being or have been disrupted and from which we can begin to predict disruptions that will come our way soon. Some may already be on our other networks.

As Hill and Lineback comment in their Harvard Business Review article: "You need a strategic network because the forces that drive change in your field will probably come from outside your current world."

Our strategic network is our most eclectic and difficult to develop. It will contain colleagues from all walks of professional life and industries, and most (but not all) will be external to our organization.

Having a diverse group of people within this network is a key value factor. The wider and more diverse the backgrounds and perspectives of those we are connected to, the more likely we are to be in a good position to adapt to future changes and tackle challenges.

The strategic network is often where most of the future-proofing of our networks will occur. These individuals may be stakeholders who we don't yet know of, have not yet met, or who, if known, seem so far outside our current weekly work interactions that we may hesitate to include them on our stakeholder map. Our advice is to aim high. Almost certainly, efficient future-proofing of our networks means establishing relationships with more senior and far-removed colleagues than we do now.

Networking Events: The Basics

MANY EXPERTS ARE NATURALLY reticent about attending networking events. Many of us find these events inauthentic, and they're a challenge for those of us who are introverts. Like everything else about being a Master Expert, mastering intelligent networking is about being clear on your purpose and techniques.

Purpose is typically about organizational, market and future intelligence. We therefore need to plan ahead of time who we want to connect with at particular events and what we hope to learn from them, and also have some questions pre-prepared that will enable us to capture their knowledge and insights.

Deploying a technique can make us feel more comfortable and relaxed whilst networking. Three helpful techniques are involved: the *one-minute introduction*, the *one-minute interrogation*, and the concept of *paying it forward*.

If you're a confident networker, feel free to skip over the rest of this chapter. If, however, you hate networking, these pages are most definitely for you.

The One-Minute Introduction

This technique helps us effortlessly and smoothly introduce who we are. It means we have prepared a couple of sentences about ourselves that we're entirely comfortable with and that address the needs of the person we're meeting for the first time. They are:

> ## *THE ONE-MINUTE INTRODUCTION*
> ### *Who am I?*
> ### *What do I do?*
> ### *Why am I here?*

Who am I? Remembering our own name shouldn't be too hard, but typically, in external networking situations, we'll have to say where we're from (from an organizational perspective). It's a mistake to assume that everyone knows your organization's name. If you don't describe what your organization does, expecting the other person to know it comes across as pride. Using one of our clients as an example, instead of saying, "I work for Dulux. I'm sure you know who we are," a gracious and respectful alternative might be, "I work for Dulux. We make all sorts of home and industrial paints and many other products that we're less well known for." In this instance, you're providing some information that might be new to the person you're networking with (therefore adding value) and allowing them to ask about the other homeware brands, because as it turns out, in most markets, Dulux does a lot more than make and sell paint.

What do I do? How do we intend to introduce the work we do? We experts have a habit of being too self-deprecating about ourselves. This is a mistake because we at least want to present ourselves as someone interesting to talk to: "Oh, I do routine maintenance in the IT team." Or we might overdo it, which we would want to avoid: "I'm the expert who builds and maintains complex Unix servers across the region and leverages their efficiency to provide a seamless service to the organization." Early on, this is too much detail. Finally, we might go for a plain-language version that presents us in too good a light, which comes across as arrogant, even if the description is actually quite accurate. For example, "I'm the person in the organization who keeps all the systems running. You wouldn't be able to work without me."

> *"That's not being inauthentic or self-promotional – that's professionalism."*

Experts also tend to introduce themselves to others in a way that gives the other person nothing to work with, such as "I'm in IT." This last example is so short and abrupt that the other person isn't likely to ask us any qualifying questions. To them, it feels like we don't want to share or we think what we do is so complicated that they wouldn't understand. Somewhere in the middle is about right: "I work in the IT team as part of the group working on back-end systems. I help keep the lights on."

The content above isn't rocket science, right? But actually, the best networkers work hard to make sure that their introductions are informative, true, and have something of interest in them but are also relaxed, natural and accurate. First impressions do count, so don't let anyone tell you they don't. Our advice is to really think about how you would introduce yourself to someone external to the organization and test it out on friends.

For internal networking events, you will probably need a slightly different script. If you're in the finance department and are speaking to someone from operations, for example, we'd encourage you to find a connection between your work and the work of operations. "I help manage cash flow so you always have funds available for those spare parts you frequently need." Internally, we want to establish a connection and partnership.

Note: some of the best talks on the planet are TED talks (*ted.com*). These vary in length these days, but generally, speakers are given 18 minutes to present their interesting idea. How long do they spend preparing for what they say during that 18 minutes? Months. Practice makes perfect. Experts should apply the same discipline and importance to getting that first impression just right. That's not being inauthentic or self-promotional. It's professionalism.

Why am I here? Assuming we're attending an external event, we may get asked why we have chosen to be at this particular event. It looks bad to not really know. Many people, not expecting the question, might ad-lib "Oh,

I'm not sure really." This is derailing behavior. What goes through the other person's head, subconsciously, is "Gee, you don't know why you're here? You must have time to kill. If you don't know why you're attending the event, then it's unlikely you're tuned in or valuable to know." There almost certainly is a rational reason we're at the event, so we should be prepared to state it. One of the authors, Alistair, is regularly invited to speak at conferences, often on the topic of Expertship. His rule is never to state first that he's a speaker and that's the only reason he's there. This feels like an arrogant answer to him. He's likely to respond that he's interested in the theme of the conference, wants to meet new people, and is *also* speaking on a topic dear to him later in the conference.

> ### THE ONE-MINUTE DISCOVERY
> *Who are you?*
> *What do you do?*
> *Why are you here?*

We've told this story elsewhere in the book, but it's worth repeating. Many experts leave our programs having, with some trepidation, committed to going to speak to senior removed stakeholders, often for the first time. They later report in our coaching sessions that, much to their surprise, the senior removed stakeholders were really pleased to see and talk to them. As experts, we're generally far more interesting to other people than we think we are—assuming we start the conversation right.

Why should they care about speaking to us? That's a great question, and those of us who lack social confidence worry about this far too much. Most people like talking to other people, provided that (a) we look like we're listening, (b) we're actually paying attention to them and not looking over their shoulder for someone more interesting to speak to, and (c) we're either asking about them or telling them something about ourselves that is relevant to them.

The objective is to find common ground as quickly as possible. Where do our roles or industries intersect or have similarities? Is there someone of interest this person knows about who I would like to know about in order to get their perspective? Many of the best questions for discovering this can be found in the next technique.

The One-Minute Discovery
This technique helps us plan a series of questions that gets the person we have just met talking comfortably with us. The questions are similar to those in our one-minute introduction (with a few extras), but our text here describes how to really get the person engaged by asking follow-up questions

that gather intelligence for us and make the person feel at ease. We use the word "discovery" deliberately, as many of the questions are the type we might ask in a consulting discovery interview with a stakeholder (Chapter 42). They are:

Who are you? Almost certainly, they'll tell us their first name and the name of their organization. There are two lines of discovery here.

- Firstly, history: "How long have you been there?" If it's a short period of time: "Where were you before?" "How has the transition to the new organization gone?" "How are you enjoying the new role?"
- Secondly, the organization is checking up on what you know about them: "Is that the company that produces paint?" "How big is the company?" "What is its ownership structure? Is it owned here? Or is it internationally owned, private or publicly listed?"

Many of their answers will naturally offer opportunities for more questions. If we make it feel like the Spanish Inquisition, then the questions will make our newfound colleague uncomfortable. On the other hand, if the questions are asked in a measured, relaxed way with genuine interest and curiosity, a conversation will begin.

"You can ask this question to any profession."

What do you do? When someone tells us they're in IT, engineering, marketing, or sales, it's easy for us to almost immediately make assumptions about them, subconsciously adding our bias to the conversation.

The myths that surround different professions are extraordinary. All IT people are no good with people, which is total rubbish. All lawyers love conflict, which is incorrect. Every salesperson is pushy and aggressive, even though the best ones are great listeners and allow us to make up our own mind about whether or not we want to buy something.

Exploring what someone's role involves and what the challenges are, is great *intelligence* for us and interesting for others to talk about. "So, I don't know much about sales. What is a typical week like?" "In sales, eh? Is it as pressured an environment as it seems from the outside?" Note, you can ask this question of *any* profession. "What challenges do you face in that role?" "How do you deal with them?" At some stage, most people are likely to ask you the questions in reverse. Suddenly, you're in a natural conversation, not a discovery interview.

Why are you here? As previously discussed, we always find this question illuminating. "What made you attend this event? What were you hoping to get out of it? How are you finding it so far? What have you found interesting so far?" All of these questions provide you with a lot of context about the person, including what they're hoping to learn, what their challenges are, where they are in their professional growth. They also allow you to practice the next technique: *paying it forward*. If you're coming out of a session at a conference or workshop, the easiest question in the world to ask to get a conversation started is "What did you think of that session?" Just make sure you have an opinion as well.

Paying It Forward

INSTEAD OF APPROACHING NETWORKING with a "what value can I get from the people I meet?" philosophy, we should consider *reverse networking*. This requires a different perspective: a "how might I *assist* the people I meet?" philosophy. The best way to think of this concept is *paying it forward*. By taking this approach, we're immediately positioning ourselves as a helper, not a taker—and for most of us, that is authentically who we are. Our objective is to be a valuable member of their network, not a drain on their time.

Paying it forward happens after we meet someone. On our way back from the event we have attended, we might contemplate the people we've met and ask some reverse networking questions:

- Who do I know who might be able to help them?
- What do I know that might be able to help them?
- How did someone help me, and how might I do the same for people in my network?
- What did they tell me their biggest challenges were, and how might I help them solve them?
- If I can't help, do I know someone who they might get value from meeting or talking to (or just connecting with)?

> *"The most valuable networking has, at its center, mutual benefit."*

In the authors' line of work as consultants, our conversations often result in us sending an article we may have read to the person we networked with. Perhaps an article on intelligent networking! Or maybe we send them a case study that we felt might be of interest. In order to make this authentic, which is one of the guiding principles of reverse networking, we only send that which we genuinely feel would be useful.

The most valuable networking has, at its center, mutual benefit. But someone has to add value first. Traditionally, networking has been seen as extracting value from those you meet. As experts, we're probably all much more comfortable adding value first, so that if, in the future, we do need advice or a favor, we've created an environment and a connection that has positive foundations.

The most fundamental question we all have to answer is: As an expert, how can we use networking creatively to become more expert?

In a program we held in Oxford in the United Kingdom a while back, we ran a session on intelligent networking toward the end of the day. Unbeknown to us, one of the participants, Andrew, was being forced (his word!) by his organization to attend an industry networking event that very night.

Later, Andrew confided in us that he had an absolute abhorrence toward networking events. He would feel completely like a fish out of water at them. Typically, in the past, he had handled this dread by finding someone he knew at the event and sticking to them like a limpet for 45 minutes, then making a rapid exit.

On the way to the event on this particular evening, Andrew practiced his one-minute introduction, his one-minute discovery, and contemplated who might be there that he would like to get to know.

The following morning, before our program recommenced, he approached us looking very serious. "I attended a networking session last night and used all of your questions," he informed us. Then he smiled. "They worked a treat. I had the best time at the networking event ever."

Andrew met four new colleagues who worked for other organizations in a similar field to him, one a senior engineer who suggested a follow-up meeting to discuss cooperation between their organizations. From one new contact, he learned that they were far more advanced than his organization in solving a particular engineering problem. From another, he discovered that his own organization was far more advanced. This became very valuable information for him as he prioritized work in the next few months.

Andrew is typical of many experts we meet. He's interesting, engaging, honest, and quite brilliant at what he does. But he had over-invested so much in his technical skills and under-invested in simple techniques, such as feeling comfortable with and getting value from networking events. Like most of the content in this book, intelligent networking isn't rocket science. It's simply advanced common sense. Master Experts apply it every day.

TAKING ACTION

Growing Our Networking Skills

IF THIS IS A capability in which you believe you could add greater value by growing your skills, here is a high-level suggestion for an action to take:

▶ ADOPT A "PAY IT FORWARD" APPROACH TO NETWORKING

- Get away from the "what can they do for us" approach to networking. Whether it's internal or external networking, we know it comes across as inauthentic, vaguely manipulative and distasteful. We need to change our mindset and adopt the principle of paying it forward. Some questions we might like to ask ourselves:
- To what extent can I switch from "what can this person do for me" to "what can I do for this person?" Is there a connection they need? Or an article I can send them?
- Have I asked questions in our conversation that helps me understand how I can help them? Have I sufficiently asked myself how I can add value to this person?
- Have I made it clear that by offering to do something for them, I am not expecting anything in return?

Random acts of kindness and consideration are much more powerful than we might imagine. They keep you front of mind across your network and build a positive brand. We may be positively surprised at how many of our colleagues, and which ones, find ways to reciprocate, regardless of that not being our objective.

Most experts are hardwired to help people. We need to consider networking as a huge opportunity to do so.

MASTERING COLLABORATION

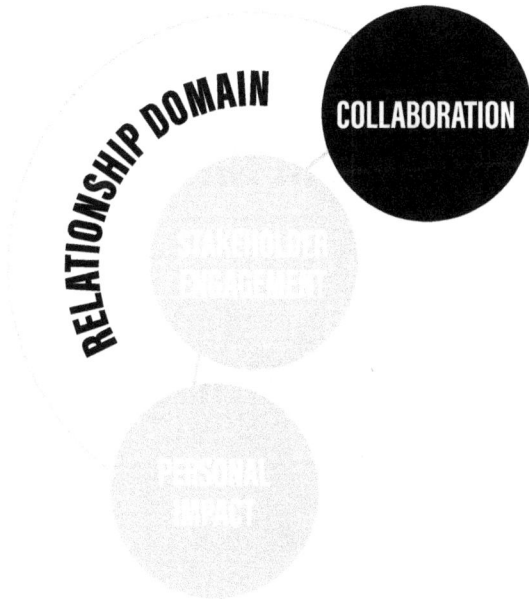

RELATIONSHIP DOMAIN

COLLABORATION

STAKEHOLDER ENGAGEMENT

PERSONAL IMPACT

The Master Expert acts as a valuable member of the team, whether virtual or co-located, taking on an Expertship and/ or leadership role when required and appropriate.

"Learning to collaborate is part of equipping yourself for effectiveness, problem solving, innovation and lifelong learning in an ever-changing networked economy.**"**

Don Tapscott

"The idea of disciplined collaboration can be summed up in one phrase: the leadership practice of properly assessing when to collaborate (and when not to) and instilling in people both the willingness and the ability to collaborate when required."

Morten Hansen

CHAPTER | 19 |

The Barriers to Collaboration

How modern organizational structures get in the way of us working effectively with others

---

IN THIS CHAPTER, WE WILL EXPLORE:

- What are the main barriers to collaboration in modern organizations?
- How do we recognize them, and why is that important?
- Why is collaboration a critical expert skill?
- How do we begin to overcome these barriers and forge truly collaborative, valuable relationships with our colleagues?

AS ORGANIZATIONS BECOME MORE global and adopt complex matrix organizational structures, the role of the expert becomes ever more complex. Products and services are offered in many territories, and as a consequence, those who support them, whether in IT or manufacturing or legal, are expected to do so from many places.

A further trend resulting from this dynamic is that outsourcing non-strategic functions has become a common way for organizations to reduce costs. This adds a series of mission-critical supplier organizations into the mix, with whom experts need to interact.

Because of different time zones and the need to maintain consistent service across the world, communication between colleagues is 24/7. There is a constant avalanche of meetings, emails and tele- and video conferences that add further complexity to an expert's life and drains their energy.

- The customer relationship management system that was once only operating in Canada is now deployed in 14 countries and needs to be supported by a core team dotted around those jurisdictions.
- Customer service, once a series of teams in distinct countries, is now operated out of three global hubs so we can call any time, from anywhere, and have our concern dealt with.
- Learning and development needs to operate programs and initiatives consistently across the world because talent is constantly on the move. The next key role in manufacturing in China could, for example, be filled by an executive from any region in which the business operates.

Not all experts are experiencing this internationalization of their roles, but according to our research, the majority are. In a recent survey we conducted, 65 percent of experts reported they had "international" responsibilities. And even if our responsibilities remain local, it's more than likely that standards and policies are being set at a regional or global level. Our ability to undertake independent action without reference to others in other locations is severely reduced.

> *"Speed is of the essence. This often creates a situation*
> *where task overtakes everything."*

All of this impacts the way in which most experts must now behave and consult. Most importantly, it means that our ability to collaborate across teams, divisions, borders, cultures, and organizational entities is now a critical skill. If we're to have an impact at the senior, strategic level that we aspire to, we need to master collaboration.

But, as every expert knows, collaboration is not easy. There are many conflicts we need to learn to resolve.

The term *expert* might suggest an autonomous individual who is somehow distinct from everyone else. Certainly, many professions encourage experts to develop and maintain an objective independence. So, on the one hand, we need to be able to think for ourselves and not be constrained by policies and procedures if we're going to help our organization innovate and stay current. On the other hand, we need to respect and involve other colleagues in faraway places. These colleagues will, of course, have different expertise, experiences and perspectives.

We're encouraged to act quickly and solve problems or produce new processes that make the organization more efficient. Speed is of the essence. But the process of involving and communicating with colleagues who are spread out around the country or around the world is time-consuming and slows us down. This creates a situation where the short-term imperative to complete the task overtakes everything. The time we need to build relationships and understand one another, including what contribution we all might be able to make and our various perspectives, is usually a casualty of such a "task focus."

There are many new technology tools available that allow us to collaborate virtually and through digital platforms. But there is still a desire to connect in person or via video conference and to build face-to-face relationships so we can provide new and better solutions.

The authors have encountered this scenario frequently. People who have had many interactions via email and video-conferencing platforms finally meet face to face at a conference or workshop, and the relationship quickly moves to another level of effectiveness, collaboration and warmth.

What is Collaboration?

THE DEFINITION OF COLLABORATION is "the action of working with someone to produce something." For example, Dominic and Alistair collaborated to write this book. Other words associated with collaboration are *cooperation, alliance, partnership, participation, in concert,* and *compromise.*

There is a second definition of collaboration, which is "traitorous cooperation with an enemy." *Colluding* and *conspiring* are similar words. This second meaning implies working illegally or immorally with someone who is "not on our side" or is in opposition to us. This second definition of collaboration comes into play far too often in today's modern and complex organizational structures.

Often, the competitive nature of senior careers in large organizations gets in the way of positive collaboration. In many respects, the culture of larger organizations is not aligned with nor ready for the behaviors that collaboration requires.

> *"Silo syndrome is one of the biggest barriers to collaboration in most larger organizations and government departments."*

Zac was an editorial expert at a large publishing company that produced several major publications. His general manager tasked him with developing a new application for readers that would allow them to conduct smart searches of the publications' archives for a very modest fee. The objective was to create a new revenue stream for the publication.

As part of his discovery process, Zac researched how other publications around the world were tackling this opportunity.

This, of course, included talking to the other publications in Zac's own organization. He found one other publication in the group was about to embark on a similar project. He approached his general manager with the suggestion that the two groups work together on producing the application.

Zac's general manager was furious. "This is *our* idea, *our* project," the GM told him passionately. "I want an application that is specifically designed for our readers, not a generic application that is a compromise. And I want us to be first with these types of initiatives. You're not to work with them; they'll slow us down. We have a reputation for being the most innovative division here, so under no circumstances will you allow another division in this company to beat us to it."

The publishing group had partnership as one of its core values. The CEO constantly talked about banishing the silo mentality and how the different divisions in the organization needed to work together on breakthrough ideas. This message was constantly being reinforced in messaging from the senior leadership team.

Zac realized he was faced with an unfortunate truth: his general manager was competing against other general managers in the organization to be the next CEO, and this internal career ambition was getting in the way of the organization working collaboratively.

As we'll see a little later in this chapter, *silo syndrome* is one of the biggest barriers to collaboration in most larger organizations and government departments, even though we're all supposed to be working toward the same goal(s).

The general manager's instructions put Zac in a difficult position. It would cost the organization at least double, maybe more, to have two divisions working on a similar application separately. If Zac was to be sure to get the app to market first, he would have to ask for additional resources to get the work done more quickly than anticipated. And he'd have to hurt an existing stakeholder relationship with a colleague in another department—one that both parties had been nurturing in the spirit of sharing and collaboration.

If Zac and his colleague from the other division were to collaborate in the way the CEO of the organization wanted them to, which is based on the first definition of collaboration we discussed, Zac would be collaborating with an enemy, more in line with the second definition, as far as his boss was concerned.

As many of you reading this will know, something like this happens much more often than it should. The truth is that the old command and control leadership styles of many senior leaders in large organizations aren't aligned with the new matrix-style structures that are more common today.

We'll explore Zac's options at the end of this chapter.

Collaboration Skills and Mindsets

WHAT COMBINATION OF SKILLS and mindsets is needed to achieve highly effective collaboration in medium to large organizations? These skills and mindsets equally apply in smaller or start-up organizations because their operating model favors more external partnering, which requires advanced collaboration.

In the next few chapters, we'll explore the following questions:

- Listening: why is empathetic listening an essential foundational skill in effective collaboration that experts find challenging?
- Influencing skills: what are the most effective influencing tactics when it comes to finding the balance between action and a highly consultative approach?
- Building trust: how do we build trust across boundaries, such as divisions, regions, nationalities and cultures?
- Communication skills: how do experts provide clarity and enable an understanding of complex issues for non-technical stakeholders so as to foster collaboration and decision-making?
- Conflict: by the very nature of the competitive and dynamic market context in which many of us operate, how do we manage and diffuse conflicts, and what is the special role of senior experts in doing so?

In each of these topic areas, we'll see that operating at Master Expert level requires us to work on the way we think (mindset) as much as how we behave (skills and knowledge).

But before we discuss how to achieve first-class collaboration, we need to explore the challenges we're facing, including the typical barriers to collaboration we all face, whether we're experts or not.

Barriers to Collaboration

IN THE USA SOME years ago, there was an interesting study conducted by a range of security agencies following the destruction of the Twin Towers in New York by a terrorist cell. "Could we have prevented the disaster?" they asked. "What got in the way?"

Compellingly chronicled in his 2009 book *Collaboration*, researcher Morten Hansen describes in detail how each of the many agencies tasked with looking after the safety of US citizens had separate intelligence that, if combined, would have given the authorities a clear picture of what was planned, and in all likelihood, the 9/11 disaster could have been avoided. What got in the way was a *lack of collaboration*.

In Figure 19.1, we describe the four barriers to collaboration. We have adapted Hansen's model to resonate with experts, but the thinking is most definitely his.

Barrier 1 - Silo Syndrome

In our early example, Zac was faced with this barrier to collaboration. The concept of organizations operating in silos has been around for many years, and interestingly, it's one that hasn't gone away. It's still alive and kicking, as many experts can attest. Note that siloed thinking is a mindset and a culture—it has nothing to do with skills and knowledge.

Silo syndrome shows up in a variety of ways. Firstly, **insular culture**. This problem is often synonymous with organizational growing pains.

Capability: **COLLABORATION**
Barriers to Collaboration

SILO SYNDROME	Insular Culture	Ownership
	Hierarchies	Fear
HOARDING HABIT	Competition	Workload
	Misaligned Incentives	Loss of Power
SCALE BARRIER	Organisation Size	Information Overload
	Distance	Poor Networks
TRANSFER PROBLEM	Informal Knowledge	Poor Transfer Skills
	Poor Transfer Systems	Lack of Relationships

Adapted by Expertunity from Morten Hansen, author of *Collaboration* (2009)

FIGURE 19.1: Barriers to Collaboration

As what were once small departments get larger and become divisions, they become more focused on delivering competitive value in their sector and stop talking to other divisions in the same organization.

They'll argue that they "don't have time" to share information and insights as they're simply too busy hitting their top-priority internal deadlines. Silo thinking may be created by the ambition of leaders, but more often, it's simply the way things develop. When we see silo syndrome in action, we also often see power struggles and an unwillingness to cooperate. The implications are a reduction in productivity and efficiency for people like Zac, as well as a decrease in morale and, crucially, missed opportunities.

Secondly, **hierarchies** get in the way of collaboration. In organizations where the culture is communicating information and making decisions through the chain of command, these hierarchies get in the way of fast and flexible collaboration.

It's a classic "bow-tie" configuration of communication inside the organization rather than a diamond (see Figure 19.2). Collaboration requires, at a minimum, colleagues at all levels of the organization having the permission, and indeed the mandate, to communicate with whoever they want in order to get things done more efficiently. We come back to the attitudes of senior leaders here. If the leader is "old school," they'll want to control everything that happens in their division, including what information other parts of the organization get to know. In this environment, mistakes are typically hidden, not shared.

Raj was charged with setting up a new call center for his global organization due to extra demand. It would be the first call center established by the manufacturing giant in India, so there was a lot of pressure to ensure it was successful.

Raj recognized that this could be his big break—his opportunity to demonstrate his ability, and indeed the ability of his nation, to deliver fantastic service. The requirement was to use the same software platform used by the other major call center his organization had established in the Philippines.

Raj is ambitious and smart. In order to make sure the center opened successfully and on time, he recognized that the implementation of the software platform was critical. He reached out to his counterparts in the Philippines to gather insights from their experience since they had implemented the new platform just a year before.

The time difference made contact difficult to organize, but Raj eventually spoke to Vedasto in the Philippines. Raj asked him how the implementation went and asked him if he had any suggestions for how to go about it since he was using the same global supplier to implement the system.

Capability: COLLABORATION

Collaboration Needs Diamonds

THE BOW-TIE COMMUNICATION CONFIGURATION

- Pre-matrix
- Silo culture
- Inter-division communication controlled by committees comprising only senior leaders
- No direct communication between general employees

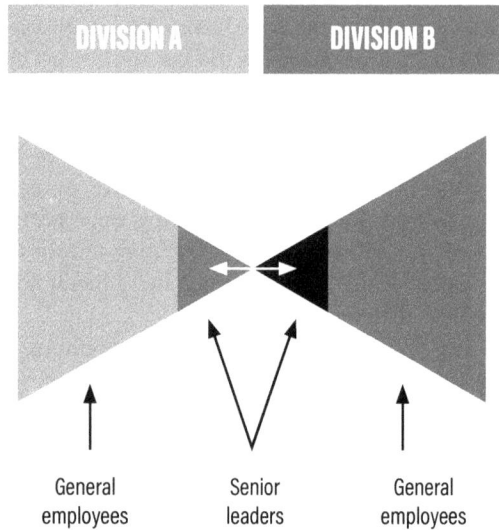

DIVISION A   DIVISION B

General employees   Senior leaders   General employees

THE DIAMOND COMMUNICATION CONFIGURATION

- Designed for matrix
- Collaborative culture
- Inter-division communication mostly by general employee; multiple contacts and interactions
- Senior leaders communicate at strategic level

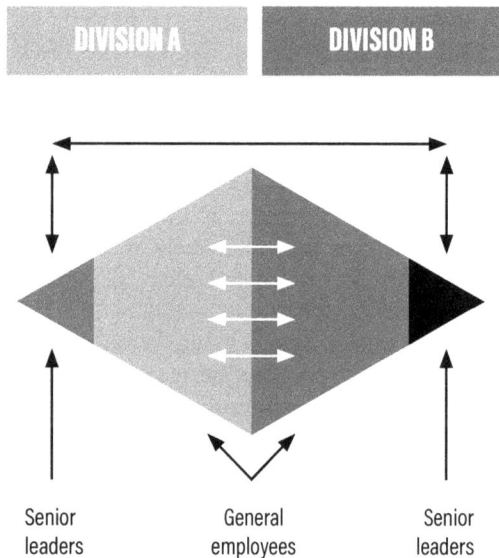

DIVISION A   DIVISION B

Senior leaders   General employees   Senior leaders

FIGURE 19.2: Bow-Tie Versus Diamond Communication

Vedasto was conflicted. He was under strict instructions from his manager not to share much about the Philippine experience with India because his division was very disappointed that they didn't win the extension of the call center.

Vedasto had taken heat from global headquarters about how long it had taken to implement the new platform. It wasn't really in his interest to help the Indian team implement the system quicker than they had. In truth, Vedasto could've provided Raj with a whole range of valuable advice—advice that he and his team had literally reflected on just a few months before at a post-implementation review meeting. They concluded they would've changed many things about the way in which the implementation was handled.

But Vedasto chose not to share the mistakes his team had made or the fact that the global provider put consultants on the implementation who had never implemented the system before, which was exactly what was planned in India.

Raj eventually implemented the system, although he ran behind schedule and encountered many of the same issues and challenges that his colleagues in Manila had faced. This lack of sharing of mistakes cost the organization time and money, and it also created a lot of stress for Raj and his team. Vedasto had passed up the opportunity to be a collaborative corporate citizen.

As Figure 19.2 shows, a diamond communication model allows faster and far more efficient communication at the relevant levels. But even this representation, we accept, is a hugely simplistic articulation of the true complexities of communication that most experts on projects face.

> *"Fear is an underlying contributor to many of the other characteristics of silo mentality."*

The third way silo syndrome shows up is **ownership**. This is the belief that we should fix our own problems internally and not burden others by asking for their assistance or to share their expertise. We got ourselves into the predicament, the argument goes, and we have to fix it. There is an underlying feeling that the division doesn't want to air its dirty laundry in public.

The alternative argument is that, almost certainly, someone somewhere in the organization has faced a problem similar to ours. They've ended up fixing it, probably by trial and error, and if we can leverage their experience, we're going to save a truckload of time and energy. This focus on being self-reliant, as if it's a positive characteristic, is now old-fashioned.

The fourth way silo syndrome shows up is **fear**. This is not wanting to reveal problems because we feel it'll impact the reputation of our division and its leaders. This is an underlying contributor to many of the other characteristics of silo mentality.

Barrier 2 – Hoarding

Many of the characteristics of hoarding described in Figure 19.1 are discussed in Chapter 46, *Knowledge Transfer.*

These might include experts worrying about sharing key knowledge that somehow reduces their importance or the dependence of the organization on their expertise. Or claiming that "we're just too busy" to spend time sharing knowledge. Or further claiming that there is no one to whom we can delegate our expert knowledge and wisdom. Either there are no candidates at all, or we claim that those who are around simply aren't smart enough (certainly not as smart as we are, at any rate).

But one characteristic of hoarding is well worth discussion here: **misaligned incentives.** Very often, project groups or whole divisions are incentivized to deliver specific value in their own area. Their incentive plan offers no motivation to add value anywhere else. This leads to the view that everyone within the division should focus on hitting their own key performance indicators (KPIs) and not worry about helping colleagues in Division B hit theirs.

Increasingly, helping out colleagues in Division B and seeing what they're up to actually *does* contribute to colleagues in Division A hitting their KPIs. Divisions are often focused on solving similar problems in different contexts, and if colleagues can get past the "but we're different" mantra, there is more commonality than we imagine in the challenges we face.

Because experts regularly operate across divisions by the nature of our work, we have a huge opportunity to be the catalyst for sharing between divisions. We often talk to executives in IT, for example, who say to us that they're in an optimal position to see what's going on across the whole of the organization. Experts from HR have said the same thing to us. These are positions of influence.

Do we proactively use them to encourage collaboration between others? The best incentive schemes take into account the modern necessities of matrix operations.

We have a client who, after finance finally backed down on technical grounds, has allowed double counting of revenue toward the targets of salespeople. Division A salespeople used to be incentivized on what they sold in Division A. Division B salespeople had the same arrangement. But Division A had clients that Division B was trying to win and vice versa.

Neither sales team was incentivized to help the other division win clients. Indeed, they actively didn't want the other division to win the client because they were worried that their own *share of wallet* might reduce. In our experience, this is a common phenomenon.

The client fixed the problem by changing their policy and building a new culture. Anything a salesperson in Division A helped a colleague in Division B sell would be counted toward their own target. Suddenly, helping colleagues in other divisions became a source of new revenue, not a threat.

> *"The scale of the business is often a major barrier to employees being able to collaborate effectively."*

But the organization still had to work on getting salespeople in both divisions to trust each other with their clients. Salespeople in Division A were worried that, overall, the organization's reputation might suffer if the salesperson from Division B did a bad job, was too pushy, or sold the client a product or service they didn't need. And of course, Division B colleagues were worried about exactly the same thing.

This is a classic example of changing the policy or structure but not the mindset, and it keeps us from reaching a truly collaborative state.

Barrier 3 - Scale

The authors work with a client organization that has over 51,000 employees, most of them based in a single country. Its millions of customers buy multiple products and services from the organization, which means there are many opportunities for collaboration. But the scale of the business is a major barrier to employees collaborating effectively.

> *"The scale of the business is often a major barrier to employees collaborating effectively."*

Scale plays out in several ways. **Organization size** is one. Let's imagine we're looking for some information. In a business the size of this client, the information could reside in hundreds of different places. Where do you look? There's no single database of anything in this organization.

If we're looking for a particular person with a particular knowledge set, the barriers are immense. There's no single database of employees with their roles and responsibilities. The organization is attempting to develop an internal LinkedIn, but a thousand staff leave and join every month, so it's a huge undertaking.

An expert in project management within the organization told us: "I know there are people who I should be collaborating with on my latest project, but I can't find them. It would take too long. I actually don't know where to look, never mind actually finding someone who is relevant. If I do find them, they're sinking under a deluge of their own projects and have no time to contribute meaningfully to mine."

If **organization size** is a problem, then **physical distance** is another. The organization we're talking about operates mostly in Australia, where distance is important. From Perth to Sydney is more than 2000 miles, which, for context, is the same distance from London to Tel Aviv.

The cost of travel between these cities for employees, and the impact of different time zones, is significant. Even if you find the right people, communication is via telephone or video conference and is difficult to organize.

Information overload is the next substantial barrier to effective collaboration. In many collaborative environments, colleagues have become very generous with their sharing, and all of us have been in a situation where we might consider their sharing too generous. We're routinely inundated with reports and minutes and articles and slide decks and project plans, and there is no possibility of reading or understanding all of it.

> *"The scale of the business is often a major barrier to employees collaborating effectively."*

The very information we seek may be buried in this avalanche of information but we miss it because it's mixed in with so much other stuff. This is what happened to the security agencies after 9/11 in the USA. There were so many reports coming from so many sources that operatives didn't have a system to qualify that was quality information and possibly useful and what was "run of the mill" and of little value. Most experts' inboxes are very similar.

Poor networks are another significant barrier to collaboration. We discuss stakeholder mapping and building networks in many other chapters of this book. Our intelligence gathering capability is usually only as good as our networks. Networks don't just help us connect; they contain people who might know people who know. This is the classic dynamic of social media. Many organizations are gradually getting better at leveraging the concept of social media at the corporate level.

Barrier 4 – Transfer Problem

The final barrier to collaboration that we will need to overcome, as if the others aren't enough, is the **transfer problem**. In Chapter 46, *Knowledge Transfer*, we discuss these difficulties extensively. Much of the knowledge of the organization is held in personal memory ("tacit" or informal knowledge) rather than in a database or a wiki. There isn't a common way of storing, labeling, or indexing information, so even if we come across the right file, we might not recognize it as such. Luckily, modern retrieval systems, when implemented, are starting to solve this problem. The same issue is described differently in different divisions. We don't have strong enough contacts or motivations or incentives or skills to share information successfully in a timely manner.

How Well Does Our Organization Rate? And How Well Do Our Colleagues Rate?

WHICH OF THESE BARRIERS do we face in our organizations? Which are most prevalent? Which would we most benefit from breaking down? Where do our own opportunities to assist in the mindset and skill changes required reside?

While reviewing an early draft of this book, one of our colleagues made the comment that the biggest barrier to collaboration he's seen in the many organizations he's worked for is the capacity and knowledge of his colleagues to collaborate. They just don't know *how*. As organizations have changed and collaboration has become more important for operational success, everyone has just assumed collaboration skills will come naturally to everyone. His view is that everything *but* collaboration happens if people aren't conscious of the skills and mindsets they need to apply to be collaborative.

In the following chapters, we take a deep dive into what those required skills and mindsets are. But first, let's revisit the problem faced by Zac.

Zac's Dilemma

IN THE CASE STUDY earlier in the chapter, Zac faced a difficult dilemma. On the one hand, the organization and the project required Zac to collaborate with other parts of the business. On the other, his ambitious and territorial manager had forbidden him from doing so. What should Zac do?

There is no simple answer, of course, but there is a simple principle: Zac needs to find a *collaborative alignment to purpose* among his various stakeholders. In our programs, we call this "going to 70,000 feet" (see the altitude model, Figure 48.5).

Most organizations have a defined purpose or vision and a strategy employees are expected to follow to achieve the long-term goal. It's really the true north of all Master Experts because alignment to purpose is what usually solves disputes over both resources and priorities.

In Zac's situation, he has a host of stakeholders to align. Firstly, his manager, whose ambition is to secure the top job in the organization. Secondly, there's the overall organization itself. What would be a good outcome for all employees? Thirdly, there's his colleague in another division. Fourthly, there's the senior leadership group of the organization. They don't appear to be a player currently, but they will eventually become a player when the group's CFO discovers inter-departmental ambitions are creating unnecessary costs. But Zac has one other stakeholder who is usually a super card to play in this game: the customer and what they want. By developing two applications separately from each other, the two publishing divisions will require readers to have two applications on their mobile devices, possibly two interfaces, and with no connectivity between them. If the competing sides each take a holistic view and bring only their own brands together on one application, then Zac's organization will be making a significant strategic mistake that will cost them readers, revenue and reputation. This is Zac bringing the market context (see Chapters 26 to 29) into play. There may be other stakeholder groups we've not mentioned.

When Zac makes a list of all the major stakeholders and considers what the right policy decision would be for all of them, the score is 4 in favor of the collaborative approach and one (his manager) against.

4:1 is no good. It needs to be 5:0. Zac has to find a way to present the collaborative option to his manager so he will want to adopt it, too.

To find this alignment to purpose, Zac has to consider what his manager's strategic objective is. He knows it's to be in the best position to inherit the CEO's role when that person moves on. Currently, Zac's manager believes that being first to market with an app is the best way to prove that he has the credentials. But clearly, if being CEO of the whole group is the long-term objective, then Zac's manager has to start thinking like a group CEO *now*. This means thinking about what's best for the whole organization, not just short-term tactical wins against other candidates for the CEO role.

In fact, Zac might argue that by refusing the collaborative approach, his manager is proving himself unworthy of the CEO role.

With some careful thinking, this is easy enough to work out, provided, like Zac, we have clarity about the organization's purpose and have the needs of our customers firmly in mind.

The challenge will be framing the discussion in such a way that Zac's manager listens and changes his approach. How Zac goes about this will depend on his relationship with his manager, his status in terms of the overall organization, and his ability to utilize other executives to influence his manager. As we discuss in the coming chapters, understanding the motivations of his manager is also crucial.

In the end, Zac revisited the conversation on the basis of having new information to share and that this information made the "go it alone" strategy look riskier than the downsides of the "collaborate" approach. Zac had also asked colleagues about their impressions of the motivations of his manager. They told him that being first was very important to Zac's manager, but at heart, Zac's manager was really risk-averse. Being known to have made a poor decision was a worse outcome for him than having to collaborate with a rival general manager.

In this case, Zac won the day.

An Insurmountable Challenge?

SO, AFTER THIS DEPRESSING listing of all the challenges we face in collaborating effectively, is collaboration an insurmountable challenge that we'll never be able to achieve?

The good news is that, as experts, we don't have to find solutions to the overarching challenges of creating a collaborative culture across the whole organization. We simply have to find solutions that work for us on the projects that we're responsible for or involved in.

This means focusing on the skills and mindsets that'll help us, as experts, be as good at collaboration as we can possibly be. And if our experience of experts in the past few years is anything to go by, there are plenty of opportunities to significantly step up in this area for most of us.

The next few chapters deal with the critical skills we need: listening, running truly collaborative meetings, and polishing our influencing skills.

TAKING ACTION

Growing Our Collaboration Skills

IF THIS IS A capability in which you believe you could add greater value by growing your skills, here is a high-level suggestion for an action to take:

▶ RUN A "WHAT GETS IN THE WAY HERE?" COLLABORATION SESSION

Share the Hansen model from this chapter with colleagues and ask them the questions we've posed:

- To what extent do the barriers described by Hansen exist in our organization? How do they show up?
- Which specific barriers are most prevalent? Why?
- What could we do to eliminate these barriers?
- What would the payoffs be?

A general discussion about these issues and those raised by the model can be transformative. The trick is for groups to contemplate why these barriers exist and what could be done about them.

"We have two ears and one mouth, so we should listen more than we say."

Zeno of Citium,
as quoted by Diogenes Laërtius

CHAPTER | 20 |

The Power of Listening

How much time would we all save if we learned how to really listen?

IN THIS CHAPTER, WE WILL EXPLORE:

- What gets in the way of experts really listening to colleagues?
- What are the different forms of listening, and why is empathetic listening an important skill to master?
- How do we master empathetic listening?

STEFAN IS A SENIOR systems architect at a large services organization. He's been with the organization for nine years and thus has a breadth of experience in how the organization operates. He's widely acknowledged as having a brain the size of a small planet. With several successful projects completed, Stefan is considered a senior expert within the information technology team.

A new project is underway, so a team has been assembled by the project manager, Uwe, who is taking them through first thoughts on how the project might be executed. He asks for ideas and suggestions.

He looks to Stefan to start proceedings, but Stefan says nothing. In fact, Stefan looks very much like he doesn't want to be in the meeting or on the project. He has his arms crossed and he's frowning. Even during Uwe's opening remarks, he clearly checked his cell phone several times in view of everyone else. He's slumped in his chair, the very picture of an unengaged participant in a meeting.

In the absence of any comment from Stefan, Uwe looks around the table and encourages contributions from others. Marieke makes a suggestion.

Almost immediately, Stefan puts down his phone, leans back in his chair, and clasps his hands behind his head. Marieke is unnerved by his body language. She knows from study that this is the body language of someone who feels superior, is about to disagree with whatever is being said, and is almost completely disrespectful to the person speaking.

To counter Stefan's movements, Uwe leans toward the table, makes eye contact with Marieke, and tilts his head slightly, as if wanting to hear more effectively. He doesn't say anything, but Marieke instinctively turns more directly to Uwe and continues her point. As Stefan lets out a loud sigh, Uwe nods encouragingly at Marieke.

This is a scene played out hundreds of times in meetings every day. Stefan is exhibiting all types of derailing behaviors as an expert, but the number one thing is that he's not really *listening*. Listening requires us to properly understand what the other person is saying by paying full attention.

Empathetic listening, which we will describe in detail shortly, means we need to investigate why a colleague has a particular point of view. What evidence have they used to come to this viewpoint? Listening requires us to respect the person who is talking, regardless of their seniority and whether we agree with them.

> *"Starting the new project meeting with a task focus rather than a relationship focus is a mistake."*

If we're to be truly collaborative with other team members, basic human respect rather than egotism has to be at the center of how we interact with our colleagues. Stefan is completely failing this test on many levels. Unfortunately, we've frequently observed that the (superficially) "smarter" and more experienced the expert, the less likely they are to *really* listen to others who have less status.

The outcome of any collaborative effort depends on well-developed personal relationships among the participants. By starting the new project meeting with a task focus rather than a relationship focus, Uwe is not allowing time for this and is making what might be a costly mistake.

Stefan, for example, has no idea who Marieke is. He knows she is new to the organization (therefore, what can she possibly know?) but doesn't know that she has just come from an external consulting role where she worked for a major management consulting firm on four global projects similar to the one about to be embarked upon.

Stefan is assuming he's the most experienced project team member, when actually he might not be. If Uwe had started with a conversation about what each team member brought to the project and provided some time for introductions, backgrounds and working styles, a classic starting point for projects (using the Stakeholder Health Check template in Chapter 13 as an agenda), some of the immediate negativity that Stefan's behavior is generating could have been avoided.

This doesn't excuse Stefan's behavior, of course. But it does mean it could have been prevented.

We'll get better results if we give our group time at the beginning of the project to get to know one another, to discover each other's strengths and weaknesses, to build personal ties, and to develop a common understanding of the project. Additionally, understanding everyone's personal motivations for being part of the project and what they hope to get out of it helps with alignment, openness, and the group finding common ground. These objectives would be, in addition to the key outcomes from a start-up meeting, the project's purpose and how success will be measured.

Stefan is displaying a mindset common among experts who aren't operating at Master Expert level. He believes that when it comes to his area of technical specialty, where he's the expert, his view should be listened to above all others.

Experts with this mindset aren't known for their capacity to listen. So why would we expect it from Stefan? From his perspective, who else has something more considered, significantly informed, duly evidenced and effectively reasoned to say than him?

While serving as the definitive truth on technical matters has its uses, it also has its limitations. What about when the subject matter is not purely technical? Or when there's a relationship at stake? Or when there's a need to get everyone aligned, not only around which facts are relevant but pulling together around shared goals? This is when the mindset and skill set of listening with empathy can be especially useful.

> *"It's simply assumed that we've learned how to listen to other people. Few people have formally developed listening as a key skill."*

When we listen, not just to the facts but also to the emotional make-up of people's messages, they feel valued, understood and heard in a manner that builds trust and goodwill, which creates an atmosphere that fosters engagement, commitment and, most importantly, increases collaboration.

Listening Fundamentals

ALL OF US HAVE been schooled on how to read and how to write. We may even have had some training in how to get a point across. But it's simply assumed that we have learned how to listen to other people. Few people have formally developed their listening as a key skill.

Effective listening is a defining and critically important skill for the Master Expert. It's not only about gathering information. It's just as much about building relationships and trust.

There are a number of reasons why experts tend to be poor listeners.

- Experts usually have fast intellects. They can often tell where a person is headed with a thought process long before that person finally gets to the point. Being busy, experts often jump in with their observations before they have really heard the other party say all they want to say. Notwithstanding that this is interrupting, which is very rude, it's also what we call jumping to the solution (see our chapters on Solutioning).
- By definition, the expert is usually the person most informed about their area of specialty. It can be somewhat frustrating to hear a person try to articulate something that they don't seem to fully comprehend. An expert might step in early to put them out of their misery, thus denying them the chance to have their say. Experts who do this are usually trying to help, but their actions are often perceived as arrogant and rude.
- Like everybody else, the expert is busy and feels like they can't afford to give others their complete and undivided attention.

> *"It takes both effort and discipline to put aside other preoccupations and completely focus on what another human being is saying."*

Listening properly involves the willingness to give our time and attention to another person. Time and attention are very scarce resources, so many of us are instinctively reticent to offer them freely, especially when we're feeling the pressure of handling multiple priorities with pressing deadlines.

Under pressure, most of us revert to instinctual survival thinking. Our capacity and our willingness to give time to others diminishes. Expediency dominates our thinking. It takes both effort and discipline to put aside other preoccupations and completely focus on what another human being is saying or not saying.

And other people don't always make the job of picking up their meaning easy. They waffle on or speak indirectly. They don't get to the point they want to make quickly. They obscure their true message by only dropping hints about what they need or what they're unhappy about. And some unload with such emotional intensity that what they really want gets lost in all the noise.

True listening, with full attention and emotional objectivity, requires a commitment of time and a level of self-control, both of which are difficult for most of us. Yet being able to listen is one of the most useful relationship building activities of all. It accelerates our insight into people's true needs and requirements. It's crucial to engaging with them effectively.

Five Levels of Listening

STEPHEN COVEY, AUTHOR OF *The 7 Habits of Highly Successful People*, created a helpful construct about listening. His five levels of listening help us assess whether we really are listening or not and also allows us to identify the extent to which others are listening to us.

Capability: COLLABORATION
Covey's 5 Levels of Listening

1. **IGNORING**

2. **PRETEND LISTENING**

3. **SELECTIVE LISTENING**

4. **ATTENTIVE LISTENING**

5. **EMPATHETIC LISTENING**

FIGURE 20.1: The Five Levels of Listening

In Figure 20.1, we can see the progression:

- **Ignoring** is when we give the other party and what they're saying absolutely no attention.
- **Pretend listening** is when we feel some sense of moral obligation to listen, but we aren't particularly engaged.
- **Selective listening** refers to the human brain's tendency to filter what it hears. We engage with certain parts of the message and disregard others.
- **Attentive listening** is what most of us do when the topic resonates with our pre-existing interests and beliefs. But we rarely set aside our own agendas, opinions and beliefs.
- **Empathetic listening** is the highest level. It's when we put ourselves in the speaker's shoes. It is, of course, Master Expert territory.

Let's take a very close look at what it takes to be a highly proficient empathetic listener.

A Guide to Empathetic Listening

IN FIGURE 20.2, WE outline the Expertship model of empathetic listening. It is, as we might expect, only advanced common sense. As experts, we intuitively know how to do every stage of this listening process, but how often do we actually do it properly? The nine steps to mastering empathetic listening are

1. Commit to listening

We need to decide that the person we're listening to is worthy of our time and attention. If this isn't our entry point, nothing else we do matters. We will, like Stefan, unconsciously communicate this lack of interest to everyone else in the room.

We have to be prepared to accept that the stakeholder is important either now or in the future, deserves respectful listening, and that the conversation is worthy of investment because we intend to learn something from it. This is all about our mindset.

The words of the late Larry King, a famous broadcaster in the United States, are relevant here. "I remind myself every morning that nothing I say this day will teach me anything. So, if I'm going to learn, I must do it by listening." Master Experts listen so intently that they're capable of learning something from nearly every conversation.

If, for example, a key stakeholder is, from our perspective, talking complete rubbish about a subject, the typical expert will dismiss not only their comments but also perhaps the person as unworthy of their time.

A Master Expert, on the other hand, will wonder how this key stakeholder came to be so ill-informed? *Is that my fault? Or hang on a second, am I the one who is ill-informed? What data did this stakeholder base this opinion on? Is it the same or different to mine?*

Not only will the Master Expert listen intently, but they'll probe with additional questions before expressing an alternate view.

2. Be present

We need to push aside any distractions and be really present and attentive. It means setting down our phone and closing out of our email inbox. It means forgetting about the issues discussed in the previous meeting. We're in *this* meeting *now*. It means ignoring, for a short time, the huge to-do list that's been a heavy weight on our shoulders. It means leaning in, not leaning back.

We also need to be patient and willing to invest our time into uncovering the truth without rushing anyone or showing irritation if they don't know how to cut to the chase.

3. Seek to understand

Having concluded that the person we're listening to is deserving of our focus and that they likely have something of potential value to say, our objective is to understand what they're saying and why they're saying it. We want to deeply understand where they're coming from.

4. Open-minded and curious

We need to be open-minded and curious. We need to be willing to learn and to put aside our own convictions and prejudices, at least until the other party feels heard or understood. This can be challenging if their point of view clashes with our own. This includes putting aside the instinct to defend ourselves if we find their perspective unfairly accusatory. It's merely a commitment to "walking in their shoes." The most confronting aspect of this is suspending, even temporarily, our own deeply held opinions.

We need to put aside the things we already know that get in the way of things we might learn. The lessons may or may not present themselves as being technical or professional in nature.

5. Suspend judgment

We need to temporarily suspend our judgment and our instinctive desire to solve the problem. We need to get rid of the presumption that the other party is seeking our expertise rather than just emotional support. We need to be able to subjugate our instinct to disagree and express our own point of view until we have their permission to proceed and know that they've felt heard and understood.

Capability: COLLABORATION

Empathetic Listening

1	**COMMIT TO LISTENING**	· Our colleague is important · The topic is important to them · This is a good investment of our time
2	**BE PRESENT**	· I will eliminate distractions · I believe they deserve my focus
3	**SEEK TO UNDERSTAND**	· I believe what they have to say is valuable · I know it is important that I completely understand
4	**BE OPEN-MINDED AND CURIOUS**	· I am willing to learn · I will walk in their shoes · I will remove my own (deeply held opinions)
5	**SUSPEND JUDGMENT**	· I temporarily suspend judgment · I will fully understand their argument before considering my viewpoint
6	**PARAPHRASE**	· I will repeat and summarize to ensure I understand fully · I will seek to delve deeper – what and why
7	**REFLECT EMOTIONS**	· I will seek to understand their feelings not just their point of view · I won't judge – how they feel is real to them
8	**TRUST THE PROCESS**	· I won't jump to solution · I understand that taking time is saving time · I know solutions will emerge given time
9	**LISTENING IS VALUABLE**	· I know the process is value in itself · I know we are building trust not just understanding

FIGURE 20.2: Empathetic Listening

6. Paraphrase

We need to summarize and play back what we're hearing. This discipline forces us to be attentive and consider what's at the very heart of everything that they're saying. How well can we encapsulate the essence of what they've said? Apart from making the other person feel understood and safe to continue speaking, by doing this, we'll get instant feedback on whether or not our understanding is accurate and complete.

This enables us to check that our intuition is on target. "It sounds like you're worried that this will add a bunch of extra workload and delays in meeting customer needs without adding commensurate value. Is that right?"

Chances are that more information will come from them through this process of voluntary disclosure, due in part to our supportive and empathetic responses, than might otherwise have been yielded from our probing.

This is not to say that artful questioning has no place. Used in masterful tandem with empathetic paraphrasing, emotionally intelligent questioning where no defensiveness is triggered is particularly powerful. Most people are so busy disagreeing with what they've heard or feeling compelled to offer advice or solve the problem that they lack the self-discipline it takes to effectively paraphrase or summarize what they've heard.

7. Reflect emotions

We need to play back the feelings we detect. Sometimes the speaker's meaning is found more in the emotions being expressed than the literal content of their words. Often, there's an emotional component to their message, especially if it's one of those emotions that can hijack the rational brain's smooth operating, such as intense frustration, a sense of dread, or ongoing stress.

In such cases, merely reflecting back the literal content of their words might not convey that we've really understood. What they want to hear is that we've picked up just how put out they're feeling, how anxious, how drained, and so on. In such cases, it's better to make a statement like "You sound skeptical or doubtful..." or "It sounds like you have some worries..."

8. Trust the process

We need to understand that even without progressing to a solution, the very act of listening often holds intrinsic value. We need to trust the process—trust that a solution may naturally emerge once the other party feels understood. Frequently, the other party is perfectly capable of solving their issue once they've unburdened themselves of their predicament. They're often helped by our emotionally intelligent questions.

If we have cultivated an empathic mentality, then the techniques are more likely to come naturally. And if the other party feels you have an empathetic spirit, they can often be forgiving of a less than ideal technique.

9. Listening is valuable

We need to understand that the very act of listening—investing time in hearing the views or challenges of a colleague—has value beyond what we might have learned or an issue we might have solved. It's about building a relationship and mutual trust.

There will be instances when we listen to a stakeholder and simply can't help, although we might be able to suggest someone who can. But fifteen minutes spent listening to an issue we can't solve isn't a waste of time. It's an investment in knowing that the next time we have a problem we would like to discuss with this stakeholder, they're likely to listen because they remember us listening to them.

TAKING ACTION

Growing Our Listening Skills

IF THIS IS A capability in which you believe you could add greater value by growing your skills, here are two high-level actions you can take:

▶ LET THE SILENCE DO THE HEAVY LIFTING

There are times when it's more effective not to express an opinion, defend our position, or try to persuade someone to change their mind. This is particularly the case if we've already passionately backed a position but others are resistant. Continuing to argue can actually weaken our case, as it implies that we still feel the need to justify our position.

A word that we often hear associated with being a trusted advisor is "gravitas." The word implies a calm self-assuredness—someone who is not overly anxious to have others agree and does not depend on others' approval. When we lack gravitas, we tend to try too hard to rationally convince someone to see things our way.

Letting the silence do the heavy lifting (a phrase coined by Susan Scott in her book *Fierce Conversations*) has many applications. It can take considerable restraint not to feel compelled to show you've got things all figured out.

If we've asked a colleague a really good question, one that requires them to think before answering, the worst thing we can do is interrupt their thinking by asking another question, or ask the same question another way, or provide a list of possible answers. We simply need to be quiet and give our colleague the time to think and respond. Much deeper insights usually come from this approach.

▶ PUT ASIDE OTHER AGENDAS

It isn't a crime to have an agenda. We all have specific things we want to achieve. But when we enter a conversation with our agenda front of mind, it impedes empathetic listening. We're looking for our colleague to say things that advance our agenda, and we're dismissive or negative about those who do not. With empathetic listening, we're trying to understand our colleagues' agendas rather than just thinking about our own.

"You're short on ears and long on mouth."

John Wayne

CHAPTER | 21 |

The Madness of Meetings

How appalling meetings lead to appalling collaboration, and how we all think we should fix the problem.

IN THIS CHAPTER, WE WILL EXPLORE:

- What do we most hate about meetings?
- Why are meetings so universally poorly run?
- How can experts finally make all their meetings and collaborative interactions efficient and effective?

ONE THING THAT EXPERTS tell us about the cost of collaboration is that it usually requires a lot of time spent in meetings. Unfortunately, due to an increasing lack of meeting discipline these days, much of this time is unproductive.

Meeting culture is something experts can significantly impact in a range of practical ways. Most choose not to do so, preferring complaint and "not my responsibility" to action. As aspiring Master Experts, our time is valuable, just like everyone else's. Making sure we attend the right meetings for the right reasons and for the right length of time helps ensure we get the right outcomes and is a critical productivity measure. It also builds collaboration rather than destroys it.

Poor meeting culture gives collaboration a bad name. Hours wasted in meetings sharing information that could've been shared in other ways is collaboration at its worst, and attendance at such meetings quickly tails off. Making poor decisions, or no decision at all, after plenty of discussion because not all the attendees have the right information means experts make decisions independently and away from the group, thus negatively impacting collaboration.

Poor meeting culture is a direct contributor to experts saying they "don't have time to collaborate." It's time experts stood up and made a difference. Here's how many groups of experts we've worked with have changed their departments' meeting culture.

Typical Complaints About Meetings

IN MANY SESSIONS WITH all types of experts, the following complaints about poor meeting quality are remarkably common:

- **Volume**: There are too many meetings, with a considerable number being of questionable value.
- **Structure**: A loosely defined or completely undefined agenda often means meetings lack structure and time discipline.
- **Preparation**: A lack of a well-shaped agenda leads to poor circulation of documents prior to meetings.
- **Governance**: There is often no one chairing or properly facilitating the meeting and keeping to the agenda and time. This leads to poor behavior, such as talking over others or someone hijacking the meeting.
- **Late or non-arrival**: Wasted time at the beginning and sporadic attendance.
- **No accountability**: No minutes circulated means there is no accountability for actions or consequences for non-delivery.
- **Lack of purpose or objective**: No clear purpose or the purpose of the meeting has been lost in time.
- **Duration**: They're too long.
- **Frequency**: Regular meetings occur too often.
- **No protocols**: Even when people attend, they're often not fully present and focused because they're doing email or jumping out of the meeting to take calls.

Across hundreds of sessions run by the authors, these same ten problems with meetings come up time and again.

We ask "If everyone knows these are the issues, why doesn't anyone do anything about them?" The typical answer seems to be that everyone is waiting for someone else to fix the problem.

The right meeting culture saves experts time and encourages proper collaboration. Every one of these issues has an easy solution that will transform the way in which our colleagues work with one another.

Let's have a look at how experts can improve our meetings, thus improving collaboration and our value within the organization.

Volume: Too Many Meetings

WE CAN'T STOP SOMEONE from inviting us to meetings they want us to attend, but there's an easy, polite and effective way to cull the number of invites we accept.

Firstly, we need to be clear about why our colleague wants us to attend. We should ask them which specific items on the agenda they think we need to be there for. If there is no agenda, we simply ask for one and explain to our colleague that we don't attend meetings that have no agenda. After all, how will we know whether it's a good use of our time or not without an agenda?

Secondly, if it's for "information purposes" or "to keep us in the loop," then we ask for the minutes of the meeting to be sent to us, as well as any documents that were circulated at the meeting. We don't have time for "in the loop" meetings.

Thirdly, we might ask the convener of the meeting to excuse us because the last meeting wasn't productive. Perhaps it started late, only half the people were there, most hadn't read the document, there were no documents, previous meetings agreed actions but no one followed through, or it was poorly chaired. As a result, we didn't get through the agenda to the bits we were interested in. It's reasonable to question whether our time is being well spent at meetings that don't appear to be productive.

> *"A simple rule: if there's no agenda for a meeting, then we won't attend."*

This may sound quite assertive, but let's be clear: the people convening such meetings are wasting our time and not adding any value. They don't deserve to have our time invested with them while there are other more pressing matters to be dealt with. In pushing back, we're actually helping the convener by providing robust but fair feedback. If they improve the organization and conduct of the meetings, we'll happily attend.

Capability: COLLABORATION

The 10 Reasons We All Hate Meetings

1	**VOLUME**	• There are simply too many of them
2	**STRUCTURE**	• No agenda = no structure = meetings that meander
3	**PREPARATION**	• No agenda and no supporting = chaotic debates
4	**GOVERNANCE**	• No chairperson, poor chair, wrong chair, no conduct rules
5	**NO ACCOUNTABILITY**	• No minutes, no action lists, no action, no consequences
6	**LATECOMERS/ NO-SHOWS**	• People arrive late, meetings start late, Interruptions, repeats
7	**PURPOSE**	• No clear purpose or objectives for the meeting
8	**DURATION**	• They are too long
9	**FREQUENCY**	• They are too often
10	**NO PROTOCOLS**	• No rules are set so anarchy rules

FIGURE 21.1: The 10 Reasons We All Hate Meetings

Another tactic is to explore the agenda and negotiate partial attendance. If there are six topics on the agenda and we're interested or required for only two of them, ask for these to be put at the beginning or end of the agenda so that we can perhaps attend for 20 minutes rather than the full hour. If they aren't urgent topics, ask them to be pushed out to the following meeting, which we will attend because most of the topics will be relevant to us.

We don't get time back, so we need to use it carefully.

We've all had the wonderful experience of being expected to attend a meeting only for it to be canceled at the last moment. Wow! It feels great to suddenly gain that time back. This is something we can make happen much more often by being discerning about which meetings we'll attend and why, and which ones we'll politely but assertively decline.

Structure: No Agenda

AS WITH THE PREVIOUS section, the rule is simple: if there is no agenda, then we won't attend. We have many competing priorities, so if there's no agenda, we simply can't assess whether the meeting is a good use of our time. And the fact that there's no agenda suggests that the meeting is either not well organized or not important. Or both.

We get asked a lot about whether it's okay to push back on meeting requests from more senior people, even our managers. Frankly, they should know better. We encourage experts to have a conversation with their manager about whether it's really how the manager wants to spend thousands of dollars of people's time. Is attending meetings with no agenda alongside colleagues who don't know why they're there or what decisions they're being asked to make really a good use of our time? Really?

Several groups, many in IT as it happens, have adopted this rule and reported great success. Firstly, agendas have started appearing. Secondly, people are better able to decide which ones to attend and which to pass on. It's common for three people from the same department to be invited, which makes it easy for one person to attend and also represent the interests of their colleagues.

Preparation: No Documentation

THERE ARE MEETINGS THAT don't really require documentation, although we'd argue that including it is a very good discipline to encourage. Even a report of performance, if circulated before the meeting, can save a lot of time. If someone spots a mistake, it can be rectified before the meeting, rather than spending 20 minutes arguing about whether the data is right or not before actually discussing the issue at hand.

But some meetings absolutely require documentation. For us, any meeting that has to make a decision needs a document. What's the decision? Why do we need to make it? What are the relevant facts? What options do we have in front of us? What is the recommended option? Why is the author of the document proposing that option? What impact will the decision have? How will we measure whether that decision was a good one or not?

Many public sector organizations have this discipline as part of their culture, and it works brilliantly. It gives every participant in the meeting a chance to weigh up their opinions prior to the meeting. It provides everyone with an opportunity to do their own research beforehand and to see how thorough the author has been. It allows us, as experts, to consult with other colleagues to get their views on the matter.

All of this means that when we get to the meeting, the discussion is about the decision, the pros and cons of each option, and coming to an informed and considered but efficiently quick decision.

Without documentation, most of the meeting is spent discussing what's important and what isn't. It becomes an information-gathering meeting rather than a decision-making exercise.

What has the way we run our meetings got to do with the way we collaborate?

In this chapter, we have focused on explaining, at some length, what it takes to run meetings properly. This is because the experts we work with complain endlessly about the time in their typical working week that is wasted in meetings. This chapter suggests to all experts that we do something about reducing that wasted time.

But there's a broader point to be made here. The principles that are described here can be directly applied more widely to the way in which we collaborate with colleagues. Let's explore the connections:

Purpose. Do all parties involved in the collaborative initiative have absolute clarity about how this initiative is going to make a difference, by when, and how this success and impact will be measured? Is everyone working toward the same outcome? Is this regularly reviewed as the initiative moves forward?

Structure. Have we established rules on what collaborative behavior actually looks like? What are the expectations? How quickly should colleagues respond? What simple mechanisms are in place to enable collaborative behavior? Has the organization even conducted a discussion about this and agreed, at a high level, minimum expectations?

Governance. Once begun, how many collaborative initiatives fail because of poor governance? How many fall apart because there's no impartial facilitator of the initiative, time is managed poorly, or some personalities dominate discussions without input from the whole group? If two parties are trying to collaborate but there are no agreed rules and processes, the initiative is almost certainly doomed to failure.

Accountability. Are there any consequences agreed ahead of time for one party not delivering on actions that were agreed? How are those involved in the collaborative venture held to account and by whom?

Preparation. No documentation. How many collaborative initiatives fail because they're simply poorly described, vague, amorphous propositions to work together or share?

Volume. Collaborating across departments and divisions of organizations is seen as slowing things down because there's so little precision about the way we do it. If collaboration was run like a well-oiled meeting, not too often but with high impact, would we collaborate more?

Could experts lead the way by starting a productive conversation with other colleagues about how to streamline and enhance collaborative efforts across the organization? We think they could.

Project meetings should be the same. We don't want to waste time in meetings learning what has been done, what deliverables were already agreed, and what hasn't been done. We can get that information from an up-to-date professional project plan. Instead, we need to spend time in the meeting discussing why actions were not completed, the impact this delay has had, the reasons for non-delivery, and whether or not those reasons are valid. And we also need to discuss what it'll take to get things back on track.

These types of conversations change the culture quickly. People arrive at meetings knowing they aren't going to be subjected to an interrogation for non-delivery. We're all accountable, but, as senior experts, we have a critical leadership role in making sure the right culture operates in our teams.

The rule is simple: if we're being asked to attend a meeting to make an important decision, we ask where the decision paper is? When can I expect it? Will I attend a meeting to make an important decision without having the decision laid out for me? No, I won't.

Governance

THERE ARE MANY CRITICISMS of meetings that come under this banner:
- There is no chair (rare).
- The chair is hopeless and ineffectual (unfortunately, quite common).
- The chair allows louder participants to dominate the discussion (all too common).
- The chair doesn't manage time well (all too common).
- The chair is the subject matter expert, does most of the talking, and has selective listening disorder (very common, particularly when the chair is the project manager or the boss).
- The agenda is a mess, the chair doesn't follow the agenda, there are no times allocated for each topic on the agenda, and so on (very common).

Why do we have so much trouble governing meetings? What would best practice look like? We regularly ask this question to groups of experts, and pretty much every group we have asked has definitive answers. The problem is that the meetings have been set up without agreeing the role of the chair and without agreeing on the conventions that need to be followed by all.

The rules are simple. Make sure the chair is not the most senior person in the room. The most senior person should be listening, not busy chairing a meeting. Their second-in-command or another experienced person should be asked to chair the meeting. They should also be responsible for preparing and sending out an agenda, in conjunction with the meeting owner, who is usually the most senior person in the room.

The best teams we've seen operate like this circulate the chair role every few months. Everyone gets a go, the workload is shared, and everyone develops respect for everyone else.

The chair is there to help the meeting achieve its goals. This person will ensure things are discussed effectively in the time allotted and will manage the agenda so everything gets discussed. The tactics a chair can use are very well documented on a million websites, so why don't we insist upon them?
- If we're running over time on a topic, the chair stops the discussion and asks us whether we want to spend more time on it? If we do,

which topic do we want to delay until next time or reduce in time allotment?

- If two people are arguing with one another about a specific point, the chair interrupts and asks them whether they can continue the discussion after the meeting and let us all know what they've finally decided. This prevents us all from having to listen to a disagreement we aren't involved in.
- The chair stops one person from dominating the discussion. The chair specifically asks others to enter the conversation. The chair actively encourages the introverts to make a contribution and always asks the person who has said nothing whether they have anything to contribute. Often, the most valuable contributions to the meetings are made by using this technique. Extroverts' contributions need to be proportionate.
- The chair helps the group move to a decision. Is there anything else material anyone wants to add? Are we ready to vote on this now? Are we ready to make a decision? If the group wants to delay the decision, the chair asks the meeting exactly what steps, by whom and by when need to take place so that a decision can be made next time. What are the impacts and consequences of delaying the decision? Who should be informed of the delay, by whom, and what reason do we wish to give them?
- If a decision or action is agreed, again, the chair should ensure that the minute-taker records who will do what and by when.
- The chair is responsible for meeting conduct. They need to stop meeting participants who interrupt others or talk over them. They need to close down secondary conversations. They need to ask people to remain calm when things get heated. They need to defuse conflict between people by asking third parties in the room what their opinion is.
- If the chair wishes to get involved in a topic, they can vacate the chair for that topic and allow someone who is not involved in that topic to sit in. This ensures that the same rules apply to the chair when they're involved in a topic as everyone else.

> *"Minutes should be circulated— including agreed actions— as soon as the meeting finishes."*

None of this is rocket science. These rules and protocols are known to almost all of us, and we would all readily sign up for all of them because they make meetings more effective. And while some people are naturally better at chairing meetings than others, it's an easily learned skill when the responsibility for chairing is being rotated.

No Accountability

THIS ONE DRIVES MOST of the experts we work with crazy. The group sits around for an hour or so and agrees on a set of tasks to be completed by, say, next week's meeting. When the meeting rolls around, most of the tasks haven't been completed. Why bother, many experts ask?

This generally happens because accountability processes are missing. Minutes should be taken at every meeting. In our view, given modern technology, they should be taken as the meeting progresses in the form of an email or on the collaborative platform of our choice. The email should then be circulated to all attendees, including those who apologized for non-attendance and those who wanted minutes. This should be done *as soon as the meeting finishes*. The minutes should record decisions, actions agreed to be taken, as well as by whom and by when. In the instances where an important decision is made, the reasons for the decision being made are a useful addition. This adds clarity to everyone present about why the decision was made.

> *"Attendees arrive late and no one holds them to account."*

Occasionally, it brings out disagreement, and that's actually healthy *during* the meeting rather than long after, when multiple versions of the decision emerge, confusion reigns, and we have to have another meeting about the previous meeting.

At the start of the next meeting, the minutes are very quickly reviewed and what wasn't achieved, by whom, and why is typically discussed.

Like everything else, we feel it's best practice to rotate this responsibility.

Latecomers or No-Shows

ONE OF THE MAJOR irritations we have with meetings is that they consistently start late. Many attendees arrive late and no one holds them to account. This disincentivizes those who arrived on time to do so next time, and so the culture perpetuates. It also means that late arrivals ask what they've missed, so the whole meeting stops and everyone who was on time has their time wasted again while we explain to the person who wasn't on time what was discussed so far.

Our advice to stop late arrivals is threefold.

First, stop updating people who arrive late. That's their bad. It interrupts the meeting. If they don't know what's going on, that's fine. If they think they have missed something important, that's fine. It might encourage them to be punctual next time.

Secondly, always start the meeting on time. If the chair hasn't arrived, appoint a new one and start on time. If you do this every time for three or four meetings in a row, everyone will know it starts on time and make an additional effort to be punctual.

It's amazing how well this works and yet how few teams actually deploy these tactics. One of the authors at a program a couple of years ago asked the participants in the workshop to be back after lunch at 2.00 p.m. At 2.00 p.m., one person out of 15 was in the room. We started. As the other fourteen wandered in over the next four or five minutes, imagining that we wouldn't start until they came back, they were startled to find they'd missed five minutes of content—content that we never revisited. The group returned from lunch right on time for the following few days. We didn't say a thing, but they got the message.

Thirdly, choose a precise and memorable time. Typically, in workshops, we attempt to give people an unusual time to be back. "Can we come back at 2.02 p.m., please?" People don't remember 2.00 p.m. or quarter-to or quarter-past, but they remember 2.02 p.m.

As you'll see later on in this section, we suggest radical retiming for meetings, which works a treat.

Non-attendance at meetings is another challenge. The critical person needed to make a decision isn't in the room but had said they would be.

There are two dynamics here. First, someone says they're coming and is then late. Is the person coming or not? People jump on texts and emails to see, wasting time and being completely disrespectful to the group. Senior people, by the way, are famous for this poor behavior. And senior experts.

The first rule is to start, even if it's just going through minutes or dealing with other items on the agenda that don't need that person in the room. The second rule is to have a rule that if we're going to be late or not make it after saying yes, it's our responsibility to let the rest of the team know. It isn't their responsibility to chase us.

Also discuss whether the team can make an interim decision without the "important" person there. This decision can be communicated to the others who didn't make the meeting, and if they have a problem with the decision, they can communicate with us. But it means that as a group, we're moving forward and not waiting for someone who "got stuck in another meeting", which is a common excuse offered by senior people or experts with poor time-management skills.

Purpose

THERE ARE SOME MEETINGS where the original purpose of the meeting has been lost in the mists of time. Best practice is, at the very least once a year, to revisit its purpose. What are we all doing here? Marketing strategy meetings become sales campaign task-fests. IT strategy meetings end up discussing tactical approaches to current problems. Global risk forums suddenly become a venue for other groups to promote their services or requests. Annual meetings of organizations become listless talk-fests for senior people who already spend half their lives together in meetings. These events don't re-energize the organization and the wider team as they were supposed to.

How many meetings actually get discontinued in your organization because they're no longer necessary? Obviously, this happens to project teams when projects are completed, but do we really need a weekly work-in-progress meeting? In our organization, all of the staff collectively agreed that every two weeks would be fine. Half the agenda was moved to smaller group meetings because they weren't relevant to the wider group.

We encourage you to start meetings with a clear statement of what we're here to achieve and check that everyone is on the same page. It helps quickly clarify what all participants are hoping to achieve.

Meetings have legitimacy when they:
- Build a common understanding among mutually accountable stakeholders about direction, performance outcomes, alignment around expectations, agendas and parameters to be observed.
- Build relationships.
- Share information.
- Make key decisions.

The key is to ask for which of these purposes does this particular meeting exist, and to what extent does the meeting successfully fulfill that? If not, why not?

"Change every one-hour meeting to a 45-minute meeting."

A classic example of a meeting that isn't really needed is one of those torturous sessions where one person after another delivers a verbal update whilst others listen, mostly without interest. The only person whose needs are typically served is the "inquisitor," who is usually the manager of the group or the project. Such information could easily be gathered and submitted ahead of any meeting, thus either making the meeting unnecessary or allowing the agenda to be something much more engaging for all attendees.

Duration

ALL OF THE ABOVE lack of protocol and processes means most meetings go on far longer than they were supposed to or needed to. They become back-to-back, so our heads are still in the last meeting we attended as we rush from one to another.

The following suggestions may appear radical, but they work.

Many meetings are an hour long. Why? Will we be dictated to by MS Office default settings? Who was it who said an hour was a good length of time for a meeting, especially since research suggests it's not? Our suggestion: change every one-hour meeting to a 45-minute meeting. If they're chaired properly and have structured agendas, 45 minutes is all that is needed. These shorter meetings have a whole range of advantages:

- It focuses people's attention on time. With slightly less time, people are less likely to waste it, so fewer irrelevant contributions are made.
- It gives participants 15 minutes at the end to get from one meeting to another or even action some of the things they were allocated in the meeting. If we agreed to send emails to a couple of stakeholders about particular tasks, we could probably achieve this before the next meeting. This can be life changing.
- It means other meetings start on time because people have time to get to them. At the very least, they have no legitimate excuse for being late. This saves more time.

As we discussed earlier, the right chairperson conducting the meeting properly will also shorten meetings.

Frequency

THIS IS A DERIVATION of the too many meetings complaint. Perhaps that weekly meeting could be done fortnightly, or that monthly meeting could be held quarterly. This is usually the case when reporting and communication are possible through other systems and communication platforms.

The reverse can also be true. Rather than a horrific all-day meeting once a month, we could change to four two-hour meetings spread throughout the month and deal with each part of the agenda separately.

Best practice here is to focus on purpose and outcomes. What do we want to achieve with these meetings, and how do we make sure that we do so in the most efficient manner possible? Just because we've always had monthly meetings doesn't mean we need to continue to have them. Every six weeks might work just as well.

No Protocols

MEETINGS NEED A SET of rules and processes that all parties have agreed to and that are reviewed from time to time. Meetings where almost no rules have been agreed are generally the worst of all.

What actually needs to occur is a meeting about meetings, as uncomfortable as that may sound. For example, many projects start off with getting straight into the work that needs to be completed. But the best first meeting will have an agenda like the ten points above. How will we work together, what rules will be applied to each other, how will we hold each other accountable, how will we communicate in-between meetings, what platforms will we use to collaborate and share information, and what does success look like if we're working really well together? Just 45 minutes spent discussing these issues will save 450 minutes or perhaps many more downstream.

TAKING ACTION

Growing Our Meeting Management Skills

IF THIS CHAPTER RESONATED with you, don't delay. Act! Waiting for everyone else to raise these issues is why no progress has been made in many organizations. Here's how:

▶ CHANGE ONE MEETING AT A TIME

Which meeting drives you most crazy? Perhaps it's the one that wastes most of your time? This is the meeting to revolutionize. Actions you might consider:

- Talk to other participants. Are they happy with the way the meetings are run and organized? Would they support a discussion about how to change the meeting for the better?
- Is there a clear mandate for the meeting? Is it really clear what the purpose of the meeting is? It may be possible to ask the organizer, chair of the meeting, or the person who has sponsored the meeting these questions. If these two things are clear, which is quite unusual, then question when they were last reviewed.
- Deal with the worst bits first. Hitting everyone up with all ten changes might be overkill. Choose two or three changes that make the most difference and sell the benefits of these first.
- After the changes have been made and implemented in several meetings, check in with the group. Is it better? Should we be deploying these new rules to other meetings?
- Good luck—and good meetings!

"The most hateful human misfortune is for a wise person to have no influence."

Herodotus

CHAPTER | 22 |

The Many Team Roles of Experts

Just playing the mono-dimensional role of technical expert relegates experts to marginal roles. It's time experts stepped up and played broader roles.

IN THIS CHAPTER, WE WILL EXPLORE:

- Besides their role as a subject matter expert, what other roles should experts be playing?
- Can experts play a leadership role when they have no formal leadership authority? Should they?
- How can we make a difference to accelerating team outcomes beyond just providing our technical expertise?

ONE OF THE THREE expert roles in the Collaboration capability is that of **Team Worker.** This expert role deals with the extent to which experts are proactive, collaborative contributors to many teams, are working across all boundaries, and are developing and maintaining highly effective relationships with all co-workers.

Our research shows that experts are regularly members of more than one team, occasionally members of many more teams, and they're called in when their expertise is needed. Therefore, although some of us do work on a highly autonomous basis, we frequently need to interact with teams and project groups.

This expert role covers our ability to make those interactions highly effective, as well as our ability to proactively contribute to the success of these teams, even though we may not be the team leader. In fact, experts are less commonly the leaders of teams, with the exception of possible superior seniority and technical capability.

Crucially, this doesn't mean we can't contribute to leadership. In most teams, there are *formal* leaders (those given the authority) and *informal* leaders (those who, by their behavior, show leadership and help teams succeed).

The behaviors at each level of Expertship for the expert role of Team Worker are described in Figure 22.1.

Some of the work that a subject matter expert is engaged in by the organization involves providing information or advice to others who are pursuing some kind of organizational outcome. The rest is doing stuff others can't do.

> *"Master Experts will be masterful at working globally in virtual, multi-national, and multi-cultural teams."*

The immature expert may not perceive it as their role to contribute any further than the provision of relevant information or advice, preferring to remain detached. As a result, they're seen as aloof and indifferent. They're likely to act as an *individual contributor* to a team and to work mostly alone on allocated tasks. They'll understand and respond to their own motivations and needs rather than actively consider those of others. Experts operating at this immature level will be most comfortable working with familiar nationalities and cultures.

Derailing experts will work autonomously, focusing on their personal agenda rather than worrying about the team outcome. Indeed, they're likely to deliberately keep their distance from the collective focus of the team. They won't want to seek or be saddled with ownership of team outcomes.

They're likely to be competitive rather than collaborative, wishing to be seen as the most expert. They may be culturally insensitive or uncaring and are likely to demonstrate higher levels of engagement with their technical profession than with their colleagues or the organization. Critically, they won't be perceived by those working with them as good team players.

The highly evolved Master Expert will consistently act as a valuable member of numerous teams. They're encouraging and contribute to a collaborative culture, demonstrating a focus on team outcomes. They'll be adept at working across organizational boundaries in a highly effective manner. They'll demonstrate a keen understanding of and interest in individual and team member goals and motivations. Increasingly, Master Experts will be masterful at working globally in virtual, multi-national, and multi-cultural teams.

Master Experts feel a sense of ownership of the team's performance and objectives. They intentionally collaborate with other team members through a variety of roles, consistently progressing toward the realization of those outcomes.

Capability: COLLABORATION

Expert Role: TEAM WORKER

MASTER EXPERT

- Acts as a valuable member of many teams, encouraging collaboration and a focus on team outcomes.
- Works across organizational boundaries in a highly effective manner.
- Has a keen understanding and interest in individual and team member goals and motivations.
- Masterful at working globally in virtual, multinational and multicultural teams.

EXPERT

- Acts as a senior individual contributor on one or two teams, playing the role of expert advisor rather than active team player.
- Works collaboratively with many stakeholders.
- Understands the motivations of all team members and works to align with own motivations.
- Beginning to work effectively with multiple nationalities and cultures, embracing diversity.

SPECIALIST

- Acts as an individual contributor on a team.
- Works mostly alone on allocated tasks.
- Understands and responds to own motivations.
- Comfortable working with familiar nationalities and cultures.

- Prefers to work alone and may appear disconnected and distant from teams.
- Works autonomously with a focus on personal agenda. Competitive rather than collaborative; wishes to be seen as the most expert.
- May be culturally insensitive or uncaring.
- Demonstrates higher levels of engagement with technical profession than the organization.

DERAILING

FIGURE 22.1: Network Manager Behaviors

Being More Than An Expert

THERE ARE MANY OPPORTUNITIES for experts to exercise a more deliberate and significant influence on their teams, other than just being the resident expert. Below are some of the many roles we may play (see Figure 22.2).

Role 1: The role of Expert

This is the role that is usually the basis of our inclusion in a given team. Given the depth of our professional or technical knowledge in a particular field, our perspective—and therefore inclusion in a team—is often considered essential when related matters are being discussed.

There is a significant risk that such a role inclines us to be more of a naysayer, judge or critic than an enabler. Often it's less about generating ideas than evaluating the relative merits of the ideas put forward by others.

This role can be very limiting. As the expert, we contribute only when our expertise is required, rather than voluntarily expanding our contribution to include some of the other roles described below.

There are several additional roles (listed below) that, as an expert, we can play beyond this limited, default persona of "technical advisor."

Role 2: The role of Catalyst

A critical role for a Master Expert is that of Change Catalyst. In this role, we act as the initiator of change and set the change agenda. We discuss this in detail in Chapter 36.

The team role of catalyst can be associated with large-scale change projects, with experts contributing at the genesis of major transformations. However, this is not what we mean here. Being a catalyst on a team or as part of a project usually takes the form of challenging the status quo, challenging enterprise and market assumptions, or challenging the way we have always done things. It means the expert is playing the role of catalyst, compelling the team to think differently, think outside their bubble, and find new approaches and new ideas. A simple but penetrating question can add huge value. Of course, in some instances, we'll be called upon to invent a new way of tackling a complex challenge.

This team role is an expression of our desire to help drive organizational outcomes rather than remain aloof as a detached technical advisor. It means that we have to be prepared to contribute to the team outside the domain of our technical knowledge.

Capability: **COLLABORATION**

The Team Roles of Experts

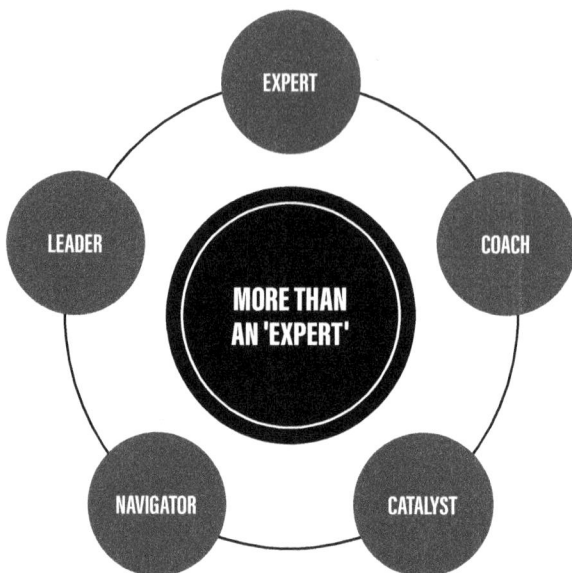

FIGURE 22.2: The Team Roles of Experts

Role 3: The role of Navigator

We've discussed how a Master Expert could play an active and valuable role in many teams by promoting and encouraging collaboration and focusing on accelerating team outcomes.

The team role of navigator comes when a team gets stuck and the nominal group leader, perhaps a project manager, needs assistance in moving forward. Teams sometimes get stuck in the details and struggle to progress from exploring conceptual ideas to implementing decisive actions and realizing the benefits.

An outcome-minded expert can take responsibility for helping the team to move forward by navigating the way. We can facilitate the shaping of the team's direction and timeline, the development of clear criteria and a process for timely decision-making, and instill a sense of urgency and a bias for action. This demonstrates informal leadership. Navigation may require the expert to act as a diplomat by negotiating and facilitating win-win outcomes when teams are faced with competing priorities or deadlines. This requires the ability to influence without authority and foster great teamwork between individual team members and separate teams. Often, the expert is in a unique position to play this role. We discuss the role of Diplomat in detail in Chapter 25.

Role 4: The role of Coach

A further team role for a Master Expert is that of Knowledge Coach. This involves deploying a question-based, collaborative coaching style. Coaching is often considered a standalone activity, but in reality, team meetings and teamwork provide ample opportunities to coach in the moment. We discuss this in detail in Chapter 48.

> *"The team navigator can instill a sense*
> *of urgency and a bias for action."*

Experts have an opportunity to contribute to the team culture as well as the skill sets and mindsets of other team members. This is a great way to demonstrate responsibility rather than seeming hands-off and unaccountable for the team's performance or the growth of the team members.

Master Experts use every interaction available to share knowledge and explain the *why* behind approaches in order to build greater understanding. Master Experts can model the key behaviors of high-performing team members, demonstrating an ability to listen closely to other team members, facilitate respectful brainstorming sessions, and illustrate the power of great questions to penetrate difficult problems.

Role 5: The role of Leader

Experts are often the most experienced person on a team but they rarely the formal leader. To ascend to the role of Master Expert, we can take on informal leadership responsibilities in a diplomatic way.

There will be times when the team needs increased leadership, even when a team has a formally designated person in charge. Working in tandem with any powers that be, we can assist and drive the team's development of a clear focus and goals, help it progress through project phases, look out for the welfare and development of team members, and so on. We discuss some aspects of this in Chapter 48, *Building a Talent Factory.*

TAKING ACTION

Growing Our Team Worker Skills

IF THIS IS AN expert role in which you believe you could add greater value, here are some high-level suggestions for actions to take:

▶ ADOPT ONE OR MORE INTENTIONAL VALUE-ADDED ROLES IN YOUR TEAMS

- Without taking up a deliberate and expanded role within our teams, we can often sit back and do nothing more than provide detached technical advice. This can make us appear aloof, one-dimensional, or even unwilling to share responsibility. And the teams we participate in miss out on the additional value that we can often add.
- Questions we might like to ask ourselves:
- What is the expectation other team members have of me? Is there an implicit expectation that I am there only to represent my field of expertise?
- Am I adopting a passive level of participation by leaving the role of driving the meeting's optimal outcomes to others? If so, am I limiting my contribution in this way?
- What opportunities are there for me to add greater value by helping to steer meetings efficiently and effectively, championing relationships, and coaching and facilitating more junior team members?
- How would I go about experimenting with greater contributions? How would I communicate my intent to the team? Would they welcome this additional contribution? If not, why not?

▶ CLARIFY YOUR TEAM'S PURPOSE

The team's purpose isn't just clarified when the team comes together for the first time. Things change, so checking back in on purpose is a critical component of maintaining energy, direction and engagement. It's not uncommon for the original reason for existence to get lost amidst business-as-usual demands. It doesn't have to be the sole responsibility of the team leader to suggest revisiting the team's purpose. Senior experts on the team can lead the way, too. Questions we might like to ask ourselves:

- How clear is each team member's understanding of the purpose of the team? How clear is mine?
- Does my work and the work of the team clearly align with the organization's strategy? Have we updated this alignment since the latest strategy review was handed down by senior leaders?
- Do we have zombie projects underway (not quite dead but very nearly) that need to be re-assessed? Is more important work not being undertaken because such projects limp on?

Teams that routinely revisit and refresh their sense of purpose tend to have increased vitality and productivity. They also avoid mission drift.

"A well-known principle of human behavior says that when we ask someone to do us a favor, we will be more successful if we provide a reason. People simply like to have reasons for what they do."

Robert B. Cialdini,
Influence: The Psychology of Persuasion

CHAPTER | 23 |

The Desire to Influence

Influencing is a skill, not the efficient presentation of facts. Without establishing personal credibility and emotional connection, most experts will fail to effectively influence.

IN THIS CHAPTER, WE WILL EXPLORE:

- Why is mastering influencing skills so important for experts?
- Different influencing strategies and their impact and effectiveness.
- Which influencing strategies do we use as our default tactics?
- Which tactics do our stakeholders generally deploy with us, and why?

MANY EXPERTS FEEL THAT they don't have the degree of influence that their expertise necessitates. Yet they haven't given much thought to what methods of influence they can use, nor the relative effectiveness of the available methods. Given that they rarely have the formal authority to compel others to act, influencing others is a vital success factor for experts.

Experts often report their frustrations about having their opinions heard and their recommendations adopted. We sometimes imagine that having more formal authority would be the answer because then people would have to listen to us. This is why borrowing strength from others' authority is so heavily relied upon, despite being correlated with triggering high levels of resistance.

We may occasionally experience surprise, wonder and envy when seemingly less informed people in the organization who happen to have positions of authority have their ideas taken up, even when they have comparatively dumb ideas in our opinion.

> *"Aristotle's Pyramid of Influence describes the three key factors in persuasion."*

We might be tempted to seek the sponsorship of a senior business leader to lend weight to our recommendations and give them extra clout. Let's explore some useful strategies that might help us to influence others and examine how effective they are.

Getting Cut-Through

RICHARD HAS BEEN MAKING slow progress on advancing his initiative to update the organization's records management system. He feels that the proposal he prepared was well argued, covering the regulatory requirements for thorough record-keeping, some documented issues that the organization has had with adequate storage and retrieval of key records, the average (and excessive) amount of time spent looking for files, the irritation this causes customers, the features and benefits of the proposed system, and alternative quotations from three separate capable suppliers.

But, for reasons that aren't apparent, the senior managers to whom Richard has been proposing the purchase of a new records management system have been taking forever to make a decision. Even though they asked him to prepare the proposal, they've not yet moved on it, so he's been asked to rework his proposal several times.

Richard's challenge is not unique. Many experts find that they routinely have to influence decisions, others' behaviors, and request support from other departments without having any formal authority to require or compel others to act. Like Richard, they put together the relevant facts and reasoning and then wonder why this fails to provoke the anticipated response. Are people impervious to sound logic and evidence? Because sometimes it seems nigh on impossible to move decisions forward despite one's best efforts.

So how does one effectively influence others?

Research suggests that most people's instincts are to try and rationally persuade others, perhaps followed by applying pressure in some way. Such methods fail to take into account how most people make the decision to commit to a course of action.

Aristotle's Pyramid of Influence

MORE THAN TWO THOUSAND years ago, the great Greek philosopher Aristotle created what has become known as Aristotle's *Pyramid of Influence*. It describes the three key factors in persuasion.

Aristotle is regarded as the father of rhetoric, which is the technique of using argument to convince. He wrote many works on this topic and greatly influenced the other Greek philosophers and the Romans. His influence continues to this day.

The pyramid has three layers, each denoted by a Greek word: Logos, Pathos and Ethos (see Figure 23.1).

Logos: Intellectually Convincing

Logos is the essential, logical, convincing nature of what you're saying. Is your case well structured? Is your case logically sound? Is it convincing intellectually? Is it meaningful?

Pathos: Emotionally Compelling

Pathos is to do with relationships. Are they in place? Are the feelings right between everybody? Did our presentation evoke the right feelings in the other person that will prompt them to take the desired actions? Is the relationship in a good state? Because if that's not right, it doesn't matter how compelling your *logos* is. You're going to run into resistance.

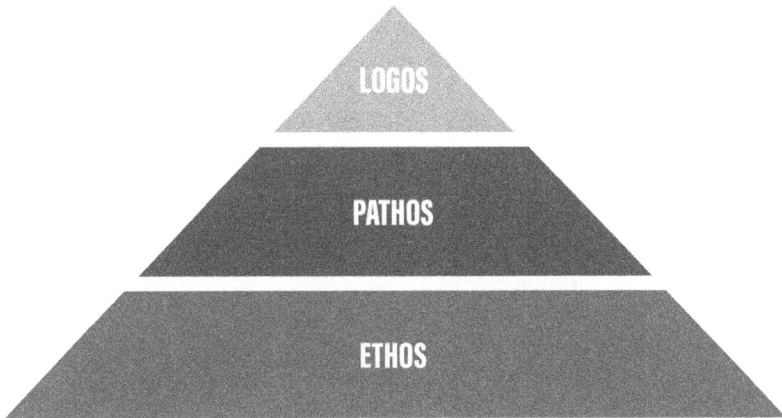

FIGURE 23.1: Aristotle's Pyramid of Influence

Ethos: Ethically Credible

Ethos is your own integrity. Are you aligned with your message? Are you the living example of its truth? Have you provided adequate proof? Because even if your relationship is right and your message is logically sound, if people don't feel your intent is right or sense that you're ethically suspect, then they'll still reject the message.

The Pyramid of Influence is used to graphically demonstrate the relative importance of each of these three elements of influence.

At the base, with the most volume and therefore argued by Aristotle as the most important, is *Ethos*. Are we credible? Are we worth listening to?

We've all had the experience of coming out of an all-day meeting only to find our inbox flooded with emails. Do we read with each email from the bottom up? Typically, we will selectively choose which emails to open and read based on two principles. Firstly, who sent it? There are people we're more inclined to prioritize. Secondly, what is in the subject line? If we're interested in what the message is about, we're far more likely to open that email first.

Emails from our manager are likely to get priority treatment. But if we take a group of random colleagues, are we selective in prioritizing emails from some colleagues over others? Most of us certainly are. We'll choose to answer emails from those we like, those we feel are credible, valuable, and who don't waste our time. We'll avoid opening emails from those who never really add value or those who always want something from us but never provide any value in return. Such decision-making represents our instinctual assessment of others' ethos and the degree of pathos that we feel toward them.

At the middle level, again with much more volume than rational persuasion (*Logos*) at the top, is *Pathos*. This is really about whether the topic the person is talking to me about creates an emotional connection. Do I care?

If someone from human resources is talking to us about compliance with the development planning process or something we have little interest in, we'll most likely switch off. If HR is talking about a new structure for bonuses, we may or may not switch off, depending on the extent to which we feel this will impact us. However, if the HR team starts talking about how to apply for grants to attend an overseas technical conference for a week to hone our expert skills, we may well sit up and take serious notice. Maybe we'll even note the deadline for submissions.

> *"It's as much about client experience as it is about a rational argument."*

Once we feel the person in front of us is worth listening to and is talking about something that interests us, we're prepared to listen to their rational argument. For many experts, we imagine the pyramid to be the other way up. Rational argument comes first.

Applying the Pyramid

A WHILE AGO, THE authors were coaching a group of accountants at a professional services firm that was trying to win a big contract. It was the day before the first important meeting. They had rehearsed over and over again their responses to each anticipated question. Their technical content was very sound. Compelling, in fact. They could demonstrate their technical expertise comprehensively. Any rational decision-making group would be persuaded.

However, the reason we were involved was because the firm kept missing out on winning contracts. Irritatingly, the partners told us, this was often to firms that they knew had less technical expertise and experience than they did.

We undertook a rehearsal, with us playing the clients. We asked a range of questions about their technical capability and credentials, all of which were answered with clinical efficiency.

Then we asked the partners about *how* they worked with clients, including which relationships seemed to work and how they adapted their services to clients with different operating styles, history and culture. Here, the answers were vague and delivered with a certain disdain, as if these aspects were of much less importance.

In our debrief, we asked the partners why this was so. Did they think about account management, adapting different styles to different types of companies, and so on? The answer was "no." They hadn't thought about this. Did they have client testimonials that highlighted how well client accounts were managed? No. Did they understand what their existing clients liked and perhaps disliked about the way the relationship worked? No, they had never thought to ask.

In effect, the partners focused on *logos* and assumed that this was the most important criterion a prospective client would use.

> *"Which of the nine influencing*
> *strategies do we tend to use most?"*

We had a long discussion about the importance of the client experience and introduced pathos and ethos into their pitch. It turned out their clients had plenty of positive things to say and many good stories to tell about how the organization's team went above and beyond their duty to serve their clients. One particular aspect came up repeatedly from existing clients: if the organization had ever made a mistake, which was rare but possible, the partner would be on the line to the client immediately to inform them. Clients didn't like the mistakes, but they loved the way the organization responded. These became important aspects of their new pitch to the prospective client.

And they did win the contract. The client's feedback was telling. "We were sure you were technically competent, but then so were the other parties we evaluated. But we felt like you were people we could work with, and you shared our values: be real, say it like it is, and quickly fix problems."

He was a clever fellow that Aristotle.

Influencing Strategies

HERE ARE NINE SPECIFIC influencing strategies that are commonly used, often unconsciously (see Figure 23.2).

Which ones do we tend to favor? Which do we most or least commonly encounter in our workplace? Which work best for us? Which aren't effective?

Rational Persuasion

The person uses logical arguments and factual evidence to persuade us that a proposal or request is viable and likely to achieve the task's objectives. This is a tactic frequently used by most experts.

Inspirational Appeal

The person makes a request or proposal that arouses enthusiasm by appealing to our values, ideals and aspirations or by increasing our confidence that we can do it. This is a tactic rarely used by experts. After all, why bother when we have a winning rational argument? It also requires us to have significant market context and an understanding of what might inspire those we're seeking to influence.

Consultation

The person seeks our participation in planning a strategy, activity or change. Our support and assistance are desired, or the person is willing to modify a proposal to deal with our concerns and suggestions. The very nature of the work experts do in complex environments means we probably spend a lot of time trying to do this, often with mixed results.

Ingratiation

The person seeks to get us in a good mood or to think favorably of him or her before asking us to do something for them. Most experts we've worked with dislike this approach. It comes across as inauthentic, so we also dismiss it as an influencing tactic when it's deployed against us.

Exchange

The person offers an exchange of favors, indicates a willingness to reciprocate at a later time, or promises to share the benefits if we help accomplish the task. Often, the fight for resources in larger organizations requires us to participate, usually with some disdain, in this type of horse-trading.

Capability: COLLABORATION
Influencing Strategies

FIGURE 23.2: The Nine Influencing Strategies

Personal Appeal

The person appeals to our feelings of loyalty and friendship toward them before asking us to do something. This is very much a relationship-based approach, and it can be very conscious (open and obvious) or subconscious. We don't realize we're using this tactic or being swayed by it.

Coalition

The person seeks the aid of others to persuade us to do something or uses the support of others as a reason for us to also agree.

Legitimizing

The person seeks to establish the legitimacy of a request by claiming the authority or right to make it or by verifying that it's consistent with organizational policies, rules, practices or traditions. A typical example of this is "Head Office told us we have to do it."

Pressure

The person uses demands, threats or persistent reminders to influence us to do what he or she wants. This is most typically top-down, coming from the senior leaders (or even our own leader). But it may also come from external suppliers or customers who have found some leverage to hold us to ransom.

Influencing Culture

IN OUR PROGRAMS, WE ask participants to rank these nine influencing strategies by how often they're used (rank 1 is most frequently used and rank 9 is least frequently used). Then we ask participants to choose which three of the nine strategies attract the most resistance, compliance, or commitment (buy-in). We ask participants to simply choose three and not worry about ranking them.

We encourage you to undertake this exercise using Figure 23.3.

Think about how emails, project meetings, meetings with your manager, or with your manager's manager play out when tasks are being allocated, deadlines are being set, or performance is being discussed. How do people in your organization try to influence you? In Figure 23.4, you can assess your own default influencing strategies. Which do you use most?

This list of nine influencing tactics was developed in 1990 by Cecilia Falbe and Gary Yukl, two American academics who undertook a very large study of influencing tactics in large organizations in the US. The results included responses from employees working overseas for the organizations surveyed, but for all intents and purposes, we should recognize the data they produced is very Western by nature.

> *"Most of us instinctively use one or two strategies…*
> *without assessing their effectiveness."*

Their very comprehensive study developed the most commonly used influencing tactics and then sought to understand the impact of these tactics on those subjected to them. Did the tactics gain commitment from employees (the highest level of effectiveness), or did they instead attract compliance (a reasonable outcome) or resistance (a problem outcome)?

Each of these influencing tactics potentially has a legitimate use in a specific context. It's very likely that until we've read these pages and completed the reflection exercise, we may not have contemplated that there are actually nine options to choose from when deciding on how to influence a stakeholder.

Capability: **COLLABORATION**
Influencing Strategies: my work?

Rational persuasion: The person uses logical arguments and factual evidence to persuade us that a proposal or request is viable and likely to result in the attainment of task objectives.
Inspirational appeal: The person makes a request or proposal that arouses enthusiasm by appealing to our values, ideals and aspirations or by increasing our confidence that we can do it.
Consultation: The person seeks our participation in planning a strategy, activity or change for which our support and assistance are desired, or the person is willing to modify a proposal to deal with your concerns and suggestions.
Ingratiation: The person seeks to get us in a good mood or to think favorably of him or her before asking us to do something for them.
Exchange: The person offers an exchange of favors, indicates a willingness to reciprocate at a later time, or promises to share the benefits if we help accomplish the task.
Personal appeal: The person appeals to our feelings of loyalty and friendship toward him or her before asking us to do something.
Coalition: The person seeks the aide of others to persuade us to do something, or uses the support of others as a reason for us to agree also.
Legitimizing: The person seeks to establish the legitimacy of a request by claiming the authority or right to make it or by verifying that it is consistent with organizational policies, rules, practices or traditions.
Pressure: The person uses demands, threats or persistent reminders to influence us to do what he or she wants.

1	**ATTRACTS MOST RESISTANCE**
2	1.
3	2. 3.
4	**ATTRACTS MOST COMPLIANCE**
5	1.
6	2. 3.
7	**ATTRACTS MOST COMMITMENT**
8	1.
9	2. 3.

FIGURE 23.3: Influencing Strategies—At My Organization?

Most of us instinctively rely on or utilize one or more of these methods without giving conscious consideration to whether it's the most appropriate or useful, whether it has proven effective or not in the past, or whether the person or situation one is seeking to influence is likely to be open, malleable and responsive to such an approach.

In our discussions with many groups of experts and leaders over the years, we've found something consistently comes up here: the ordering of which influencing tactic is most frequently used varies enormously by organization, country and culture. There is significant variance from the Yukl research in the first task, where we're asked to order the tactics by use from 1 to 9. But interestingly, we've discovered that regardless or organization, country or culture, there is a very high level of consistency with the way in which we react when subjected to the tactics, as well as which ones produce resistance, compliance and commitment.

Does Pressure Work?

IF WE'RE UNDER PRESSURE — feeling worried or anxious, for example— then we may pass that pressure on to others. Since the pressure prompts us to make the situation a priority, we may reasonably assume that if others simply realized how catastrophic or desperate a given situation is, they too would understand the significance and urgency of the situation and naturally mobilize to address the matter. Such a tactic may seem both reasonable and necessary.

Quite often, such a tactic is effective in mobilizing action, although just as often, it would appear that it triggers resistance.

Figure 23.4 shows the results from the Falbe and Yukl research.

Pressure rates highest on generating resistance when deployed as an influencing tactic. This shouldn't be that surprising, really. People typically have enough pressure of their own and, at a primal level, wouldn't thank us for loading them up with more.

"The results of the survey are
quite counterintuitive."

Even if they begrudgingly comply because they accept the stated threat as real and legitimate, they're unlikely to commit wholeheartedly. And they may, if it happens frequently enough, develop an impression that "here comes the person who always brings unwelcome pressure and hassle into our lives." In other words, that compliance may be secured at a high cost if it adversely impacts goodwill in the process.

Pressure can take many forms. It's highly unlikely that anyone nowadays will resort to actual threats. We sometimes encounter managers, experts or project managers with low self-awareness, empathy and self-control who believe that the only way, or the most effective way, to motivate somebody is to put the squeeze on them. But they are a dying breed.

> *"If we rely on this method, we're pounding people into submission but not making many friends."*

And, since most experts have no authority to make or carry out actual threats, putting the squeeze on others tends to take a more subtle form. For example, painting doomsday scenarios:

"If we don't get this data into the report, we'll lose our biggest client."

"If you don't update our infrastructure, we'll lose all our data."

"If you don't follow the process we've defined, we'll have delays, major cost-blow outs, and I'll have to escalate to senior leaders."

Sometimes the pressure tactic is merely hounding someone with persistent follow-ups until they give us what we're after. It might even take the form of a notification trigger that a particular email requesting something has now been read, and therefore the clock is ticking, thus forfeiting plausible deniability.

If we rely on this method of influence—hassling, escalating, and so on—we may succeed in pounding people into submission, but we're unlikely to make many friends. We'll fail to secure a higher level of commitment.

In other words, the people we're seeking to influence are likely to develop no intrinsic sense of the value of what's being asked of them. They'll just do the bare minimum to get us off their back. Pressure rarely seems to inspire true ownership or commitment, where people don't need chasing.

Pressure is often implied in some of the other methods of influence, such as coalition (peer pressure), legitimizing (borrowing authority from elsewhere), exchange or ingratiation ("I've done such and such for you, so now you should feel obliged to reciprocate").

Surely Rational Persuasion Works?

ANOTHER OF THE SURPRISING findings involves the relative effectiveness of rational persuasion. It ranks third in resistance, with nearly half of people surveyed saying they find themselves resisting when the tactic is used.

Capability: **COLLABORATION**

Influencing Strategies: What Works?

1 Rational Persuasion	**ATTRACTS MOST RESISTANCE**	
2 Pressure	**1.** Pressure	
3 Exchange	**2.** Coalition	
	3. Rational Persuasion	
4 Legitimizing	**ATTRACTS MOST COMPLIANCE**	
5 Personal Appeal	**1.** Legitimizing	
	2. Coalition	
6 Coalition	**3.** Pressure	
7 Ingratiation	**ATTRACTS MOST COMMITMENT**	
8 Consultation	**1.** Inspirational Appeal	
	2. Consultation	
9 Inspirational Appeal	**3.** Personal Appeal	

Source: Falbe, C.M. & Yukl, G

FIGURE 23.4: Influencing Strategies—What Works?

It's not particularly surprising that it's the most common strategy employed in a business context, especially amongst experts, as we might suppose that rationality would play a huge role in determining the best way forward. After all, most experts in various fields have spent many years in rationally oriented learning in a rationally based field. Our technical and professional discipline has favored a rational way of operating. In fact, anything not rationally sound might constitute incompetence, unprofessionalism, a regulatory anomaly or failure. It might be easy for an expert with this conditioning to assume that all decisions are reasonably informed by a sound argument and the logical weighing of pros and cons.

The purely rational argument seems to assume that all we're dealing with when engaging with a stakeholder is their neocortex (see the description of emotional intelligence inChapter 5), which will make a logical, fact-based decision based on the evidence.

This influencing strategy and way of thinking fails to recognize the role of the emotional or limbic brain, which all too often filters information based on emotional biases.

These include biases like "I like Jennifer more, so I'm not going to subject her proposal to the same burden of proof that I'm going to apply to Geoff's."

Or "Roger has me feeling boxed in. His rationale appears to be irrefutable, but I nonetheless feel uncomfortable about what making this decision will mean for the business. Perhaps he has pitched an idea which favors his preferred outcomes in some way. I think I'll ask him to do some more research."

> "The limbic brain filters information
> based on emotional biases."

Deploying Consultation and Inspiration

WE SHOULD, OF COURSE, always ensure our case is soundly reasoned. But we should not be surprised if this tactic alone doesn't guarantee stakeholder buy-in. We'll likely need to supplement a well-reasoned argument with additional tactics that predispose the other parties toward feeling emotionally compelled and inspired to accept it.

Do they get to feel consulted with? Have they had a chance to air their concerns, feel heard and understood? Have they had the opportunity to share their ideas about how things might look going forward?

Inspiration creates no resistance and only a small amount of compliance. Nine out of ten people in the research said it attracted commitment or buy-in. Consultation ranked second, with more than half of respondents saying it attracted commitment. In working with many groups of experts, these results have been broadly validated across various cultures, organizations and locations.

Of course, deploying consultation and inspiration as influencing tactics requires skill and is often more time-consuming. But at least we're actually making an effort to engage with the other person rather than trying to be hyper-rational.

Attempts to be inspiring can also be quite confronting. "Do I believe I can sell the stakeholders a compelling vision? Do I have insight into what they would find inspiring? What if I fail to provoke such inspiration? At least if I have just prepared a clinical, logical case based on flawless reasoning, if they reject it, then there's nothing lacking in me, only in their deficit of having sufficient smarts to recognize the flawless logic I've presented."

Is the ability to inspire purely a matter of charisma? Is it some kind of X-factor that some people are born with and others are not? What makes something inspiring?

> *"We're not trying to convince ourselves.*
> *We're trying to convince a stakeholder."*

Experts who are successful at deploying these tactics ask themselves these questions:

- Is there an engaging purpose or vision that I could credibly articulate?
- Does our solution or recommendation address a strongly felt need from the perspective of a given stakeholder?
- Does life get better for someone as a consequence of what I am seeking to gain their support for? Who and how specifically? How might these anticipated advantages be credibly conveyed and felt?
- Is there some kind of noble principle at stake?

Inspiration certainly takes thought and effort. We need to put ourselves in the shoes of others and consider how they'll then relate to what we're saying. "Is there anything emotionally compelling about what I am asking of them?" At the very least, we can explore the idea that they're more likely to positively engage with us if we give them a compelling upside rather than bludgeon them into submission using some of the other methods.

Master Experts think very hard about using the right influencing tactics for the right reasons with the right people. They'll take some time to consider what has worked in the past, which arguments and tactics have had the most impact, and which tactics, when used, have meant efforts to influence have crashed and burned? They'll remove themselves from the very limited context of thinking, *what would convince me?*

We're not trying to convince ourselves. We're trying to convince a stakeholder who has a whole different set of needs, motivations and responses to particular influencing tactics. Ingratiation doesn't, in our experience, work very well on most experts, except perhaps those who are heavily ego driven. But that doesn't mean it won't work on some of our stakeholders. As experts, we might be skeptical of colleagues trying to inspire us, but inspiration is quite likely to work very effectively on many other stakeholders.

In our programs, after asking participants to identify critical stakeholder relationships, we then explore those that are either broken or not working well. We ask them to consider what influencing tactics they've been deploying with that stakeholder. Very often, it's a combination of rational persuasion and, failing that, legitimizing. And if even that fails, pressure. These are exactly the tactics that the wider organization or senior leaders often use on us! So, it's no surprise that these tactics don't work or fail to achieve a deeper buy-in than mere compliance.

Most experts want to be more influential. The ability to master each of these influencing techniques and then deploy them for the right reasons at the right times with the right stakeholders will hugely enhance our influencing effectiveness.

Richard's Records

AT THE BEGINNING OF this chapter, we described a typical expert dilemma being faced by Richard: getting a proposal approved. Richard, you may remember, had recast the proposal several times, as requested, but there was still no decision forthcoming.

After exploring the concept of influencing strategies and becoming acquainted with a 2000-year-old philosopher, Richard re-examined his business case. He realized many things that could have been included but were not specifically asked for were missing. These included:

- His and his team's credentials in records management and their experience in improving and updating systems in the past, thus reducing the risk of project or implementation failure.
- Any mention of the time and effort wasted by the organization due to using the current system, as well as the consequences. For example, people didn't update records as often as they should. A whole new section about the risks of poor record-keeping and new compliance regulations was inserted.
- No "what's in it for the employees" argument. Richard had just stated the clinical functionality of the new system and the costs, but he had not connected the impact of this easier-to-use system on everyday employees. A further small section on this was added near the start of the proposal.
- No "how this will improve customer service" argument. This was quickly rectified and put right at the start of the proposal.
- And finally, he'd had a discussion with his manager about the delay and had been told that senior leaders didn't see the project as "urgent." It was only viewed as a "nice to have." In response to this, Richard included a short paragraph on the cost to the organization and associated risks of doing nothing.

Richard re-submitted his new business case. Just a few weeks later, he was asked to present it to senior leaders, where it quickly got approval.

TAKING ACTION

Growing Our Influencing Skills

IF INFLUENCING SKILLS IS a capability you want to grow, here are some high-level suggestions for actions to take:

▶ EXPLORE YOUR DEFAULT INFLUENCING TACTICS. HOW EFFECTIVE ARE THEY WITH KEY STAKEHOLDERS?

If we aren't deliberate in choosing which influencing tactics we use, we default back to the two or three we're most comfortable with. These are the tactics we use all the time. Questions we might like to ask ourselves:

- Which influencing tactics are my default setting(s)?
- Do I tend to rely heavily on rational persuasion, quickly followed by escalation to formal authorities (legitimizing) when my stakeholders fail to respond?
- Are there alternative strategies that I've never even considered using or testing?
- What tactics do I think might work best on particular stakeholders?
- What experiences do I have of others using tactics that seem to work on my major stakeholders?
- What experiences do I have of influencing tactics that definitely don't work and that I need to avoid using?
- Do I have a clear influencing strategy for my most important five or six stakeholders?

▶ IDENTIFY THE INFLUENCING STRATEGIES BEING USED BY KEY STAKEHOLDERS

Start reviewing how you're being influenced by those you work most closely with. Some questions we may wish to ask ourselves:

- Am I resisting or complying, or am I doing work for stakeholders because I have bought into the task and its impact?
- How do I respond to various tactics?
- How could I ask questions of stakeholders so they use different tactics on me? For example, if I wanted to be more inspired, I could ask questions about how tasks and initiatives connect to strategy, like why are we doing this, how does it affect the big picture? I could ask about the difference a particular task might make.
- Are there particular influencing tactics that generate a very negative response from me, and how might I convince my stakeholders to avoid using those tactics?
- How do I push back on pressure? (see Chapter 10, *The Art of Saying No*).

CHAPTER | 24 |

Next-Level Communication

Delivering knowledge and advice very effectively is a core component of being a Master Expert.

IN THIS CHAPTER, WE WILL EXPLORE:

- How a careful consideration of framing a message can make all the difference in great communication.
- How to use talking points to professionalize the impact of our communication skills.
- How to polish our presenting skills.

THE SECOND EXPERT ROLE in Collaboration is Communicator. This expert role deals with the extent to which experts have the ability to be highly professional and effective communicators, using storytelling, knowledge of our audience, advanced framing skills, and promotion of inclusive processes to inform those at all levels in the organization.

Nearly every chapter of this book is about our ability as experts to communicate well with others, whether in our own organization or beyond. This expert role looks closely at some of the tactics we need to master to do this effortlessly and brilliantly in almost every meeting and interaction with stakeholders. It's not possible to be a Master Expert without highly developed communication skills.

The behaviors at each level of Expertship for this expert role are described in Figure 24.1. At immature levels, experts communicate predominantly using technical language. This makes it difficult for non-technical groups to understand. They'll typically use rational and policy arguments when influencing technical groups, describing any proposed action's difficulties first and the positive outcomes second. They'll rarely consult with the wider organization, and if required to do so, they'll be uncomfortable with it. As a consequence, they rarely take the lead in technical presentations at this stage of their development.

Derailing experts in this expert role communicate almost exclusively using technical language or jargon. They'll favor rational persuasion as their primary influencing strategy, not considering others' perspectives, feelings or objectives. They'll be perceived by those who work with them as closed-minded and opinionated, either by talking far more than listening or by being non-communicative.

The reliance upon or overuse of technical language not only represents an indifference toward others' grasp of the concept but could even represent a power play—a way of asserting our own superior understanding over others.

Resorting to rational persuasion can similarly be intellectually combative, as if the expert is using their own supposed superior reasoning and command of information in their specialist field to bulldoze others into submission.

> *"The Master Expert inspires and consults, promoting inclusive processes in which everyone is heard."*

Thus, such derailing experts often fail to build the goodwill required to get others to work collaboratively with them.

The Master Expert, on the other hand, brings to life complex technical concepts and terms via compelling storytelling in language that has been adapted to the audience they're addressing. The Master Expert inspires and consults, promoting inclusive processes in which everyone is heard. Because of these skills and approaches, they'll often be an in-demand presenter across the organization due to their ability to combine technical and business concepts. They'll exhibit advanced listening skills.

As a result, other stakeholders find such Master Experts a joy to work with, and collaboration flows as a natural consequence.

In the next few pages, we'll explore the three tactics that master communicators use all the time to get their message across most effectively: framing, talking points, and presentations.

Capability: COLLABORATION

Expert Role: COMMUNICATOR

MASTER EXPERT

- Brings to life complex technical concepts/terms via compelling storytelling in accessible language.
- Inspires and consults, promoting inclusive processes whereby everyone is heard.
- In-demand presenter across the organization and externally due to their ability to combine technical and business concepts.
- Advanced listening skills.
- Embraces diversity of thought when discussing complex issues.
- Communicates assertively, balancing courage with consideration.

EXPERT

- Translates technical concepts/terms into practical and accessible language to increase others' comprehension.
- Employs a variety of influencing techniques to gain commitment to ideas and plans.
- Takes the lead in delivering effective presentations on behalf of function.
- Good listening skills.

SPECIALIST

- Communicates predominantly using technical language.
- Uses rational and policy arguments when influencing technical groups; rarely consults with the wider organization.
- Rarely takes the lead in technical presentations

- Communicates almost exclusively using technical language/jargon.
- Favors rational persuasion as primary influencing strategy.
- Comes across as closed-minded and opinionated, either by talking far more than listening or by being non-communicative.

DERAILING

FIGURE 24.1: Communicator Behaviors

The Art of Framing

NEXT TIME YOU VISIT an art gallery, ignore the actual artwork for a few minutes and study the frames. Picture framing is an important art in its own right. The more we look, the more we realize that the selected frame has the ability to bring out the best in an artwork or get in the way of us enjoying it. The same can be said for the "framing" we put around conversations.

Dipesh is a senior finance business partner allocated to service the IT department of his organization. He helps the chief information officer, Tamsin, and her executive team develop and manage their budgets and supplier arrangements, as well as shape their business cases for investment made to the organizational executive team.

Dipesh has just received a business case from Tamsin for purchasing and deploying a new cybersecurity application that will cost $400,000 in the first year. In Dipesh's professional view, the business case has large holes in it because it was *only* based on technical considerations. He knows that business cases are usually assessed by the finance team before they become recommendations to the senior executive team.

He needs to break this news to Tamsin, who is more senior in status but not as expert or experienced as he is when it comes to shaping business cases that get accepted. There are several ways in which Dipesh could frame his feedback to Tamsin.

"There are many different ways to frame a message."

Option 1. One option is to judge the work dispassionately and critically. This is the option many experts choose by default. "The business case is very poor, Tamsin. Costs beyond the first year aren't clear. There are no alternative applications canvassed and assessed, so how will the executive team know you've chosen the right one?

"Furthermore, the actual business case template has not been filled in properly. There are no obvious benefits outlined, and a return on investment has not been calculated. This proposal stands no chance of success whatsoever. Your team needs to rework it."

Option 2. A second option might be to frame the feedback as tactical concern. "Tamsin, thanks for the business case. I'm concerned that the executive team might not see the benefits as you and your team see them. I know they're obvious to anyone from a technical background, but I wonder whether the busy executive team will be able to join the dots.

"Would it be worth me spending some time with your team to really draw out the benefits and the organizational risks that are being addressed, and perhaps develop some simple return-on-investment measures? Also, I feel we'd save a lot of time if we showed the executive a cost request for several years, not just year one. It would mean we don't have to go back for more investment later."

Option 3. A third option might be to frame the feedback as strategic concern. "Tamsin, I have some technical concerns about the business case, but I'm happy to manage those with the relevant members of your team. However, I also have a strategic suggestion. I know how important this application is for the organization, but I worry that the executive team may just see this as an IT initiative or the IT team wanting yet more resources.

"Given that the application will significantly help decrease the risk of cyber intrusion, I wonder whether the business case would be best put forward by either the legal team or the risk team. It seems to me both of these teams have more to gain from the application, since they're the ones asking for it. I know this is more work and may delay the presentation for a month, but what do you think of us trying to partner with those other departments?"

In the first instance, Dipesh's framing positions him as a technical roadblock. His criticisms may be absolutely fair and accurate, but he isn't coming across as adding value. And of course, there is no offer of help or of partnering, which is what business partners are supposed to be doing. They aren't supposed to simply be policy police.

In the second framing option, Dipesh is making most of the same criticism but framing the argument as concern that the current document doesn't do the recommendation justice and he's worried it might be rejected. The work that the IT executive team needs to do on the business case is the same, but they'll approach it with a different motivation. And they'll approach this work armed with Dipesh's offer of help.

> *"Thoughtful framing helps experts make the message more palatable, interesting, and more likely to succeed."*

As we might expect from something at a strategic, Master Expert level, the third option is transformational. Dipesh takes a 70,000-foot view, linking it to the organization's strategy, risk tolerance and reputation. He's also suggesting that the recommendation shouldn't be framed as coming from IT at all, but from the department heads that have the most to gain from the application's implementation.

Dipesh's suggestion is actually pure genius. He'll get other executive members arguing for the recommendation, not IT. This is truly adding value at the highest level. With three departments clamoring for the proposal, its chance of success skyrockets. Plus, IT is seen as adding strategic business value.

This is the power of framing. We're wrapping the same message in a different colored paper and consequently making the recommendation more interesting, palatable, and eventually, of course, more likely to succeed. You can serve a cup of tea in a dirty and chipped enamel mug. Or you can serve it in a beautiful bone china cup. We all know which one people will choose to drink, and which one, for no logical reason, will taste better.

As experts, we have several framing choices. We can frame our messages and recommendations from:

- a technical perspective
- a stakeholder perspective
- an organizational perspective
- a customer perspective.

The more we consider the framing that will work for our removed stakeholders, the more likely our opinion and suggestions will get traction at a senior level. This means our ideas and proposals will have a greater chance of success. These removed stakeholders might be larger or more strategic groups, such as the organization as a whole or our organization's customers or clients.

We might also re-read the three framing options that faced Dipesh and consider the language he used in each.

In the first option, much of the language was *negative*: very poor … not clear … no alternative … not been filled in … no obvious benefits … not been calculated … no chance … rework. This is unlikely to inspire anyone. It's depressing.

In the third option Dipesh used positive language: happily … suggestion … important … significantly help … best … gain … partner.

Of course, there are some negative words used in the third option, but in the main, Dipesh is describing an extended opportunity to do better. We sense that the CIO will be much more likely to engage and think about the positive message than she would the negative one.

The Art of Talking Points

IN MOST COUNTRIES, EXECUTIVES and politicians use talking points extensively. Talking points are a core set of messages leaders utilize when communicating with stakeholders. If you work with public relations firms, they'll be talking you through key messages, the language they contain, and what messages to use with which audiences. If you have an unlimited budget, you can work with research firms to test messages on different audiences to see which resonate most.

Seasoned professionals have spent time building an outline of a series of messages that they keep coming back to. Perhaps the best example is during elections, where at the beginning of each week or stage of the campaign, you can see all the candidates suddenly talking about the same issues, all making the same points, and in some instances, using exactly the same language. They're using their talking points.

> *"There are many opportunities for experts to work with colleagues to develop talking points."*

Master Experts use this same technique to make sure everyone has got the message.

If Dipesh followed up his great framing with talking points for his internal clients (the CIO, the CRO, and perhaps the General Counsel), they might look like this:

- Implementation of this system will reduce the risk of us having customer data stolen.
- Implementation of this system will reduce our risk of being sued because we didn't take sufficient precautions to secure customer data.
- Implementation of this system will make it far less likely that we'll end up in the media as the victim of a hack.

By developing talking points, each of these executives can go forward and promote the proposal to various stakeholders using a consistent message, discussing the positive impact of the application, and explaining how it will mitigate many organizational risks.

There are many opportunities for experts to work with colleagues to develop talking points. A new HR system—what are the talking points? Implementing new remuneration arrangements—what are the talking points? A new strategic direction for this division—what are the talking points? A change in engineering protocols, legal terms, finance regulations… you name it. There's always a good case for making sure the experts know why we're pushing the initiative and for having talking points gathered to make sure everyone else is equally well informed.

The Art of Presentation

OUR EXPERIENCE OF SUBJECT matter experts when it comes to making presentations is varied:

- A high proportion of experts dislike public speaking and presenting to large groups, especially on a stage. In fact, many tell us it's their worst nightmare.
- Many presentations from top subject matter experts are difficult to understand because the experts go into too much detail, make assumptions about the audience's knowledge, or use the experience to prove how smart they are.
- Many experts have never really had any training on presentation skills, which is evident by the way they present.

Experts have to attain at least a basic proficiency in presentation skills Whether it's presenting a critical plan or recommendation to the executive team or helping a professional audience at an industry conference raise their professional standards, experts need to be able to present competently.

In the Expertship model, these skills are described as follows:

- MASTER EXPERT: Is actively sought out by a wide range of stakeholders to provide highly engaging, pragmatic and effective training and presentations.
- DERAILER: Presentations are unengaging and lead to few effective learning outcomes.

Ask any group of experts and they will quickly develop a comprehensive list of elements they've noticed about good versus poor presentations. They can do this even if they aren't proficient themselves (see Figure 24.2).

Like many things in this book, giving good presentations is all about process and structure, with some simple behaviors thrown in.

There are many worthy organizations around the world that provide high-quality courses on presentation skills, and these courses usually involve many opportunities to practice.

We would encourage every expert to attend such a program and prioritize polishing these skills.

"The big question for most audiences in the first two minutes is: Is this person worth listening to?"

What's the point of having great knowledge that will help teams and organizations succeed if you can't clearly present this knowledge in various situations?

As you can see from the list of best versus worst, there are some clear planning principles that successful presenters use. We've taken a brief look at some of these below, particularly in reference to the type of presentations experts often have to make. Like much of this book, they're simply advanced common sense.

BEST PRESENTATIONS	WORST PRESENTATIONS
· Gets the audience involved	· Monotone, flat language
· Natural/authentic	· Bad and long stories
· Clear about what the point is	· Insensitive
· Good storytelling	· Too aggressive in mannerisms
· Credible, connection, logic	· Too detailed
· Conversational style	· Too many tools and frameworks
· Simple visuals	· Too many slides
· A little humor	· Slides are too complex
· Good timing, not too short or long	· No eye contact
· Knows and engages the audience	· Repetitive
· Eye contact	· No engagement/involvement
· Emotional connection, inspiring	· Me, me, me, me – self-promoting
· Good preparation	· Poor choice of language, offensive
· Clear agenda and takeaways	· Boring
· Comfortable in own skin	· Reading notes
· Layman's language	· Mumbling
· Relevant	· Crackly voice
· Context	· Pacing
· Realistic	· Arrogant
· Smiles	
· Complex made simple	
· Projection of voice	
· Knows the subject	

FIGURE 24.2: Best Versus Worst Presentation Skills

1. Know your audience

Ask yourself "How much do the audience know about my topic?" and "How can I link my topic to their business goals or personal aspirations?" This will inform how much background information we should provide and will help us formulate an interesting presentation linked to specific business issues.

Outstanding presenters do plenty of pre-work to understand who is in the audience and why they're there. These presenters will assess the audience's current knowledge and figure out what most of the attendees are hoping to get out of the presentation. A great question to ask is NOT "what do I want to tell them?" but "What would they like to know?"

By way of a simple example, in days gone by, the authors ran conferences for senior technical leaders (leaders of experts). We quickly learned that the most valuable presentations were case studies. We also learned that after spending 20 minutes explaining to the audience what went right, attendees got the most value from listening to presenters telling the audience what went wrong. These are the mistakes we all want to avoid. Some presenters didn't want to admit that things had occasionally gone wrong, so we reframed the question (see earlier section!) to "If you had the chance again, what would you do differently?" This understanding of what made presentations very useful to the audience was part of these conferences' success and was why many attendees came back year after year.

As experts, demonstrating that we have reviewed what we did, worked out what didn't go as well as planned, and have planned for what we would do differently next time creates a very positive professional brand. Being prepared to share openly with our colleagues is generous and usually very much appreciated by our peers. It's not seen as a weakness that we made mistakes. It's seen as honest, engaging and humble. All attributes of a Master Expert.

2. Introducing yourself is very important

As Aristotle taught us in the previous chapter, the big question for most audiences in the first two minutes is "Is this person worth listening to?" This doesn't require us to say how great or important we are. It requires us to explain that we've had these experiences, and we intend to share them in an unvarnished way because we believe they may be valuable to you.

Many experts are far too shy or humble to big-note themselves, but this shouldn't get in the way of you explaining who you are. In our experience, most audiences are less interested in how fancy our job title is or how senior we are and more interested in what we've done and how we got to where we are. This also provides us with an opportunity to relax ourselves and the audience.

One of the authors, Alistair, uses a technique that he noticed was used by all of the most successful speakers at several conferences he attended. Each really great speaker started with a single slide that showed the stages of their career.

Alistair's own slide has these bullet points:
- Student Leader
- Corporate Executive
- Successful Entrepreneur
- Unsuccessful Entrepreneur
- Missionary

These are how this author sees the five stages of his working life. He talks about his slide for perhaps 30 seconds while the audience is reading it. When the audience gets to reading the fourth bullet point, there is usually a chuckle. The fourth bullet is very important. It's true. It's where Alistair says he learned the most, and it demonstrates something straight away: he's going to tell it like it is. The fifth bullet point leads into what he typically talks about, being a Missionary, which is being an advocate for Expertship.

There are no job titles, no organization names, and no timelines here. Just a very quick explanation of the experiences that have shaped his thinking. That is, where he's coming from.

This slide isn't incidental to the presentation. It's a critical component of the setup. These five bullet points are the result of maybe 20 revisions until it felt right.

3. Start strong

It's important to start strong, so our audience has confidence that we're going to use their time wisely. We need to clearly outline what we'll cover, what the desired outcome is, and why it's important. We can establish credibility by also giving a short story about our background or sharing an experience that relates to the presentation.

If you hear a presenter start by saying something like "I am going to share our three key lessons from this experience, and two of these were a real surprise to us...", then there is every likelihood that the audience will stick around because now they're curious. We'll need to actually have three lessons, and two of them will need to be counterintuitive.

4. Start with WHY, not WHAT

In the book, *Start with Why: How Great Leaders Inspire Everyone to Take Action*, Simon Sinek argues that to get others on board, we need to start with the goal or mission before describing the solution.

Starting with why a project was undertaken, or even why you agreed to speak at this meeting or conference, helps people understand where you're coming from and what you are/were hoping to achieve.

5. Keep it simple—remember the rule of three

Our audience will likely remember only three things from our presentation. We need to plan out what these will be and structure the main part of our presentation around them.

Remember that our presentation has three parts: the beginning, middle and end. To create an easy-to-digest message, use a similar technique to storytellers:

- Beginning: Discuss what is and what could be.

- Middle: Keep playing up the contrast between what is and what could be.
- End: Wrap up, end with a call to action, describe our vision of action and the impact these actions will have. Close positively and firmly, then thank the audience and accept questions and feedback graciously.

6. Practice

Fear of public speaking is often caused by low confidence and or a low level of control, which typically stem from inadequate preparation or minimal experience. To increase our confidence and sense of control, we need to rehearse our presentations and seek opportunities to present to others.

We can't possibly emphasize enough how valuable this is. We suggest experts do this first in environments where they feel relaxed, such as with people you know, and then later to a group where you feel less comfortable, such as people who are safe but who you don't know. Practicing our introduction until it becomes second nature will also help make that strong first impression, which will benefit us throughout our presentation. Early feedback from these groups enables us to polish and refine our messaging, change language, get rid of jargon, and sometimes re-order things, so it's easier for the audience to understand.

Most of us have seen very impressive TED talks. These 18-minute presentations have typically been practiced 20 or 30 times before the people at TED let a speaker anywhere near their stage.

7. Be aware of body language and remember to breathe

Taking a few deep, slow breaths to relax before we present is a good tip, and many presentation trainers advocate embracing a "power pose." Getting someone to video us presenting is a key part of preparation. Yes, we know, it's excruciating watching ourselves. But it teaches us a lot. One of the authors discovered he spent the entire presentation not looking at the audience but looking at his shoes. Not a very engaging technique. The other discovered his nervous energy had him racing back and forth across the stage, making the whole audience nervous and detracting from the message.

For many introverts, making eye contact with an audience is totally nerve-racking. Professional presentation trainers can help us with this, but a great tip we've learned is to choose a spot on the back wall, just above the audience's heads. This means you don't have to look at people, but it looks as if you are.

8. Accept silence

Pausing seems like ages when presenting. We do it sometimes because we've either lost our way or were so busy making point 2 that we've forgotten what point 3 is. But the audience won't think a pause is a mistake unless you draw attention to it. Think of pausing as a helpful way to put emphasis on what you say next. It's a moment for you to gather your thoughts and for your audience to reflect on what you've just said.

9. Smile

Smiling eases your nerves. It ensures you speak more clearly and confidently. It engages the audience. It can also demonstrate your passion for the topic.

10. Remember: The audience wants you to succeed!

The audience is on your side. When you're a presenter, you're in control. Eleanor Roosevelt once wisely said, "No one can intimidate me without my permission."

11. Know the room

Become familiar with the place where you will speak. Do this by arriving early, walking around the room, including the speaking area. Stand at the lectern, speak into the microphone, walk around the area where the audience will be seated, and then walk from where you will be seated to the place where you will be speaking. No surprises.

12. Don't apologize

Most of the time, our nervousness does not show at all. If we mention our nervousness, we'll only draw attention to it and, of course, make our audience nervous.

13. Concentrate on the message

Focus your attention away from yourself and concentrate on your message. You're there to help the audience, to simplify something, help them make an informed decision, prepare them for something, make their jobs easier, prevent them from making a mistake, or to share information that is useful to them. It's about them, not you.

14. Failing to prepare is preparing to fail

Prepare, prepare, prepare! We've all heard this saying many times. A colleague of ours has a mantra he works by. The night before a presentation, he imagines getting a call the next morning, the day he's supposed to present, telling him that the event is canceled or delayed. He asks himself: *am I disappointed or relieved?* He argues that if he's disappointed, then he knows he's properly prepared. If, on the other hand, he's relieved, he knows he hasn't prepared properly and often stays up all night until he knows he has.

TAKING ACTION

Growing Our Communicator Skills

IF THIS IS AN expert role in which you believe you could add greater value, here are some high-level suggestions for actions to take:

▶ PRACTICE YOUR PUBLIC SPEAKING—BOTH PLANNED AND IMPROMPTU

If we lack the confidence or ability to present our ideas fluently, cohesively, intelligibly and impactfully, then we're unlikely to influence effectively. Questions we might like to ask ourselves:

- Have I considered actively working on my presentation skills via a training program or speaking group (e.g., Toastmasters)?
- What opportunities do I have to practice my speaking?
- Where might I get good feedback about my current skill level?
- Are there interesting books I could read to hone my knowledge of effective techniques before practicing?

▶ DEVELOP A "PRINCIPLES" PRESENTATION

We all have our specialties. And we all have a series of mantras or principles we apply to the work we do. Some of these may be common practice, but many are tacit or informal concepts stored in our memory bank, pulled from our many experiences.

Our specialty is likely to be the thing we're most confident speaking about, and as a consequence, it's a great place to start when practicing our speaking skills. Questions we might like to ask ourselves:

- What is the unique knowledge and experience that I have, and how would I go about sharing it?
- What are my ten golden rules for what I do, and how did I come to shape these rules?
- Which audiences would be interested in me sharing my approach to my work with them? How would I make it valuable to them? What forums might be available for me to present to them?

- Am I motivated enough to want to become a proficient speaker and presenter? Am I willing to put myself out there and start speaking on my chosen topic of expertise?

▶ CONSIDER TAKING A COURSE ON PRESENTING

We've found that experts who have taken a presenting course build their overall communication confidence, not just their presenting confidence. These programs also help you curate content, and most training providers provide a safe place to make the mistakes so you can shine when you get back to your workplace.

CHAPTER | 25 |

The Expert as Diplomat

How can experts be the catalyst for facilitating win-win outcomes and defusing conflict?

IN THIS CHAPTER, WE WILL EXPLORE:

- How to master the skill of negotiation.
- What process can we use to build structure into managing conflict and bringing parties with different agendas together?
- How to use advanced questioning techniques in negotiation.

THE THIRD EXPERT ROLE in the collaboration impact area is that of **Diplomat**. This expert role deals with the ability to diplomatically negotiate and facilitate win-win outcomes across highly complex organizational and external teams and lead effectively without authority. This is often called political savvy.

The dictionary definition of a diplomat is "a person who can deal with others in a sensitive and tactful way."

This expert role flies in the face of the concept of "I'm the expert, so I'm right and everyone else is wrong." It requires experts to see the bigger picture. We need to combine our technical arguments with organizational objectives and desired customer outcomes, while at the same time taking into account everyone else's agenda, as well as our own.

This expert role requires a combination of many of the skills we've discussed throughout this book, but in particular, negotiation skills and the ability to deal with conflict. As opposed to avoiding conflict, the Master Expert deals with conflict head-on, taking a conflict-resolution, win-win perspective. The behaviors at each level of Expertship for this expert role are described in Figure 25.1.

An expert who is derailing in this role is a master of throwing oil onto the fire rather than trying to put the fire out. They'll adopt a combative style when negotiating for outcomes. They'll approach disputes from an entirely technical standpoint, focusing only on issues and priorities. They'll seek to get outcomes that are personally favorable rather than considering broader organizational needs.

With limited or non-existent diplomatic skills, a derailing expert is often committed to pursuing a professional or technical ideal, oblivious to whether they're forging alliances with other stakeholders or instead burning bridges. At their worst, experts displaying these derailing behaviors really don't care what others want or think.

At immature but not necessarily derailing levels, experts tend to be involved in making decisions but rarely take a leadership role. They see issues from a narrow and technical perspective but don't aggressively demand adherence to their views or agendas as they're unlikely to have yet developed the confidence to do so.

> *"Negotiation is a phrase that comes with some baggage."*

On the other hand, a Master Expert who has evolved diplomatic skills will skillfully negotiate and facilitate win-win outcomes when faced with competing priorities, interests or deadlines. They'll focus on organizational outcomes. They'll become an expert at leading without authority, assisting their teams with making good decisions that accelerate results and foster great teamwork. They'll demonstrate political savvy to get things done.

The Art of Negotiation

AS DISCUSSED IN CHAPTER 12, *Expert Stakeholder Strategy*, a Master Expert carefully cultivates mutually rewarding relationships with a vast array of stakeholders. Engaging and maintaining relationships with such stakeholders requires us to understand and address their needs. However, within such complex structures as the modern organization, invariably, there will be times when the various stakeholders' needs and interests are in inherent conflict with each other.

Capability: COLLABORATION

Expert Role: DIPLOMAT

MASTER EXPERT

- Diplomatically negotiates and facilitates win-win outcomes when faced with competing priorities or deadlines.
- Focuses on organizational outcomes.
- Expert at leading without authority, helping teams to make good decisions that accelerate results and foster great teamwork.

EXPERT

- Uses formal decision-making techniques to arrive at good decisions about priorities and solutions that balance the needs of stakeholders.
- Tends to focus on technical outcomes.
- Takes on a leadership role when required, comfortable leading with or without authority.

SPECIALIST

- Is involved in making decisions but rarely takes a leadership role.
- Sees issues from a narrow and technical perspective

- Adopts a combative style when negotiating for outcomes.
- Takes an entirely technical view of issues and priorities.
- Seeks to get outcomes that are personally favorable rather than considering broader organizational needs.

DERAILING

FIGURE 25.1: Diplomat Expert Behaviors

There might be times when a stakeholder's view about how to approach solving a particular problem differs from ours. Should we assert our expertise and bulldoze them into submission at the risk of burning the relationship? Or should we negotiate and collaborate?

There might be times when one stakeholder group wants us to implement something in a particular timeframe, but we have prior commitments to another stakeholder group. Should we choose purely what suits us based on tribal loyalties? Should we just defer the less powerful of the two stakeholder groups in order to earn the favor of the more powerful group? Or should we seek to negotiate the best possible outcomes with all parties and the overall business in mind?

So far, we've just spoken about the internal conflicts that can arise among stakeholders who are, at least theoretically, all aligned to the same organizational purpose and strategy. Once we get into the complex world of managing relationships with stakeholders in supplier and client organizations, the ability to act diplomatically to resolve conflicts comes into even sharper relief. In these instances, we're attempting to synthesize a good outcome between parties that may have quite different agendas, needs and interests. Perhaps our organization wants to buy the service for the least amount of money, while the supplier wants to charge us as high a figure as they think they can get away with. These are complex negotiations.

"Compromise is an easy way to make a bad decision."

The reality is that we actually have to consider what strategies and goals we want to achieve as we begin to manage conflict and try to find solutions. We have several options (see Figure 25.2). The grid we have included is an adaptation and synthesis of several models of conflict resolution. We would encourage readers to look at the work of Kenneth Thomas and Ralph Kilmann on conflict and conflict modes.

When faced with a difference of opinion or a conflict of interest, we can respond in any number of ways, as the chart shows. Some of these approaches are ineffective in the long term.

- **Win-Lose:** This is where we view the situation as inherently adversarial and strive to win the argument, thus defeating our opponent and asserting the superiority of our own point of view and needs over theirs.
- **Lose-Lose:** This is where we lack the confidence or courage to represent our own ideas or challenge others' constructively. We might avoid the uncomfortable conversation, thus not meeting our own

needs, whilst continuing to prevent others from getting their needs met.

- **Lose-Win:** This is where we might be too eager for others' approval, so we acquiesce or capitulate to the other party's needs, point of view or interests, abandoning our own.

These common strategies don't lead to enduring or effective outcomes. If we push our own point of view with our stakeholders, even if we happen to have a more informed opinion, we'll end up sacrificing goodwill. If we always give ground to others, then we're not representing our expertise adequately. And although we might think that we're earning others' favor, in reality, we're losing their respect. And, of course, lose-lose behaviors meet nobody's needs or interests.

So, typically, the above strategies are sub-optimal when the goal is to pursue long-term, mutual benefit. Although, arguably, giving ground (lose-win) or pushing our own point of view (win-lose) might occasionally have merit if there's no expectation of or requirement for achieving long-term mutually satisfying outcomes.

Capability: **COLLABORATION**

The Negotiation Matrix

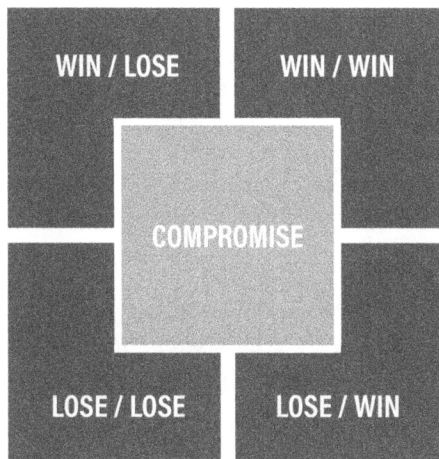

FIGURE 25.2: The Negotiation Matrix

Another common strategy that many confuse with win-win is **compromise**. You get a bit of what you want but give up a bit to do so, and I also get a bit of what I want but give up a bit in return. People tend to think of compromise as a form of win-win because there is, on the surface at least, a sense of commitment to fairness as no one should prosper or lose entirely at the expense of another. But compromise isn't fully satisfying to either party, and it rarely delivers the optimal outcome organizationally. Compromise is sometimes the easiest way to make a bad decision. This is why, on our grid, compromise is positioned nearer to lose-lose than win-win.

Rather than implementing either the expert's or the stakeholder's approach, there's a compromise whereby some combination of approaches is executed. Rather than choosing which needs to prioritize and having all stakeholders agree on which needs take precedence over others, there's a risk of everybody feeling frustrated because, in attempting to be fair, no one's preferred deadlines, for example, were delivered to.

Compromise has its place. Sometimes it's the only fair approach. But all too often, it's the default option rather than a mature exploration of a courageous and considerate negotiation toward outcomes that all stakeholders accept as optimal, i.e., win-win. It's sometimes a strategy to avoid anticipated conflict. We propose an early settlement with some wins and losses for both parties so as to avoid what might otherwise be drawn-out wrangling in an adversarial win-lose spirit by both parties.

The term *negotiation* also has some baggage. We often associate it with the cunning and lengthy thrashing out of terms of business between two contracting parties. Typically, both parties seek the best possible deal for their interest group and hope to have to sacrifice the least.

There's typically all kinds of game playing, with inflated requirements at first on the presumption that in the inevitable trade-off toward the end of the negotiation, one can end up settling on an outcome closer to one's true starting position than might have otherwise been accomplished. When exploring negotiation as Master Experts, this is not the style of negotiation we are referring to.

> *"Negotiate in a spirit of collaboration with all stakeholders' success in mind."*

Win-win negotiation, as the term implies, involves a deep commitment on the part of the negotiator to each party's legitimate needs and interests. This includes both the stakeholders with whom the Master Expert is negotiating, as well as those who aren't present in the negotiation, such as organizational shareholders or consumers.

The Master Expert negotiates in a spirit of collaboration with all stakeholders' success in mind. "It's counter-productive if I win the argument at this other person's expense, even if that's merely wounded pride" or "What's the point of our two departments agreeing on a course of action if it's suboptimal for consumers and will, as a result, negatively impact profitable growth?"

The win-win negotiation starts out as a mindset. It's a deep concern that all stakeholders have their needs met as much as possible and have their points of view heard, acknowledged and considered.

It takes into account empathy for others' situations. Others' views, needs and interests may not always be well articulated, so it takes humility, as well as a willingness to listen and learn. "I may not have the complete picture about what constitutes optimal long-term outcomes. Let's see where my valued stakeholders, including the other party in the negotiation, stand." And it also takes resilience and courage to represent one's own needs, interests and perspectives appropriately.

But, beyond these essential mindsets, there is a process of win-win negotiation to follow. These steps are based on Ury and Fisher's *Getting to Yes* and *The Seven Habits of Highly Effective People* by Stephen Covey (see Figure 25.3).

1. Understand

Try to understand the desired outcomes of the other stakeholders. As experts, we sometimes fail to negotiate effectively because we start out by describing the outcomes that we want or expressing the opinion that we hold. Others assume, whether rightly or wrongly, that we're trying to win an argument. They think that if they agree with us, they'll lessen the likelihood of their own needs being met.

> *"We let them know explicitly that win-win is our intention."*

Seeking to understand their point of view, needs or interests first assures them that we're committed to the other party "winning." We initially put aside our own convictions, points of view, needs and concerns—not forever, just until the other party feels heard and that their needs are understood.

- "What's driving that deadline? What do you worry might happen if it was missed?"
- "What is it that's important to you about doing things that way?"
- "What does success look like from your perspective?"

Capability: **COLLABORATION**

Negotiation: Win/Win **AGREEMENT FRAMEWORK**

DESIRED RESULTS	· What deliverables will each party commit to? · What are the standards or measures of success? · What outcomes are both parties committed to?
GUIDELINES	· What parameters will both parties agree to abide by? · What protocols exist if there is any variance from the target deliverables? · How much of a variance is acceptable?
RESOURCES	· What resources will each party need reasonable access to in order to successfully discharge its responsibilities?
ACCOUNTABILITIES	· What happens when and how should progress (or performance to target) be reviewed?
CONSEQUENCES	· What happens in the event of success? Over achievement? Underachievement? · What corrective measures may be appropriate if required? When and how do they kick in?

FIGURE 25.3: The Win-Win Agreement Framework

Consider the needs and interests of stakeholders who aren't present to participate in our negotiation and what reliable information sources we have that describe them.

Our purpose in learning about others' needs and interests first is twofold. If we're truly committed to win-win, then we have to learn of all our stakeholders' success criteria. And also, it's psychological. By finding out directly from them what they consider a win, we're dissolving any resistance. They'll see that we're as committed to fighting their corner as we're our own.

We let them know explicitly that this is our intention. That we're seeking win-win outcomes that satisfy everybody's needs as much as possible. We might find it helpful to summarize, with a focus on accuracy and precision, what we've heard them outline as their desired outcomes.

2. State Your Position

Once we understand others' positions and they feel understood, we can describe our own perspective, needs and interests. We can feel free to explain our rationale. It's important for us to remember to both do justice to what we have to say and what we need while also not coming across as trying to win the argument. Our goal is to articulate our needs or views without triggering defensiveness. Using subjective language makes it clear that we're simply expressing our own view, not one that we believe they should already be signed up to:

- "My perspective is..."
- "Our team's needs are..."
- "The rationale for our thinking is..."
- "The outcomes that we're accountable for are..."

Enduring, healthy relationships are founded on the mutual satisfaction of win-win. It's important that both sides "win," i.e., have their needs met. It's our responsibility to ensure that our voice, perspectives and needs are heard and acknowledged. Our case needs to be sufficiently articulated.

3. Work Together

Invite the other party or parties to work with you toward identifying and adopting win-win outcomes.

Steps 1 and 2 are about ensuring that the legitimacy of all parties' needs have been articulated and acknowledged. Now it's time to collaboratively explore ways in which all parties' needs and concerns can be addressed. Of course, that's not always possible. Sometimes it's an either/or situation, so settling on an appropriate compromise in the spirit of win-win is the best way forward. We treat this like the Options phase of an I-GRROW conversation (see Chapter 48).

- "Let's brainstorm all of the possible ways we could move forward before we decide together which courses of action to pursue..."
- Then... "What do you like/dislike about Option 1, Option 2,...?"
- "Are there any circumstances under which Option 1 might be acceptable to you?"

The idea is to maintain an attitude of trying to find ways forward that meet all parties' needs, perspectives and interests. Even if it's not possible to always tick every box, your stakeholders will deeply appreciate the spirit in which you collaborate with them.

TAKING ACTION

Growing Our Diplomat Skills

IF THIS IS AN expert role in which you believe you could add greater value, here are some high-level suggestions for actions to take:

▶ SET UP SERVICE-LEVEL AGREEMENTS

- In the absence of aligned expectations between us and stakeholders, it's easy for trust to become strained as one or both parties' needs aren't adequately addressed. Questions we might like to ask ourselves:
- Is it possible to develop a mutually beneficial service-level agreement (SLA) with a key stakeholder (or team of stakeholders) in order to ensure that each other's needs are better understood, communicated and met?
- How can I explain that I'd like to ensure that expectations and needs are clearly understood on both sides in order to support mutual benefit? What would be their likely reaction?
- A helpful framework might be the win-win agreement framework (See Figure 25.3).
- How do I ensure that conversations aren't carried out in a litigious fashion? How do I ensure the goal is to develop a mutually rewarding relationship and not set up walls or the basis for future recriminations?
- How would I, from the outset, clarify expectations and deliver accordingly, creating a great basis for excellent stakeholder relationships?

▶ DON'T TAKE CONFLICT PERSONALLY

Conflicts arise naturally. If we don't proactively deal with them, they often fester, wearing away at stakeholders' goodwill and disrupting collaboration. Questions we might like to ask ourselves:

- Am I experiencing tension with another team or key individuals?
- Have I undertaken a quick "needs/situation analysis" by asking what kind of conflict is this? Is it a clash or misalignment of interests? Is

it someone's unmet needs? Is it a clash of ideologies and beliefs? Is it because we all have different styles, standards or values?

- How do I use any emerging insights to help me facilitate working conjointly for mutual success?

▶ CONSCIOUSLY INVEST IN YOUR EMOTIONAL BANK ACCOUNT

The emotional bank account is a metaphor developed by Dr. Stephen Covey. It likens every relationship we have to a bank account in which our every interaction either builds a balance of increasing trust (deposits) or reduces it (withdrawal). If we aren't actively taking the initiative to foster high trust relationships, then the general trend is one of entropy—a gradual deterioration in the natural levels of trust. In extreme cases, where, for instance, one or both parties' needs aren't being addressed, there can even be resentment or antipathy, which undermines collaboration. Questions we might like to ask ourselves:

- Do I have specific stakeholder relationships that I feel need to be improved?
- How would I objectively assess the historical balances (both ways) of deposits and withdrawals into the emotional bank account? (See Figure 25.4).
- Can I identify some deposits (trust-building activities) that I can make and withdrawals (trust-eroding activities) I can reduce, eliminate or at least offset? See Figure 25.4 for examples.

It's likely that, if a particular relationship isn't working well at present, we will have some grievances with the other party's historical conduct. This framework invites us to take the initiative to improve the relationship. That doesn't mean that we entirely overlook our own needs. But it means that we start making deposits into our emotional bank account with the other party, even if they don't seem initially deserving or responsive.

Capability: **COLLABORATION**

The Emotional Bank Account

Examples of deposits and withdrawals

DEPOSITS	WITHDRAWALS
· Taking the time to listen to people, attending to – or at least sensitivity toward – their needs	· Interrupting, not listening, judging, being callous toward their needs, sparing them no time
· Making and keeping commitments, accepting responsibility, taking ownership and initiative	· Resisting making commitments, breaking commitments, excuses, blaming, an unwillingness to accept responsibility/ownership
· Eliciting, clarifying, and honoring expectations	· Making assumptions, violating expectations
· Common courtesies, thoughtfulness, sincere apologies	· Rudeness, indifference, oversight.
· Being trustworthy, honorable, reliable, loyal to the absent, honest, authentic, candid, courageous	· Being untrustworthy, dishonest, unreliable, gossipy, fake, cowardly

Adapted from Stephen Covey, *7 Habits of Effective People*

FIGURE 25.4: The Emotional Bank Account

PART | 03 |

THE VALUE DOMAIN

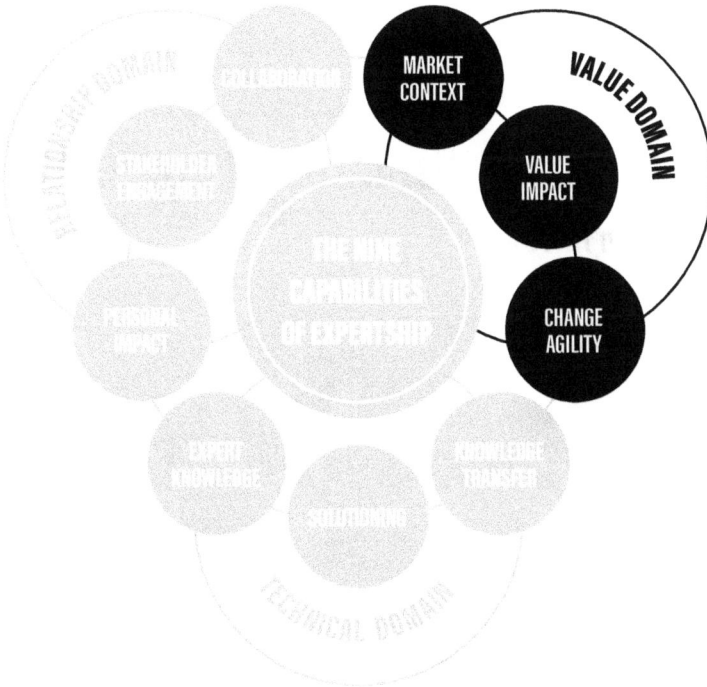

"Priority is a function of context."

Stephen R. Covey

MASTERING
MARKET CONTEXT

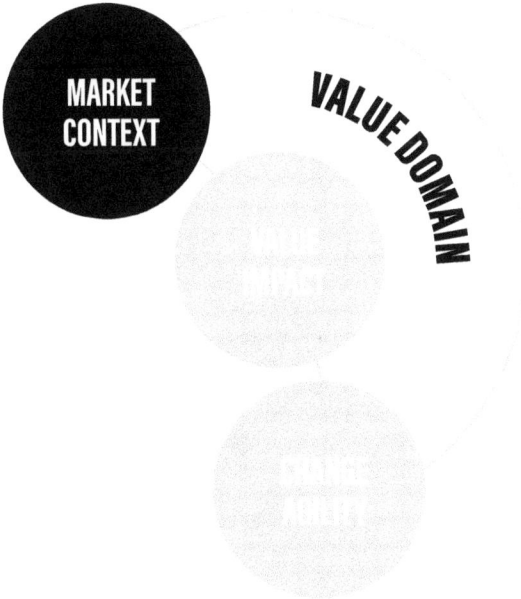

MARKET CONTEXT

VALUE DOMAIN

The Master Expert acquires, retains, refreshes and leverages contextual organizational, competitive and customer knowledge effectively.

CHAPTER | 26 |

Why Market Context Matters So Much

What is our purpose and desired impact? How do we quantifiably contribute to our organization successfully executing its strategy?

IN THIS CHAPTER, WE WILL EXPLORE:

- Why is market context a vital contributor to being a Master Expert?
- Why are experts often insufficiently informed about market context? How informed do we need to be?
- How do we quickly and efficiently get up to speed on market context and change the way we're perceived across the organization?

THE MODERN ORGANIZATION IS a complex beast. It contains subject matter experts because there are many areas of specialty relevant to the organization's functioning. Experts are hired because of their technical knowledge and experience, but they can only operate at a Master Expert level if they have developed a holistic understanding of how the entire organization functions and the external environment in which it operates.

The Master Expert needs this *market context* in order to see the role their expertise plays in creating value. Without this broader context, we're likely to be operating in a technical bubble, disconnected from the rest of the organization.

The benefits of mastering market context are very significant. Think of it as having a foot in both camps. On the one hand, we're technically very capable and can communicate and align easily with our technical colleagues, both within our organization and beyond it. On the other hand, we're comfortable working closely with the wider organization as we understand their context, what they're trying to achieve, and how their work gets measured. When and where required, we can speak their language. We can empathize with their challenges, and we have a reasonable knowledge of what they're talking and worrying about. They see us as being equally committed to the same organizational successes that they're striving to achieve rather than being indifferent or oblivious boffins or technocrats.

Experts who are able to traverse the technical and wider organizational world with ease are in high demand, are well respected, and get the best gigs. They get invited to the right meetings, and their views are listened to with more intensity.

This last point is particularly interesting. Master Experts' technical views, which might be the same as ours, are listened to more. Why? It's not because their technical views are necessarily more accurate or insightful than ours, but because they position their technical opinions and recommendations within the market context of the organization. They help people realize how important the technical contributions are for the organization as a whole. None of this is news to most readers. The big question is: if we don't currently feel comfortable and confident talking about our organization's market context, how do we master this capability?

> *"Experts who are able to traverse the technical and wider organizational world with ease are in high demand."*

Experts often haven't taken the time to complement their technical brilliance with a good working knowledge of the broader organization. Many experts we've worked with struggle to accurately answer some of even the most basic questions about their organization (*organizational knowledge*) and look at us blankly when asked about the external environment in which the organization operates (*competitive knowledge* and *customer knowledge*).

In our programs, for example, we ask experts why potential customers of their organization choose to buy the products and services from rivals. If you can't answer this question with at least some data and insight, you're certainly not operating at Master Expert level. This question raises another: how do you know you're creating new competitive value if you don't know what you're competing against? Answer: you don't, and it's very likely you can't.

One of the authors was asked by a client to address the *"enabling services"* staff at an annual get-together. There were more than 200 people in the room, including legal, finance, risk, HR, facilities, business planning and so on. Collectively, nowadays, most of us call these *"shared services"* functions.

The vast majority of the people in that room would qualify as "experts" under the definition we use in this book. Highly technical, highly capable backroom value-adders. The first speaker was extremely upbeat as they had had a very successful year. There were new systems put in place, on time, on budget. Major renovations to a more collaboratively designed workplace? Completed, occupied, and embraced by the employees. Revitalized talent strategy? Done. Streamlined risk and legal processes? Completed. It was a to-do list that most shared services teams would be (and should be) envious and proud of, and with good reason. But there is one issue.

Figure 26.1 presents the typical environment in which most experts operate within their organizations. The central circles describe the internal environment for most experts. It includes themselves, their manager, their technical cohort, and their immediate and removed stakeholders. These last two being a typical expert's internal customers. Immediate stakeholders are those from whom experts take a brief or those upon whose services the expert immediately depends. Removed stakeholders are the eventual recipients of the expert's work. They're usually out in the business and often much closer to the customers, are "suppliers" further upstream, or are other senior influencers in the ecosystem. The outer ring describes the external environment: competitors, customers, and industry trends.

> *"Can you put your hand on your heart and tell us your work has delivered competitive value?"*

Our talk with the shared services group about their achievements during the year was designed to be a little more challenging. "Did the streamlining of systems you carried out in the risk and legal processes," we asked the risk and legal team, "mean that colleagues who needed decisions from you got better answers faster than their counterparts in your rival competitive organizations?" There were a few feisty comments from the lawyers present about the decisions being made much faster, but they couldn't tell us conclusively that these processes were faster than those enjoyed by rival firms.

"Are the systems you put in place," we asked of the IT department, "better than those in place at your two main competitive rivals? Do these systems make it easier for internal stakeholders to work with your customers than the corresponding systems in competitor organizations?"

They weren't sure, they told us. This means they didn't know. It also means they had never really thought to ask.

We asked the facilities people whether the newly designed office space created an environment that allowed more collaboration between departments than was happening in rival companies? We took their silence to mean they didn't know.

"Can you promise us," we asked the HR team, "that top talent in this organization is looked after far better than top talent in competitive, rival companies?" There were some honest shakes of the head from the HR team.

You may think we were perhaps being a little unfair to the assembled group, who had done a fine job completing important projects that were no doubt difficult and complicated and had required a huge effort. But the simple message was that none of the 200 people in the room could put their hand on their heart and tell us they had delivered *competitive value*. That is, made work easier for their staff to do than their competitors, enabling them to serve their customers faster or better than their competitors.

The targets and projects had been set looking at their *internal* context, not taking into account both the *internal* and the *external* environment. This is remarkably typical when it comes to experts (and, unfortunately, shared services).

This story highlights one of the common ways experts are marginalized: through their lack of perceived knowledge or concern about commercial aspects of the organization. Experts are often aloof, disconnected, oblivious to normal organizational metrics, such as profits, losses, acceptable margins, customer wins and losses. Our performance focus is more likely to be measured by technical metrics associated with our technical fields. Consequently, people on the business side of the operation don't take technical experts seriously. After all, we don't appear to be interested in or committed to the wider purpose of the entire business. Such beliefs are occasionally fueled by comments from experts themselves, who at times can be dismissive of organizational metrics because they don't see themselves as impacting, or able to impact, these metrics. *Let others worry about the bottom line,* many experts think. They typically observe "I'm not responsible for them. My role is to concentrate on my specific domain, which also happens to be a lot more interesting to me."

Capability: **STAKEHOLDER ENGAGEMENT**
The Expert Operating Environment

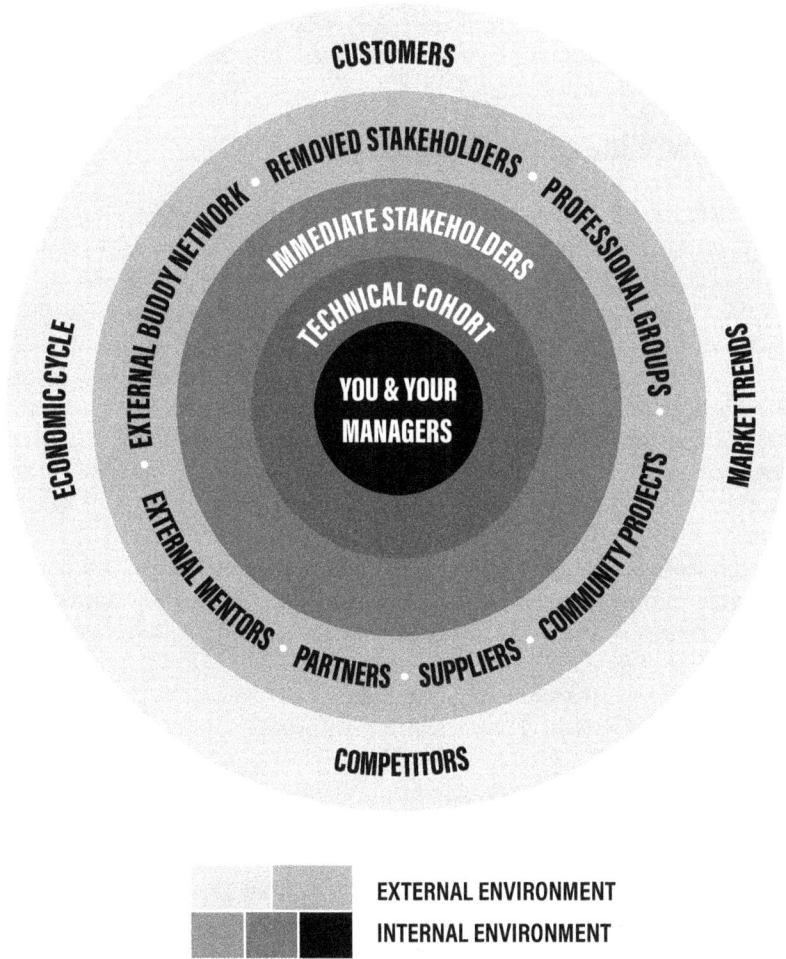

CUSTOMERS

REMOVED STAKEHOLDERS

EXTERNAL BUDDY NETWORK

IMMEDIATE STAKEHOLDERS

PROFESSIONAL GROUPS

TECHNICAL COHORT

YOU & YOUR MANAGERS

ECONOMIC CYCLE

MARKET TRENDS

EXTERNAL MENTORS

COMMUNITY PROJECTS

PARTNERS • SUPPLIERS

COMPETITORS

EXTERNAL ENVIRONMENT
INTERNAL ENVIRONMENT

FIGURE 26.1: Organizational Navigator Behaviors

We work with a large number of experts, and this is a very common blind spot. We call this *observer syndrome*, where the expert exudes a condescending detachment from those in the organization who do what the expert considers the dirtier, more commercial work. It amounts to "sitting on the sidelines" and not being prepared to "roll their sleeves up" or be part of the solution rather than a detached, judgmental observer. This is a classic derailing, negative brand behavior.

The Downside of Disengagement

THE IMPACT OF NOT being confident and informed about the wider organizational and market context is far-reaching. It has a negative impact on how experts and their contributions are perceived by the organization.

The disengagement becomes self-fulfilling. Having declared or at least shown no interest in wider organizational issues, experts are often simply left out of the communication loop when it comes to discussions about things like the organization's key performance metrics and strategy statements. There's an assumption on behalf of the rest of the organization that experts simply aren't interested. This, in its own right, means experts have less access to the critical information and discussions that they need in order to add value.

This leads to experts being less able to frame their recommendations and proposals in the context of precisely how they'll benefit the organization or in such a way that others can readily appreciate the pragmatic value of what they're putting forward.

We're less exposed to the language of the wider organization, so we retreat into our own technical language, which makes getting our point across even harder. It's a vicious circle.

Because experts don't typically fit neatly into the operationally focused structures of many organizations, we often find ourselves in what is termed a *support function*, such as, for example, legal, HR, finance, IT. This often means that our work is routinely seen as a *cost* to be subsidized by others (those generating revenue), with no clear connection made to how our activities contribute to the organization's operational performance.

In fact, most experts we've worked with, even when pressed, struggle to articulate a credible and compelling connection between their daily work and how the organization executes its strategy.

Even fewer experts are able to articulate the difference their daily work makes to increasing the *competitive advantage* of the organization against rivals, or in the case of government organizations, the compelling value improvements the organization is creating for the community.

Disappointingly, many experts are also unable to comprehensively list the organizations' main competitors or explain the competitive positions, strengths and vulnerabilities of each organization in relation to one another. This suggests a huge deficit in market context knowledge. Three years' worth of survey data from the experts we've worked with backs up this point, as market context is the Expertship capability most experts score lowest on.

> *"It's vital that experts couch ideas in terms of how they specifically impact the organization, its strategy, and it's customers."*

All of these aspects have consequences that reduce the status, effectiveness, and scope of the work of the expert.

The lack of external context relegates the expert to being an internally focused, lower-level functionary who appears to be (and, let's face it, often actually is) disconnected from the real competitive world that most of their colleagues face every day. Most of our major stakeholders are experiencing these pressures. We can't afford to be unaware of them if we want to have a significant positive impact or even be taken seriously.

Such stakeholders may not see or appreciate the connection between the work that the expert does and real-world outcomes, so as experts, it's vital that we learn how to couch our ideas in terms of how they specifically impact the organization, its strategy, and its customers. That way, our colleagues will recognize the significance. Otherwise, our ideas, particularly when they're couched in technical language that others find inaccessible, unintelligible or abstract, will naturally be seen as somewhat irrelevant.

A Lack of Context

ROGER, ONE OF THE senior risk experts in the corporate finance team, was delighted when the chief risk officer (CRO), who is his manager, called him into his office a day before going on annual leave.

"We have an executive meeting coming up next week and we've been asked to give an hour's presentation aimed at getting the executive team to better understand risk. What it is, why it matters, what best practice risk culture looks like, how it's a key part of being competitive, and how our risk profile and systems compare to our competitors."

"It's what we've been talking about trying to get them to engage with for months. I'm on leave, but I've been trying to get a discussion about risk on the agenda, as you know, and Margaret, the CEO, has finally agreed, so you'll have to prepare it and present it."

Roger had been lobbying to get more exposure to the organization's executive level, and here was his chance. He had lots of questions for the

CRO, but the CRO was heading out to another meeting, and that was the last he saw of him.

Roger had been working in risk for 15 years, and he wondered how he could cover such a big topic in such a small amount of time.

Since he joined the organization two years previously, he'd seen firsthand lots of poor decisions being made due to a lack of a properly conducted risk audit. One highly visible example was the acquisition of an organization called AKZ Metrics. Another was the calamitous outsourcing of customer complaints handling. Roger and the CRO had been working hard to try and get some traction on, and compliance with, a proper risk culture in the organization.

> *"The presentation was a train crash. Roger was unprepared to answer very specific questions on the right approach to acquisitions."*

Roger's key challenge now was his lack of sufficient market context. As discussed, this is not uncommon with experts in many different fields. They know their subject matter inside out. But they're often insufficiently familiar with the market context that shapes their stakeholders' worlds of meaning and priorities.

As he began to prepare a comprehensive overview of how risk works, global best practice, and the risk team's agenda, it didn't occur to him to ask any of the executive team what they would like to know and, crucially, why. Roger was concerned that asking these questions might reveal that he does not understand the business as well as he should. The chief executive officer, Margaret, would have been the obvious person to ask about this.

Behind the CEO's request for a session on risk culture was a key business requirement: the organization needed to grow more rapidly, and the Board had approved funding to accelerate acquisitions. But Margaret and her CFO, Anand, didn't want a repeat of the disaster that was the AKZ Metrics acquisition, where key staff left immediately after the acquisition, several irregularities showed up in the forward forecasts, and several supplier contracts proved unenforceable. Hence the executive team's interest in understanding how the risk team could strengthen the organization's decision-making and reduce risk on targeted acquisitions.

It would have only taken a few well-directed questions from Roger about exactly what the chief executive wanted to achieve to refine his presentation's focus. Or he could have done a bit of background research on the key issues the business was facing, in which case he would have discovered the following vital piece of market context information: acquisitions are a central theme in the new strategy.

In the absence of such insights, Roger put together a generic rather than acquisition-targeted presentation examining risk culture and best practice. While this may have addressed some of the business's felt needs, it failed to grab the executives' attention as being a pivotal business issue at the heart of their strategic intent.

> *"Mastering market context boils down to the fact that experts need to develop and signal their willingness, capability and commitment to improving organizational performance in comparison to other organizations."*

Roger saw this as an opportunity to convince senior management to take more seriously the risk team's many requests to use the variety of risk tools the team had developed.

So Roger worked all weekend. It was his big chance to explain everything he could about risk culture and why it's important. Models, stats, research, the difference between good risk culture and bad risk culture in organizations, its impact on business performance, and so on.

Roger arrived at the boardroom and was quickly told he had only 30 minutes, rather than the promised 60 minutes. This isn't unusual in board meetings. Might he have anticipated that?

On his sixth slide, Anand leaned forward and said, "This theory is all very well, but how does this apply to our organization when it comes to acquisitions? What are you recommending we do exactly to avoid problems, like those we had with AKZ Metrics?"

Roger immediately realized that the expectation of the people at the meeting was very different from the brief he received to "tell us about risk culture."

The presentation was a train crash. Unprepared to answer very specific questions on the right approach to acquisitions (even though he had several views, he didn't feel *prepared enough* to share them), Roger stumbled through a range of possible options. Margaret cut him off. "You're the risk expert. We want to know how to make sure our due diligence of any new acquisitions is completely watertight. That's what we need from you."

With that, Margaret proposed they move on to the next topic, and Roger's presentation came to an abrupt end. Many experts have been in similar positions and had similar experiences.

Roger's initial reaction was to feel betrayed. He didn't feel that the failed presentation was his fault. He'd delivered in line with the brief, which turned out to be different from what the executive team expected or really needed. *It's their fault,* he told himself. *They didn't give me a proper brief. They didn't give me enough time. They didn't tell me they wanted recommendations.*

What could Roger have done differently? Why didn't he think of doing it differently? What got in his way?

He should have realized that a risk expert mildly berating the executive team, moralizing that they should perhaps take their risk assessment responsibilities more seriously, was not exactly an engaging approach. His approach also made risk assessment seem like a peripheral finance-centric activity rather than a core business activity.

Roger didn't have the *market context* he needed to frame the presentation in the right way for this senior business audience. And he'd failed to properly probe what the executive team wanted to know and why. The epilogue to this case study can be found at the end of Chapter 29.

Similar challenges are felt by experts in other areas, such as finance, HR, compliance, legal, IT, and all across the board.

Experts need a clear and elevated view of how they can add value to themselves, to their teams, to their departments, to their organizations, and to the organization's customers. They need to understand the competitive context in which their organization operates, and even its position within the wider community. That's what market context means.

So what exactly does an expert really need to know about the market context of their organization?

Mastering Market Context

MASTERING MARKET CONTEXT BOILS down to the fact that experts need to develop and signal their capability and commitment to improving organizational performance *in comparison* to other organizations. There are a number of tools and frameworks that allow us to do this.

To get to Master Expert level, we must become a student of the organization, of its competitors, and of its customers.

Then we can see how our own specialty is adding value to the organization's bottom line.

Figure 26.2 and Figure 26.3 describe the Expert **Market Context Canvas**—one for commercial organizations and one for community or public sector (government) organizations. It describes the things we need to know about our organizations from both an internal and external perspective. This will enable us to truly understand and leverage the market context of our organization.

Capability: **MARKET CONTEXT**

The Market Context Canvas
COMMERCIAL VERSION

ORGANIZATIONAL PROFILE · STUDENT OF YOUR ORGANIZATION

DESCRIPTION	PURPOSE	CULTURE
History, size, geography, provenance	Vision, mission	Values, operating style, ethos

PERFORMANCE	PRODUCTS & SERVICES	STRATEGY
Revenue, profit, market share, growth profile	What? Which are hot and which are not?	Where are we going? Why?

COMPETITIVE LANDSCAPE · STUDENT OF YOUR COMPETITORS

COMPETITORS	COMPETITOR PERFORMANCE	COMPETITIVE STRATEGY
History, size, geography, provenance	Revenue, profit, market share, growth profile	How do we believe we compete effectively?

CUSTOMERS · STUDENT OF YOUR CUSTOMERS

CUSTOMERS	VALUE PROPOSITION	INDUSTRY TRENDS
Who, how many, key accounts	Why do customers buy from us?	What will they buy in the future, why, and who from?

FIGURE 26.2: The Market Context Canvas—Commercial

Can you pass the Market Context Canvas test? All you have to do, without visiting the Internet or checking on what the organization's values are on your phone, is to answer the questions in an informed and insightful way. We ask many of the experts we work with on our programs to do this as a way of introducing their organization to everyone else in the room.

It's instructive to see how much most experts can and cannot articulate meaningfully. How do you think most experts perform when assigned this task? How about colleagues in your wider team? Would they find this task easy or difficult? As you can see from the graphic, the questions get progressively more difficult, requiring external knowledge. The Canvas is organized into three distinct parts: organizational profile, competitive landscape, and customers.

Organizational Profile describes the knowledge we need to know about our organization in order to operate at a strategic as well as a tactical level.

Competitive Landscape describes what we need to know about our competitors and how they relate to our own organization so we can think about adding competitive value.

Customers describes what we need to know about our various range of customers, internally and externally, in order to understand future requirements.

We explore knowledge and insights for each of these sectors in the following pages. If you're in the public sector, mission is often a challenging area because the legal mandate is often different from community expectation. Making sure these are aligned and that citizens are just as well informed about the mission and scope or mandate of your organization is very important.

There are three roles an expert must play in order to master market context:

- **Organizational Navigator**: the extent to which the expert is able to use their knowledge of the organization, how it works, its strategic direction, and its internal landscape, such as its structure, key movers and shakers, to get things done.
- **Competitive Analyst**: the extent to which the expert has a pragmatic, well-informed view of the strengths and weaknesses of the organization in comparison to competitors offering alternative products and services.
- **Customer Strategist**: the extent to which the expert has an intimate understanding of the organization's current and future customers' met and unmet needs, expectations, experiences, and so on.

These three roles equate closely to the different sections of the Market Context Canvas, and in the following chapters, we'll deal with each one in turn.

Capability: **MARKET CONTEXT**

The Market Context Canvas
COMMUNITY VERSION

ORGANIZATIONAL PROFILE   STUDENT OF YOUR ORGANIZATION

DESCRIPTION	PURPOSE	CULTURE
History, size, geography, provenance, status	Vision, mission, mandate	Vision, mission, mandate

PERFORMANCE	PRODUCTS & SERVICES	STRATEGY
Service metrics, performance to mandate	What? Which are in demand and which aren't?	Where are we going? Why

COMPETITIVE LANDSCAPE   STUDENT OF YOUR COMPETITORS

COMPETITORS	COMPETITOR PERFORMANCE	COMPETITIVE STRATEGY
History, size, geography, provenance	Service metrics, performance to mandate	How can we become more productive?

CUSTOMERS   STUDENT OF YOUR CUSTOMERS

CUSTOMERS	VALUE PROPOSITION	INDUSTRY TRENDS
Who, how many, key accounts	Why do customers come to us?	What will they want in the future, why, and who from?

FIGURE 26.3: The Market Context Canvas—Community

TAKING ACTION

Growing Our Market Context Skills

IF THIS IS A capability in which you believe you could add greater value, here is a high-level suggestion for action to take:

▶ GET INFORMED ABOUT AND ALIGN WITH THE ORGANIZATION'S STRATEGY

Getting a good understanding of the organizational strategy is key to navigating the organization successfully and understanding what it's trying to achieve. We want to avoid our function being considered, at best, a necessary evil, or at worst, a burdensome cost or distraction from the main game. This would reduce the value and relevance of whatever recommendations we're putting forward. Here are some critical questions we might want to ask ourselves:

- Have I properly read, thought about, and understood the current organizational strategy?
- Have I reached out and connected with the people involved in shaping the strategy, i.e., the strategy team? Do I understand why this is the strategy, including which alternative options were rejected and why?
- Have I reached out to my manager to ask for their thoughts, interpretation, and advice on aligning our activities with the organizational strategy?
- Have I considered and understood the market context factors that have contributed to the organization choosing this strategic path?
- Can I familiarize myself with the organization's underlying analysis of the market, which likely means getting my hands on the customer data, competitor analysis, and other data sources that informed the organization's strategy? The strategy team will have typically gathered all kinds of data to help inform their thinking about the strategy, and they're often willing to share such data if you're trustworthy and make a reasonable case for it.

- Do I feel committed to helping execute the strategy? Do I think it's the right strategy? If not, why not? Have I diplomatically challenged those who shaped it with my alternative views?
- Do I need to practice articulating the strategy, its underlying rationale, and the connection between it and what I do as an expert? As experts in a support function, how easy is it for us and others to make a connection between our daily activities and the organization's highest priorities?

CONTEXT
noun

"The circumstances that form the setting for an event, statement or idea, and in terms of which it can be fully understood."

CHAPTER | 27 |

Becoming a Student of Your Organization

What do we really need to know about our organization to become capable of delivering expert value? How deep and broad must our knowledge be?

IN THIS CHAPTER, WE WILL EXPLORE:

- What is the value of deeply understanding our organization? How does this add value to our work as experts?
- What information do we specifically need, and how do we gather it?
- How do we build networks that enable us to easily maintain the value of our knowledge of and insights into the organization?

THE FIRST OF THE expert roles in Market Context is **Organizational Navigator.** This expert role deals with the extent to which experts are able to use knowledge of the organization, how it works, its strategic direction, and the internal culture it deploys in order to get things done. The behaviors at each level of Expertship for this expert role are described in Figure 27.1.

Typically, experts operating at the specialist level of Expertship will have knowledge of how the organization operates, but this is limited to their immediate environment. In other words, how the organization works with their department. They'll have a very siloed view of their role and department, and they'll be completely focused on the task and short-term outcomes rather than long-term goals.

An expert operating at Master Expert level will have much greater knowledge and superior navigational abilities. They'll have an advanced understanding and comprehensive knowledge of the global organization, with an ability to understand, articulate and demonstrate commitment to global and local strategy. Armed with this knowledge, the Master Expert will have the ability to navigate complex political landscapes within the organization to achieve their goals.

In the context of the Expert Market Context Canvas, the first six boxes deal with being an Organizational Navigator and our knowledge of the internal organization. Looking at each of these in detail will give us an overview of what we need to know to leverage this knowledge into creating value.

Organizational Profile

EXPERTS NEED TO KNOW about their organizations, beyond the specialist roles they operate in. Figure 27.2 reproduces the Organizational Profile component of the Market Context Canvas described in the previous chapter.

Description

Here we ask experts to describe:
* History: When was the organization established, by whom, and why? The organization's history is increasingly important to understand as enterprises experience growth spurts, combine, pivot, change funding models, shift to new mandates, develop and change culture, face and overcome challenges, and so on. Knowing the history is one thing, but Master Experts *understand* the history. They have clarity about why things happened and why decisions were made, which often helps inform future decisions. Organizational history also usually has a significant impact on culture.

Capability: MARKET CONTEXT

Expert Role: ORGANIZATIONAL NAVIGATOR

MASTER EXPERT

- Advanced understanding and comprehensive knowledge of the global organization.
- Understands, can articulate and demonstrates a commitment to global and local strategy.
- Navigates complex political landscapes within the organization to achieve goals.
- Fluently articulates their function's essential contributions toward the organization's strategy.

EXPERT

- Comprehensive understanding and knowledge of the immediate organization.
- Understands and clearly communicates current local strategy.
- Interacts with other departments and functions with clear understanding of their objectives.

SPECIALIST

- Knowledge of how their department contributes to the immediate organization.
- Understands the departmental plan.
- Knowledge of how the organization operates is limited to immediate environment.

- Siloed view of role and department.
- Focuses on task and short-term outcomes rather than long-term goals of the department or organization.
- Uninterested and uninformed about wider organizational context.

DERAILING

FIGURE 27.1: Organizational Navigator Behaviors

- **Size**: By any relevant metrics, such as revenue, number of employees, physical attributes and status. A hotel employee will tell you how many rooms the hotel has and how many stairs. An employee at a major publicly owned organization will tell you theirs is a Top 100 index organization, and so on. Size is another core lever on the past, present and future of an organization. The scale of the business also contributes to defining culture, and often, as organizations shift from small energetic start-ups (and we include government departments in this description) to mainstream service/product providers, size matters and changes things. Understanding these pressures and pivotal moments of scale can help inform decisions and even transform the way in which experts think about delivering their expertise to the organization.
- **Geography**: In what markets does the organization operate? How do these help shape its profile? In a globalized economy, many organizations are constantly seeking new markets, which often have very different financial and social dynamics. It's important to understand these.
- **Provenance**: Where has the organization come from? A famous example is the Australian mega-company BHP Billiton. Originally started by a small group of miners in the outback town of Broken Hill (the company name stands for Broken Hill Propriety Limited), it has since teamed up with UK super-miner Billiton, which itself was started as a small mining company in Indonesia. How companies have developed, i.e., their corporate story, is usually of great interest to people.

Generally speaking, experts are pretty proficient at completing the Description box on the Market Context Canvas.

"While many experts are simply too busy to worry about exploring these types of questions, doing so transforms them."

Purpose

HERE WE ASK EXPERTS to explain their organization's vision and mission. As most experts will know, confusion between vision and mission in most organizations is common. And depending on how these items were shaped, they can often be the target of hilarity, disgust or inspiration. We wish we could tell you it was mostly the latter, but we can't.

Expert Role: ORGANIZATIONAL NAVIGATOR
The Market Context Canvas
COMMERCIAL VERSION

ORGANIZATIONAL PROFILE   STUDENT OF YOUR ORGANIZATION

DESCRIPTION	PURPOSE	CULTURE
History, size, geography, provenance	Vision, mission	Values, operating style, ethos

PERFORMANCE	PRODUCTS & SERVICES	STRATEGY
Revenue, profit, market share, growth profile	What? Which are hot and which are not?	Where are we going? Why?

FIGURE 27.2: Organizational Profile

Purpose (or vision) answers the questions "Why do we exist?" and "Where do we want to get to?" It describes the difference an organization wants to make long-term in the community it serves. Mission answers the question "What do we do?" Strategy answers the question "How do we plan to get there?" For example, "Put a computer on every desk" was an early Apple vision. If the words talk at all about the organization and how big it is or wants to be, or its target market position, then that's the mission. Vision is external and related to impact on the community. Mission is internal and focuses on how the organization will contribute to this goal. And strategy is how we're going to achieve the mission.

All three of these elements, vision, mission and strategy, act as a "true north" setting for everyone in the organization. As a consequence, they're crucial for experts who are working in complex organizations, where many conflicts can exist. Sometimes, the vision and mission, as well as the values we discuss shortly, can be the tie-breaker. What do these statements tell us about the direction we should move in? How should we work with each other and our customers?

Often dismissed by cynical experts as marketing blurb from the senior management, purpose is actually very important in organizations that have a meaningful and actionable vision and mission. It drives motivation, culture and outcomes. It's often why colleagues choose to work there.

While many experts are simply too busy to worry about exploring these types of questions, doing so elevates them from Expert to Master Expert status. Suddenly, we're being future-focused, are looking at a longer horizon, and are thinking strategically about how to create value. This is how to make a difference.

Culture

DESCRIBING AN ORGANIZATION'S CULTURE is a challenge for most of us because we all experience culture in a very personal way. Some experts, for example, enjoy the clarity that comes with a command and control leadership approach. Others detest this style and want the freedom to work out what needs to be done by themselves, unencumbered by a micro-manager.

In describing culture, we might take the following elements into account: values, operating style and ethos.

> *"Ethos is the characteristic spirit of a culture, era or community, as manifested in its attitudes and aspirations."*

Values describe the way in which people work together. How do they behave with one another, with external stakeholders and with customers? In most large organizations, a set of values are usually stated explicitly. It's important to remember that values describe how the organization *intends* or *aspires* to operate, rather than necessarily how it does.

In our programs, our experts can usually remember three of the four values and look up the last one. Once that's achieved, we tend to ask experts whether or not their department *lives the values*. That is, does the behavior of the team comply with what the values stand for (collaboration, trust, empathy, and so on)? A supplementary question is whether colleagues in the wider organization comply? There's often a disparity in the answers from experts from the same organization. Values should be our ethical true north. They should guide employees to do the right thing when there's no one else around to ask.

Increasingly, we're seeing technical groups develop their own values, i.e., "the way we work around here," which are often aligned with corporate values. These are distinctly customized to their specific aspirations as a technical team. For example, the concept of "one team" comes up a lot in IT teams where different functions have previously operated in a very siloed way. By collaboratively developing a shared set of values, chief information officers hope to instill a more collaborative, networked approach to delivering services. One CIO told us: "The business can't differentiate whether one of my IT specialists is from applications development or desktop infrastructure— to the business, we're all from IT." By implication, the objective is to create a single experience for the business dealing with IT, regardless of which part of IT they're dealing with.

> *"If your organization produces an annual report, all of the relevant second-level metrics will be described and discussed there."*

Operating style describes the leadership and governance culture of the organization. Some organizations have a very controlling operating style, where everything has to be triple-checked and triple-signed-off. It's an operating style that's risk-averse and usually slow to make a decision. Others have a very *laissez-faire* operating style, with a lot of authority delegated to more junior teams and senior leadership offering broader direction and perhaps boundaries. However, leadership doesn't wanting to direct specific actions, preferring to let those closest to the customer make decisions. Others have an entrepreneurial spirit, with a focus on growth at all costs. Some are very innovative, others the antithesis of innovation.

Ethos is the characteristic spirit of a culture, era or community, as manifested in its attitudes and aspirations. Examples might be an entrepreneurial ethos, a service-oriented ethos, a competitive ethos, or a risk-averse ethos. Often, the behaviors of employees in the organization may not all be in sync with the organization's ethos.

Performance

We're all interested in how our organization is performing. Great performance possibly means greater opportunities, salary increases, bonuses, and investment in projects we're interested in executing. Poor performance often means the lack of all of these things, fear about continued employment, and increased workload as costs are cut because the organization is not hitting its key measures.

The metrics used to measure organizational performance vary. Public sector or not-for-profit (NFP) organizations will have performance metrics around service delivery standards, the number of community members served, efficiency and productivity, and the extent to which the mandate of the organization is successfully executed.

Not-for-profits will still be keen not to make a loss. Income generation and grants, along with the delivery of services, will be typical metrics. Perhaps also the number of volunteers engaging with the organization and the number of donors.

Commercial organizations have a different set of metrics. The simple and typical metrics revolve around revenue, margin (profit) and market share. Are these metrics reporting stable performance (the same as last month or year), improving performance (happy days, if this is revenue and margin) or worsening performance (unhappy days). Public companies are expected to grow, so the speed of growth is important. In particular, the speed of growth in comparison to rivals is an essential metric that moves share prices.

"Is your organization in a sunrise or sunset industry? How does this affect decision-making and resource allocation?

There is a second level of metrics that those of us who aspire to be Master Experts should familiarize ourselves with. Return on capital is an important metric in capital-intensive industries. Productivity metrics, which vary dramatically depending on the industry, are also considered crucial by the market as they indicate how well run the organization is. A gold miner, for example, will measure the cost of extracting an ounce of gold from the ground. A retailer will measure the level of sales per square foot of retail space.

If your organization produces an annual report, all of the relevant second-level metrics will be described and discussed there. We highly encourage all experts to both read that report and master these metrics.

Why? Because doing so gives us four advantages. Firstly, by reading these reports, we learn the language of the organization's senior leadership. Secondly, we learn the key metrics that are considered the most important. They'll be headlined in the early part of the report. Thirdly, we'll learn which accomplishments the senior leadership team is most proud of in the previous year. This is valuable information. Did our function even get a mention? If so, why? Was it for our most significant achievement or something we felt was business as usual? If we didn't get a mention, why not? Fourthly, annual reports are also future-focused. What do the chairperson and senior leaders describe as the most important aspects of the organization's performance that they'll be focusing on in the years to come? This is extremely valuable information for experts as it enables us to plan how we add value to match these aspirations.

Products and Services

HOW WELL DO WE understand our organization's products and services and their relative performance? In large organizations, this can be very challenging because the range of products and services can often be large. However, division by division, it's a good idea to understand which parts of the organization are doing well and why, and which ones aren't.

This helps us understand what's keeping the various stakeholders we have in these divisions awake at night, and it hints at what their agenda might be, which helps us align our service to their individual needs. The leader of a division that is growing rapidly won't be worrying about costs. They'll be worried about fulfilling demand and continuing to innovate to stay ahead of the competitors. The leader of an underperforming division will be worrying about costs and productivity and business simplification.

> *"What is required of us, as experts, if we want a seat at the strategic table?"*

It's also important to understand what part of the business cycle each division is operating in. Are they in *sunrise* industries, where they can expect decades of high growth because they're just starting out and are involved in a new sector of customer demand (for example, biotech firms)? Are they in *sunset* industries (for example, coal), where the business cycle is coming to an end, substitutes are now viable and affordable, and customer sentiment has shifted away from old products to new ones?

The stage of the cycle will be important in terms of whether the organization is over- or under-investing in that division. The business imperatives will be different as well. In sunset industries, the objective is to reduce costs as much as possible to squeeze the last profits out of customers before they jump to new alternatives. In sunrise industries, the imperative is to be the first to market with the latest breakthrough, thus attracting hordes of new customers away from sunrise competitors and sunset alternatives.

Strategy

WHAT IS REQUIRED OF us, as experts, we want a seat at the strategic table?

Most senior experts want to have more influence, and part of that is a desire to be involved and accepted as a valued contributor when the big decisions impacting our department, and our organization overall, are being made. Very few experts get an invitation to these strategic conversations. There's a range of reasons for this. Perhaps they aren't considered valued contributors to these decisions or are perceived as being "too technical." The implication is that experts are always "down in the details" and not really capable of thinking strategically. Perhaps the experts in question haven't demonstrated their strategic thinking abilities. Perhaps their head of department believes they can represent experts' views at a more senior level better than the experts themselves. Perhaps the expert works in an organization where the senior leadership team see strategy as their province, and theirs alone. Whatever the reason, we're back to waiting for Godot. As experts, we have to demonstrate that we can add value at the strategic level first, and then we'll be invited. If we wait to be invited, the invitation is very unlikely to arrive. So how do we start making a case for a seat at the strategic table?

A Master Expert knows three things about strategy. Firstly, what a good strategy looks like—and conversely, what is simply a list of business imperatives in disguise. Secondly, they'll know what the organization's strategy is, and *why*. And thirdly, they'll know what the department's strategy is and how it aligns with organizational strategy.

Strategy is simply a plan of action designed to achieve a long-term overall aim. The experts we work with who are respected by the wider business get traction with innovation and other projects, and they're always invited to meetings with the top level of their organization.

> *"In our experience, a vanilla connection to strategy won't cut it. Retrofitting won't work either."*

There's a simple reason why they get this traction: supporting an initiative is often a binary decision for many on the executive team. Does the initiative being proposed, including the accompanying expenditure and resource allocation, help us execute our strategy from our perspective or not? If yes, approve. If no, argue and vote against it. The complication is that different executives will have different perspectives on what "aligned with the strategy" means. Senior finance executives are more likely to be concerned with containing costs and increasing margins. Meanwhile, senior sales and marketing executives are likely to be more concerned with growing customer numbers. But this complexity shouldn't get in the way of experts making a direct connection in their proposals to strategic outcomes.

In our experience, a vanilla connection to strategy won't cut it. By vanilla, we mean a strategy slide early in the slide deck that is barely referenced again throughout the presentation. The alignment must be crystal clear and, obviously, valid. It needs to be evident that the proposal was born and shaped with the organizational strategy in mind, not retrofitted because someone somewhere told us "don't forget to link it to the strategy." For those of us in support services of one description or another, this can sometimes be a difficult connection to make. Let's take a look at how Master Experts do it.

> *"Knowing what the strategy says is one thing, but understanding why it's the strategy is Master Expert territory."*

Since there is a lot of confusion about what strategy is and isn't, let's start with a definition. Figure 27.3 provides a simple way of looking at strategy. At its very essence, it involves the straightforward answering of a few simple questions:

- Where are we now? What is our current state? (In Figure 27.3, we refer to this as Point A.)
- What is the organization's goal, destination or target state? Where precisely do we intend to arrive? Why do we want to get there? (In Figure 27.3, we refer to this as Point B.)
- When do we want to get there? This is referred to as the "strategic horizon." This is usually two or three years in the future.
- Which specific routes or choices will take us there? How will we best get from where we are now to where we want to be? (In Figure 27.3, we label these choices as C.)
- What obstructions, constraints or risks are we likely to encounter? And how will we navigate these?

Capability: **MARKET CONTEXT**

Understanding Strategy
ORGANIZATIONAL STRATEGY

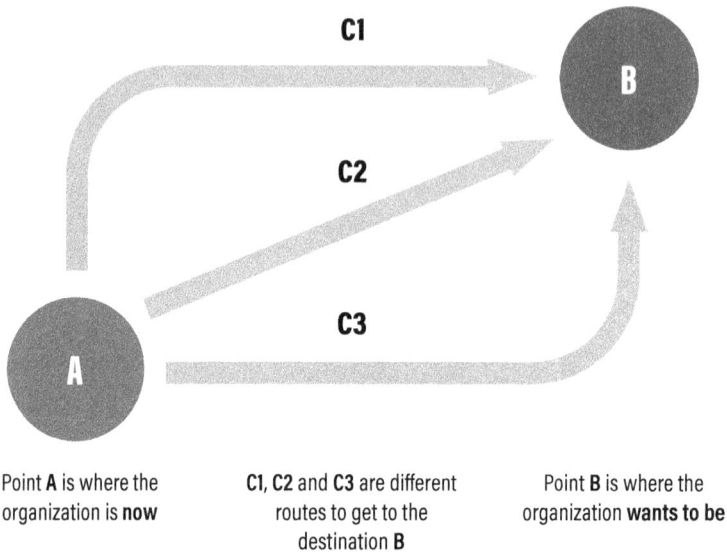

| Point **A** is where the organization is **now** | **C1, C2** and **C3** are different routes to get to the destination **B** | Point **B** is where the organization **wants to be** |

FIGURE 27.3: Understanding Strategy

The term *strategy* is unfortunately used in many different ways. The resulting confusion generally ends up unresolved with few true strategic insights about how one organization might successfully win out over its competitors. In the commercial world, this tends to be the focus of strategy. In the public sector, strategy is more likely to be about achieving better community outcomes, although the government sector is increasingly adopting rigorous benchmarking against national and global service delivery standards, driving individual government entities to aspire to be the best.

The term *strategy* is often misused to the point where it simply represents the means by which we hope to achieve this year's financial targets or spend this year's budget. The development of a strategy has been largely eclipsed by the organization's need to meet its targets in a process most commonly referred to as business planning. The annual business planning cycle provides an excellent opportunity for the evolving expert to engage more fully with their market context and key organizational stakeholders.

We believe that a workable understanding of organizational strategy can be achieved in approximately two hours. That is a very achievable goal for every expert. Be prepared to spend another couple of hours on adjacent reading (rival's annual reports, media reports of organizational performance, and so on) to become highly informed on your organizational strategy.

This may sound like an academic point, but it's actually the whole point: *knowing* what the strategy says is one thing, but understanding *why* it's the strategy is Master Expert territory. It provides a window into the thinking of the organization's senior leaders or those who shaped the mandate a public sector department may be operating on. It implies knowing which strategic choices were made and why, and why other options were rejected.

TAKING ACTION

Growing Our Organizational Navigator Skills

IF THIS IS AN expert role in which you believe you could add greater value, here are some high-level suggestions for actions to take:

▶ BE PROACTIVE ABOUT NETWORKING OUTSIDE YOUR DOMAIN

Many experts interact with a very narrow group of people within their organization, which is heavily influenced by what tasks they're working on. This creates a siloed and head-down domain focus rather than a strategic, head-up focus. Here are some critical questions we might like to ask ourselves:

- Am I taking the time to talk about the organization and its market context with my stakeholders?
- Do I regularly take the initiative to call them or visit them, if only briefly, to ask them to clarify the context of things I have been asked to do and inquire about what they see happening in the organization?
- Am I actively reducing the amount of rework I have to do by getting ahead of organizational requirements, so I know what they'll ask me for next month and the month after, thus enabling me to shortcut future requirements?

▶ BE SAVVY ABOUT PERFORMANCE BENCHMARKS

Whether in a commercial or a public sector organization, understanding performance benchmarks is critical. There are two levels to this knowledge: how well is my department performing compared with similar departments in other organizations? And how well is my organization performing against rivals? Here are some critical questions we might want to ask ourselves:

- Do I have a clear idea of how the performance of my department ought to be measured?
- Am I measuring it this way? Do I have the data feeds that allow me to benchmark against rivals? How would I get access to this data? How

often do I conduct a reality check on how well we're really performing against rivals?

- Do I have a clear idea of how the performance of my organization ought to be measured?
- Am I aware of how well it's performing?

▶ MAKE EXPLICIT REFERENCE TO THE ORGANIZATIONAL STRATEGY

In the absence of explicit linkages to the organizational strategy, people may not see the critical relevance or value of the work we do.

Once we have understood the strategy and figured out how we contribute to its execution, it's important to use our knowledge to bring the strategy to life for ourselves and those we regularly work with. This is what being "strategic" actually means in an organizational context. Here are some critical questions we might want to ask ourselves:

- Do I practice translating the strategy in terms that other experts and stakeholders will appreciate and relate to? Can they clearly identify their contribution to it? Translating the strategy simply means describing the implications of the strategy for whichever group of people we happen to be addressing, i.e., how they can best contribute to it. The idea is to illustrate precisely how our particular activities support the realization of the organization's goals.
- Do I align my priorities with the strategy? This means that if an activity doesn't appear to be essential, or is perhaps contrary, its validity might be questioned.
- As a golden rule, do I make explicit links to the strategy in any reports or recommendations I write?

CHAPTER | 28 |

Becoming a Student of the Competition

The competition (or alternatives) can be a powerful source of inspiration and angst. Knowing your competitors helps experts create real value.

IN THIS CHAPTER, WE WILL EXPLORE:

- Why is understanding our organization's competitors (private sector) or alternatives (public sector) important?
- Given they are competitors/alternatives, how can we find out real information about them? What opportunities do we have?
- Once we have this information, what would a Master Expert do with it?

THE SECOND EXPERT ROLE of Market Context is **Competitive Analyst.** This expert role deals with the extent to which experts have a pragmatic, well-informed view of the organization's strengths and weaknesses in comparison to those offering competing products and services.

Many experts, of course, work for community-based organizations, such as the government, the not-for-profit sector, and so on. As such, the term *competitive* might not sit right with those of you from that sector. Instead of *competitive,* you might want to use the word *alternative.* Those who use government services have alternatives, or substitute services, that they might use from the private sector, for example, or the alternative option not to use any service at all.

If we use the example of an Electoral Commission, experts employed here will know that they're in a competition in many ways. This could be to increase the number of voters who actually vote, to increase the percentage who vote online, thereby saving the taxpayer money, or to create a system and process that maximizes outcomes, minimizes costs and ensures privacy and validity, as measured against other Electoral Commissions around the world. Best practice and next practice exist in the public sector just as much as in the private sector, and it might be argued that in the public sector, these metrics are under greater public scrutiny. The behaviors at each level of Expertship for this expert role are described in Figure 28.1.

At immature levels, the expert will have limited knowledge of the competitive environment in which the organization operates. They may know the names of competitors but have no detailed understanding of them (unless, of course, they previously worked there). An expert operating at the specialist level won't really be thinking about competitors. They'll be more focused on their competing work priorities and how to get all of their workload completed within the desired timeframes.

> *"Master Experts will also worry about where the next competitors might come from, and why."*

An expert who is derailing in the role of Competitive Analyst will have a head-in-the-sand approach to the role, with limited knowledge or interest in external factors. Derailing is characterized by a dismissive, "nothing to do with me" attitude toward their organization's challenges in the wider competitive landscape.

At a mature level, the Master Expert will boast an advanced knowledge of the competitive environment in which the organization operates, including current and insightful knowledge of one competitor's relative positioning versus another. This ability to assess their own organization's relative strengths and weaknesses versus competitors is a critical strength that allows them to leverage market context to create new value.

Capability: MARKET CONTEXT

Expert Role: COMPETITIVE ANALYST

MASTER EXPERT

- Advanced knowledge of the competitive environment in which the organization operates.
- Assesses relative strengths and weaknesses of the organization versus competitors.
- Considers the genesis of future competitors.
- Constantly referencing the threats and opportunities that face the organization.

EXPERT

- Developing knowledge of the competitive environment in which the organization operates.
- Good knowledge of own organization's competitive position.
- Aware of the threats and opportunities that face the organization.

SPECIALIST

- Limited knowledge of the competitive environment in which the organization operates.
- Limited awareness of the threats and opportunities that face the organization.

- Siloed approach to the role with limited knowledge or interest in external factors.
- Limited knowledge of organizational competitors.
- Internal focus.

DERAILING

FIGURE 28.1: Competitive Analyst Behaviors

Let's take a look at this knowledge and insight in detail. In the Market Context Canvas, three sets of competitor data and insights are described: competitors, competitor performance, and competitive strategy (see Figure 28.2).

Competitors

IN THE NEXT CHAPTER on Value Impact, we ask how experts can add new value to internal clients and external customers. Logically, it's impossible to add *new* value unless we know what existing value is available to these client groups, either from our own organization (Organizational Navigator) or from competitors (Competitive Analyst).

Rather like understanding our own organization, Master Experts will be familiar with the history, size, geographical footprint and provenance of the organization's major competitors in the marketplace.

Master Experts will also worry about where the next competitors might come from, and why. They'll scour other industries and markets for clues about where the next challenger might come from. Many large organizations, for example, are being seriously disrupted by completely new, and often very small and nimble, start-ups.

Competitive Performance

AT A HIGH LEVEL, experts will also seek to understand the performance of known competitors. How are these organizations performing against our own organization and other operators in our markets? We would use the same metrics that apply to our organization's performance to measure this, unless we saw from reports that competitors were using different metrics. This would be of significant interest. Why are they using alternative metrics, and are theirs more relevant than those being used by our organization?

If we were smart, we'd also seek to understand the trend data, not just what is being reported today. Are there competitors rapidly gaining market share against us or others? Or losing market share? And why is this so? Which rivals are growing rapidly, and which have stalled? Why? In which customer segments do rivals perform better than our own organization, and why? And is that something our expert team could help do something about?

Capability: **MARKET CONTEXT**

The Market Context Canvas
COMMERCIAL VERSION

COMPETITIVE LANDSCAPE   STUDENT OF YOUR COMPETITORS

COMPETITORS	COMPETITOR PERFORMANCE	COMPETITIVE STRATEGY
History, size, geography, provenance	Revenue, profit, market share, growth profile	How do we believe we compete effectively?

FIGURE 28.2: Customer Strategist Behaviors

Competitive Strategy

FINALLY, MASTER EXPERTS SEEK to understand their competitors' strategies—or alternative suppliers' strategies, in the case of the public sector—and compare these strategies against those of our own organization.

As experts, if we want to establish commercial credibility with the wider organization, being an informed Competitive Analyst is a great place to start. We might assume that customer-facing departments in our organization are completely up to date with competitive intelligence and leverage it every day, but in the authors' experience, this is often not the case. Indeed, we sometimes see customer-facing departments in denial about current market share trends, particularly if they're declining. Occasionally, we'll see a sales team blaming the loss of market share on their competitors discounting, when the competitors have actually either found a more efficient way of delivering the service or the service is simply better. As experts, we have the advantage of being able to look at the evidence about competitive performance very objectively so we can gain insights and ideas that might be more difficult for departments closer to the action to understand or accept.

An important aspect of competitive strategy is thinking about how our rivals' strategies help us predict what they'll do next or how they'll respond to any strategic initiatives we launch. One of our esteemed colleagues uses chess as an example of this. The best players are planning four or five moves ahead, anticipating how the other player will respond to the moves they make.

TAKING ACTION

GROWING OUR COMPETITIVE ANALYST SKILLS

IF THIS IS AN expert role in which you believe you could add greater value, here are some high-level suggestions for actions to take:

▶ CONDUCT A COMPETITOR ANALYSIS

- In the absence of having a clear sense of the organization's competitors, the landscape in which they're competing, and their respective strategies, we'll be viewed as internally focused, unconcerned with and largely irrelevant to the organization's "main game." Undertaking an analysis of one or more of our competitors enables us to talk confidently and think creatively from an informed point of view about how we can contribute to improving the organization's market position against this competitor. Questions we might like to ask ourselves:
- Via my relationship with the "strategy team," have I built an understanding of the alternative strategies at play with my organization's competitors?
- Have I identified and can I articulate the strategies through which my organization's competitors are hoping to win more business?
- Have I identified the competing value propositions that each competitor, and my own organization, appear to be offering?

▶ CONDUCT A SWOT ANALYSIS

Without a clear understanding of the relative **strengths** and **weaknesses** of our organization compared to its competitors and the **opportunities** and **threats** that apply, it will be difficult to identify the highest priority needs of the organization for the prudent application of our expertise. Questions we might like to ask ourselves:

- Have I identified the organization's respective Strengths? The existing positive attributes that provide it with a potential competitive advantage? Note that this is not merely a positive attribute. It's one that affords us an advantage because it's something that our competitors don't have—at least not to the same degree.

- Have I identified the organization's respective Weaknesses? The existing vulnerabilities, shortfalls or handicaps that don't apply to competitors and result in a competitive disadvantage?
- Have I identified the organization's respective Opportunities? The potential moves that the organization could make in order to increase its competitive advantage? Unlike Strengths and Weaknesses, these can be common to all organizations being compared.
- Have I identified the organization's respective Threats? The potential exposures that could adversely impact the organization's competitive performance? As with Opportunities, Threats can be common across all organizations in your comparison.

One goal of such an analysis is to identify ways to create a new strength in order to increase the organization's competitive advantage. This will be a positive attribute that our competitors don't have. It might perhaps further strengthen an existing strength, making us immune to competitive threats. Another is to eliminate or at least reduce a weakness or better exploit competitors' weaknesses. A third objective is to take advantage of one or more opportunities identified, and a fourth is to protect the organization against risks.

CHAPTER | 29 |

Becoming a Student of our Customers

What can we learn about the value we can create from our existing customers? And can we learn more from those who aren't yet, or once were, our customers?

IN THIS CHAPTER, WE WILL EXPLORE:

- Customer centricity is a common phrase we hear these days, but what's it got to do with experts?
- While sometimes difficult to find, sources of information and insight on customers, current, past and future, contribute strongly to those aspiring to operate at Master Expert level.
- How do we quickly and efficiently get up to speed on customers without getting diverted from our existing workload?

THE LAST OF THE expert roles in Market Context is **Customer Strategist.** This expert role deals with the extent to which experts have an intimate understanding of the organization's current and future customers' met and unmet needs. In the public sector, customers might be translated to citizens.

We hear a lot these days about the concept of *customer centricity*, i.e., putting the customer at the center of organizational design and processes. We also hear the term *customer intimacy* used a lot in relation to knowing the customer very well so as to be able to predict immediate and future behavior.

Some experts concerned with the collection and analysis of big data are heavily involved in helping produce these insights. Many experts, however, are significantly removed from interactions with external customers of the organization and have to rely on often anecdotal, and therefore unreliable hearsay about what their needs are. The behaviors at each level of Expertship for this expert role are described in Figure 29.1.

An expert operating at an immature level might focus on delivering services that match the existing needs of the organization's customers without much thought as to future needs. They'll generally be more focused on professional insights within their technical domain than market insights. An expert who is derailing in the role of Customer Strategist might operate in a technical bubble, with little interest or knowledge of changing customer (or citizen) needs or the trends that are impacting them.

An expert operating at the Master Expert level, however, will demonstrate a deep understanding of why existing, past and future customers (or citizens) will do business with the organization or gain value from interacting with it. They'll devote time to exploring the future unmet needs of existing and future customers (or citizens). And, most importantly, Master Experts will have a holistic knowledge of and insight into the meta-trends that will inform and frame the future of the organization and industry.

Let's take a look at this knowledge and insight in detail. In the Market Context Canvas, three sets of data and insights are described: customers, value proposition, and industry trends (see Figure 29.2).

Customers

FOR EXPERTS, THE CONCEPT of *customers* means many things. We typically do work for internal customers. These are either immediate stakeholders, who usually give us the brief and who we work with to deliver a solution, or removed stakeholders, who are the eventual recipients of our work. They're usually out in the wider organization and very often in customer-facing functions.

In Market Context terms, we mean *external* customers, i.e., the consumers of the organizations' products and services. In the public sector, that will mean various groups within the community.

Who are our customers? Do we really know? It may seem like a simple question, but in our experience, experts tend to have a superficial understanding of who their customers are and sometimes lack an understanding of why they are our customers (see value proposition in the next section).

Capability: MARKET CONTEXT

Expert Role: CUSTOMER STRATEGIST

MASTER EXPERT

- Has a deep understanding of why existing, past and future customers will do business with the organization.
- Explores future unmet needs of existing and future customers.
- Holistic knowledge and insight into the meta trends that will inform and frame the future of the organization and industry.
- Regular interaction with external customers.

EXPERT

- Demonstrates awareness of the needs of existing, known external customers.
- Knowledgeable about current trends impacting the organization and industry.
- Some exposure to external customers

SPECIALIST

- Focuses on delivering services that match the existing needs of the organization's customers.
- Focuses on professional insights rather than market insights.
- Limited exposure—if any—to external customers.

- Operates in a professional and technical bubble with little interest or knowledge of changing customer needs and the trends that are impacting them.

DERAILING

FIGURE 29.1: Customer Strategist Behaviors

Capability: **MARKET CONTEXT**
The Market Context Canvas
COMMERCIAL VERSION

CUSTOMERS STUDENT OF YOUR CUSTOMERS

CUSTOMERS	VALUE PROPOSITION	INDUSTRY TRENDS
Who, how many, key accounts	Why do customers buy from us?	What will they buy in the future, why, and who from?

FIGURE 29.2: The Market Context Canvas: Customers

For most experts, customers are typically other organizations and the specific job roles within these organizations responsible for purchasing our organization's products and services (business-to-business products and services – B2B) or consumers (business to consumers – B2C).

Our products and services will appeal to specific demographics and psychographics (the classification of people according to their attitudes, aspirations, and other psychological criteria). They'll appeal more in some geographies than others. Although we may have market leadership in some customer segments, we're often also trying to win customers in new target segments. Do we have lots of customers? Or just a few very large, important accounts?

> *"There is a wealth of information about clients circulating in most organizations, but experts often aren't on the circulation list."*

All of these characteristics of our organization's customers impact senior executives' thinking and behavior, particularly in sales and marketing. This mindset about customers is important to understand because it very often directly affects the work we do and how we are resourced.

As an example of how it might affect us, imagine a relatively small and apparently unimportant piece of work that we're briefed on that may be something we're inclined to leave until later because other major projects need our attention. But if that small piece of unimportant work turns out to be for a very large and important key account, we need to know about it and probably prioritize it.

As a point of best practice, in the B2B space, the Master Expert will be aware of who the organization's key accounts are, and what stage of the customer cycle they are in (recently acquired, stable, approaching re-bid, flight risk). Super-smart Master Experts will also be aware of which accounts the organization is attempting to win, and they'll be asking how they might help.

In the B2C space, Master Experts will be aware of which segments the organization is progressing in, indicated by actively building market share, and which ones it's struggling with, indicated by a loss of market share or an increasing number of new entrants or new products that challenge the organization's market position.

There is a wealth of information about clients circulating in most organizations, but very often, experts aren't on the circulation list. If, as experts, we want to develop a 70,000-ft view (much higher than helicopters—we're talking U2 spy planes!) of how we can add value, then there is no more strategic a way to do so than winning new customers and hanging on to existing ones. We need to know who they are and where help is required.

Because experts are often once or twice removed from the actual sale, this strategic help is frequently backroom help, such as new systems, perhaps new processes, or sometimes the ability to offer product enhancements. We'll explore our options in the next chapter.

Value Proposition

NEXT, DO WE PROPERLY understand our organization's **value proposition?** Value propositions come in two flavors: imagined and real. An imagined value proposition is how we describe internally why our customers buy products and services from us. What value are they purchasing? How is our value different from alternative choices? The real value proposition is why our customers actually buy from us.

> *"By understanding the activities that add or subtract customer value, we're better able to prioritize work on our overblown to-do list."*

We make the distinction between these two flavors because, in our experience, many organizations don't understand as well as they should what customers value about working with us (buying our products or services). This, incidentally, is especially true of experts. We imagine that it's simply our knowledge or problem-solving abilities that our stakeholders find most valuable. In many cases, however, it's a cocktail of these things combined with other attributes or value we bring to the table.

By way of example, in a survey of our own clients some time ago, we asked those taking our leadership development programs why they chose us as a supplier and why they continue to choose us. Note, these are two different questions.

The answer to the first question was what we might have expected and hoped for, such as good design, a modern approach, and so on. But most of our clients made the point that we actually were very similar to many other organizations in this respect, and it was a tight call, but they decided to try us out. We, of course, had imagined that we impressed new clients because of how different and innovative we are. It turned out, this wasn't true.

The answer to the second question provided a really valuable and surprising insight. They continued to choose us because, as an organization, we were easy to work with. One client told us: "You're great consultants and everything, and we like working with you, but we know lots of other great consultants with whom we also like working. But what differentiates your organization from others is your project management team. You're by a distance the easier supplier to work with, and enable us to do many other things because you have project management under control." We work hard to make sure this is still true.

If your organization provides multiple products and services, the value proposition will obviously be different for each one of these offerings. Fundamentally, we're asking:

- Why do customers buy from us? What do they value about our products or service?
- What is the value proposition for those customers who choose alternative products and services?
- What elements of value will become more important to customers over time, and which will become less important?

Why is it important for experts, perhaps those working in risk, IT, or HR, to intimately understand value proposition? Firstly, our intent should always be to do work that increases our organization's success (or nullifies threats), and by understanding what customers value, we may be able to identify opportunities to add more value. Secondly, and possibly more importantly, by understanding the activities that add or subtract customer value, we can prioritize important work on our overblown to-do list, such as strategic value-adding work rather than tasks that may or may not add customer value. Thirdly, when we're making a business case for more investment, greater resources, or approval to make a significant change, if we can link the change to the value proposition, we're much more likely to get airtime with senior leaders.

Industry Trends

WE ASK EXPERTS TO describe the trends that are currently impacting their industry and therefore their organization, and then also speculate about what trends might affect their industry in the future. The key questions are:

- What products and services will customers want to buy in the future that are different from today?
- What will drive this change in purchasing habits?
- Will the same industry players supply these products and services or will new entrants be better positioned to provide them?
- How well-positioned is our organization to succeed in these new market conditions in the future?

Once these questions are considered, the next set of questions play very much into the role of the Master Expert. What role will experts play in shaping a successful future for the organization? Is our current strategy and project pipeline sufficiently future-focused? Are we starting from the point of what customers will want in three years and working back from that scenario, or are we simply incrementally improving what we do today, assuming there will be no major change in customer needs?

One of the exercises we ask our program participants to undertake is called History Wall. We ask experts to analyze a historic moment—the most significant game-changing event in their industry in recent years. How did it arise? A technological innovation? A change in customer purchasing habits? A change in customer demographics or preferences (psychographics)? Regulatory change? Once the group of experts has worked out what this industry-shaping event was, and what drove it, we ask them to work on predicting what the next big thing will be. Is there a change brewing? An unmet need that customers are highly motivated to address? An imminent regulatory change?

> *"Getting to grips with industry trends is less difficult and more entertaining than we might think."*

This is a form of scenario planning. Once we have imagined a possible change, the next stage is to understand the implications for the market and our organization's position in it. We ask the question "How could we successfully respond?" In the exercise, we ask our participants to come up with one recommendation or initiative that, as experts, they could make and drive to help their organization capitalize on this imminent development.

Readers may be surprised to know that we complete this exercise in five minutes, and the insights and recommendations from the group are usually extremely helpful and valid. But this is a team sport. Doing it alone is much more difficult. People feed off their colleagues' ideas and opinions.

Our organizations conduct these types of activities regularly, often driven by the strategy or business planning teams. Experts rarely get invited, and if they do, they're expected to only contribute to the technical trends part of the equation. Master Experts take a more holistic approach, and they get invited back because they added more broad value. They can only do this by understanding the organization's customers (current and future), value propositions (current and future), and broader industry trends (current and future). In other words, they have to be a very competent Customer Strategist.

Undertake a Trends Binge

GETTING TO GRIPS WITH industry trends is less difficult and more entertaining than we might think. Here is a suggestion. Once a year, perhaps at the turn of the calendar year, many commentators, industry groups, global consulting firms and think tanks publish lists of the top ten trends for the new year, or for the next three to five years. Any Google search will garner a huge number of these decks.

Stage 1 of executing a trends binge is taking three or four hours to collect a folder full of these decks from every source possible. Indeed, it's important *not* to stay within your domain or even just adjacent sectors. Instead, go wide and go long. The more diverse and eclectic the sample, the better.

Stage 2 is to read them, but do so from the perspective of looking for commonalities and trends within trends. If, for example, almost all the soothsayers talk about customers wanting a personalized service and the ability to customize what they purchase, then we can be reasonably sure that it's a broad trend that's likely to come to fruition. More importantly, we can surmise that it's likely to impact our industry in the near future. Personalization, of course, was a trend from 2012-2015 that has clearly come to pass in most industries. Build a list of trends that many different groups identify; a list that we can be reasonably certain is likely to come to fruition.

Stage 3 of this process is to take this list and ask ourselves how and when these trends will occur in our sector. Are there already signs that the trends are materializing? Which of the current players are currently best placed to service these new customer needs? How well does our organization stack up? What initiatives will we need to implement to be ready to serve these new customer needs effectively? How can we build a competitive advantage in advance (or at least just in time)?

Stage 4 is taking a look at our specific function and asking what obligations we have to make our organization ready for the new customer requirements or other changes, such as technology, that will change the way business is done in our sector?

> *"By having studied what everyone else thinks might happen in their markets, we're capable of using examples and referencing comments from accepted authorities to challenge thinking and set the agenda."*

This type of scan takes a day at most to complete, but it gets us thinking further into the future, rather than just focusing on the work we have immediately in front of us. It helps us begin to imagine our organization's future market context, which assists us with making more informed, strategic contributions to meetings and projects. It also helps us to be on the lookout for evidence that either confirms or is contrary to the manifestation of some of these new trends.

Finally, it significantly helps us shape insightful and informed questions for our stakeholders, so we're better able to have longer term conversations with them about what changes they see occurring in our sector in the next few years. By having studied what everyone else thinks might happen in their markets, we're capable of using examples and referencing comments from accepted authorities to challenge thinking and set the agenda.

TAKING ACTION

GROWING OUR CUSTOMER STRATEGIST SKILLS

IF THIS IS AN expert role in which you believe you could add greater value, here are some high-level suggestions for actions to take:

▶ BECOME FAMILIAR WITH THE ORGANIZATION'S CUSTOMER DATA

Without a working knowledge of the customer statistics, such as their needs, preferences, service experiences, issues and concerns, and so on, we'll appear to be out of touch with the organization's primary business. Here are some critical questions we might want to ask ourselves:

- Do I have access to a constant stream of any customer research or profiling that my organization gathers?
- Am I familiar with the customers' expectations, needs, preferences and experiences, whether good or bad?
- Do I know what kinds of things customers find especially satisfying? What is it that the organization does that keeps customers coming back?
- Do I know what kinds of things customers find dissatisfying? What threatens their loyalty or actually causes them to take their business elsewhere? What are their common complaints?
- Do I know how customers, whether current or emerging, describe their needs?
- Do I have a combination of quantitative (measurable) and qualitative (stories and examples) data? Have I considered how these data points inform (or might inform) my own team's vision, priorities and provisions of advice or services?

▶ LEARN YOUR ORGANIZATION'S CUSTOMER VALUE PROPOSITION

Organizations or functions that don't refresh their sense of what customers or stakeholders value can suddenly lose relevance. That can result in loss of funding or a drop in the necessary engagement levels to remain viable going forward. Here are some critical questions we might want to ask ourselves:

- Though there might be a written statement of the organization's customer value proposition somewhere, have I gone further than merely reading those words? Am I able to fluently and convincingly articulate precisely what it is that the organization offers to customers that they may find more compelling than our competitors' equivalent offers?
- Am I able to convincingly articulate how my expert function contributes to the customer value proposition and what my function's value proposition is to my stakeholders?
- What does the organization's advice, products, services, and so on allow them to achieve that is of value to them and wouldn't otherwise be possible? How precisely do my team and I offer them a compelling best option?

▶ CONDUCT TREND ANALYSES AND DEVELOP SCENARIO PLANS

Without the foresight to anticipate emerging needs, issues and opportunities, we can find ourselves being reactive and playing catch up, as well as providing little guidance to the organization as to how it might capitalize on favorable opportunities. Failing to have insightful contingency plans in place provides no inoculation for the organization or our departments against critical incidents manifesting, along with all the associated ill effects.

Study the meta-trends that might impact your industry and customers. As with all of these recommendations to conduct an analysis, they can be performed as a solo activity or performed conjointly with other stakeholders. They can be conducted simply to prompt insight or, better still, to stimulate insight-driven actions.

One popular framework for conducting such analysis is the PEST framework:

- **Political**: what kind of developments are emerging in the regulatory arena and what implications might these have for our function, organization, industry and customers?
- **Sociological**: what kinds of trends are emerging when it comes to societal or workforce demographics, and what are the implications for our function, organization, industry and customers?
- **Environmental**: as the world becomes more concerned with climate change, what implications might this have for our function, organization, industry and customers?
- **Technological**: what kinds of technological innovations are emerging, and what implications might these have for our function, organization, industry and customers?

Sometimes people add Legal and Economic factors to create PESTLE. In addition to this structured analysis, there are some specific meta-trends that we might want to consider. These include:

- The rise of artificial intelligence and other technological breakthroughs, such as driverless cars, augmented reality, machine learning, cloud computing, blockchain, increased digitally enabled remote working/learning, and so on.
- Data analysis and data mining.
- Cryptocurrencies.
- Generation Z entering the workplace.
- The aging population.
- The burden of chronic disease.
- Sharing economies, such as ride-sharing, shared accommodation, P2P marketing, lending, insurance, and so on.

▶ UNDERTAKE A TRENDS BINGE

As we describe in detail above, we can undertake a scan of what experts in other expert domains are thinking about the future and start gathering our own insights as to what trends are likely to impact our industry in the future. Here are some critical questions we might like to ask ourselves:

- What drove major change in my industry previously?
- What impact did these changes have?
- How did we react as an organization?
- How did we react as an expert group? What were the trends in my expert profession, e.g., HR, finance, IT, engineering?
- What would I do differently now?
- What is likely to be the next big change to arrive?
- Do I have a plan? What can I learn from previous experiences?
- What preparations can I start making now for disruption in the future?

Consider spending time on tools and websites that monitor trends for you. The website *trendwatching.com* is recommended, along with keeping an eye on the big global consulting firms that regularly publish trends-based reports and thought leadership. Consider doing a trends binge as a project with friends or colleagues to share the workload. Friends who operate in other industries are particularly valuable as they'll have a very different perspective, which is usually valuable.

Epilogue: Roger's Presentation

AFTER A FEW DARK days, Roger reflected upon the lessons he had learned about his disastrous presentation to the executive team on risk. He approached the CFO and asked what specifically the leadership team wanted to know about risk and received a clear brief. "We can't afford to make any more underperforming acquisitions because our funding will dry up and we'll lose market confidence," the CFO told him. "We want to know what the risk team suggests we should do to ensure we minimize the risk of future acquisitions underperforming."

Roger went back to the drawing board. He researched all the literature about why so many—nearly 80 percent, he discovered—acquisitions fail to achieve the projected gains for the acquiring organization. He researched how enterprises are valued and which metrics were most critical in acquisitions. He made a list of the top ten risks associated with acquisitions, which included losing key talent, contracts becoming void at the change of ownership, negative brand impact, and so on. He spoke at length to the finance managers who developed the business case for the AZK Metrics acquisition and explored what assumptions they had made that turned out to be false. He spoke to the ex-managing director of AZK Metrics, who unexpectedly left shortly after the acquisition, to get her perspective.

Then he prepared his presentation and persuaded Margaret, the CEO, to give him 15 minutes at the next leadership meeting.

On the day, Roger presented just four slides. He had tested these slides with two non-risk colleagues to make sure they did not contain risk-related jargon. They were:

- Slide one: globally, what are the statistics on acquisitions achieving the business impact projected at acquisition?
- Slide two: what are the top ten risks associated with acquiring an organization?
- Slide three: AZK Metrics: what risks did we spot during due diligence and what risks did we miss? What assumptions did we make that turned out not to be true?
- Slide Four: a proposed due diligence process for future acquisitions, designed to illuminate the top ten risks, along with a scoring system to help the leadership team decide whether an acquisition was a low-risk, medium-risk, or high-risk decision.

After ten minutes of providing a high-level overview of the four slides, he sat down and asked if there were any questions. There were. Seventy minutes of questions, in fact. Roger was able to leverage all of the research he had undertaken in preparation of his four slides to answer these questions. He peppered his answers with real-life examples of acquisitions that had worked, and why, and acquisitions that hadn't worked, and why not.

Eventually, Margaret said the same thing she had a month earlier. "Okay, we need to move on," but this time, she thanked Roger for a highly insightful presentation.

Six weeks later, Roger received an email from the CFO. It was a request. They had identified another acquisition. Usually, finance ran the due diligence process, and indeed would be heavily involved again this time. However, the executive team wanted Roger to oversee the due diligence process. Would he be prepared to do this, and would he be able to delegate some other tasks in order to make time to do it? It was urgent.

Roger's role in the organization had suddenly grown significantly.

"Knowledge is of no value unless you put it into practice."

Anton Chekhov

MASTERING
VALUE IMPACT

VALUE DOMAIN

MARKET CONTEXT

VALUE
IMPACT

CHANGE
AGILITY

The Master Expert identifies, articulates and realizes tangible ways of adding commercial or community value, demonstrating an active engagement in improving overall organizational performance.

CHAPTER | **30** |

Understanding Value Impact

What is an expert's role in creating value? How do we create compelling and lasting impact by imagining and delivering new value?

IN THIS CHAPTER, WE WILL EXPLORE:

- Why are so many experts frustrated that they don't have the opportunity to add value to their organization?
- How do experts go about delivering on the fundamental promise of a Master Expert: the ability to add new value to our organizations?
- The Three Domains of Value Creation, and how experts can impact value creation in each area.

WHEN WE FIRST MEET our colleagues in our new workplace, it's reasonably typical to ask them what they do. In our Expertship programs, we ask a slightly different question: "As an expert in your organization, how do you *add value?*"

This is, if we think about it, the central question for experts. Do we just do stuff, or do we add value? Are we just doing the same old stuff, adding the same amount of value year after year, or are we committed to adding new value, extra value, extended value? And if we could add extraordinary value to our organization, how might that come about, and how would we go about doing it? What different approach might we need to commit to?

In a survey we conducted among experts, 82 percent said they could add more value to their organization if they were given the opportunity to do so. This result was no surprise to us, as we work with experts every month who are similarly frustrated. Very many of these experts can see opportunities to add more value, but for one reason or another, they are unable to do so.

> *"Like beauty, value can be in the*
> *eye of the beholder."*

Perhaps they're too busy dealing with the repetitive work processes they're tasked with. Perhaps they can't make a successful business case for the extra resources needed to undertake the initiative. Perhaps they fail to properly articulate how the proposed initiative might create organizational value, whether that be value for customers or competitive value.

This chapter is about delivering on the fundamental promise of a Master Expert: the ability to add *new* value to the organizations we work for.

In the Expertship model, we define three types of new value that experts can bring to their organization (see Figure 30.1):

- Operational value: the ability to generate initiatives that allow the organization to conduct its activities more efficiently.
- Customer value: the ability to generate initiatives that allow the organization to create new value for its external customers. It's important to note that these are not the expert's internal customers, who are included more in our first value-add category.
- Competitive value: the ability to generate initiatives that assist the organization in improving its current and future competitive position in the marketplace.

> *"Establishing what is and is not valuable to customers*
> *is a great skill to master."*

The definition of what value looks like in each of our experts' worlds is a complex question—one that experts who master Value Impact are good at exploring, finding answers to, and effectively articulating. Like beauty, value can be in the eye of the beholder. The ability to objectively establish what is and is not valuable to either internal or external customers, for both today and tomorrow, is a great skill to master. It requires a lot of discovery, insight, inspiration, and sometimes luck.

Let's consider the story of Priscilla, a financial reporting accountant. The main part of Priscilla's job is to send a large number of financial reports to the global head office. When we met her, the count had reached 41 reports per month. The nature of some of these reports were profit and loss management accounts, aged debtors, accounts payable, reconciliations, cash flow, headcount, and so on. Others were more obscure.

Priscilla's Story

WHEN WE MET PRISCILLA, she was about to join a cross-organization change initiative. She was to be the representative of the finance function on a sales and marketing improvement project. Working on such an inter-departmental project had been a long-standing aspiration, but she was stressed. "Being involved in all those meetings will not give me time to complete all the reports," she told us.

After some discussion, Priscilla decided on a plan of action. The best solution was to figure out which of those 41 monthly reports were *least valuable* to the organization and then stop producing them. A secondary criterion for no longer producing reports might be assessing which reports consumed the most time for not much value.

Of course, Priscilla was about to learn that in order to save time, you have to take time. So, she embarked on a military-style campaign of insight gathering. Where she knew the stakeholders, she went to talk to them about each report. How do you use it? What is it specifically about the data in the report that is insightful for you? Do you need all of the information or just a summary? Is there information not currently included in the report that would be useful to you? Pricilla had some doubts about asking that last question because it would likely generate more work for her rather than less, but it was the right question to ask, so she persevered.

Priscilla also bravely added one final tactic to her plan. When she could not find an owner, she would produce the report but not send it to the usual recipient list. There were 12 reports in this category.

Within six weeks, Priscilla's workload had changed completely. Of the 12 "unowned" reports, only two people contacted her asking why the report hadn't arrived. She immediately sent these reports to the respondents. The other ten reports turned out to be *zombie reports*. The recipients of the reports had either moved on or didn't require the information anymore, but the reports lived on. Perhaps they were requested by someone at head office years ago, but now no one knew or cared whether the reports were produced.

Capability: **VALUE IMPACT**

Creating Value as an Expert

THE THREE DOMAINS OF VALUE CREATION

Operational Value

The ability to generate initiatives which allow the organization to conduct their activities more efficiently.

Customer Value

The ability to generate initiatives which allow the organization to create new value for its external customers.

Competitive Value

The ability to generate initiatives which assist the organization to improve future competitive position in the marketplace.

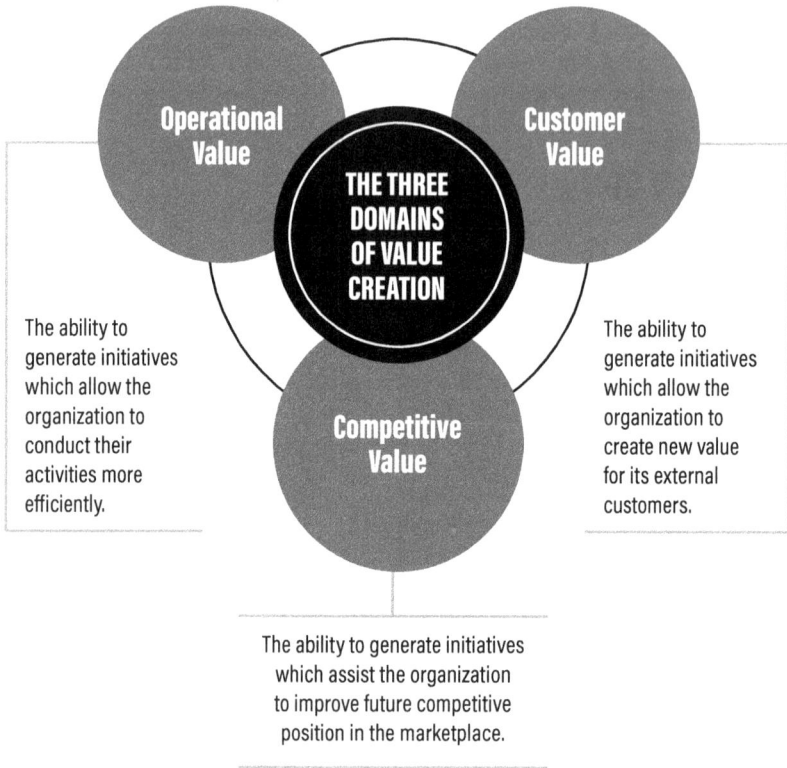

FIGURE 30.1: Creating Value as an Expert

Priscilla also bravely added one final tactic to her plan. When she could not find an owner, she would produce the report but not send it to the usual recipient list. There were 12 reports in this category.

Within six weeks, Priscilla's workload had changed completely. Of the 12 "unowned" reports, only two people contacted her asking why the report hadn't arrived. She immediately sent these reports to the respondents. The other ten reports turned out to be *zombie reports*. The recipients of the reports had either moved on or didn't require the information anymore, but the reports lived on. Perhaps they were requested by someone at head office years ago, but now no one knew or cared whether the reports were produced.

These ten reports included one that was very time-consuming to produce. This represented a very big productivity win for Priscilla, freeing almost two days a month that was previously spent producing a report that no one valued. Who knew? In the case of the two executives who reached out to Priscilla about the reports she didn't send, they only really used part of the report she produced and said they would actually value the data provided in a slightly different form. A further win.

> *"Ten of these reports turned out*
> *to be zombie reports."*

The discovery process Priscilla had embarked upon yielded a much better understanding of what the data was used for, and this helped Priscilla produce higher value reports in less time. Priscilla also reported that she now *enjoyed* producing those reports because she knew the value her stakeholders got from them.

Conversations with all the other reports' stakeholders shed a further five reports from the monthly roster. Recipients told Priscilla "Yes, I occasionally look at it, but it doesn't really add much value," and "I'd prefer to be able to ask for specific ad-hoc reports rather than receive a generic regular report." Most importantly, Priscilla told us that the conversations with stakeholders who did need the reports generated a raft of improvements, making the data more useful to the recipients.

The Power of Periodic Triage

IN EFFECT, WHAT PRISCILLA had undertaken was a triage exercise. Triage is defined in medical use as the assignment of degrees of urgency to wounds or illnesses to decide the order of treatment for a large number of patients or casualties. In other organizations, it's the process of determining the most important people or things from a large number that all require attention. Figure 30.2 explains this concept of value triage. It maps the cost of producing a product or service (resources, time, money) from high to low against the value the customer perceives from low to high. Note that the indices run in opposite directions.

Capability: **VALUE IMPACT**

Value Triage: Cost-Benefit Analysis

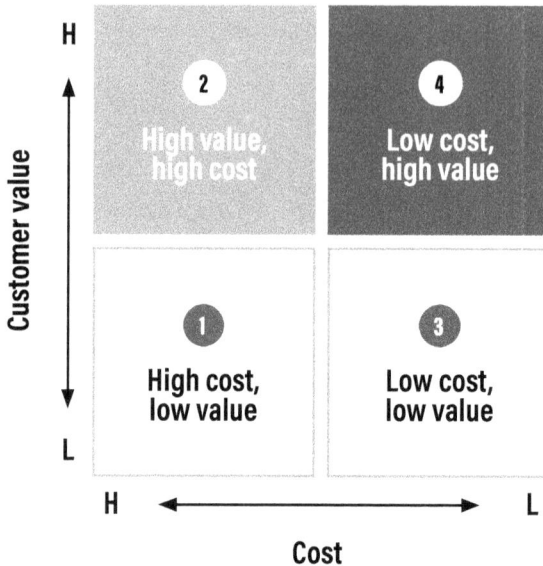

FIGURE 30.2: Cost-Benefit Analysis

After the discussions with stakeholders, Priscilla allocated all of her 41 reports to one of these four boxes. At least one was high cost as it took lots of time to produce and of very low value. It was actually of no value since no one came forward to say they missed receiving the report, so she allocated this to Box 1. As a general rule, anything in Box 1 should be stopped, and we should be on a perpetual crusade to find such activities and delete them from our to-do list.

There were some reports that fell into Box 2. They took a lot of time to produce but were of extremely high value to the customer. Sometimes, from a regulatory perspective, these were mandatory. They remained on Pricilla's list and needed to be completed.

Box 3 presents some opportunities for us. In Priscilla's case, these are reports that the customer didn't really get much value from but also didn't take much effort to produce. Overall, we'd recommend eliminating these reports because they represent time that could be used more productively. In one instance, however, Priscilla wanted to build a better stakeholder relationship with the report recipient, so she decided it was strategically worth the effort to continue producing the report.

Box 4 is where the gold is found. These are reports that take less effort to produce than those in Box 2 but are very highly valued by the customer. Priscilla reported that, as a consequence of her discussions, some reports she produced got moved from Box 3 to Box 4 because she could adapt the report to make it more valuable to the customer. At the same time, she reduced the time it took to produce that report.

If we take a simple example of this phenomenon, let's consider electricity bills. Receiving an invoice from our electricity supplier is not exactly the highlight of our month. Indeed, many of us dread the event. It's Box 3 territory because producing it is low cost for the electricity company and it's of low value to us. We'd prefer it if they forgot to send it to us.

But since electricity companies have started including helpful hints in this document on how to save money on your invoice, such as switching off plugs at the wall, putting timers on certain appliances, running dishwashers and washing machines after 9 p.m. to get off-peak rates, and so on, the invoice has become something of greater value. Did it move from Box 3 to Box 4? Well, maybe not. But for the electricity companies supplying this information, it was easy and cost almost nothing at all, yet it adds value to their customers and enhances their brand. "They're trying to help me save money, so they must be nice people." The first company to implement this gained the most in terms of brand recognition and customer loyalty and was lauded in the media for doing so. Now nearly all suppliers provide similar data and insights.

"The impact we describe in this chapter is the hardest work in this book, but it's also the most self-defining."

Organizations are always on the search for opportunities of this type. And as experts, we should be, too.

Priscilla, by being proactive, changed how she added value to the organization. She made the time she spent doing things more valuable and created time to participate in growth initiatives, such as the cross-organization project. She undertook this exercise because another project had suddenly arrived, so she had to find the time. Priscilla could also spend more time analyzing the reports' content, adding valuable additional commentary and helping stakeholders gain more immediate value from them. By doing so, Priscilla had found a way to *add more value*.

We'd encourage all experts to regularly undertake this value triage exercise. Because stakeholder X wanted that report last year does not mean they want the same report this year.

A CIO colleague of ours undertook this exercise on active IT projects across the Asia-Pacific region in his organization. He allocated a team to build a set of categories for these projects and then spent two months traversing the region, asking the same types of questions Priscilla asked. As a consequence of undertaking value triage, one-third of the projects on his current list were closed down. The productivity gain and the sense of relief among his team were immense.

Bringing It All Together

THE IMPACT WE DESCRIBE in this chapter is the hardest of all the work we discuss in this book. But it's compelling and the most self-defining. This is where the rubber meets the road. It's where we can position ourselves as not just experts but truly valuable executives in the organization's eyes.

Later in this chapter, we'll look at some specific techniques and tactics to create more value. But the first thing to say is that those who are successful and are building a track record of consistent value creation do so by bringing many other parts of the Expertship model to the table.

It's almost impossible to create new value in our expert domains unless we're doing a very competent job in the Expert Knowledge capability. In other words, seeking knowledge effectively, curating knowledge professionally, and then using innovative ways of creating new knowledge and insights. These insights are what lead to value creation (see Chapters 38 to 41).

Similarly, if we aren't operating at a Master Expert level in Market Context, we have little chance of finding meaningful new value. Market Context capabilities—a deep organizational knowledge and navigation abilities, a broad understanding of the competitive environment, and a close understanding of how customers think and choose products and services—lead directly to us seeing gaps and opportunities in value creation. Mastering Market Context is a precursor to mastering Value Impact (see Chapters 26 to 29).

All of the skills of Solutioning need to be brought to the table as well, including superb discovery skills, making sure we move off solution, exploring the deeper causes of problems and challenges, and using expert problem-solving skills. All of these contribute to finding new, innovative, deployable solutions that add great value (see Chapters 42 to 45).

Many of the skills we talk about in this book regarding personal impact and collaboration and advanced stakeholder engagement skills are also foundational requirements. To find new value means doing things in a new way, often changing how we and others think about the way things should be done or considered. Only with terrific interpersonal and influencing skills can we bring our colleagues along for the ride.

Value Impact is the ultimate objective. It's creating new value. We'll need to bring our A-game in our technical skills and our enterprise skills in order to operate at the Master Expert level in this capability. It's the ultimate test of just how expert we are.

The Secrets of Value Creation

IN OUR PROGRAMS, THE creation of new value, particularly experts operating proactively rather than reactively, is accepted as a major challenge for many participants. Putting aside finding the time, experts usually aren't quite sure how to go about auditing the value they're already creating, just as Priscilla did, or how to then look for opportunities to extend that value.

In our view, the six secrets of value are, like most of the concepts in this book, simply advanced common sense. They're nowhere near as complicated and difficult as many experts might imagine. Figure 30.3 describes our six secrets to success.

1. Develop a clear value definition

As an expert, we must understand how we create value through our work. This ability means being able to clearly differentiate between high-value work and low-value work. Without clarity on this, we can't begin to transition from too much low-value work to a higher percentage of high-value work. In publicly traded companies, work that contributes to financial performance (current and future profits) is at the center of this definition. Many experts are actually doing work that is more focused on tomorrow's profits. In not-for-profit organizations, value will most likely be determined by community impact.

2. Align to strategy

Understand your organization's strategy. As we discuss at length in the chapters on Market Context, understanding the *what* and the *why* of organizational strategy is really a ticket to the game in value creation. It acts as a road map for how to create value. It determines how the organization will allocate resources, so we will only be allocated some if our request is properly aligned and effectively articulated.

3. Understand value creation choices

Understand the several competing ways to create value: operational value, customer value and competitive value. Usually, in organizational roles, there are tensions between these three. Expert are, however, typically in a good position to both recognize these tensions and help resolve them.

4. Identify value drivers

Value drivers are the levers that the organization can activate in order to increase value. They'll be subtly different in each organization and relatively unique in each expert domain. In operational value, for example, the key value drivers include high-impact operational improvement initiatives to either cut costs, drive revenue enhancement, or allocate resources (such as capital, talent) more effectively. What is our ability to move the dial on these drivers?

5. Develop metrics

Develop appropriate measures of success for adding value. How will we measure Value Impact? Organizational measures are usually publicly available and easily understood. Personal success measures are harder to define but no less important. Some metrics, such as monthly financial reports, are very *rearview mirror*. That is, they report on something that has already happened. In value creation, we might need metrics that are like *headlights*, lighting the way forward. Customer satisfaction data usually provide clues as to whether or not customers will buy again in the future. The metrics we're looking for answer the question "Did I meet or exceed my organization's expectations of value creation?"

6. Develop a bias for action

The best value creators move very rapidly. They urgently seek to implement new ideas as soon as they possibly can. As agile methodology teaches us, learning and value creation is an iterative process. Starting to implement will, in itself, create more ideas and thoughts on solutions. These insights aren't available until we begin. Most importantly, we need to avoid the trap that many experts fall into: paralysis by analysis. Behaviors we often see are experts waiting until the perfect solution is formulated. Or waiting for yet more data to arrive. Each of these behaviors is a recipe for inaction and generates a poor personal brand. The idea of failing fast to succeed sooner is now standard operational policy at many innovative organizations.

Aligning Departmental Strategy

IN PREVIOUS CHAPTERS, WE discussed the importance of all experts understanding the *what* and the *why* of organizational strategy. The next step is to make sure our departmental or function strategy is aligned with the wider organizational strategy.

Figure 30.4 describes how Master Experts shape and then prioritize the key inputs that support organizational strategy. These inputs vary dramatically from one expert domain to another.

One organization may have an aggressive acquisition strategy. A strategically aligned legal team in that enterprise needs to be ready to quickly and effectively support best practice legal services during acquisitions. This probably also means that the legal team, even when not under strict, heavy deadlines, need to urgently and efficiently clear business-as-usual legal work so that they have bandwidth when acquisitions land unexpectedly and suddenly.

Capability: **VALUE IMPACT**

The Six Secrets of Value Creators

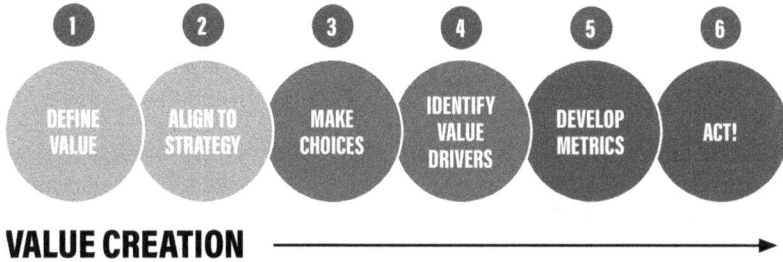

FIGURE 30.3: The Six Secrets of Value Creators

A Master Expert in this field would also ensure that the team reviewed what went well and what didn't after every acquisition, followed by a detailed discussion with the wider organization about what extra value legal could possibly add next time.

Another organization may have a strategic plan that involves overseas expansion and requires the setting up of new offices in other markets. Before the first office opens, a strategically aligned IT team would need to consider what changes to architecture and security might be required to provide new employees with immediate, trouble-free, and secure access to all IT services. In this instance, they would need to "get ahead of the business" to add new value by having planned and designed solutions ready for rollout when the business says it's ready.

Another organization may be planning to launch several new services in the next few years. A strategically aligned HR team would look at that organizational strategy and recognize that it will need to rapidly upstaff. And they would, quite possibly, need to start hiring professionals they have never hired previously. The HR team would need to plan processes to handle this new recruitment volume, possibly re-fashion and modernize its induction and onboarding processes, then talk to the business ahead of time about updating success profiles. Success profiles are descriptions of the attributes, skills and knowledge that the most successful people in roles have, so that the new staff exhibit the same qualities. Again, the HR experts will be getting "ahead of the business" by planning and designing so they can be highly responsive to the organizational need as soon as it arrives.

In many of these instances, there may be requirements to build business plans and business cases for new resources so that the pre-work is completed in a thoughtful and timely manner. There may also be a necessity to consider organizational redesign to handle new and possibly expanded responsibilities. In the legal team's case, perhaps they would take a senior lawyer and ask them to specialize in due diligence. In HR's case, recruitment was a small team with a steady amount of work, and that team is not properly structured or resourced to handle a sudden increase in volume, so new people and reporting lines may have to be put in place.

Institutionalizing Value Checks

WITH INTERNAL CLIENTS, IT'S important to conduct a value check as often as possible. We discuss this in detail in the chapters on stakeholder engagement (Chapters 12 to 15). We ask our internal clients "What is it that our advice, products, services, and so on allow you to achieve that is of value to you and wouldn't otherwise be possible?"

We're seeking to understand precisely how we and our team offer them a compelling best option. And if we aren't, in which areas do we need to step up?

Capability: **MARKET CONTEXT**

Aligning to Strategy
ALIGNED EXPERT STRATEGY

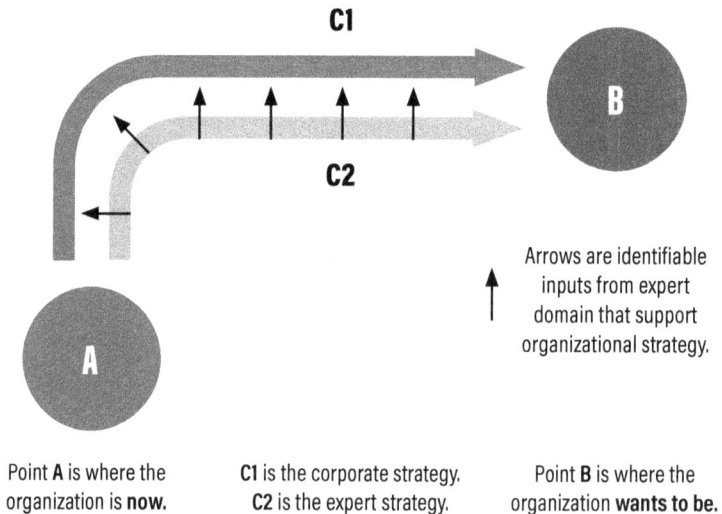

Arrows are identifiable inputs from expert domain that support organizational strategy.

Point **A** is where the organization is **now**.

C1 is the corporate strategy.
C2 is the expert strategy.

Point **B** is where the organization **wants to be**.

FIGURE 30.4: Aligning Expert Strategy with Organizational Strategy

In these times of outsourcing and technological disruption, it's important to realize that our clients very likely have alternative options to utilizing our expertise, even if they don't happen to be actively considering them at present. Ensuring that we have a compelling value proposition gives us some insurance against becoming obsolete or our roles and/or activities being outsourced going forward. And it also ensures that our services and advice remain relevant and on target, which is excellent value for money. At the very least, we should be less constrained by cost.

Brainstorming Out-Of-The-Box Ideas

WE'VE ALL HEARD OF brainstorming as a technique for generating creative ideas. But it's also a very useful technique for coming up with ideas for generating new value. The objective of brainstorming is to get people "thinking outside the box." There are two ways for experts to contribute here. You can be the catalyst for organizing a session and then facilitate it, or you can be invited to and participate in a session organized by someone else.

"Thinking outside the box" is a concept created by the psychologists running the nine-box experiment. In this experiment, participants are asked to connect the nine dots by drawing only four straight lines, without retracing or removing their pen from the paper (see Figure 30.5).

Thinking Outside the Box—Can You Complete This Exercise?

Problem: connect the nine dots by drawing only four straight lines. You cannot retrace or remove your pen from the paper.

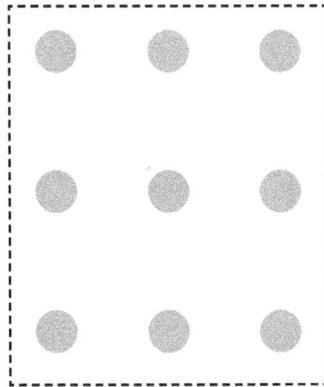

FIGURE 30.5: The Nine Dots and Thinking Outside the Box

Solution: On the next page — no cheating!

Most people can't do it because it requires them to look beyond the illusory spatial constraints created by the nine dots.

The same might be said of trying to imagine new value. It requires us to be prepared to reconsider what we had thought impossible or an idea where success is at least improbable.

Experts, as a rule, aren't good at brainstorming. But we need to be. We have natural constraints built into our DNA. The majority of experts are introverts, and research shows that extroverts are much more likely to contribute positively to brainstorming than introverts. This is because, as we have witnessed many times, extroverts speak without thinking things through. And that is the secret of success here: generating wild ideas and then gradually paring them back to something that is doable and creates new value.

As experts, we naturally tend to concentrate on the practicality of how something might get done and the detail of implementation and design. This can get in the way of us applying our imagination. The creator of brainstorming and its first rules, Alex Faickney Osborn, called his 1963 book *Applied Imagination*.

The rules of brainstorming are well known, and we list them in our primer in the Appendices of this book. We also give insights and advice on how to run a brainstorming session, which is a useful capability for most experts to master.

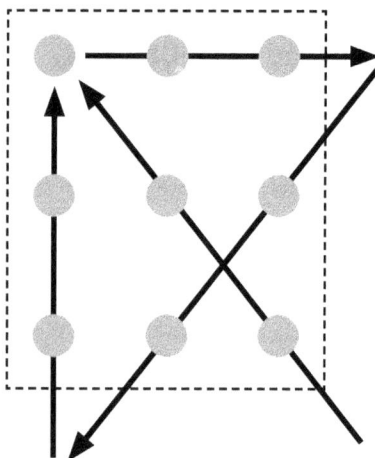

FIGURE 30.6: The Nine Dots and Thinking Outside the Box

Solution: think outside the box

Introverts can, of course, contribute significantly to brainstorming if the sessions are structured properly. Participants might be asked to work in pairs first or to write down ideas during a quiet period before sharing and discussing them with the wider group. Reflection periods might be scheduled, with each participant sharing elements of ideas they like and support, as well as the ideas they worry about. It's important and very beneficial to cater for everyone in these sessions.

The Expert Roles of Value Impact

VALUE IMPACT DESCRIBES THREE roles an expert must play:

- Operational Value Creator: the ability to provide long-term, organization-wide new value by creating effective operational efficiencies.
- Customer Value Creator: the ability to provide significant new value for internal and external customers.
- Competitive Advantage Creator: the ability to provide solutions to the business that positively impact competitive advantage.

The following three chapters address how Master Experts operate in each of these roles.

TAKING ACTION

Growing Our Value Impact Skills

IF THIS IS A capability in which you believe you could add greater value, here are some high-level suggestions for actions to take:

▶ INTENSIFY STUDY OF EFFICIENCY BREAKTHROUGHS IN OUR DOMAIN

As a member of our profession, there are usually multiple opportunities to explore which organizations are making the biggest efficiency breakthroughs worldwide and how they're doing so. This data and insight will enable us to spot possible efficiencies in our own organizations. Some questions we might like to ask ourselves are:

- When I attend events or consume newsletters and website content, am I specifically searching for information about operational efficiencies?
- How often do I take 30 minutes to really explore a much narrower search, and what impact might such an investment in time generate?
- Do I really study operational efficiency breakthroughs in other industries, especially those that have similar dynamics to mine? Am I actively trying to draw parallels and consider how breakthroughs elsewhere might be applied to my organization?

▶ SPEND MORE TIME OUT IN THE WILD

By out in the wild, we mean outside our technical bubble, either in the wider organization or external to our organization. Getting out into the wild allows us to observe our current work's impact and provides ideas for highly impactful future work. If we don't get out in the wild often enough, we end up simply doing business as usual, losing focus on priorities, and doing work that people ask us to do rather than work that moves the needle. Some questions we might want to ask ourselves:

- To what extent do I think spending time out in the wild is a waste of time? How do I change my mindset so I can see that it eventually prevents me from wasting time by doing the wrong work for the wrong reasons?
- How might spending time out in the wild help me prioritize my work based on real customer needs?
- Who do I need to spend time with outside my technical bubble? Who would add the most strategic thinking and perspective? How do I ensure a variety of viewpoints and perspectives?
- How do I make sure I get the most value out of these meetings—listening rather than problem solving?
- What systems do I need to implement to make sure I do spend time out in the wild and it doesn't just get forgotten?
- How do I assess the value of spending time in the wider organization, so I gradually build a good case for spending more time thinking and listening rather than just doing?

"Value creation in the future will be based on economies of creativity."

Jack Hughes

CHAPTER | 31 |

Creating Operational Value

How do we significantly impact our organization's operational efficiency?

IN THIS CHAPTER, WE WILL EXPLORE:

- How to ascertain which activities in our organization are value-adding and which are commoditized.
- Understanding the value drivers in our organization and how they can be impacted.
- The concept of total cost of ownership, and why it's important for many experts.

THE FIRST OF THE three expert roles in Value Impact is **Operational Value Creator.** This expert role deals with the extent to which experts provide new, long-term, organization-wide value by creating effective operational efficiencies. This expert role involves creating tangible value, ranging from delivering incremental technical initiatives to delivering organization-wide efficiencies or other tangible outcomes of material advantage.

The behaviors at each level of Expertship for this expert role are described in Figure 31.1.

At immature levels, experts will make recommendations for action based on only short-term, technical, departmental and tactical considerations. They'll rarely deploy commercial reasoning when presenting ideas or thinking about adding value. Their contributions to improvements in operational efficiency are likely to be limited to a departmental scope.

Experts that are derailing in this role will be delivering technical solutions with little connection to organizational budgets, goals or strategic direction. They'll rarely deploy commercial reasoning when presenting ideas. This may lead to them proposing ideas that are impractical from a commercial or community perspective or that exhibit little community dividend or commercial awareness.

In contrast, the Master Expert makes recommendations based on long-term, commercial, organizational and strategic considerations. In the public sector, commercial would mean cognizant of budgetary opportunities and constraints, or improvements that achieved a quantifiable community dividend. Master Experts consistently demonstrate reasoning focused on long-term commercial or community dividends when presenting ideas. They can be found leading visionary, innovative, organization-wide outcomes around operational transformation.

> *"Total cost of ownership (TCO) is a concept that is highly relevant to most experts."*

The value creation choices in the expert role of Organizational Value Creator revolve around identifying and prioritizing opportunities to eliminate redundant and inefficient activities. The purpose here is to explore which activities undertaken in the organization add value and which are low-value, commoditized activities (value than can easily be replicated by many parties). One strategy that many organizations choose is to outsource non-value-adding operations so that the organization can focus on core value-adding activities. Essential operations that are retained by the organization internally are optimized.

As experts in operational efficiency, part of our work is to drive down costs, automate and simplify processes, and focus on doing the unique things we do well as an organization brilliantly—faster, cheaper, more effectively than anyone else.

Those of us involved in systems development have a huge opportunity to add value here. Those of us in global organizations will be heavily involved in standardizing processes globally to find efficiencies and reduce the cost of ownership.

Total cost of ownership is a concept that is highly relevant to experts in most domains but is little understood by many in the wider organization.

We know a financial service firm that took 19 different database applications across the Asia-Pacific region and replaced them with one that

Capability: VALUE IMPACT
Expert Role: OPERATIONAL VALUE CREATOR

MASTER EXPERT

- Recommendations made on business, long-term, organizational, and strategic considerations.
- Demonstrates compelling commercial reasoning when presenting ideas.
- Leads visionary, improved, whole-of-business outcomes around operational transformation.
- Implements solutions that deliver tangible operational performance uplifts.
- Is pivotal in helping the organization making timely and well-informed decisions.

EXPERT

- Recommendations made on technical, business, medium-term, functional, and tactical considerations.
- Demonstrates commercial reasoning when presenting ideas.
- Delivers significantly improved functional outcomes around operational efficiency.

SPECIALIST

- Recommendations made on technical, short-term, departmental, and tactical considerations.
- Rarely deploys commercial reasoning when presenting ideas.
- Contributes to improvements in operational efficiency on a departmental basis.

- Delivers technical solutions with little connection to organizational budgets, goals, strategic direction.
- Never deploys commercial reasoning when presenting ideas.
- Proposes commercially impractical ideas and shows little commercial awareness.
- Displays indifference or antipathy towards the commercial agenda.

DERAILING

FIGURE 31.1: Operational Value Creator Behaviors

was significantly more modern. The IT team undertaking this change fielded screams of anger and protest from nearly all 19 jurisdictions. The Vietnamese wanted to support a local software developer in their fledging software development industry. The Thai team wanted the application to be in the Thai language. Internal customers in Hong Kong had a special functionality that they needed because of local regulations. And the list goes on. Each national stakeholder could only see the cost of the change and implementation (which they had to pay for) and a consequent reduction in the functionality and ease of use for their teams. Why would a local enterprise agree to such a decision?

> *"Determining what the key value drivers are in each organization is what operational value creation is all about."*

The simple answer is total cost of ownership. What each individual country could not see was the very significant cost of having to manage 19 different vendors, having to support 19 different applications, and the serious cost of have a single point of failure. What if the only person in Vietnam who intimately knew the application left the organization? What about the huge cost of sharing data across 19 different platforms or the organization's ability to see a single view of a regional client (the organization's main commercial focus and sweet spot). What about the inability to report organizational performance back to headquarters in North America? And increasingly, in today's world, what about the cost of adding robust security and data protection functionality to all 19 applications?

All of these elements make up a *total cost of ownership* calculation. While some of those who were using the system were losing perhaps 10 percent of the functionality they had enjoyed while using country-specific applications, by combining the region as a whole, the organization could save 59 percent a year on maintenance. Furthermore, the upgrades that delivered future functionalities and great efficiencies could now be implemented quickly and efficiently by a very small team. The broader corporate advantages were huge and long term but less visible. In comparison, the local pain was small and short term but very visible.

> *"Despite the many constraints, Master Experts make things happen anyway."*

Of course, it's the expert's responsibility to properly articulate the total cost of ownership to individual stakeholders and help them see the need to think strategically (the whole region, plus today and tomorrow), rather than tactical (my country, now). Unless we can show these stakeholders the whole picture and elevate their thinking, protest and push-back will continue. This push-back will cost the implementation team time, effort and stress, damaging relationships.

In this example, the IT team was responding to the key value drivers the organization operated on. Those value drivers included the ability to service a client seamlessly across the whole of what is a very complex region with many different languages, cultures and operating environments. The business had many local competitors, but an increasing number of larger clients in each of these 19 countries wanted the ability to operate easily in multiple jurisdictions. This organization saw that the thing that would drive value for clients was a single operating environment that was cheaper to run and would provide a more seamless service.

Determining in each of our domains what these key value drivers are and then prioritizing and implementing projects to create greater efficiency in these key value drivers is what operational value creation is all about.

As we will see in the following chapters on Change Agility, it requires Master Experts to not only visualize opportunities to achieve significant decreases in the total cost of ownership of systems and processes but also to sell and deliver the change effectively, taking our stakeholders on the journey with us. In fact, a Master Expert will inspire stakeholder support.

In most of the organizations we work with, these organizational efficiencies are not rocket science. An informed scan of what best practice looks like worldwide usually creates a long list of things that could be done more efficiently. Due to their size and slow decision-making, many large organizations lag behind the super-efficient processes and systems deployed by smaller or even start-up organizations who, of course, start with no legacy processes or systems (or stakeholders!) at all.

Having a bias for action is a critical Master Expert trait. Making a case for inaction is easier. The initiative will take too long, upset too many people, require retraining, and so on. It requires greater skill, courage and commitment to articulate a breakthrough total cost of ownership that will benefit the whole organization rather than individual departments or territories. This courageous articulation is the territory of the Master Expert means understanding the constraints but being determined to make things happen anyway.

TAKING ACTION

Growing Our Organizational Value Creator Skills

IF THIS IS AN expert role in which you believe you could add greater value, here are some high-level suggestions for actions to take:

▶ FAMILIARIZE YOURSELF WITH THE ORGANIZATION'S PRIMARY METRICS AND HOW IT'S PERFORMING

We need to be aware of the performance metrics that the organization, its leaders and the majority of its employees are focused on and accountable for.

- If we aren't, we'll miss out on some significant organizational context, and we might inadvertently send the signal that we're not interested in or are indifferent toward organizational performance. We'll seem like just another mouth to feed rather than a creator of value. Some questions we might like to ask ourselves are:
- What are the organizational performance metrics used across the organization? How well do I intimately understand them and what they mean?
- Does benchmarking data exist that tells us how well we're executing particular functions (IT, HR, finance) versus other similar organizations in our field? Am I utilizing these data?
- Are the standard reports that senior leaders look at available to me, and if not, what could be done to enable my access?
- If I have access to these data, am I successfully assessing how the organization is performing so that I can identify opportunities to add value? Is this business performing well? Is it improving, standing still, or going backward? Is it generating more revenue than last year? What's driving its growth? Or what explains its declining numbers? How's profitability? What is the variance between budgeted performance and actual performance? Are there any metrics that are concerning? Which metrics are senior managers most focused on (and why)?
- In the public sector, what community standards need to be met, what operational metrics are in play, how well does our organization do

this in comparison to similar organizations around the world? Is the taxpayer's money being put to the very best use, or not?

▶ EXPLICITLY APPLY COMMERCIAL REASONING (OR COMMUNITY DIVIDEND THINKING) WHENEVER YOU MAKE A RECOMMENDATION

When experts make proposals or recommendations that exhibit a lack of commercial reasoning, not only are those proposals or recommendations unlikely to be approved or adopted, but the experts will also be seen as impractical and out of step with reality. Proposals that don't have clearly defined organizational and commercial benefits can't be quantifiably measured, and thus their effectiveness is not realized. Some questions we might like to ask ourselves:

- Next time I make a proposal or a recommendation, how will I aim to convey the anticipated payoff in commercial terms? Do I have the knowledge and skills to do this? If not, how do I acquire them?
- Who is successful at putting forward business cases to the organization and getting them approved? How do I leverage their secrets of success into my own proposals?
- How will I measure any uplifts or savings and produce an impact report post-implementation? How can I demonstrate that I'm a trusted steward of scarce organizational resources and will deliver the promised return on investment?

"Get closer than ever to your customers. So close that you tell them what they need well before they realize it themselves."

Steve Jobs

CHAPTER | 32 |

Creating Customer Value

How do experts create new internal and external customer value?

IN THIS CHAPTER, WE WILL EXPLORE:

- How do we master adding new value to our organization's internal and external customers?
- What barriers get in the way of us thinking externally?
- How do we quickly and efficiently get up to speed on internal and external customer needs and feedback?

THE SECOND EXPERT ROLE for Value Impact is **Customer Value Creator.** This expert role deals with the extent to which we as experts provide significant new value for internal and external customers.

The behaviors at each level of Expertship for this expert role are described in Figure 32.1.

In this context, by external customers, we mean the external customers of the commercial enterprise or members of the community in the instance of a not-for-profit or public sector organization. This is an extension of the internal clients that experts usually focus on. Creating value for customers could mean anything from delivering incremental internal customer value-adds all the way up to delivering value creation breakthroughs for external customers.

At immature levels, experts will mainly focus on internal customers. They'll consider internal customer feedback when making recommendations regarding technical solutions. They'll usually react positively to requests for new solutions but are unlikely to be proactive. Derailing experts will be totally internally focused and will demonstrate very little awareness of, or interest in, external customer needs.

> *"The opportunities for us to add value to external customers can sometimes be difficult to see."*

Derailing experts will be focused on local, immediate pressures and requirements. They'll be focused on delivering for the internal customers who shout the loudest and/or are the most senior. They'll rarely assess which work should be undertaken based on value to customers. They'll typically advocate solutions that are consistent with the way things have always been done. Note that they'll advocate this approach based on their belief that it's the correct low-risk option. But, as experts, we can't create new value by doing it the way it has always been done or not being open to incremental or even stepwise improvements.

Master Experts, on the other hand, will make recommendations and implement solutions that deliver long-term product and service benefits to the organization's customers. They'll consistently demonstrate a strong commitment to understanding and reacting to changing customer needs, both today and in the future. As a matter of routine, they will deliver new value to internal customers, while their strategic focus lies in doing so for external customers.

> *"Seeing our organization 'from the outside in' is a critical success factor."*

It can sometimes be difficult for experts to see the opportunities to add value for external customers because most of us work at least one stage removed from external customers—and sometimes two or three times removed.

But we must not use this as an excuse. Those of us operating at Master Expert level study customer trends in the wider world (see Chapters 26 to 29) and consider what new value customers will need from our organization in one or two years' time. The question then becomes: how does my expert domain contribute to delivering that value?

So how do we get hold of customer knowledge to create new customer value?

Capability: VALUE IMPACT

Expert Role: CUSTOMER VALUE CREATOR

MASTER EXPERT

- Demonstrates a strong commitment to understanding and reacting to changing customer needs today and in the future.
- Recommendations made deliver long-term product/service benefits to the organization's customers.
- Routinely delivers new value to internal customers.
- Tracks global customer trends in order to predict future customer needs.

EXPERT

- Recommendations made deliver short-term product/service benefits to some of the organization's customers.
- Demonstrates an understanding of current customer needs.
- Responds effectively to requests for added value from internal customers.

SPECIALIST

- Main focus is on internal customers.
- Will consider internal customer feedback when making recommendations around technical solutions.
- Reacts positively to requests for new solutions.

- Is focused only on internal immediate internal customers.
- Demonstrates no awareness of external customer needs.
- Advocates doing it "like we've always done it," pushing back on requests for innovative solutions
- Lacks customer service skills and mindset.

DERAILING

FIGURE 32.1: Customer Value Creator Behaviors

Getting Perspective

EXPERTS ARE OFTEN IN roles that aren't client-facing. In fact, we may even have no contact at all with client-facing people in the organization. It's possible we may even avoid such colleagues. As experts, we often can't see the customer's perspective. We see the organization *"from the inside out."* If we're not careful and don't take steps to counter this perspective and intentionally broaden our view, we can become oblivious to what constitutes value to the organization's customers.

> *"The team didn't see this as a customer value creation opportunity. They saw it as risk minimization."*

Customers, of course, have a different perspective on our organization. They see it *"from the outside in."* In order to create value for customers, it's essential that we walk in their shoes. In particular, we need to understand what constitutes value for them. By the way, what they regard as value is not necessarily informed by what internal client-facing teams tell us they value. Sales teams and product teams, in particular, can overestimate their sense of what the customers value, describing instead their own opinions. Sales teams, for example, will often explain that the reason customers are not buying from us is because our competitors are discounting prices. As experts, we would not be doing our job if we took this type of narrative at face value. Sales teams may actually believe this, but that doesn't make it true. Product teams, flush with the excitement of inventing a new feature, will tell you that the new feature is the entire reason why customers are swinging toward our product. The reality in customer land, in our experience, is rarely that binary.

We described earlier (Chapter 29, *Becoming a Student of our Customers*) the authors' personal experience of surveying our clients about what they found most valuable about our services. We discovered that we inaccurately assumed what they valued. This was a perfect example of us believing one thing when another was true. We don't believe that this mistake is unique to us. In fact, organizations are often hugely impacted when competitors redefine value for customers with new products or services. As experts, we have to ask customers truly open questions to get deep insights into their current and future definitions of value.

So those of us who are naturally removed from direct contact with external customers face a challenge: is there a way to legitimately spend time with customers, talk to them or observe them? Or, could we at least delve into all the customer data that helps us understand where their passions and interests lie?

As a further example, let's take a corporate legal team. Their task is to rewrite the terms and conditions of use for a new product or service that the organization's product development team has conceived and designed.

The legal team may not approach this as an opportunity for customer value creation. They might be more focused on risk minimization as they have to ensure the terms and conditions defend the organization from the small number of customers who will attempt to sue it. We've all seen the kinds of terms and conditions such a mindset produces. It's classically the small print in a document that no one actually reads until something goes wrong.

As an example, did you know that buried in the fine print of the terms and conditions of your mileage plan with your airline, they have the right, at any time, for any reason or no reason at all, to cancel the scheme and cancel your points and you have no recourse whatsoever? This is a condition that the airline obviously doesn't want you to read, but the lawyers must make sure that it's in the small print somewhere.

However, we believe there is an opportunity here for the legal team to add value for the customer. They could take the time to write the terms and conditions in plain language, therefore making it more accessible and transparent. Most legal teams don't. They're too busy, or it's too hard, or it involves risk, or they didn't even think about the customer. They think inside-out, not outside-in.

> *"Where does feedback come into the organization,*
> *and is anyone looking at it?"*

We recently purchased a service from an organization in the US where their terms and conditions were in fine print and legalese. However, someone had decided to write a plain English preamble that explained the principles upon which the terms and conditions were built.

One was "If it doesn't work properly after you have followed the instructions properly, that's our fault, and we'll fix it. If it doesn't work because you didn't bother to read the instructions properly, and it breaks as a consequence, we think that's your fault, and we won't. Please read the instructions!"

We absolutely loved this. It was like one person talking to another, not a large corporation hiding behind impenetrable legal jargon. It articulated a clear and pretty fair principle.

Another principle espoused was "If you're having difficulty using the product as you had hoped to, we want to hear from you straight away. Please use our hotline or email us. We promise to be responsive. All the new features we're proud to include in this version of our product have come from great feedback from our customers. Please help us provide a better product for you by telling us what you think."

Again, the message is framed as one to one. It's open, transparent and encourages feedback. Most organizations don't want to know what's wrong with their products. This one did, which is why, of course, they're doing so well.

With a spot of brainstorming and a minimal amount of research, a legal team could get a sense of how customers interact with their terms and conditions and decide to act to make this process easier for customers. Very likely, since most lawyers are pretty smart people, they'll also be able to combine this new customer value they're creating with an operational efficiency, such as the customer service team getting far fewer calls asking them to explain the terms and conditions, for example. Perhaps they'll streamline the feedback process. Or maybe they'll think about where feedback comes into the organization and whether anyone is looking at it.

Customer experience is at the center of growth services worldwide, such as Uber. Initially, passengers may have been attracted to the service because of the lower price, but ask most Uber users these days (or users of the many equivalents currently available) and they'll tell you that it's the superior customer experience that attracts them to the service. They can see where their driver is on approach and help them find the location. They're offered water. The driver always speaks to them nicely because they know that the customer has the ability to rate the service (and of course, we behave very well because we know the drivers rate our behavior as customers.) There is no messing around with payments at the end, so we can just jump out. It's a fixed price ahead of the ride, and so on.

This is very different from many taxi organizations worldwide, where it's a closed, heavily regulated market. Although Uber has changed this in many instances. The service can range from wonderful to terrible, and there's no way to easily inform the taxi service of this difference in experience. Prices vary, and you have no way of knowing how much it will cost ahead of time. And, of course, occasionally, a taxi driver decides the bigger fare nearby is more worthwhile so your ride doesn't arrive.

But consider this: did traditional taxi companies around the world know that customers were frequently disappointed with the service they provided? In many cases, they did. Complaints about poor service were rife. Every year, thousands upon thousands of people complained, and many taxi companies did little or nothing about it because they didn't feel they needed to. Then Uber arrived and the taxi industry complained that this new competition was unfair and illegal. Eventually, laws were changed. Uber and other rideshare services were legalized, and the traditional taxi companies realized that their survival depended on them raising their game and listening intently to customers again.

Listening To Customers—Yes or No?

CLEARLY, LISTENING TO CUSTOMERS is very important, and *how* we listen is more important still. Talking frequently to a variety of customers is a key advantage in delivering value. Researchers have found that it's important for us to listen to exactly what the customers are saying. Customers will know what is needed to make them more satisfied with products and services. They'll also be able to tell you, if you ask the right questions, what types of improvements they're willing to pay extra for.

But there are times when listening to customers doesn't, in and of itself, provide adequate direction. If we're in the business of developing a completely new product or service, customers' opinions and preferences may be misleading because they're stuck in a current or historic mindset and can't necessarily envisage a completely new breakthrough product or service.

Research shows that companies that listened too much to what customers said were less successful with radical innovations than those that placed less emphasis on the content of conversations. This dynamic is neatly encapsulated in Henry Ford's famous quote: "If I had asked people what they wanted, they would have said a faster horse." In his excellent book on innovation, *The Innovator's Dilemma*, Clayton Christensen emphasizes this point. Customers are often happy with what they have until they see a new version that they could never have imagined.

The focus on customer experience and how it could be improved is an area every expert can focus on and add value to. After all, we're all customers of other products and services every day, experiencing the good, bad, ugly and hopefully, every now and then, the awesome.

TAKING ACTION

Growing Our Customer Value Creator Skills

IF THIS IS AN expert role in which you believe you could add greater value, here are some high-level suggestions for actions to take:

▶ USE CUSTOMER-CENTRIC REASONING

Stuck in their old ways, departments, and the experts who work there, use two main excuses for their approach: "we've always done it this way" and "this is the easiest way for us to do it." Experts have to deploy customer-centric thinking rather than department-centric thinking to avoid lapsing into this mind-numbing, internally focused claptrap. Some questions we might like to ask ourselves are:

- Many things will have changed in customer land in the last twelve months. Do I know what they are? Have I considered the impact they might have on what I deliver?
- Do I position all recommendations in terms of the positive impact that they'll have on the organization's customers? Or am I overly internally focused? Is what I propose likely to have an impact on customers? Do I not explicitly state the impact it will have on customers because I assume everyone else will be able to join the dots?
- How can I credibly create a connection to positive customer impacts? What do I need to know? Who do I need to know?
- Looking at the most recent recommendations and proposals I have made, do they sufficiently link to customer benefits? If I had my time again, how would I shape them differently?

▶ PROMOTE AND USE SCENARIO PLANNING TO VISUALIZE NEXT PRACTICE

Scenario planning, if used in a future-focused situation, helps us begin to imagine what the opportunities and challenges of our role, as well as the value we add, might look like in two or three years' time. It helps us develop a viewpoint on what next practice looks like. Some questions we might like to ask ourselves:

- What would my objective be if I were to undertake such an exercise? Am I clear on an ideal topic area? Who might I collaborate with to refine the topic and goals?
- Am I up to date on the latest techniques for scenario planning? How do I adopt a process that seems right for our team and for me?
- Which colleagues should be involved in the process? How would I invite them? How would I make it compelling for them to accept?
- Which specialists do I need to engage from other departments to make sure the process is focused on the entire organization rather than individual departments?
- What will I do with the insights once the session has occurred? What are my options for action?

▶ SPEND TIME WITH CUSTOMER-FACING TEAMS

In order to avoid the constraint of only being able to see issues from our specialist point of view, we need to get other perspectives. In adding customer value, the obvious candidates are customer-facing teams in our own organization. They're aware of how issues look from our customers' perspectives. Some questions we might like to ask ourselves:
- How do I make a case with customer-facing teams that I will be able to serve them better by spending time observing what they do and how they interact with customers?
- How will I build trust with them over time?
- If I spend valuable time away from other tasks, am I clear on what I am trying to achieve and how this will add commensurate value? To what extent do I need to update my knowledge of how things currently work and why they're designed this way?
- What type of insights am I hoping to gain that will enable me to be better able to think through incremental changes that would redefine customer value?

▶ ASK "WHAT WOULD GOOGLE OR AMAZON DO?"

There may be other innovative industry titans you might want to reference, but it's an interesting exercise to ask ourselves what world leaders in innovation and disruption might do with the problem we're facing. How would they think about the issue, capture customer insights or explore new value, and what approach would they take to test these new ideas?

"Experts need to get ahead of standard business requirements to offer timely new value."

CHAPTER 33

Creating Competitive Advantage

Whether private, public or not-for-profit sector, every organization has competitors or alternatives. How do experts contribute to making their organization the best choice?

IN THIS CHAPTER, WE WILL EXPLORE:

- How thinking competitively, whether in private business or public service, helps us ideate ways to create new value for customers.
- How to seek out rich sources of customer intelligence to build our knowledge and ideas.
- How to get out of our technical bubble and make a sustainable difference.

THE THIRD EXPERT ROLE in Value Impact is **Competitive Advantage Creator.** This expert role deals with the extent to which experts are able to provide solutions to our organizations that positively impact competitive advantage (or alternative advantage). The behaviors at each level of Expertship for this expert role are described in Figure 33.1.

At immature levels, experts will shape technical solutions for departmental improvements. They'll apply their focus to an immediate action list that has been presented to them. They'll make recommendations for small, short-term, incremental improvements that are important but don't result in major competitive advantage value.

Derailing experts here will focus on work from a purely technical perspective without considering broader enterprise goals or competitive positioning. They'll be reactive rather than proactive in making recommendations. They may not even know who the competitors are.

Conversely, the advanced Master Expert will actively shape and refine solutions to deliver significant business impact. They'll focus on understanding and delivering in line with the future needs of the organization to extend its competitive position. They'll make recommendations that align with long-term strategic goals and competitive advantage.

As we discussed in the previous chapters on Market Context, we need to be (and be seen to be) a highly proficient competitive strategist in order to be able to create value here.

Connecting Better With The Organization

IT'S A CHALLENGE FOR most experts to connect effectively with their colleagues who are actually competing day to day with the organization's competitors. Or colleagues who are striving to provide public sector services that are as good as or better than those provided by similar organizations anywhere in the world. Please note: this is still a competitive environment, particularly as global public sector benchmarking continues to grow in advanced countries.

"Put another way, we need to get outside of our comfort zone."

"I know I need to go out and connect with the wider business so I can really add strategic value, but I don't know how to go about it, and I'm pretty sure they wouldn't be interested in spending time with me." We hear this regularly from experts.

Other excuses (yes, sorry, that's what we believe these to be) are that "those customer-facing colleagues are too busy to spend time with me" or "I would have no idea what to say to them" or, more subliminally, "I don't initially want to show how ignorant I am about the sales process and our external customers." See our chapters on Market Context for a whole raft of questions we have available to us as experts to build our understanding and knowledge in these areas and get rid of these excuses.

Capability: VALUE IMPACT

Expert Role: COMPETITIVE ADVANTAGE CREATOR

MASTER EXPERT

- Actively shapes, refines and implements solutions to deliver significant business impact.
- Focuses on future needs of the organization to extend competitive position.
- Makes recommendations that deliver against long-term strategic goals and competitive advantage.
- Implements solutions that measurably improve the organization's competitive position.

EXPERT

- Actively shapes solutions to add technical and organizational advantage.
- Focuses on near-term initiatives to maintain competitive position.
- Makes recommendations that deliver against immediate organizational priorities.

SPECIALIST

- Shapes technical solutions for departmental improvements.
- Applies focus to immediate action list.
- Makes recommendations for small, short-term, incremental improvements.

- Applies focus from a purely technical perspective without consideration to broader organizational goals or competitive position.
- Is reactive rather than proactive in making any recommendations.
- Displays indifference/antipathy towards or ignorance of the organization's competitive landscape.

DERAILING

FIGURE 33.1: Competitive Advantage Creator Behaviors

The truth is that in order to be able to achieve Master Expert status, we need to be able to contribute to the generation of competitive advantage, and to do that, we have to start operating outside our technical bubble. Put another way, we need to get way outside of our comfort zone.

"Meeting removed stakeholders … the majority of reports were overwhelmingly positive."

To help experts get over these barriers, here are our three favorite tactics for engaging with people who we think might not want to engage with us.

Tactic 1: "Need your advice…"

"We're thinking of doing something different and want to get your take on it before we do it." Choose a likely future change. Most people worry about changes that might upset their current situation and that they won't be consulted about these changes. By talking to them about changes that might be coming down the line, you're consulting with them and building a positive relationship at the same time.

After exploring the possible change for five minutes, use the meeting to ask questions that build the relationship. Your biggest challenges? What keeps you awake at night? What are competitors doing that scare you? What problems would you love to solve? Then figure out how to deliver long-term strategic value to this part of the business. Tricky but effective!

Tactic 2: "I've been instructed to get feedback…"

"We've been instructed to undertake a business audit of our department's impact, and you're on the list." The pitch is: "We need feedback, and we've been told it has to come directly from the business, not via our intermediaries. You're on my list. Can you spare 30 minutes?"

This approach can gather some really good data. Make it real by getting a mandate to do this from your boss. Key questions include: "What do we do that you value, and what do we do that adds no value to you?" "What would you like us to do differently, and why?"

Tactic 3: "I'm a dumbass. Can you help me be less dumb?"

This tactic requires us to admit someone else might know more than us (gulp!). As it's such an unexpected approach, choose a topic that you can plausibly appear slightly ill-informed about, then appeal to their greater ego. The pitch is: "I'm not sure I fully understand this area, and I really want to be able to before we go to work on a solution."

The experts who attend our programs are expected to develop a Personal Growth Plan. Many of them include an action to "meet more removed stakeholders," by which they mean the wider business. These stakeholders are the eventual recipients of the value experts look to create but who they rarely meet. The level of nervousness about arranging and then attending these meetings is usually very high. And when we ask experts to report back on how the meetings went, the vast majority of reports are overwhelmingly positive. Experts report their surprise at just how welcomed they were, and how useful the broader perspective they gained from making this effort to meet removed stakeholders has been.

It takes courage, but it's an unavoidable task. Eventually, we need to get out of our bubble and go meet the people to whom we can add the most value. We have to stop depending on intermediaries to tell us what stakeholders want. We need to go and ask them ourselves.

Defining Competitive Advantage

IN OUR EXAMPLE IN the previous chapter of the Asia-Pacific IT team implementing a region-wide database application, the team had determined what its competitive advantage was: customers wanted to be able to operate seamlessly across the region.

This insight would have come from client-facing colleagues reporting back what they were hearing from customers. As a central function, which, as experts, we're often part of, the trick is to find opportunities (or channels) to listen to as much of this feedback as possible. It helps us discern where the message is consistent and therefore where it presents an opportunity.

The most high-level (and high-impact) question we're asking here is "How could our organization create value that would make our competitors' customers choose to buy our products and services instead?" And a further critical question is "What role does my expert domain have in helping shape this new value?"

Our organization's strategy deck should indicate where our organization anticipates future value can be found. But the real data is embedded in what customer-facing colleagues hear.

> *"Our client was soon the beneficiary of positive brand stories at dinner parties."*

We consider *customer-facing* a broad term. In most organizations, this isn't simply sales people or marketing people. Customer service teams are often a rich source of intelligence. The complaints department even more so, given that much of what they hear are the factors driving existing clients to leave our organization and choose our competitors. The digital team will be able to tell us what existing and prospective clients click on when visiting our websites and what they don't.

One of our client companies determined that resolving insurance claims faster and more efficiently than rivals would create a significant competitive advantage. They concluded that every organization has products that break, so the one highest-rated for customer experience is usually the one that fixes problems fastest and communicates best while doing so. Our client was soon the beneficiary of positive brand stories at dinner parties because they had upgraded their response times, communications, and overall service levels when it came to claims.

Using a combination of experts from product development, customer service, claims and the finance team, they realized that the process they put customers through was designed to address the 10 percent of customers trying to gain an unfair advantage. For example, those trying to get a replacement when the product was worn out rather than broken.

The complaints process did not cater for the 90 percent of customers whose product had broken and who had a completely valid complaint. They changed the process in favor of the majority and got a significant brand lift nine months later.

Sometimes, in the minds of some experts, competition is a dirty word. Some experts argue that competition is a low-end activity generally executed by sales people, not something experts should get involved in. In the minds of Master Experts, however, competition is an opportunity to make a difference and demonstrate our significant worth.

TAKING ACTION

Growing Our Competitive Advantage Value Creator Skills

IF THIS IS AN expert role in which you believe you could add greater value, here are some high-level suggestions for actions to take:

▶ LEVERAGE BREAKTHROUGH IDEAS IN OTHER INDUSTRIES TO CREATE NEW COMPETITIVE VALUE

If we can be the first in our industry or specialism to adopt new ideas that have worked in other industries, we'll be at the vanguard of creating new value and competitive advantage. We also want to avoid being surprised by new customer requirements, which are often generated by new services and features they're being offered in other areas of their life. Questions we might like to ask ourselves:

- Am I reading widely enough to know about these breakthroughs? Am I choosing what I read carefully enough to specifically look for these breakthroughs?
- Am I contemplating in enough detail the products and service my family and I am consuming and why I prefer them. Am I considering how these principles might apply to my organization's customers?
- Am I open enough to becoming a student of the "breakthrough," not worrying about the personal stardust associated with entrepreneurs who are changing markets? Am I exploring what thinking got them to the "new" and "breakthrough"? Am I thinking about how their thinking and concepts might apply to my organization? This thinking and analysis is the prelude to action.
- Have I considered which internal stakeholders have the most to gain from any similar breakthrough in my organization? How would I approach them with a view to starting a pilot or some other way of testing the new ideas in their environment? What would bring them to action?

"The world as we have created it is a process of our thinking. It cannot be changed without changing our thinking.**"**

Albert Einstein

MASTERING
CHANGE AGILITY

The Master Expert acts as a change catalyst and leads change initiatives effectively.

CHAPTER | **34** |

Change Agility

**One of the key measures of being a
Master Expert is the ability to consistently
drive innovation and change.
How well do we rate in change agility?**

IN THIS CHAPTER, WE WILL EXPLORE:

- Why is change so difficult for most organizations?
- What does modern best practice in change agility look like?
- Are we born with a change mindset, or can it be developed?
- What is enlightened change management, and what role do experts play in its execution?

KIRSTEN WORKS AS A specialist assessor in the claims department of a major global insurance broker. She deals with highly complex claims, often involving hundreds of thousands of dollars. It's a challenging role that requires intricate negotiations between the broker's clients and the insurer.

Kirsten has just learned that she and other members of the claims team will no longer have assigned desks and offices. Going forward, they will be hot-desking. An automated booking system will allocate a different desk to them every time they visit the office.

She is told this is part of the organization's global strategy of shifting to an agile work environment. It's being promoted as a way to better enable collaboration and knowledge sharing.

While Kirsten can see that this might have advantages for some roles, she doesn't see how it works in her situation. She mostly works alone, needs greater privacy given the nature of her work, and requires easy access to the central filing system.

She doesn't believe that her needs have been adequately understood or considered by the people making this change.

"Typical," she thinks. "No one thinks of our team." Kirsten goes on to bemoan the decision repeatedly—even in the presence of other members of the claims team.

She fires off an angry email to the facilities management manager, challenging the decision and complaining about not being involved or consulted. Kirsten states for the record that this is yet another example of no one understanding the importance of her work, how much money she routinely saves the organization every week, and how her special needs as an expert are yet again being overridden to meet the needs of the wider organization.

"It can also be argued that Kirsten's response to the change leader may be counter-productive."

Rhonda, the facilities manager in question, receives the email with disdain. Kirsten's email is one of many Rhonda has received from technical specialists claiming their needs are unique. It has the same "you don't know what you are doing" message that is typical of the way the organization's specialists communicate. There is no attempt at a conversation or an exploration of the issues—just a straight-out refusal to accept the change. *Typical of experts,* Rhonda thinks.

Consulting On Change

ON THE FACE OF it, Kirsten's organization has made one of the most basic errors when it comes to effective change leadership. It has overlooked how disruptive change can be. It does not appear to have taken into account that in any change process, people need to go through an adjustment period. The majority of people automatically resist change unless someone has made a compelling case for why the change is a good thing.

If organizations—or experts—do not give enough thought to how employees and other stakeholders will be impacted by a particular change, they can expect to encounter resistance. (We note that some organizations and people very quickly embrace change, but these are, in our experience, very much in the minority.) Because no consideration has been given to the impact of a change on specific individuals or groups, organizations typically do not customize their communication of this change for different groups and employees in different roles or circumstances. In this case, it appears that there has been a lack of consultation, and perhaps those implementing the change (the introduction of hot-desking) have not really considered how different categories of employees might react.

However, it could also be argued that Kirsten's response to the change leader—Rhonda, in this case—may be counter-productive. The style with which Kirsten's message is delivered and the content—outright condemnation of the change and the way it has been communicated—cause her message to be discarded. Kirsten has not created an environment in which her concerns are going to be properly considered. Therefore, the email is a waste of effort and a missed opportunity to influence the outcome.

Those leading change initiatives in organizations often forget that people need a period of time to adjust and that they often need to voice their concerns. Investing time in such a process frequently accelerates the engagement of hearts and minds in the new direction. People will begin to work through their emotions about the change more swiftly and constructively. This reduces resistance and positively engages people in supporting the change. The change itself gets done faster.

> *"The irony is that change aggressively imposed will almost guarantee fierce resistance."*

But many involved in sponsoring or implementing the change argue that there's no time for consultation. The typical excuse made is that "We need to make the change now, or else…" The irony is that change aggressively imposed will almost guarantee fierce resistance, which ends up taking much longer to address. By not taking the time to consult with the affected individuals and groups upfront, organizations tie up resources and make the implementation of change much more time-consuming.

This lack of consulting by senior management is extremely common in the West. There is almost a parent-child relationship at play. The failure to treat employees like adults by asking them to also think about the problems faced by the organization and help shape solutions speaks to a leadership attitude that believes employees won't understand, or they will resist anyway, so there's no choice but to impose solutions on them—or worse, an attitude of "we know best."

Another common mistake is that the benefits of a particular change are often expressed by senior leaders and change managers purely in terms of various organizational outcomes, rather than how the change will affect employees. Individuals—quite naturally and understandably—tend to be concerned with what the changes will mean for them. In situations like this, the organization needs a well-argued communications plan with alternative strategies for different stakeholder groups. This might include an upfront consultation about people's needs and concerns.

In workshops with senior leadership teams on shaping change processes, when we discuss the benefits of prior consultation, leaders often ask us "… but what happens if employees come up with a plausible alternative strategy?" Then subtext is: How should we, as leaders, react? Employees coming up with a possible plausible alternative strategy is going to derail us further!

Questions like this one from senior leaders reveal two common beliefs: Firstly, that the consultation process is being done "because we have to be seen to be consulting" even though "we've already decided on the best action." Secondly, the question implies that leaders do not believe it's possible for employees to come up with a better option. Is this the ultimate statement of senior leadership arrogance? In our experience, conversely, employees are often those closest to the challenge or to customers, and they frequently make valuable contributions that improve change ideas. We'd also argue that you won't find this poor senior leadership attitude in new, fast-growing corporations. They listen as closely to their employees as they do to their customers.

When employees like Kirsten are worried about the changes, they often display problematic behaviors in front of their colleagues, such as resistance, disillusionment, and antipathy toward the change. This in turn affects other people's attitudes.

But Kirsten is also at fault. She did not take the time to try to understand the rationale behind the organization's decision to make this change. She immediately assumed that her circumstances hadn't been taken into account without checking in to see if others had been consulted.

> *"We have met many experts who are in denial about the rate of change."*

She didn't need to turn it into a personal attack on the capability of a colleague. She should have focused on the issue. She made an assumption that additional collaboration between herself and others would add no value to the organization and its clients.

By imposing her opinion about these changes and automatically opposing them, Kirsten has made exactly the same mistake that she was accusing Rhonda and her team of making.

Change is the New Normal

OVER THE PAST FEW years, we have worked with hundreds of organizations all around the world. Change is happening in every one of them. Change is, as they say, the new normal.

There are a few organizations where change isn't happening, and these are the companies most at risk of being disrupted. They're the new Kodak, the new Novell, the new BlackBerry.

Some organizations are so overcome by the constant rate of change that they're suffering from change fatigue, or out-of-touch senior executives are simply unable to adapt their worldview and their market strategy quickly enough to survive.

Many of us, as experts, have the same problem. We get so wrapped up in our own way of doing things that we cannot see beyond it. We've met many experts who are in denial about the rate of change and how it'll impact them, even though we're clearly living in times when the ability to change and adapt to change has never been more important.

> *"Positive conviction needs to be earned*
> *—it cannot be demanded."*

Given the importance and prevalence of change, we need to realize that it's something that experts cannot avoid. More than that, we need to embrace it, and even lead it, if we are to deliver value optimally. As experts, we're likely to be active players in the changes happening around us.

The Master Expert understands change and operates as a senior influencer in many ways. This chapter examines how experts at various levels view their own sense of responsibility for and sense of agency in engaging with change projects.

Enlightened Change Management

ENLIGHTENED CHANGE MANAGEMENT SHOULD begin before any decisions are made about how that change will be implemented. It involves identifying who to include in the decision process, who is likely to be impacted and how, and how they're likely to feel about the proposed change.

Unenlightened change management is a rearguard action aimed at damage control to lessen the effects of the emotional reactions that have been triggered by the failure to anticipate them and offset them with intelligent planning, communication, and engagement.

Shock and disbelief are the most commonly occurring initial reactions to learning of an unanticipated change, just as they're often the initial reactions to learning of the death of a loved one.

"No! That can't be! Why would the organization make such a ridiculous and unenlightened decision?" Denial is a common form of defensiveness. It's a form of non-acceptance, a form of self-protection. By denying it's happening, the mind tries to avoid any accompanying trauma.

When experiencing feelings like shock and denial, our rational brains are temporarily suspended, and we're rendered incapable of constructively thinking through what we need to do to progress through the change or even evaluating what it means objectively. Typically, such disabling feelings not only impair our attention and engagement but are the prelude to more resistant emotions, such as fear and anger.

Once it becomes clear that the change is actually happening—that it's undeniable—then antipathy toward it triggers stronger and stronger resistance. We instinctively feel that we should oppose this threat that has unsettled us. Enlightened change management practices recognize that these are natural human responses to the unfamiliar and to perceived threats. It allows for people's need to process such feelings for a period of time. It anticipates such responses and provides proactive support to aid them in processing such feelings in the most constructive and expedient manner possible.

Unenlightened change management, on the other hand, fails to envision or anticipate the natural and legitimate concerns that people will have. When these feelings are expressed, they not only remain unacknowledged but are often actively suppressed. "You shouldn't feel like that! Come on! Get with the program!"

When people feel that they can air their concerns and express their worries or outrage and that the decision-makers are hearing their concerns and taking them into account, then the intensity of such feelings typically subsides. That allows their rational brain to take over the controls again. They can start adjusting rationally to the proposed change. But if, when expressing their doubts and worries, people don't feel that they're being heard, then they often dig their heels in. They become even more resistant and unreasonable. They get stuck.

When applying some of the effective change management practices outlined shortly, it's not reasonable to expect that you'll have everyone's buy-in from day one. It's more realistic to anticipate some natural resistance. But when anticipated and planned for, when empathy is applied to hearing people's concerns and allowing their expression within reasonable limits, the resistance can quickly give way to openness—a willingness to cautiously move forward.

> *"As many as 70 percent of change initiatives*
> *fail to realize the anticipated benefits."*

Over time, this caution can also make way for a more wholehearted commitment. But such positive conviction needs to be earned—it can't be demanded. To insist on the buy-in of others while they're still expressing reservations will likely only compound the resistance. When managed skillfully, resistance can be dissolved relatively swiftly, perhaps even in the course of one artful and empathic conversation.

But when people don't feel that their expressions of concern have been heard and taken into account, they can get stuck in a resistant, cynical, hostile, oppositional state, sometimes for years. So, with each new change the organization embarks on, it faces an increasingly hostile resistance movement. Morale and engagement inevitably tank and performance sinks, wiping out any of the anticipated benefits of the change initiative.

As many as 70 percent of change initiatives fail to realize the anticipated benefits. That's usually not because the idea wasn't sound in principle. Rather, such "benefit realization" shortfalls are typically the result of poor execution of change management and a failure to win the hearts and minds of the people who needed to be brought on the journey.

The Stages of Change

IN OUR WORKSHOPS, WE conduct an exercise where we invite participants to recall two changes that they have experienced:
- One that they embarked on of their own volition, such as a change of job or career direction, buying a house, getting married, having children, taking up a new diet or exercise program.
- One that was determined by others, such as an organizational restructure, a new boss, the introduction of new processes or procedures.

We ask them to describe the feelings at the outset of the change, during it, and at its conclusion. We then ask them to estimate how long it took them to become sufficiently accustomed to the change so that it felt like the norm again, with no further adjustment required of them.

In just about all of these cases, they describe the experience of undertaking change of their own volition as the most preferable of the two experiences. They had ownership of the intended outcomes. They were making changes to achieve some self-determined benefits which no one else had to sell them on. They were the intended beneficiaries, with no trust issues about whether or not they were being told everything or whether there was some undisclosed agenda at play.

> *"The change curve describes emotional*
> *reactions, not logical ones."*

They also felt that they had probably estimated what kinds of challenges there might be in making the transition to the new way of operating. Even if there were occasional surprises—after all, they were charting new waters— they were prepared to accept responsibility for them because they owned the decision. No one else was to blame for any unanticipated challenges.

Sometimes, as participants considered this self-imposed experience, there was a recognition that they had perhaps suffered from uninformed optimism. The change had proved harder to implement than they'd envisioned, it was more unsettling or disruptive, and the new reality wasn't everything they had hoped for. But nonetheless, they owned it.

Most participants had quite a different experience when change was imposed upon them as a consequence of others' decisions. Participants' descriptions of this aligned with a typical progression of emotions.

We call this the change curve (see Figure 34.1). As you can see, there are various stages, which we describe below.

Denial, anxiety and shock

Participants usually say that the announcement of the change was a surprise, and the impact it might have on them was a shock. Denial follows quickly afterward—that "this isn't really happening" feeling.

We're not describing logical reactions here. The response from most participants is that their comfortable world is being disrupted, even ended. These are *emotional* reactions.

Fear and anger

In the next stages, people become angry and then fearful. "Why didn't anyone warn us? Whose fault is it that we have to change? Why can't others change while I stay the same?"

This anger is quickly followed by fear of an unknown future. "Is my job safe? Will I lose valuable colleagues and friends? Will I be successful in my new role? Will I enjoy the responsibilities? Did I do enough in the last year or so to survive this change?"

Capability: **CHANGE IMPACT**

The Change Curve

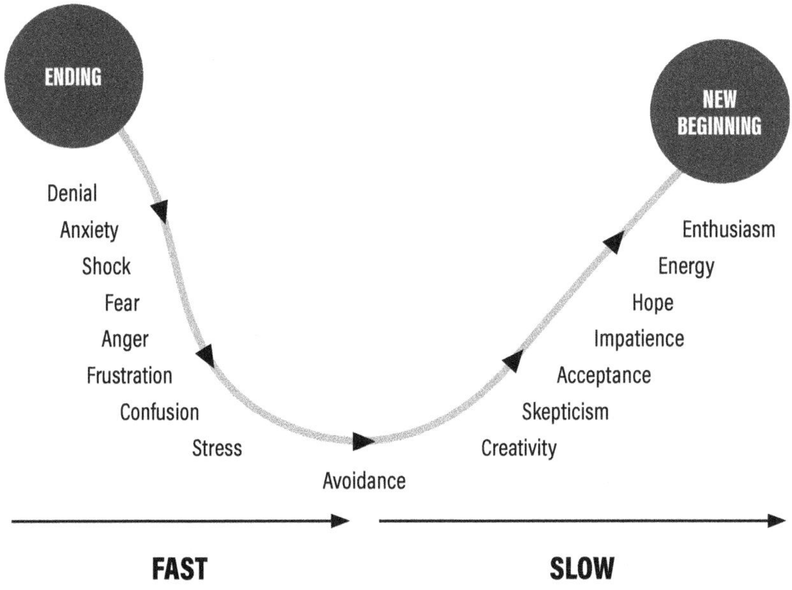

FIGURE 34.1: The Change Curve

Skepticism and acceptance

The next stages of dealing with change lead to acceptance. This is the turning point that's reached after anger and fear have been exhausted. It takes more time for some people than others, and in some cases, it's never achieved.

This stage often manifests as ambivalence—no longer caring one way or the other. Whatever will be, will be. But, gradually, skepticism gives way to acceptance that the change is going to happen whether we like it or not, and we might start thinking about what part we might play in this new world.

Enthusiasm

The final stage is enthusiasm. In this stage, we're prepared to get on the bus and accept the change. We might even start to feel enthusiastic about it because we can see some of the benefits.

By this stage, participants are getting used to the change and recognizing that it was necessary. They may also see the potential for personal and professional growth. The memory of how things used to be fades. It feels like a new beginning.

Ending and new beginning

One last observation about the change curve represented in Figure 34.1. At the top left of the curve, we see Ending. Participants often ask us why the ending is actually positioned at the beginning of the curve.

The ending is a stage that is very often ignored by those driving the change. But it's far more difficult to ignore if you're the one having change imposed upon you. The whole concept of change is that "now things will be different." What was normal for me before will no longer be normal for me going forward. In work life, this sometimes means a change of team members (often team member losses), changes in responsibilities, or perhaps even relocation. Our life up to that announcement was X, and now X will be replaced by something else. There is a significant feeling of loss.

> *"Different individuals navigate the change journey at different speeds."*

As an aside, senior leaders often compound this sense of loss by inadvertently laying blame. "We've been approaching this process all wrong, and we now need to do it differently," comes the cry. The response, usually muttered under the breath, is "Well, it was you lot who told us to do it that way…" Most particularly, the participants have often experienced a lack of recognition for their previous work—no "thanks for all your efforts so far and for the fact that your hard work and great teams have got us here." This accentuates the sense of loss and starts generating the more aggressive emotions, like anger and fear, that are to come.

The New Beginning is actually signaling that we're moving from the "change in progress" stage to accepting and normalizing the new arrangements, whatever they may be.

Changing Insights

WE'VE CONDUCTED THIS DISCUSSION with thousands of participants over the years, and also more recently with many hundreds of subject matter experts. The consistency with which these descriptions arrive is quite remarkable.

Not everyone has negative reactions to the initial announcement of change. We estimate about 10 percent of people are ready to embrace change straight away and are excited about it. Typically, upon exploration, these participants have either a remarkably positive disposition, or have benefited from the last few changes and therefore see change as a good thing.

But for most people, their initial response to change travels through these four steps. By the end of the story, about 90 percent of participants say the change they were initially worried about turned out well for them. About 10 percent say it ended up being a complete disaster, as they initially predicted.

Several other insights usually emerge from these discussions. Firstly, most people agree that different individuals navigate the journey at different speeds. Some participants could easily accelerate from one stage to another, while others took much longer to progress. It's a mistake to believe that everyone should move along the curve at the same speed. This also implies that, as experts leading change, we need to be prepared to dedicate more time to helping some of our colleagues than others.

> *"TINA (There Is No Alternative) communications have had their impact."*

Secondly, every group tends to agree that by the time the change is announced, those making the announcement are at stage four of the curve—positive, passionate, believing in the change. This is typically senior management, of course, and this helps explain why while the rest of the organization are in shock and denial, the managers (who had their shock and denial stage months ago, prior to shaping the change solution) are impossibly and irritatingly happy and committed.

Thirdly, most groups agree that those in stage four—those leading change—tend to want to drive people through the *disturbed* stages far too quickly. Communication has a great deal to do with this, as insufficient thought, time and attention are allocated for questions from those upon whom the change is being imposed.

Communication emanating from those leading the change is typically one-way during these initiatives. Those who don't immediately agree that the change is a great idea are quickly labeled detractors or negative people. They're told sternly to get on the bus, or that the train is leaving the station, or some similar, highly annoying metaphor.

In addition to communication, the way in which organizations decide to handle change projects is a common problem. Change teams are created and given tight deadlines to complete the change process. These change teams are often populated by professional change managers and are driven by project Gantt charts rather than audience emotions.

And they're rewarded for on-time delivery and achieving milestones rather than winning the hearts and minds of the employees. By the time these change professionals are appointed to the change project, the key mistakes of lack of consultation and TINA (There Is No Alternative) communications have had their impact. The resistance movement has already formed and is armed and ready for battle.

While the journey along the change curve is reasonably consistent, different people travel through the curve at different speeds. Management, who announce the changes, for example, are often already through the curve before the staff they announce it to have even started. And different personalities have different reactions. The glass-half-full versus glass-half-empty reaction is well documented.

In the next few chapters, we focus on the three roles a Master Expert plays in change agility: that of Change Leader, Change Supporter, and Change Catalyst.

- Change Supporter: the extent to which experts have the ability to promote a positive change culture by modeling supportive behaviors toward change.
- Change Catalyst: the extent to which experts have set a change agenda by consistently looking for opportunities to make positive changes.
- Change Leader: the extent to which experts have the ability to step up into a leadership role on change projects when required, constructively engaging others in change.

These chapters form a detailed primer on how to manage change through the change process for those experts who may have to lead a change initiative.

The Expert Roles of Change Impact

CHANGE AGILITY DESCRIBES THREE roles an expert is in a strong position
to play:
- These are shown in Figure 34.2

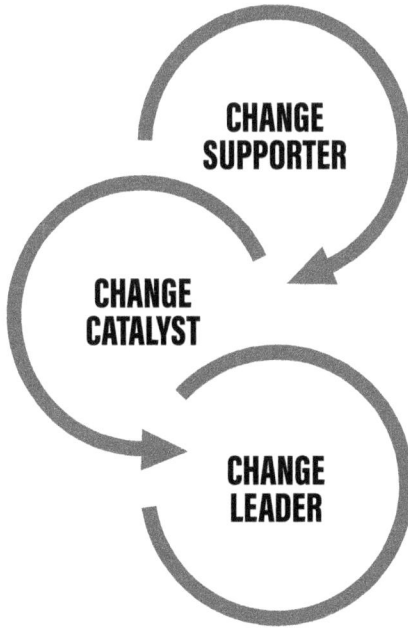

FIGURE 34.2: Change Agility Expert Roles

CHAPTER 35

Being a Change Supporter

What are our default attitudes toward change? Where did they come from?

IN THIS CHAPTER, WE WILL EXPLORE:

- What attributes, often found in experts, assist us in being change supporters, and which get in the way?
- What should the role of experts be in supporting change?
- How do we become a light, not a critic?
- How do we build our change agility?

THE FIRST OF THE expert roles in the Change Agility capability is **Change Supporter.** This expert role deals with the extent to which experts have the ability to promote a positive change culture by modeling supportive behaviors toward change.

This expert role is about our default individual change settings. Do we naturally embrace change or typically resist it, and how do these behaviors play out in our role as experts?

The behaviors at each level of Expertship for this expert role are described in Figure 35.1.

At immature levels, experts are developing an ability to embrace and participate in change. They're able to envisage and articulate the individual change benefits. Derailing behaviors include the expert exhibiting a very closed mindset toward change. Their default reaction when change is proposed is immediate and often very overtly resistant.

In contrast, the Master Expert will promote and model a positive change culture and is able to envisage and articulate not just the individual and departmental benefits of change, but also the organizational benefits of change.

Change As An Expert

MANY OF THE MINDSETS and capabilities that make us great experts actually get in the way of our being effective change agents.

All of these challenges can be summed up in the observation of a client of ours, a chief information officer (CIO), who told us that, in his experience, his IT experts were attitudinally fine with change when demanding change of others. However, they were much less enthusiastic when change was being imposed on them. We observe that this is not a situation that is unique to experts. In the next few pages, we'll look at this specifically from the perspective of experts.

There are many factors that contribute to experts being wary of change:

1. Love of order

As experts, we're generally used to working in an orderly world. A change, by its nature, is not orderly—or at least it's rarely experienced as such. Change is about systems, but systems are used by people, and people are messy.

Understanding this and planning to win hearts and minds is a challenge for many of us. We tend to prefer the cold, hard logic of rational arguments for a system change. No gray areas, please!

> *"Experts may not consider their actions as arrogant, but others will see them that way."*

As many of us may have done at times, Kirsten reacted emotionally to the change of office arrangements. Although she believed she was acting rationally, she was not. A person acting rationally would seek to get all the facts before making up their mind about the benefits, or otherwise, of the change. Kirsten, under the guise of using logic, made many assumptions about the way her role was viewed, how she was being treated, and the intellect of the people advocating the change. These are all emotional reactions, as per the change curve.

Capability: CHANGE SUPPORTER BEHAVIORS

Expert Role: CHANGE AGILITY

MASTER EXPERT

- Promotes and models a positive change culture.
- Able to envisage and articulate organizational change benefits.
- Constructively and proactively engages in change.
- Is an early adopter

EXPERT

- Models a supportive mindset towards change.
- Able to envisage and articulate departmental change benefits.
- Constructively engages in change.
- Is an early follower.

SPECIALIST

- Models a developing ability to embrace and participate in change.
- Able to envisage and articulate individual change benefits.
- Actively seeks to understand the benefits of change.

- Closed mindset toward change.
- Immediate resistance when change is proposed.
- Publicly dismissive of change initiatives.

DERAILING

FIGURE 35.1: Change Supporter Behaviors

2. Staying in our comfort zone

As experts, we're most comfortable when we're concentrating on our own specialty. Unless it's a change we ourselves are advocating, we often feel that participating in or facilitating a wider change is not part of our role. We don't consider it our responsibility. We often have a sense of detachment from change.

Kirsten perceives the new office arrangements as something relevant to others rather than herself. But consider this: finding ways of collaborating more effectively across the organization is very likely to benefit the organization, its customers and its commercial success. There are even benefits for Kirsten.

It's arrogant of Kirsten to assume that collaboration with other parts of the organization will have no value. She may not consider her actions arrogant, but others will most definitely see it that way.

3. Lack of ambiguity

Many experts are not good at ambiguity. Accuracy, predictability and exactitude are important in our world. Otherwise, computer code wouldn't run, bridges would fall down, and poorly worded contracts would open the organization up to significant risk. We like things to be definite and consistent, which is the very antithesis of change.

Kirsten's resistance to change is mainly because it creates uncertainty about how things will be. How does she make private phone calls? The new design has privacy booths, but she didn't wait to find this out. Will the filing system be further away and therefore require her to walk more? Yes, which means that she will be bumping into colleagues and connecting in a way she doesn't currently. Will she enjoy sitting somewhere else with a different view and with different colleagues around her? It will take her a little out of her comfort zone, but she might even get a window view on some days. Will the agile workspace mean that more colleagues witness the challenges she faces in her role, how professionally she handles them, and therefore respect her and her function more? Most likely, yes.

Often, it's an expert's natural instinct to think of all the things that might go wrong in any process. In fact, this negativity bias is true of all humans. For example, if you explain the changes you're planning to an expert in a related field, that expert may well tell you all the things that could possibly go wrong. As experts, we've learned the hard way to be very good indeed at identifying and isolating risks. In fact, as previously discussed, it's something experts are famous for, and not usually in a good way.

But once our expert friend has finished listing the challenges and issues, we might ask "So, you're not in favor of these changes?" Our expert will look up, surprised, and say "No, I didn't say that. I'm just telling you all the things that could go wrong. I'm supportive of the change, provided we plan to mitigate the risks properly."

Who would've guessed? This natural deep-dive analysis often comes across as resistance to the idea, when the expert in question is simply thinking out loud. We've all experienced such a conversation. And we've all been guilty of being that expert.

> *"As experts, we're often at the other end of this groupthink."*

4. Wariness of Nirvana

As experts, we've all learned to distrust the glorious promises of nirvana promoted by the change team or by the enthusiastic missives from senior management.

Our distrust of change might be quite rational. "The last six change programs this organization attempted have all failed to deliver the benefits, and they have taken far longer to execute than initially claimed," we might say, with some justification. Why would we imagine the seventh initiative be any different? Logic dictates it's unlikely.

Kirsten immediately channels previous experiences of failed change initiatives to describe the new one Rhonda and her team are advocating. Kirsten is judging this idea based on poor execution of other ideas. Again, while Kirsten believes she is being rational, she's actually exhibiting an emotional response.

We have seen this often. An expert has had a poor experience with someone in the wider organization (not one of their technical group, so let's use sales as an example) and thinks all people in sales are morons. Someone from our technical group has a bad experience with payroll, so all of payroll's activities are immediately branded inefficient.

As experts, we're often at the other end of this sloppy thinking. Someone in the wider organization has a problem with a laptop, so instantly, the whole of the IT department is seen as incompetent. One lawyer in the legal department pushes back on an unrealistic timeframe. Very quickly, it's common knowledge that every lawyer that has ever worked in the legal department is slow and uncooperative. As experts, this type of thinking annoys us a lot, but we might be guilty of the same crime more often than we think.

Overcoming Personal Barriers

MANY EXPERTS HAVE A deep-seated dislike of the change process, and of change in general. It's best to explore this mindset before it becomes a derailer for us.

Our ability to challenge ourselves and our close colleagues around these mindsets is a trait of a Master Expert. Our ability to become thoughtful, objective change supporters is more and more likely to be a critical success factor for us professionally, given that change is the new normal and will be ongoing.

> *"Experts should be the thought leaders stimulating change."*

The ability to manage and adjust our change orientation will help us be successful. The most disruptive personal settings we've heard from experts are these:

"I hate change."

Change is an opportunity to develop and exercise increased emotional intelligence. It can increase self-awareness if we ask ourselves why the change provokes antipathy and other negative feelings.

We need to ask ourselves what we're afraid of losing. Why do we feel this degree of discomfort? Is there anything new we can do to feel or at least show up differently so that we're not seen as resistant to change, even if it's our natural instinct?

"I don't really have an opportunity to take more of a change leadership role. I have no formal responsibility for leading others. Why would anyone care what I think?"

Experts need to be constructive participants in change. There are often opportunities for experts to play a much bigger role in shepherding the organization's people through change.

We can do this by anticipating the likely impacts on and responses from various stakeholders, by helping to formulate appropriate communications and engagement strategies, by working to build compelling cases for change, and by offering reassurance where needed.

Experts should be thought leaders stimulating change. As with most of the Expertship framework's competencies, any lack of formal authority can be offset by well-thought-out and well-implemented influencing strategies.

"I've had a bad experience with change in the past."

It's only natural that if we've had previous bad experiences with change that we'll naturally anticipate similar outcomes in the future. We may still be carrying trauma and triggering defensive reflexes.

With the appropriate use of emotional intelligence, we should be able to identify how this is playing out, rather than simply reacting irrationally and fiercely resisting. We can then adopt a more open mindset and get actively involved in shaping the change initiative so as to lessen the likelihood of any bad outcomes or experiences.

"I don't agree with the change."

If we don't agree with the change, the biggest problem is usually not expressing our concerns responsibly. We either keep them to ourselves or we're critical of the project to everyone except those who can do something about it.

We need to be willing to have our minds changed. We need to consider the thinking behind the new direction. If we have a counter-argument or evidence that the change might not work, we need to offer it in a respectful fashion and in a spirit of dialogue. Under stress from change, we may (like many others groups) revert back to type, meaning we will state something overtly in a way we imagine is being constructive and honest but in fact may be considered oppositional or aggressive. This is where the influencing skills (Chapter 23) and the power of really listening (Chapter 20) come into play.

We need to work to have our concerns and suggestions for improvement heard, but we don't want to wreck our relationships or brand image by coming across as a stubborn naysayer or an intransigent critic.

TAKING ACTION

Growing Our Change Supporter Skills

IF THIS IS AN expert role in which you believe you could add greater value, here are some high-level suggestions for actions to take:

▶ BE A LIGHT, NOT A CRITIC

Experts who respond negatively to change by expressing high levels of opposition, resistance or criticism often end up alienating and marginalizing themselves. They get others offside (particularly the senior people who have initiated the change) and sometimes entirely sabotage or undermine change initiatives. If there is a danger we could be falling into these traps, here are some questions we might want to ask ourselves:

- Next time there's a change, how can I, even if I feel skeptical and resistant, be as open-minded as possible? What does it require of me? How do I learn to suspend judgment?
- If the change has been poorly communicated to me, how do I proactively seek out the reasons for the change?
- If I conclude that the change being proposed is fundamentally flawed, how do I frame my concerns in a positive way? How can I avoid being simply negative about the idea? In this instance, could I come up with a better way of achieving the objective?

▶ UNDERSTAND AND DEVELOP OUR OWN CHANGE AGILITY

When it comes to our ability to embrace change, we all have different default settings. These are based on our personality and past experiences. We often allow our personal biases, either as a change cynic or a change advocate, to determine our response to change. Building our capability to assess change initiatives on their merits is a critical Master Expert skill. Some questions we can ask ourselves are:

- What is my change history? In the past, what have been my typical first impressions on the numerous occasions when change has been imposed on me? What does this tell me about my default settings?
- Why are my default settings as they are? Is it the result of my personality, or is it the result of the experiences I've had with change?
- What would be a useful set of questions that I can ask neutrally about any change initiative? How do I explore the rationale behind the change?
- Is doing nothing an option instead of the change being proposed? If not, and I feel resistance, what would I do instead?

CHAPTER | 36 |

Being a Change Catalyst

What attributes and impact does a change catalyst have? Do we have the courage to become one?

IN THIS CHAPTER, WE WILL EXPLORE:

- Should we be careful of what we wish for because being a change catalyst means we'll upset colleagues by suggesting changes?
- What are the key attributes of change catalysts, and why?
- What are some derailing behaviors of change catalysts?

THE SECOND EXPERT ROLE is Change Catalyst. This expert role deals with the extent to which experts are able to set the change agenda by consistently looking for opportunities to make positive changes. The behaviors at each level of Expertship for this expert role are described in Figure 36.1.

At immature levels, experts can identify and promote individual change opportunities, usually within their limited operational area. Experts who are derailing will be very comfortable with the status quo and rarely consider the case for change.

At Master Expert level, experts act as a catalyst for change, setting the change agenda. They continuously seek better ways of executing and adding value across the organization. Master Experts will objectively question enterprise and market assumptions and challenge the status quo.

Being future-focused, they'll anticipate possible disruptions to their own organization and see opportunities to disrupt others.

> *"Be careful of what you wish for, lest it come true." - Aesop's Fables*

Attributes of a Change Catalyst

MORE THAN 2,200 YEARS ago, an author called Aesop (of *Aesop's Fables* fame) authored this now-famous quote: "Be careful of what you wish for, lest it come true."

The moral of the story is that we often fail to consider the implications of our wishes coming true. And that may be true for some of us reading this book. Many experts (the authors plead guilty immediately) have always wanted to be known as a change catalyst, a thought leader and someone who made a real difference. But how many of us have considered the significant pain we'll have to go through to achieve this? Pain and gain will be a theme throughout this chapter.

In Chapter 34, we describe the change curve—that emotional rollercoaster that gets unleashed when a change catalyst has a lightbulb moment and convinces key influencers it's a change worth making. There are easier ways to become popular. If we become a successful change catalyst—that is, if we ideate the change and then drive it to happen—then we will, by definition, risk upsetting lots of peers and colleagues in the short term. Below, we offer a short list of key attributes Master Experts need to acquire in order to be a successful change catalyst, and while the list is in no particular order, we thought it sensible to start with courage.

Change Catalyst Attribute #1: Courage

It takes courage to suggest change because most people, most of the time, initially resist change. Even if you work in an organizational culture that encourages and rewards innovation and change, some colleagues won't like *your* change. Stepping up to this plate means that we understand there will be pain before there is gain. And we need both types of courage. The personal courage to be resilient and not take things personally, as well as the courage of our convictions, which means knowing it's worth doing and trying to make it happen.

Capability: CHANGE AGILITY
Expert Role: **CHANGE CATALYST**

MASTER EXPERT

- Acts as a catalyst for change, sets the change agenda.
- Continuously seeks better ways of executing and adding value across the organization.
- Objectively questions enterprise and market assumptions; challenges the status quo.
- Anticipates opportunities for disruption and to disrupt.
- Effectively designs and implements vital change initiatives.
- Institutes effective strategies that constructively engage people in change.

EXPERT

- Identifies and promotes departmental change initiatives.
- Continuously seeks better ways of executing and adding value within function.
- Objectively questions departmental assumptions and challenges the status quo.
- Encourages people to engage with change initiatives.

SPECIALIST

- Identifies and promotes individual change opportunities.

DERAILING

- Comfortable with the status quo.
- Rarely considers the case for change.
- Intentionally or unintentionally undermines change efforts.

FIGURE 36.1: Change Catalyst Behaviors

Change Catalyst Attribute #2: Asking Tough Questions

Being courageous entails challenging the status quo by asking tough questions. As we discuss in other chapters (Chapter 5, *The Brand Power of Emotional Intelligence* and Chapter 11 *Mastering Courageous Conversations*), it's often the manner in which we ask the tough questions that makes all the difference. The tough questions always seek to find the pain first and then understand the value of the gain.

> *"As every risk manager knows, but few of their colleagues properly understand, risk is a continuum."*

A remarkable number of our working processes haven't really been designed. Instead, they've just developed. They're the way we do things and have always done them. These are the processes and habits that change catalysts ask about. The good news is that smart change catalysts make this tough questioning part of business as usual. They incorporate curious questions about what issues are causing pain and what the gain would look like if that pain was gone in their normal, everyday stakeholder engagements. The more questions we ask as a matter of course, the more people get used to us asking those questions. And the best part is that they also get better at answering those questions.

Change Catalyst Attribute #3: Dedicate Thinking Time

If we're allowing ourselves to be 200 percent busy, we can't find the time to think, and that means we can't find the time to ideate. Change catalysts find themselves making time in their schedule for thinking. This doesn't need to be hours, but it does require quiet time (or perhaps time when exercising) to mull over problems and possible solutions.

Change Catalyst Attribute #4: Taking Measured Risks

As every risk manager knows, but few of their colleagues properly understand, risk is a continuum. Doing nothing at all, for example, is a risk. In some industries that are being disrupted, doing nothing is a huge risk. Similarly, changing everything at once increases the risk of failure. Successful change catalysts take measured risks, where the gain significantly outweighs the pain and this insight is evident to everyone, so they want to support the change.

Change Catalyst Attribute #5: Becoming a Gain Beacon

Change catalysts are champions of painting a very clear picture of a better situation for stakeholders. They often do this by describing a powerful and desired vision of the future, where the gain will be experienced. They most likely explain the *why* of a change better than most. Consequently, they're able to build a coalition of those willing to execute the change and achieve the benefits.

Change Catalyst Attribute #6: Become a Center of Trust

The authors are involved in running a business that almost wholly depends on trust between ourselves (designers and facilitators of professional growth programs for experts) and our clients (the participants and program organizers in the client organization). With almost every program we run, we innovate. We make changes along the way. Our clients are happy with this because the first few times we suggested a different way of doing things, it worked. Phew. But that was by design. We all need to pick early winners. Build trust. Then people will trust us to go further.

Change Catalyst Derailers

CHANGE CATALYSTS ALSO MANAGE to avoid some derailing behaviors. While this list may seem obvious, sometimes we fall into these traps subconsciously.

Trap #1: Putting Problems in the "Too Hard" Basket

The self-talk goes like this: *Um, not right now. That's tomorrow's challenge. I need to wait until a few more people are speaking the same language as me. My boss isn't looking supportive, so perhaps now's not the time.* Of course, what we're really doing is saying this idea, right now, is being put in the "too hard" basket. If we have the courage of our convictions (see above) and we're convinced we're right, then, actually, this initiative is going to happen at some stage in the future because it's needed. The question then becomes: do we tackle it now, when we have time to do it right? Or do we wait until it's probably too late to make the change, and it will be rushed and ruined.

Trap #2: Critical Thought Bubbles

In our enthusiasm to transform our colleagues' world of pain into a world of gain, we might come across as, well, a little critical of why on Earth they have been doing this in the first place. We need to position our intent very clearly, and that doesn't include a very informed treatise on the stupidity of the current process and the people executing it.

TAKING ACTION

Growing Our Change Catalyst Skills

IF THIS IS AN expert role in which you believe you could add greater value, here are some high-level suggestions for actions to take:

▶ SEEK OUT WHAT'S NOT WORKING

- We're seeking to find meaningful and actionable ways to do more with less, and as a change catalyst, we're expected to seek these opportunities out regularly. We try to avoid getting into a situation where our processes and knowledge are stale and we require others to generate change suggestions.
- How hard do I listen to what colleagues and stakeholders are saying about the challenges they face in the workplace and in serving customers?
- How curious am I? Do I take the time to understand why processes and systems are the way they are? For how long have these processes been the same? How might they be improved? Is the latest technology and systems thinking being applied to the issue? What barriers to change and improvement are claimed? Are they legitimate barriers or signs that my colleagues simply don't want to change?
- How competitive am I? Am I genuinely interested in helping my organization win or improve?
- If I have a good idea, do I act on it? Or do I consider it too difficult or too much additional work?
- If I am a lot more curious, will more ideas be generated by taking this investigative and curious approach?

▶ BECOME A STUDENT OF EMERGING COMPANIES

Ideas don't grow on trees. We get inspiration from what others are doing and by applying their ideas to our own situations. Perhaps we combine several ideas we've read about from different sources to create something unique that works in our situation. Some questions we might like to ask ourselves:

- How much time do I spend learning about emerging companies and the innovative products and services they're bringing to market? To what extent do I understand their underlying customer and competitive assumptions?
- Do I have an informal diverse buddy group that I periodically talk to about these organizations? Do I use these discussions and their diverse perspectives to refine my thinking and consider their relevance to my own situation?

▶ BECOME AN EXPERT AT MAKING A CASE FOR CHANGE

To be an effective catalyst for change, we need to master the process of shaping a compelling case for and narrative around the change we're proposing. Some questions we might want to ask ourselves:

- What constitutes a best practice case for change? How do successful change catalysts illustrate the problems inherent in making no change? How do they describe the benefits of changing? How do they communicate a compelling future state?
- Which of my colleagues could I actively engage with to learn how this is best done? What mistakes do I need to avoid?
- How would they benefit from helping me master these skills and processes?

CHAPTER | 37 |

The Expert's Role in Leading Change

How do we best lead change, even if we're not the formal project leader? What positive impacts can we have?

IN THIS CHAPTER, WE WILL EXPLORE:

- Whether experts still have a responsibility to contribute to leading change, even if we're not the formal change leader?
- What process could we deploy to make sure we're thinking about the right steps for leading change in the right order?
- How do we leverage our knowledge of the change curve to make a positive difference?

THE THIRD EXPERT ROLE in the capability Change Agility is **Change Leader**. This expert role deals with the extent to which experts have the ability to step up to a leadership role in change projects when required, constructively engaging others in change. The behaviors at each level of Expertship for this expert role are described in Figure 37.1.

At immature levels, experts contribute dutifully toward change initiatives. They'll raise concerns diplomatically and objectively, and seek to manage themselves effectively through change. They may be naturally open to or resistant to change. Experts who are derailing will be actively fighting change initiatives, often playing a blocking role. They will react subjectively and emotionally to change initiatives.

In contrast, Master Experts lead change with insight, providing direction and instituting effective strategies to constructively engage people in change. In particular, they'll step up to the plate when change leadership is needed, whether or not it's their formal responsibility. Master Experts understand how organizational stakeholders may be impacted by change and proactively assist others in dealing with it.

Leading Change

NOT SO LONG AGO, senior management in one of the Big Four professional consultancy firms decided to move the risk consulting team, which had sat within the consulting division, into the assurance division (the auditors). It was felt that positioning risk advisory services within the suite of auditing services would make more sense to customers and perhaps result in more cross-selling.

But convincing the risk team of the merits of this change—and keeping them constructively engaged throughout the transition—was painful and problematic. This was purely because the need for emotionally intelligent change management was underestimated.

On the surface, it may not have appeared to the decision-makers that too much was occurring or that it would adversely affect the risk consultants. "All we're doing is redrawing the organizational chart, changing one reporting line, and changing the way we present the team to clients," management said. "It might also mean physically relocating the team to a different floor of the same office block."

But that's not how the risk consultants saw it at all. They took great pride in being an integral part of the prestigious consulting organization. To them, being placed within the audit function felt like a demotion.

> *"The decision-makers did not consider how the people affected would feel about it."*

"Our work won't be valued the same. The work will come to us in a different way—perhaps merely as a service add-on (a freebie) offered by the auditors. We want to work as consultants, developing bespoke solutions. Now we're going to be reporting to an auditing function that doesn't understand what we do, nor the kind of resources or representation we need."

Capability: CHANGE AGILITY

Expert Role: CHANGE LEADER

MASTER EXPERT

- Leads change with insight. Provides direction and institutes effective strategies to constructively engage people in change.
- Effectively identifies and engages organizational stakeholders impacted by change.
- Proactively assists others in dealing with change.
- Shapes and articulates a compelling case for change.
- Exercises an inclusive approach to leading change.

EXPERT

- Helps execute change initiatives with professionalism and commitment.
- Understands how departmental stakeholders may be impacted by change.
- Assists others in dealing with change.

SPECIALIST

- Contributes dutifully toward change initiative.
- Raises concerns diplomatically and objectively.
- Seeks to effectively manage self through change.

- Actively fights change initiatives or plays a blocking role.
- Reacts subjectively and emotionally to change initiatives.
- Leaves all the responsibility for change leadership to others.

DERAILING

FIGURE 37.1: Change Leader Behaviors

When the risk consultants first learned of the organization's intentions, it came as a shock because they had zero involvement in the planning process prior to the announcement. There was an immediate and palpable sense of outrage.

It quickly became clear that the executives who had made the decision hadn't considered how all the human beings impacted by the decision would view it. They didn't consider how the people affected would feel about it, nor the implications that the decision would have on business.

Even the partner who headed the risk consulting team wasn't told. They were presented with a *fait accompli*, which only added insult to injury.

This is an example of senior leaders deciding upon change with little or no consideration for those being affected, ensuring that resistance was almost inevitable. It's terrible change management from an organization that claims to be able to advise the rest of us on change.

Change Leadership That Works

THERE IS AN ALTERNATIVE to poor change execution. It's another conversation we regularly have with groups of subject matter experts from all types of technical domains, including change managers, by the way, which is interesting and informative.

We ask participants to think of a change process that has recently been run in their organization and which they've been exposed to. On a scale of 1 (very poor) to 10 (brilliant), we ask them how they'd score these various change initiatives. Typically, we get 4s and 5s across a large group, but with the odd outliers—some 8s and 9s, a few 1s and 2s. One of our favorite examples was the data scientist who scored his organization's change initiative a minus 5. After twenty minutes of exploration into how they'd handled the process, most of the group agreed that the data scientist had been generous with his score—it could've been worse!

We then ask about the change processes the organization deployed. "What could've been done better?". "Better" is defined as making the change initiative less painful and stressful for employees and helping the organization move from past to future more quickly.

> *"Without creating a compelling case for change, there will be no momentum to overcome any resistance or inertia."*

It won't surprise you that this exercise produces a large list of extremely sensible and doable initiatives that would've helped everyone concerned. Many revolved around really open communication, honesty and real transparency (for example, senior leaders admitting "Yes, some people will lose their jobs"). While these discussions are likely to be confronting, they'll build trust and demonstrate a mindset that says senior leaders and change managers are going to treat the employees like adults and really attempt to collaborate with them—taking on board some of their good ideas—to make the changes more effectively.

Kotter's Eight-Step Change Model

JOHN KOTTER IS A renowned thought leader on the topic of change and has written several bestselling books on the topic (see further reading). Here are his eight best practice steps that contribute to a successful transition from the "current state" to the "target state" (see Figure 37.2). While the headings are Kotter's, we have written our own assessment of the critical insights.

1. Create Urgency

Since most people resist change, i.e., moving from the known to the unknown, there needs to be a compelling case as to why the change is necessary. This should talk about the problems of staying as we are versus the compelling upside of changing. Those initiating the change need to win over hearts and minds.

The perceived benefits of changing need to outweigh any perceived disadvantages. Without creating a compelling case for change, there will be no momentum to overcome any resistance or inertia. It's about convincing people that the proposed change is necessary and immediate.

If action isn't taken, then they'll be foregoing a particular advantage or will be subjected to some kind of avoidable inconvenience. Even if you aren't the one initiating the change, you can always help build the case and help get people's buy-in.

Capability: CHANGE AGILITY

Kotter's Eight Steps

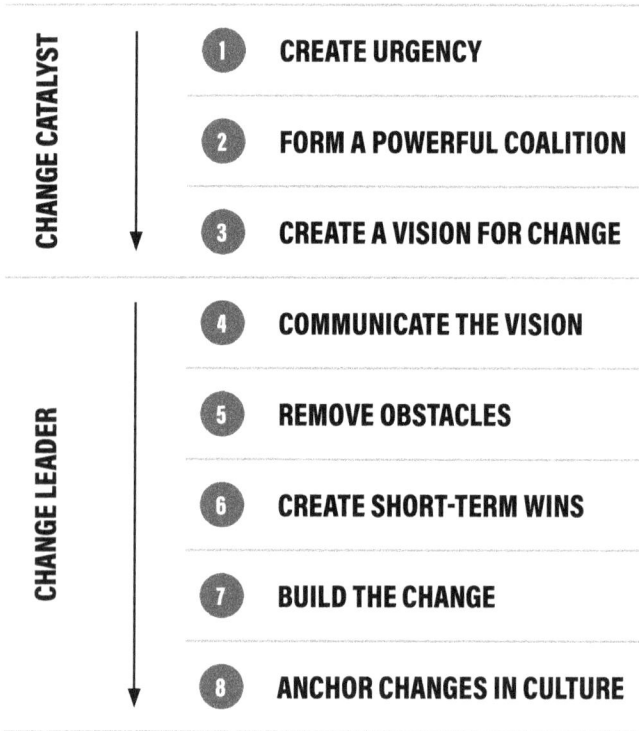

CHANGE CATALYST
1. CREATE URGENCY
2. FORM A POWERFUL COALITION
3. CREATE A VISION FOR CHANGE

CHANGE LEADER
4. COMMUNICATE THE VISION
5. REMOVE OBSTACLES
6. CREATE SHORT-TERM WINS
7. BUILD THE CHANGE
8. ANCHOR CHANGES IN CULTURE

The Expertship Roles are indicated on the left of the graphic.

FIGURE 37.2: Kotter's Eight Steps of Change

Most organizations don't make cases for change very well. Occasionally, the organizational benefits have been reasonably well identified, but there's rarely much discussion of the advantages that might come to the individual participants in the change process. There's no perceived upside for them. The perception is that the organization gains and they lose.

> *"All too often, experts are asked to support initiatives that they themselves do not yet understand."*

If we're initiating a change, it'll be very useful to conduct a stakeholder analysis. Who will be impacted by the change and how? What might they be concerned about? What do they potentially stand to lose—or how might they perceive it that way? How receptive to the proposed changes are they likely to be? Is there an upside for them? What's the compelling rationale as to why this change is necessary? What evidence do they need to be convinced that a change is necessary?

To build a compelling case for change, we need to:
- Identify potential threats and develop scenarios showing what could happen in the future.
- Examine opportunities that could be exploited.
- Start honest discussions and give dynamic and convincing reasons to get people talking and thinking.
- Ask for support from customers and outside stakeholders to strengthen our argument.

These can be compiled into a document or a slideshow. We need to practice speaking about them, even testing our hunches to see how stakeholders will react. If we notice that we fall short of making an emotionally compelling case for change, we can work with the leaders to see how the case could be strengthened rather than taking a critical and detached stance.

2. Form a Powerful Coalition
Kotter talks about building on this initial momentum by gathering support from key opinion-makers. This can have the effect of accelerating the change initiative. He advocates identifying early adopters and others with influence who can become positive advocates for change and sway others.

Most experts we work with are familiar with this tactic since they're often the people who change managers come to seeking this coalition support. It only works effectively if the opinion-makers really do believe in the change, are committed to it, and can articulate the benefits. All too often, experts are asked to support initiatives that they themselves don't yet understand.

To be a good change leader, the Master Expert will gather information about the initiative and its benefits by asking lots of questions. They'll then consider the proposed change initiative through three lenses:

- Strategic: is it good for the organization and its external stakeholders?
- Tactical: will it make the organization operate more effectively, with measurable productivity gains?
- Personal: will it help employees and teams work more effectively?

To be a good change leader in this respect, we need to be able to identify the true leaders in our organization, as well as our key stakeholders. These may be senior leaders or very influential experts. As Master Experts, we'll have been working on building relationships with key stakeholders for some time. We don't suddenly appear and demand support for a project from someone who is effectively a stranger. At some stage, we're going to need to ask for an emotional commitment from these key people, which requires trust and belief.

> *"A shared vision is a way of positively mobilizing our coalition and other stakeholders through inspiration."*

Ideally, any change team we lead will have the right connections and networks to mine great relationships and supporters in all the important parts of the organization. As we pull together the skills needed on the project team, we'll also need to consider what relationships will be required.

Well-led change requires the change team to have a diverse mix of people who represent the constituencies being affected. That way, all views and perceptions are represented and can be taken into account as the project team more successfully executes the change.

3. Create a Vision for Change

The creation of a shared vision is a way of positively mobilizing our coalition and other stakeholders through inspiration.

Much is made of the need for a "burning platform"—the supposition that people won't move unless the ground beneath them is on fire. But it's even more important to clearly define the destination to be arrived at by outlining a compelling vision that evokes positive feelings in all those impacted by the change. The idea is to develop and articulate a goal or end state that people will feel compelled to move toward, overcoming the inertia of staying where they are. We should also be clear about what is *not* changing. People need to know what success looks like and feel that it'll be worth the effort. This is needed to offset any inconvenience involved in the change itself and the transition period.

> *"With the entire coalition broadcasting the vision, momentum will build and people will climb aboard."*

If we're feeling the pressure to make change happen, it can be tempting to get straight into planning the logistical aspects of what needs to be changed, who needs to do what and when they need to do it, all the while forgetting that we need to mobilize people. Kotter recommends working with key stakeholders and coalition members to:
- Determine the values that are central to the change.
- Develop a short summary (one or two sentences) that captures how we see the organization's future.
- Create a strategy to execute that vision.
- Ensure that our change coalition can describe the vision in less than five minutes.
- Practice our vision speech often (so that it flows naturally and evokes others' commitment).

4. Communicate the Vision

It's not enough to simply develop a vision. Engaging the entire coalition in advocating for the change and selling the vision is vital. People often have to hear a message several times before it connects and they recognize that your commitment to change is serious, non-negotiable and definite. It's always helpful if people hear the message through many different mediums, such as email, Town Halls, video, discussion groups, social media, and so on.

It's a numbers game. If the recipient of the message hears it from numerous trusted sources, they're more likely to believe it than if there's only one or two advocates. If the coalition has been intelligently constituted, there will be trusted opinion leaders representing various levels and disciplines, meaning that there's someone visible advocating for the change so everybody can get behind it.

With the entire coalition broadcasting the vision, momentum will build and people will climb aboard. It's important to observe that this is not one-way communication. It's the initiating of a *conversation*. It's less to do with "has the vision been communicated?" than it is to do with "have people started buying in? Has their resistance started to dissolve?"

The idea of resistance *dissolving* rather than being worn down is important. To wear down resistance implies an adversarial dynamic, in which case resistance often increases. Communicating the vision entails:

- Talking often about our change vision.
- Addressing peoples' concerns and anxieties openly and honestly.
- Applying our vision to all aspects of operations, from training to performance reviews. Tie everything back to the vision.
- Leading by example.

5. Remove Obstacles

Change requires more than talking a good game. The change process itself also has to work smoothly. Master Experts anticipate and identify potential obstacles in advance. They take countermeasures so that their change efforts don't get derailed or held up.

"People's sustained commitment will be enhanced if they experience the benefits of the change early and often."

If implementation feels too hard, then people's commitment to see the change through may waver. They may doubt our commitment to achieving the vision and assume that we're all talk. The naysayers may feel empowered to mount increased resistance.

In their minds, the very presence of obstacles is evidence that it's all been poorly thought through and is likely to play out disastrously. A smooth transition, on the other hand, tends to encourage more conviction. Key actions for us to consider are:

- Identify change leaders whose main roles are to deliver the change.
- Look at the organizational settings (systems, structures, rewards, etc.) to ensure they're in line with our vision.
- Recognize and reward people for making change happen.
- Identify people who are resisting the change and help them see what's needed. (And listen to them.)
- Get the entire coalition to take visible action to quickly remove barriers (human or otherwise).

6. Create Short-Term Wins

Even if we and our coalition initially succeed in winning people's hearts and minds, there's no guarantee that we'll sustain the levels of commitment necessary for the duration of the transition period from the old to the new.

People's sustained commitment—especially over a longer timeframe—will be enhanced if they experience the benefits of the change early and often. This requires design thinking (a methodology for creative problem solving) and planning, such as identifying opportunities to prove that the changes are working and bringing about the desired results.

It minimizes the sense of fruitless disruption or chaos that sometimes accompanies unsettling change. It's all about eliminating the need for leaps of faith and reducing the risk of skepticism derailing people's focus and perseverance. Key actions we could consider are:

- Look for sure-fire projects that we can implement without help from any strong critics of the change.
- Avoid early targets that are expensive. We want to be able to justify the investment in each project.
- Thoroughly analyze the potential pros and cons of our targets. If we don't succeed with an early goal, it can hurt our entire change initiative.
- Reward the people who help us meet our targets.

> *"Stanford University's design thinking process involves five steps: Empathize, Define, Ideate, Prototype, and Test."*

7. Build the Change

Wait to celebrate success. The change needs to be truly bedded in. The change initiative is best seen as an endurance event—a marathon rather than a sprint. Until the benefits are being realized and new habits have formed, we can't afford to lose momentum.

Many experts we talk to describe change as being a journey, and that truly is what change is like. Good change processes flex and add components all the time. The trick is to make sure everyone on the journey understands that progress is being made.

For example, a mistake we see time and again is the change team (or IT team) believing the project is finished when the application they've been implementing goes live (that is, users can use it). In truth, the change is complete when the benefits are realized. That usually only happens when the users embrace and use the new application's functionality as the designers intended.

As Master Experts, our role is to continually remind ourselves and our colleagues how much we've learned, how much extra value we're now capable of adding, and how much more we know about our customers.

Specific actions we can take include:

- After every win, analyze what went right and what needs improving.
- Remember to give credit to those who have made suggestions that work and are adopted by the change team.
- Set goals to continue building on the momentum we've achieved.

- Learn about and apply *kaizen* (a Japanese business philosophy of continuous improvement of working practices). The direct translation of *kaizen* is "good change."
- Keep ideas fresh by bringing in new change agents, experts and leaders for our change coalition.

8. Anchor the Change in Culture

It's not over until the change is embedded into new everyday habits and behaviors.

Once they become everyday, it can be easy to lose sight of how far we have come.

Recently, we attended an event where a CFO pointed out the accomplishments of the shared services team during the year but also pointed out that such a large list of on-time, on-budget, "realizing the return on investment" projects would have been very unlikely two years previously, when the team had a reputation for under-delivering and being over budget.

They changed the processes, got tougher on business outcomes, and were now operating as a team at a much higher level. You can lock in the new way of operating through practices such as:

- Talking about progress every chance you get. Tell success stories about the change process and repeat other stories that you hear.
- Including change ideals and values when hiring and training new staff.
- Publicly recognizing key members of your original change coalition, ensuring the rest of the staff, both new and old, remember their contributions.
- Publically recognizing people who initially were not on board but came on board and made a great contribution.
- Creating plans to replace key leaders of change as they move on. This will help ensure that their legacy is not lost or forgotten.

TAKING ACTION

Growing Our Change Leader Skills

IF THIS IS AN expert role in which you believe you could add greater value, here are some high-level suggestions for actions to take:

▶ BE A STUDENT OF THE CHANGE CURVE

- Typically, many people experience a range of emotions when disruptive changes are announced in their organization. These are often described on the change curve, which is based on the stages of grief people feel when they lose a loved one.
- Understanding where different individuals and whole teams are on the change curve significantly helps change leaders adapt their tactics and messaging to assist colleagues through the change process. Some questions we might want to ask ourselves:
- How well do I understand the change curve, and how well can I apply it to change projects I am leading? Can I recognize how the different stages manifest as personal behaviors in my colleagues?
- What support will colleagues need, depending on what stage of the change curve they're at? How capable am I of offering this support? Am I prepared to offer this support?
- What opportunity do I have to influence the way in which change in my projects is being implemented? Do I have an opportunity to help smooth the way?

▶ UNDERTAKE A STAKEHOLDER ANALYSIS

Failing to anticipate how stakeholders impacted by the changes we initiate will respond typically means that we will face considerably more resistance than is helpful in the smooth and timely execution of our plan(s), which may in turn detrimentally impact—or at least delay—the intended benefits expected from our change initiative. Some questions to ask ourselves:
- Recognizing that the change will impact others, could I conduct some prior analysis of which stakeholders will likely be impacted and how?

- Could I better consider how I'll position the rationale for the change in a fully informative and compelling fashion? Do I take a collaborative and consultative approach by facilitating two-way discussions with stakeholders to hear and resolve their questions and concerns? Or am I resistant to negative feedback?

▶ VOLUNTEER TO BE A CHANGE CHAMPION

Even if we haven't initiated a change, you could miss the opportunity to play a constructive role in helping shepherd others through change. Neglecting to grasp such opportunities can result in being seen as one further non-differentiated "passenger" to be brought on the journey, rather than as an active crew member committed to the realization of organizational objectives. Some questions we might like to ask ourselves:

- What gets in the way of me volunteering my services as a change champion when the next change initiative kicks off?
- What benefits might I get from putting my hand up for such a role? What lessons might I learn, what exposure to the wider organization might I get, and how might I positively build my network as a consequence of stepping forward?

PART 04

THE TECHNICAL DOMAIN

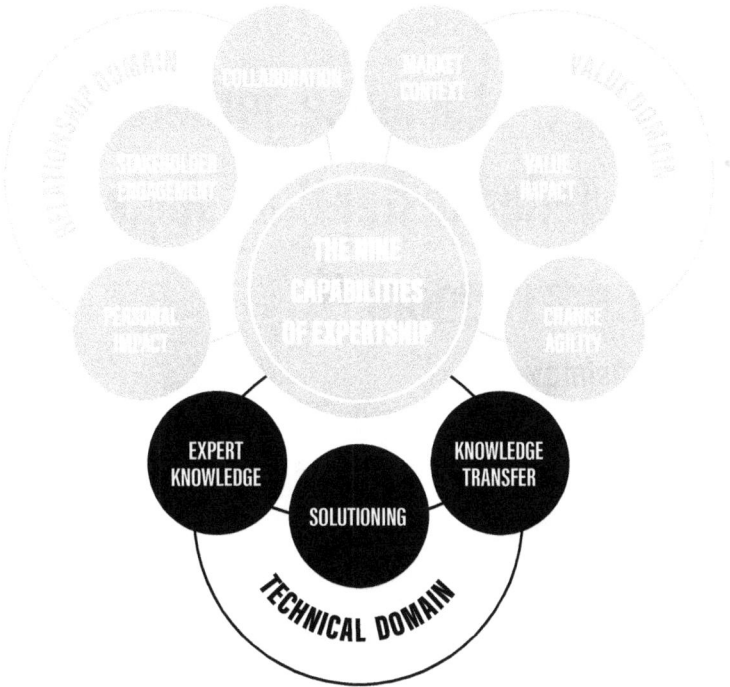

THE NINE CAPABILITIES OF EXPERTSHIP

EXPERT KNOWLEDGE

SOLUTIONING

KNOWLEDGE TRANSFER

TECHNICAL DOMAIN

"The saddest aspect of life right now is that science gathers knowledge faster than society gathers wisdom.**"**

Issac Asimov

MASTERING EXPERT KNOWLEDGE

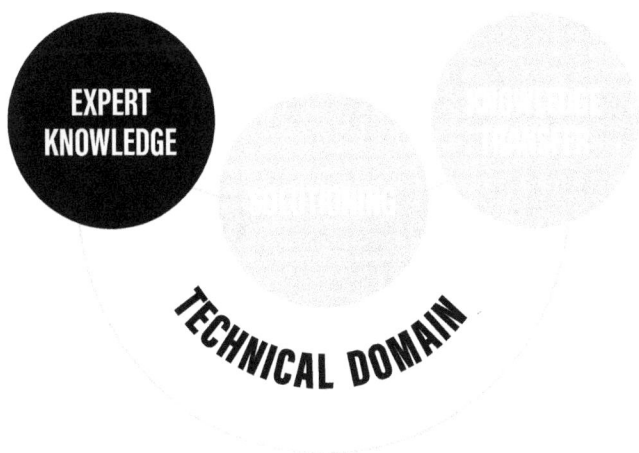

EXPERT KNOWLEDGE

TECHNICAL DOMAIN

The Master Expert acquires, retains and grows deep specialist knowledge and experiences effectively.

CHAPTER | 38 |

Leveraging Expert Knowledge

The very best experts have mastered the skill of strategically managing and leveraging their expert knowledge.

IN THIS CHAPTER, WE WILL EXPLORE:

- Why do we need an expert knowledge strategy? What are the payoffs for experts, their organizations and stakeholders?
- Whether our expert knowledge can get in the way of us successfully partnering with the wider organization.
- What does an expert knowledge strategy look like?

A CENTRAL THESIS OF this book—and indeed, one of our main reasons for writing it—is that most of us who believe we're experts in a particular knowledge domain are often not as expert as we think we are.

We're surrounded by evidence every day that suggests to us that our expert knowledge is outstanding and unmatched. Colleagues repeatedly ask our advice. They come back for more, so we assume they must have been happy with our previously offered wisdom. They ask us to solve difficult technical problems that they believe only we have the knowledge to solve, and we encourage that belief.

Now, rather than make any effort to solve issues themselves, they come directly to us *all the time*. When called into meetings to deliver our wisdom, people—some quite senior and probably paid much more than us—hang on our every technical word. Surely the evidence that our expert knowledge of our chosen domain exceeds that of the rest of our colleagues is to be celebrated, not questioned, here?

We beg to differ.

Let's take a look at a real-life example of where "expert knowledge" is poorly defined.

> *"An investment in knowledge pays the best interest."*
> *– Benjamin Franklin –*

Patricia is a compliance expert at a large financial services firm. It could be just about any organization. With ten years' experience in her present organization and fifteen years as a compliance expert, Patricia is the real compliance deal. She has the qualifications and association memberships to prove it, along with a plethora of conference speaking credits to her name.

Attending one of our programs, Patricia became the subject of a conversation about expert knowledge. We asked a question to the group, which comprised experts from many different domains, including law, information technology, marketing, risk, engineering and, of course, compliance.

"Do we all agree that the compliance person in the room, Patricia, knows more than everyone else in the room about compliance?"

Patricia answered with some modesty. "Well, I certainly hope so." Others seemed to be comfortable with this response.

> *"Does the compliance expert really know everything*
> *there is about getting people to comply?"*

"What is it," we asked, "that Patricia knows about compliance that the rest of us don't know?"

The group quickly agreed that Patricia is likely to know the most about the internal organizational rules and regulations to do with compliance, about the current legislation, the organization's obligations, and so on. When it came to this type of information, the group was more than prepared to pronounce Patricia a Master Expert.

We then asked the question "What does the wider organization know about compliance that the compliance expert does not?"

After a short interval of thinking, several theories emerged. One participant argued that the wider organization was likely to have a more realistic view than the designers of the process of how easy or difficult it is for individuals and teams in the organization to comply.

Building on this theme, others suggested that the wider organization would know how easy or difficult it would be to find time to comply. The participants argued that it might be the case that the wider organization better understood what motivations or incentives would likely persuade people to comply and, conversely, which would not work.

Patricia wasn't so sure. She stated that her profession had data on which incentives worked and why. One participant suggested that the wider organization would certainly know best how much of the compliance material was really read and understood and the level of buy-in generated by these information campaigns.

We then asked "Is the wider organization or the compliance expert better at figuring out what would make the wider organization comply?"

A lively debate ensued. At the end of this discussion, the majority view was that the compliance department might have some best practice case studies, etc., but the wider organization would probably have a better idea of what would deliver the greatest amount of compliance in a short time period and what would not.

> *"Knowledge has to be improved, challenged, and increased constantly, or it vanishes."*
> *- Peter F. Drucker -*

The conversation moved on to other topics, but Patricia later shared with us that the discussion had a big impact on her. She found herself challenging the amount of time she spent talking to the wider organization about the compliance initiatives she and her colleagues designed. Her view was that she and her colleagues spent hardly any time doing this. Patricia also challenged her mindset about the organization and her belief that she and her colleagues in compliance knew how best to implement compliance changes. She said her "ah-ha" moment was when she realized that the compliance team was expert in what needed to be implemented and why, but it should take a partnership approach with the organization to design the rollout of these campaigns.

She had believed that the business was resistant to and showed little interest in compliance, so she hadn't even contemplated seeking their help in design.

So, whose fault is that? Why is the business not engaged?

Patricia and her colleagues should spend more time working with the organization, and even *in the organization*, to better understand the extent to which messages were being received, understood, embraced and acted upon. Further exploration of why partnering with the organization hadn't occurred to the compliance team led to a further insight: the organization was typically so resistant to any compliance initiative and showed such little interest in their work that the team had concluded the organization wouldn't be interested in partnering with them.

When we hear this type of broken relationship described, we always ask "Whose fault is it that this state of affairs exists? Is it the fault of the experts or the organization?"

The default response from experts, stated almost before we have finished asking the question, is that it's "the wider organization's fault for not understanding the value of our work." This is often quickly followed by an admission that perhaps the experts didn't position the value of the initiative as well as they might have done. This is a modest acknowledgment of some fault. Eventually, experts will typically concede that the wider organization can't be expected to understand the value of a compliance initiative on their own because they aren't the experts.

"New examples of horror stories were posted every week."

Patricia had concluded, in effect, that she and her colleagues were not the sole custodians of expert knowledge on compliance they had imagined.

Patricia's case is not an isolated event. We've seen two separate experts tackle the task of persuading a large organization to take cybersecurity seriously. With similar expert knowledge, one expert succeeded in a huge change in mindset, and the other did not. Why was this the case?

The more successful expert did four things his colleague didn't. He used advanced persuasion techniques. He partnered with the business on deployment. He developed a range of different versions of documents, from very technical to simple briefing documents, making the knowledge component very digestible for different audiences. Finally, he made these documents easily accessible to the wider organization (the knowledge curation component, see Chapter 47).

In one instance, an easy-to-find folder in the corporate intranet was populated with short sharp *why* and how-to articles about cybersecurity.

These were written in simple business language, with easy-to-understand case studies of what happened if you didn't take precautions and were attacked.

New examples of horror stories were posted almost every week on the front page of the portal, meaning cybersecurity was front of mind. This approach had been co-created by leveraging the marketing department and a selection of colleagues in the business that the expert wanted to influence. Every email on this topic was tested by this business group before it went out, and often small but key changes were made that very positively impacted open and click-through rates.

The less successful colleague used an alternative approach that focused on the expert talking to people at meetings and providing discussion guides for managers to run their own talks about cybersecurity. While fine in theory, both of these initiatives felt like impositions on the managers, who already had full meeting agendas.

Further, managers found that the "here is what you must do" approach from the expert didn't connect with people at the meeting. And, more importantly, these talks didn't translate into action, which made the whole exercise feel like a waste of time. The lack of action was also frustrating for the expert, of course.

These examples show us that we might be a little complacent in thinking that we're naturally operating at Master Expert level when it comes to our Expert Knowledge capability. True mastery involves the effective deployment of knowledge so that others take up its application.

Developing a Knowledge Strategy

A FURTHER METHOD TO reduce complacency might be to consider how actively we're engaged in continuous learning and sharing.

As experts, we might believe that what we're doing is running a knowledge practice. We know about a specific topic, about solutions, and about rules and processes to a greater degree than most people. If we have an expert knowledge strategy, we have a deliberate and outcome-focused plan to use and disseminate this information for the betterment of ourselves, our colleagues, and the organization as a whole.

The expert knowledge strategy model (see Figure 38.1) describes the four typical stages for getting this impact area right: seeking, curating, generating and sharing. The model is a generic guide to the types of issues experts must consider when developing our own knowledge strategy. Each expert's strategy model will be unique to their own situation.

Best practice is to develop and execute this strategy with adequate planning and deliberation. Most experts we've worked with don't have a formalized plan for continuous learning and sharing, let alone a fully formed strategy. The Expert Knowledge capability described in the following pages might set our sights a little higher when it comes to acquiring, organizing, creating and sharing our knowledge.

> *"A huge part of the payoff for experts is in the sharing part of the knowledge strategy."*

And there is a strong imperative to do so. Many experts are constantly frustrated by the amount of time they have to spend doing basic knowledge work rather than the higher value activities they would prefer to be devoted to. They wish there were others, perhaps more junior, who could take over some of the basic work.

Help needs to be trained. But training is both time-consuming and a lot of work.

Take a look at the model in Figure 38.1. The real payoff for experts is in the Sharing part of the rollout. Imagine if those we consult for could resolve basic problems by themselves? Imagine if the large number of daily interruptions by people asking "where do I find this" was hugely reduced. Imagine if, as a consequence of being able to quickly find knowledge that is easy to understand and actionable, our stakeholders found that fixing problems themselves was quicker and more efficient than waiting for us to respond.

All of these things would be wonderful, but unless we carefully gather, organize and provide easy access to what we know, this will never come to fruition.

You may not have come to this book seeking answers on how to manage your knowledge better than you currently do, but you very likely arrived here wanting to add more value by devoting more time to higher order activities. Your expert knowledge strategy, if properly planned and executed, is a critical pathway to this personal and professional growth.

The Three Roles of Expert Knowledge

THE KNOWLEDGE EXPERT MUST play three roles:
- **Knowledge Seeker.** Ensuring that the organization has correct and current knowledge in their technical and related domains.
- **Knowledge Curator.** Making sure that the relevant knowledge is easily accessible and available in meaningful versions to stakeholders and colleagues who need it.
- **Knowledge Generator.** Taking existing knowledge and experience and leveraging insights into new knowledge.

In the next three chapters, we explore each of these expert roles in detail.

Capability: **EXPERT KNOWLEDGE**

An Expert Knowledge Strategy

Capability: **KNOWLEDGE EXPERT**	**SEEKING**	**SCOPE**	· Internal / External · Local / Global · Current / Future
		TACTICS	· Info Feeds, Associations, Events, Partners, Exploration
Capability: **KNOWLEDGE EXPERT**	**CURATING**	**SCOPE**	· Internal / External · Local / Global · Language / Voice
		TACTICS	· Audiences, Versioning, Access, Storage, Renewal
Capability: **KNOWLEDGE EXPERT**	**GENERATING**	**SCOPE**	· Internal / External · Local / Global · Current / Future
		TACTICS	· Data feeds, Analysis, Insights, Experiences, Brainstorming
Capability: **KNOWLEDGE TRANSFER**	**SHARING**	**SCOPE**	· Internal / External · Local / Global · Push / Pull
		TACTICS	· Frequency, Channels, Platforms, Quality, Quantity, Broadcasting, Narrowcasting, Media

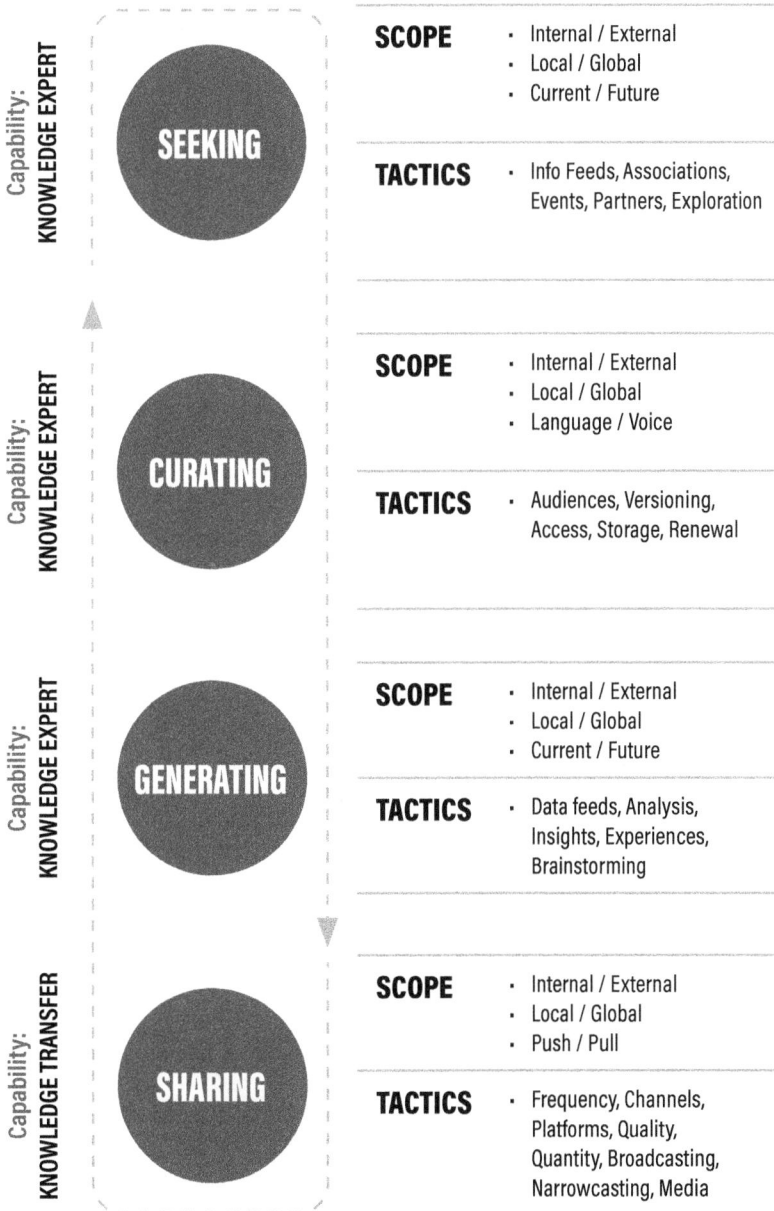

FIGURE 38.1: An Expert Knowledge Strategy

TAKING ACTION

Growing Our Expert Knowledge Skills

IF THIS IS AN expert role in which you believe you could add greater value, here are some high-level suggestions for actions to take:

▶ DEVELOP AN EXPERT KNOWLEDGE STRATEGY

Most experts we work with have a knowledge strategy that is in their head, haphazard, and executed sporadically when (and if) there is spare time. Master Experts don't work this way. They plan out what time needs to be taken to seek, curate and generate knowledge. Using the above chapter, build a winning knowledge strategy that makes you even more expert and builds skills and knowledge in those around you. Questions for us to ask ourselves:

- Do I have a distinct, documented plan for seeking, curating and generating knowledge? If not, why not? If I have one, is it sufficiently comprehensive? Am I executing it?
- How efficient are my systems for capturing and retrieving knowledge when I need it? Or for disseminating knowledge effectively? What systems do I need so I can do this really well?
- To what extent do I partner with colleagues to share and leverage expert knowledge?
- How current is my expert knowledge? How current should it be?

"If knowledge is not put into practice, it does not benefit one."

Muhammad Tahir-ul-Qadri

CHAPTER | 39 |

The Art of Knowledge Seeking

Ensuring currency, comprehensiveness, and clarity in our knowledge seeking will secure success.

IN THIS CHAPTER, WE WILL EXPLORE:

- While knowledge seeking is something most experts do, why aren't we more deliberate about it?
- The key principles underpinning advanced knowledge seeking.
- The importance of diverse information feeds.

THE FIRST EXPERT ROLE in the Expert Knowledge capability is **Knowledge Seeker**. This set of behaviors relates to ensuring that we have the right information, both specialist and non-domain, and that it's comprehensive and current.

An expert's knowledge really is their ticket to the game. Without great knowledge, combined with skills and experience, it's unlikely that we'd be considered experts in our technical field. Ideally, an experienced expert's knowledge should be at the forefront of their field. Master Experts commit to continuous learning in their domain, the broader industry, and related global trends.

The quality of an expert's knowledge is judged by three things. The three Cs of knowledge are *currency*, *comprehensiveness* and *clarity*. The behaviors at each level of Expertship for this expert role are described in Figure 39.1.

At immature levels, there's a danger that the knowledge is tired at best and outdated at worst, without the expert being aware of these facts. Experts who have "always done it this way", or who have analyzed a problem assuming past solutions will work as well today as they did in the past can often be caught out by rapid changes in information, best practice, and next practice.

In contrast, the Master Expert is constantly worried about not having the latest information, and that's why this role uses the word *seeker* in its title.

The Master Expert Knowledge Seeker has information flowing to them from a broad range of sources, keeping them up to date on the latest innovations, developments, versions, practices and case studies in their immediate domain and those adjacent to their knowledge area.

> *"Currency is assisted by curiosity,*
> *which is another key factor."*

The Master Expert is always challenging past assumptions, always asking what has changed that we know about, and what might have changed that we don't know about. They're intensely curious about trends and how the world, and customers in particular, are changing. Master Experts have wide networks of like-minded experts who share information and sources. They're always seeking new channels of valuable information. They don't rest on their laurels. They fidget and fuss over their information sources.

Derailers. Given that many of the experts we've worked with consider the breadth and currency of the knowledge they possess to be one of the biggest contributors to their personal brand, there's probably no greater crime than an expert's knowledge being outdated. With the increasing speed of change and new ideas and approaches to business, technology and customers, accidentally becoming outdated is now a greater danger than ever. In Figure 39.2, we look at the Knowledge Seeking aspects of a Master Expert's Knowledge Strategy.

Capability: EXPERT KNOWLEDGE

Expert Role: KNOWLEDGE SEEKER

MASTER EXPERT

- Continuously updates existing knowledge from traditional and new domain sources, maintaining very high specialist knowledge currency.
- Continuously challenges existing knowledge assumptions.
- Actively seeks new sources of knowledge from domain and non-domain sources.
- Demonstrates commitment to extending skills and knowledge beyond the edge of existing expertise.
- Models life-long learning across a breadth of topics.

EXPERT

- Ensures knowledge remains immediately current by continuous engagement in professional development activities.
- Actively seeks new sources of knowledge from domain sources.
- Can challenge well-established and accepted assumptions within technical domain.

SPECIALIST

- Ensures knowledge remains current by periodic participation in professional development.
- Relies on well-established and accepted assumptions without challenge.

- Relies on out-of-date knowledge; little time spent on increasing currency.
- Dismisses new sources of knowledge as irrelevant.
- Completely reliant on narrow domain information sources.

DERAILING

FIGURE 39.1: Knowledge Seeker Behaviors

Knowledge Currency

LET'S TAKE A LOOK at what constitutes Master Expert behavior when it comes to information sources and maintaining currency.

Currency is very important. It's about being up to date all the time. This requires experts to seek out new developments in relevant specialized technical fields and in the organization's industry. It's vital that expertise remains current.

Currency is assisted by curiosity, which is another key factor. Knowledge Seeking is an attitude. Curiosity always trumps certainty or knowing. As we know, some people are naturally curious, and others are not. Most experts we meet are curious. They want to know the *why*, not just the *what*. Curiosity can also be developed. Key questions a very curious expert might ask include:
- What are the emerging challenges in my field?
- What innovations are taking place in my field?
- What implications do these developments have for the field?

The Master Expert has a deep thirst for learning. They experience a raging curiosity rather than a complacency that they're already knowledgeable about everything.

Depending on our level of Expertship, we collect valuable information through either a narrowly focused set of information feeds or a very broad and eclectic set of feeds. By *feeds*, we mean channels of information, such as colleagues, suppliers, blogs, podcasts, websites, journals, newsletters, video and other media, experiences and so on. In the expert knowledge strategy model (Figure 39.2), we've listed other obvious categories, such as associations we might be members of, events we might attend, partners we work with, and our past, current and possibly future experiences.

Master Experts have broad, multi-topic, global, internal and external information feeds. As Master Experts, we should constantly be looking for new feeds to inform *next practice* and *future practice*, as these will enable us to make a strategic contribution to our organization.

Knowledge Comprehensiveness

OUR EXPERIENCE OF WORKING with many experts is that they have gradually come to rely on reliable, trusted, comfortable information sources that are mostly within their expert domain.

Capability: **EXPERT KNOWLEDGE**
An Expert Knowledge Strategy

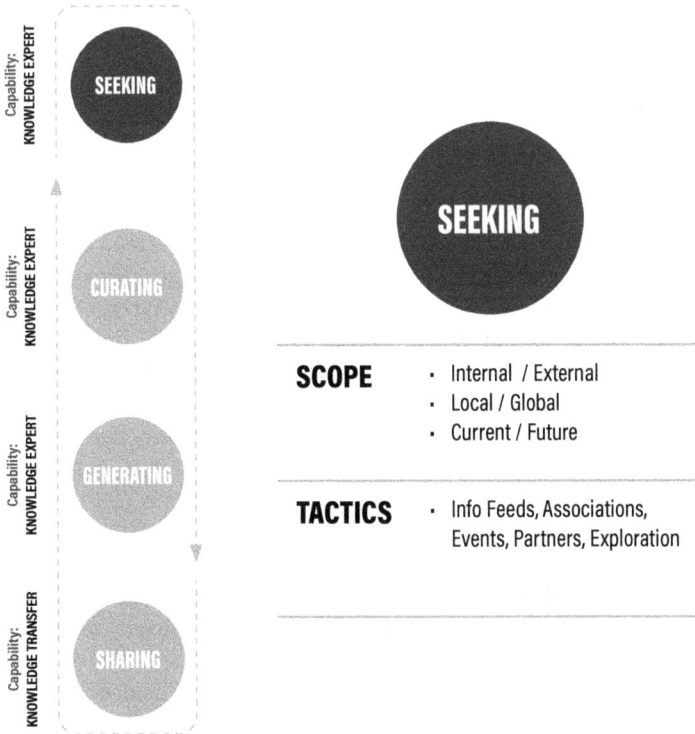

FIGURE 39.2: Knowledge Seeker Strategy

Roger, a very experienced IT specialist, at our prompting, did an analysis of his information sources. He discovered that they almost exclusively covered his two passions: very targeted IT information and music. Roger aspired, however, to spend more time working with executives and influencers outside the IT department on shaping the organization's strategic direction. If he was to be credible, this required that he spend some time looking at the information these executives regularly consumed and relied on.

As a consequence of his audit, he reduced his IT-related information feeds and replaced them with broader business and society feeds that would help him contextualize where his organization was, and where it needed to get to in the future. His list now includes marketing blogs that talk about customer centricity, a chief digital officer's newsletter, and various feeds regarding changing consumer behaviors and attitudes.

This means that Roger now has a much more comprehensive breadth of knowledge, giving him insights into how his technical craft can add value to the organization and its customers.

"The balance between mainstream and contrarian is harder to define, but we value it highly."

Finding the balance between internal and external sources is also important. If we're an expert in a large organization, it's tempting to only read the internal communications about the progress of the organization. There's a lot of this information, but it's the equivalent of drinking the organization's Kool-Aid. We're only getting one view of the world, and it's often one that paints an over-enthusiastic picture of our organization's position. We need to know what our competitors are saying about themselves and our organization.

The balance between local and global is a more obvious consideration. What is happening in our backyard is one thing, but understanding what is happening elsewhere, particularly in places where consumers are early adopters of new ideas and technologies, is vitally important. Since so many experts now work in international roles and very large global organizations, this has become essential.

The balance between mainstream and contrarian is harder to define, but we value it highly. Mainstream is the reporting of established norms, processes and mindsets. Contrarian is the reporting of radical and alternative ideas and thinking. As senior experts in organizations, we can't really afford to be on the bleeding edge in terms of policy or practice. But on the other hand, we can't afford to be blindsided about the future by only consuming information feeds that tell us what we want to hear.

A Master Expert is keen to discover information feeds that contain content that runs contrary to the accepted view. This provides the expert with balance, as listening to those who have a completely different view to us is helpful. It allows us to understand how others think. It helps us clarify why we think the way we do about issues.

It's dangerous to only read information streams that strongly focus on one view of an issue. In Australia recently, there was the view, promoted by mainstream media, that property prices couldn't possibly fall. They did. A small number of expert economists had been predicting the fall for a while.

There are information feeds that focus on climate change being a myth, and there are those that wholeheartedly accept it as a reality. If we only read one side of the story, we wouldn't be much of an expert. Of course, there may be some we believe are higher quality or more accurate, so we'll give more weight to those sources than others.

The Master Expert has a balanced set of information sources, many of which constantly challenge common thinking. This is a sensible approach to Knowledge Seeking.

There is no absolute right or wrong list of information sources. But there is a right or wrong way to manage them. Regular audits, killing feeds that are no longer relevant, seeking out new feeds that offer different perspectives or thinking, regularly checking in with colleagues about what they're finding most interesting—these are the behaviors of a Master Expert.

> *"Senior experts focus on information feeds that*
> *enable them to see into the future."*

Our objectives are maintaining currency and relevance, as well as achieving breadth and diversity.

In the last decade, many highly successful emergent companies have achieved scale and relevance because they combined a customer need with a new business or value model and clever technology. It's the combination of these things that creates success.

If Roger had continued to only read IT news feeds, he couldn't have become the innovative and creative Master Expert he is today.

Knowledge Clarity

THE TROUBLE WITH INFORMATION feeds is that there are far too many of them, and they're of variable quality.

We encourage the experts we work with to develop real clarity about the variety of information they're consuming. We ask them why they are consuming the information they do, and what they do with it afterward. We talk about knowledge curation in the next chapter.

In the expert knowledge strategy model, we suggest three measures that help ensure the information being consumed is balanced:

- Internal versus external: more junior experts will focus on absorbing all the relevant internal informal. This is also true of more experienced experts who have just joined an organization. Master Experts will have a balance that favors external feeds.
- Local versus global: more junior experts will be concerned with understanding what's going on around them. More senior experts want to know what's going on everywhere.

- Current versus future: more junior experts will focus on current news and developments. More senior experts will focus on information feeds that enable them to see into the future.

In addition to knowing *what* information we're consuming and *why*, knowledge clarity also requires us to have clarity about *how* we consume it. Are we consuming information with a high degree of curiosity? Do we want to know why things are developing as they are, and what it means for our organization, our job, our craft and our customers? This type of active reading helps us to get the most value out of our knowledge seeking.

Finding Time to Knowledge Seek When We're Flat-Out

THE POINT OF HAVING a strategy is that we're being deliberate about gathering knowledge and putting it to use. But most experts we work with tell us they're already extremely busy, so finding time to consume more new information is difficult.

The development suggestions below offer some guidance, but we'd also suggest you consider applying some of these principles:

- Don't overwhelm your knowledge gathering with multiple information feeds on the same topics. Cull your list down to one or two trusted sources and one contrarian view.
- Schedule your consumption of these feeds. Make them part of your everyday work. One of the authors consumes new information by listening to audiobooks on the long drives he has to take for work. The other author makes lunchtime his time to catch up on economic and learning feeds.
- Use one of the many great digital tools that now exist for aggregating and collecting content so that the hard work is done for you.

TAKING ACTION

Growing Our Knowledge Seeking Skills

IF THIS IS AN expert role in which you believe you could add greater value, here are some high-level suggestions for actions to take:

▶ AUDIT CURRENT KNOWLEDGE SOURCES

- When did you last do a review of your reading habits and your most trusted information sources? If it was a while ago, doing a review is always worthwhile. Here are some critical questions we might like to ask ourselves:
- Have any of my long-term trusted information sources been superseded by more up-to-date information feeds?
- Do my information sources reflect the future direction of the organization, or the past?
- Are they sufficiently global in scope?
- Have new thought leaders emerged that I should be following (even if I disagree with their point of view)?
- Do my information sources reflect a huge technical bias, or are they broad enough to include reading about my organization, its rivals, and the industry it operates in?

▶ CHALLENGE CORE BELIEFS ABOUT BEST PRACTICE AND EXPLORE NEXT PRACTICE

We all use assumptions to underpin our opinions, policies and approaches to the expert work we do, but there's a risk that changing market dynamics or indeed customer needs will render these assumptions obsolete, or only partially relevant. Here are some critical questions we might ask ourselves:

- When did I last objectively document my evidence-based assumptions about best practice?
- When did I last objectively challenge these assumptions?
- When did I last explore alternative assumptions, processes and approaches?
- What new approaches are likely to supersede the ones I'm using now?

"Content curation is the process of gathering information relevant to a particular topic or area of interest, usually with the intention of adding value through the process of selecting, organizing, and looking after the items in a collection or exhibition."

Wikipedia

CHAPTER | **40** |

The Art of Knowledge Curation

Making our knowledge accessible to those who need it.

IN THIS CHAPTER, WE WILL EXPLORE:

- How curating knowledge saves us time by making our expert knowledge available to our colleagues.
- What are the key success factors in knowledge curation?
- What examples of great knowledge curation can we learn from?

THE SECOND EXPERT ROLE described in the Expert Knowledge capability is **Knowledge Curator.** This set of behaviors relates to ensuring that we have our information stored and versioned so that it's accessible, easy to consume, and actionable by those who need it. As every expert reading these words will know, this is a lot easier said than done.

If much of our knowledge resides in our head, or on servers where no one can find it, or on the organization's intranet but headlined in such a way that only other experts would understand how to find it, then we'll have a never-ending line of interrupters outside our cubicle or office asking us to complete basic tasks for them. This wastes our time. It saps our energy. It distracts us from creating real new value.

Accessibility is the key here. This means organizing the available information to make it retrievable, relevant and user-friendly. The real skill of a Master Expert who plans and executes Knowledge Curation well is the extent to which a broad audience in their organization can access, understand and act upon the knowledge we have gathered.

> *"Knowledge Curation is about seamlessly getting the right information into the right hands at the right time."*

We recommend that experts undertake a proper audit of how effectively their knowledge curation is being organized. The key questions to consider are as follows:
- Is the information easy to find? Do the documents and guides have titles that users will actually search for, or are they in our arcane technical language?
- Have different versions been developed for audiences with different levels of understanding and expertise?
- How well-developed and audience-friendly is the distribution strategy when it comes to an expert's domain knowledge?

The behaviors at each level of Expertship for this expert role are described in Figure 40.1.

At immature levels, experts are the recipients of knowledge sharing. They're still learning where to find good information. They'll exhibit a good understanding of common concepts, practices and approaches. But experts operating at the specialist level of Expertship won't be in the business of curating anything more than their own information resources and library.

> *"The way we curate knowledge for different audiences is, in effect, marketing."*

The Master Expert, in contrast, will preside over an advanced, comprehensive knowledge bank. They will be focused on making sure that the variety of stakeholder groups served can easily access suitable material when they need it and this material is customized to their needs and skill levels. In short, they'll be concerned with getting really useful information into the right hands at the right time, seamlessly.

Derailing behaviors include having little or no regard for the information needs of the customer groups being served, and possibly a disorganized and haphazard approach to organizing information.

Knowledge curation provides an opportunity for all experts to positively promote what they do and how it adds value, provided that we all take into account what methods of communication, language and levels of detail are appropriate to each group we serve (or want to influence).

Expert Knowledge Curation

LET'S TAKE A LOOK in more detail at what top-class knowledge curation looks like inside a modern, matrix organization. How do we organize, evaluate and store our hard-won knowledge? This is typically an opportunity for significant improvement among most experts we've worked with.

As experts, the challenges we face to get the curation part of our knowledge strategy executed are actually very significant. This is because there are many barriers we need to overcome, with the most significant barrier being ourselves. How we see the knowledge in our technical domain is typically from an *expert perspective*. We'll almost certainly use complex jargon (or acronyms) to describe, categorize and file knowledge artifacts.

This makes the information we need easy for *us* to find. But use of specialist language and referencing means that for others in the organization, our knowledge base becomes an impenetrable minefield.

> *"Marketers love to define audiences or personas."*

As experts, we can make the mistake of assuming our colleagues have foundational knowledge that actually isn't there.

Artifacts that appear very simplistic in their approach may be of no interest to us as seasoned experts but offer a very valuable introduction to a topic for a colleague in the wider organization who is not an expert.

If we consider ourselves running a knowledge practice, one that we wish to promote and have colleagues throughout the organization find useful, then we have to consider that the way we curate knowledge is, in effect, marketing, and we should therefore take a few leaves out of marketers' books.

Marketers love to define audiences (or personas). An audience is a specific group of people we're trying to inform and/or influence.

Capability: EXPERT KNOWLEDGE

Expert Role: KNOWLEDGE CURATOR

MASTER EXPERT

- Manages a well-curated, advanced, comprehensive knowledge bank that is easy to access.
- Develops effective versioning of knowledge, making knowledge easy to find and digest by a variety of audiences.
- Promotes and models adaptive and innovative usage of existing knowledge and practices, making knowledge actionable and value-creating.

EXPERT

- Has a comprehensive knowledge bank of both common and uncommon concepts, practices and approaches.
- Shares knowledge effectively with technical cohort.
- Systematic usage of existing knowledge and practices.

SPECIALIST

- Sound understanding of common concepts, practices and approaches.
- Shows developing use and application of knowledge.

- Significant knowledge acquisition still required.
- Knowledge is undocumented and not shared.
- Inconsistent and arbitrary storage of knowledge.
- No consideration given to the information needs of others, particularly those outside their technical domain.

DERAILING

FIGURE 40.1: Knowledge Curator Behaviors

A marketer will spend deliberate time trying to understand a particular audience, its concerns and interests, the language the group uses and understands, and what captures the audience's attention (and what does not). Then all information targeted to that audience is customized to maximize interest and engagement.

> *"Senior executives are typically only interested in high-level pragmatic advantages to the organization."*

Let's take the example of a group of colleagues most senior experts are trying to influence: senior executives in our organizations. They're interested in the strategic realm of thought. They want to know what our competitors are up to, how to develop a compelling value proposition for customers, the latest industry innovations, and so on. They're less likely to be interested in the details of our methodologies, technologies, policies or procedures, but they may be interested in reading about the high-level pragmatic advantages that these initiatives offer the organization.

Knowing this, we're in a position to curate our knowledge so that it's both easy-to-find and compelling information for our prioritized stakeholder group—senior executives.

Let's consider the case of the cybersecurity expert we introduced in Chapter 38. Saanvi is responsible for promoting risk products (what the rest of us call insurance) to corporations who might suffer cyber-attacks.

When we were working with Saanvi a few years ago, the risks and the associated disruption and financial and reputational loss a cyber-attack could cause was not well-understood by senior executives in her prospective client companies.

Saanvi's strategy was threefold. Initially, she needed to educate her first target audience, senior executives in large organizations, about cyber risks, so they would authorize investments in cyber insurance. Then, she had to convince her second target audience, corporate risk managers, that the organization she represented was best positioned and had the best products and services to meet this need. Since Saanvi was working in an insurance company, she had a third target audience: insurance experts in her own firm who were selling different types of insurance to the same risk managers in Saanvi's second target audience group. Saanvi had to persuade her colleagues to make introductions. This involves getting one division of a large firm to work collaboratively with another division, which as anyone who has worked in a large firm knows, ought to be simple but rarely is.

Over time and many conversations, Saanvi came to understand that each group's information needs were radically different.

We all know that case studies about the success other organizations are having will greatly appeal to senior executives. In Saanvi's case, she collected disaster stories about what happened to firms and their leading executives because they hadn't properly accounted for cyber risk.

> *"Knowledge versioning makes complex content accessible to busy executives."*

We know they're far more likely to consume information if it's written in business language—*their* language. We know not to inundate them with technical mumbo jumbo that they won't understand. Saanvi went one step further and versioned these case studies. She circulated very short and sharp summaries through social media and emails. These contained links to a longer version of the case studies. This *knowledge versioning* makes the content far more accessible to busy executives.

Saanvi carefully crafted the headings and descriptions of these information artifacts so that they could be easily understood and later retrieved by this audience.

She circulated the simplest case studies first. This meant dealing with issues like viruses, then data theft, and then the more complex denial of service attacks. She understood that she needed to educate executive teams gradually on the issue rather than overloading them with an all-at-once approach. This is called *knowledge sequencing*.

For the risk managers, Saanvi took a different approach. She circulated technical papers and articles describing how risk managers might deploy a best practice cyber-risk framework. She listed, at some length, all the types of cyber risks that existed, the potential damage of each, and how to mitigate these risks. Saanvi took this approach because risk managers are technical specialists, and Saanvi had learned that they want all the detail immediately.

Capability: **EXPERT KNOWLEDGE**
An Expert Knowledge Strategy

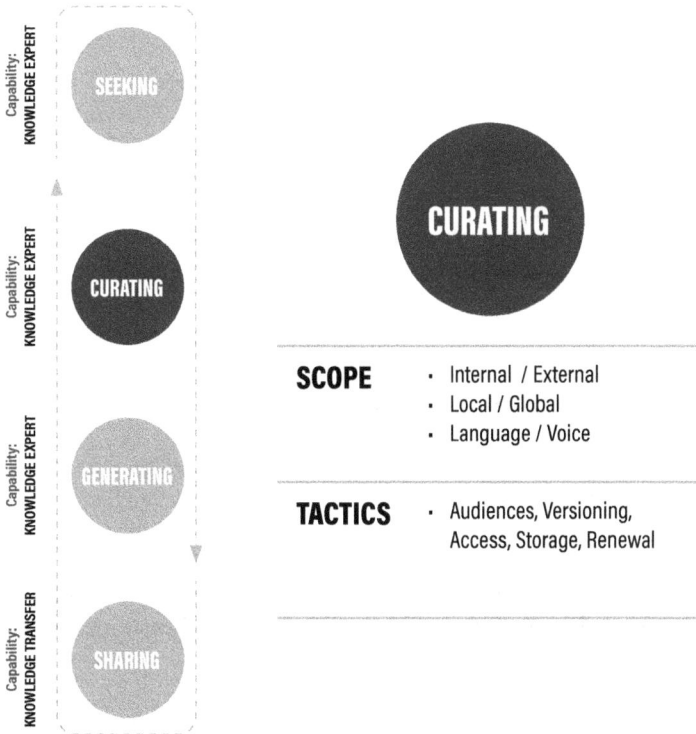

FIGURE 40.2: Knowledge Curator Strategy

For internal colleagues from other divisions, Saanvi worked hard to shape the right message. Typically, colleagues don't like to potentially jeopardize their successful relationship with a client by introducing a colleague who may negatively impact that relationship. So, Saanvi needed to help her colleagues from other divisions, who perhaps didn't know her so well, to feel safe (and possibly that they might benefit from) making an introduction. She understood that any corporate directive ("You must cross-sell between divisions") was always going to be subservient to individual comfort levels. Saanvi leveraged several network connections (see Chapter 14 and Chapter 18) that she had previously made in other divisions and ran pilot sessions with clients. She asked her internal colleagues and the clients involved to provide testimonials on the value of the meetings and the information and insight Saanvi had provided. She leveraged these testimonials into new pilots with associated colleagues or her network friends. She built a collection of strong endorsements from internal colleagues and their external clients, then circulated these to a much wider audience of internal colleagues. The result: colleagues she didn't know came forward requesting her attendance at client meetings.

None of this is rocket science. It just requires some careful and informed thought. And, of course, some effort. In particular, it helps if we understand what types of materials different groups will respond to positively.

"How and where do we store our various versions of our expert knowledge?"

A respected colleague of ours offered this example for the versioning of language. He suggested these three classic versions, describing the release of a new version of software implemented at an organization:

- **The Technical Statement**: Version 7.2 will allow 78 percent more simultaneous interactions while cutting unnecessary record locks by 51 percent (spoken by an expert to an expert).
- **The Business Statement**: A new version of our software will reduce costs by cutting the time required for order entry by an average of 8 percent. It will also enhance service quality by ensuring the data is updated correctly (spoken by an expert to most internal business stakeholders).
- **The Executive Statement**: This investment will improve the bottom line because of lower costs in our back office and fewer customer returns due to incorrectly entered orders (spoken by an expert to senior leaders, board members and any external stakeholders).

The three statements above all say the same thing, but as they say in Singapore: "Same, same but different." Each is framed to connect with the specific concerns of the target audience. Each uses the language of the target audience. Each offers the right amount of detail.

The solution to successful knowledge curation is therefore simple: know your audiences, then knowledge version and knowledge sequence accordingly. For colleagues at our Expertship level, we might share a very complex paper that is riddled with jargon, but it's jargon that we all understand.

For more junior colleagues, we might share that paper but add an introduction explaining in simpler terms what the paper is about, or find a simpler but still technical exposition of the topic. For our senior executives, we might have to write a much shorter, business-oriented explanation.

Access to Expert Knowledge

HOW AND WHERE DO we store our various versions of our expert knowledge? And how do the people who want access to this information find it?

Making very specific decisions about where items are stored is crucial. Where will our target audiences naturally look? Making very specific decisions about what the documents are called is a further critical success factor. What will our audiences actually be searching for? What will they call the topic or how will they describe the issue?

As an example, let's imagine that Oracle, the enterprise applications software company, has made large changes in its security settings in the latest release of its software. Our organization is a big user of various Oracle applications. Senior technical colleagues will want to understand the detailed architecture and thinking behind the changes because this will impact how, internally, we design things in the future.

More junior technical colleagues will want to know what has changed and how they need to recalibrate various applications and user manuals as a consequence.

> *"How do we get people interested in a topic they are not initially excited about?"*

The executive team, on the other hand, will want to understand how these changes will affect our organization's security against attacks and the cost of the changes the IT team will have to make. They won't be interested in the technical nuts and bolts.

The headings on all three of these versions will be entirely different. And most likely, they will be stored in different places. The more technical content might be on a wiki, and the more business-oriented content could be in a business case or be a paper attached to specific decision-making meetings.

As we discussed earlier in this chapter, if we curate knowledge well, then we have the opportunity to achieve a number of strategic objectives: a self-service model for the wider organization, development opportunities for more junior technical experts, and an opportunity to build our personal expert brand and add value higher up our organization's value chain.

Think Creatively

HOW DO WE ENGAGE people's interest in a topic they're not initially excited about? Perhaps we could take a leaf out of Cameron's book. One of our Expertship participants supplied us with this great example.

Cameron is an asset valuer. Most of us will be familiar with property experts who value properties for the banks so they'll loan us money to buy residential property. Cameron and his team are engaged by clients to value things that are really difficult to value. This might be the machinery in a factory (easy, he says) or the value inherent in a brand name (maybe not so easy).

Cameron is honest about the work he does. While he and his team find it fascinating, most people don't. A further complication is that, rather like your dentist, you only really look for another one when you move location, or if your current dentist underperforms in some way. To build his practice, Cameron had to come up with a strategy that would engage clients and non-clients alike, keeping his practice front of mind when a new opportunity arises.

Cameron and his team found that a classic knowledge distribution strategy worked best. They developed a series of postcards that were sent out to a database of existing and prospective clients every couple of months. On one side was a picture of a really unusual (and therefore interesting) asset. On the flip side, headlined, was how much is this asset was worth. They also briefly told the story of how they went about valuing the asset.

Cameron was good enough to share some of these with us, and while we have virtually no interest in asset valuation, the picture and story behind it was a fascinating three-minute read. We also found, as was the case with Cameron's clients, that the postcards were difficult to throw away. They tended to go into a drawer because they were interesting enough that we subconsciously knew we might want to revisit the content again someday. Or they were shared: "Hey, look what we just received. Isn't this interesting?"

Cameron and his team had achieved three goals with one small idea. They had gained the interest of a broad audience, showed how complex the work is (i.e., how difficult it is to value some complex and unique pieces), and also showed their professionalism and process by sharing the story of how they valued it. It was a simple but unbelievably powerful knowledge curation idea.

Cameron and his team thought about what would interest the client, not want he and his team wanted to tell the client. This is Marketing 101 beautifully executed.

TAKING ACTION

Growing Our Knowledge Curation Skills

IF THIS IS AN expert role in which you believe you could add greater value, here are some high-level suggestions for actions to take:

▶ DO A STAKEHOLDER ACCESS TEST

When did we last do a review of what information our stakeholders would actually like to have access to and consider whether that access appropriately exists or not? Here are some critical questions we might like to ask ourselves:
- Can my key stakeholders find what they need from me?
- Can I quickly find what I'm asked for?
- Is information saved in a variety of locations that only I can navigate? If I'm serving a multi-national stakeholder group operating in different territories, is the information I curate appropriately internationalized?

The way to complete this test is to directly ask our stakeholders and request that they be robust in their feedback to us.

▶ REVIEW OUR KNOWLEDGE REPOSITORY

We may be spending lots of time producing insightful information for the organization but presenting it in such a way that it doesn't reach its target audience. Here are some critical questions we might ask ourselves:
- Am I bringing my knowledge to life by using multi-media, stories, case studies, videos, quizzes, challenges?
- Which of my knowledge artifacts are used frequently by my stakeholders? Which are never used? Why?
- Does anyone ever open my newsletters and emails? What do the results tell me?

CHAPTER | 41 |

The Art of Knowledge Generation

Generating new knowledge and then applying it is the trademark of a Master Expert and thought leader.

IN THIS CHAPTER, WE WILL EXPLORE:

- How does new knowledge get created? How do experts go about generating new knowledge?
- How does knowledge generation sit at the epicenter of innovation?
- How do experts develop sufficient knowledge generation skills to become seen by colleagues and peers as thought leaders?

THE THIRD EXPERT ROLE described in the Expert Knowledge capability is the challenge of being a **Knowledge Generator**. This set of behaviors relates to ensuring that we contribute value by creating new information by being forward-looking, curious, and by encouraging a learning culture. Leading the way in knowledge means being involved in the generation or creation of new knowledge and insights.

Evolving in this capability involves shifting from being a passive recipient of new knowledge, where we slavishly rely on new data and insights presented to us by our industry, professional associations, or generous colleagues. Or we might be experts who believe there is nothing new to learn in our areas of specialization. The goal is to evolve into an expert who, through our knowledge capture systems, almost automatically creates new knowledge and insights.

"How do we avoid being seen as a thought loser?"

The value created by being the first to realize that a key business assumption or rule has changed, and being the first to understand the implications of this change (both the inherent dangers but also the opportunities), cannot be understated. It leads to us attaining a status that many of us aspire to: being considered a *thought leader* in our domain.

The professional implications of being the last to realize and understand key changes in our domains can be career-ending. Think of it as being a *thought loser*.

The behaviors at each level of Expertship for this expert role of Expertship are described in Figure 41.1.

At immature levels, almost no knowledge generation occurs, although experts operating at the specialist level may be involved by those more senior in some research or information capture activities. Experts at this level demonstrate a sound knowledge of and strong adherence to existing knowledge practices.

"This is an area of Expertship where we have a clear leadership role."

The Master Expert, in comparison, will be involved in actively contributing to the generation of new knowledge, engaged in anticipating long-term future knowledge requirements, and will be building systems and processes that enable knowledge breakthroughs to occur. Aggressively curious, the Master Expert will be eager to be at the vanguard of industry breakthroughs, introducing innovative solutions and seeking to operate at *next practice*. Remember, best practice is just catching up. Next practice means everyone is following us.

Furthermore, Master Experts bring everyone else along with them. They create an environment that prompts others to engage with knowledge generation and be open to new ideas, and they encourage appropriate experimentation.

Experts with derailing behaviors in this role, which we've labeled *thought losers*, won't be contributing to knowledge generation. They'll quite possibly be resisting the introduction of any new practices. Needless to say, those derailing here will fail to anticipate or embrace future needs or developments.

This is an area of Expertship where we have a clear leadership role. Open-minded, innovative, adaptive and curious, we have the opportunity to add significant value to our colleagues, teams and organization by providing well-researched opinions about where the organization or the field of expertise might go next and the emergent needs and opportunities.

Innovation and Generating New Knowledge

AS MIGHT BE EXPECTED, successful knowledge generation requires planning, effort, inspiration and a bit of luck. What does next practice look like?

As Knowledge Seekers, we have sought to acquire relevant information so as to keep our skills and insights honed. As Knowledge Curators, we have set up a system for ourselves and others to easily access and utilize the most relevant information. As Knowledge Generators, it's now time to decide what additional knowledge might be advantageous for us to create and disseminate. Is there a unique perspective that we can provide based on our particular vantage point that could be advantageous to the organization? Are there developments in our specific (professional or technical) field that could present game-changing opportunities for the organization—ones that no one other than us is likely to be aware of?

> *"Genius is 1 percent inspiration and 99 percent perspiration." - Thomas Edison*

Many of the world's largest consulting firms routinely produce thought leadership publications as a way of ensuring that they always have something to talk to clients about, to provoke clients' interest, and to demonstrate the value they can add. Master Experts adopt a similar mentality with creating content to stimulate their stakeholders' thinking. This involves looking at emerging trends and considering the impact that these may have on the organization, whether political, environmental, sociological, technological (a process known as PEST analysis) or examining unmet needs, gaps or issues and then proposing that the organization pursue an appropriate course of action.

Capability: EXPERT KNOWLEDGE

Expert Role: KNOWLEDGE GENERATOR

MASTER EXPERT

- At the vanguard of industry breakthroughs, introducing innovative solutions and seeking to operate at next practice.
- Actively contributes to the generation of new knowledge.
- Anticipates long-term future knowledge requirements and makes suitable and timely provisions.
- Regularly authors and shares new knowledge.
- Creates an environment that stimulates others to engage in knowledge generation.

EXPERT

- Seeks and adopts new effective knowledge management practices and seeks to operate at best practice.
- Anticipates near-future requirements and makes suitable and timely provisions.
- Creates an environment for others to engage in knowledge generation.

SPECIALIST

- Demonstrates sound knowledge and adherence to existing knowledge management practices.
- Participates under direction in the generation of new knowledge.

- Does not contribute to knowledge generation.
- Resists documenting any new practices.
- Fails to anticipate or embrace future needs or developments.

DERAILING

FIGURE 41.1: Knowledge Generator Behaviors

Knowledge generation is all about innovation. Knowledge is an intangible thing. It's governed by very different laws than physical objects. Knowledge itself, when employed innovatively, creates more knowledge. That is its great power. And contrary to popular belief, innovation is rarely about lightbulb moments. The inventor of the lightbulb, Thomas Edison, is credited with this now-famous quote: "Genius is 2 percent inspiration and 98 percent perspiration." The argument is that breakthrough ideas and insights do come, but usually only after the exhaustive collection of data, synthesis of information, and development of insights. The literature on innovation supports this view.

> *"Experts are often at the fulcrum of where innovation is expected to be delivered."*

Innovation is a word that is thrown around a lot in most organizations. It's frequently misused, and there is often little understanding of what the term actually means. *Innovation* can cover many activities and outcomes, which may result from different pressures on a business to renew itself and its products and its services or propel itself successfully into the future. Much of the misunderstanding and confusion comes from the belief that there is only one type of innovation. In fact, there are three types. We discuss each of them below.

This means that different types of innovation processes may be required for different types of innovation. And most importantly, different types of technical leadership are required to make each type of innovation come to life. In today's dynamic market, an understanding of innovation and how businesses can improve their innovation performance is essential to survival. Indeed, it has become a critical leadership capability. This is particularly true for experts since we're often at the fulcrum of where innovation is expected to be delivered.

The three types of innovation are incremental (or sustaining) innovation, strategic innovation, and disruptive innovation (see Figure 41.3). Let's look at each of these in turn and examine the contribution experts can make in each category.

Most experts have more opportunities to be involved in the process of innovation than they might realize. In particular, in the area of incremental innovation, there's nearly always an opportunity to continuously improve things. Is the process sufficiently efficient or lean? Is it user-friendly?

But even in the area of disruptive innovation, it could be that the expert identifies unmet customer needs or frustrations, technology trends, developments in regulatory oversight, and so on, that could allow the organization to better differentiate itself or take advantage of opportunities.

Incremental (or Sustaining) Innovation

INCREMENTAL INNOVATION IS DIRECTED at existing products and services, with the objective of making small but important changes to obtain the greatest extension to the life cycle of the product or service. The Japanese call this type of innovation kaizen (change for the better, or improvement).

These innovations are commonly designed to respond to customer requests, competitive threats, regulatory changes, and service and support issues. They often also incorporate technical improvements. These are normal product improvements that some businesses currently accommodate.

Many experts are involved in incremental innovation every day. This is particularly true of experts in the IT domain, for example, who constantly add system improvements requested by the organization or update systems and processes to achieve efficiency.

> *"Our rule of thumb for incremental*
> *innovation is the 10 percent rule."*

However, whether in IT or not, experts have a fundamental role to play in driving incremental innovation. Is there a better way to do something? A faster, cheaper or higher value way? Our clients want what we have today, but what will they want tomorrow? Can we make assessments and have small changes ready?

At one time or another, we've all been the expert who gets in the way of incremental change. This happens when we're so wedded to our way of doing things that we dismiss or resist any proposed changes to systems and processes made to us by people who are "less expert." Have we ever been guilty of seeing all the difficulties of small changes and questioned whether the effort would be worth it before considering the positive outcomes that the change would create? Like it or not, experts have a reputation for sometimes being blockers when it comes to innovation.

Most of us have the opportunity to be the opposite and help build a culture of challenge and ambition when it comes to finding new ways of creating value. Most of us have years of experience and have seen innovation projects succeed and fail. We can leverage this experience to help our teams succeed in delivering incremental innovation.

Capability: **EXPERT KNOWLEDGE**

An Expert Knowledge Strategy

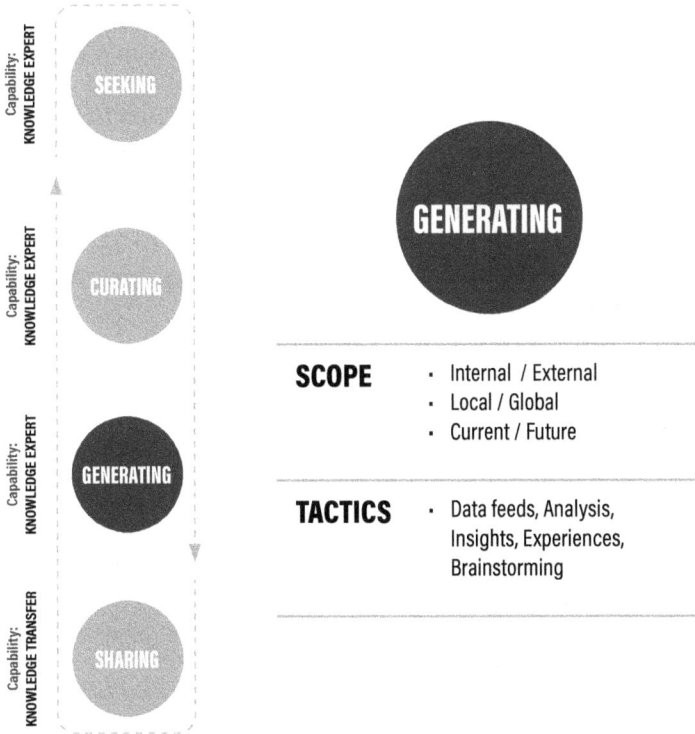

FIGURE 41.2: Knowledge Generator Strategy

Our rule of thumb for incremental innovation is the 10 percent rule. Can we, every month, find a way of delivering a 10 percent improvement? This might be producing the same product but for 10 percent less. Or making the product 10 percent better but at the same cost. Or finding a way of making the same product for the same money but somehow 10 percent faster? Or can we find a way of reducing product failures by 10 percent?

Much of this thinking comes down to looking at the data—or knowledge—that tells us how well we're delivering value.

Strategic Innovation

STRATEGIC INNOVATION IS USUALLY directed from the Board level in recognition of a longer term vision of the direction in which the business should proceed. It may be an extension of the existing product range or it may be significantly different (for example, to capitalize on a particular distribution or manufacturing or technology strength).

Often, strategic innovation means moving into an adjacent market or expanding the scope of our products and services. An organization, for example, that has many contracts for cleaning hospitals may decide that the core skill set they have can also be deployed in cleaning stadiums, and they either build or acquire a new division to do just this. An organization specializing in negotiating leases for cars for their customers may decide to branch out into negotiating other types of leases.

> *"We can't expect our customers to know what they want." - Steve Jobs*

While the initiative may be directed at Board level, experts can often be highly influential in spotting the opportunity, particularly if we have a very broad set of information sources.

Strategic innovation can sometimes require a more radical culture shift and leadership challenge than incremental innovation. It could also incorporate our third category of innovation: disruptive innovation.

Disruptive Innovation

DISRUPTIVE INNOVATION SIGNIFICANTLY CHANGES the business model of the whole organization, or at least a large part of it. A good example is Apple's decision to get into the portable music business in 2001, a completely new mass-market business model, which led to over 20 million iPods being sold in 2005 alone.

It may also come about as a result of new ways of doing things. Henry Ford's comment that if he'd asked people what they wanted, they would have told him "faster horses" illustrates this point. It's remarkably consistent with Steve Jobs' view that "we can't expect our customers to know what they want."

Disruptive innovation is often driven by new technologies, not by market intelligence. It's usually underpinned by a new business model (or way of delivering value). The iPod's success was driven by iTunes, which enabled us to buy one song at a time rather than in albums as the music industry had insisted upon for so long. It might also be underpinned by new ways of working and new business models, with the sharing economy producing new companies such as Uber.

Experts from all domains find themselves at the center of such innovations, whether seeing an uncaptured opportunity, writing code, or building new models of working from vast amounts of knowledge. But in similar ways to incremental innovation, we can be blockers of disruptive innovation because our status as experts is being undermined.

Large parts of the wisdom and knowledge that make us valuable could be swept away as obsolete by a successful disruptive technology. Lawyers, for example, used to charge a lot to produce common sales contracts, but now various disrupters provide similar services for a fraction of the cost and in a fraction of the time.

Brokers of all descriptions used to charge for their ability to intelligently compare complex service offers from multiple vendors. Now smart AI engines can do the same on a website in a matter of seconds. Travel agents used to be the font of all knowledge about travel. Now TripAdvisor helps us crowd-source experience from visitors who have actually recently visited our potential destination.

> *"Some disruptive innovation challenges our own value as experts."*

Any expert reading these paragraphs and thinking *this can't happen to me* is in dangerous denial. It's a matter of *when*, not *if*. Master Experts don't worry about being made obsolete as they're actively working on helping it happen. And in the process, they're creating new knowledge and insights that make them the new experts that people will seek out and value.

- Spend years doing this, sharing your thoughts and working collaboratively with others to shape new thinking and ideas.
- Wait for someone else to call you a thought leader as it's not something that can be self-labeled.

Almost certainly, thought leaders have devoted time and energy to knowledge generation and to developing unique insights from unique knowledge collections. This concept of collection is important. Any study of the success of the iPod shows that Apple didn't invent either the MP3 player (the hardware of the iPod) or the online buying platform that leverages third-party content (iTunes). But they did build on and perfect both the hardware and the buying platform, and by combining these two ideas, they changed the way most people buy and listen to music in the world today.

Capability: **EXPERT KNOWLEDGE**

The Three Types of Innovation

DISRUPTIVE

- Directed at new markets, creating new customer needs
- Driven by innovators
- New future vision, new imagining of the enterprise, time to market varies (very fast to longer incubation)
- Creation of new value proposition, creating new 'blue ocean' opportunities; makes competitors obsolete
- Driven by wanting to change the rules of the game (or change the game completely)

STRATEGIC

- Directed at new products and services, or adjacencies
- Driven by the Board or investors
- Longer term vision, where is the future of the enterprise, longer to market
- Major changes that impact the positioning of the company and its competitive environment
- Can be reactive or proactive changes (responding to opportunities, changes in buying patterns, or leverage capabilities, competitor moves)

INCREMENTAL

- Directed at existing products and services
- Driven by people working on the product or service, and close to the customer
- Short term and fast to market
- Small but important changes that sustain or extend the life cycle of a product or service
- Often reactive changes (responding to competitors, regulations, etc)

FIGURE 41.3: The Three Types of Innovation

Becoming a Thought Leader

MANY EXPERTS DREAM OF becoming a thought leader, and many do within their own organizations. To become a thought leader outside our organization is much harder. The web is crowded with "become a thought leader quick" articles, but the best ones make the case that the only way to become a thought leader is to:

- Do a lot of original thinking based on a review of a great deal of evidence (knowledge seeking and knowledge curating).

TAKING ACTION

Growing Our Knowledge Generation Skills

IF THIS IS AN expert role in which you believe you could add greater value, here are some high-level suggestions for actions to take:

▶ CREATE A "NEXT PRACTICE" PLAN

As experts, we hope we're operating at best practice level in our technical domain. But to get to Master Expert level, we need to be focused on getting to *next* practice level as quickly as possible. For this, we need a deliberate and documented plan. Here are some critical questions we might like to ask ourselves:

- What obvious trends are going to force me to change the way I do things in the future?
- What drove the most recent changes in the way my domain operates, and how could I learn from that to predict where the next inflection point will come from?
- What changes have I been hoping to make in the way I go about things, and what have been the barriers? How do I overcome them?
- To what extent is the whole team thinking and worrying about the future of what we do? How do I encourage and facilitate that thinking?

▶ BE OBSESSIVE ABOUT RESEARCHING CUSTOMER, STAKEHOLDER AND ORGANIZATIONAL NEEDS

It's not possible to generate new knowledge, insights, ways of working, or new value unless we're seeking to understand the subtle or major changes to the way our services are being currently consumed, or how they may be consumed in the future. And new insights come from research. Here are some critical questions we might ask ourselves:

- What information is collected by the organization that might help me gain insights about current and future trends?
- What are customers complaining about and why?
- As a team, how much time do we spend on "what if…" scenarios based on what we've learned? How often do we ask the question "How would this trend play out in my industry, organization or technical domain?"

MASTERING SOLUTIONING

SOLUTIONING

TECHNICAL DOMAIN

The Master Expert solves complex technical problems effectively and quickly via insightful diagnosis and shaping long-term solutions that improve processes and create opportunities.

CHAPTER | 42 |

The Expert Art of Solutioning

How might the careful utilization of a consulting approach facilitate better outcomes and be more rewarding for you and your stakeholders?

IN THIS CHAPTER, WE WILL EXPLORE:

- How deploying an advanced consulting model helps experts build and implement solutions that create quantifiable and reported value.
- Why does the way we ask discovery questions matter?
- What barriers get in the way of experts deploying advanced consulting techniques?

MANY EXPERTS DESCRIBE THEIR work as handling others' requests all day. Fielding such requests isn't always the optimal way for us to spend our time. Our expertise is best directed toward activities delivering greater business impacts. It's natural that our know-how is sought out to solve problems. It's our conviction that the judicious use of consulting mindsets, processes and techniques can help us and our stakeholders to focus on and address the right problems, build more impactful solutions, deliver the sought value, and measure and report progress.

High-impact solutioning, i.e., using our curiosity and critical thinking skills to understand complex issues, is something every expert relishes. It requires us to combine our technical and industry know-how (market context) to design imaginative solutions. The best of us engage stakeholders along the way. However, all too often, solutioning feels like we settle for a so-called expedient but sub-optimal approach.

So many of the experts we work with express frustration with how this problem-solving aspect of their role currently works. They report being asked for the same fixes time and time again. Many complain that their stakeholders engage them too late in the process and provide incomplete briefs. Experts report that their stakeholders don't seem to be clear on what exactly they want. They're fed up of having to rework solutions time and again because when they deliver what they were asked for, the "solution" is not on target.

A very common complaint among experts we work with is that they often feel they're not given sufficient context.

> *"We need to become expert in resisting the*
> *instinct to jump to the solution."*

And finally, many experts report that they're unable to demonstrate the true value of the contributions they could make because stakeholders push them to implement already decided solutions without sufficient assessment or diagnosis. Although experts do their best to make sense of requirements and build solutions accordingly, they often end up looking like chumps because they've received a bad steer.

This chapter and the following three look at the consulting mindset, the phases of a consulting assignment, skills, and even specific questions to ask so experts can transform transactional requests into real opportunities to add business value and move our contribution up the value chain.

Let's first explore what we mean by "adopting a consulting mindset and approach" in contrast with simply "taking the order."

A Consulting Mindset

IN A PERFECT WORLD, solutioning would look like this: deploying our best expertise in determining what outcomes our stakeholders wish to achieve and why, and how to best pursue those advantages so as to co-create a solution with our "client."

Any time we don't do our own analysis and simply build the solution that someone else has asked us to build, we're colluding in our own sub-optimal engagement. We're failing to consult. We have succumbed to becoming non-value-adding order takers. We have left the shaping of the solution to individuals who lack the full know-how to do so alone. It needs to be a partnership, a co-creation. Our stakeholders should bring their contextual knowledge, such as the issues as they see them and the business outcomes being sought. We should bring our diagnostic and design skills, our content knowledge in our areas of specialism, and our grasp of market context. Then, *together*, we can shape and implement a solution that elegantly addresses the defined needs.

Shifting to a consulting approach involves numerous skills and processes. In the first instance, we need to become expert at resisting the instinct to solve the problem, and jump to the solution, before we adequately understand the issues at hand or gather relevant information.. This would include understanding precisely how the issues show up in concrete organizational results. Secondly, we need to master selling the requesting stakeholder on the importance of doing so. We have to persuade them we're not going slow, insulting their thinking (by not accepting their conclusion about what's needed), or being difficult to work with. We'll explore with our stakeholder's the idea of "moving off the solution", carefully transitioning the conversation to "what is it we're trying to do exactly?" and away from "please implement such and such."

> *"As experts, we have to earn the right to open up a broader organizational conversation."*

If we don't master "moving off the solution," we run the risk of stakeholders thinking we're wasting their time with these broader questions. This may be because they believe they've already figured out what's needed, whereas it's likely that we would find their analysis far from exhaustive. In most cases, it's not just that they've already decided on the solution they want us to implement, but they've also become psychologically and emotionally committed to their "solution."

Another risk when we start asking questions about broader organizational requirements is that our stakeholders might find this presumptive of us, as if their own "joining the dots" thus far is regarded by us as inadequate. They ask themselves, "what would a technical expert, coming from a very specialized knowledge domain, know about organizational strategy, competitors, and long-term requirements?" They expect us to stick to and operate within our technical bubble, leaving the big-picture organization-wide expertise to them. In reality, our stakeholders may also have an underlying concern (usually subconscious) that the technical experts are asking questions that they should've *already* asked but didn't. These types of questions often mean our stakeholders aren't sure of the answers, and this both embarrasses and irritates them.

The truth is that, as experts, we have to earn the right to open up a broader organizational conversation. Moving off the solution requires emotional intelligence and skill. We need to ask the questions that will enable us to see how the issue affects the organization. And we need to ask them in a way that will engage our stakeholders rather than put them offside. We'll go into more depth on this in the next chapter.

The third issue is one of our own making. If we're going to explore underlying issues, we have to move beyond merely understanding the technical requirements by also asking questions that adequately explore all potential outcomes.

The Dangers of Jumping to a Solution

LET'S LOOK AT A real example of how a stakeholder wanting us to simply implement their solution proved problematic.

Melinda is the organization development manager at Perfect Providores, a large grocery wholesale and distribution business. Her boss is Arnold, the HR manager. One day, with no prior discussion, he asked her to develop a one-day workshop on "commercial acumen" over the next week or so. The natural response of an expert, particularly when a request like this comes from a superior, is to agree that we'll do it. The first thing we might do is gather requirements, so we ask questions like:

"Who is the workshop for? How many will attend? Exactly what areas of commercial acumen do you want them to know more about?"

Questions like this are *necessary*, but they're not *sufficient*. We need to ask more. The answers tell us about the *informational* or *content requirement*, which is the knowledge and/or skills gaps to be addressed. But they don't tell us about the specific underlying business rationale for such skill-building. As Master Experts, that is where we need to go, and this is where Melinda went.

"I'd love to develop a commercial acumen program for you. I did that at my previous company," she told Arnold. "Out of curiosity, what are some of the business issues you're hoping to address by increasing your people's abilities in this area?" This is an example of how to elegantly "move off the solution." Melinda assured Arnold that he would get his program but then transitioned the conversation to exploring the underlying business issues.

> *"By asking one simple question in the right way, Melinda shifted the focus from means to ends."*

Such questioning gets to the heart of what's driving the request. By understanding the desired underlying business outcomes, Melinda got the opportunity to *deliver measurable business impact* rather than merely *delivering a workshop* (Arnold's proposed solution) as requested. Without exploring the desired business outcomes, even a well-delivered workshop could fall short of the intended impact.

In response to Melinda's question, Arnold explained that competitive pressures in the grocery retail market were creating problems for the organization's customers—independent grocery retailers. Perfect Providores' account managers could no longer simply take orders for groceries for the retailers to sell. They needed to become strategic advisors on how those businesses could better compete with the large supermarket chains. Unless those retail businesses improved their sales performance, they would soon become unviable, which in turn would very negatively impact Perfect Providores' entire business.

Note that Melinda asked an emotionally intelligent question. She asked "what business issues are you hoping to address?" She didn't ask "Why do you want to do this?"

Why questions can be confronting. By asking Arnold what business issues he was hoping to address, Melinda was not challenging him or asking for a justification, she was just making an inquiry. She moved off the solution. She shifted the conversation from the solution (discussing the design of a workshop on commercial acumen) to the underlying business needs that the solution is intended to address. Melinda managed to do this by asking just one carefully composed question.

Once she teased out the underlying business issues, Melinda then explored evidence and impact. This not only allowed her to explore the entire context of the request but her subsequent questions also helped Arnold further flesh out his thought process. She quickly discovered that Arnold actually wasn't the best person to comprehensively address all her questions about underlying business issues. Arnold was actually only an intermediary for those who actually "owned" the requirements.

As we'll see shortly, Melinda needed advanced consulting skills to persuade Arnold to give her access to the senior business leaders who had the complete answers.

> *"There are four consulting phases to pass through.*
> *In order, these are Discovery, Designing,*
> *Implementing and Evaluating."*

If we ask the right questions in the wrong way, this can still go badly. We worry the client will feel challenged if we ask "why do you want a commercial acumen solution?" in a blunt manner. We can see that by Melinda simply changing a *why* question to a *what* question—an emotionally intelligent choice because Melinda is thinking about how the client will emotionally respond to the nature of the question—she transformed the conversation from *means* (a workshop) to *ends* (improved business performance). This is Master Expert behavior.

An Expert Solutioning Model

BY RESPONDING TO THIS request in this way, Melinda is initiating the first phase of a classic expert consulting model: Discovery. The model is described in Figure 42.1. There are four phases to apply, and these are in a strict order: Discovery, Designing, Implementing, and Evaluating. We'll provide an overview here and go into more depth in subsequent chapters.

Capability: SOLUTIONING
An Expert Consulting Strategy

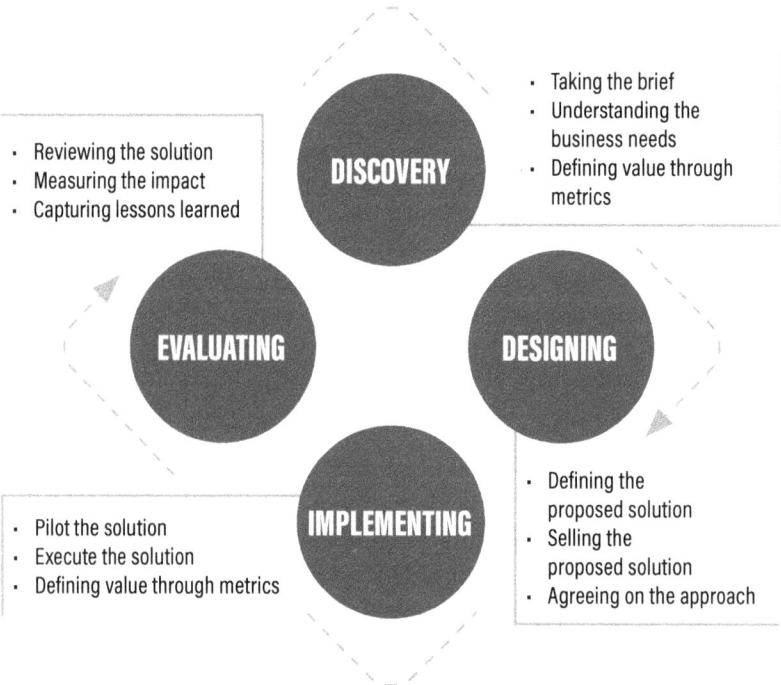

- Taking the brief
- Understanding the business needs
- Defining value through metrics

- Reviewing the solution
- Measuring the impact
- Capturing lessons learned

DISCOVERY

EVALUATING

DESIGNING

IMPLEMENTING

- Defining the proposed solution
- Selling the proposed solution
- Agreeing on the approach

- Pilot the solution
- Execute the solution
- Defining value through metrics

FIGURE 42.1: An Expert Solution Framework

Discovery

THIS INITIAL PHASE OF Solutioning goes by different names in different environments, such as *diagnosis, needs analysis* or *requirements gathering*. Experts who operate below Master Expert level often limit this to a technical needs analysis. For example, "What do you want the software to do?" At best, they learn only about the technical specifications the stakeholder has identified. This limits the expert to returning to the stakeholder with a technical answer to what is often a deeper enterprise question.

Master Experts, on the other hand, try to discover the underlying organizational rationale behind the stakeholder's request or the business outcome(s) the problem is meant to address. When they've fully understood the underlying organizational needs, the Master Expert will then come back and propose a holistic solution that addresses the organizational outcomes the stakeholder is really concerned with.

Properly handled, the Discovery phase should provide us and the stakeholders with the conviction that no specific solutions should be implemented until we have gathered the relevant baseline data. Neither party should feel bound by the initial solution ideas the stakeholder has put forward. Rather, we'll use our full expertise to thoroughly diagnose what's needed and then design accordingly.

Design

DESIGN REFERS TO THE formulation of recommended solutions to solve problems or address needs, and the positioning of those recommendations with key decision-makers. If we have conducted a thorough discovery, we'll also have worked out precisely who the key decision-makers are, as well as their decision criteria.

> *"No plan survives its collision with reality."*
> *- Susan Scott*

We'll have gathered sufficient data to make compelling arguments as to how our proposed solution will effectively address the requirements and why the related expenditure and effort represent a good investment. We'll have also unearthed any likely risks or complications, which will also be addressed by our proposed solution.

As part of the Design phase, it's essential to consider any likely challenges to the implementation. After all, our recommended solutions don't exist in a vacuum. If our stakeholders lack the skill or time to successfully implement our ideal solution, then we may have to adjust the solution or include upskilling or additional staffing.

We'll also need to consider the role we'll play during the implementation. Are we the project manager or overseer? If we're not in this role, who is? Are they a suitably skilled, committed and available individual? How will we remain informed about implementation progress and any issues arising? Will we be able to actively respond if necessary to address anything that might threaten the successful implementation?

Are we prepared to tweak our solution to better realize the benefits rather than stubbornly insist that our solution is the best one, even in the face of evidence to the contrary?

Implementation

ASSUMING THAT OUR RECOMMENDATION for the solution we've designed is adopted, we then need to implement it or oversee the implementation. If our Discovery has been thorough, there should be very few surprises during the Implementation phase. It's vital that we get the implementation right because the first two phases create expectations. A failure to realize the anticipated benefits may reflect poorly on our diagnosis and/or design, even if the true culprit happens to be poor implementation.

The Implementation phase is where actual value needs to be delivered and where our expertise is confirmed. People may never appreciate that we recommended a perfectly relevant solution if inadequate implementation fails to deliver the promised results.

The Implementation phase is reasonably straightforward, or it should be. It's simply the execution of the agreed solution according to the documented plan, adapting as and where necessary (with the achievement of the agreed aims in mind). In the first instance, the implementation often takes the form of a proof of concept, where we only roll out the solution to a clearly defined and limited set of users and compare their results to a norm or control group.

> *"Failure to conduct a PIR means that the team*
> *fails to learn from the mistakes made."*

There's a saying that "no plan ever survives contact with the enemy," attributed to the famous WW1 Prussian General Helmuth von Moltke. In modern organizations, this has become "no plan survives its collision with reality," a quote attributed to Susan Scott. It may become obvious in the early stages of implementation that the plan needs refining. In that case, we should liaise with stakeholders to ensure we have their support in tweaking the process, documenting any changes in the evaluation report.

All too often, the Implementation phase is where things can come unstuck. This is where our tendency to be more of a detached advisor rather than an active driver of outcomes can be the cause of our undoing. No matter how thorough our diagnosis, no matter how well designed our solution, there will almost inevitably be unforeseen implementation issues.

These can be appropriately addressed if the implementation is properly monitored and managed by someone with sufficient expertise and skin in the game. If the implementation is left in the hands of people who lack the requisite skills or commitment, it's very likely we'll end up shouldering the blame when things don't turn out as the stakeholders expect.

Many organizations have now adopted an Agile methodology, a prototyping approach that assumes things won't be right the first time out of the box. This has its advantages and disadvantages, but its flexibility is very beneficial, and some of the concepts can be usefully applied in many situations.

Evaluation

THE EVALUATION STAGE MEASURES and reports the effectiveness of the solution. We evaluate whether our implementation delivered what we intended (and likely said) it was going to. This is often achieved via a post-implementation review (PIR), which can be formal and multi-staged or informal and simply a conversation checking back in with pre-agreed outcomes and measures described in the business case.

In our experience, PIRs are rarely carried out, and if they are, they're not done effectively. It's worth briefly exploring why every project doesn't have a PIR. Some PIRs don't happen because of circumstances like:
- The team delivering the implementation is quickly disbanded and re-allocated to other projects, thereby making a post-implementation review (PIR) difficult.
- There is no specific milestone to say the project is finished, so it's never quite the right time to conduct a PIR.
- The team may have radically changed since the inception of the project, so the initial business case and measures have been lost.
- There is no proper leadership and accountability loop associated with the project to make a PIR happen.
- The senior sponsor is just "too busy" (i.e., doesn't place much value on gauging whether the intervention and associated time, expenditure and effort delivered the anticipated benefits).

The persons typically most disadvantaged by the lack of reporting quantifiable progress are the experts whose hard work and insights end up going unrecognized.

> *"No PIR means we are missing an opportunity to communicate our full expertise."*

Because this is a book about being a Master Expert, we'd argue that no self-respecting expert would collude with such lightweight thinking. Even if it's 30 minutes on a video conference, or even an email exchange, a minimum standard ought to be that the results are matched against expectations. There are some very good reasons for this, which we'll describe shortly.

But before we do that, let's explore the more Machiavellian reasons post-implementation reviews don't occur.

- Measurable organizational requirements were not adequately discussed or uncovered in the Discovery phase.
- Clear measures to track, which are necessary to evaluate whether the solution makes a difference, were not clearly defined or baselined— or unhelpful measures were defined (e.g., subject to so many other variants that the specific impact of the implemented solution is impossible to verify).
- No one can find the original business case. This happens much more than you might imagine, either deliberately (it was buried) or accidentally. Often, such cases are not adequately documented.
- Those responsible for conducting a PIR won't do so because they know that the report will show a failure to deliver the projected value or outcomes.

Whatever the reason, failure to conduct a PIR means that the team and the leading experts fail to learn from the mistakes made. They don't identify the incorrect assumptions built into the solution or implementation plan, which means it's possible, and maybe even likely, that the organization will make the same errors again. In a world where every organization has limited resources, this is a very poor process. It suggests the lack of an adequate performance culture in the organization.

In a perfect situation, the Master Expert is able to produce a post-implementation report, along with the colleagues involved, that demonstrates:

- How the need identified in the Discovery phase has been satisfactorily addressed.
- Whether the solution recommended in the Design phase has had the desired impact.

- What results have been produced.
- Any lessons arising.

Without the production of such a report and a cogent articulation of the impact of the solution, it's likely that the value created by the solution will remain unknown and thus unappreciated. The stakeholder who asked for the solution doesn't know with any certainty what they got out of the exercise, but they'll certainly be aware of the costs and the disruption associated with the solution's implementation.

> *"Effective solutioning is also about providing our stakeholder with a superior service experience."*

If we don't commit to and insist on this final Evaluation step, which stems from an effective Discovery phase, we're missing an opportunity to communicate our full expertise or worth. We're failing to prove to all stakeholders that the solution we've implemented actually addressed their intended outcomes.

Moving Up The Expert Value Chain

MOVING UP THE VALUE chain means working with stakeholders to get closer to the underlying business requirements. This is the case even if the owner of the business issue(s), who has the most to gain or lose from a solution or opportunity, isn't the one who directly engages us. In our example, Arnold was not the owner of the business issue. He was the messenger.

Effective Solutioning is not only about asking penetrating questions. It's about providing our stakeholder with a superior service experience. That's why you'll notice that we refer to the owners of the needs that we're being asked to address as "clients." We want to provide them with an optimal "client experience."

The intention behind our questions is to discover how to provide them with what they're really after, not just with what they're asking for.

When we make inquiries about the desired organizational outcomes, it often becomes apparent (both to us and the Arnolds of this world) that:
- It's vital to find answers to the legitimate questions asked.
- It's necessary to connect the inquirer with the person who can satisfactorily answer their questions.
- It's important that we don't put "Arnold" offside, making him feel inadequate, deficient, or like someone to be bypassed.

He may say, "I don't know the answer to the question." Our emotionally intelligent response needs to be something like "Who might be able to provide such information, and when might I be able to talk to them?"

He may say, "Don't bother the business leaders with this. They're too busy." And we might persist intelligently with "I am worried that without such a proper understanding, we might end up wasting even more of their time with a poorly thought through solution that fails to deliver."

When the Master Expert has perfected the art of asking the right questions for the right reasons, the stakeholder will welcome them and find value in the exploration that the questions prompt.

Developing a Dual Identity

AS EXPERTS, WE TEND to have a strong sense of identity, with strong points of view about our technical specialty. That means listening is often not our first instinct, which can give the impression that we lack empathy and social skills.

We all want to increase our effectiveness within our organization and for our stakeholders. To do this, we need to develop the capacity to listen and empathize. For Master Experts, this is a foundational enterprise skill upon which many other capabilities rely, including consulting, coaching, influencing, leading change, identifying other people's motivations, and engaging in difficult conversations.

In the mind of our business stakeholders, we need to develop a dual identity, being seen on the one hand as a highly proficient technical expert, and on the other hand, as a well-informed, value-adding business partner.

In the next few chapters, we'll explore the three expert roles of Solutioning:

- **Problem Identifier:** ensuring that underlying causes of problems are comprehensively identified and diagnosed.
- **Problem Solver:** ensuring that the right solutions are identified and implemented, which future-proof the organization and realize long-term benefits for internal and external customers.
- **Active Responder:** ensuring that the technical function is proactively responsive to the organization's needs, and that limited resources are deployed on the right tasks for the right reasons.

TAKING ACTION

Growing Our Solutioning Skills

IF THIS IS AN expert role in which you believe you could add greater value, here are some high-level suggestions for actions to take:

▶ ADOPT A CONSULTING APPROACH

When engaged to address a particular problem, deploy the Discovery phase to undertake a detailed discovery of the related issues, including gathering relevant evidence of how those issues show up and their impact on the organization's key performance indicators (KPIs). Some questions we may wish to ask ourselves:

- Am I guilty of merely "taking the order" or just seeing problems from a technical perspective?
- To what extent am I regularly very well-informed about the underlying organizational outcomes and impacts, and to what extent do I remain ignorant of the organization's underlying intent?
- Can I articulate the case for taking the time to step away from the solution to investigate the underlying issues? How might I build my stakeholders' trust and get them to devote the time to this process?
- What data will provide me and my stakeholder with greater insight into the exact problem we're being asked to solve? What questions do I need to ask and answer in order to have a holistic understanding of everything that needs to be in place for the underlying organizational issues to be addressed?

Considering these questions will allow you to bring more of your expertise to bear and ensure that your solutions are holistically designed and focused on the intended organizational impact. This will positively enhance your brand. You'll be perceived as more strategic and more focused on outcomes.

▶ LOOK BEYOND TO ANTICIPATE FUTURE PROBLEMS

If we aspire to operate at Master Expert level, we have to become very future-focused. This means being able to see around corners. Our ability to detect early warning signs for emerging problems that may negatively impact our organization (or, indeed, offer an opportunity) enables us to be far more effective when dealing with them. Questions we might wish to ask ourselves:

- It's almost certain that somewhere in the world, someone is already experiencing a "future" problem, so how do I tap into this information? Where is it likely to be?
- Are there forums I can join to participate in that discussion and predict future problems?
- Are there insightful people in my network who can be leveraged?
- Do I regularly run future risk discussions that enable me and my colleagues to be more prepared for future issues?
- Am I sufficiently plugged into what is happening outside my technical domain so that problems experienced by other industries are visible to me and can be considered in my own context?

"You are either part of the solution, or you're part of the problem."

Eldridge Cleaver

CHAPTER | **43** |

Identifying Problems

How might we evolve from fixing the "technical" issues stakeholders throw at us to delivering quantifiable organizational value through the art of discovery?

IN THIS CHAPTER, WE WILL EXPLORE:

- The issues arising from simply "taking the order" and how we miss opportunities to deliver greater quantifiable value.
- The structure and sequencing of questions that result in discovering underlying business requirements (beyond the technical requests).
- How to earn the right to engage stakeholders in a deeper needs analysis when they might believe they've already figured out what needs to be done.

THE FIRST EXPERT ROLE in the Solutioning capability is **Problem Identifier**. This set of behaviors relates to ensuring the underlying causes of problems are comprehensively and accurately identified and diagnosed and the associated impacts are addressed.

Inherent in the use of the word *solution* is the assumption that you have clearly and accurately defined or identified a problem or issue that is worth fixing, and that your proposed method of solving it does indeed do so.

Analytical skills are a key success factor in Solutioning. No matter which field we're working in, true mastery entails developing expertise in analyzing situations, issues, problems, needs and requirements. Only then can we be sure that any subsequently proposed and implemented solutions actually deliver the desired improvements. The ability to drill down and understand the underlying issues that are creating the problem is the only way to shape a lasting solution, as we discussed in the overview of the last chapter.

Advanced listening skills are also important (see Chapter 20). There is little point asking the right questions if we don't actively listen to the answers. For many professionals, listening—really listening—is a major challenge as we've often already decided what we want to hear. This is possibly because we're under pressure to fix problems as quickly as possible. Additionally, the list of problems to fix is extremely long and they all appear to be urgent.

The behaviors at each level of Expertship for this expert role are described in Figure 43.1.

> *"A Master Expert will always be seeking out new ways of looking at current problems."*

At immature levels, the expert will be able to accurately identify common problems and be able to analyze complex problems. But they'll only occasionally consider the underlying causes. If they are derailing, experts will conduct problem identification from a narrow or wholly technical point of view. They may not have the skills to properly investigate underlying issues.

A typical defense mechanism for derailing experts is to jump as quickly as possible to a solution. "I know what the problem is. Leave it to me. I'll fix it."

By contrast, the Master Expert will be highly skilled at identifying nearly all problems, regardless of complexity. They'll be at pains to accurately identify all likely underlying causes and potential implications, and they'll face pressure from stakeholders to immediately come up with a solution.

Master Experts do this because they're concerned with shaping a long-term, sustainable solution that adds value to the organization and its customers. They're prepared to take time to save time. No quick fixes here. As we discussed in the last chapter, stakeholders can sometimes see this as prevarication, or avoiding dealing with the issues.

Master Experts are also always on the lookout for new ways of looking at current problems. Crucially, Master Experts assume their own ignorance, especially if they already know a lot about a subject. They realize that this is when they can become blind to new information and be possessed by their biases. Master Experts park what they know until they have adequately understood things like:

- What issues are showing up? What has prompted the need for a solution?
- How are the issues showing up? What is the scale and nature of the issues? What impacts are they having? Who specifically is impacted and how? Can the associated costs (or missed opportunities) be quantified?
- What has caused the issue? What solutions have been attempted to date? What was their level of success? Why did they fail?
- How committed are other stakeholders to addressing the issue? What kinds of resources are they prepared to commit? Based on what decision criteria?
- What are their desired measures of success?
- How might we collectively determine that the issues have been satisfactorily addressed?

The Discovery Process

MASTER EXPERTS SUSPEND THEIR instinct to start applying solutions until they have satisfactorily resolved these questions. They do this through an important process called **Discovery**.

They ask questions that are not always easy to answer. Unresolved issues can cause discomfort, which is why people often end up jumping to premature solutions.

> *"When experts operate from the assumption of superior intellect, this can be experienced as arrogance."*

During Discovery, we're likely to ask questions that have the chance of making us feel dumb or uninformed. We might also make others feel dumb, especially if we're asking a perfectly reasonable question to which they have no immediate answers. We often experience the pain of unmet needs or dysfunction in the Discovery phase, whereas when we're formulating and implementing solutions in the Design (or problem-solving) phase, we get to feel clever or productive.

Capability: SOLUTIONING

Expert Role: PROBLEM IDENTIFIER

MASTER EXPERT

- Promotes new ways of looking at current problems.
- Highly skilled at identifying all problems, regardless of complexity.
- Addresses symptoms and accurately identifies all likely underlying causes and likely implications.
- Conducts rigorous analysis to get to the heart of key "business"/enterprise/organizational issues, identifying business requirements not merely technical requirements.
- Challenges standard thinking by exploring alternate ways of looking at difficult problems.
- Proactively identifies problems before they materialize.

EXPERT

- Accurately identifies common and uncommon problems.
- Analyzes complex problems effectively.
- Addresses symptoms and accurately identifies likely underlying causes.

SPECIALIST

- Accurately identifies common problems.
- Developing ability to analyze complex problems.
- Unlikely to consider underlying causes

- Struggles to identify common problems with consistent accuracy.
- Cannot analyze complex problems or consider underlying causes.
- Conducts problem identification from a narrow, wholly technical viewpoint.

DERAILING

FIGURE 43.1: Problem Identifier Behaviors

Master Experts adopt, formally or informally, a staged consulting process so that the urge to solve (or jump to the solution) is deferred until a proper understanding of the matter requiring resolution has been arrived at. And it's not just their own understanding that they're seeking. It's a shared understanding with the stakeholders experiencing the problem.

In the Discovery phase, the positioning of the relationship with those we're questioning is vitally important. Master Experts avoid the seductive trap of the doctor-patient dynamic, whereby the requesting stakeholder is viewed as ignorant and helpless, and we view ourselves as an all-knowing and unquestionable authority.

This game doesn't do anyone any favors. When we operate from an assumption of superior intellect or understanding of things, this can be experienced as arrogance or intellectual snobbery.

The Discovery phase also helps apply process and discipline to identifying problems (and eventually the solutions) when experts are in danger of paralysis by analysis. This is where experts spend too much time over-analyzing the issue or getting the solution absolutely perfect before implementation.

Best Practice Discovery

DISCOVERY IS NOT JUST an elegant way of ensuring that we end up with the right solutions that are likely to produce the right impact. It's also a process of managing stakeholder expectations and the stakeholder experience.

> *"An insightful diagnostic report will create value in itself."*

The expert and requester, along with other stakeholders, have a shared understanding of precisely what organizational issues they're seeking to address with the requested or proposed solution.

- They'll have a shared understanding of how, in measurable terms, those business issues are playing out and their causes and effects.
- They'll have a shared understanding of what kind of budget and other commitment levels are available for tackling the issue and the parameters they must work within.
- Ideally, this will be documented and explicitly agreed upon, including assumptions, evaluation criteria, and baseline levels of the agreed measures before intervention. This should detail all the relevant specifications and requirements.

For a major request, this may include a report that documents our findings. An insightful diagnostic report will create value in itself. When the stakeholder accepts our findings and recommendations, they give us the green light to proceed with the design of the solutioning. It's unwise to proceed otherwise, or to assume that there is agreement.

There's always a risk that the stakeholder who has requested the solution doesn't feel that rigorous analysis is necessary. They may say that developing and tracking metrics is too much work. They may say they already know what's going on, or that they don't have time.

It may also be the case that they're concerned that hard data will dispossess them of their preferred approach. But the risk of skipping this stage or not doing it properly is that we might not identify all of the factors inhibiting success and the benefits that will flow from it.

Our implementation may succeed or fail, but it may also end up where nobody can tell whether or not it has worked. As a result, people might think that all the work that has gone into the design and implementation of a solution was not worth the effort. A rigorous Discovery process minimizes the chances of this happening.

Discovery in Action

LET'S RETURN TO OUR example of Melinda, the organization development specialist who was asked to design a workshop on business acumen by her manager, Arnold.

Melinda had successfully moved off the solution and started a conversation with Arnold about the underlying business issues driving the request for "more business acumen" for Perfect Providores' account managers.

Melinda asked Arnold a very important question: "I'd love to develop a commercial acumen program for you. I did that at my previous company. Out of curiosity, what are some of the issues you're hoping to address by increasing your people's abilities in this area?"

"The key tactic to master is moving off solution."

You will remember that Arnold explained that competitive pressures in the grocery retail market were creating problems for the organization's customers—independent grocery retailers. Perfect Providores' account managers could no longer simply take orders for groceries for the retailers to sell. They needed to become strategic advisors to those retailers on how they could better compete with the large chains.

In subsequent discussions between Melinda and Arnold, it emerged that the commercial acumen workshops were just one of a series of strategic moves that Perfect Providores was taking to strengthen its customers' ability to compete in a tough market.

The strategy was based on two key hypotheses:

- That there was a need and opportunity to build more effective competitive strategies in the independent grocery businesses for small retailers to remain viable. Without this, they would lose ground to the big chains.

> That the independent grocers would be willing to share their data with the account managers, and that the account managers would be able to interpret the data, identify opportunities to improve sales and profits, and convince the grocers to successfully adopt and implement such strategies.

The building of commercial acumen would only partially address this need, and it would also involve some critical dependencies. Account managers would need to become, in the eyes of the store operators, strategic advisors rather than order takers. How would the account managers foster sufficient trust regarding their strategic acumen among the retailers to successfully accomplish this? How could they build their credibility with store operators to convince them to share their data and regard them as potential strategic advisors, not just as the salespeople they had previously been regarded as?

As Melinda increased her understanding of the underlying business issues, it became clear that the commercial acumen workshops would only add value if they resulted in improved sales and margins. In other words, if they satisfied the ultimate business intention. It would be entirely possible for the program to technically improve the commercial acumen of workshop attendees and yet fail to deliver a sales uplift.

In that case, Melinda would have addressed the original request (building business acumen among account managers) without adding any quantifiable value. In fact, by investing in the workshops, Melinda would have simply increased operating costs through both the direct cost of running the workshop and the opportunity costs of taking the account managers off the job for the duration of the workshop. Conducting more comprehensive discovery helped her avoid such risks and allowed her to build and implement a solution that positively impacted business performance.

Derailing Discovery

MOVING OFF THE SOLUTION is a rapid and elegant way of building an understanding of your stakeholder's business issues and engaging in advanced problem identification. It takes us beyond the requested solution's "technical" specifications to the underlying commercial or community imperatives.

Melinda was executing the Discovery phase well. She was operating at Master Expert level. A less mature expert might have presumed that she knew what Arnold wanted, particularly if she had previously delivered a program to build commercial acumen before, as Melinda had.

> *"The mantra of issues, evidence and impact should guide our questions and thinking."*

Let's look at some of the more common responses to Arnold's request for a workshop on business acumen—less intelligent responses than Melinda's strategy of moving off the solution. We could have:

- **Told the stakeholder what they need.** This runs the risk of us both being wrong because we haven't found out the precise details of the scenario. We also risk alienating our stakeholder. Some stakeholders might be happy to hear that we've everything in hand, but this only increases the risk that it's all blamed on us if our solution doesn't deliver the desired outcomes.

- **Guessed.** After all, if we've not really engaged in more detailed discovery (issues, evidence, impact), then we're essentially guessing. If we don't know precisely what the stakeholder means when they say they want to improve people's commercial acumen, and if we don't know what the consequences of the gap in applying commercial acumen are, then we're shooting in the dark. We need to explore the consequences: what the targeted increase in commercial acumen is expected to mean, how we might measure success, what's been put in place to assist people in applying commercial acumen historically, and a host of other things.

- **Just taken the brief.** How could we be taking any risk if we simply ask the stakeholder for the specifications and give them exactly what they're asking for? We're supposed to be the experts. Surely, since the stakeholder may not have the same in-depth knowledge as we do, we have a responsibility to ensure their expectations are realistic. What if the stakeholder's brief is incomplete or based on wrong assumptions or unrealistic expectations? Aren't we then at least partially liable for any subsequent mismatch between expectations and results? If we simply take the brief and carry out the stakeholder's request while remaining ignorant of the business imperatives, we have failed to exercise our professional responsibility. And we only have ourselves to blame for our expertise being underutilized or for failing to deliver the desired outcomes.

Expert Questioning in the Discovery Phase

THE CHALLENGE IS THAT we often feel that our initial consulting questions will be too blunt, too challenging, or make us seem dumb. "Why do you want a commercial acumen solution?" We worry that the stakeholder will either feel challenged—as if we're questioning the validity of what they've asked us to do—or they'll conclude that they're dealing with an idiot who should have already known the answer to such an obvious question. That's why we must ask questions in a more intelligent way.

Fortunately, there is a good process for doing this. We follow three steps in our questioning: **Issues**, **Evidence** and **Impact**. The process is described in Figure 43.2. Consulting skills are enterprise skills, and this the focus of this model.

1. **Identify the underlying issues**

    The critical thing here is to get a quick list of underlying issues. Since we have requested that the client temporarily suspend solving their problem to allow us to first understand the issues that they're hoping to address, we don't want them to feel that we're not interested in solving the problem. We want to move quickly to get into depth on the most important issue.

    The quicker we can get into depth on the most important issue, the quicker we'll learn what's really needed and the more productive the "client" will find the exchange with us. The art is to quickly tease out the list of issues or opportunities and present them as an *a la carte* menu from which the client can choose which items to go into more depth on.

    It's important to check for completeness—has anything material been missed on the list? "And if we addressed these issues and nothing else, would that constitute a solution that exactly meets your needs?"

2. **Select priority issues**

    Going into depth is where we're likely to learn what's truly required. And if we ask good evidence and impact questions, the client will likely learn, too.

Capability: SOLUTIONING

Discovery Process

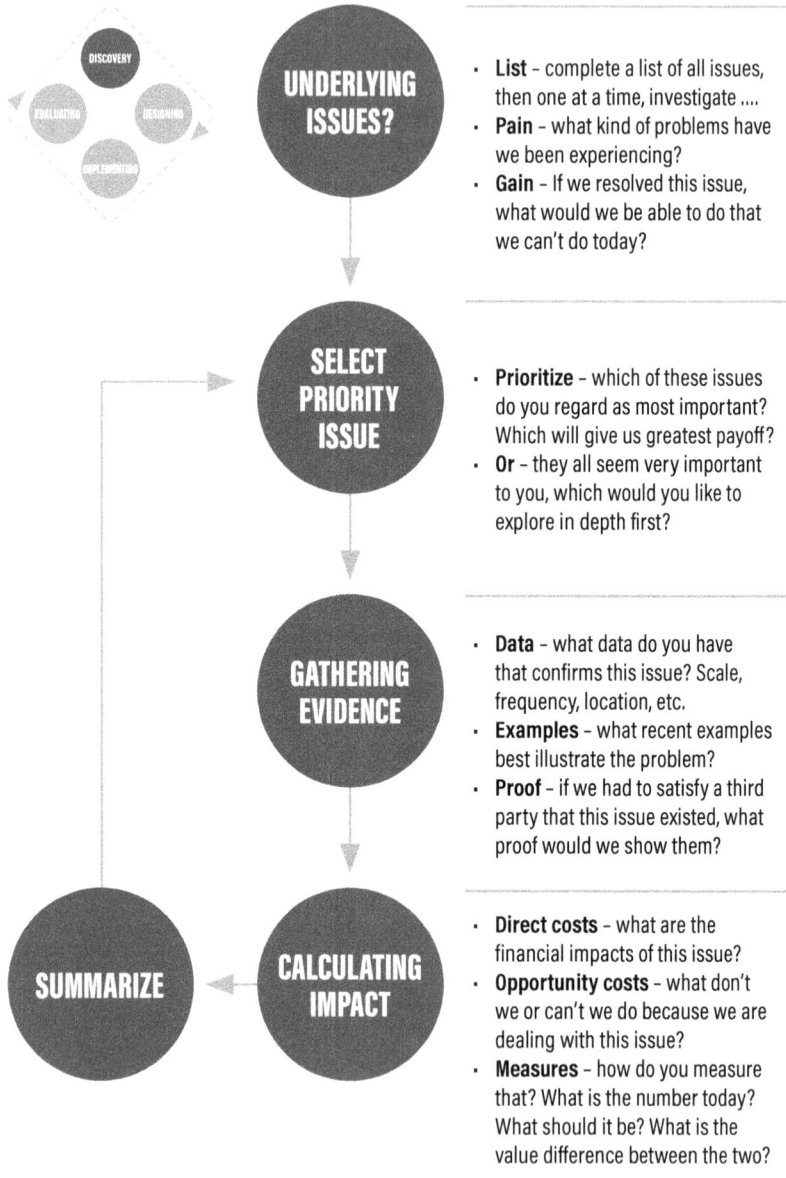

UNDERLYING ISSUES?

- **List** – complete a list of all issues, then one at a time, investigate ....
- **Pain** – what kind of problems have we been experiencing?
- **Gain** – If we resolved this issue, what would we be able to do that we can't do today?

SELECT PRIORITY ISSUE

- **Prioritize** – which of these issues do you regard as most important? Which will give us greatest payoff?
- **Or** – they all seem very important to you, which would you like to explore in depth first?

GATHERING EVIDENCE

- **Data** – what data do you have that confirms this issue? Scale, frequency, location, etc.
- **Examples** – what recent examples best illustrate the problem?
- **Proof** – if we had to satisfy a third party that this issue existed, what proof would we show them?

SUMMARIZE ← **CALCULATING IMPACT**

- **Direct costs** – what are the financial impacts of this issue?
- **Opportunity costs** – what don't we or can't we do because we are dealing with this issue?
- **Measures** – how do you measure that? What is the number today? What should it be? What is the value difference between the two?

FIGURE 43.2: Discovery Process

In such a case, you've started adding value through the conversation, even before you've delivered a solution.

It's important to pick the right thing to go into depth on. There's nothing worse than picking the first item on the list and spending a whole bunch of time exploring the issue in depth only to find out that the time would have been better spent on list item #4, and now you're out of time. Since the goal is to co-create (and thus co-own) solutions with your client, invite them to identify the most critical items to explore in depth first.

Depending on the time available, you can always repeat the in-depth discussions with other issues as energy, interest and time allows.

Some key questions are: "Which of these issues do you regard as most important?" "Which of these will give us the greatest payoff?" "These all sound pretty important. Which would you prefer to explore in a bit more depth first?"

3. Gather evidence

If we don't know exactly how the issue is showing up, then we may not possess sufficient insight on to how to best address it. Finding the appropriate measure often illuminates how to fix the issue, how to prove that it's fixed, and even how to quantify its worth. Both qualitative and quantitative evidence might be useful to us and our stakeholders.

Key questions: "How does that issue show up in the business exactly?" "How many instances? How frequently? In which scenarios?" "Which customers in particular have been experiencing problems?"

4. Calculate impact

Whenever we have measurable evidence, there's likely a value in converting such measures into an explicit dollar value. Doing so can often help provide the basis of a commercially sound business case. The organization's investment should be proportionate to the potential return. Calculating this will help inform our business stakeholders of what it's actually going to take to fix the issue, no more trying to solve everything "on the smell of an oily rag," and will start signaling that we're commercially minded, not purely technically obsessed. Be aware that this process may be new to the stakeholder, so the answer might be that there's little financial impact, or perhaps a lot. Either could be a surprise to your stakeholder.

Key questions: "How do you measure that?" "What is the measure now?" "Ideally, what should the measure (or number) be?" "What's the value of the difference between the two (current and target)?" "What timeframe is an appropriate time period for us to measure the impact and execute a solution?"

5. Summarize

After playing back everything that we've heard, we then check with the client that we've understood accurately and completely. This helps them feel understood. It also helps you confirm that you've understood, and it often elicits new information. We both feel productive.

Key summation comment and question: "It sounds like you're keen to (insert solution) in order to address (key issues) that are showing up as (evidence) and having this (impact) on the business. Did I understand you correctly and fully?"

Deploying this process helps us overcome our instinct as experts to solve problems as quickly as possible. It's slowing down in order to speed up. If we jump to solution quickly, thinking we're being responsive, the impact on our stakeholder is more likely to be that they think we haven't listened to them and heard the whole story. It might stop others from seeking us out because they don't see us as supportive and easy to work with.

It's our responsibility as experts to provide a rewarding engagement experience for our stakeholders.

If we're simply taking the order, the worst-case scenario is that the "solution" that the requesting stakeholder has asked us to implement may prove ineffective. And in failing to consult with them on the underlying issues, evidence and impact, we would at least be partly liable for the ensuing problems or missed opportunities.

TAKING ACTION

Growing Our Problem Identification Skills

IF THIS IS AN expert role in which you believe you could add greater value, here are some high-level suggestions for actions to take:

▶ COMMIT TO SUSPENDING JUDGMENT AND LISTEN INSTEAD

Master Experts exhibit a constant curiosity to discover what we don't know but could or should. They're also constantly re-checking to see what's changed. As busy experts, this requires us to avoid jumping to quick conclusions and making assumptions. Questions we might want to ask ourselves:

- Am I prepared to commit to listening carefully to everything my clients and colleagues are telling me, interrogating them to check carefully that I have understood before moving to the solution?
- Can I commit to doing the above, even if it sounds like the same issues I've heard about many times?
- Am I prepared to accept this approach will take extra time in the first instance but will eventually save me time (and possibly rework)?
- Am I convinced that suspending judgment is good for my brand and the quality of my work?
- Have I decided how I will measure the effectiveness of my deployment of this new behavior? Whose help will I need to provide feedback and encouragement? How will I know when I have finally embedded the behavior as a habit?`

▶ CONDUCT A PATTERN ANALYSIS

Spending a disproportionate amount of time fixing the same old issues while higher value and less routine activities receive insufficient attention is poor Expertship.

Identifying examples of where this occurs requires us to undertake a pattern analysis. Some questions we may wish to ask ourselves:

- Do I have a list of the most common problems that I'm asked to address or the most frequently raised requests?
- Have I recently analyzed whether or not there are any patterns to the sorts of needs people have and what kinds of issues they face?
- Is there a disproportionate number of the same kind of request? Do issues stem from the same process, piece of software, and so on. Does the disproportionate number of problems arising indicate some kind of common cause? Is there a need to re-engineer the process? Or would a training program, for a finite investment of time, get a large percentage of these requests to go away going forward?

"No problem can withstand the assault of sustained thinking."
Voltaire

CHAPTER | **44** |

Solving Problems

Which universal principles will allow us to not only solve technical and business requirements but quantifiably prove them to everyone's satisfaction?

IN THIS CHAPTER, WE WILL EXPLORE:

- Design principles and the choices experts face.
- How true solutioning does not end with our recommending a particular approach, and why we need to ensure all elements of implementation are explicitly identified and driven through to benefits realization.
- How so many excellent diagnoses and designs go unrecognized due to a lack of effective implementation controls and inadequate implementation reviews and reporting.

THE SECOND EXPERT ROLE in the Solutioning capability is **Problem Solver**. This set of behaviors relates to ensuring that the right solutions are shaped and delivered, thus future-proofing the organization and realizing long-term benefits for internal and external customers. Building this capability involves making the shift from providing technical, short-term solutions to delivering organization-wide solutions.

The behaviors at each level of Expertship for this role are described in Figure 44.1.

At immature levels, experts tend to rely on their past experience to solve problems. Maslow famously said, "If all you have is a hammer, everything looks like a nail." Typically, experts operating at the specialist level have a favored method that they're familiar with. It can be daunting for experts to find themselves in unfamiliar territory, as many believe their sole value proposition is knowing with certainty what needs to be done. So, there's a temptation to fall back on tried-and-tested solutions without fully exploring how the new requirements are subtly or completely different than last time.

At the specialist level, experts are likely to conduct problem solving from a narrow, wholly technical viewpoint. They might be guilty of applying their methodologies in an overly rigid and uncompromising fashion, regardless of the nuanced context and its requirements.

By contrast, the Master Expert will focus on shaping long-term solutions from a holistic perspective, taking into account technical, organizational and systemic perspectives. The Master Expert will promote new ways of looking at existing solutions. They'll challenge current practices, including their own. This isn't always a comfortable experience for the experts, their colleagues, or even their stakeholders sometimes. They'll proactively put in place strategies to future-proof against known problems.

Most importantly, Master Experts commit to seeing solutions through to realizing benefits. In doing so, they focus on delivering lasting solutions for the business rather than simply getting (broken) things working again.

Problem Solving covers the Design and Implementation phases of the consulting model (see Figure 44.2).

Best Practice Design

DESIGN REFERS TO FORMULATING recommendations to solve the problem, then positioning those recommendations with key decision-makers. The goals of the Design phase should be:
- A documented and agreed holistic approach, including a rollout plan with specific milestones, timings and costs, risks, assumptions, evaluation process and criteria. It should show how the proposed solution addresses the requirements.
- That all key stakeholders are signed up to the approach before progressing to implementation, and specifically to the contributions of time, effort and resources that the implementation requires from them.

Capability: SOLUTIONING
Expert Role: PROBLEM SOLVER

MASTER EXPERT

- Expert in all common and uncommon problems.
- Shapes and implements long-term solutions from a technical, business, and systemic perspective.
- Promotes new ways of looking at current solutions and challenges current practices.
- Proactively puts in place strategies to future-proof against known problems.
- Sees solutions through to realizing benefits.
- Deploys deep experience as appropriate to the issues at hand..

EXPERT

- Collects experience of common and uncommon scenarios.
- Provides accurate solutions to common and uncommon problems.
- Seeks to future-proof against regularly occurring problems.
- Approaches solutioning by considering both technical and business perspectives.

SPECIALIST

- Collecting experiences of common scenarios.
- Provides accurate solutions to common problems.
- Approaches solutioning from a mostly technical perspective.

- Relies on past experience to solve problems.
- Conducts problem solutioning from a narrow, wholly technical viewpoint.
- Jumps to solutioning before properly understanding all requirements and context.
- Overly rigid and uncompromising application of methodologies.
- Addresses symptoms not causes.

DERAILING

FIGURE 44.1: Problem Solver Behaviors

The mistakes experts often make at this stage include:

- Implicitly taking all the responsibility for the successful realization of the benefits by failing to outline the limits of what our inputs should deliver.
- Failing to explicitly call out the commitments that others need to make (including the budget).
- Failing to think holistically and to identify all the elements necessary for the benefits to be realized. This underprices the total cost of the solution and fails to identify others' contributions and time commitments.
- Failing to identify risks and assumptions and how they might be addressed.

Approaches to Design

DEPENDING ON THE SIZE of the problem, our approach will vary:

- How inclusive do we want to be?
- Is solutioning a team effort or a solo situation?
- To what extent does the design process become consistently applied and business as usual?

In Melinda's case at Perfect Providores, account managers could no longer simply take orders for groceries for the retailers to sell. They needed to become strategic advisors to those retailers about how they could better compete with the large chains. Melinda extended her discovery to include a wider group of interviewees. She clarified that the "new" account managers' skills would need to be very different from those of the current order-taking account managers. She asked this question of a key decision-maker: "How many of the account managers do you believe will successfully make the transition?" She then listed the skills that needed to be developed and also the experience required. You don't learn business acumen from a book—you need case studies and examples. She then created a dummy store and invited store owners to be involved in the training process. Without extended discovery, this solution, which worked brilliantly, would never have been imagined, designed or implemented.

Implementation

THE GOALS OF THE Implementation phase should be:

- Execute the proposed solution as per the agreements arrived at in the Design phase.

Capability: SOLUTIONING
An Expert Consulting Strategy

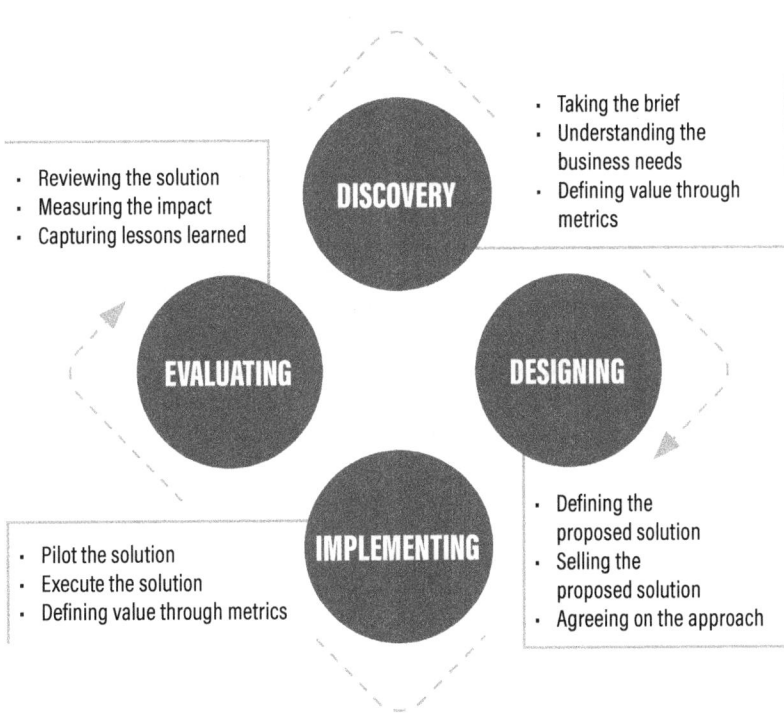

Taking the brief
- Understanding the business needs
- Defining value through metrics

Reviewing the solution
- Measuring the impact
- Capturing lessons learned

DISCOVERY

EVALUATING

DESIGNING

IMPLEMENTING

- Defining the proposed solution
- Selling the proposed solution
- Agreeing on the approach

- Pilot the solution
- Execute the solution
- Defining value through metrics

FIGURE 44.2: An Expert Solution Framework

- Develop a pilot implementation, if appropriate, to trial the solution in a limited and manageable way.
- Monitor the implementation, flexing as necessary with the desired results in mind. Document any problems or deviations from the plan and advise stakeholders.
- Ensure adequate metrics are in place and data is being captured for the Evaluation phase.

> *"This is why so many become zombie projects."*

Pilots for very large projects just make sense. With nearly all our new programs, we run a pilot (sometimes internally, sometimes with a willing client) to test version 1.0. Version 1.1 is always so much better as a result of this test.

Most well-run projects have regular project meetings to focus on tasks. But we would also advise interim post-implementation reviews (more details on how to execute PIRs in the next chapter).

Interim PIRs are a discussion about the big picture, focusing on questions like "Is the project on track to succeed? Will it deliver on its main objectives and benefits? What is the current likelihood of the project succeeding? As a consequence—gasp—should the implementation proceed as planned, or should we stop the project?" These last two questions, from what we hear from countless experts every year, rarely get asked. This is why many projects become *zombie projects*. They're dead but still shuffling along. While most team members can see the failure clearly, few can muster the courage to call it out and say, "we should consider stopping."

There are many telltale signs of a failing project, too many to list here. But the lack of engagement from sponsors or the wider organization is a telling sign. Key project members consistently prioritizing other work ahead of this projects' work is another. Constant moving of the goalposts is a further indicator, as are our own energy and engagement.

We don't want to accept that we have failed, and this mindset makes us avoid challenging whether or not projects should continue. But we'd argue knowing we're failing and doing nothing about it is a worse failure.

TAKING ACTION

Growing Our Problem Solver Skills

IF THIS IS AN expert role in which you believe you could add greater value, here are some high-level suggestions for actions to take:

▶ CONDUCT AN IMPACT ANALYSIS

Without conducting an impact analysis, all too often, even when our solutions have added value, that value is hidden and therefore less appreciable in concrete terms. This is where we have an opportunity to demonstrate our value and to improve the quality of our solutions by carefully gathering and citing evidence. Questions we might like to ask ourselves:

- When someone brings me an issue to be addressed, do I ask evidence questions, e.g., "how (or where) precisely is the issue showing up?" If such a question doesn't directly elicit a measurable phenomenon, do I follow up with an impact question, e.g., "and then what happens?"
- Do I insist on identifying the KPI that I'm being asked to help the organization improve?
- Do I clarify how the impact of the change/work is to be measured? By measuring the relevant KPI prior to the implementation of my solution and then again afterward, I would be in a position to compare how far the "needle has moved." By comparing such a shift to the same measures for a concurrently tracked control group, I could assert with reasonable confidence that any difference between the two groups might reasonably be attributed to my solution.
- Do the questions I ask and the data and measures I insist upon mean I am much more committed to the work? That is, do I know how my effort will be rewarded by my organization or colleagues?

▶ PREVENTION IS BETTER THAN CURE.

If we fail to engage in sufficient prevention, we'll end up locked into a reactive cycle, perpetually mending things after the fact. It can be regarded as heroic to be the person or the team who rescues a project or the organization from imminent disaster. It can also be exhausting. And, tackling problems once they've already begun to impact the organization or its stakeholders is not as effective as identifying them ahead of time and preventing them. Presumably, someone still suffers the ill effects of the issue until it gets resolved. And we may end up with a reputation for being the person to engage in a crisis rather than the person to engage early on in conceptualizing what course to pursue. Questions we might like to ask ourselves:

- Having resolved a problem, particularly if it's a significant one, do I insist on and action the conducting of a review?
- Do I engage the right individuals in this process?
- Do I ask what the likelihood is of the problem recurring? If it's likely and the impact is significant, have I identified how exactly the problem arose and how it might be prevented from happening again?
- Am I aggressive enough in expediently mobilizing an effective response to issues that minimizes adverse effects?
- As a consequence of adopting these behaviors, am I gradually spending less time "fighting fires"?

▶ DEPLOY "OUTSIDE-IN" THINKING

Coming at problems from the same angle all the time will mean that solutions that might be viable from alternative angles remain invisible to us. This reduces our problem solving effectiveness and leaves us open to being superseded by competitors' solutions derived from a fresh perspective. Solving problems from the "inside-out" means we deploy our current understanding of all of the issues. When we start thinking "outside-in," we put ourselves in the customer's shoes and see the problem from their perspective. Questions we might like to ask ourselves:

- Am I working hard enough to create this change of perspective, so I can see solutions that might not otherwise be visible to me?
- Am I asking future "outside-in" questions, where I imagine the value being delivered to the customer in three years' time, or perhaps by a competitor unencumbered by my organization's legacy systems and responsibilities?
- Am I exploring whether I need to change my approach entirely?
- Am I still fixing incremental issues that don't really solve the long-term customer problem?
- Have I, as a consequence of adopting outside-in thinking, increased my ability to think more holistically about customer value, thereby increasing my personal brand?

"Human beings are great at solving problems but they're not always solving the right problems."

Matt Taylor

CHAPTER 45

Actively Responding

Besides the essential arts of identifying and solving problems, how does masterful solutioning ensure an optimal client experience?

IN THIS CHAPTER, WE WILL EXPLORE:

- While we solve clients' needs, what's the optimal experience that we want them to have throughout the entire engagement?
- What are we like to engage with from a client's perspective? How would we know?
- Why is the net promoter score important, and how might we improve it?
- The enormous benefits of utilizing post-implementation reviews.

THE THIRD EXPERT ROLE in the Solutioning capability is **Active Responder**. This describes the extent to which experts ensure that the technical function is proactively responsive to the organizations' needs and that limited resources are deployed on the right tasks for the right reasons. Building this capability involves a shift from being exclusively responsive or reactive toward being proactive, anticipatory, preventative and ahead of the game.

For many experts, defining precisely who our clients and customers are is complicated. We've used the term *clients* here as a catch-all for internal and external stakeholders who consume our services, whether directly or indirectly. Very often, the final recipients of the value experts create are one or two stages removed from our work.

> ## *"Master Experts will work hard to anticipate the future needs of clients."*

However, this shouldn't stop us from concentrating on fulfilling or anticipating their needs—or from considering how we contribute to their experience of the organization's services.

At an immature level, experts will respond to problems reactively and as they occur. They're likely to respond sequentially to problems as they're raised rather than prioritizing (because they don't have the big-picture view that enables them to prioritize effectively).

Those who are exhibiting derailing behaviors will respond to problems reactively and possibly in a highly selective manner, doing the work they like doing (or for stakeholders who they like) rather than strategically choosing work to be done based on its importance or impact. They'll simply be unresponsive to some stakeholders.

> ## *"What opportunities are there for me to improve the service my clients experience?"*

On the other hand, the Master Expert will be a very active responder, utilizing advanced prioritization skills to do the most important or critical work first. They'll facilitate responses from others by leveraging their network. They'll proactively uncover or predict emergent requirements to facilitate real-time responses to market changes. That is, they'll work hard to see around corners, anticipating what their clients are likely to ask for in the future. And they'll be ready to provide it quickly. They'll initiate contact with those who are likely to experience problems in anticipation of emerging requirements. Overall, they'll consider how they might contribute to a superior engagement experience with clients.

Capability: SOLUTIONING
Expert Role: ACTIVE RESPONDER

MASTER EXPERT

- Active responder, advanced prioritization skills.
- Facilitator of responses from others, leveraging network.
- Proactively uncovers or predicts emergent requirements to facilitate real-time responses to market changes.
- Initiates contact in anticipation of emerging requirements.

EXPERT

- Responds to problems as proactively as possible seeking longer term solutions and immediate fixes.
- Responds with appropriate speed congruent with the criticality of the problem.
- Routinely updates needs analysis to address changing requirements.

SPECIALIST

- Responds to problems reactively but in a timely fashion.
- Tends to respond sequentially to problems as reported rather than prioritizing.

- Responds to problems reactively, selectively and in either a reluctant or slow manner.
- Unresponsive.
- Difficult to deal with.

DERAILING

FIGURE 45.1: Active Responder Behaviors

Understanding Client Experience

HOW ARE CLIENTS EXPERIENCING our services and interactions with us? To what extent are we meeting their expectations or missing opportunities to delight them further? How do we know? Are people's expectations of us on target? Are they met or routinely violated? Do they know which issues not to bring to us or how we prioritize or approach their requests?

> *"The questions they ask are*
> *laudable but wrong."*

Continually increasing our clients' positive engagement experience takes work, but most of all, it takes organized systems. The very best experts have systemized the collection of feedback, which enables them to continually improve the service they're offering to their clients. In various chapters of this book, we've mentioned ways to do this. They include:

- **Stakeholder health check** (see Chapter 12): this is where we explore the extent to which both parties, us and our clients, are fulfilling each other's current needs. We briefly discuss how to explore what our client's future needs might be and how we might be proactive in order to meet them.
- **Informal feedback loops**: many experts use a set of two or three questions at the end of meetings or interactions to check in on how we're meeting expectations. Questions might include "Did you get out of this meeting or discussion what you were hoping to?", "Is there anything else that you had hoped we might cover or resolve?", "If we could have improved this interaction or transaction, how might we do so?" These questions model a continuous improvement mindset, which is a key behavior of the Active Responder.
- **Formal feedback loops**: scheduled, structured processes that capture feedback, learnings and possible improvements to process and outcomes. Many organizations have pulse checks that run quarterly or half-yearly to check in on customer satisfaction. Master Experts might deploy a similar mechanism to check in on a group of clients. These systems capture general feedback rather than specific feedback on projects or initiatives. We propose post-implementation reviews to deal with such matters (see later in this chapter).

All of these tactics, when well designed, are simple to run and provide various levels of feedback that answer two key questions: how good a job am

I doing in the eyes of my clients, and what opportunities are there to improve the service they're receiving?

In our work with experts, we've noticed some barriers that get in the way of these processes working well. Often, the first barrier involves experts failing to suspend judgment and being unable to see the service levels and outputs from our clients' perspective. We've all been guilty at some point of dismissing feedback. Our clients tell us that such and such process was a bit slow or not quite right, and we quickly rationalize away the criticism. "Our clients don't understand how difficult our work is. Our clients don't realize that this is a proven process we've used for many years. Our clients don't realize that we have to do it that way for various other reasons they can't see. Our clients don't realize how much extra work that would create for us." And so on.

> *"The net promoter score is the toughest and most relevant measure around."*

Many of these rationalizations may well be true, but simply dismissing clients' concerns is derailing behavior. Master Experts understand things from the clients' perspective first and then ask what they could do about it.

The second barrier we see experts struggle with is choosing the right questions to ask. As an example, organizations that service vehicles often have processes to determine whether we were happy with our recent service. Typically, this is a phone call or an emailed survey form. The questions they ask in these interviews are laudable but often wrong. For example, they typically ask:

"Were the staff polite to you when you first arrived?" (Answer: yes.)

"Did the staff explain the invoice in detail?" (Answer: yes.)

"Were you happy with the cleanliness of your vehicle when you collected it?" (Answer: yes.)

"Did the vehicle get serviced to your satisfaction?" (Answer: yes.)

At the end of these questions, the servicing organization might conclude that they'd done a great job. But what if they had added these questions?

"Were you happy with the cost of the service?" (Answer: no, in fact, I had a major price shock. The price was much higher than I had imagined it would be.)

"Would you use us again?" (Answer: I would have to think about it. I worry that you find expensive parts to replace as a way of making money.)

"Would you recommend us to a relevant colleague?" (Answer: no, not yet. I'm not confident enough in the service you provide to do so.)

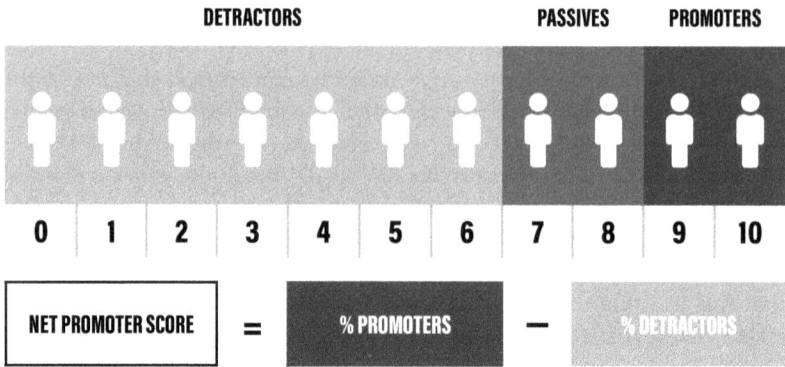

FIGURE 45.2: Net Promoter Scores

At the end of these questions, the servicing organization would conclude that we're actually not a happy customer, and perhaps they're in danger of losing us. This is despite the staff being polite, the service being technically proficient, the invoice being explained, and the vehicle being cleaned well.

The takeaway here is that we have to give careful consideration to the questions we ask. If we're asking about the transaction from *our* perspective, what our standards say must happen (politeness, technical proficiency, invoice explanation and cleanliness), then we may be missing the point. If we don't ask open-ended questions, such as "How could we have improved your experience?", we won't capture broader issues that may be important.

The final question we suggest adding is the net promoter score question. Why? Because we think it's the toughest and most relevant measure around. There are various wordings available, but essentially, we're asking our clients "To what extent would you recommend us to a relevant colleague?" If you're using the net promoter score (NPS) methodology (see Figure 45.2), you provide the client with a scale of 1 to ten, where 1 is "I would absolutely not recommend you" and 10 is "I would absolutely recommend you."

NPS scores are calculated using the following metrics:
- Any client scoring us between 1 and 6 is a *detractor*. They're considered to be a negative testimonial of the quality of our service, and each respondent is scored with a minus point.
- Any client scoring us a 7 or an 8 is a *passive*. They're considered a neutral testimonial. They're lukewarm and unlikely to actively promote our service to friends. Each of these respondents is allocated a zero score.
- Any client scoring us a 9 or a 10 is a *promoter*. They're a client who will actively and positively promote our services to relevant colleagues and friends. Each of these respondents is allocated a single point.

Net promoter scores help us really understand what it takes to get people actually recommending our services. Let's say Uri surveyed a group of ten of his clients and got one 6, three 7s, and six 8s. Uri might imagine that he has have done pretty well. However, using the calculation in Figure 45.2, Uri would end up with a net promoter score of -**10**. That's not good. The data is saying that Uri has one client who might warn a colleague away from his service and has nine who wouldn't warn against or actively promote. To get a good net promoter score, Uri needs to be scoring 9s and 10s.

> *"The net promoter score forces us to think beyond average.*
> *It forces us to think about outstanding."*

The authors like NPS and use it in every interaction we have with our clients and participants because it forces us to ask a simple question: "What would we need to do differently in order to get a 9 or a 10 from a client? That is, delight them." Truly great service levels come from exploring this question. NPS forces us to think beyond average and beyond okay. It forces us to think about outstanding.

So, what is a good NPS score? The worst score is -100, with every respondent being a detractor. The best score is +100, with every respondent being a promoter. NPS averages vary dramatically between industries, so often the "best" NPS score is one that outscores relevant competitors.

The net promoter score was created by Frederick F. Reichheld, a fellow at Bain & Company. It's now used extensively throughout the world as one of the most accurate predictors of customer loyalty. Any NPS score above 0 is "good." It means that your audience is more loyal than not. Anything above 20 is considered "favorable." Bain & Co, the source of the NPS system, suggests that above 50 is excellent, and above 80 is world class. If readers will excuse a small amount of self-promotion by the authors, our *Mastering Expertship* programs, which are delivered around the world, regularly receive NPS scores from participants of above 80.

Evaluation of Specific Contributions

ACTIVE RESPONDERS CONSTANTLY WANT to assess the impact of their contribution so they know how to respond more effectively next time around. This is, in effect, the Evaluation stage of the expert consulting model. This final stage measures the effectiveness of the solution we've designed and implemented. We evaluate whether our specific implementation did what we said it was going to do.

In our experience, when we ask experts about this stage of a project, we discover that it's rarely executed, and even when it is conducted, it's rarely carried out well. This is a shame as these reviews are usually the source of significant learning when done properly.

The goals of the Evaluation phase are as follows:

- An impact report demonstrating, in measurable terms, the extent to which the solution has positively addressed the business issues that it was designed to impact. This should be issued to and signed off by all stakeholders.
- A process implementation review involving key stakeholders that explores and documents any lessons learned and recognizes all contributors.

"Did our solution move the needle?"

There are a number of benefits in identifying and tracking key measures at the outset and at the conclusion of rolling out a solution. The very fact that we're attempting to measure the results will make us much more conscious of the fact no change means the endeavor has been a waste of time, resources and energy. Just knowing that the exercise is being evaluated in quantitative terms focuses our and our stakeholders' minds on ensuring everything is in place to guarantee the needle moves.

Knowing that we're aiming to move the needle and publicly reporting any improvement will most likely ensure the more rigorous upfront discovery that we discussed in detail in Chapters 42 and 43. What exactly is the issue that we're trying to fix? How is it showing up, both qualitatively and quantitatively? What's causing such effects to happen? What are the business impacts? Who and what else is affected? What measures could we reliably track that would indicate that our solution is improving the situation?

When we inquire about the organizational context and show a commitment to improving real-world results, we improve our brand. We're not just peddling a methodology or using technical jargon and remaining indifferent to the final results. We're people who deliver real-world results.

We're much more likely to be seen as key organizational contributors rather than experts on the margins. We'll be able to clearly report how results have improved, backed by objective proof of delivering value to the organization.

Until we have demonstrated a clear return on the investment, we'll be viewed as organizational costs or overheads. If people can't see how expenditure delivers organizational value, then they have only an abstract estimation of our worth to the organization. Metrics are tools that move us from being seen as abstract and marginal *technical* contributors to being viewed as vital and trusted *organizational* contributors.

Post-Implementation Reviews

A KEY FACTOR IN proving our real-world value is mastering the art of effective post-implementation reviews. What is the role of experts in conducting a highly effective post-implementation review (PIR), particularly as we're not the senior project managers, owners of the project, or sponsors?

> *"The purpose needs to be stated up front:*
> *it's learning."*

Let's first explore what the attributes of an effective PIR are. In order to execute a PIR successfully, these conditions need to be met:

- **The right people in the room**: every contributing group associated with the project needs to be represented, and in particular, the end recipients of the project. Sorry, but safety people sitting around and congratulating themselves on a recent initiative doesn't cut it if those whose behavior they were attempting to influence aren't at the table, too.
- **The original business case needs to be front and center**: this would, of course, contain the objectives of the project, how success or otherwise would be measured, and other key performance indicators, such as budget, timeline, return on investment and possibly return on effort. This usually requires a data-gathering exercise on whether the outcomes and results were properly measured.
- **A spirit of learning, not blame**: the purpose of the PIR needs to be clearly stated up front: learning. If the PIR is going to be about apportioning blame for projects that didn't completely deliver on expectations, then those who attend will do so in a defensive frame of mind, and many important stakeholders simply won't attend at all. The culture of understanding what happened and being able to learn from it is a key success factor in most dynamic growth organizations. Where blame culture dominates, real learning rarely occurs.
- **Core questions framed**: gaining a clear sense of what questions we're trying to answer and why they are important. What did we do that worked, and why? What did we do that didn't work, and why not? How could we do this better next time? What would it take? What assumptions did we make at the beginning of the project that turned

out to be accurate? Which didn't? What could we do to improve the accuracy of our core assumptions in the future?

- **A bias for action**: how are we going to act upon the insights and learning from this process so that we and others can produce better results next time around?

On the web, there's many high-quality resources we can access to provide agendas and advice about how to conduct a post-implementation review. But the key principles above are primarily attitudinal and behavioral rather than process-oriented.

"Lessons from projects often get lost in time."

As we discussed in Chapter 42, there are many reasons why PIRs don't occur, some situational and some Machiavellian. But what can experts do to ensure PIRs are used and we all benefit from the lessons learned?

Firstly, we can make sure it's on the project plan from the very beginning. We can begin a discussion about how this project's success will be measured. In everything we do, we should be asking "what will success look like, and how will we measure it?" In Chapters 26 to 29, we discuss tangible and intangible measures in some detail.

Secondly, we can insist upon interim PIRs, which are quick check-ins along the way at key milestones in the project to ensure that the project is tracking well. These interim PIRs are vital. As discussed in Chapter 44, they enable project teams to ask a fundamental question that, in our experience, is rarely asked: at this stage of the project, what's the likelihood of the project succeeding in achieving its objectives, and as a consequence, should implementation continue as planned or would it be better to discontinue or modify it?

Thirdly, in the absence of a properly constituted review, we can ensure we at least review our own performance and publish and share the results.

Learning From Reviews—It's Easier Said Than Done

THE NEXT CRITICAL QUESTION is what we do with feedback that comes from either feedback loops or PIRs. In other words, how can we embed learning? How do we share what we've learned with others who might be making the same mistakes or missing opportunities for improvement? How do we make sure we remember to deploy new processes and behaviors ourselves? In our experience, none of this is easy.

There are many constraints that make it difficult. Project teams get broken up and quickly dispersed around the organization on new projects. We move on quickly from dealing with one set of stakeholders to dealing with a new set of stakeholders. We make the mistake of believing that what happened on the last project isn't relevant on this one. And even if we do, colleagues may not. The lesson we've learned may only be deployable a year from now, when we repeat the project (by which time, in the absence of capturing the learning, key lessons can get lost). And the essence of learning is that we need to persuade people to think differently and act differently. This is always a challenge at the best of times, but it's significantly harder when there's a big project and a short deadline looming.

> *"Expert leadership inspires constant improvement and an openness to feedback."*

Active Responders who we've seen be very successful in capturing and deploying learnings have used the following tactics:
- **Embed the 10 percent rule in start-up meetings**: we discussed this in Chapter 41 on Knowledge Generation. It's answering the question "How can we do this project 10 percent better than the last project we ran?" That 10 percent might be faster, cheaper, better results, and so on.
- **Leverage lessons from everyone on the team**: deliberately ask project team members to share recent results of post-implementation reviews; what was learned, and why? Might those insights be applied to the current project?
- **Create wikis or other repositories where lessons learned are captured**: ensure everyone on the team regularly visits the knowledge bank and considers what lessons are applicable.
- **Regularly share lessons broadly across the expert group**: don't leave it to chance that colleagues may explore knowledge banks. Send out the lessons to anyone who might be relevant. This might take the form of informal "what we learned in the last two months" sessions or experts constantly referring to lessons from previous projects.

Master Experts create an environment where colleagues are keen to learn and keen to deploy these learnings. Their informal leadership in this regard inspires constant improvement and openness to robust feedback.

Seeing Around Corners—Anticipating Future Needs

PROACTIVE EXPERTS PERIODICALLY TAKE the time to try to identify future directions, requirements and potential problems for their most important clients or stakeholders. We describe this as seeing around corners because, by its very nature, the process attempts to discern what is not yet visible but will be at some stage in the future. And like everything else in this book, seeing around corners doesn't require some extraordinary time-bending powers. It simply requires discipline and process.

As we discussed in our chapter on knowledge generation (Chapter 41), the clues to the future are actually all around us if we observe carefully.

It's worth thinking conceptually about what we're trying to achieve here. In effect, we're attempting to imagine and create our service of the future before anyone else in order to delight and amaze our clients and stakeholders.

> *"Do nothing, and we'll be responding in crisis mode.*
> *Not a comfortable place to be."*

One of the authors' largest clients, a global oncology health firm, does this better than anyone. They have vast numbers of their employees, from the front line to strategic positions, engaged in incrementally imagining and then creating the future in what is a highly dynamic environment. Advances in the equipment used, both hardware and incredible software, to treat cancer are extraordinary. And by being an early adopter of these new technologies, our client has to invent new administrative and procedural processes to ensure the new technology is deployed effectively. They do so by having teams from around the world working in large numbers of work streams (in addition to their day jobs). A new process could be developed in Queensland, Australia and deployed only weeks later in Michigan, USA. A streamlined service model can be tested in Nottingham, UK and deployed only weeks later in Madrid, Spain.

The central part of this very effective process, and which makes them world leaders in innovation in their service, is identifying areas where capabilities are changing and then working through what that means for a doctor, patient or patient services officer on the ground.

For most experts, we're regularly seeing changes in three main areas:
- The capability of technology to do things differently.
- The often rapidly changing requirements of clients and stakeholders, i.e., what they want us to do.
- The changing expectations of clients and stakeholders and how they want us to do things.

This last one is sometimes the most challenging. One supplier somewhere on the planet finds a way to offer a new and enhanced service level to a customer, and then we almost immediately expect every supplier we buy things from to be able to do so, too.

There is a big payoff in finding the time to peer around a corner near us. Without taking the time to identify, anticipate and prepare for emerging requirements, opportunities and problems, we can find ourselves having to respond in crisis mode once those issues or opportunities are already upon us—usually with insufficient capacity or time to respond effectively. That's uncomfortable for our brand and makes us much less likely to respond effectively. Forewarned is forearmed!

One simple methodology we might want to deploy is SCAN-FOCUS-ACT (see Figure 45.3). This methodology lends itself to an annual application. Its purpose is to identify emerging issues and opportunities, brainstorm anticipated future requirements, and then plan for timely provision. It can be conducted individually, although it's typically more fruitful if we involve a diverse set of stakeholders.

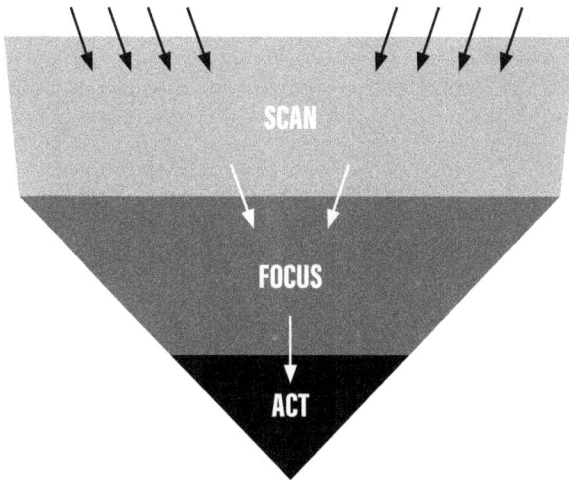

FIGURE 45.3: The SCAN-FOCUS-ACT Model

Getting everyone together—interacting and building off each other's ideas—will tend to elicit more ideas and insights. It's also possible, and sometimes better logistically, to interview or survey stakeholders and other interested parties separately with a common set of future-focused questions.

The SCAN-FOCUS-ACT process has three steps:

- *Scanning* focuses on exploring all the possible future scenarios, such as strategic choices the organization is contemplating, moves from competitors or other players in the industry, the evolution of various meta-trends (political, environmental, sociological, technical), and so on. The purpose is to explore all emerging trends and suspend judgment on whether they might be relevant at this point.
- *Focusing* is zeroing in on the potential issues or opportunities that you consider most likely and highest impact. It's prioritizing all the possible actions you could take as a consequence of the *scan*.
- *Acting* is determining precisely what proactive initiatives you will undertake, either to immunize yourself and the organization from emerging problems or to capitalize on opportunities and, of course, take timely action.

It's often helpful to provide colleagues with some notice, particularly of the Scan phase. What sort of material are we looking for, and why? Providing a central place to capture this information and the insights is also essential.

TAKING ACTION

Growing Our Active Responder Skills

IF THIS IS AN expert role in which you believe you could add greater value, here are some high-level suggestions for actions to take:

▶ LEARN OF STAKEHOLDERS' PLANS AND EMERGING REQUIREMENTS

Part of the secret of responding quickly is understanding what is coming down the line from stakeholders and planning to be ready and able to support those requests when they arrive. This also helps us avoid being called to join projects too late and having to unwind some of the work and thinking already done by stakeholders. Some questions we might like to ask ourselves:

- How often do I schedule proactive discovery conversations with key stakeholders to learn of their emergent challenges/initiatives so as to anticipate requirements and make timely provision? In such instances, we may want to stress that we're not seeking to lock down an exact prediction of future requirements. We're just trying to get a general indication of their direction.
- What other steps can I take to start to predict what requirements my stakeholders may have?
- How closely am I monitoring trends that might help me predict the types of changes coming?
- Will their requirements stay mostly the same? Do they have any new strategies planned? Are there any market changes that might dictate a revised approach (and new requirements)? Once we have built up a picture of likely future requirements thus, we can take the necessary steps to prioritize the team's focus on the most significant requirements. This might include readying processes and systems, upskilling, planning resources, and so on, so that we can respond efficiently and effectively when the requirements surface.

▶ MAKE IT EASY FOR STAKEHOLDERS TO ACCESS AND BENEFIT FROM OUR EXPERTISE

Sometimes stakeholders' experiences of engaging experts are not what we would wish, leading to the souring of relationships or disincentivizing them from approaching experts in the future. Questions we might like to ask ourselves:

- How easy is it for my stakeholders to engage me? Do I have any default responses that they might take issue with? These could be problematic default responses like long waits or the expert appearing hassled or annoyed. In an ideal world, how would I like those moments of truth to play out?
- If it transpires that my default responses are less than ideal, what can I do to respond in the future in a manner consistent with stakeholder needs and expectations? How clear am I on stakeholders' expectations and their subjective view of what I'm like to engage with (and responsiveness)? Should I be surveying them about how they view my responsiveness? Are they generally satisfied with what I do? Or, if not, is there a pattern to what they're dissatisfied with?
- Have I identified and removed any problematic hurdles?
- Have I worked on designing and engineering the ideal stakeholder experience—their journey from first contact through to total satisfaction? (This is a common practice in customer experience initiatives. Create a flowchart starting with the point of first contact right through to the confirmation of a successful resolution. Determine precisely how you would like each step of the process to be experienced by the stakeholder. For example, when they raise a ticket, what type of response would you prefer they experience for them to think positively (and realistically) about you and the team? How should they be kept informed whilst you're working on their problem? How would you like them to experience the closing out of the issue? And so on. Once you've mapped the ideal stakeholder journey, organize everyone and deliver it consistently.)

▶ IDENTIFY FUTURE DIRECTIONS, REQUIREMENTS AND POTENTIAL PROBLEMS

Without taking the time to identify, anticipate and prepare for emerging requirements, opportunities and problems, we can find ourselves having to respond in crisis mode once those issues or opportunities are already upon us, usually with insufficient capacity or time to respond effectively. As described above, apply the SCAN-FOCUS-ACT methodology.

MASTERING KNOWLEDGE TRANSFER

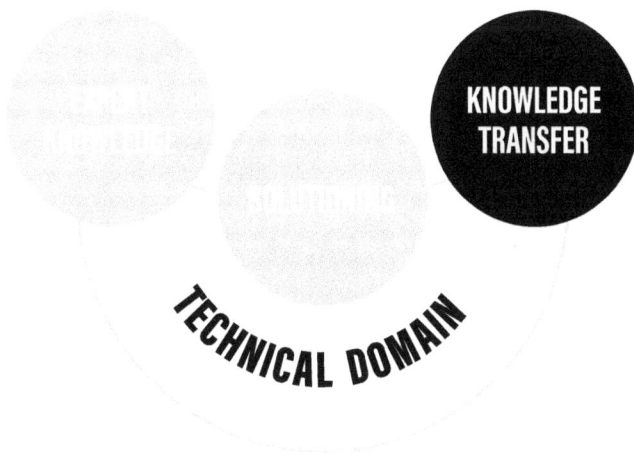

KNOWLEDGE
TRANSFER

TECHNICAL DOMAIN

The Master Expert develops increased expertise in others so they can apply specialist knowledge, which increases overall organizational capability.

CHAPTER 46

Knowledge Transfer

What are the benefits and barriers to experts passing on their expert knowledge?

IN THIS CHAPTER, WE WILL EXPLORE:

- The benefits for all experts, stakeholders and organizations, of being effective at knowledge transfer.
- The common barriers experts typically face in achieving effective knowledge transfer.

KNOWLEDGE TRANSFER DEALS WITH increasing the ability of others to apply specialist knowledge, which facilitates overall increased organizational capability.

In the previous four chapters covering Expert Knowledge, we introduced the concept of an expert knowledge strategy (see Figure 46.1). The fourth and final stage of this strategy is the *knowledge sharing* component, which we cover in this capability of Knowledge Transfer. It's a critical capability to get right if an expert aspires to operate at the Master Expert level.

Many experts we meet are hugely frustrated with having to do the same work year after year, dealing with low-level requests that interrupt higher order work, and being constantly under pressure as the single go-to person for particular tasks or work. There are also significant advantages, for both stakeholders and the organization, to equipping others to be more capable and responsible so they can avoid delays and be more autonomous.

When done effectively, sharing knowledge with others is the solution to all of these problems. It allows us to transfer or delegate work to other colleagues and make them more self-reliant. Some of this work may be the less taxing problem-solving and administrative tasks.

Of course, knowledge transfer is not simple or easy. In our experience, many senior technical experts aren't very good at it, either due to neglect, stubborn refusal, or an inability to master the relevant techniques. We're often concerned that sharing our expertise in some way could jeopardize our job security or career opportunities. Lack of technique comes into play if experts aren't familiar with how people learn, or the available options and methods to build capability. Experts sometimes believe they have no colleagues to delegate activities to (none that are obvious to them, anyway).

But the benefits of successfully sharing knowledge are twofold. It either allows others to solve their own problems rather than being dependent on us, or we build our colleagues' ability to solve problems for others instead of relying on us to do so. Many knowledge transfer initiatives achieve both of these benefits. These are game-changing achievements.

Why? What's in it for us?

Firstly, building others' abilities and responsibilities allows us to shift our focus to higher impact areas. Very often, the fact that we're the only person who can do a particular thing, or are the only one with a particular knowledge set, ensures that we get tied up with all the associated requests, which may not always be the best use of our skills, experience, time and efforts. If know-how and responsibility are distributed, then we can focus our attention on higher order priorities. We get to do the fun stuff and the high-value stuff.

> *"If we are the only person who can do something, we don't get offered more interesting opportunities."*

Secondly, helping our colleagues and team members become more expert fosters higher morale, autonomy, commitment and confidence. Though we might justify holding on to certain activities so as to "not bother people," developing our colleagues' capabilities often triggers higher levels of engagement because they feel they're growing and progressing. It also demonstrates our leadership and commitment to being a team player. In short, knowledge sharing is extremely good for our personal brand. Also, building redundancy into what we do—that is, others can do the work if we're not available—allows us to be available for other things. This can include high-value projects, broader roles within our area of expertise, working on cross-domain teams, secondments to other parts of the organization or other parts of the world, and promotion opportunities. If we're the only person who can do certain things, most organizations will choose not to offer us these opportunities because we're seen as irreplaceable.

Thirdly, in committing to effective knowledge transfer, we're fostering others' increased self-reliance. By building our colleagues' capability, we're contributing to their personal and professional growth and to the overall capability of the organization. We're playing a role in talent development, something we discuss in detail in Chapter 49.

Fourthly, enabling others reduces single-point sensitivity. There can be a significant risk that the organization is exposed if we're the only person who has a particular expertise and we become indisposed for any reason.

Finally, by enabling others, we're able to work on higher level tasks and projects and add more value to the organization.

> *"There may be a tendency among experts to hoard their knowledge."*

Making Excuses—Real or Imagined?

WHEN WE TALK ABOUT knowledge transfer, many experts offer excuses for why they don't help with the training and development of their colleagues. The sorts of things we hear experts say are:

- No one else can do it as well as me. (There's a tendency among experts to hoard their knowledge.)
- It won't get done properly unless I do it.
- None of my colleagues are interested or have the time to help me with my workload.
- It'll be much quicker if I do it myself.
- I've tried to train people before to do some of my more complex work, but they just can't do it.
- I don't have time to train someone.
- It would take too long to train someone. It's not worth the effort.
- There is no one here to train. I don't have anyone to delegate to.
- It's not my job to train people.
- This is my favorite part of my work. I don't want to give it to someone else.

Do any of these reasons resonate with you? Have you heard yourself say them? Or think them? Deep down, subconsciously, might there be some inner voice telling you that some of these are valid in your situation? At some stage or another, most of us justify not delegating or sharing knowledge based on some of the reasons described above.

Capability: **EXPERT KNOWLEDGE**
An Expert Knowledge Strategy

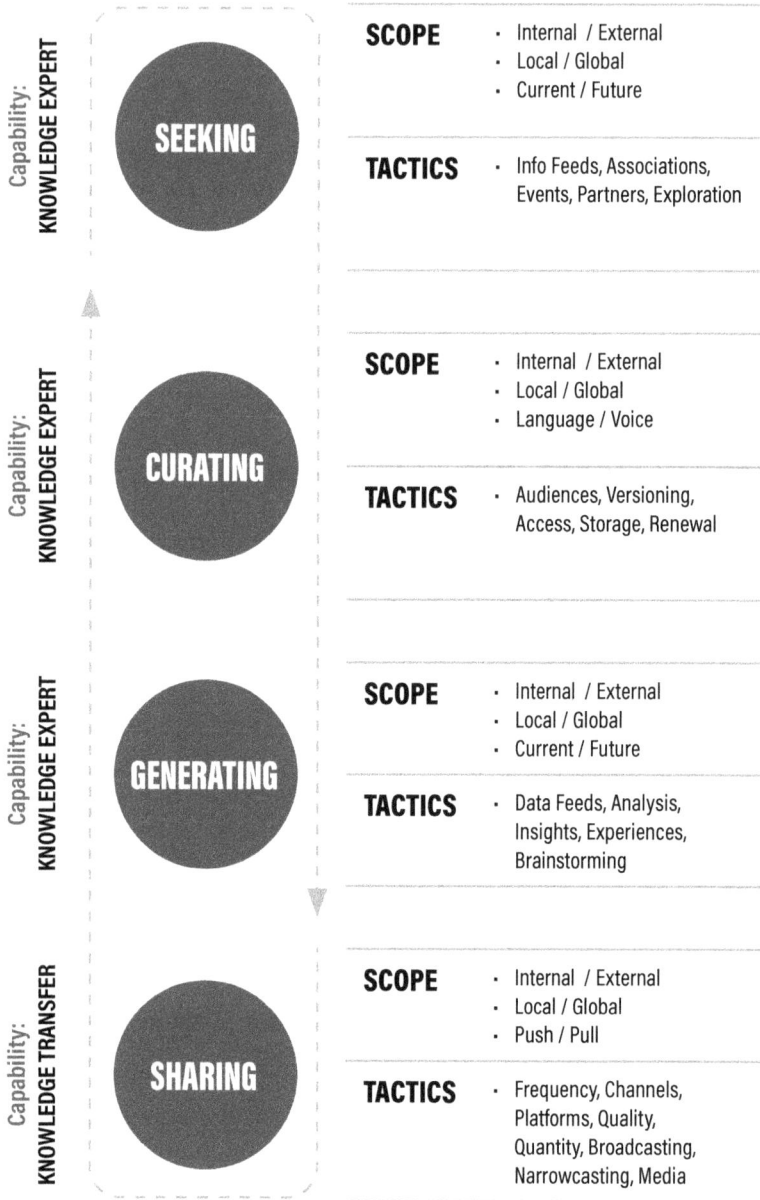

	SCOPE	TACTICS
Capability: KNOWLEDGE EXPERT — **SEEKING**	• Internal / External • Local / Global • Current / Future	• Info Feeds, Associations, Events, Partners, Exploration
Capability: KNOWLEDGE EXPERT — **CURATING**	• Internal / External • Local / Global • Language / Voice	• Audiences, Versioning, Access, Storage, Renewal
Capability: KNOWLEDGE EXPERT — **GENERATING**	• Internal / External • Local / Global • Current / Future	• Data Feeds, Analysis, Insights, Experiences, Brainstorming
Capability: KNOWLEDGE TRANSFER — **SHARING**	• Internal / External • Local / Global • Push / Pull	• Frequency, Channels, Platforms, Quality, Quantity, Broadcasting, Narrowcasting, Media

FIGURE 46.1: An Expert Knowledge Strategy

Of course, if you're the only person who knows how to do something, this may appear to be to your advantage. Experts have recounted stories to us of colleagues who shared their expertise with more junior colleagues and were then shown the exit. The more junior (and cheaper) expert was deemed a better option. As a consequence, there may be a tendency among experts to hoard their knowledge.

Working as we do with many organizations, we hear this often, but we find evidence it happens to be scarce. In our experience, most experts who demonstrate the ability to develop others, educate colleagues to solve simple problems themselves, and motivate technical colleagues to rapidly advance their expertise are typically either promoted or quickly asked to do higher order activities. Because they have delegated to others, they're free and available for more interesting work and projects. Transferring knowledge also tends to demonstrate their mastery of critical enterprise skills, as well as technical skills.

To master the knowledge transfer skills and techniques we'll describe in the following three chapters, we have to first overcome a few natural barriers (see Figure 46.2).

> *"Knowledge transfer requires us to take time to save time."*

The first barrier is that our tendency as experts to want to solve things is ingrained. We're here to help, and we want to be seen to be doing so. Though seemingly efficient and service-oriented, this desire to help ultimately inhibits growth, both our own and that of the colleagues we can empower with improved skills and knowledge.

The second barrier to effective knowledge transfer is that we tend to underestimate our less experienced colleagues' learning agility. Colleagues (even junior ones!) are often far more capable of thinking things through, solving problems, and taking effective action than we give them credit for. Rapid development is typical, even with quite limited coaching. Part of this is psychological: our self-worth dictates that we perceive the work we do as complex and taking years to master. This may be true for *everything* we know and have experienced, but *selected* knowledge and experience may be easier to pass on. We transfer knowledge one task or challenge at a time.

The third barrier is a further misconception: we believe knowledge transfer typically takes far longer than doing it ourselves. As busy experts, as much as we mean to get around to building capability in our colleagues, this week is just never the right week to take the time to devote to it. We have too much on. It's quicker in the short term for us to fix it ourselves. But this is a false economy. Put it off, and we'll always be stuck in the responsive fixer role. Knowledge transfer requires us to *take time to save time*, and for many experts in highly responsive roles (with lots of regular unplanned troubleshooting), that's not easy. But it's possible. And there is a large payoff once successfully completed.

The fourth barrier is more difficult for us accept: we might not be as good at knowledge transfer as we think we are. Knowledge transfer is a skill in its own right. It's difficult to deploy the right processes and planning, particularly if our colleagues have a very low base of knowledge. This requires us to go back to basics and not over-complicate things too quickly. For an expert who can see twenty different possible answers to a simple question, this can be challenging, so it requires discipline. Part of this dynamic is an underlying and often unconscious wish to show how much we know, to demonstrate how expert we are to those we're training.

This instinct gets in the way of effective transfer. We make the expertise sound too complicated, and this undermines the student's confidence. They begin to doubt that they'll ever master the work and the knowledge. They then tell us it's too hard, which confirms our bias that only we can do it. Unfortunately, this is a common story.

A fifth barrier is worrying about our personal brand. If we're asked to fix something for a colleague and instead of doing so, we start asking them whether they read the documentation or followed the troubleshooting process, we can be perceived as avoiding our responsibility to help or being obstructive.

Our colleagues sometimes can't see the long game, which is that our objective is to help them save time and build their capability (fixing things themselves without having to wait for us to arrive). We have to manage expectations carefully and be clear about our intent. Why we're taking extra time to try and upskill them has to be understood.

In some circumstances, we want to hold on to work that we really enjoy doing, or work that we feel defines our value to the organization. We're concerned about lessening our status and perceived value by delegating tasks that others could do but that we get kudos for when we do them. It can be flattering to seem indispensable. And who doesn't get a kick out of demonstrating a high level of mastery?

Finally, there's an underlying worry among some experts that what they do is so dry and mundane that no one will be interested in learning it.

Capability: KNOWLEDGE TRANSFER

6 Barriers to Expert Knowledge Transfer

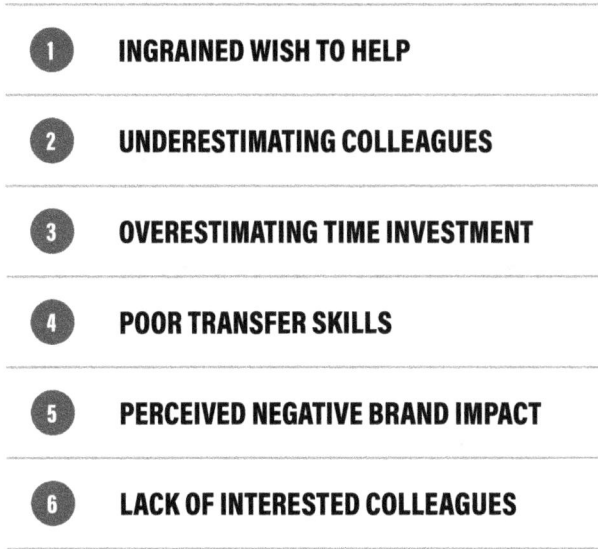

1 INGRAINED WISH TO HELP

2 UNDERESTIMATING COLLEAGUES

3 OVERESTIMATING TIME INVESTMENT

4 POOR TRANSFER SKILLS

5 PERCEIVED NEGATIVE BRAND IMPACT

6 LACK OF INTERESTED COLLEAGUES

FIGURE 46.2: Six Barriers to Knowledge Transfer

Mastering Knowledge Transfer

IN THE FOLLOWING CHAPTERS, we'll suggest new ways of thinking about knowledge sharing and delegation and their role in our journey to becoming a Master Expert.

The capability of Knowledge Transfer deals with developing others' ability to apply specialist knowledge, facilitating an overall increased organizational capability. Knowledge Transfer describes three roles an expert must play:

- **Knowledge Sharer:** ensuring knowledge is disseminated effectively across the organization to relevant parties.
- **Knowledge Coach:** helping colleagues understand and make the best use of our specialist knowledge.
- **Talent Developer:** ensuring that we and colleagues are involved in continuous learning, and actively identifying and developing future talent.

TAKING ACTION

Growing Our Knowledge Transfer Skills

IF THIS IS A capability in which you believe you could add greater value, here is a high-level suggestion for action to take:

▶ PLAN TO OVERCOME KNOWLEDGE TRANSFER BARRIERS

As discussed in this chapter, we all experience multiple barriers to the effective sharing of expert knowledge. Master Experts focus on initiatives that overcome these barriers.

Questions we might want to ask ourselves:
- To what extent are there opportunities for people to self-solve rather than me explaining or doing everything for my colleagues? How might I position these in a positive way with colleagues?
- To what extent do I underestimate the capability of my colleagues? Which tasks or projects give me the best opportunity to test their capability without major risk? How will I convince myself that taking a small risk for a big gain is worth it?
- How do I provision slightly more time to get the training message across to colleagues? Rather than me just doing it myself, should I be planning and scheduling specific times to do this?
- What is my current approach to transferring knowledge? Am I as effective as I could be? Do I rush things or assume knowledge that colleagues don't have? Am I patient with people as they learn? What needs to change in the way I approach knowledge transfer to make it a positive experience for my colleagues and myself?
- What is my "what's in it for you" pitch to colleagues who aren't stepping forward to learn things but who I know are capable? Who else could help me persuade willing helpers to step forward?

"Thinking is difficult. That's why most people judge."

Carl Gustav Jung

CHAPTER | **47**

Knowledge Sharing

With so much to share and so little time, how can we best make every knowledge sharing moment count?

IN THIS CHAPTER, WE WILL EXPLORE:

- What constitutes a sensible, workable knowledge sharing strategy?
- How do we leverage different communication channels effectively?
- What are the Four Levels of Learning, and what do they tell us about our approach to training other experts?
- What are the secrets of success when facilitating learning from experts?

THE FIRST EXPERT ROLE in the Knowledge Transfer capability is **Knowledge Sharer.** This set of behaviors relates to ensuring that we disseminate our knowledge effectively, taking the initiative to ensure the wider organization knows our knowledge and uses it. The behaviors at each level of Expertship for this expert role are described in Figure 47.1.

At immature levels, the expert is mostly a recipient of knowledge sharing activities. Occasionally, they might assist in sharing knowledge when asked, which is a reactive approach to this expert role. Experts who are derailing in this role will actively hoard information and resist sharing their knowledge and experience with anyone, especially other technical colleagues they believe could usurp their position as an unrivaled authority in their technical domain.

In contrast, the Master Expert will model a culture of knowledge sharing within their technical cohort, as well as across the wider organization, by actively, freely and effectively sharing all current and relevant information in order to empower others and enable self-reliance. Additionally, Master Experts motivate a broad network to participate in and deploy learning. They regularly check in to see if this is happening effectively. They oversee the creation and maintenance of a highly accessible knowledge repository.

> *"Experts are often unconsciously competent, and counter-intuitively, this is a problem."*

What Knowledge Sharing Techniques Work?

IN OUR PROGRAMS, WE have rich discussions with experts about learning and their role in it. For example, we ask experts how they learned what they know. The answers are typically that experts learned through a complex combination of:

- Self-study, including research and observation.
- Practice, experimentation (trial and error), repetition and teaching others.
- Visualization.
- Formal education, including internal and external courses.
- Learning from others, such as asking, being coached, handovers and watching skills being demonstrated.

This concept is called *blended learning*. It means using multiple techniques to acquire expertise, which we can then convey to others. This is particularly useful when we have a diverse group whose learning preferences may vary.

When we asked them how they go about running training sessions for colleagues, "death by PowerPoint" appears to be a frequently practiced option, or "I just told them how to do it." Upon reflection, for many experts, the juxtaposition of how they learned and how they teach is an "aha!" moment. They said they realized that the way others will likely best acquire expertise is very different from the way they currently or historically taught it. This is an extremely common insight, and one that can be easily addressed.

As experts, we have focused on attaining technical skills in our specialized area, not acquiring and practicing teaching skills. Any proficiency we've acquired in this area will have been absorbed from positive experiences with great mentors we've had in the past or even high school teachers who particularly inspired us.

Capability: KNOWLEDGE TRANSFER
Expert Role: KNOWLEDGE SHARER

MASTER EXPERT

- Actively champions and role models a culture of knowledge sharing within the organization.
- Actively and freely shares all current and relevant information in order to empower others and enable self-reliance.
- Motivates very broad network to participate in and deploy learning, and regularly checks in on deployment.
- Deploys a deliberate and consistent promotional effort to leverage their knowledge repository and make it front of mind for those who need it.
- Engages relevant stakeholders to deepen stakeholders' expertise.

EXPERT

- Understands the importance of sharing knowledge but doesn't make it a priority.
- Communicates current and relevant information on a "need to know" basis.
- Motivates immediate network to participate in and deploy learning.
- Contributes to the knowledge repository.

SPECIALIST

- Is mostly a recipient of knowledge sharing activities.
- Occasionally assists reactively with sharing knowledge across the organization.

- Provides information to others, but only when requested to do so. Tends to hold information close.
- Resistant to handing over knowledge. Conceals and withholds vital information.

DERAILING

FIGURE 47.1: Knowledge Sharer Behaviors

Many experts exhibit numerous derailing behaviors when it comes to knowledge transfer:
- The teacher being more focused on wanting to impress the audience than teach them anything. This is an exercise in emphasizing seniority and mastery.
- Not understanding the skill level of the audience and shooting too high too early. Or, conversely, insulting their intelligence by not taking into account their existing knowledge level.
- Assuming the audience knows stuff they don't.
- The teacher explaining the *what* and the *how*, but not the *why*.

All of these mistakes are made because we haven't clearly articulated (a) what we're trying to achieve (learning outcomes), (b) the benefits for all parties if the learning is successful (what's in it for me and those being taught), and (c) we haven't properly analyzed our starting point. This is considering what stage of learning both ourselves (as teachers) and our colleagues (as students) are currently at.

> *"For many experts, the juxtaposition of how they learned and how they taught was an 'aha!' moment."*

A useful model to discuss this is the Four Levels of Learning (see Figure 47.2). Leveraging our extensive experience of working with experts, we can map experts' knowledge transfer twice in Figure 47.2. Firstly, when it comes to their teaching ability, we'd argue many experts are at level 1: unconsciously incompetent. Many experts just don't realize what poor teachers they are. This translates into badly planned and delivered learning experiences that drive potential students away. Secondly, when it comes to experts' knowledge and experience, we'd argue many experts are at level 4. They don't know (or have forgotten) just how much they know. This translates into poor learning experiences because the expert continually references knowledge that the students don't have. The students, on the other hand, may fit into categories 1 or 2. They either don't know what they don't know, or they do know what they don't know. Tangentially, business planning uses similar language: what do we know, what do we know we don't know, what don't we know that we know and what don't we know we don't know? This latter category is only discovered when the business actually starts a project and learns as they go. Rapid prototyping is based on this construct.

Like everything else, the application of strategic thinking and careful planning and the use of a range of techniques are the secrets to knowledge transfer success. This translates into compelling and engaging learning experiences that are fulfilling and enjoyable for teachers and students alike.

Capability: **KNOWLEDGE TRANSFER**

The Four Levels of Learning

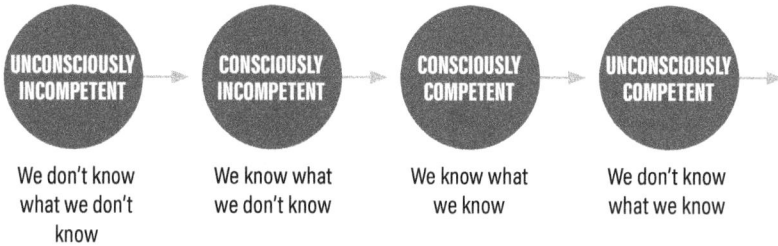

UNCONSCIOUSLY INCOMPETENT	CONSCIOUSLY INCOMPETENT	CONSCIOUSLY COMPETENT	UNCONSCIOUSLY COMPETENT
We don't know what we don't know	We know what we don't know	We know what we know	We don't know what we know

FIGURE 47.2: The Four Levels of Learning

A Case Study: This Book

THE AUTHORS ARE THE first to admit how difficult and complex a task knowledge sharing can be. This book is a case in point. It is, in some ways, the biggest knowledge sharing project that we have attempted—and we've attempted lots! In our attempt to disseminate the information, skills, experiences and insights on Expertship we've gathered in these many pages, there were a host of decisions and assumptions we've had to make. For example:

- Who is the book for? (Several target audiences presented themselves, but in the end, we chose experts themselves.)
- Why would they pick it up and bother reading past the introduction? (A very fine question, and we hope it's because most experts want to be the best they can possibly be.)
- What type of book would experts want to read? (After considering a very academic approach to the topic, and the classic message by fictional story approach, we opted for a practical guide, deploying lots of examples of real experts doing expert things.)
- Should we include pictures—well, graphics? (Of course!)
- What type of voice should we use through the text? (We chose the voice of opportunity over a more directive voice, i.e., *you should do this* and *you must do that.*)
- How should we position ourselves? (We chose to refer to ourselves as "authors" throughout, while making it clear that we're also experts in our technical domains and face the same daily challenges as all experts. So, we use the word "we" rather than "you" throughout the book.)

In each chapter, we faced more micro knowledge sharing conundrums. In the next chapter, for example, we introduce the I-GRROW model. How many experts will have heard of it? How much should we write about it? If we write too much, we'll lose the reader. If we mention it in passing and experts don't know of it, they'll be confused and/or frustrated. We were wary of making this a short book that glossed over the important details. We've learned from working closely with experts that they want the detail.

In the end, we chose to make the book many (50) relatively short and (we hope) accessible but detailed chapters, with highly descriptive titles and introductions so readers can delve into the chapters they're most interested in. We've added various indexes to allow experts to easily find the content or graphics they want. We've tried to imagine the different ways in which readers might approach the book, such as reading first page to last page, reading selected chapters, only looking at the pictures, and so on. We've tried to make it accessible to all these typical styles. If you only look at the pictures, you're in luck—we have over one hundred of them!

"Understanding our audience was vitally important."

You might imagine that, had we chosen to write this book for managers of experts, almost all of these concerns would have been slightly different. If we wrote the book for people in organizational development, the people charged with the talent development of experts in their organizations, then once again, our editorial concerns would have different.

These are the decisions and conundrums experts all over the world face every day when trying to share their knowledge across their organization, made up as it is of disparate groups with differing levels of comprehension, interest, perspective and time. It's why understanding our audience, whether in a training session or a conference speech, is critically important. It impacts every decision we make about content, style of delivery, sequencing, rationale and so on.

Given the complexity of knowledge transfer and the effort it takes, it's no wonder some of us give up and don't bother. This book, for example, has taken three years to write.

But there are ways to make knowledge transfer easier and more effective, and the payoff for those experts who can, with some upfront effort, get this right is huge.

Getting Sharing Right—A Strategy

AS WE REVISIT THE expert knowledge strategy (Figure 47.3), we see that the Sharing component talks about frequency, channels, platforms, quality, quantity, broadcasting, narrowcasting and media. These are publishing terms that apply equally to the work that experts running a knowledge practice need to deploy to share knowledge.

Disseminating information needs to be a combination of three aspects:

- Regular communication and keeping stakeholders abreast of recent events and changes. These are usually presented in a regular cycle, such as monthly. They need to be delivered over multiple platforms, including social media.
- An information repository, whether a wiki or database or portal, where stakeholders can find information on an as-needed basis, updated on a cycle, possibly quarterly.
- In-the-moment communications, either campaigns to launch new services, updates or initiatives, or newsletters to comment on a particular important happening, occurring as required.

> *"Once communication channels have been selected, the question becomes what content goes where?"*

By their nature, the first two of these should be planned and scheduled, whereas the third category would very much be at the discretion of the Master Expert to decide when, how and why. Smart Master Experts act as catalysts to get the first two components happening but delegate these elements' maintenance and execution to more junior experts as part of their professional growth.

Once these channels are established, and we may have many more to leverage than the three described above, then the question is "What content goes where?" Which information artifacts lend themselves to a pull strategy? In other words, made available to colleagues in a portal or on an intranet so that they can easily access them (and make good use of them to solve problems) without any interaction with us as the expert?

And which artifacts lend themselves to a push strategy, where we push out the content through newsletters, alerts and internal social media so that changes and innovations in our technical domain can be successfully communicated to those who might be interested or impacted?

Capability: **EXPERT KNOWLEDGE**

An Expert Knowledge Strategy

FIGURE 47.3: An Expert Knowledge Strategy
This graphic is a deliberate repeat of Figure 38.1.

Which delivery mechanisms do particular information artifacts lend themselves to? The trend is to be as digital as possible these days, but there are times when delivering a printed-out article works better and has more cut-through. We're all aware of the very low open rates on e-newsletters or emails. Just because we've sent an email to someone doesn't mean they've opened it, read it and understood it. Assuming that would be a huge mistake. Even if our colleagues have opened the email, it certainly doesn't mean they have contemplated the implications for them and the organization.

> *"The golden rule is to think about what they would want to know, not what we want to tell them."*

Multiple channels appear to work very well, though they can be very time-consuming. Frequency is a big issue. Disseminate too often and we alienate our audience. Not often enough, and when we do communicate, they've forgotten who we are, what we do, and even why they should be interested. There are hugely conflicting views on how often it's okay to send someone information, and indeed how often it's okay to send them roughly the same information. In our experience, the data is hugely contextual. It has a lot to do with who is sending the information and what historic quality their communications have possessed. As we discussed in Chapter 24, *Next Level Communication*, how we frame information is critically important. The golden rule is to think hard about what the audience would want to know, not what you want to tell them.

What alternative channels are available to us to reach key audiences with critical information? For example, other departments also communicate with senior executives, so can we piggy-back on their efforts to get our message out? Can we persuade a senior executive with a wide reach to comment on one of our posts, thereby significantly increasing the likelihood of it being opened and read by other stakeholders?

As we discuss in detail in Chapter 16, *Managing Our Networks*, making sure we have a relevant and up-to-date list of stakeholders is also a critical component. Who needs to know this, and who doesn't? Is a personal and perhaps even face-to-face or phone interaction required? Who simply needs to be briefed electronically? Are the right people on our distribution lists for the right reasons? And are they in the right categories? This seems like an administratively painful waste of time, but categorizing audiences carefully maximizes impact and minimizes people getting fed up with us.

Versioning is the next big challenge. It means choosing different approaches for different audiences. It can be a lot of work, but it pays dividends. Senior executive audiences need something very simple and directly linked to the strategic and competitive questions that keep them awake at night. Technical groups will require the detail and the analysis. Financial audiences will check to make sure the figures add up correctly before they read a single word, so we need to make sure that they do, and then make sure the numbers tell a story that makes the finance team *want* to read the words.

> *"Someone applying pedagogical theory to a classroom full of*
> *professionals might find that their efforts read as child's play."*
> *– Jack Makhlouf*

Facilitation Versus Training

THE AUTHORS ARE REGULARLY asked for tips on facilitation skills— something we spend a large proportion of our time doing. There is plenty of excellent general material on this topic, so we'll limit our suggestions to a few points we think are most relevant to working with experts.

Our top ten tips are (see Figure 47.4):

1. **Acknowledge prior expertise.** Regardless of whether we think we know more than the participants, it's important we acknowledge that our participants collectively know a lot. We're not going to treat them like children or young adults. We're not going to take a *pedagogical* approach with them (the method and practice of teaching, which translates from Greek to *guiding children*). With pedagogy, the teacher is in charge, determines the curriculum, knows best, is in charge of assessment, and so on. Instead, we're going to take an andragogical approach (the method and practice of learning applied to an adult audience, which translates from Greek to *guiding man*.)

With andragogy, the learners take responsibility for their own learning and influence the curriculum. The teacher is simply the person who creates an effective learning environment. As Jack Makhlouf explains in his excellent article on the subject, "Someone applying pedagogical theory to a classroom full of professionals might find that their efforts read as child's play."

2. **Park egos at the door.** By implication of the above, the facilitator cannot be seen as all-knowing and seeing, so the biggest tip we have for experts who are helping other experts learn is to leave the ego where it belongs in andragogical learning: outside. This is easier said than done. We're so keen on our subject, and so keen our colleagues learn about our subject, that we can unconsciously get carried away, serving up large dollops of wisdom at great length. (Additional free tip: glazed eyes in participants is a warning sign.)

Capability: KNOWLEDGE TRANSFER

Top Ten Tips for Facilitating Expert Groups

1   **ACKNOWLEDGE PRIOR EXPERTISE**

2   **PARK YOUR EGO AT THE DOOR**

3   **MULTIPLE ANSWERS ARE AVAILABLE**

4   **ASK GENERATIVE QUESTIONS**

5   **ENGINEER CONVERSATIONS**

6   **MANDATE EVENNESS**

7   **BE EXPERIENTIAL**

8   **MAKE IT REAL NOT CONCEPTUAL**

9   **ACCOMMODATE ALL LEARNING STYLES**

10   **EVIDENCE OR DIE**

FIGURE 47.4: The Top Ten Tips for Facilitating Expert Groups

3. Multiple answers are available. Gather any typical group of 10 experts together in a room (say with an average of 10 years' working experience, including student jobs at 16), and you'll have at least 100 years of experience in the room. That's over 23,000 days of working experience. However experienced and smart we think we are as an individual, we can't match that. Theirs is the experience we need to leverage, and that means that 99 percent of the answers someone comes up with are deserving of respect and consideration. Facetious inputs from learners suggest that we haven't adequately fostered constructive engagement with the subject matter or that we might have a participant who is not committed to learning. If we ask questions where we're fishing for and only willing to accept one narrow response, we've gone back to pedagogy again, where the only answer that matters is the one we've pre-determined. When presented with participant input that appears problematic, a simple but effective tactic is to ask the room "Who agrees with that thought, and who has an alternative idea?" We're facilitators, not judges.

> *"A typical expert group of 10 participants has 23,000 days of working experience between them. However old and smart we think we are, we can't match that."*

4. Ask generative questions. Generative questions are those where we're exploring what might be. In facilitation terms, it means being prepared to ask questions when we've no idea what the answer might be. In *To Kill A Mockingbird*, Harper Lee famously espoused the opposite (the context being a courtroom): "Never, never, never, on cross-examination ask a witness a question you don't already know the answer to, was a tenet I absorbed with my baby-food." As facilitators, we're obligated to do the opposite. The goal is to shift the responsibility for the discussion and the development of best practice and next practice to the participant group.

5. Engineer conversations. This goes hand in hand with the point above. Our philosophy as facilitators of experts is that the answer is in the room. That is, not (only) in our heads where we might presume we have the definitive truth. So, we have to generate meaningful conversations so that the participants can arrive at useful conclusions that they feel ownership and commitment toward. Given the 23,000 days of working experience in the room and the group's many very different experiences, we can expect a variety of views at first. You'll be surprised at how often (and how quickly) the collective wisdom of the room comes to the fore. This also means letting the participants do the heavy lifting. Our job as facilitators is to come up with interesting questions. The participants' job is to come up with amazing answers. And don't let experts off the hook by filling the silence. If you ask a great question, you'll often get a period of silence because the participants are thinking! Smile, nod and relax. Eventually, someone will give a response, and off the conversation goes. Remember, participants are used to being *taught*, so it'll take them an hour or so to realize that you're approaching them differently and you really are interested in what they think. If the silence continues unabated, then it's worth contemplating whether the question was confusingly worded or somehow "unsafe," which would make participants reluctant to risk being wrong or looking silly.

> *"A facilitator is responsible for creating a respectful, inclusive learning culture."*

6. Mandate evenness of contribution. Possibly the only area in which we might get a little strident is making sure everyone in the room is evenly heard. This is particularly important with groups of experts, which tend to have a higher proportion of introverts (thinkers!) in their ranks than extroverts (talkers!).

One of the authors routinely plays this trick on extroverts: he asks the group (our groups are usually 10 or more participants) an open question: "What do you think you might be feeling if you were an introvert in a large group like this?." The answer is almost always answered quickly by an extrovert. They just can't help themselves.

The rules around evenness of contribution must be agreed by the group and rigorously enforced early on. Extroverts are often unaware of how dominating they can be in conversations. Talking over people before they have finished is also a common habit that has to be broken. The facilitator is not responsible for controlling the conversation, but we're responsible for controlling a respectful, inclusive learning culture. One helpful technique is to give introverts notice. Give them a minute or two to think about the question (or even to discuss in pairs) before the confronting proposition of having to first share their thoughts out loud in front of a large group.

7. Be experiential. Our first major design tip. Designing a single one-hour workshop or a four-day program requires the facilitator to develop a run sheet. This is a document that contains the learning elements in the order in which we anticipate delivering them. The sequence is important. You can think of it as building a house. Sometimes we have to spend a while longer than we might like waiting for the foundations to set, but once they are in place, we have a strong base upon which to build. A key element of our design philosophy with experts is making the workshop or program *experiential*. This means they can practice, engage in doing, acquire practical experience, and learn by this experimentation rather than everything being abstract and theoretical. Sometimes experts' preference for theorizing means that they'll feel more comfortable with abstract frameworks or want to be shown "the right way" of doing things. However, without practicing applying the associated skills or reasoning, they can mistake their theoretical understanding for actual proficiency. It's only when they're presented with a real-world challenge (outside of the workshop) that they realize they're out of their depth. Generally, however, experts love figuring things out for themselves, so design experiences to enable them to do so. Create nearly real situations and puzzles for them to work through and come up with the best answers. While there are many learning styles available, we've found the majority of experts have learned their craft by trying and failing and trying again. The best program designs for experts will reflect this.

8. Make it real, not conceptual. This is our second design tip. This takes a little longer to prepare, but it's worth the effort. Focus your design around giving participants real problems to solve. Take an example of something that actually happened, that routinely happens, or is likely to happen (perhaps changing details slightly to protect the guilty). Ask the group to solve the problem and then debrief the various approaches they could have taken, including the pros and cons of each. Finally, arrive on a set of principles to be deployed when these types of situations occur. This is learning that lasts. And engages. Additional free tip: If you're doing roleplaying, make the scenarios as real (something that really happens) as possible. And ignore the eye-rolling and moaning that occurs every time you hand out the roles. The truth is, and we have the data to prove it, most experts hate roleplaying, but they also grudgingly agree that they learn the most from it.

> *"Models and frameworks help experts structure*
> *thinking, decisions and conversations."*

9. Accommodate all learning styles. There are many types of learning styles, so it's worth identifying our own learning styles to make sure we're not designing content and delivery that only suits us. Every group will contain many styles, so it makes sense to include learning tactics that help everyone. Yes, we'll include experimentation, roleplaying and the like. But we'll also have sufficient time set aside for reflection. We'll discuss a topic live, but we'll also offer the participants extensive notes to take home and read. We'll sometimes cover concepts and topics twice, in different ways, to embed learning and revise. Models and frameworks that help experts structure thinking and conversations are vital (but see next tip). Of course, you'll have been exposed to many such models in this book. Some you'll have found extremely useful. Others simply hold no appeal. This is a typical learning experience. Perhaps the least catered for learning style is that of the pragmatist, who needs planning time to consider how what they've learned about will be applied in the real world. We're often so committed to our content and methodologies and frameworks that we starve learners of the time, opportunity and impetus to think through how, when and with whom they'll specifically apply the ideas in their everyday worlds. Reflection time built into learning helps everyone, especially pragmatists.

10. Evidence or die. Experts are, by and large, a data-driven bunch. We want to see evidence, and insufficient or unreliable evidence is likely to trigger resistance (even if that resistance has more to do with emotional discomfort than objective logic). Our advice here is not to allow any group to get too hung up on evidence. That said, it should be referenced, and participants ought to be able to go off and source the data for themselves if they wish to post-session.

We have focused our tips on facilitating learning, but there is another type of facilitation to consider: helping groups come to decisions or facilitating conversations. Sometimes we're asked to facilitate mediations between parties in conflict. By definition, these can't be planned and designed in detail, although careful consideration of sequence and the discussion's core questions can be pre-planned. We'd encourage you to read Chapter 20 (*Power of Listening*) and 19 (*Barriers to Collaboration*) as preparation for these sorts of facilitation.

One last tip: practice makes perfect. Make sure you gather feedback from your sessions. What did the participants enjoy? What did they get value from? What did they not get value from? What were their key takeaways? What would they like to see covered in addition to this session? The authors have built a successful business on the back of asking thousands upon thousands of participants for feedback and listening carefully to what they have said. Everything we do has been improved as a consequence.

TAKING ACTION

Growing Our Knowledge Sharing Skills

IF THIS IS AN expert role in which you believe you could add greater value, here are some high-level suggestions for actions to take:

▶ RUN A DEPLOYMENT TEST

We might read a book about Expertship, but will we actually act upon its contents? The authors may offer extra content on our portal, but will anyone ever go to that site and use the material? These are the questions that go to the central issue with any information sharing. Are people consuming it, and are they then deploying the knowledge as expected? The only way to find out is to run an audit. Some critical questions we might want to ask (and try and figure out how to answer) are:

- To what extent are the collateral, knowledge sessions, individual coaching sessions, workshops and other knowledge sharing activities I have been involved in delivering being deployed by those I have disseminated information to?
- What metrics can I build and monitor that will tell me whether the application of my expert knowledge strategy is actually working?
- Once I publish something, from whom do I seek feedback as to its usefulness and ease of application, and do I do this regularly enough?

▶ HABITUALIZE INCIDENTAL LEARNING

Encouraging teams of people to learn and create new knowledge is very much part of the role of a Master Expert. We might be producing new knowledge and insights ourselves, but it's our ability to motivate a wide group around us to also do so that makes us a knowledge creation champion. Here are some critical questions we might like to ask ourselves:

- Competitive advantage is all about constantly seeking to do things in a more productive way. To what extent is this part of my team's culture, and how do I make it so?
- Incidental learning happens for experts almost every day, but because we're so busy executing tasks or fixing problems, we never have time to share the information. How might I create an environment where these learnings get regularly shared?
- How often do I ask "What did I learn today?" Do I ask stakeholders "How could I have done this better for you?" at every opportunity? What other learning questions can I regularly ask?

▶ PRESENT OUR EXPERTISE TO DIVERSE GROUPS

The ability to explain things in simple but meaningful terms to diverse groups of stakeholders is a critical skill of a Master Expert. Some essential questions to ask ourselves:

- How well do I rate when I present? Do I challenge myself by asking for feedback anonymously at the end of presentations or training sessions (feedback forms)?
- Do I encourage robust feedback by asking colleagues to suggest at least two ways I could improve my presentation, or am I just looking for compliments?
- How often do I reflect on presentations that I have attended that engaged me? What did the presenter do that won me over? What techniques did they use? When did I last study up on how the best presenters build and then deliver their presentations?
- Attend conferences and study which speakers get good reviews and strong audience attention and respect. Which ones don't, and why?
- How well (and often) do I adapt my content and delivery based on the audience? Have I spent enough time thinking about what is in this presentation for them? How will I measure whether my presentation has been effective for this particular group of colleagues? What do I want them to think or do differently, and how will I measure this?

"A teacher is one who makes himself progressively unnecessary."

Thomas Carruthers

CHAPTER | 48 |

Becoming a Knowledge Coach

How might coaching be the key to experts building others' expertise and self-reliance, freeing more time to create long-term value?

IN THIS CHAPTER, WE WILL EXPLORE:

- What is coaching, and how might it be a useful skill and mindset for experts to master?
- What are the key skills involved in coaching, and why do they matter?
- What organizational and personal benefits might experts gain by deploying effective coaching as part of the execution of their role?

THE SECOND EXPERT ROLE in the Knowledge Transfer capability is **Knowledge Coach.** This set of behaviors relates to ensuring that colleagues understand and make best use of our specialist knowledge, and doing this in an engaging and effective manner. Sharing our knowledge is an important part of the process, but making sure it's understood, properly applied, and that our colleagues can use it with confidence to both their and the organization's maximum advantage is the next step. This is where being a knowledge coach comes in.

By using the term *coach*, we're describing a broad set of behaviors where the senior expert helps a wide range of stakeholders to develop their capability, from individuals in one-on-one conversations to groups of stakeholders in workshops and project meetings. Coaching is a process and a mindset, not a specific event.

The behaviors at each level of Expertship for this expert role of Knowledge Coach are described in Figure 48.1.

At immature levels, the expert will deploy a directive communication style. Technical knowledge will be communicated via confident assertion and will usually be focused on the *what*, not the *why*. Very little coaching goes on in this style of knowledge transfer. It comes across as similar to a teacher in a classroom talking to students. As a consequence, this "teaching" style of communication often leads to presentations that are unengaging and ineffective in terms of learning outcomes.

In contrast, the Master Expert always deploys a question-based, collaborative coaching style. There is a strong focus on the *why* to ensure others understand the business value and context. Deploying a coaching style leads to interactive and engaging sessions that are in demand and oversubscribed. People enjoy the sessions and learn a lot from them.

In our experience, moving to a coaching and collaborative style of working with stakeholders, particularly in the context of knowledge transfer, is one of the most challenging transitions an expert has to make. It's because coaching can be an unnatural style for many experts. Let's explore why.

> *"We need to believe something fundamental: that our objective with our stakeholders is to build independence and not dependence."*

Why Experts Find Coaching Difficult

LET'S CONSIDER WHY COACHING can, at first, feel unnatural and seem difficult to master.

Firstly, coaching requires the expert to take a hands-off approach rather than being "hands-on." Hands-on is what experts do. We get stuck in, solve problems and take an expedient approach. Time is money and we have lots of other things to do, so the shortest and quickest way to get this done or fix this outage is to either do it ourselves or tell someone precisely how to do it.

Coaching requires us to step back and ask questions. Instead of saying "I think I know what has happened here," we ask our coachee (the person who is being coached, whether they know it or not) "What do you think has happened here?"

Capability: KNOWLEDGE TRANSFER
Expert Role: KNOWLEDGE COACH

MASTER EXPERT

- Always deploys a question-based, collaborative coaching style.
- Shares the why to ensure others understand the business value.
- Proactively provides information sessions about domain knowledge to colleagues from outside the technical domain to assist with their understanding.
- Is actively sought out by a wide range of stakeholders to provide highly engaging, pragmatic, and effective training/ presentations, insights, coaching and mentoring.
- Coaches others toward increased self-reliance.

EXPERT

- Deploys a combination of "asking" and "telling" when coaching on technical knowledge to develop other technical experts.
- Provides pragmatic and effective training/presentations, particularly to less qualified technical colleagues. Shares the how to support capability development.

SPECIALIST

- Interacts from a learning perspective almost exclusively in the technical domain with technical colleagues.
- Shares the what (i.e., the tasks and goals) when training others.

- Deploys a directive, "telling" training style.
- Presentations are unengaging and lead to few effective learning outcomes.
- Frequently neglects "coaching opportunities."

DERAILING

FIGURE 48.1: Knowledge Coach Behaviors

And then comes the hard part: waiting patiently for the coachee to have a think about it and come up with an answer. The answer is unlikely to be right the first time—after all, it's taken us years to be able to diagnose such problems in milliseconds. So, coaching requires us to ask another question. "Okay, that is one possibility. What other things might have caused this problem?" Coaching requires us to step back, not judge the first answer, and leave it in play.

These behaviors don't come naturally to most experts. We're hired because we know stuff and can act fast. We typically think having a theoretical conversation with someone who clearly doesn't have a clue is a waste of time. We have to make a significant conceptual leap to accept that coaching is an important and appropriate approach. We need to believe something fundamental: that our objective with our stakeholders is to build independence, not dependence. As we've discussed before, if we're the only go-to person for a particular skill or knowledge bank, we'll never have peace, and we'll never be able to reach our full potential by adding ever-greater value to our organization. We'll be up to our necks in fixing routine issues every day, every week, for years on end.

The short-term objective is to fix the problem as fast as possible. This is the place where experts play. But the long-term objective, the place where Master Experts play, is to build the confidence and skills of our colleagues so they can fix the problem *themselves*. Independence, not dependence. You don't give them the day's catch; you teach them to fish. This requires a more time-consuming learning curve, but you're *taking time to save time*.

> *"There are opportunities for coaching
> all around us every day."*

The second reason experts find coaching difficult is that, in many expert circles, coaching has a bad name. The term has acquired a number of different connotations—some helpful, others not so much. In many organizations, a statement like "she would benefit from some coaching" typically means "a manager should have a word with her and improve her attitude or performance."

In this context, coaching is viewed as a remedial activity, an intervention in which the coachee is the unwitting recipient of some unsolicited direction. But there's also another meaning. Coaching can mean a facilitated process of a well-intentioned and skilled individual aiding the growth of another. These days, most coaches are deployed to help people reach the next level of capability, not as a fix. And it's definitely in this context that we promote the Master Expert as a master coach. But note that being a master coach also means that you have to point out when someone has erred; however, there are both effective and ineffective ways to do this.

The third reason experts find coaching difficult is probably the most difficult to overcome: most experts have had little experience of being coached. This means most of us have little understanding or experience of how to do it well. To build independence among key stakeholders, you need to coach and not instruct. In the next few pages, we provide an overview of an effective coaching technique.

In summary, although coaching may appear, on the surface, to require more time, the investment should pay off in the long run.

We'll build others' capability, making them increasingly self-reliant, especially if the task in question isn't the best use of our time, energy and expertise. As a result, we gain the time and freedom to focus on making higher value contributions.

Coaching Opportunities: The Expert Context

HOW DOES COACHING PLAY out in the life of an expert? We might assume that by its nature, coaching is delivered in a pre-organized session, with two people facing one another as a very formal, structured conversation takes place. As Figure 48.2 describes, the reality is that there are opportunities for coaching all around us every day, and most of them are informal rather than formal.

The chart isn't a comprehensive list, but we're sure that by thinking about a typical week, most experts could customize it to describe many of their coaching opportunities.

The transfer of skills and knowledge are two obvious opportunities to use coaching techniques to build our colleagues' confidence and capability. These opportunities might take the form of a planned event, like a workshop, for example, introducing some new cybersecurity rules and materials to help colleagues spot rogue emails before opening them. Or perhaps it could be helping a colleague find a key document on the intranet using the question technique ("Where do you think it's most likely to be filed, and why?") so that the next time they try to find a document, they can remember the logic of how these files are organized and stored.

The first example might take an hour to deliver and several hours to plan and prepare. The second example might take less than two minutes. They are both valuable coaching opportunities for experts.

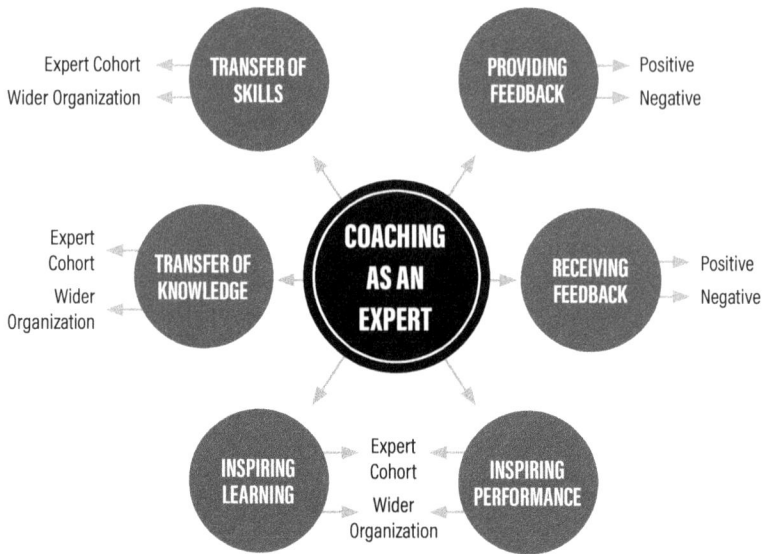

FIGURE 48.2: Coaching Opportunities as an Expert

Inspiring learning and inspiring performance are also opportunities for deploying coaching skills. We might, for example, decide to deploy the telling approach and tell a junior colleague that he/she must learn the XYZ protocol. This instruction from a senior expert may or may not be welcomed by our junior colleague. They may or may not take this advice. It may be one of many such edicts we've communicated to them in the last few months.

Alternatively, we could take the questioning (coaching) approach. We could ask a series of questions. "How much do you know about the XYZ protocol? Why do you think we use it? To what extent, as you progress as an expert here, do you think that mastering the XYZ protocol would be helpful? What do you think might be the best way of going about mastering it? What help would you need, and from whom? When do you think would be a good time to start this learning? How can I help?"

This coaching approach gets our junior colleague to do all the heavy lifting. They'll need to think hard about the importance of mastering the XYZ protocol, how they might go about it, how urgent it is, and whose help they will need. In this conversation, as the senior expert, we're not only *coaching* our junior colleague toward committing to a learning outcome, we're also exposing them to a series of questions they can use again and again to help them assess the importance and urgency of key learning outcomes. One result is certain: if our junior colleague decides to prioritize the mastery of the XYZ protocol, they're much more likely to reach the objective because it was *their* decision. They know why they're doing it and what's in it for them.

Conceptually, in coaching, this is called *ownership*. The likelihood of them carrying through with the learning is consequently much higher.

What did it cost us? Five or six intelligent questions.

So, inspiration is possible via coaching. By asking these questions, the likelihood is that, as an expert coach, we've inspired our junior colleague into action, as opposed to having told them in a perfunctory fashion to learn something. The same principles apply to inspiring performance.

Providing feedback, whether positive or negative, is another coaching opportunity. In the case of negative feedback, we could choose to simply tell our colleague that they've done something wrong and point out the right way to do it. This would take perhaps a minute.

> *"Providing feedback is a particularly important component of knowledge transfer, and a critically important coaching technique."*

Or we could ask, via the question technique, why they chose to do the activity in the way they did. We could ask them how time-consuming it was and whether the end result was robust. Then we could ask them to think of other ways they might have completed the task. Would any of these alternative approaches have been easier, safer or quicker? This coaching interaction might take ten minutes, which is five times as long, but it will contain lessons that will last forever because our colleague has had to do the thinking. This is building independence rather than just passively complying with the instruction of an expert, not knowing why, not having to think about why, learning nothing, and being likely to make the same mistake again.

If we consider how we've learned what we know today, many of the most complex things we've learned were mastered by doing them ourselves—by practicing, experimenting and thinking rather than just slavishly following instructions.

> *"Many experts are introverted by nature. They're wary of conflict and tend to avoid it if they can."*

A handy guide that allows us to check whether we're coaching or telling is described in Figure 48.3.

Capability: **KNOWLEDGE TRANSFER**
Are You Really Coaching?

COACHING IS NOT ...

- Telling someone how to do something.
- Giving instructions.
- Laying down guidelines on how to accomplish a task.
- Avoiding giving feedback.
- Limiting options to be explored.

COACHING CAN BE ...

- **Proactive** – which identifies opportunities for people to grow and extend their skills.
- **Reactive** – which focuses on getting people back up to speed when they have fallen behind.

A GREAT COACH ...

- Has empathy.
- Is willing to take risks.
- Has a commitment to developing others and themselves.
- Shows patience.
- Demonstrates understanding of when to challenge and when to support.
- Recognizes effort, contributions, achievements and progress.
- Helps people track their own progress.
- Believes in openness and sharing.
- Establishes a climate of trust that encourages others to seek coaching.
- Does not take over.

FIGURE 48.3: Are We Really Coaching?

The Power of (Ineffective) Feedback

PROVIDING FEEDBACK IS A particularly important component of knowledge transfer and an extremely useful coaching skill. Our experience of how effective experts are at giving feedback is mixed. We've found experts are either very direct or very avoidant. And yet, without feedback, few of the people we're hoping to upskill can learn effectively.

Let's take the direct example first.

Alice, a corporate lawyer, works for a large public sector organization, which means it's bound by a whole range of rules and regulations about what it can and can't do. The sales team has asked Alice to review a contract. In a meeting to explain the changes Alice feels need to be made to the contract so it aligns with corporate governance rules, Mark, a sales director, suggests rewording a particular clause to make it less specific. Alice is blunt and brutal. "No, you can't do that," she says. As she moves on to the next clause, Mark leans back in his chair, irritated by a more junior member of the organization rebuffing him in such a direct manner.

Alice is, of course, right. The suggestion Mark made would have been difficult to enforce in the future and was therefore impractical. It was also against organizational rules and opened the organization up to material risk. It was a definite no. Alice knew the law and corporate governance rules, and as a consequence, she felt very sure indeed of her ground. In this scenario, she felt comfortable giving very direct feedback.

This is a dynamic we see play out regularly. The more certain of their ground the expert is, the more likely it is that the feedback will be delivered with brutal honesty. As no doubt Alice in the example would have, many experts will argue that she was just trying to save everyone's time. There's no point in having a debate about something that is a clear non-starter.

"Trust me," Alice is saying to the room. "I'm the expert." Another expert we recently worked with described to us how he tends to put people down in meetings for being uninformed. "Have you actually read the law?" he asks them, no doubt with an icy look.

Alice has, unfortunately, delivered her message so bluntly that she has inadvertently put Mark offside. This might not matter much in this meeting, but it's likely to have an impact on their stakeholder relationship.

In contrast, given that many experts are introverted by nature, they're wary of conflict and tend to avoid it if they can, particularly if they are not certain they possess all the relevant facts and insights. In these instances, they tend to hint indirectly at changes they might want to see.

Later in the meeting, Alice came to a clause that contained the level of volume discounts proposed for the client. Alice was not an expert in sales and didn't understand the underlying commercial issues involved with offering different magnitudes of discounts. But Mark was only one of the sales directors she dealt with in the organization, and she'd seen plenty of these contracts before. From her perspective, the discounts looked much higher than those being offered to other clients. She hesitated and then asked, "Are these discounts correct? They seem very high?"

> *"The principle here is courage and consideration."*

Mark's response was immediate. "Why don't you stick to law and leave the commercial side to us." Mark was as direct as Alice had been. It was, after all, his area of expertise. As a fellow expert, Alice left her misgivings unsaid, did not give Mark the reason behind her question, and the meeting moved on.

Well, he's been warned, Alice thought. And later, when it turned out the contract was massively unprofitable for the organization, Alice had the luxury of thinking *I tried to say something but he wouldn't listen.* Listen to what? Alice had valuable information that wasn't communicated.

Imagine this scene replayed.

Mark: "What about this clause. Could we reword it so it's less specific?"

Alice: "Well, we could, but that would make it ambiguous. How might that ambiguity play out for us, or for the client?"

Mark: "Well, it would give us some wriggle room, which would be great. It would mean we could increase prices downstream. But it would also mean the client could ask for a discount downstream as well."

Alice: "I think finance is likely to want a definite price on the value of the contract for the shareholders, as well, especially given the size of this deal. I'm not sure the CFO would want that ambiguity in there. What do you think?"

Mark: "I agree. Let's leave it as it is and see if the client pushes back."

And later …

Alice: "Are these discounts correct? They seem very high?"

Mark: "High? Why do you say that?"

Alice: "I only ask because on other recent contracts, the highest I've seen us offer as a discount has been 9 percent. At 15 percent, these looked high to me. But this is your area; I'm just sharing what I've seen elsewhere."

Mark: "I only see what discounts we've historically offered in this division. I'll check around with other sales directors to see if we've been too generous. Thank you."

The principle being described here is courage *and* consideration. The key is to summon the appropriate amounts of courage (the willingness to confront) and a balancing amount of consideration (the art of challenging gracefully) so that stating our observations is genuinely appreciated.

Courage involves a willingness to risk getting the feedback recipient offside, to represent our opinion without compromise, to challenge, and to insist that our boundaries or needs are recognized and respected.

Without being prepared to fully show up, it's pointless to get frustrated or complain that someone isn't behaving as they should. To provoke a change in someone else's behavior or attitude, we need to be prepared to take a stand and to say it like it is.

> *"Given that conversations can get off track*
> *very easily, using a template to plan and*
> *execute conversations is helpful."*

But that forcefulness needs to be tempered with consideration. We need to be aware that we're probably dealing with a person whose emotional response to the feedback will likely have more to do with their decision to accept or reject it than their rational brain. So, the message will be most effectively delivered by balancing these two attributes: courage and consideration.

Too much courage with too little consideration and the message gets lost because the mode of delivery feels too hostile. It will provoke a defensive reflex. The other person will feel harshly judged.

Too much consideration with too little courage and the person may not even realize that their behavior or attitude is viewed as problematic and in need of changing.

Coaching: Using the I-GRROW Model

IF THESE ARE THE types of coaching interactions we wish to have with our stakeholders, then what is best practice in terms of what happens in the conversation?

Let's introduce one of the models that many experts have told us positively revolutionized the way they plan and execute conversations and meetings: the I-GRROW model (see Figure 48.4). As we have seen with the earlier example featuring Alice and Mark, conversations can get off track very easily, so having a template to plan and execute conversations is helpful.

For planning, the model helps us imagine how the conversation might progress, and clarifies our motivations (intent) and purpose (goals). It helps us think about what facts the other party may know (their reality), facts we know (our reality), and also helps us contemplate all of the options for action or problem solving.

When we're actually having the conversation, the model helps us navigate it and acts as a checking mechanism in case a key stage has been missed. As experts, we might be very quick to state the facts as we see them but forget to ask what facts the other party is seeing (their reality). Or, halfway through the conversation, we might realize we failed to properly communicate our motivation for having the conversation (intent: "I am trying to help") or agree the goal of the conversation.

By having the I-GRROW model in the back of our minds, or even sketched on a sheet of paper in front of us, we can check in and see if we have covered steps 1 to 4, which lay the basis for an effective conversation. We need to have covered steps 1 to 4 before getting on to steps 5 and 6.

Capability: **KNOWLEDGE TRANSFER**
The I-GRROW Model

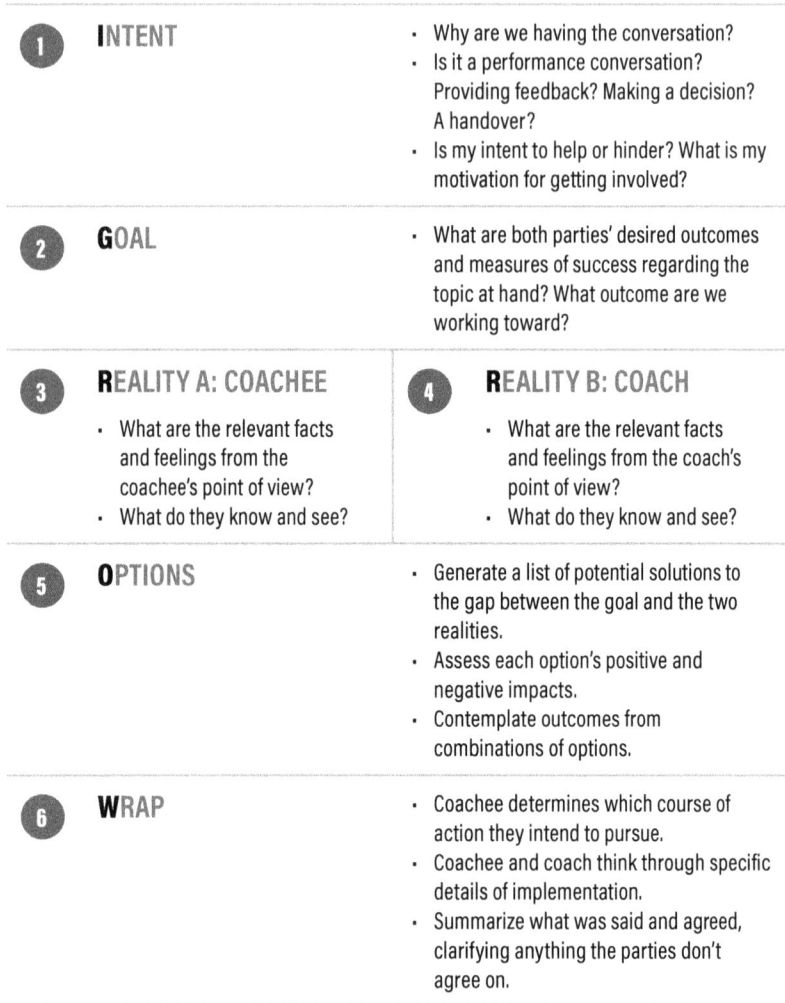

1	**I**NTENT	• Why are we having the conversation? • Is it a performance conversation? Providing feedback? Making a decision? A handover? • Is my intent to help or hinder? What is my motivation for getting involved?
2	**G**OAL	• What are both parties' desired outcomes and measures of success regarding the topic at hand? What outcome are we working toward?

3	**R**EALITY A: COACHEE	**4**	**R**EALITY B: COACH
	• What are the relevant facts and feelings from the coachee's point of view? • What do they know and see?		• What are the relevant facts and feelings from the coach's point of view? • What do they know and see?

5	**O**PTIONS	• Generate a list of potential solutions to the gap between the goal and the two realities. • Assess each option's positive and negative impacts. • Contemplate outcomes from combinations of options.
6	**W**RAP	• Coachee determines which course of action they intend to pursue. • Coachee and coach think through specific details of implementation. • Summarize what was said and agreed, clarifying anything the parties don't agree on.

FIGURE 48.4: The I-GRROW Model

Intent

SOME READERS MAY BE familiar with the GROW model, which Sir John Whitmore introduced in his 1992 book *Coaching for Performance* (still an outstanding book). The GROW model has become a widely used standard structure for coaching conversations globally.

The authors have had the temerity to build on Sir John's model. One change is adding *intent*, and another is adding a second "R."

> *"We believe that stating your intention—and making sure your intention is pure—is particularly important for experts."*

By intent, we mean our motivation for having the conversation. Intention is different from a goal, which is a concrete outcome that can be measured. During childhood, we spent our days being told not to do things by our parents, which made us believe their intent was to make our lives as boring and miserable as possible. Of course, our parents' main intent—well, in most cases—was to keep us safe and healthy. If our parents had started every conversation by stating this intent, then perhaps we would've listened to their instructions more often.

As an expert, if we want to give advice to a more junior colleague, we need to ask ourselves why we're doing so. Is it because that junior expert is approaching a task differently from how we might approach it? In this case, our intent is to ask them to comply with established processes. Is the junior colleague approaching a task in a way we've approached it many times and failed?

In this case, our intent might be to share our experience of that approach or possibly save our junior colleague time. Let's, for a moment, imagine ourselves as that junior colleague. We can see from understanding the two different intentions in this example that we're likely to respond differently to the senior expert's input because we now know what their intent is. Many junior experts we know would consider the latter intent as being helpful and collegiate, and the former intent as getting in the way of progress.

Over the years, as we've watched thousands of leaders and experts execute simulated conversations (roleplaying), we've seen so many conversations crash and burn because the leader or expert has a positive intention, but the other party assumed their intention was negative (being critical, admonishing, personal and so on).

We believe that stating your intention—and making sure your intention is pure—is particularly important for experts. We often provide feedback, input and advice to people who don't report to us, so they don't have to do what we suggest or even listen to what we have to say. Making sure that we clarify our professional intent upfront helps to lubricate the early part of the conversation and reduce the defensiveness of the person we're talking to.

Goal

DEFINING THE GOAL OF the conversation (the desired outcome) is an obvious step in planning a conversation, but, over the years, we've found that many experts struggle to define an appropriate goal. In Figure 48.5, we describe moving from *transactional* to *tactical* to *strategic* through the idea of altitude. The concept is that the higher we are, the further we can see. The model works like this:

- 1,000 feet describes the expert's thinking as being almost on the ground. There is no medium- or long-range visibility. It's simply head down, doing very low-level transactional thinking.
- At 30,000 feet, we can see a reasonable distance, and we're looking into the near future. We're being tactical (medium-term thinking).
- At above 50,000 feet, we're being more strategic (that is, very long term) in our thinking.

> *"Depending on the goal, the conversation*
> *will be entirely different."*

In our experience, we see experts setting goals for conversations or coaching discussions that are far too close to the ground. For example, in our programs, your task is to talk to a junior colleague who doesn't report to you about the fact that they used to come in early and leave late, but now they are arriving late and going home early. This impacts the work they need to do for you, so you've made the call to have a conversation with them. What's your objective? You have several choices:

- Transactional: the goal is to get the colleague to turn up to work on time and not leave early. This is compliance. *Drone* level: 3,000 feet.
- Tactical: the goal is to understand what has generated the change in behavior in our colleague and see if the problem can be addressed. We're seeing their timekeeping as a symptom of the real problem. *Airliner* level: 40,000 feet.
- Strategic: the goal is to re-motivate and re-engage this colleague so they recover their long-term commitment to their work and the organization, and so they can have the stellar career once predicted for them. *Spy plane* level: 70,000 feet.

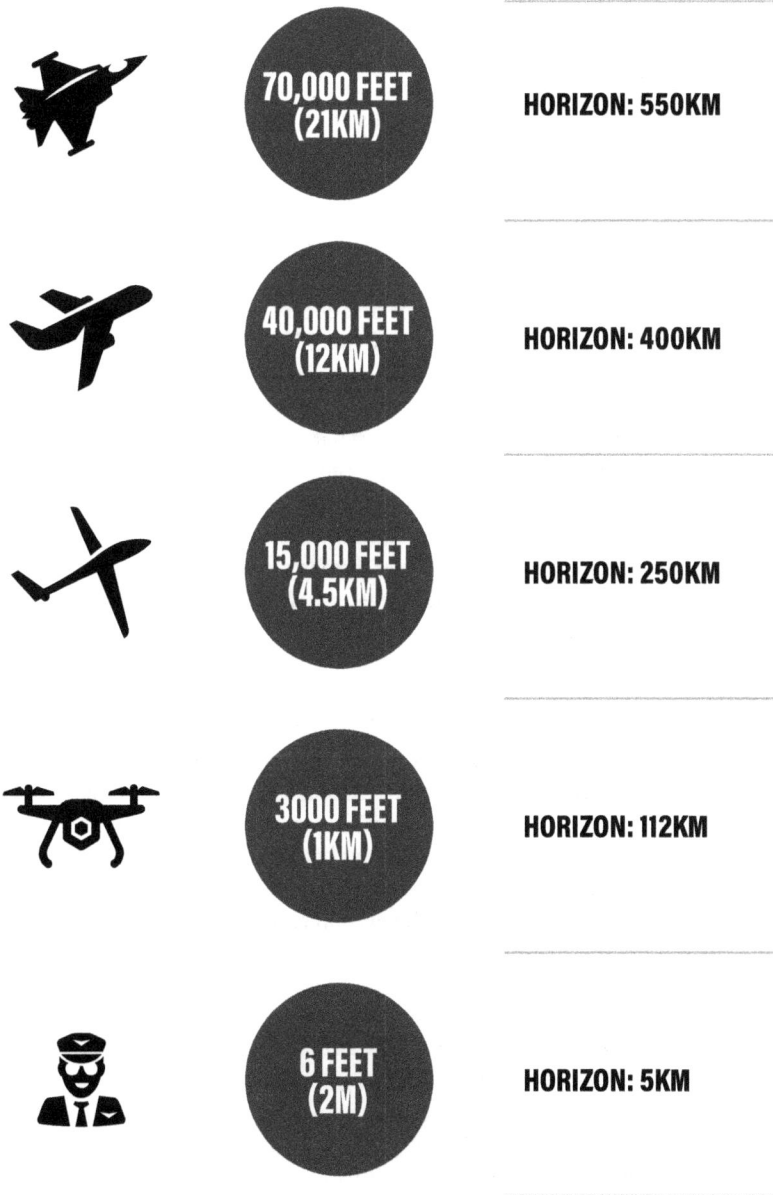

70,000 FEET (21KM) — HORIZON: 550KM

40,000 FEET (12KM) — HORIZON: 400KM

15,000 FEET (4.5KM) — HORIZON: 250KM

3000 FEET (1KM) — HORIZON: 112KM

6 FEET (2M) — HORIZON: 5KM

FIGURE 48.5: The Altitude Model

Depending on the goal, our approach to the conversation—the intent we communicate, the questions we ask throughout the conversation, and our tone—will be completely different.

If we took a transactional approach, we'd probably be short, sharp and to the point. We'd ask closed questions that are possibly challenging and aggressive in tone, and we'd demand compliance.

If we took a tactical approach, we'd take longer and ask more open questions. We'd be neutral or positively supportive, but we'd still be addressing an issue (lateness), so the likelihood of an initially defensive response from our colleague would still be high.

If we took a strategic approach, our first question might be "Where do you see yourself professionally in two years' time?" In this type of conversation, the lateness that sparked our need to have the conversation may never be mentioned. The conversation will revolve around the aspirations of our colleague, how they think they're doing, what they need to do to reach those career goals, how we can help, and what types of behavior might get in the way of achieving these goals (for example, turning up late to work).

Very often, we see experts take a transactional or tactical approach to setting goals for conversations. Master Experts operate consistently at the strategic level, contemplating the long-term impacts and implications of policy, action, behaviors and motivations.

Reality

IN WHITMORE'S ORIGINAL MODEL, there was just one "R," which stands for reality, but we've added a second. This stage is all about finding out the current state of play—the real situation. As an example, the goal might be for us to be a market leader. The reality is that we're running third. The goal might be to be operating at Master Expert level. The reality is that we're only doing so in a few of the nine Expertship capabilities, and in at least one capability, we're operating at the specialist level.

> *"A strident statement of the expert's reality tended to shut down the other party."*

So, the question is: What is the reality of the current situation?

We've found it helpful to have two "Rs"—one for us and one for the other party in the conversation. In a corporate negotiation, this might be the client or a collaborative external partner. We've also structured the model so that establishing the other party's reality comes first, which is the order we recommend. In some complex conversations, there might be three or four parties involved, and therefore three or four realities to explore.

Referencing the thousands of conversations we've witnessed, we realized that a strident statement of the expert's reality tended to shut down the other party. Or worse, it started an argument from which the conversation, and sometimes the relationship, could not easily recover. In any sort of personal one-to-one coaching or more general business conversation, enquiring after the wellbeing of others first seems to be the accepted norm. When meeting people, we tend to ask "How are you?" We rarely say "Hello, I'm really fine. I just got promoted, I'm building a new house, and I have a birthday coming up—and how are you?"

The Master Expert will always ask about the other reality first because it creates a strategic advantage. Knowing what data the other party has used to come to their point of view helps us consider (a) if they have all the facts, (b) if they have all the facts, have they interpreted them differently than we have, and (c) if they have facts we don't have that perhaps we need to take into consideration.

To hark back to our example about timekeeping, if we go strategic and ask "How are you, and what do you aspire to be in two years?" and get the answer "I'm in a bad way. I've put all my career aspirations on hold because one of my children is really ill," then we can see how putting the other party's reality before our own can be a conversation-saver. Suddenly, in the light of this information, we need to offer time off to our junior colleague, not attack them for being 15 minutes late every morning.

> *"Extracting a list of possible solutions from colleagues is often more difficult than we might think."*

On a broader note, as we say to the experts we work with in our programs, it's just technique. Master the technique, such as leveraging the I-GRROW model, and you'll be amazed at the difference it makes to your effectiveness.

One final point on reality. Very often, we enter into the conversation without a clue about the other party's reality. For these situations, we can start to build up a set of killer questions that we can ask in order to find out, and these can, of course, be pre-planned. We talk in detail about discovery questions in Chapter 37, *Solutioning*.

Once we have firmly established an agreement on what our two realities are, it's not necessary to agree with each other's viewpoints. However, it is necessary to know what that is and, if at all possible, understand it. Then we're ready to move on to finding a solution.

Options

IN THE VERY BEST coaching conversations, the parties develop a comprehensive list of what *might* be done to address the issue or solve the problem. Ideally, the coach asks the coachee to come up with suggestions. As a rule, the coach, whether we're an expert or not, is not supposed to ask leading questions and make suggestions. In order to avoid doing so, we might want to think about what our list of options would look like and then consider what questions, which aren't leading, we might ask to put the idea in the coachee's head.

Once the coachee has generated a number of options, there's usually little harm in volunteering a couple of one's own ideas. But if this is done before they've exhausted their thinking, there's a risk that they'll believe you're pushing those solutions and that you still retain ultimate ownership of the issues being discussed. Teasing out a list of possible solutions from colleagues is often more difficult than we might think. Generally, colleagues can only produce one or two solutions, and these are likely to be the most obvious or the most recently deployed solutions. But developing a comprehensive list is advised as the solution is usually three-quarters of option C and one-quarter of option F.

These combined solutions end up being far more effective than simply doing the first thing the colleague thought of. Once the list is formed, each option is reviewed for positive and negative impacts, and then a decision must be made as to which action will be taken, by whom, why, and when.

Wrap

THE FINAL STAGE IS the Wrap stage, where we decide on an action, document the decision and the responsibilities, and then check back with the goal of the meeting to see whether this has been achieved or not. Many coaches exchange the word *Wrap* for *Will*. What *will* we do as a consequence of this conversation?

Our experience tells us that motivated experts can quickly master the I-GRROW model and start using it to plan and execute critical conversations. It's easy to apply this model to simple decision-making and to understanding and resolving roadblocks in projects. It's just a *technique*, but it's a powerful one.

Death by PowerPoint

PART OF THE SKILLS of a knowledge coach, someone who is expert at sharing knowledge widely and effectively across the organization, is being able to present well. Our experience of subject matter experts' capabilities when it comes to making impactful presentations is varied:

- A high proportion of experts dislike public speaking and presenting to large groups. In fact, many tell us it's their worst nightmare. Although there are some experts who love the sound of their own voice and fail to notice that their audience lost attention early on in their diatribe.
- Many presentations from top subject matter experts are difficult to understand because experts tend to go into too much detail, make assumptions about the audience's knowledge, or are using the occasion to prove how smart they are. None of these mistakes result in effective knowledge transfer.
- Many experts have never really had any training on presentation skills, which is evident in the way they present.

Experts should be reasonably proficient at giving presentations. Whether it's presenting a critical plan or recommendation to the executive team or helping a professional audience at an industry conference raise their professional standards, experts need to be able to present competently. In the Expertship model, we describe the Master Expert level of this capability as being actively sought out by a wide range of stakeholders to provide highly engaging, pragmatic and effective training and presentations. In short, they want us back. And soon.

We offer a very short overview of presentation skills for experts in the Appendices of this book. More importantly, the concepts described in the Value Domain chapters (Chapters 26 to 37) offer huge value when it comes to how deciding what to say, how to say it, and how to connect your comments with the strategic intent of your organization by using language tailored to the audience.

There are many resources available for making good presentations. These address the topic far better than we could do here. For those who feel ill at the thought of giving a presentation to a large number of important stakeholders, we encourage you to seek out these resources and use them.

TAKING ACTION

Growing Our Knowledge Coach Skills

IF THIS IS AN expert role in which you believe you could add greater value, here are some high-level suggestions for actions to take:

▶ TAKE A COACHING APPROACH TO KNOWLEDGE AND SKILLS DISSEMINATION

The best way to hone your coaching skills is ask yourself some questions:

- To what extent do I need to practice the "ask, not tell" mantra of coaching, and who might be a safe and suitable candidate for my first pilot coaching assignment?
- How will I use the I-GRROW model to plan my questions and remind myself to listen to the answers?
- What typical situations, either current or historical, can I leverage to bring to life expert challenges that will form the basis of excellent "what would you do" coaching sessions?
- How will I measure the success of the intervention, and what time frame am I going to give myself?

▶ DEVELOP A CAPABILITY TRANSFER WISH-LIST

Delegating activities and tasks to others is just a theoretical exercise until we've made a sensible plan for what we want to transfer, why, to whom, and how we're going to do it. Some questions we might like to ask ourselves:

- What capabilities or knowledge would I like to make available to others?
- How did I acquire my level of expertise? Was it by reading books or manuals? Experimentation, practice, trial and error? Perhaps my knowledge transfer methodologies ought to replicate what I know works.
- To what extent do I believe others—those in my knowledge transfer target group—will necessarily learn in precisely the same way as I did?
- How will I engender the learner's positive engagement with the capability or knowledge being acquired? What's in it for them? What felt issues does the new knowledge or skill resolve? What real-world advantages does the new knowledge or skill offer to the learner?
- How clear am I on the gap between current knowledge, skills and activity levels and the desired levels? What impact do these have on the organization?
- Given that the knowledge uplift is usually to enable new behaviors, to what extent will I be able to ensure that the learner has an opportunity to actually practice utilizing the knowledge or skills so that the likelihood of real-world application is increased?
- What tools will I need to deploy to help the learning occur (e.g., the I-GRROW model)?

CHAPTER | 49 |

Building a Talent Factory

What is our role in building expert talent across our organization? How do we identify and grow those with potential?

IN THIS CHAPTER, WE WILL EXPLORE:

- Is developing expert talent part of a typical expert's job description? What value can experts add in the area?
- How do we spot potential? What are the signs and symbols we should look for?
- What is the difference between coaching and mentoring?

THE THIRD EXPERT ROLE in the knowledge transfer capability is **Talent Developer**. This set of behaviors ensures both we and our colleagues are engaged in continuous learning and are actively identifying future talent and supporting their development.

The behaviors at each level of Expertship for this expert role are described in Figure 49.1.

At an immature level, an expert shows little interest in and spends no time on helping emerging technical talent develop. If the expert is derailing, they may consider developing talent a threat to their status and employment.

Capability: KNOWLEDGE TRANSFER
Expert Role: TALENT DEVELOPER

MASTER EXPERT

- Owns their own personal growth plan and makes continuous professional development a priority.
- Oversees junior colleagues' personal growth plans and provides timely feedback to support execution.
- Creates challenging and stretch opportunities for colleagues that are aligned with their career goals.
- Actively identifies and prepares a successor.
- Actively contributes to the nurturing and growth of future talent.

EXPERT

- Owns their own personal growth plan and makes continuous professional development a priority.
- Ensures more junior colleagues have personal growth plans and provides timely feedback to support execution.

SPECIALIST

- Owns their own personal growth plan and makes continuous professional development a priority.

- Shows little interest in, and spends no time on, helping emerging technical talent develop.
- Considers developing talent a threat to their status and employment.
- Competes to be the smartest "in the room."

DERAILING

FIGURE 49.1: Talent Developer Behaviors

In comparison, at Master Expert level, experts actively identify and help grow future talent and successors. They typically own their own Personal Growth Plans and make continuous professional development a priority. Their learning focus is visible to the rest of their technical cohort and stakeholders. They informally oversee junior colleagues' Personal Growth Plans and provide feedback to support execution. Master Experts take the time to create challenging and stretch opportunities for colleagues that are aligned with their career goals and assist in their professional growth.

Is Talent Development Really My Job?

IN OUR YEARS OF working with experts, it's become quite clear that many hold a range of beliefs and attitudes contrary to our view of what makes a Master Expert when it comes to being a talent developer.

We could summarize these views as follows:

- Many experts believe being a talent developer is not their job. The authors argue it's a core responsibility that helps experts add value in many ways.
- Many experts believe developing new talent carries with it the inherent risk that we'll be training cheaper successors. The authors argue that if we don't train junior people, we won't create the space we need to deliver a higher level of value.
- Many experts believe that they aren't any good at training. This may be true, but if we feel that it's important, we'll make the effort to master it. The authors have seen this argument used as an excuse to avoid responsibility.
- Many experts believe they don't have the time to train someone, even if they wanted to. The authors argue that time constraint is often of our own making. We haven't trained up junior staff to do the mundane stuff that is holding us back from more senior and more interesting work, which is precisely the reason we don't have time to train successors. The proverbial Catch-22.

> *"We encourage experts to consider talent development an opportunity rather than an obligation."*

By taking on the role of talent developer, we can:

- Increase the general capability levels within the organization in a particular area of expertise.

- Increase the job satisfaction of those who are gaining new skills by giving them the opportunity to tackle fresh challenges and assume greater levels of responsibility.
- Increase our own job satisfaction by actively helping others grow and freeing up our own bandwidth for work that requires higher order skills (and the more appropriate use of our expertise and experience).
- Increase our own effectiveness by focusing on the highest value contributions, confident in the knowledge that other matters aren't being neglected.

We accept that the notion of experts spending time developing other experts is a contentious point. What we're proposing here is that we take some responsibility for developing talent, even if those individuals don't report to us. Generally, experts are not directly accountable for managing talent, setting performance expectations, assessing the performance of talent, working on their development plans, or succession planning. (We might even have actively avoided management positions so we wouldn't need to do these tasks.) We have no formal authority, so there's no reason for people to listen to us or accept our input. In fact, they might consider any such attempt by us to be a form of intrusion.

But we encourage experts to view talent development as more of an opportunity than an obligation. There's no reason why we can't propose to the formal leaders (to whom the relevant others report) that we assist them in shaping the performance expectations for various roles, if there's a need or value in seeing increased competent execution of pertinent skills.

> *"If we invest time, we must ensure our trainees have potential."*

In fact, we'd argue it might be very much in the expert's interests (as well as the organization's) to reduce the risk of single-point sensitivity, where the organization and its stakeholders might be left high and dry in the event of the expert leaving the organization for any reason.

The importance of building a talent factory is a common strategic objective for many of the world's fastest growing and influential organizations. And we often find that senior experts are engaged at the center of such initiatives.

The Expert Talent Continuum

IN THE PAST, IT was difficult to contemplate what development our more junior colleagues might need and how we could assist them with these aspirations. But today, experts have a range of tools that make this far easier, less time-consuming, and a more effective use of our time. Remember, we're trying to make sure we have capable experts coming on stream. We want them to be able to pick up some of our more foundational work because, for them, it's advancement.

The first of these tools is the knowledge we have as senior experts. We've been using our knowledge to help more junior colleagues for years, but if we can organize, structure and document this knowledge to make it more accessible without our input, we're winning the battle to reduce disruptions to our more important work.

We would strongly recommend using more junior colleagues to organize all this knowledge and create versions for less technical groups of stakeholders. It's directly in their interests to be involved in this work.

The second of these tools is the Expertship model, which is described in detail throughout this book. The Expertship model provides an ideal framework for experts to use to assess and convey where colleagues sit in terms of their capability on the path to being a high-value expert, and what type of development they need to address any shortfalls or gaps. Indeed, this whole book acts as an assessment and guide for development.

The third set of tools available today are a variety of 360-degree multi-rater surveys that gather feedback for experts on their overall effectiveness, as perceived by their managers, their peers, and their various stakeholder groups. Expertunity offers such a tool. It's called *Expertship360* and it has been used by a rapidly growing number of experts to assess their current level of Expertship.

The fourth tool is a meaningful and actionable Personal Growth Plan. We discuss how to build such a plan in detail in the next chapter.

Who Has Potential, and Who Doesn't?

IT'S CRITICAL THAT THE effort we're expending in building the capability of colleagues, particularly junior experts in our domain, produces results. Are the people we're investing time and effort into worth it? Do they have what it takes to grow quickly and be the assistance and stress relief we need?

> *"Potential is a combination of aspiration, ability and engagement."*

The question we're really asking here is: *do they have potential?* As senior experts, we really don't have time to invest in colleagues who are not motivated, not cognitively capable, or will merely pick up a few things from us and then leave the building. Several years ago, a management research organization, The Corporate Executive Board, now part of Gartner Inc., came up with what is widely accepted as a very robust definition of potential. It's graphically represented in Figure 49.2.

As you can see, potential in this model is defined as a combination of aspiration, ability and engagement. Someone who has high potential has all three. These are the colleagues we hope to find and are worth investing in.

Aspiration deals with whether our colleague wishes to progress, either via reputation or promotion, and is willing to invest time and energy in their own development (self-improvement). If they lack such motivation and drive, we would be wise to leave them out of our coaching plans.

Ability deals with whether our colleague has the innate intelligence and the learned capabilities of technical knowledge, enterprise skills, emotional intelligence, and interpersonal skills to learn quickly and be able to deploy effectively. If they don't, we should probably deprioritize the time we're willing to invest in them.

Engagement deals with whether our colleagues are committed to staying with the organization and working hard so that both we, as senior experts, and our organization will see the fruits of our investment. Engagement can quickly increase and quickly decrease, but we may have the ability to re-engage disenchanted junior experts simply by investing in some learning time with them.

As a way of understanding the model, it's useful to consider our own employment histories and the mood swings we've encountered. We've all probably felt very engaged at times, especially when we're doing really interesting work for capable and respectful managers. And we've all probably felt the opposite at other times.

We've all aspired to grow in influence, perhaps via promotion, and also had times when we've seen the pressure more senior managers are under and decided we want no part of that dynamic. It's also instructive for us to consider what influences have changed our levels of aspiration and engagement, and to what extent we can make a difference in these areas to our colleagues.

Colleagues with good potential are harder to spot than we might think, and there are some red herrings to be wary of. Figure 49.3 describes the three classic profiles of colleagues we've probably all experienced. Maybe we've even been these people at some stage.

Capability: **KNOWLEDGE TRANSFER**
Talent Spotting: What is Potential?

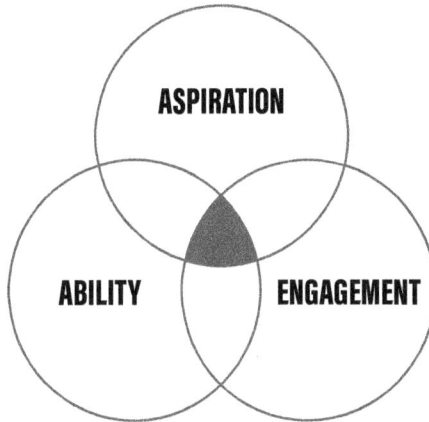

ASPIRATION

ABILITY   ENGAGEMENT

ASPIRATION
The extent to which a colleague wants or desires:
- Prestige and recognition in the organization
- Advancement and influence
- Financial rewards
- Work-life balance
- Overall job enjoyment

ABILITY
A combination of the innate characteristics and learned skills that a colleague uses to carry out his/her day-to-day work: Innate characteristics
- Mental/cognitive agility
  - Learned skills
- Technical/functional skills
- Emotional intelligence
- Interpersonal skills

ENGAGEMENT
Engagement consists of four elements:
- Emotional commitment – the value and belief they have in the organization
- Rational commitment – the belief that it is in their self-interest to stay in the organization
- Discretionary effort – colleagues' willingness to go above and beyond the call of duty
- Intent to stay – colleague's desire to stay

FIGURE 49.2: What is potential?

Capability: **KNOWLEDGE TRANSFER**

Talent Spotting: Which are they?

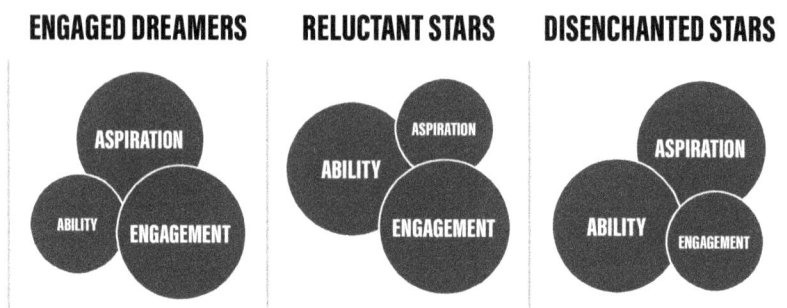

FIGURE 49.3: Talent Spotting: Stars or Dreamers?

Engaged Dreamers have the aspiration and desire to learn and progress but might lack the horsepower. This won't mean they can never progress, but it means they'll take longer and may not have the cognitive ability to successfully contribute to high-end strategic problem solving or innovation.

Reluctant Stars, of which we have met many as we've undertaken Expertship initiatives in our client organizations, are a rich vein of talent, but they're difficult to spot. They won't typically put themselves forward for things, and they'll lack confidence in themselves. With coachees like this, we need to build their confidence slowly and carefully at first, then gradually accelerate the pace of learning as they become increasingly motivated to progress. It's common to get huge personal satisfaction from transforming reluctant stars into fully formed high-potential experts.

Disenchanted Stars are those who have the capability but have, for one reason or another, become disinterested in putting in the effort to contribute to the team and the organization. Using highly developed coaching skills, we can get to the bottom of why they are disenchanted and determine whether or not we can rekindle their engagement.

Many experts we meet fit this category. They feel undervalued and disrespected. They're isolated from the mainstream activity of the organization and can't connect their work to the difference the organization is attempting to make. They're often waiting for the organization to change rather than getting on the front foot and making the first move to change themselves. We hope our book will encourage experts in this category to re-engage.

In summary, carefully selecting the talent we invest time in is important. They need to be motivated to learn. They need to have learning agility—the horsepower to learn complex things quickly. And they need to want to stick around and deploy these new skills.

Even if our high-potential junior colleagues have all the attributes required to grow their capabilities quickly and make our effort worthwhile, we need to acquire the skills and knowledge to provide learning that engages and inspires this audience.

What's the Difference Between Coaching and Mentoring?

THERE ARE MANY DEFINITIONS available for what coaching is and isn't, and the same applies to mentoring. What confuses matters is that mentoring also generally involves coaching, but, in simple terms, it includes something that coaching purists actively avoid: providing advice. In the previous chapter, we talked in depth about how to coach as an expert. Coaching methodologies are designed to help our colleagues find their own way, and the best way for this to occur is for the coach not to provide direction.

Mentoring is a little different. Very often, mentoring is a relationship between a senior colleague in an organization and a more junior colleague. Typically, the mentor sits outside the junior employee's line of control, perhaps in a different department or division of the organization. The purpose of the relationship is for the senior colleague to assist the junior colleague in the following ways:

- **Help navigate the organization.** This is particularly helpful if the organization is vast. Sometimes, getting things done is a function of who you know, not just what you know. Mentors can make introductions to helpful contacts and offer suggestions on how to build internal networks. They can sometimes provide context, which is more difficult for a junior colleague (or recent arrival at the organization) to acquire. An example of useful context is that the senior person might be able to describe how decisions are made or how funding is won in the firm.
- **Advice regarding career choices.** For junior colleagues, it's often difficult to ask their direct managers for advice about career choices. Our managers are unlikely to be completely neutral (unless we're very lucky). They'll not want us to move to another department or leave the organization. A mentor can take a more objective, long-term view and provide sound advice.
- **Help navigate the industry.** Senior colleagues of long standing will have extensive external networks, associations with professional bodies, and possibly a more global network. They can advise more junior colleagues on how to develop similar networks and emphasize the value of such relationships.

When we help organizations set up mentoring networks internally, which we strongly support, we also provide mentors with some advice on offering advice. The choice of what to do, in mentoring as in coaching, should always lie with the mentee. The mentor may share their experiences, but these will be specific to their own circumstances, occurring in the past (sometimes the distant past), and may or may not be relevant to the mentee in the present situation.

The best technique is to share openly. "A few years ago, I was facing a similar (note: not the "same") conundrum. This was the approach I took, and here were the reasons I took such and such a path rather than others. What are your options for action today? Are they different from mine? What makes you lean more toward one option than another? What's your next step?"

In this example, the mentor is sharing their own experiences, which the mentee can decide to use as a guide or ignore. They're then following up with coaching questions.

Mistakes that mentors often make include taking undue levels of responsibility and ownership for the career progression of their mentees. This should not be their role. The concept of taking someone under one's wing is an old-fashioned, patriarchal and dangerous concept. What worked for the mentor 15 years ago is very unlikely to work for the mentee today. For instance, the time that the mentor waited until being promoted might have been reasonable 15 years ago, but now mentees don't need to wait.

Many experts tell us they don't have the time to mentor more junior colleagues, which is a shame because they're missing out on the benefits of mentoring. The benefits don't just accrue to the mentee. In feedback at the end of mentoring programs, the senior mentors report they got at least as much value out of the mentoring arrangement as the mentee. Much of this value is in *reverse mentoring*, the concept that senior executives learn a lot about new ways of thinking and working from their junior counterparts.

In an expert's role, the difference between mentoring and coaching is subtle, and indeed both approaches may be deployed in a single conversation. But it's important for experts to understand the distinctions and make a conscious decision about which hat, that of mentor or coach, they should be wearing at any one time.

Mentoring is an ideal way to practice the coaching and question technique, empathetic listening, and giving back to our professions. It's also a good way to spot talented colleagues who might be able to take some of the more junior work off our desks.

TAKING ACTION

Growing Our Talent Developer Skills

IF THIS IS AN expert role in which you believe you could add greater value, here are some high-level suggestions for actions to take:

▶ DEVELOP AN EAGLE EYE FOR POTENTIAL TALENT

- Investing in succession planning, particularly our own, will become easier if there is a vibrant pipeline of trusted talent ready to step up and take on more responsibility. It's easier for the organization to give us new and interesting roles or projects if they know we've competently groomed successors who can backfill the great work we're doing. Some questions we might like to ask ourselves:
- Do I have a clear description of what it takes to be defined as talent with potential in my technical domain? Do I need to work with other senior colleagues to develop such a profile?
- How do I make time for and frame aspiration discussions with junior talent as I interact with them on tasks and projects? What are the most effective questions I could ask them in these conversations?
- How aware am I that many experts find it difficult to articulate what professional growth is? Am I aware that I might need to help them by socializing the Expertship model and by sharing this book with them?
- What opportunities for professional growth via shadowing or places on projects might periodically be available that I can offer to high-potential talent?

▶ CHOOSE A COLLEAGUE TO MENTOR

Assist more junior colleagues with effectively planning their careers and professional development. This will help them fulfill their aspirations, and you'll build your positive personal brand as a Master Expert.

- What assistance will junior colleagues need to successfully navigate our domain specialty, our industry and the organization?

- Who might benefit most from my mentorship, bearing in mind their aspirations, aptitude and learning agility? Which departments outside my own would value my offer of mentoring time?
- How will I establish the rules of engagement early on and make sure we're both aware of what is and isn't acceptable in a mentoring situation?
- What approach will I take to establish some clear goals for the connection early on? What is the mentee hoping to get out of the relationship, and what am I hoping to gain from it?
- How will I ensure that the mentee is doing most of the hard work, arranging meetings, suggesting topics, and completing the post-session actions they said they would?
- What are reasonable terms to agree for an exit strategy, right from the beginning?
- How will I measure the success of the relationship for both parties? Am I clear on what success would look like?

▶ MODEL THE RIGHT BEHAVIOR AND CREATE A PERSONAL GROWTH PLAN

If our objective is to create a dynamic learning environment where sharing knowledge, experience and skills is part of the culture, we have to model this behavior for others to follow. Here are some questions we might like to ask ourselves:

- Have I shaped a meaningful and actionable Personal Growth Plan (PGP) in order to set an example and demonstrate the standard I will be asking everyone else to follow? (The next chapter details how to do this.)
- Once shaped, how will I bring my PGP to life and make it visible to those who work around me?
- How will I bring it to life by sharing it with the broader group as something I am consistently working on?
- How will I get buy-in and support from my manager for the plan?
- How will I measure my success?

CHAPTER 50

Building a Personal Growth Plan

How can we hold ourselves accountable for our own development? The answer is by building a Personal Growth Plan and *executing* it.

IN THIS CHAPTER, WE WILL EXPLORE:

- Why do we need to build a Personal Growth Plan?
- What makes a Personal Growth Plan meaningful and actionable?
- How do we motivate key stakeholders to help us successfully execute a Personal Growth Plan that will take us to the next level of Expertship?

EVEN THOUGH THIS CHAPTER is the last in the book, the authors hope it's a **new beginning** for most readers. This is where the real work begins. On ourselves. For ourselves. Because, as experts, we matter. Because we know we can make a *greater* difference.

Most experts we meet are so busy helping others and growing others that they forget to help themselves and grow themselves. They're so busy helping their organization become more effective that they forget to spend time helping themselves become more effective. Just like those announcements on airplanes that tell you to fit your oxygen mask first and then help others, our message is to take the time to help yourself. If we really want to help our organizations succeed, delight more customers, and help the community sustainably prosper, we have to build our own capabilities. To make the biggest difference for others, we need to spend time on making ourselves the best experts we can be. This is the journey to Master Expert.

"If it doesn't get measured, it doesn't get done."

The journey starts with us shaping a Personal Growth Plan. Here's why. Here's how.

In Search of Personal Growth

IN MOST ORGANIZATIONS, PERSONAL Growth Plans are called *development plans.* They're promoted aggressively by enthusiastic HR teams as a template you must fill in. Their intention is to help us, but it somehow comes across as just another unnecessary administrative task that takes us away from the real expert work we need to get done. Well, that's the easy excuse many of us have used for not completing our development plans. The truth is somewhat more complicated.

One of our key sponsors, Mark Smith, the CIO of Asia-Pacific at a significant global financial services firm, told us: "For years, I couldn't get my senior technical specialists to complete a development plan. I'd get into trouble every year with HR because my team was the least compliant."

Among the experts we've worked with, the excuses for not completing a development plan were as colorful as they were consistent. Technical experts didn't see the need for development plans because, as far as they were concerned, they were already fully developed.

"What does a good growth opportunity look like?"

They were *experts,* after all. In addition, they were already undertaking technical courses to build their technical capability, which, of course, they chose because only they would know what courses they needed, and they didn't need HR or anyone else to tell them how to do that.

What we now know, having worked with thousands of experts, and as this book articulates, is that technical experts need to *grow* their enterprise skills as well as their technical skills if they want to *grow* the impact and influence they crave. Growth is the theme here.

Hence, we encourage experts to shape and then execute a Personal Growth Plan, and this chapter is dedicated to showing readers how easy that is. Why have a plan? Because if it doesn't get measured, it doesn't get done. By documenting what skills, knowledge and experiences we're going to grow, how we intend to do so, and how we'll measure these achievements, we're creating a tool with which we (and others) can hold ourselves accountable.

CREATING AND ACTIONING
Your Personal Growth Plan (PGP)

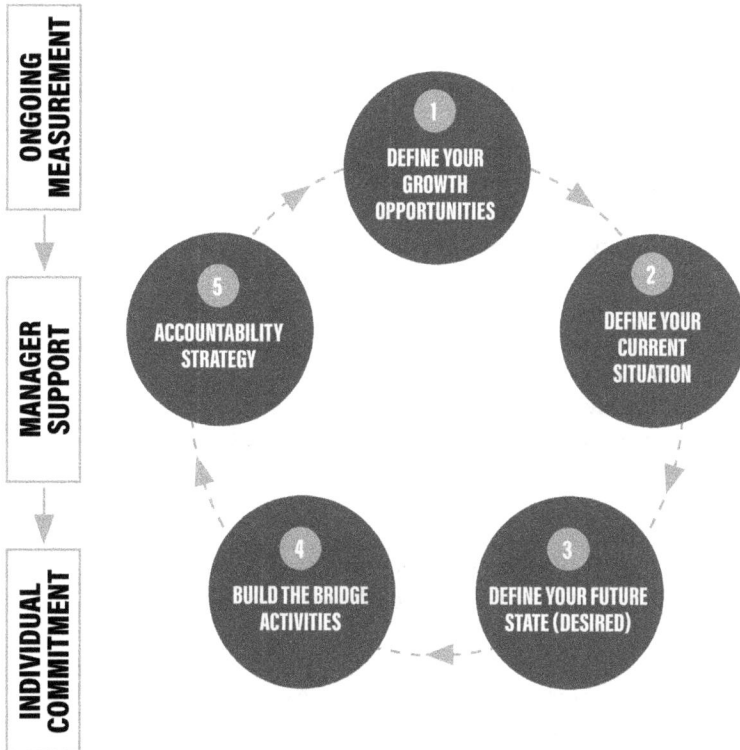

FIGURE 50.1: Creating and Actioning Your Personal Growth Plan

Steps to Creating a Personal Growth Plan

FIGURE 50.1 DESCRIBES THE five steps to creating a Personal Growth Plan, hereafter called a PGP.

STEP 1: DEFINE OUR GROWTH OPPORTUNITIES

Most of us have multiple areas in which we would like to grow our skills (new behaviors) and experiences. As readers have progressed through this book, many options for actions will have presented themselves. The key question is which actions and opportunities are we going to work on first, and why?

What does a good growth opportunity look like? It will typically have the following important attributes:

- **It will be doable**: that is, it isn't so ambitious that it's unlikely to be completed. If we choose a growth opportunity we think we can't successfully execute, we'll never follow through on it.
- **It can be completed in 6 to 12 months**: our preference is to plan for six months as it's a reasonably long period but the deadline is not too far away, which provides us with an impetus for action. If the opportunity that most appeals will take longer, we suggest breaking it up into smaller parts.
- **It will have a significant, sustained impact**: that is, the impact of achieving the goal far outweighs the effort expended to do so. The principle is one times effort for at least three times impact. The opportunity will help us increase the value we add as experts over and over again. This attribute is possibly the most important. We have to choose something that has a visible and long-lasting payoff. If we can't envisage a significant impact, we're unlikely to stay the course and complete the action.
- **It will be measurable**: we can construct a set of measures that indicate when we have achieved it. We need to be able to answer the question: "What does success look like?"

"Without knowing how good it will feel at the end, we'll never finish."

Not every opportunity will fulfill all of these criteria. A typical process we encourage is to make a list of all the opportunities we think are worthwhile and then chose the three that we believe will be the easiest to execute but provide the most worthwhile return. There may be, of course, an opportunity that requires very high effort and has a high degree of difficulty that we choose because the payoff is also very high. Importantly, we don't want to over-extend ourselves by choosing opportunities that are too hard and require time we don't have, and then we fail to execute them.

At the end of most of this book's chapters, we suggest actions experts can take if they could benefit from building their skills in that area. These might be a good place to start.

To demonstrate how to shape a Personal Growth Plan, we've chosen an opportunity we believe fulfills the criteria above. The example we'll use is this: We've decided that we want to become a better listener. This sounds simple, but it isn't. It has an impact on many aspects of our work if we can achieve it. It feels like a small change with a very large impact.

STEP 2: DEFINE OUR CURRENT SITUATION

Figure 50.2 describes this process in more detail. We have to analyze the impact of our current behavior.

To use the example of listening, let's imagine we've realized that we actually don't listen well when interacting with stakeholders. We've explored the concepts in Chapter 20 (*The Power of Listening*), understood that we're guilty of selective listening and pretend listening (Figure 20.1) and want to progress to the high-level capability of empathetic listening (Figure 20.2).

In Box 1 of Figure 50.2, we own up to our current behaviors. In Box 2, we need to describe the impact of these current behaviors.

We urge readers to take the time to do this because a detailed examination of how this behavior is getting in the way of us being the best experts we can be helps drive our will to change. In this instance, we might conclude:

- Selective and pretend listening can lead to us missing important information, which leads to rework, personal brand damage, and occasionally poor outcomes for all parties.
- By not practicing empathetic listening, we're not really understanding what our stakeholders' motivations and underlying needs are. This gets in the way of us creating solutions that really delight the stakeholder.
- Current listening behaviors may give the stakeholder the sense that we're not really interested or invested in trying to help them.

With such analysis, we create a burning platform for change as the effort appears to be worth it.

STEP 3: DEFINE OUR DESIRED SITUATION

In Box 3, we state the behavior we desire to master and deploy. In this case, empathetic listening. And in Box 4, we describe the impact we expect these new behaviors to have. Again, this is an important step because without knowing how good it'll be at the end, we won't find the energy and determination to finish. In this instance, we might conclude that the impacts are:

- Much better relationships with stakeholders.
- Less rework.
- More opportunity to do outstanding work that delights our stakeholders.
- Ability to strengthen our personal brand.
- Taking time to save time.

Readers might notice that we haven't yet discussed what we might do to make this change. We've restrained ourselves from jumping to a solution—a theme throughout this book. Instead, we've focused on the outcomes. And the final stage of doing is to determine what measures we'll use to establish that the growth opportunity has delivered the positive impacts we planned (completing Box 5). This is possibly the part of personal growth planning experts struggle with most. Data-driven as we are, we tend to want to find a hard number that we can apply. With a growth opportunity, such as improving our listening, hard numbers are difficult to come by.

Analyzing the Impact of Behaviors

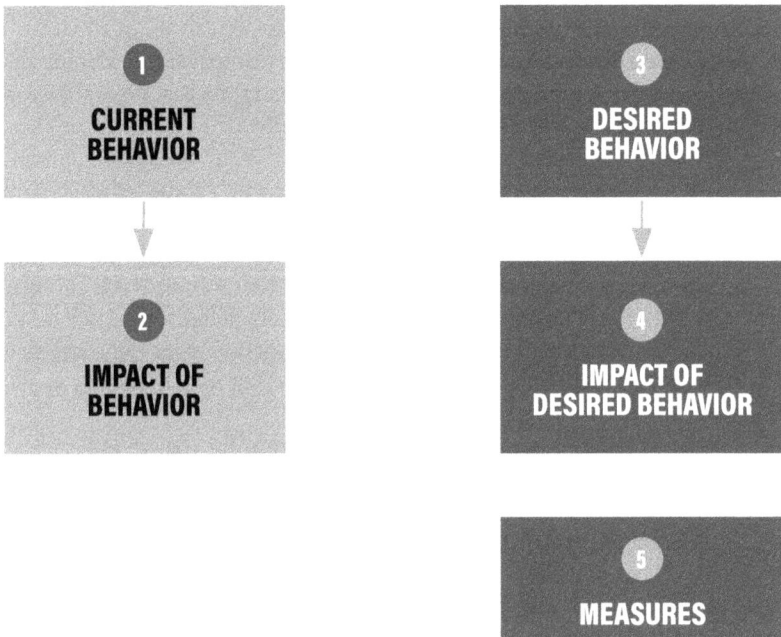

FIGURE 50.2: Analyzing the Impact of Behaviors

In this instance, we might consider a range of measures, some tangible and some intangible. Let's consider each of the positive impacts we've defined:

"What activities are we going to use to bridge the gap?"

- *Much better relationships with stakeholders.* We could use the Stakeholder Health Check audit (Figure 13.2) to assess whether, at the end of this plan, we're better able to answer the questions about our stakeholder than we are today. We could make a note today of how well we understand the stakeholder and their challenges and revisit the list in four months' time. These are meaningful measures, even if they remain subjective. We could ask the stakeholder in four months' time whether they think we listen more effectively to their needs, which is a courageous but powerful measure.
- *Less rework.* This would be a concrete measure. How much rework has been required in the last four months? Let's imagine it's six instances. What would we want to get that down to? Let's say two instances. That's a hard measure.
- *More opportunity to do outstanding work.* This might be a subjective measure from our own perspective, or it might be a structured, more objective measure if we're conducting proper post-implementation reviews with a broader stakeholder group (Figure 45.2).
- *Ability to strengthen our personal brand.* We would have to ask some colleagues to observe our behavior and provide us with feedback on whether they have noticed us listening more effectively. We'd probably want to engage people we trust, both to respect our confidentiality and to provide us with robust and honest feedback when we need it. Colleagues such as these are enormously valuable. If we're producing more outstanding work more regularly, we'll be in increasing demand, which is a sure signal that the organization has positively revised its view of the value we contribute.
- *Taking time to save time.* This ought to be a hard measure that is consistent with rework. How much time have we been wasting, and to what extent do we now have time to do higher value work? In Chapter 9, where we discuss the Expert Energy Engine, we suggest some processes to help experts measure what they actually spend their time on and consider what they would like to spend their time on.

Having completed Box 5, we're ready to move to stage four of shaping a Personal Growth Plan.

Building the Growth Bridge

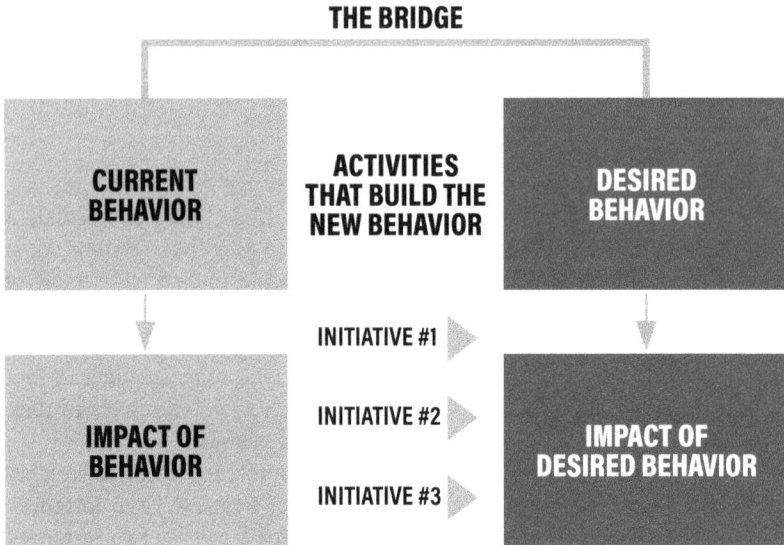

FIGURE 50.3: Building the Growth Bridge

STEP 4: BUILD THE BRIDGE—ACTIVITIES

Having defined our starting point, and also our finishing line and the positive impacts we hope our growth opportunity will realize, it's time to consider what activities we're going to undertake to achieve this growth. How do we bridge the gap between the two sets of behaviors (current and desired)? We have to build a *growth bridge* (see Figure 50.3).

We're looking for activities that help us master new behaviors. Typically, we choose two or three initiatives that we believe will help us achieve this objective.

> *"Finishing sentences for colleagues is disrepectful,*
> *stupid and arrogant all at once."*

In order to achieve our goal of mastering and consistently deploying empathetic listening, we might want to consider the following activities:

- **Ask more questions.** Throughout this book, we've emphasized the power of asking the right question at the right time in the right way. Listening is all about gaining a deeper understanding of needs, opinions or proposals. In this instance, we might spend an hour considering what questions would enable us to get a deeper understanding of what our stakeholders are looking for. For example, when gathering the needs of a stakeholder, what set of questions can we prepare and then deploy? A further example: when a stakeholder proposes a solution to us, which additional questions can we ask to truly understand why they are proposing that particular approach?

- **Increase our listening intensity.** We'll try to be much more consistent about leaning in and really listening to what someone is saying. We'll hang on their every word. Wait until they've finished speaking. Pause even because they might voluntarily have more to say. Poor listeners tend to listen to the first half of the sentence and then complete it in their own mind, not actually listening to their colleague while doing so. Or worse, they regularly interrupt and finish colleague's sentences for them. This is possibly one of the most annoying traits a colleague can have—it's disrespectful, stupid and arrogant all at once. Letting a colleague finish and listening intently to what they are saying will significantly improve our precise understanding of what they're trying to communicate to us.
- **Listen to feelings as well as facts.** Focus on the emotional side of the conversation, as well as the verbal side. Try to accurately pick up on whether a stakeholder is frustrated, angry or sad. Each of these emotions means something different (and requires a slightly different response from us). Remember, we're trying to master *empathetic* listening.
- **Paraphrasing.** This is a technique all good listeners deploy to ensure they have understood a colleague correctly. We could decide to deploy it regularly in conversations. "So, what I heard you tell me was A, B and C. Is that right?" Our colleagues almost always want to embellish what we've paraphrased back to them, thereby deepening our understanding, which means we've listened more effectively.
- **Seek to understand why, not just what.** Colleagues tell us things, and as poor listeners, we just take those things at face value and move on. But what we're hearing is just that: the *what*. If we're truly to listen properly, we'll need to understand the *why* as well. More questions are required. "Can you help me understand…"

Phew—quite a lot there! But each initiative in its own right is doable, and in combination, they will transform our listening skills and our ability to understand, connect with and do great work for our stakeholders.

STEP 5: ACCOUNTABILITY STRATEGY

The final stage of shaping a PGP is to determine an accountability strategy. Who is going to hold us accountable for executing the plan, and how? The best way to do this is to engage key stakeholders in the process. Our managers may be an ideal contributor here if they regularly see us in action. Or perhaps colleagues who see us working with stakeholders every day.

The best PGPs are the ones that are alive, looked at regularly, checked weekly, discussed fortnightly, constantly revised and updated as items get ticked off, and have new opportunities added to them.

The most crucial element of any accountability strategy is our own individual commitment to executing the plan. This is why we emphasize that the payoff—the benefits and positive impacts that accrue from our effort—must be visible and worth fighting for.

Take our example of increasing the quality of our listening and consider what we're attempting to change: the habits of a lifetime. Yes, we discussed deploying techniques to make us a better listener, but in reality, this is a significant mindset change. On paper, the individual initiatives appear easy to execute. But in the day-to-day hurly-burly of our working environment, they're very hard to apply consistently. We'd better be committed.

Additional help

IN THE FOLLOWING PAGES, we've created a list of all of the Group Opportunity actions included in this book for your easy reference. We have an online *Expertship Growth Guide* at *expertship.com* which contains nearly 200 suggested growth opportunities for experts. We also have accredited Expertship coaches around the world who can help you shape a meaningful Personal Growth Plan, which is a small investment in your career that will be transformational. The coaching component of our programs is often the part participants tell us they valued the most.

A further level of commitment is to undertake an assessment of your current Expertship capabilities. A survey completed by stakeholders and colleagues called the *Expertship360* is available worldwide. You'll find details of your local supplier at our Expertship website above.

Not long ago, there were almost no resources available to experts to help them be the best experts they can possibly be. That's no longer the case. No more excuses. The world is out there, so let's go forth and change it for the better, as only experts can.

"The beautiful thing about learning is that no one can take it away from you."

BB King

PART | 05 |

ADDITIONAL
RESOURCES

"Learning never exhausts the mind."

Leonardo da Vinci

Master Expert Action List

Index

F

G

H

I

J

K

Knowledge Curator 65, 544, 559, 562, 565
Generator 544, 571, 574, 577
Knowledge Generator 544, 571, 574, 577
Knowledge Seeker 65, 544, 549, 550, 551, 553
Seeking 100, 112, 131, 147, 179, 189, 193, 220, 299, 336, 340, 341, 344, 372, 402, 448, 452, 516, 525, 542, 543, 544, 546, 549, 550, 555, 556, 572, 574, 580, 582, 592, 595, 602, 619, 631, 663
Knowledge Sequencing 564
Knowledge Sharer 66, 643, 647, 649
Knowledge Strategy 539, 543, 544, 546, 552, 555, 561, 637, 653, 662
Knowledge Transfer 29, 64, 66, 284, 287, 635, 637, 643, 644, 647, 665
Knowledge Versioning 564
Knowledge Worker 19
Kodak 491
Kotter, John 523, 524, 525, 527
Kotter's Eight-Step Change Model 523

L

Laërtius, Diogenes 292
Law 19, 25, 540, 673
Leadership 11, 12, 17, 32, 45, 50, 62, 82, 124, 163, 181, 240, 254, 262, 272, 274, 278, 288, 312, 321, 322, 326, 327, 366, 367, 404, 405, 406, 408, 426, 428, 435, 436, 488, 489, 490, 498, 506, 519, 520, 521, 572, 573, 575, 578, 595, 627, 638
Leadership Pathway 17
Learning and Development Team 45
Lee, Harper 658
Left- Versus Right-Brained 24
Legitimizing 337
Lewis, C.S 119
Limbic Brain 98, 110, 342, 343
Lineback, Kent 224, 260, 262
LinkedIn 75, 240, 285
Logos 333, 334
Lose-Lose 368
Luft, Joseph 83

M

Makhlouf, Jack 656
Management Skills 22, 24, 201, 315
Market Context 12, 23, 36, 44, 63, 124, 227, 236, 259, 279, 288, 336, 383, 384, 388, 389, 390, 391, 392, 394, 396, 410, 412, 416, 431, 588, 589
Market Context Canvas 392, 393, 394, 395, 400, 402, 418, 424, 426

Marketing 11, 19, 131, 151, 234, 236, 238, 266, 403, 408, 426, 434, 443, 481, 540, 543, 553, 560, 561
Master Expert 3, 12, 13, 22, 27, 29, 32, 33, 36, 38, 41, 45, 47, 50, 51, 52, 53, 55, 60, 65, 70, 81, 83, 89, 94, 106, 107, 116, 128, 130, 136, 143, 156, 157, 174, 176, 183, 186, 187, 188, 193, 199, 203, 214, 218, 224, 226, 227, 234, 236, 259, 262, 272, 279, 295, 296, 298, 299, 323, 325, 326, 327, 349, 350, 353, 356, 358, 366, 370, 371, 382, 383, 384, 385, 392, 400, 404, 408, 409, 411, 415, 416, 423, 424, 427, 429, 440, 441, 442, 448, 449, 451, 460, 463, 468, 478, 480, 486, 487, 491, 498, 502, 506, 509, 511, 526, 538, 540, 543, 550, 552, 554, 555, 560, 571, 572, 581, 586, 592, 593, 596, 598, 600, 592, 598, 608, 618, 636, 637, 643, 648, 653, 663, 666, 668, 680, 681, 683, 689, 697, 702
McClelland, David 94
Medical 11, 19, 445
Meeting Culture 305
Meetings 20, 23, 25, 55, 76, 86, 87, 144, 150, 155, 156, 167, 173, 185, 195, 200, 218, 219, 236, 239, 248, 275, 289, 294, 305, 306, 307, 309, 310, 311, 312, 313, 314, 315, 316, 317, 318, 319, 327, 328, 338, 384, 391, 408, 431, 443, 457, 481, 540, 543, 565, 566, 567, 612, 620, 627, 666, 673, 675, 698
Mentoring / Mentor 57, 78, 81, 695, 696
Mind Map 192, 203
Mindset 13, 31, 35, 37, 49, 64, 95, 96, 106, 107, 161, 269, 279, 280, 285, 287, 295, 298, 371, 426, 457, 469, 471, 473, 487, 502, 503, 505, 506, 523, 541, 542, 588, 612, 620, 665, 666, 710
Motivator(s) 136, 248, 252
Myers Briggs 119, 121

N

Navigator 63, 326, 387, 394, 399, 400, 401, 412, 418
Negotiation 159, 365, 366, 370, 371, 372, 680
Neocortex 98
Net Promoter Score (NPS) 617, 621, 622, 623
NPS 622, 623
Networking Events 231, 262
Networking/Network 62, 220, 225, 231, 233, 235, 239, 242, 259, 260, 262, 269, 412
Network Manager 62, 233, 235, 242
Network of Goodwill 184, 188
Neuroscience 110

Further Reading

We maintain a live list of research and resources related to this book at *expertship.com/resources*.

Visit the site for links to the books, models and tools we have discussed throughout this book.

There's also links to further Expertship downloads and our newsletters on Expertship and Expertship Research and Benchmarking.

The Expertship Portal

On the Expertship website you can also request access to the Expertship Portal, our subscriber-only support system for Expertship coaching and programs.

Growth Calculator

You'll find the growth calculator mentioned throughout this book at *expertship.com/growth*.

About The Authors

Alistair Gordon

Alistair is the CEO of Expertunity, an expert coach, speaker and author. A long-time veteran of the media and organizational development worlds, he has been publisher of one of Australia's most successful business magazines of the 00s, BRW. Through his first company, Strategic Publishing, he created some of the earliest magazines that helped experts develop their business skills. He is also CEO of Expertunity's parent company HFL, Leadership.

Dominic Johnson

Dominic is a master facilitator who, like Alistair, has logged thousands of hours coaching experts and masterminding Expertship programs. He is the co-author of *How to be a Master Expert*, and a co-designer of the processes described in the book. He has also been head of consulting for EMEA for Stephen Covey's consultancy Franklin Covey, and he has run the largest Hindu temple in Europe, Bhaktivedanta Manor in the UK.

Develop Your Expertship

You don't become a Master Expert overnight. It helps to have mentoring, advice, and a community of other experts who've faced the same challenges. Since 2017, Expertunity has offered specialist expert coaching and group programs to help you, and your organization, use Expertship to radically improve business competitiveness.

At the organizational level, we provide benchmarking and research to help leaders, CEOs, HR and organizational development leaders create peak performance in their expert teams. If you are responsible for improving expert team performance, we strongly recommend subscribing to our research, benchmarking and performance data updates at *expertunity.global/research*.

Expert Coaching - for Individual Experts

Career coaching is life changing. It challenges you to deeply re-think how you approach problems, manage your relationships, and resolve short-term career blocks. It is a great boost to early and mid-career experts, and we particularly recommend coaching for experts like Edward in Chapter 1 who feel "career stuck."

Expertunity's specialist one-on-one expert coaching is available worldwide through our network of accredited coaches. Unlike other coaching programs, it is purpose built for technical specialists who want to reach peak performance.

Mastering Expertship - for Groups of Experts

Learn how to apply Expertship problem-solving to the thorniest challenges in your career.

Our flagship program, Mastering Expertship, asks experts to work in pods of four with a coach. Each session, participants bring their real-life challenges to the group to solve within a structured coaching program that shows you the way to Master Expert status.

We hate the idea of PowerPoint and "chalk-and-talk," so this is a highly interactive, challenging set of workshops and learning episodes. It will transform your ambition for your work and career.

Leader of Experts - for Team Leaders

Experts are not easy to lead, especially if you're a non-technical manager who's been asked to take over a team of experts. Leader of Experts is a one-day intensive workshop to help you understand how to focus, motivate and manage expert teams, and to ensure expert ideas contribute to competitive advantage.

Expertship Community Programs - for Individual Experts

Our coaching and programs are all grounded in person-to-person learning, underpinned by our coaching and logistics platform, the Expertship Portal. Access is available via subscription. This digital service helps you build personal development plans, find Expert mastermind groups, and access additional career resources, such as extensions to this book.

Expertship Research and Organizational Development - for Organizations

Research and benchmarking are key to proving the competitive value of expert teams. Our research division works with organizational development and HR teams, and CEOs to help you answer three questions.

First, what is "good" expert performance? Second, how do my teams compare with my industry, organization or globally? And third, what levers can I pull in my organization and externally to improve the performance of my experts?

Next Steps

These services are described in greater detail at *expertunity.global/programs*, which also allows you to request coaching, programs, or research and benchmarking. We provide a number of regular update services for experts. Please consider subscribing at *expertunity.global/resources*.

Dedication and Acknowledgments

To experts - that they can realize their full potential.

To our families - Malee, Jodie, Elina, Radha, Lalita, Radheya and Rohini - thank you for supporting and believing.

The list of colleagues and friends that provided inspiration and support to the authors is too long to list here – but let it be known that every kind word of encouragement or question about whether we had finished it or not contributed mightily to this book seeing the light of day. There are very many indirect contributors as well – all those authors whose ideas and wisdom encapsulated in books and articles we have leveraged and learned from.

Possibly the most important role of all was played by all of the participants of our expertship programs from whom we have learned and were willing recipients of our ideas. These programs couldn't have taken place over the years without the extraordinary program management skills of our colleagues Cheryl Chow and Jo Bunce, who also hugely assisted in the production phase of this book. They must be sick of reading it in its many versions.

We have been assisted by two wonderful editors who converted our mumblings to concise prose, Graeme Phillipson (who tragically passed away before the first version was printed) and Susan Ryan. Any mistakes are ours not theirs. We were also assisted by two Art Directors, Jodie Laczko and the team at Ronnoco, Jodi and Raz O'Connor, the latter of which managed the layout of 732 pages against horrendous deadlines. Thanks to those who made us look good.

We were assisted from first version to last by incredible feedback from colleagues, including Bob Hayward, Darin Fox, Kim Ambor, Tony Horton, Craig Healy, Dale Robinson, Divya Maheshwari, Ross Exton, Vas Varousiadis, Kim Mundell, Ken Davison, Hamish Reeves, Jack Su, Kirsty Allen, Jo Bunce and Steve Kimmens. Grant Heinrich took on the role of Publisher and this book would most definitely not have seen the day without his enormous efforts. His advice and clarity has been both welcome and essential.

We have been encouraged in our efforts by some extremely supportive and early-adopter clients, again who are too numerous to name, but some stand out: Mark Smith, Cath Proud, Kim Johnson, Scott Prosser, David Fryda, Annabelle Larkham, Lindsay Jenkin, Leahna Hardie, Stewart Fotheringham, Rachael Grant, and Mal Reason. We should perhaps finally offer some thanks to each other – without our collaboration the book would never have happened. Thanks Dominic. Thanks Alistair.

ALISTAIR GORDON & DOMINIC JOHNSON